INTERNATIONAL HANDBOOK

of

EARLY CHILDHOOD EDUCATION

Garland Reference Library
of Social Science
(Vol. 598)

INTERNATIONAL HANDBOOK

— *of* —

EARLY CHILDHOOD EDUCATION

Edited by

Gary A. Woodill, Ed.D.

Judith Bernhard, Ph.D.

Lawrence Prochner, M.A.

School of Early Childhood Education

Ryerson Polytechnical Institute

Toronto, Canada

GARLAND PUBLISHING

New York & London 1992

Library of Congress Cataloging-in-Publication Data

International handbook of early childhood education / edited by Gary A.
Woodill, Judith Bernhard, Lawrence Prochner.
     p. cm.—(Garland reference library of social science; vol. 598)
     Includes bibliographical references (p.) and index.
     ISBN 0-8240-4939-X
     1. Early childhood education—Handbooks, manuals, etc. I. Woodill, Gary.
II. Bernhard, Judith. III. Prochner, Lawrence. IV. Series: Garland reference
library of social science; v. 598.
LB1139.23.I68   1992
372.21—dc20   92–23846
                                                CIP

Printed on acid-free, 250-year-life paper
Manufactured in the United States of America

CONTENTS

• • • • • • • • • • ◆ • • • • • • • • •

PREFACE

• • • • • • • • • • • ◆ • • • • • • • • •

The idea for an *International Handbook of Early Childhood Education* started in recognition of a need. As teacher educators, we found that many of our students were interested in the organization and curricula of early childhood education in other countries, but often had difficulties finding such material. It is hoped that the original articles in this volume will begin to meet the needs of students and researchers in comparative early childhood education.

While the origins of this handbook were relatively easy, the process of getting the work to publication was not. First, authors with both knowledge and experience of early childhood education in their country had to be located. This was accomplished through a "call for papers" mailed to almost every university with an education department outside of Canada and the United States (in Canada and United States, we relied on colleagues who had demonstrated a thorough background in the history and organization of early childhood education). The result was multiple potential authors from most countries. In many cases, the final selection of authors was based on their credentials, previous publications, and experience. In a number of cases, we asked that people collaborate with each other, or divide the subject matter into preschool and primary education so that we could use the input of several well qualified individuals. We believe that the contributors' list for the handbook represents an outstanding group of authors in terms of achievements and experience in this field.

Several countries were not included due to political difficulties in each country. Civil war and unrest prevented mail reaching at least three potential contributors, and their contributions will have to await a subsequent volume. During the two years the handbook was being prepared, the Berlin Wall fell, governments and political systems changed in Eastern Europe and the USSR, and the two Germanies were reunited. In spite of all this, authors in these areas were able to write articles, even though their countries were involved in massive changes.

In a work of this size and scope, there are bound to be a number of errors and omissions. We apologize for these, and will try to make corrections in subsequent printings and editions. The logistics of coordinating articles from 45 countries on five continents, written in three languages, proved to be an immense task, and took much longer than we expected. In order to have the chapters fit the criteria set out in the Call for Papers, extensive editorial changes had to be made to a number of articles.

We were very fortunate that Garland Publishing had an outstanding copy editor in Paula Grant, from whom we learned many lessons on improving the English language, and who caught mistakes that had passed us several times. Marie Ellen Larcada, the editor at Garland who commissioned this work, and Kevin Bradley, production editor at Garland, deserve a thank you for their patience, encouragement, and support.

During the process of completing the book, a number of our colleagues in Toronto offered welcome comments on our ideas or on parts of the manuscript, gave us lists of contacts in other countries, or offered support for the project. In particular we would like to thank Jane Knight, Donald McKay, Kenise Murphy Kilbride, June Pollard, Monique Richard, and Gloria Roberts-Fiati of the School of Early Childhood Education, Ryerson, for their suggestions and information. We also thank the Faculty of Community Services Research Committee at Ryerson for seed money for developing the original book proposal to Garland Publishing, and the Dean of Community Services, Jennifer Welsh, for supporting research projects such as this book.

Much of the work of putting the manuscript together was carried out by our research assistant, Lori Schmidt, whom we sincerely thank. She typed the manuscript, wrote letters to authors, and kept the project moving, all while completing her Bachelor's degree in early childhood education at Ryerson. This project would not have been completed without her.

Finally, Lawrence Prochner wishes to thank his wife Barbara McPherson and daughter Isabel for their support and encouragement. Gary Woodill thanks his wife Karen Anderson for editing and checking translations of parts of the manuscript, and giving feedback and support throughout the project.

INTERNATIONAL HANDBOOK

of

EARLY CHILDHOOD EDUCATION

INTERNATIONAL EARLY CHILDHOOD CARE AND EDUCATION: HISTORICAL PERSPECTIVES

• • • • • • • • • • ◆ • • • • • • • • • •

Gary A. Woodill
Ryerson Polytechnical Institute
Toronto, Canada

All societies have specific approaches to raising and educating young children. What we now call "early childhood education" is the pattern of creches, preschools, kindergartens, primary classes, and early intervention programs found in most countries of the world. It is a particular set of cultural and historical inventions that developed between the 16th and 19th centuries in Europe and was imported to most corners of the globe. As several authors show in this volume, in many countries, Western forms of early childhood education either supplanted or mixed with indigenous forms of child care and education, with their complex heritage of teaching the folklore, customs, and traditions of the local culture. While there is a commonality today among most countries in basic terminology about early childhood education, this may mask a diversity of forms of child care that is hard to recognize and describe given that one dominant discourse on early childhood education tends to be present in the official writing in the field, especially by academics (including the present editors) who live in Western countries or who are influenced by Western educational models.

In its Western form, early childhood education has come to mean education and care of the child in group settings outside the child's family home. The spread of this particular form of caring for and teaching children is related to both colonization of much of the world by European powers and the spread of industrialization throughout the world. This chapter briefly describes the history of the development and growth of the components of early childhood education up to the beginning of the 20th century. In the following chapter, Lawrence Prochner takes a critical look at today's early childhood education. Each of the chapters that compose the rest of this volume contains a short history of the country discussed to show how early childhood education developed there.

Extrafamilial Child Care

To survive and to grow up as members of a society, young children need a certain minimal level of care and education. It is a common Western view that in most human societies, this care and education are initially given by "loving" parents, especially by the child's mother, in the context of a "universal, bioculturally based family constructed" on a mother-child unit" (Moore, 1988:26). But this is an ethnocentric view of the matter, a romanticization of both parenting and the nature of families in previous times. Rather, the concepts of "motherhood," "family," and even "early childhood education" can be seen as historically and culturally specific "social constructions" (Dally, 1982).

The image of the child growing up in an idyllic family throughout history was first challenged by Aries (1962), who suggested that until the late Middle Ages, children were seen as miniature adults and not given special treatment. Pollack (1984) countered Aries's views, contending that while Aries may have been right about the treatment of children in certain parts of France in the Middle Ages, not all European societies treated children in this way. The image of peaceful childhood has also been challenged by recent historical research that documents widespread infanticide (especially of girls); abandonment of children (Boswell, 1988); and child abuse, neglect, and the use of harsh discipline (de Mause, 1974; Miller, 1983; Greven, 1991).

It is probable that most human societies in the past have had some alternative arrangements for child care when the parents, for whatever reason, were unable or unwilling to care for their child, but these arrangements are culturally and historically specific and quite varied. A full cross-cultural study of this subject has not been undertaken, but a few examples can be cited to indicate that alternative child care arrangements occur in most cultures, past and present. In *The Roman Mother*, Dixon (1988) describes how, from the early second century B.C. to the early third century A.D., "the usual social practice among the well-to-do—and perhaps also among the lower social orders—was probably to give babies over to a slave or mercenary nurse" (p. 141). Dixon comments that "the mother's presence and intimate physical involvement with the small child was [sic] not prized as much by the ancients as by modern experts" (*ibid.*).

In many societies, child care is undertaken by close kin as a way of "covering" for the parents while they are working. Mead (1963) tells how small children of the Arapesh tribe in New Guinea would hold infants while their mothers worked in the garden. Black migrant women workers in Botswana send their children back to their own mothers (i.e., their children's grandmother) in the rural areas in order to maintain employment, especially in residential domestic service in white households (Izzard, 1985). Anderson (1991) describes how, before the 17th century, women of the Huron longhouses were supported in child care, domestic tasks, and agricultural work by strong kinship networks in a matrilineal society. There are many other examples of informal child care arrangements in the literature, including some described in the chapters of this book.

Roots of Primary Education

Alternative child care arrangements are not the same as the intentional education of young children. While attendance in early childhood educational programs for children under age 5 is optional in most countries, there is no doubt that most present-day preschool programs are intended to be educational, and that where these programs are provided, they are in high demand by parents. This, however, is a relatively recent phenomenon in the history of child care for young children.

Before the 16th century, in most countries, few children received any formal schooling, and those who did started at about age 9 or older. But, by the end of the 16th century, many "petty schools," or *écoles petites*, had been started in Great Britain, France, and some other European states. These new schools, which had pupils as young as age 6, were the beginnings of primary education as we know it today. They were followed in the 17th and 18th centuries throughout Western Europe by various "charity schools" and "dame schools" for the children of the poor; these latter schools sometimes had children as young as age 2 or 3 mixed in with the older children.

The petty school was "primarily a place for religious training. It always aimed to teach pupils to read and write, often teaching elementary accounting as well, but the religious aim was all pervasive" (Sylvester, 1970:78). Both the Protestant Reformation and the Catholic Counter-Reformation produced a zeal for teaching young children how to read. For the Protestant reformers, beginning with Luther, the goal was to produce citizens who could read the Bible for themselves.

For the Catholic Counter-Reformers, led by the Jesuits, the goal of educating young children was to get to them early, while their minds could be imprinted with the tenets of the "true faith."

With the development of the printing press came children's ABC primers and children's books. One of the first books for children was designed by the wandering Moravian Bishop, John Comenius, who, in 1628, also wrote *The School of Infancy*, a book on teaching young children. The idea of teaching children under age 6 in small groups outside the home had not yet been proposed, and Comenius wrote a section for teaching preschool children at "the school of the mother's lap."

During the 18th century in Europe, theorists proposed new schemes on how to influence children's learning without using whippings and beatings, the most common approach to school discipline to that time, to induce memorization. Melton (1988) has suggested that the Protestant Reformation resulted in a shift from outer to inner mechanisms of social control. In Luther's mind, the inculcation of inner discipline and obedience, as well as the reading of the Bible, was to be accomplished through universal education. And the 18th-century Protestant reformers who followed believed that "an enlightened subject was one who rendered obedience voluntarily and spontaneously; conversely, an enlightened ruler exacted the obedience of his subjects through love rather than force" (p. xxii). Schools were of interest "because they offered an instrument for exacting obedience in a less coercive fashion" (*ibid.*).

One influential group in the history of elementary education was the German Pietists. Pietism was a late-17th-century reform movement within Lutheranism founded as a reaction to the scholasticism of the established theologians and the perceived excessive luxury and its display by the upper classes in German society. Pietists emphasized austerity, spiritual renewal, purification of sin, and obedience to one's God-given social duties. Pietist pedagogy was characterized by the study of Christian doctrine, obedience to authority, and a strong work ethic. Regulating time was important, and every hour of the day was scheduled with activities. Institutional control of the child was strengthened by intense supervision and by compulsory attendance.

Several innovations of the German Pietist educationalists were practices that became part of modern elementary and secondary education. To break their rigid time scheduling with a little "free play," for example, the Pietists introduced morning and afternoon recesses. They also extended the French innovation of teaching children in groups according to proficiency rather than individually. The practice of hand-raising, the development of separate vocational schools (*Realschule*), and "normal" schools (to teach the *norms* of educational practice) were all 18th-century German Pietist innovations (Melton, 1988).

Also influential in establishing practices of school discipline at all age levels were the monitorial systems of education developed independently by Dr. Andrew Bell, an Anglican clergyman, and by Joseph Lancaster, a Quaker reformer. In the 18th century, there was a debate in the elite circles of European societies on the wisdom of educating the poor. For example, Bernard Mandeville, an English physician and essayist, wrote in 1723:

> To make society happy, and people easy under the meanest circumstances, it is requisite that great numbers of them should be ignorant as well as poor. Knowledge both enlarges and multiplies our desires, and the fewer things a man wishes for, the more easily his necessities may be supplied. The welfare and felicity therefore of every state and kingdom require that the knowledge of the working poor should be confined within the verge of their occupations, and never extended (as to things visible) beyond what relates to their calling (quoted in Kaestle, 1973:1).

Eighteenth-century reformers who opposed this view did so not by arguing for a universal right to education, but on the grounds that education would, as Hannah More, a Sunday School promoter, stated, "train up the lower classes in habits of industry and piety" (quoted in Kaestle, 1973:2). Lancaster offered a system of social control of the classroom that promised both efficiency (and was therefore cheap) and the teaching of military discipline to the children of the poor.

At the heart of the Lancasterian monitorial school was the use of older, more advanced students to supervise and teach the younger children. As well, there was an elaborate set of rules to instill precise discipline; a hierarchy of place decided by competition in learning; a token economy of tickets with awards of tops, balls, books, and pictures for high academic performance; and an architecture designed for maximum control of large groups of children by a single adult. While learning could be effective and sometimes fun in such a system, its main purpose was "to inculcate the values of obedience, subordination, promptness, regularity, cleanliness, thrift and temperance" (Kaestle, 1973:8). As some chapters in this volume show, the Lancasterian system spread throughout the world, to such diverse places as Bulgaria, Canada, Liberia, South Africa, Spain, and the United States. It also found its way into the dominant model of "infant schools" in 19th-century Europe.

Preschool Education

Preschool education in Europe developed its institutional forms in the late 18th and early 19th century as a response to the abandonment and mistreatment of children associated with the development of factories, smelters, and mines that employed their parents. It was his belief in the improvability of the poor and the need to rescue children that led the Protestant pastor Jean-Frederic Oberlin, in 1770, to hire 19-year-old Sarah Banzet to take care of a group of unrelated preschool children of families in the Alsace region of France (Kurtz, 1976). Soon Oberlin recruited other women to take small groups of young children into their homes and to teach them Bible stories and knitting. These "knitting schools" are often considered the first example of organized group day care where the children were all under school age.

Rescue from poverty and abandonment was also the aim of Heinrich Pestalozzi in opening an industrial school for destitute children from ages 6 to 16 on his farm near Zurich, Switzerland, in 1774. While his experiment lead to his financial ruin, and the school closed in 1780, Pestalozzi was to become famous as an innovator in elementary education in the early 1800s. From the examples of both Oberlin and Pestalozzi, who were in turn influenced by Jean Jacques Rousseau, the idea of "caring" for the child, as well as "educating" the child, is a part of early childhood education even today.

Based on the knowledge of Oberlin's pioneering work in the Alsace, Madame Adélaïde de Pastoret opened, about 1800, an *asile*, or "refuge," for children under age 3 of working mothers in Paris. Several other infant schools were founded in Europe in the following decades, the first was started in Germany by Princess Pauline of Lippe in 1802 after she read about the *asile* in Paris (Rusk, 1933). Perhaps inspired by this example, or by Maria Edgeworth's novel describing the Paris infant school, Robert Owen founded his Institution for the Formation of Character in New Lanark, Scotland, on January 1, 1816. The first teacher of Owen's Infant School was James Buchanan, who, in 1819, became the first teacher of an infant school in London, opened in Brewer's Green. A second London infant school was started by Samuel Wilderspin in Spitalfields.

Wilderspin reorganized the program for the infant schools, adding to it the monitorial systems of Bell and Lancaster (Pence, 1990). The original ethic of freedom and play in the preschools of Oberlin and Owen soon gave way to the larger custodial models of child care.

[T]he infant schools which proliferated in Britain during the nineteenth century were swallowed up in the growth of cheap elementary education for the poor. The essence of early childhood education as seen in Alsace and New Lanark had been freedom and enjoyment through play; Owen even proclaimed that children were not to be *annoyed with books*. When infants were incorporated in huge barrack-like rooms where hundreds of older children were drilled in the alphabet and multiplication tables all this was lost. Dr. Andrew Bell and others devised the monitor system of supervision by older children, the "gallery" benches to restrict movement, and offered a system of discipline and instruction (Deasey, 1978:8).

In 1825, a new type of center for young children called the *salle d'asile* was begun in Paris by Baron de Gérando and Denys Cochin. Based on the English monitorial infant schools, these new institutions held large numbers of children under age 6 (one of the first *salles d'asile* was designed for a thousand children) in order to protect them from the dangers of disease and the streets. Children sat in long rows of benches with their hands behind their backs, moved only on the sound of a whistle, and even blew their noses in unison. Count Leo Tolstoy, visiting Marseille during this time, described a *salle d'asile* as follows:

I saw the *salles d'asile*, in which four year old children, at a given whistle, like soldiers, made revolutions around the benches, at a given command lifted and folded their hands, and with quivering and strange voices sang laudatory hymns to God and to their benefactors and I convinced myself that the educational institutions of the city of Marseille were exceedingly bad (quoted in Deasey, 1978:22).

In spite of Tolstoy's opinion, the *salles d'asile* spread to Eastern Europe and Russia by the 1830s. Le Pas (1852) documents the growth of the *salles d'asile* in St. Petersbourg from 1839 (when eight establishments served 1,080 children) to 1848 (when 18 *salles* enrolled 2,255 children). The charts in Le Pas's book show that the death rate of children in the Russian *salles d'asile* declined over the ten-year period and was about one-third of the mortality rate of children not in these settings.

In contrast to the custodial nature of monitorial infant schools and day care centers, a new type of education for young children, the kindergarten, developed in Germany in the 1830s. The kindergarten originated with Friedrich Froebel, who spent two years (1808–1810) working with Pestalozzi at his school in Yverdon, Switzerland. It was there that Froebel first recognized the educational value of play. Froebel's kindergartens had spread throughout Germany and Europe and were introduced into both North America and South America by German ex-patriots in the middle of the 19th century. The first U.S. kindergarten was opened by Margarethe Schurz in Watertown, Wisconsin, in 1855.

Preschool services for the poor spread from Europe to North America because conditions the same as in Europe—rapid industrialization, child labor, and middle-class moralism—were present in both Canada and the United States. The first *salles d'asile* and the first creches were established in Montreal in the early 1850s (Schulz, 1978). Almost at the same time, the New York Hospital established its Nursery for the Children of Poor Women, which provided care for children of working parents and for the children of wet nurses. The first publicly funded kindergartens began in the St. Louis school system in the 1870s.

A 1908 health study in England showed that 80 percent of British infants were well at birth, while only 20 percent were healthy upon entering public schools (Osborn, 1980). Margaret McMillan and her sister Rachel responded to this report by establishing an open-air nursery school in the London slums in 1911. McMillan originated the term "nursery school," and these new organizations emphasized play, nurturing of children, and support for parents. The nursery school model also spread throughout the world, particularly in the form of enrichment programs (often as university laboratory schools) and parent cooperative nursery schools.

Development of Special Education

The idea of a special class or school, where students follow a different curriculum than that followed by their peers of the same age, comes first from the idea of grading, and second, from the realization that certain groups who were thought to be uneducable, could learn in a school setting.

Schools in the Middle Ages were not organized into grades (Aries, 1962). That is, students were not grouped together according to age, nor was the curricula ordered in graduated segments from the easiest material to the hardest. In France, this innovation arrived in the last half of the 16th century, but it did not become a common practice until the 18th century. With grades came the possibility of detecting failure by comparison with peers, and in the 19th century both separate special education classes in the school system (in Halle, Germany, in 1859) and the measurement of intelligence through peer group comparisons were developed in Europe.

Special education in segregated residential schools began in the 17th century in France with separate institutions and pedagogical methods for "wayward girls" and "problem boys," and in the late 18th century with special residential schools for deaf children and blind children. Special education was decidedly a product of the Enlightenment and carries with it much of the positivistic thought of the modern age of science, progress, and exploration. Francis Bacon's ideas on the domination of nature through the new scientific method were a precursor to Jean Itard's experiments with the wild boy of Aveyron. John Locke's sensationalist theory of the primacy of experience in learning, promoted in France by the Abbé Condillac, provided the philosophical foundations of the new methods of teaching blind, deaf, and mentally retarded children. Rousseau's call for a return to nature led directly to the methods of "object teaching" found in the pedagogies developed by Pestalozzi, Froebel, Itard, Edouard Seguin, and Maria Montessori.

The French *philosophes*—such as Diderot, Voltaire, Rousseau, Condillac, and La Mettrie—questioned the legal, moral, and religious foundations of the French state while at the same time believing in the idea of progress through science and reason. The ideas of progress, perfectibility of humans, individual freedom, the efficacy of empiricism, the importance of direct experience and concrete activity to learning, and many aspects of modern Western culture were Enlightenment ideas on which the new methods of educating disabled children were founded (Winzer, 1986).

The first institutions for blind children and deaf children in France were residential settings, run by members of religious orders. Blind and deaf persons were viewed as similar to those deemed to be "insane" or "idiots," in that it was thought that they could not make use of their powers of reasoning. They were seen as separate from ordinary people, therefore living and needing to live apart (Capul, 1983). They, too, were part of what Foucault (1965) has termed the "Great Confinement."

The *Institution Nationale des Sourds-Muets* in Paris was founded in 1760 by Charles Michel, l'Abbé de l'Epée. This school not only served deaf children but was also intended for children of the poor. De l'Epée promoted the manual system of communication for the deaf, while in Germany, Samuel Heinike advocated the oral method. Those who promoted the manual system (signing) believed that deaf people needed their own language. This debate, which continues today, was particularly strong in the 19th century. The major argument for the oral method was that deaf children and hearing children could be taught together, thus promoting the integration of deaf children into society. The first school for the deaf in Great Britain was started by Thomas Braidwood in Edinburgh in the early 1760s. Mr. Braidwood's Academy for the Deaf and Dumb, as it was called, took a handful of selected paying pupils to be taught to speak and read.

Valentin Haüy was the first to claim that blind persons could be educated, and the first to adopt embossed print for teaching blind children how to read. To prove his contention, he opened the *Institution Nationale des Jeunes Aveugles* in Paris in 1784. Though the school was closed for a brief time by the National Assembly, it reopened a few years later, enrolling Louis Braille, its most famous student and, later, teacher.

The development of special education for mentally handicapped children took place after a shift in the philosophy of the 17th century resulted in a new view of human learning. Locke in England and Condillac in France both proposed that learning takes place through the senses, and because of this, a stimulating environment was necessary for learning. This sensorial philosophy was a sharp break from the idealism of the day, and resulted in a new environmentalism which became the philosophical basis for special education. The Enlightenment also brought a belief in the idea of "progress," and fostered a new optimism which motivated the first efforts at trying to devise pedagogical methods for groups previously uneducated.

Special education for children who were cognitively different began in France with the work of Itard and "Victor," the wild boy of Aveyron. Itard, who worked at the Deaf and Dumb Institute in Paris, first saw Victor in 1799. He and Madame Guérin tried to teach Victor to speak and to read. They were only partly successful, but their methods, along with those evolved by Seguin, Itard's successor, started a tradition that drew attention to the importance of sense-training and stimulation in the development of the child's cognitive abilities.

Seguin's fame spread throughout Europe and North America. Influenced by his methods, the first school for "idiots" in England opened in 1846, followed by the first such school in the United States in 1848. In 1848, Seguin emigrated to the United States, where he helped set up educational programs for mentally retarded children in the newly formed "training schools."

The optimism of the 1840s and 1850s gradually turned to pessimism in the late 19th century. After 1870, a new system of institutional life emerged. The work of Itard, Seguin, and Montessori was eclipsed by hereditarian Darwinism and the belief in the immutability of intelligence, which characterized American psychology of the early 20th century. Consequently, Seguin's enlightened educational approach was replaced by the eugenics movement of the 1920s and in some countries the resulting institutionalization and forced sterilization of many of the mentally handicapped.

The development of special classes in the school system took place in both Europe and North America during the last half of the 19th century and the first decades of the 20th century, the same period that saw the growth of large residential institutions for disabled children and adults. In some cases, special education classes were seen as alternatives to the regular classroom. But early special education classes were also used as a kind of recruiting station, in which children were observed to judge their suitability for institutional placement or placement back into the regular classroom.

From the beginning of the 20th century to the 1960s, special education grew into a large-scale enterprise and became a significant part of the school system. After World War II, parental groups in the United States and Canada began to organize into "associations for retarded children"; parental groups for other disability categories were also formed. These associations were both lobby groups and service providers to children who were either excluded from the school system because they were judged to be "uneducable" (usually defined as having an intelligence quotient below 50) or because they were too young. At the same time, studies of early stimulation of both animals and young children indicated that early intervention in the lives of young children could make an immense difference in their developmental potential. The "normalization" movement, which originated in Scandinavia in the late 1960s, resulted in both the "deinstitutionalization" of many mentally and physically disabled individuals and the instituting of many "early intervention" programs for "children with special needs."

Child Study Movement

Perhaps the other most significant development in the history of early childhood education has been the growth of developmental psychology. Although books were published on child psychology in the 19th century in Europe, they were mainly based on the observation of a single child. The systematic empirical study of children began in 1880 in the United States with G. Stanley Hall's inquiries into the thoughts of the young child. In 1881, Hall published *The Contents of Children's Minds on Entering School*, which was reprinted in 1891 in the first journal of child psychology, *Pedagogical Seminary*. Around 1895, Dewey began

to develop his "functional psychology," with its accent on the practical character of human intelligence. Dewey's work was published in French in 1913 as *L'École et L'Enfant*, and the introduction to this book was written by the Swiss child psychologist Edouard Claparède, the editor of the *Archives de Psychologie*.

There were other important milestones in the development of child psychology at the turn of the 20th century. In 1902, Frederic Queyrat published *The Logic of the Child and Its Culture*, and in 1905 Sigmund Freud wrote *Three Essays on Sexuality*. In 1905, as well, Alfred Binet and Simon published their first results on the testing of children's intelligence, and Claparède's *The Psychology of the Child* also appeared in print. The years 1907 and 1909 saw publications on children in Germany by Clara and William Stern, and in 1912 Ovid Decroly and Mlle. J. Degand's "Observations relatives à l'évolution des notions de quantitiés continues et discontinues chez l'enfant" was printed in the *Archives de Psychologie*. The year 1912 also witnessed the creation in Geneva of the J.J. Rousseau Institute by Claparède and Pierre Bovet, which, after 1925, was where Piaget developed his theories on childhood.

Summary

The principal institutional forms of early childhood education in the world today, and its dominant discourse, originated in Europe between the 16th and 19th centuries. These innovations in child care and education first circulated among and were modified by various social reformers in Western Europe, and from there were spread throughout the world by missionaries, immigrants, and colonizers; now these European forms appear to be almost universal. The introduction of these ideas into various societies resulted in different local histories of early childhood education and different present-day practices reflecting local modifications of the original models. How European models of early childhood education arrived and was changed in many countries, as well as descriptions of indigenous forms of child care and education in non-Western countries, is the subject of the rest of this volume.

References

Anderson, K. (1991). *Chain her by one foot: The subjugation of women in seventeenth-century New France.* London: Routledge.

Aries, P. (1962). *Centuries of childhood: A social history of family life.* New York: Knopf.

Boswell, J. (1988). *The kindness of strangers: The abandonment of children in Western Europe from Late Antiquity to the Renaissance.* New York: Pantheon.

Braun, S. & Edwards, E. (1972). *History and theory of early childhood education.* Worthington, OH: Charles A. Jones.

Capul, M. (1983). *Internat et internement sous l'ancien régime.* 4 vols. Paris: Centre Technique National des Etudes et des Recherches sur les Handicaps et les Inadaptations.

Dally, A. (1982). *Inventing motherhood: The consequences of an ideal.* London: Burnett.

Deasy, D. (1978). *Education under six.* London: Croom-Helm.

Deller (Pollard), J. (1988). *Family day care internationally: A literature review.* Toronto: Queen's Printer.

de Mause, L. (1974). *The history of childhood.* New York: The Psychohistory Press.

Dixon, S. (1988). *The roman mother.* London: Croom-Helm.

Doll, E. (1962). A historical survey of research and management of mental retardation in the United States. In E. Trapp & P. Himelstein (Eds.), *Readings on the exceptional child.* New York: Appleton Century Crofts.

Donzelot, J. (1979). *The policing of families.* London: Hutchinson.

Fein, G. & Clarke-Stewart, A. (1973). *Day care in context.* New York: John Wiley.

Foucault, M. (1965). *Madness and civilization.* New York: Vintage.

Gibson, W. (1989). *Women in seventeenth-century France.* London: Macmillan.

Greven, P. (1991). *Spare the child: The religious roots of punishment and the psychological impact of physical abuse.* New York: Knopf.

Hunt, D. (1970). *Parents and children in history: The psychology of family life in early modern France.* New York: Basic Books.

Izzard, W. (1985). Migrants and mothers: Case-studies from Botswana. *Journal of South African Studies, 11*(2): 258–80.

Kaestle, C. (1973). *Joseph Lancaster and the monitorial school movement: A documentary history.* New York: Teachers College Press.

Kurtz, J. (1976). *John Frederic Oberlin.* Boulder, CO: Westview Press.

Le Pas, A. (1852). *Des salles d'asile en Russie.* Paris: Guillaumin.

Mead, G.H. (1963). *Mind, self and society.* Chicago: University of Chicago Press.

Melton, J. (1988). *Absolution and the eighteenth-century origins of compulsory schooling in Prussia and Austria.* Cambridge, England: Cambridge University Press.

Miller, A. (1983). *For your own good: Hidden cruelty in child-rearing and the roots of violence.* New York: Farrar, Straus and Giroux.

Moore, H. (1988). *Feminism and Anthropology.* Minneapolis: University of Minnesota Press.

Omwake, E. (1971). Preschool programs in historical perspective, *Interchange, 2*(2): 27–40.

Osborn, D.K. (1980). *Early childhood education in historical perspective.* Athens, GA: Education Associates.

Pence, A. (1990). The child-care profession in Canada. In I. Doxey (Ed.), *Child care and education: Canadian dimensions* (pp. 87–97). Toronto: Nelson.

Pollock, L. (1984). *Forgotten children: Parent-child relations from 1500 to 1900.* Cambridge: Cambridge University Press.

Postman, N. (1982). *The disappearance of childhood.* New York: Dell Publishing.

Ross, E. (1976). *The kindergarten crusade: The establishment of preschool education in the United States.* Athens, OH: Ohio University Press.

Rusk, R. (1933). *A history of infant education.* London: University of London Press.

Schulz, P. (1978). Day care in Canada: 1850–1962. In K.G. Ross (Ed.), *Good day care.* Toronto: Women's Press.

Shapiro, M. (1983). *Child's garden: The kindergarten movement from Froebel to Dewey.* University Park, PA: Pennsylvania State University Press.

Steinfels, M. (1973). *Who's minding the children: The history and politics of day care in America.* New York: Simon & Schuster.

Stone, L. (1979). *The family, sex, and marriage in England 1500–1800.* Harmonsworth, England: Penguin.

Sylvester, D. (1970). *Educational documents, 800–1816.* London: Methuen.

Tizard, J., Moss, P., & Perry, J. (1976). *All our children: Preschool services in a changing society.* London: Temple Smith.

Whitbread, N. (1972). *The evolution of the nursery-infant school: A history of infant and nursery education in Britain, 1800–1970.* London: Routledge & Kegan Paul.

Winzer, M. (1986). Early developments in special education: Some aspects of Enlightenment thought. *Remedial and Special Education, 7*(5): 42–49.

THEMES IN LATE 20TH-CENTURY CHILD CARE AND EARLY EDUCATION: A CROSS-NATIONAL ANALYSIS

• • • • • • • • • • ◆ • • • • • • • •

Lawrence Prochner
Ryerson Polytechnic Institute
Toronto, Canada

A cross-national analysis of early education reveals similarities both in terms of its history and the current provision of service. But there are also fundamental differences that bring into question many of the assumptions of Western early education. For example, in the following chapters, and consistent with contemporary thinking in Western early education, early childhood is considered to include the years of primary schooling. However, in a cross-national discourse this is problematic. If childhood is a social invention, as historians (Aries, 1962), sociologists (Damon, 1977) and anthropologists (Goodman, 1970) suggest, a universal definition of early childhood is impossible. Moreover, the divisions within the period of childhood, carefully mapped out by two generations of psychologists, are not universal. Elisabeth Singer (in this volume), for example, describes the relatively recent invention of the toddler in the Netherlands. While all of the nations represented in this volume have some mix of educational and caretaking services for young children, the philosophies and pedagogies are so varied that it is evident there is no common understanding of the meaning of childhood.

Although describing the status of early childhood education in the United States, Spodek's (1989) comments are relevant to the international situation:

The field of early childhood education reflects a number of contradictions. While it has developed as an international movement, in fact, programs of early childhood education are nation and culture-specific. While it builds on a view of the natural development of children, and programs are supposed to reflect and respond to the nature of children and childhood; in fact, it consists of contrived learning settings and invented educational methods, materials and activities that are far from natural. While the field continually articulates the importance of parents in the education of young children, in fact it generally excludes parents by mystifying practice and limiting practice to those with professional credentials. . . . The most basic contradiction might be, that while early childhood education represents a single unified field, in fact, the practice of early childhood education is set in diverse programs and services for young children—programs that might have very different goals and even different primary clients (p. 1).

Despite these contradictions, "comparative ECE" has tended to gloss over difference in favor of an optimistic belief in shared meaning and understanding.[1] In addition, the heroic view of early education serves to ignore its failures. Lall and Lall

(1983), for example, undertook a comparative analysis "to learn the strengths of each program and not to ponder on their weakness" (p. ix). The result of what Featherstone (1989) calls "playing Marco Polo," or bringing only the best back home, may create a "prophetic fiction" (p. 339) of the state of early education in a particular country. To avoid this pitfall, Phillips (1989) recommends that comparativists begin "to take into account the historical, political and cultural settings of particular systems and aspects of them . . . . Outcomes themselves should not be seen in isolation from the processes that have created them" (p. 269).

There have been several recent attempts to develop a conceptual framework for comparative analysis of early education, in which difference is used as a way of knowing, without distorting the comparative data. In the tradition of cross-cultural psychology,[2] Katz (1989) promotes cross-national analysis as a way of studying the "processes of development" (p. 403). In particular, it can call into question assumptions concerning "normal" development and point to alternative educational methods and practices.

Adopting a more ecological approach, Tobin, Wu, and Davidson's (1990) study of preschools in Japan, China, and the United States emphasizes the relationship between the form and content of preschools, societal ideas about the nature of children and families, and political and moral ideologies (p. 2). Such an approach to understanding cross-national early childhood education can be contrasted with the earlier work of Robinson, et al. (1980) to develop a taxonomy of national child care systems.

Robinson and her colleagues proposed a system of "four national models" characterized by social policies: Latin-European, Scandinavian, Socialist, and Anglo-Saxon. However, in many of the countries represented in this volume there are two or more competing models at work. In particular, a four-model system based on a Western educational tradition does not describe the evolution of postcolonial systems of early education, in which the legacy of colonial schools competes with educational reforms[3] to create a tension yet to be resolved.

Moss and Melhish (1991), also using an ecological orientation, use cross-national analysis as a way of studying the relationships among social policy, social context, and day care, and the resulting impact on children's development.[4] The cross-national approach in this case is intended mainly to highlight the role of social context in the construction of family policy. Social influences, they reason, are often taken for granted by researchers working in their own country (p. 7). Social context becomes more visible when viewed from the outside.

Finally, cross-national analysis should consider the role of children in creating their own meaning within caretaking contexts. Werner (1988), using the language of psychology, emphasizes that "infants do *not* [original emphasis] react passively to the effects of reproductive stress, deprivation, and a disordered caretaking environment. They make an active ongoing attempt to organize their world adaptively" (p. 109).

The following brief analysis of themes in international early education assumes that early education is complex, informed by multiple interpretations of methods and goals, and rooted in the lives of families and the broader interests of societies.

Ideology and Early Education

Formal early childhood education has the potential to be a radical intervention in the lives of children and their families. As Gary Woodill describes in his historical review in this volume, child and parental education cannot be separated from issues of power and control. The "mystifying" enterprise of scientific child rearing—which, as Spodek claimed, results in alienating parents from the process of early education[5]—is embedded in the ideological interests of power groups. The politics of early education—interwoven with issues of race, class, and gender—are the sum of the ideological influences that direct its provision and practice. For example, in all cultures mothers are the principal caregivers of children. That this is seen as normative is often reflected in family policy (Eichler, 1988). In the Netherlands, despite recent increases in the number of women in the labor force, governmental funds remain directed to programs that support mothers who care for their children at home. In Albania, however, where the aim of early education is to ensure women's participation in social production, children are exposed to the rigors of scientific child rearing in state preschools. Many families, however, particularly in rural Albania, resist the invitation to enroll their children. In both cases, the exigencies of government and the culture of patriarchy combine to direct family policy.

Despite attempts to redefine policy and power structures so as to make child care a normative service (Kammerman, 1985), in many countries there are few services for children from birth to age 2 or 3; and if programs exist, their use is limited. The common view continues to be that mother care is normal care (Scarr, 1987) and that young children particularly are best cared for at home.

The politics of early education are also evident in the provision or nonprovision of educational programs. Commenting on postcolonial educational policies in Africa, Chazan and her colleagues (1988) suggest that primary education has a dual purpose.

> Throughout the continent, considerable emphasis has been placed on primary education as a means of providing basic literacy to the mass of the population. This emphasis has obvious relevance to economic development and the government's ability, in the term used by modernization theorists, to "penetrate" society—that is, to ensure that the policies decided at the center reach those at the periphery of the society. (pp. 230–31)

Literacy as a means of "penetration" has an ideological use that goes beyond the development of the individual or the reduction of class or gender disparities. Moreover, despite claims in many developing countries that primary schooling is the foundation of the educational system, higher levels have fairly consistently received a disproportionate amount of the educational budget (Coombs, 1985: 72). It seems that the long-term benefits of primary education are weighed against immediate needs, that is, "to fill technical and scientific positions in the economy" (La Belle and Ward, 1990: 105).

The quality of the service is also a function of the politics of early education. As reported in this volume by Rohaty Mohd Majzub, in Malaysia a low-quality system of state preschools was developed to serve the largely rural Bumiputera (Malay) population. Chinese and Indian children, living mostly in urban areas, attend higher quality private preschools. But according to Simmons (1984), genuine reforms "must reduce inequality in educa-

tional results, not just opportunity" (p. 9). The result of the educational reform in this case is to continue racial polarization. Maintaining the racial status quo may also be the result of the early childhood educational system in South Africa, in that the training of early childhood educators, even when they are black, reflects the values of the white dominant minority, and not the black majority (Dladla, 1990).

Ideology also impacts on educational practice. Spodek (1980) comments that the field of early childhood education is united by, if nothing else, a "common belief system" (p. 11). At the level of international early childhood education one common belief is evident: young children are sufficiently malleable so as to make intervention worthwhile. Since the early 1960s and the research of Bloom (1964), Hunt (1961), and others demonstrating the importance of environmental factors on child development, scientific "child-saving" has been a major preoccupation of early education. While the type and extent of change that is possible and by what means are still debated for both developed (Kagan and Zigler, 1987) and developing nations (Halpern and Myers, 1985), that there is at least the potential for change is part of the belief system of early childhood education.

This belief has been both the promise and the burden of early childhood education. Although early intervention programs are part of many nations' plans for social and political reform, in many instances insufficient funding and an inadequate vision result in a system of understaffed, ill-equipped, and poorly housed programs. As was the case in Malaysia, instead of social reform, the result is often a substandard public system of early education that serves the needs of a few poor children and their families, and a separate usually higher quality private service for the middle and upper classes. Lucia Vilarinho (in this volume), commenting on Brazil's experience, labels this a symptom of the tendency to valorize early childhood education, while at the same time ignoring systemic causes of economic and social disparities. As Vilarinho and others (Ennew and Milne, 1990) write, families in Brazil will not be helped by isolated emergency-based child welfare programs.

Another common belief in international early education—in this case grounded in an ideology of normal child development—is the educational value of children's play[6]; in China, play is increasingly viewed as an important aspect of early education; in India, the "playway" method is officially endorsed; in Malta, the aim of the state preschools is to develop "social attitudes" through play; Swaziland's official preschool curriculum advocates learning through play; in Finland, play is the recommended activity.

Learning through play or discovery contrasts with the mastery method in which importance is placed on the learning of subjects. The shift from play to mastery may occur at the break from creche to preschool, as in France's *école maternelles*, or more often, at the start of the first level of the primary school system. Despite a push toward "back to the basics" curriculum by some educators, in North America and some European countries play continues to have a role in the primary curriculum. The method is also employed in the primary systems of New Zealand, Australia, and white South Africa.

However, insufficient numbers of teachers—in Swaziland a ratio of 60:1 at the primary level is not unusual—or a lack of appropriate "play" materials makes discovery learning impractical in many countries. Moreover, it may not be the method of choice. In developing nations, where many pupils drop out during or after the primary level, it may be necessary to provide fundamental skills in what is viewed to be the most time-efficient manner, that is, through direct instruction. Providing pupils with an "education for life" grounded in the "basics" has been part of many nations' development plans since the 1970s (Coombs, 1985: 26). In addition, pupils of widely different ages may be enrolled in the same grade level due to lateness in commencing school, repeating grades, or, in the case of children younger than grade level, the school assuming a child care function. The multi-aged large group, inconsistent attendance, and insufficient teacher training may make discovery learning difficult.

There is also variation in cultural views of the role of play in children's lives and in learning (Rogoff, 1990). The focus on children's play is a preoccupation in Western early education that may not be shared by other cultures, or in many cases, by Western parents. As a result, many parental educational programs have attempted to teach parents the value of children's play.[7] Examples of cultural differences in interpreting the meaning of play are found in the chapters that follow. In her description of the playgroup movement in the Netherlands, Elisabeth Singer notes the reluctance of Turkish and Moroccan minorities to attend the programs, which advocate a child-centered philosophy. Similarly, Anne Smith of New Zealand writes that in some "kohanga reo" (Maori-operated preschools) free play is "explicitly rejected." In Taiwan, the discovery method, introduced in a missionary spirit by the wife of a visiting scholar, was experimented with in several kindergartens in the early 1970s. However, as Hui-Ling Wendy Pan comments, it clashed with the structure and tradition of Taiwan's early education and subsequently had a "limited lifespan."

Finally, the degree to which play in an educational institution is free is rarely questioned. The widespread use of the phrase "free play" may blur the role of the teacher in managing children's experiences so that they learn to respond to what Marc Depaepe and Ferre Laevers of Belgium refer to as "internal commandments." In addition, that free play is a term used in many countries to describe what occurs during a large portion of the preschool day implies a shared understanding that may or may not exist. As Katz (1977) has noted, the void resulting from the lack of research in early education has been largely filled by ideologies of practice that preclude research. There is a need to develop critical perspectives on play (see, e.g., Michelet, 1986; Walkerdine, 1984). The slogans of early childhood education—especially when used in an international context—may have outlived whatever purpose they originally possessed.

Coming to Terms With Early Childhood Education and Care

For a variety of reasons—historical, political, ideological, and idiosyncratic—the terminology used to describe social and educational programs for young children is diverse. In Western nations, the generic term "early childhood education" is generally used to describe services for both the care and education of children from birth to age 8. A number of factors contributed to the creation of a single system of what has been termed "educare"

(Caldwell, 1989): the expansion of child care to include infants; the overlapping history of kindergartens, day nurseries, and nursery schools[8]; the professionalization of nursery education; and the rise of the idea of infant competence.[9] Nevertheless, in practice, child care in many instances is primarily custodial.

Internationally, child care in a group setting may be offered in a creche, day nursery, nursery, nursery school, school, kindergarten, day care, or child care center. Some of these terms are grounded in the history of the service. For example, since the 19th century, public kindergartens in Finland served a child care function and have assumed the name day care only in the last two decades. Others, however, describe a philosophy, for example, of the dual focus on care and education, as in the educare system in New Zealand, preschools in China, nursery centers in Great Britain, and creche-kindergartens in the Soviet Union. There are also unique services developed to meet a specific need, for example harvest creches in Russia and Taiwan, market creches in Liberia, and mobile creches for children of construction workers in India.

Not all child care takes place in group settings. As noted earlier, most young children around the world are cared for by their mothers in the home, or by older female siblings or relatives. An organized family-based system of child care, together with a more widely used informal system, exists in many countries as a cheaper, more readily available, noninstitutional alternative to group care (Deller, 1988). The caregivers are variously called "day mothers" (Australia and Austria), "child minders" (Great Britain), or "family day care providers" (Canada and the United States). In North America, providers of unsupervised child care are popularly called "babysitters" or "sitters."

There are also variations of organized family day care, primarily relating to the number of families served by a single provider and the location of care. In Finland, "three family care" is available in which a single caregiver provides a service for up to three families as a group, with the children and caregiver rotating among the family homes. Several caregivers providing care in a single location for the collective group of children is called "group care."

The service of a private nanny or nursery nurse has always been an option for wealthy families. Both professionally trained nannies and, as is more often the case, untrained nannies are reported to be an increasingly popular option for parents in Great Britain and New Zealand. Audrey Curtis (in this volume) notes that nannies provide more care than public day nurseries in Britain.

Programs with an explicit educative agenda are more uniformly called kindergartens, nursery schools, or preschools. In contrast with child care, which is almost never compulsory, a very few countries have implemented a system of universal and compulsory preschool.[10] However, in nations ranging from Hong Kong to France, Malta, and Canada,[11] enrollment in some kind of preschool—public or private—for at least one year is almost universal while not compulsory. The starting age for preschool is generally age 4 or 5 but can be as young as age 3, as in France and Hong Kong.

In many developing nations, there is a more distinct separation of child care and child education. Early childhood services are more likely to be aimed at improving the general welfare of the child and mother, while preschools or kindergartens are aimed at giving children an academic headstart. For this and other reasons, private preschools often focus on the learning of subjects in a formal manner.

Primary education—the entry of the child into the formal school system—begins at age 5 in some countries (e.g., Antigua, Cyprus, Great Britain, Malta) and age 6 or 7 in most others.[12] Although primary education is generally compulsory,[13] in many instances it is not yet universal. In particular, children in rural areas, poor children, girls (Bowman and Anderson, 1982; Smock, 1981), and disabled children are less likely to attend school.

Future Directions in International Early Education

Of the many issues concerning the future of early education raised in the following chapters, two are particularly important in the development of international early education, the education of minority group children, and the role of parents in early education.

The Education of Minority Group Children

The education of children who are different raises pivotal questions regarding the relevance and purpose of early education. In North America, early education has historically served an assimilative function for immigrant children and their families. Colonial schools in Africa, India, South America, and elsewhere also expressly promoted the interests of a dominant group, in this case, the colonizer. In both instances, little attention was given to the needs of the individual learner. "Needs" in this sense does not mean those defined by an ideology of "developmentally appropriate practice" currently popular in North America, but rather those needs met by an emancipatory educational experience.

Although currently, in early childhood education as in education in general, the trend is to acknowledge and support difference, it is not a universal goal. Moreover, the debate over what constitutes an equal education—whether for the children of "guest workers" in Germany, handicapped children in Canada, or children in one of the many refugee camps around the globe—is far from resolved. The "politics of difference" makes easy answers an unlikely possibility.[14]

The debate over the formal education of children who require something other than a "typical" program because of physical, intellectual, or often behavioral factors largely takes place within a discourse of what constitutes an equal and meaningful education. Many countries, using a philosophy of "integration," serve special needs children in regular classrooms or at least in the proximity of regular classrooms. Integration may be a relatively new phenomenon, as in Austria, or have a ten- to 15-year history, as in some parts of the United States and Canada. Other nations, and they represent the majority of those surveyed, continue to offer programs for such children in separate facilities. Most of the world's disabled children, however, have limited educational opportunities of any kind. As Venita Kaul of India (in this volume) writes, the lack of "fit" between disabled children and the regular school system results in a general pattern of leaving school early.

The education of racially or culturally different children also presents a dilemma in many countries. The politics of difference in this instance is complicated by issues of class, historical patterns of domination, and the process of nation building. In the national curricula of many countries, education for good citizenship precludes the study of minority languages or culture. In other countries, implementing a policy of multicultural education is complicated because it gives official acknowledgement to the permanence of residence of a particular cultural group.

Parental Role in Early Education

Attempts to implement multicultural education and to involve parents in the formal education and care of young children represent a departure for a field characterized by professional intervention in the lives of families. One of the most common roles for parents in early education has been as learners. Subsequently, parental or family educational programs are included within the rubric of early childhood education in many parts of the world. Whereas a progressive view of parental education sees parents as partners in the task of child rearing, the history of parental education is largely that of giving expert advice to mothers (Ehrenreich and English, 1979; Hardyment, 1984). In this tradition, parents are seen as part of the problem. Thus, while there is often a rhetorical calling for the need to involve parents in early education, as Spodek (1989) noted, the push for professional practice shuts parents out.

As one symptom of this problem, Evans (1985) points to the lack of programs to meet the "intersecting needs" of women and children in developing countries. She recommends that child care services evolve out of existing women's programs and not the other way around. In this way, mothers have a place at the core of the program and not on the periphery, thus redefining parental education as parental involvement. This will require a "demystifying" of early education and a shift in power from the professional to the parent.

Playgroup movements in Australia, Great Britain, the Netherlands, and New Zealand, among other countries, and the related parent-cooperative nursery schools, emerged partly as a result of middle-class parents wanting to take charge of their own programs. In many instances, playgroups have received state funding and have been subject to some level of professionalization. A debate is currently taking place in New Zealand over state involvement in the large playgroup movement and the perceived loss in autonomy that would result.

The question of community involvement in early childhood programs is an extension of the issue of the role of parents. The least successful programs, as noted by Ruth Monau in her profile of Botswana, are those that do not consider community and parental needs. In contrast, "grassroots," "emergent," or "participatory" programs are known to have an increased chance of survival (Simmons,

1984). A report from the Bernard Van Leer Foundation (1990) observes that in its experience, "Where communities have themselves begun to develop even the most elementary child care or pre-school systems, the barrier between school and community is broken down, the transition of children into primary school is eased and children do better when they get there" (p. 6). Although not always immediately successful,[15] programs rooted in the interrelated needs of communities, families, and children may ensure the future relevance of formal early childhood education and care.

Notes

1. See, e.g., Lall and Lall (1983), who view comparative early education as providing a "platform" for discovering "unity through diversity" (p. ix). That children are the "common denominator" (p. x) overshadows difference. Assumptions regarding the universality of children's experience is rooted in the history of early childhood education as mission work. For example, Froebel's gospel of the unity of humankind was spread throughout the world in the late 19th century. Hewes (1980) notes that by the 1880s "missionaries" had introduced Froebelian education to the Sandwich Isles, Japan, Africa, and Palestine (p. 346). The dominance of developmental psychology and stage theories as sources of knowledge in early childhood education may also contribute to the tendency to underestimate the importance of difference.

2. See Werner (1988) and Jahodd and Lewis (1988) for a discussion of the role of cross-cultural studies of child development.

3. See Chazan, et al. (1988: 229–35) for an analysis of postcolonial primary education in Africa.

4. Moss and Melhuish (1991) draw on Bronfenbrenner (1979) for the concept of the "social context" of child care.

5. In their history of experts' advice to women, Ehrenreich and English (1979) describe how motherhood came to be seen as pathological. Child rescue was then directed inward to the home, in which children were saved from mother-inflicted psychological damage by expert advice or the experts themselves.

6. See Cottle (1973) for an expression of the idea of the universal value of "self-discovery through play."

7. Hardyment (1984) describes the cult of children's play and its class and culture bias as shown in child-rearing manuals (pp. 273–77). She argues that the focus on play is a middle-class preoccupation that relies on a psychological and physical environment in which play is permitted.

8. In the 19th century, dame schools, infant schools and later kindergartens functioned to varying degrees as child care settings.

9. See Elkind (1987b: 103) for a discussion of the origins of the idea of "infant competence."

10. Four-year-old kindergarten, for example, is compulsory in New York City in the United States. In other countries, Austria, for example, a preschool year is compulsory in some parts.

11. Kindergarten attendance and provision varies from province to province. See Biemiller, Regan & Lero (Canada) in this volume.

12. In Mali, not represented in the present survey, children begin compulsory education at age 8 (UNESCO, 1989).

13. Among the countries surveyed in this volume, primary education is not compulsory in Bahrain, Botswana, Kenya, Oman, and Saudi Arabia (UNESCO, 1989).

14. See Giroux (1984) for a critique of radical educational theory.

15. See, e.g., Smith's discussion of the Maori kohanga reo in New Zealand in this volume.

References

Aries, P. (1962). *Centuries of childhood: A social history of family life* (Trans. R. Bladick). New York: Vintage.

Benjamin Leer Foundation. (1990). *The challenge of early childhood care and education: An agenda for action*. The Hague, Netherlands. ERIC Document ED 319 522.

Bernardo, M.F. (1990). Literacy and cultural identity. *Harvard Educational Review*. 60(2), 181–204.

Bloom, B.S. (1964). *Stability and change in human characteristics*. New York: Wiley.

Bogaslawski, D.B. (1973). Day care . . . an old idea a new meaning. In UNICEF, *The neglected years* (pp. 77–84). New York: United Nations Children's Foundation.

Bowman, M.J., & Anderson, C.A. (1982). The participation of women in education in the Third World. In G.P. Kelly & C.M. Elliot (Eds.), *Women's education in the Third World: Comparative perspectives* (pp. 11–30). Albany, NY: State University of New York Press.

Bronfenbrenner, U. (1979). *The ecology of human development: Experiences by nature and design*. Cambridge, MA: Harvard University Press.

Experiences by nature and design. Cambridge, MA: Harvard University Press.

Caldwell, B. (1989). A comprehensive model for integrating child care and education. *Teachers College Record, 90,* 404–14.

Chazan, N., Mortimer, R., Ravenhill, J., & Rothchild, D. (1988). *Politics and society in contemporary Africa.* Boulder, CO: Lynne Rienner.

Coombs, P.H. (1985). *The world crisis in education: The view from the eighties.* New York: Oxford University Press.

Costin, L.B. (Ed.). (1985). *Toward a feminist approach to child welfare. Child Welfare* (Special Issue), *64*(3).

Cott, N.F. (1987). *The grounding of modern feminism.* New Haven, CT: Yale University Press.

Cottle, T.J. (1973). Self-discovery through play. In UNICEF, *The neglected years* (pp. 85–94). New York: United Nations Children's Foundation.

Damon, W. (1977). *The social world of the child.* San Francisco: Jossey-Bass.

David, M.E. (1984). Parents, children, and the state. In G. P. Kelly (Ed.), *Excellence, reform, and equity in education: An international perspective* (pp. 103–35). Buffalo, NY: Comparative Education Center, State University of New York at Buffalo & Ontario Institute for Studies in Education, Toronto, Ontario.

Deller (Pollard), J. (1988). *Family day care internationally: A literature review.* Toronto: Ministry of Community and Social Services, Child Care Branch.

Dladla, Y. (1990). Rediscovering the meaning of child care. *Harvard Educational Review, 60*(1), 98–100.

Ehrenreich, B., & English, D. (1979). *For her own good: 150 years of the experts' advice to women.* New York: Doubleday.

Eichler, M. (1988). Family change and social policies. In K. Anderson, *et al., Family matters* (pp. 63–85). Toronto: Methuen.

Elkind, D. (1987). *The miseducation of children: Superkids at risk.* New York: Alfred A. Knopf.

Elkind, D. (1987b). Early childhood education on its own terms. In E. Zigler and S. Kagan (eds.), *Early schooling: The national debate.* New Haven: Yale University Press.

Ennew, J., & Milne, B. (1990). *The next generation: Lives of third world children.* Philadelphia: New Society.

Evans, J. (1985). Improving program actions to meet the intersecting needs of women and children in developing countries: A programme and policy review. In R. Myers (ed.), *Women's work and child care in the third world: A discussion* (Summary report of a meeting held Nov. 12, 1985, organized jointly by the International Centre for Research on Women and The Consultative Group on Early Childhood Care and Development). ERIC Document ED 271 199.

Featherstone, J. (1989). Playing Marco Polo: A response to Harry Judge. *Comparative Education, 25*(3), 339–45.

Gallagher, J.J. (Ed.). (1987). *The malleability of children.* New York: Brooke.

Giroux, H. (1984). Public education and the discourse of crisis, power, and vision. In G. P. Kelly (Ed.), *Excellence, reform, and equity in education: An international perspective* (pp. 135–74). Buffalo, NY: Comparative Education Center, State University of New York at Buffalo & Ontario Institute

for Studies in Education, Toronto, Ontario.

Goodman, M.E. (1970). *Culture of childhood: Child's eye views of society and culture.* New York: Teachers College Press.

Hardyment, C. (1984). *Dream babies: Child care from Locke to Spock.* Oxford: Oxford University Press.

Halpern, R., & Myers, R. (1985). *Effects of early education on primary school programs and performance in the developing countries.* Educational Resources Information Center in the USA Document ED 279 392.

Hazzard, V. (1987). *UNICEF and women, the long voyage: A historical perspective.* UNICEF Historical Series, Monograph VII. New York: United Nations Children's Foundation.

Hewes, D. (1980). The Froebelian kindergarten as an international movement. In N. Nir-Janiv, B. Spodek, & D. Steg (Eds.), *Early childhood education: An international perspective* (pp. 345–50). New York: Plenum.

Hunt, J. M. (1961). *Intelligence and experience.* New York: Ronald Press.

Jahodd, G., & Lewis, I.M. (Eds.) (1988). *Acquiring culture: Cross-cultural studies in child development.* London: Croom-Helm.

Kagan, S.L., & Zigler, E.F. (1987). *Early schooling: The national debate.* New Haven, CT: Yale University Press.

Kammerman, S. (1985). Child care services: An issue for gender equity and women's solidarity. *Child Welfare, 64*(3), 259–71.

Katz, L. G. (1989). An afterword: Young children in cross-national perspective. In P.P. Olmsted & D.P. Weikart (Eds.), *How nations serve young children: Profiles of child care and education in 14 countries* (pp. 401–06). Ypsilanti, MI: The High Scope Press.

———. (1977). Early childhood programs and ideological disputes. In L. Katz (Ed.), *Talks with teachers.* Washington, D.C.: National Association for the Education of Young Children.

La Belle, T.J., & Ward, C.R. (1990). Education reform when nations undergo radical political and social transformation. *Comparative Education, 26*(1), 95–106.

Lall, G.R., & Lall, B.M. (1983). *Comparative early childhood education.* Springfield, IL: Charles C. Thomas.

Michelet, A. (1986). Teachers and play. *Prospects, 16*(1), 114–22.

Moss, P., & Melhuish, E.C. (1991). *Day care for young children: International perspectives.* London: Routledge.

Phillips, D. (1989). Neither a borrower nor a lender be? The problem of cross-national attraction to education. *Comparative Education, 25*(3), 267–74.

Robinson, N., Robinson, H., Darling, M., & Holm, G. (1980). *A world of children: Daycare and preschool institutions.* Monterey, CA: Brooks-Cole.

Rogoff, B. (1990). *Apprenticeship in thinking.* New York: Oxford University Press.

Scarr, S. (1987). *Mother care/Other care.* Penguin: New York.

Scarr, S., Phillips, D., & McCartney, K. (1989). Dilemmas of child care in the United States: Employed mothers and children at risk. *Canadian Psychologist, 30*(2), 126–39.

Simmons, J. (1984). Reforming education and society: The enduring quest. In J. Simmons (Ed.), *Better schools: International lessons for reform* (pp. 3–20). New York: Praeger.

Smock, A.C. (1981). *Women's education in developing countries: Opportunities and outcomes.* New York: Praeger.

Spodek, B. (1980). Early childhood education: A synoptic view. In N. Nir-Janiv, B. Spodek & D. Steg (Eds.), *Early childhood education: An international perspective* (pp. 1–14). New York: Plenum.

——— . (1989). *Early childhood education in America: Consistencies and contradictions.* Paper presented at the International Conference on Early Education and Development (Hong Kong, July 31–Aug. 4, 1989). ERIC Document ED 313 101.

Tobin, J.J., Wu, D.Y., & Davidson, D.H. (1990). *Preschool in three cultures.* New Haven: Yale University Press.

UNESCO. (1989). *Statistical yearbook.* Paris: UNESCO.

UNICEF. (1990). *The state of the world's children.* New York: Oxford University Press for the United Nations Children's Foundation.

Walkerdine, V. (1984). Developmental psychology and the child-centred pedagogy: the insertion of Piaget into early education. In J. Henriques, W. Hollway, C. Urwin, C. Venn, & V. Walkerdine (Eds.), *Changing the subject: Psychology, social regulation and subjectivity.* New York: Methuen.

Werner, E.E. (1988). A cross-cultural perspective on infancy. *Journal of Cross-Cultural Psychology, 19*(1), 96–113.

Whiteside Taylor, K. (1967). *Parents and children learn together.* New York: Teachers College Press.

THE DEVELOPMENT OF PRESCHOOL AND PRIMARY EDUCATION IN THE PEOPLE'S SOCIALIST REPUBLIC OF ALBANIA

• • • • • • • • • ◆ • • • • • • • •

Bedri Dedja
Tirana University
Tirana, Albania

Albania is one of the oldest nation states in Europe. Occupied by foreign powers for centuries, it gained independence following the triumph of the People's Revolution in 1944. It is a country in which the educational influence of foreigners has a long history, beginning with the ancient Greeks and Romans and continuing through the development of schools built by the Ottoman Turks, Greeks, and Slavs.

Historical Overview of Early Childhood Education

A form of "collective" education of young children existed in antiquity in the Illyrian tribe. At age 5, children were given over to the state to begin their education. They were encouraged to develop a spirit of love for work and were given physical and military training. Attention also focused on their moral and artistic development.

The first religious schools using the Albanian language were established in the 17th and 18th centuries. The first private primary schools were founded in the early 19th century, while Albania's first lay primary school was opened in 1887 in the city of Korea. This school was soon followed by others in various towns and villages. These schools, however, were violently persecuted by the Ottoman Turks, who occupied Albania until 1912. For example, in 1909, after the Educational Congress of Elbasan, the first secondary normal school for training primary teachers was founded, only to close two years later under military force.

The ideologists of the National Renaissance movement at the turn of the 20th century—particularly Sami Frasheri, Naim Frasheri, and Gjerasim Qiriazi—made significant contributions to the modern educational system in Albania. They envisioned a system of preschool education in the "mother's school," and compulsory primary schooling in state institutions. The system was attempted in a limited manner in 1912, and in 1920, a curriculum was developed. Nevertheless, schooling for most Albanians was extremely limited. The result was that in 1939 approximately 90 percent of the population remained illiterate.

In 1913, Parasheevi Qiriazi, a school teacher, designed a model curriculum for the preschool kindergarten and primary school on behalf of the independent Albanian government. Qiriazi was critical of the educational system of the Turkish Empire because it did not provide a groundwork for the development of schools in Albania. The Turkish-influenced schools were not progressive and were based mainly on Moslem principles.

In Qiriazi's view, the purpose of the kindergarten would be to serve as a transition from family life to the school. Children ages 4 to 6 would be taught good behavior and morals, simple handiwork adapted to their mental abilities, and observations of nature, language and proper speech, as well as given physical training. The primary school would be in two phases. In the first three years, reading, writing, and arithmetic would be taught, taking care that the children "should form good habits" in these three subjects and be aware of the relevance of these disiplines to their lives. During the second three-year cycle of primary school, the subjects would include history (in the form of stories or legends), language, arithmetic, geography, poetry, vocal music, gardening, handicrafts, and gymnastics. Kindergartens and primary schools would serve both girls and boys. The minimum training for teachers would be secondary school graduation. Qiriazi's model curriculum also included special schools for children with mental or physical handicaps to provide practical work skills. Separate programs would exist for the blind, the deaf, and those with other handicaps.

Because of historical and political conditions, Qiriazi's model primary school—like the other progressive models stimulated by the Educational Congresses of 1920, 1922, and 1924—was never implemented. The years 1925–39, marked by the reign of Ahmet Zog, were a black period in Albania's history of education.

Preschools

The weakest link in the school system was preschool education. Restricted by the government, preschool and primary education had no opportunity to expand and remained unconnected to the needs of the country. For example, in 1925 there were only 11 kindergartens in Albania, which, at that time, had a population of about one million inhabitants. By 1935, only one new kindergarten had opened, and at the end of King Zog's reign there were only 22 kindergartens with a staff of 40 teachers serving 2,434 children. All other children were left entirely under the care of their families, most of whom lived in difficult economic circum-

stances. Included in the total number of kindergartens were private Catholic infant schools, which had their own methods and curricula. Until 1934, primary school teachers were not required to have qualifications at this age level. Although three teachers had taken a course at the Montessori Institute in Italy, none was employed in early education.

In this period, each teacher was responsible for an average of 60 children. In the only preschool kindergarten in Tirana in 1928, a single teacher taught 150 children in one room. Due to the state's neglect and complete lack of concern, the material conditions of the preschool kindergartens were deplorable, with unsuitable buildings and no teaching equipment.

Kindergartens were generally in the least desirable room in the primary schools and functioned as preparatory classes with a one-year syllabus with undefined aims and programs. Enrollment included children who did not meet the requirements of the first year at school, chronologically, physically, or intellectually.

The only private secular preschool in Albania, which operated under relatively good conditions, was the kindergarten associated with the short-lived "Teuta" College in Tirana (1930–33). The founders of the college sought permission to operate it as a combination kindergarten and primary school in collaboration with the Ministry of Education. However, because of a shortage of money, it operated as a private institution with relatively high fees. Enrollment was therefore restricted to children of wealthy families.

Two main educational philosophies were popular in preschools and kindergartens in Albania in the 1920s. Until the late 1920s, Freidrich Froebel's philosophy, in which children are to be diverted from their desired, natural development, dominated preschools. After 1929, the system developed by Maria Montessori became widespread, although the Froebel philosophy was not completely eliminated. According to Montessori's system, which gained increasingly broader support, primary importance is given to education of the senses. However, because of the limited training of most teachers, neither Froebel's nor Montessori's philosophy was rapidly applied.

Primary Schools

In 1925, Albania had 447 primary schools with an enrollment of 25,187 pupils and a teaching staff of 757. Each school had a small enrollment and one or two teachers. However, only one of every 36 Albanians attended primary school. At the time, the state viewed an educated populace as potentially dangerous to the ruling order.

From 1924 to 1939, only 196 new primary schools were added to Albania's educational system. This growth was well below the increase in population over the same 15-year period. There was also an unequal distribution of schools in rural and urban areas, and among rural areas in different districts. From 1921 to 1934, country schools increased at an average of six per year. In some districts, there was no increase in schools, while in others the numbers declined. For example, in the villages of the prefectures of Durres, Elbasan, and Tirana, there were fewer schools in 1937 than there had been in 1920. Of the 2,460 villages in Albania in 1938, only 472 had primary schools. Of these schools, 40 percent offered only a few years of the five-year primary program. Thus, most peasants were deprived of the opportunity to go on to secondary level schools.

Teacher training and recruitment for the primary schools during this period was an ongoing problem. Statistics show that of the country's 609 primary schools in 1938, only 65 had a complete staff of five teachers; most had only one.

The situation continued almost unchanged during World War II, when Albania was occupied by Italy and Germany. The Italian government attempted to further its ideological expansion by introducing the Italian language and fascist culture in the Albanian schools, and by opening Italian schools and clubs. The aim was to colonize and denationalize Albania. Following the entry of Hitler's army into Albania in September 1943, however, all schools were closed. Meanwhile, the liberation of Albania from foreign occupation began following the formation of the Albanian Communist Party on November 8, 1941. The struggle ended with the founding of the People's Democratic Government on November 29, 1944. In the zones liberated by the partisan army, the foundations of a socialist, universal educational system were established.

Revolution in Education

Because of the widespread devastation caused during World War II, schools in Albania did not reopen until March 1945 and they remained open until the end of July. The 1945–46 school year began normally in September. Following the proclamation of the People's Republic of Albania in January 1946, educational reform made the school system the property of the people. A unified system of four years of primary schooling was made compulsory for the first time, and intermediate (three years) and secondary (four years) systems were expanded. In addition, training programs for kindergarten and primary teachers were established. Many students were sent abroad to be trained as secondary school teachers.

To assist Albanian women to take an equal part in social production, and, at the same time, to carry out the early education of children, two other links were created: nurseries for children ages 1 to 3, and preschool/kindergartens for children ages 3 to 7 (in 1970 this age range was changed to 3 to 6). Until 1955, only the first four years of primary schooling were compulsory. After that year, seven years of schooling became compulsory. This was extended to eight years in 1963. (At the time of this writing, there are preparations to introduce compulsory ten-year schooling in the 1991–92 school year.)

The age of primary school admission was reduced from age 7 to 6 because of the accelerated psychological development of modern children, a phenomenon that has been confirmed in Albania, where children are maturing earlier. In Albania, all children of school age, including handicapped children, are enrolled in primary schools.

Preschool education, on the other hand, is widely available but not compulsory. Although there is relative harmony between family and social education in the Albanian socialist order, remnants of the old education, especially that which was patriarchal (mainly in the countryside) or liberal (mainly in the towns), is still transmitted by families. For this reason, the state tries to draw all the children into the social system of preschool education. This measure serves two major aims. First, it gives a stimulus to the emancipation of women as a major social movement, increasing their independence in economic, political, and social worlds. It permits them the possibility of participating in government and the running of the state. Nevertheless, the mother is not exempted from her function as the child's first, natural educator. Second, the early social education of children can be organized on scientific foundations in the state institutions of preschool education. Teachers are trained in the methodology and theory of early education.

Since 1944, preschool education has undergone marked development and is now including increasingly larger numbers of children, even those in remote mountainous zones. Despite this, only 56.3 percent of the children of kindergarten age attend kindergartens (49 percent in rural areas). The goal is for 80 percent of all 5-year-olds to attend state kindergarten programs by the early 1990s. It is reasoned that preschool experience enriches a child's primary school education. Children are better prepared to assimilate the more scientific approach to knowledge they will encounter in the primary school. A unified approach to concepts is adopted in all years of school.

Students are automatically promoted in the first four grades of the primary level, and marks are no longer part of their evaluation. This change is an attempt to make it possible for all children to acquire a primary school education. In addition, no streaming of students is permitted. All students in the years of compulsory schooling are promoted regardless of their ability. At this time, automatic promotion has been applied in grades 1 and 2 of the primary schools and is currently being extended to grades 3 and 4.

Philosophy of Education

Preschool programs and methods are revised in relation to social and educational developments, the enhanced level of expertise of the teachers, and the increasingly higher requirements for the admission of children to grade 1 of primary school. The general philosophy is that preschool programs should provide the social education of young children. In addition, attention should focus on overall development. This includes physical, intellectual, and aesthetic development; knowledge of socialist morality; understanding of elementary ideological and political concepts; and preparation for school.

The preschool program takes into account developmental norms and individual needs and desires of the children. The curriculum is organized around the following themes and concepts.

• *Culture, Politics, and Hygiene.* Through books and discussions, children gain elementary political notions about their country and its history and respect for work, parents, educators, and friends. Attention is given to developing children's interest in books, radio, and television, in keeping the garden and the home tidy, in cleanliness, and other proper habits connected with life.

• *Language.* The principal method of language education involves the use of fairy tales, stories, poems, recitation and recitation competitions; practice in speaking on the basis of artistic tableaux, albums, and other figurative means; and the children's own stories.

• *Mathematics.* Mathematics education includes the formation of ideas about numbers and basic mathematical reasoning.

• *Aesthetic and Artistic Education.* This is imparted through drawing, singing, dancing and performing small theatrical skits. The most talented children participate in artistic festivals involving the kindergartens of one town or district and in national artistic festivals for children.

• *Physical Education.* Physical education takes the form of morning gymnastics, age-appropriate physical exercises, traditional games in the open air, walks and excursions in parks, and simple sporting competitions. Kindergarten children perform gymnastics exercises in local or national displays in the country's largest stadiums.

• *Education Through Work.* This aspect of education involves the development of correct habits of cleanliness, hygiene, homemaking, and eating. Creating habits of work is also related to activities involving paper or cardboard "constructions."

Kindergarten lessons and activities are described in the *Program of Preschool Education*, a Ministry of Education document. The program for the nurseries for children from ages 1 to 3 is generated by the Ministries of Education and Health. In general, it includes health education, the general upbringing of children, and the development of communication skills. Programs in both the preschool and nursery are play-based and tailored to individual needs.

The guiding principle for all levels of education is derived from socialist pedagogy, that is, the best method of teaching and education is that which links the words of the teacher or the book with revolutionary practice, life, and socialist production. The degree to which this principle is applied varies among the educational institutions and with the age of the pupils. However, even children within the kindergarten are taught in a manner consistent with this principle. For example, preschool children participate in beautifying the kindergarten grounds, watering the plants and flowers, making excursions to work and production centers, and the fields (where they learn about the work of cooperative farmers and workers), giving modest aid at building sites and during the country's political campaigns, and cleaning up around memorials, historic monuments, and their own playgrounds.

Organization of the Primary School

The organization of primary schools has taken several forms. Until the late 1960s, for instance, in urban centers primary schools were generally included within secondary schools with a single director and a joint pedagogical council of teachers. The advantage of the system was that the older pupils, together with the teachers of the primary school and parents, were involved directly in the work of supervising the younger ones. However, the system also placed a great burden on the school's director and pedagogical council. In addition, the needs of the younger children were quite different from 18- to 19-year-olds. As a result, in the early 1970s the senior four years of the secondary system became independent units, with separate directors and buildings. Since then, there has been an improvement in the operation of the schools, the quality of teachers, and the general educational work.

Currently, there are three main forms of primary school organization in Albania. Most primary schools in the towns and large villages provide the full 8-year compulsory primary program. Within this program there are two cycles: the lower (grades 1 to 4) and upper (grades 5 to 8). The upper cycle is the first stage of secondary education. In the lower cycle, the students mainly work with one teacher, although experiments are being conducted with different teachers instructing different subjects.

In the upper level, teachers are subject specialists and the children are taught by many teachers. The transition from the lower level, where children have prolonged contact with a single teacher, to the upper level is often difficult for children. This problem is currently the focus of research studies.

The second major form of organization, representing a small number of villages where the number of upper-cycle pupils is small, is that of an independent lower cycle. A single full eight-year school operates for several nearby villages. If necessary, boarding is provided for pupils.

Another form of organization is found in a few villages, primarily in the more remote mountainous zones. If the lower cycle enrollment is small, grades may be combined. For example, grades 1, 2, and 3 may be taught jointly by two teachers. The upper cycle is offered at a more central location.

In this way, since the 1970s all children attend the first eight years of school. A small number of children leave school in grades 7 and 8. However, when they start to work at age 16, they are obliged to complete their compulsory eight-year schooling by attending evening classes.

Primary Curriculum

The subjects taught in grades 1 to 4 of the primary school are defined in the curriculum and are discussed below:

Language Study

The Albanian language is taught six hours each week in grades 2 and 3, and four hours in grade 4. Minority languages, such as Greek in Southern Albania or Macedonian in Southeastern Albania, receive the same amount of instruction. Reading instruction takes place two hours each week in grade 1, four hours in grade 2, and three hours in grades 3 and 4.

The study of the Albanian language is seen as one of the most important subjects in the primary school. Its purpose is to familiarize the pupils with the written language, to make them capable of using it in practice, and to train them in its correct use. In addition, children are taught to cultivate a love for their native language. Albanian is not taught as a separate subject in grade 1. Instead, the youngest pupils learn Albanian through reading and writing. The language program in the primary school includes elementary grammatical knowledge or morphology, phonetics, and syntax. The program also includes spelling, development of speech through written and oral exercises, and the writing of essays. During the lower cycle of the primary school, about 500 teaching hours are allocated to this program.

In grade 1, the reading program consists of a preparatory period (two weeks), a period of learning the alphabet (19–21 weeks), and a period of learning to read (10–12 weeks). There are separate textbooks for teaching reading in each of the lower cycle grades. In grades 2 and 3, excerpts from literature are used according to a defined range of themes—(e.g., the school; the family; the Homeland, including its past, the Antifascist National Liberation War, the socialist construction of the country, and portraits of heroes of socialist labor; the defense of the homeland, its geographic beauty, national celebrations, and the lives of other peoples).

By grade 4, more than 100 teaching hours are allocated to reading literature from a variety of sources (e.g., Albanian literature of the past, Albanian socialist realist literature, Albanian folklore, and foreign literature). There are also literary hours and discussions of out-of-school reading.

In grade 4, as in the other grades, special attention is given to the development of elocution through the recitation of the "classics," the learning of techniques of reading fluently and expressively, and enrichment of the vocabulary. The goal is not only for children to be introduced to great literature, but also to develop a sense of patriotism; socialist humanism; the proper attitude toward work and socialist property; correct habits of cultured behavior; and respect for working people, teachers, parents, and companions. To this end, Albania's finest writers and teachers are employed to write materials for reading instruction.

Albanian History

Albanian history is taught beginning in grade 4. The goal is to make pupils aware of the main historical facts of the Albanians' economic, political, social, and cultural life. In addition, students learn to appreciate the historical facts and phenomena in a logical way. Elements of history are taught in the lower classes through the use of

literature.

The history curriculum includes instruction about Illryia and the Illyrians, the ancestors of the Albanians; the Albanian resistance to the Turkish invaders; and the struggle of the Albanians under the leadership of Gjergj Kastriot-Skanderbeu against the Turkish occupiers. Also included is the history of Albania under the five centuries of Turkish rule, during which the Albanians preserved their language, culture, and traditions; the peasant uprising; the Albanian National Renaissance in the 19th century; and the proclamation of independence in 1912.

Students also study 20th-century Albanian history from 1912 until independence in 1939, the Antifascist National Liberation War of the Albanian people under the leadership of the Communist party of Albania (1941–44), and the liberation of the country. The modern period, from 1944 to the present, includes the study of the building of socialism, agrarian reform, the development of industry, and social and cultural development.

Birthplace and Homeland

This subject provides students from grade 4 with elementary knowledge of the physical and economic geography of Albania. Students study the physical and cultural geography of the country (e.g., the towns, countryside, and industries) in the context of the socialist development of Albania.

Nature Study

Nature study is taught in grades 3 to 5. The goal is to add to children's understanding of the world through observations, experiments, and practical lessons about nature. By relating nature study to production centers, students become familiar with the mechanisms of labor.

In grade 3 the program includes knowledge about flora and fauna, the properties of various natural compounds, and agricultural science as it relates to nature. In grade 4, students study the wind, changes in the weather, weather forecasting, aerial navigation, human physiology, and humans' relationship with nature.

Arithmetic

The study of arithmetic is intended to provide students with lasting mathematical knowledge.

Students develop concepts about quantity and space and perform calculations and measurements appropriate for their age. Arithmetic is believed to assist children's general development, especially the development of thinking and speech, and to better equip them for life. Lessons are practical and linked to children's life experiences. Students also study basic geometry in grades 2 to 5.

Art

The study of art is intended to directly influence the ideological and aesthetic development of primary school pupils. Students who demonstrate outstanding talent at the end of their primary schooling may compete for admission to the secondary schools of art.

In grade 1, art instruction consists of coloring (e.g., squares, the flag, the trees in autumn, cows, flourishing fields) or illustrating fairy tales.

In grade 2, students make constructions (e.g., with flowers and leaves), draw or color (e.g., poplar leaves, apples, a rainy autumn day, a round clock, and make decorations for the national celebrations of November, the New Year, May Day).

In grade 3, students draw subjects, which, for example, may include the first day of school, fruit with a leaf, a star, picking fruit, electric lamps, or terraced mountainsides planted with fruit and olive trees. Information about the figurative arts, and especially about the works of outstanding Albanian painters, is taught beginning in grade 3.

In grade 4, drawing includes themes from summer holidays, still-life (depicting, for example, vegetables and fruit, folk ornaments, corncobs, or a toy gun), the anniversary of liberation, the planting of fruit trees, the drawing of the letters PSRA (The People's Socialist Republic of Albania), Pioneer Day or Friends of the First Day, the May Day Parade, or butterflies. The talks on figurative arts continue.

Music

The study of music is intended to acquaint primary school pupils with the works of the Albanian and foreign composers most suitable for their age. Children are instructed in the art of singing as soloists and in groups. As in art, pupils who have a special talent in music can compete for admission to the art schools at a young age. The schools share the national curriculum with all schools in Albania, but there are additional lessons in music performance and theory.

The regular curriculum includes learning ten songs in each school year from grades 1 to 4 and lectures on the musical arts and classic compositions. There are also extensive out-of-school musical activities and district and national festivals for primary school children.

Handiwork

The aim of handiwork is to develop a love for all kinds of work and respect for workers and the socialist attitude to work. The view is that socially useful handiwork, together with the other subjects, is a positive factor in the overall intellectual, moral, and physical development of children. Activities covered in the syllabus include the following:

• teaching practical lessons in sewing and embroidery in grades 1 to 4 (26 hours);

• working with cardboard, pasting, and plaiting in all classes (52 hours);

• working with clay, plasticine, etc. (24 hours);

• modelling and building in grade 4 (8 hours);

• teaching agricultural knowledge in grade 4 (8 hours);

• attending field trips (18 hours); and

• participating in socially useful work in production and work centers or in the social environment (two full weeks in grades 3 and 4).

In planning the practical "socially useful work" experience, attention is given to hygiene and sanitation of the work site and to the age suitability of the work, so that children acquire the desired knowledge and attitudes.

Participating in useful work provides children with practical knowledge and an idea of the meaning of collective work. Students are taught to appreciate the productive activities of older people, to care for and protect collective property, to regard themselves as members of the collective, and to assist in the socialist construction of the country.

The syllabus for grade 1 begins with children attending to their own personal needs and keeping the classroom and playground neat and tidy. Children then learn to use scissors and fold paper to form geometrical figures. In addition, children acquire agricultural knowledge, care for decorative plants, experiment with clay and plasticine, make decorations for celebrations, acquire knowledge of textiles and the strengths of different threads, learn how to sew on buttons, and embellish clothing with folk designs.

In grade 2, children learn how paper and cardboard are made; how to place the ruler and T-square on paper; how to make paper toys; about the seasonal tasks of farm life through excursions; how to make objects from wool, cotton and synthetics; how to use a needle and to embroider the outline of a flag; how to make models symbolizing national celebrations and articles from natural materials; and how to weave straw.

In grades 3 and 4, handiwork becomes increasingly more complicated until the children are able to participate in social production, as described above, working together with the workers and cooperative peasants.

Physical Education

The aim of physical education is to assist the overall growth of children's bodies. In addition, children acquire the basic habit of independent and collective physical activity and the virtue of socialist morality.

Physical education is taught as a subject in the first four grades of the primary school. It is also integrated into the daily routine of the classroom, for example, the morning exercise before lessons commence and the minute's break for physical exercise after each hour of lessons.

In grades 1 and 2, physical education includes gymnastics (stretching and climbing, balancing, pushing, and weight-bearing exercises), athletics (running, jumping, throwing), mobile and traditional games, marches to scenic spots, and anthropomorphic measurements (70 hours per week).

The syllabus for grade 3 adds acrobatic exercises and elements of artistic gymnastics to the gymnastic program. The marches in autumn are six kilometers long, seven kilometers in winter, and eight in spring. On most school days, there are two marches (one on holidays).

In grade 4, the level of difficulty of the physical activity is increased. For example, it includes covering a distance of 315 meters, broken up into 140

meters of running, 35 meters walking, and a further 140 meters running. Runs of this type are repeated with the goal of keeping a uniform pace and regular breathing. Students march eight kilometers in autumn, nine kilometers in winter, and ten kilometers in spring.

Primary schools are provided with standard materials, including running tracks of 60 meters, jumping pits, wooden hurdles, rubber balls, high-jump bars, gymnastic mats, low horizonal bars, balance bars, skipping ropes, ladders, wooden rifles, aiming targets, spring boards, and children's uniforms.

Physical education is supported by many related community activities carried out in various institutions, (e.g., the House of Pioneers and Palace of Culture).

Special Programs of Education for Young Children

Several educational teaching institutions offer programs for children with physical or intellectual handicaps or who are orphans.

• *Dystrophic Nurseries.* The dystrophic nurseries are for young children (ages 1 to 3) with poor physical development. The focus is on maintaining their health and treatment under the supervision of doctors with pediatric training. The teaching staff promotes language development through games, physical exercises, and singing and music, with the aim that the children achieve normal psychological development.

• *Weekly Preschool Kindergartens.* Weekly preschool kindergartens for children ages 3 to 6 are available when, for various reasons, their parents are unable to care for them during the workweek. The programs of these kindergartens are virtually the same as for regular kindergartens. The educators work in three shifts over a 24-hour day.

• *Psychiatric Programs.* Kindergartens and schools for children with psychiatric problems emphasize games, music, and singing, as well as lessons connected with work. While such children are in the care of the state, their parents can visit them at any time.

• *Schools for the Mentally Retarded.* Schools and classes for mentally retarded children attempt to cover the curriculum of two or three grades of the normal primary school within four years.

• *The Institute for the Deaf, Dumb, and Blind.* The

Institute for the Deaf, Dumb, and Blind Children, with its center in Tirana, consists of a hostel and all the facilities necessary for collective life. The blind children complete the full program of the regular primary schools. The deaf and dumb children complete the program of two or three classes of the primary schools, while attention is given to the exercise of speech and to lessons connected with work in order that they acquire a skill.

• *Homes for Preschool and School-Aged Children.* Children without parents are raised in homes under the care of the state. Buildings have been designed and equipped to provide a family environment so that these children do not feel the lack of their parents. The personnel of the children's homes—consisting of educators, supervisors, and domestic staff—work 24 hours in three shifts and are employed by the state. To ensure that these children are not isolated from society and especially from children with parents, they attend the normal kindergartens and primary schools in their community. Any mentally retarded children in these homes are sent to the respective classes of the special schools.

There is a complete network to provide health and dental care for school children in Albania. Included are regular general medical examinations, vision and hearing tests, treatment for particular illnesses, regular vaccinations, and, in particular instances, long- or short-term treatment in pediatric hospitals. When preschool or primary school children are confined to hospital for long periods, their education is continued in kindergarten groups with educators.

Training Teachers of Young Children

Until the 1970s, teachers of kindergartens and primary schools were trained in pedagogical secondary schools, with courses of four years duration, following completion of the eight years of compulsory general education. At present, kindergarten teachers are trained in these schools, while primary school teachers have three years of courses of higher schooling following 12 years of combined primary and secondary schooling. There are three such facilities in Albania—in Shkidra (Northern Albania), Elbasan (Central Albania), and Gjirokaster (Southern Albania).

In addition to the general subjects of philosophy, history, geography, mathematics, physics, and chemistry, students study general pedagogy,

school hygiene, the psychology of different age groups, educational psychology, didactics, the teaching in particular disciplines such as language, the history of world and Albanian education, the methods of preschool education, and teaching in particular disciplines, such as language, mathematics, and nature study. Students also receive teaching practice in kindergartens and primary schools.

After graduation, training takes the form of in-service professional development sponsored by the pedagogical council of the institution, discussion groups, local or national meetings, special scientific sessions, and specialized periodicals (e.g., *Preschool Education* and *The Eight-Year School*).

Another aspect of in-service professional development is a series of graded tests conducted after 5, 10, and 20 years of work in the classroom. The tests measure the teachers' awareness and knowledge of new developments in the sciences of psychology and education and in the field of the individual teacher's specialization.

Parents and Early Education in Albania

Although only a small percentage of young children make use of the preschool system, early education has a special character in Albania. The goal is 100 percent enrollment of preschool children by the end of the century. Early education has emerged from the context of the family, while primary schooling is the sole responsibility of the state and includes all Albanian children.

While primary schooling is free, parents pay a small charge for preschool services (nurseries and kindergartens) calculated on the basis of the family income (the fee cannot exceed more than 0.5–1.5 percent of the income). In this way, a unified system of education has been created, which includes schools and families working together.

The advantages are many. Assistance provided to the family raises the level of supplies and services that can be provided. Second, it ensures that preschool education and primary school education have a scientific content and employ scientific methods that even the most cultured family could never ensure. However, tensions have long existed between the family and the school. Conservative patriarchal forces, as well as liberal influences, frequently exist within the family. As a result, the role of the school is both to educate children and to reeducate their families. To this end, the following six-part system of parental educational services has been developed.

1.   Personal assistance from and contact with teachers are available for parents to discuss the problems their children have with their lessons or present in their conduct.

2.   Monthly parent/teacher meetings are held to discuss the general concepts of preschool and primary education.

3.   Schools disseminate educational information through talks and lectures in order to enhance the ideological-pedagogical and psychological understanding of parents. The pedagogical propaganda is developed on the basis of an annual plan drawn up by the directors of the institutions. All teachers and educators are involved in this work.

4.   Consultations are available at medical and pedagogical centers for parents to discuss problems that arise with their young children.

5.   Educational information from around the world concerning young children is disseminated through the radio and television, the general press, and the special educational press, particularly through special bulletins that focus on the problems of preschool and primary school education.

6.   Information and programming for young children (e.g., magazines, radio, and television broadcasts; children's literature by Albanian or foreign authors) is designed to influence the whole family. Many parents read books to their children or view the television broadcast with their children. In this way, parents gain an understanding of issues in schooling and education.

Early education in Albania is subject to a variety of influences, both social and state. The aim of all educational work is to offer programs of superior quality, staffed by trained personnel, in well-equipped, hygienic physical facilities. The preschool kindergartens and primary schools are special institutions charged by the Albanian socialist society and state with the task of the early education of children using unified programs approved by the state organs. But this does not mean they are left to spontaneity. On the contrary, they are subject to a general control, both social and state, from the political organizations and the

parents themselves. In all this work, priority is given to implementating programs of the proper quality and to the qualifications of the teaching personnel for the improvement of general conditions, especially conditions of hygiene and sanitation, the combination of lessons with games, rest periods, etc.

The organizations and mechanisms of state control are numerous; the social interest in the education of young children is put into practice by:

• the Commission on Education and Culture of the People's Assembly of the People's Socialist Republic of Albania;

• the Education Sector of the Council of Ministers of the Republic (the government);

• the directorate of preschool, primary school, and eight-year school education of the Ministry of Education;

• the children's nurseries (for children ages 1–3) under the Ministry of Health, while the educational program is approved by the Ministry of Education (the former is responsible to the government for the organization of the health service in all the educational institutions);

• the Democratic Front of Albania (as the largest mass organization of the people, has commissions for the education of children everywhere and at all levels);

• the Women's Union of Albania;

• the Labour Youth Union of Albania, which has direct responsibility for overseeing the first political-social teaching of children in the three groups, Pioneers, Fatosa, and Yllka (Pioneers are primary school children age 8, Fatosa are primary school children under age 8, and Yllka are preschool children);

• the respective sectors of the Institute of Pedagogical Studies in Tirana;

• the sections of education in the districts and the Pedagogical Cabinets (i.e., groups responsible for the qualifications of the teaching personnel); and

• the chairs of pedagogy and psychology of the various institutions of higher education in the country.

The education and schooling of young children are at the center of attention of all these organizations, both from the standpoint of providing funds, assistance, and control, and from the standpoint of conducting scientific studies of early education in Albania.

EARLY CHILDHOOD EDUCATION IN ANTIGUA AND BARBUDA

Patricia Canning
Memorial University
St. John's, Canada

Edris Bird
University of the West Indies
St. John's, Antigua

Antigua and Barbuda form an Eastern Caribbean, English-speaking nation which gained its independence from Great Britain in 1981. The inhabitants are predominantly of African descent, a group comprising about 97 percent of the population. The population is estimated to be between 78,000 and 80,000 (no census has been conducted since 1960).

Significant improvements in the well-being of children have taken place over the past 40 years and particularly in the last two decades. Improvements in health and education have had positive effects on the quality of childrens' lives. Antigua and Barbuda have a well-developed health care system covering the entire population through hospital and health centers. The nursing profession, comprising nurses, assistant nurses, public health nurses, provides most of the health care services.

By 1983, 98 percent of births occurred in hospitals and were attended by well-qualified staff (Sinha, 1988). Many women attend prenatal clinics and receive postnatal care as well. Infant mortality and morbidity have been greatly reduced and are estimated to be among the lowest in the Caribbean. The reported infant mortality rate of ten per

1,000 live births is similar to that of a number of developed countries (International Planned Parenthood Federation, 1988). The fertility rate of 1.7 children per women is relatively low. Infectious diseases and diseases of childhood were either eradicated (e.g., malaria) or greatly reduced (e.g., gastroenteritis, diphtheria, tetanus) by the 1980s. By 1985, virtually all children had been immunized against poliomyelitis, diphtheria, pertussis, and tetanus (UNICEF, 1990).

Similar to the advances in the health care field, significant improvements have been made in education over the last 40 years. By the 1970s, Antigua and Barbuda had made provisions for secondary education for all children. In contrast to other parts of the developing world, women's educational achievements are similar to those of men at the primary and secondary levels. Even at the tertiary level, women lag behind men only in the science and engineering fields.

Preschool Education

In Antigua and Barbuda, preschool, which is the term used for all preschool day care and education, has existed for a relatively long time. It is generally accepted that preschool is an appropriate place for children ages 3, 4, and 5. This is also true in other parts of the Caribbean. There is a great demand for preschools not only because it is seen as desirable for children but also because many Antiguan parents work outside the home, there is a high percentage of female-headed households, and fewer and fewer family members are available as caregivers. Interestingly, the percentage of preschool-aged children in formal group care in this developing country appears to be significantly higher than the percentage in registered group care in more developed countries, such as Canada and the United States. In 1984, it was estimated that 45 percent of preschool children in Antigua were enrolled in a preschool program (Sinha, 1988). In the same year in Canada, it was estimated that 15 percent of preschool-aged children were being cared for in registered preschools or day cares (Status of Women, 1986). There are now over 50 preschools in Antigua and one on the island of Barbuda, which has an estimated population of less than 1,200.

Some of the Antiguan preschools have an enrollment of more than 70 children, but most have between 30 and 60 children. Teacher-child ratios are usually considered low by North American standards. Children usually begin preschool before their third birthday. It is estimated that currently there are approximately 2,500 preschool-aged children between the ages 2 and 5 in preschools. This represents approximately one-half of the country's children in that age group and underscores the need to ensure high quality preschool programs.

Most centers are staffed by local women and either are privately owned by them or are operated under the auspices of a local church or community organization. There is no governmental legislation regulating preschools and there are no training requirements. However, preschools are, in practice, required to obtain a basic level of service, as determined by the Coordinator of Preschool Services, of the Department of Education. Some support in the form of teachers' salaries and supplies is given by the Antiguan government's Department of Education.

There are a few locally produced toys and they, as well as imported play materials and other preschool supplies, are expensive and usually far beyond the budgets of most preschools. Fortunately, furniture, equipment, books, play materials, and funds for childrens' meals are donated by such organizations as the Christian Childrens' Fund, Canadian Development Assistance Programme, Canadian Organization for Development Through Education, UNICEF, and such church groups as The Board of Global Ministries of the United Methodist Church of America.

While there is no common "curriculum," many preschools focus on formal education rather than on providing care for children. Because parents, as well as many preschool teachers, believe that children should be able to read and print by the time they are age 4, reading and printing are taught. A common attitude is that preschool is the appropriate time for teaching reading, printing, and arithmetic and many preschools are pressured into doing this by the parents. The result is that many preschools have a "school-like" atmosphere, training children almost exclusively by a rote training method. This is of concern to many early childhood educators providing preschool teacher training and is addressed in teacher training courses and workshops and parental education courses. Many preschool teachers have taken part in formal preparatory workshops, which may result in a more play-like atmosphere in the preschools.

Preschool Teacher Training

Research in North America has shown that the education and the training of preschool teachers are important factors in determining the quality of care provided to children (Berk, 1985; Clarke-Stewart and Gruber, 1984; Howes, 1983). In Antigua, as in many other countries, until recently most early childhood educators had little or no formal training. Many did not have a high school diploma or its equivalent. Moreover, even caregivers with postsecondary education were rarely qualified in early childhood development and care.

While no legislation mandates the training of preschool teachers and many teachers have not completed high school or its equivalent, a surprising number of preschool teachers in Antigua and Barbuda have received some formal training. That this is so can be attributed to the ongoing work of a number of women in Antigua and Barbuda and recent efforts on the part of the government. Almost all of this training in early childhood education has taken place during the 1980s.

In the early 1980s, preschool education in Antigua and Barbuda began to receive significant attention from educators. One significant impetus for improvements to preschool came from the Extra Mural Department of the University of the West Indies (UWI), which was recently renamed University of the West Indies School of Continuing Studies, Antigua. Although preschool training was not officially part of the mandate of the Extra Mural Department, the development of adult education programs, both academic and skill training, was. The resident tutor, in an attempt to address the training needs of women working in preschools, began to organize workshops and short training programs for preschool teachers. In 1979, with assistance of funds donated by Sir Luther Wynter, a local physician, and supplemented by the government of Antigua and Barbuda, a preschool was established on the grounds of the then UWI Extra Mural Department to provide a model preschool and training program for Antigua and Barbuda.

Other major developments in preschool education followed quickly. With the assistance of UNICEF, a coordinator of preschool services was appointed within the Department of Education, to monitor and provide assistance to, and training of, preschool teachers. Scholarships were made available and continue to enable people to attend year-long training programs, such as those offered at the Child Welfare Training Centre in St. Vincent, at the SERVOL Caribbean Life Centre in Trinidad, and at the Caribbean Child Development Centre at UWI, Mona Campus in Jamaica.

Department of Education

The coordinator of preschool services and her assistant provide on-site training and workshops one day a month and a two-week workshop every other summer. Resource persons (e.g., experienced preschool teachers, nutritionists, drama and art teachers) are invited to assist with these workshops. In alternate summers, a similar workshop is offered by UWI's School of Continuing Studies. The coordinator of preschool services has been a significant member of Antigua's preschool community and has done much to advance the recognition of the importance of high-quality early childhood education.

University of the West Indies

In addition to offering courses and workshops, UWI has developed and offered cooperative training programs in early childhood education in Antigua and Barbuda between the Department of Extra Mural Studies and Mohawk College of Arts, Science, and Technology and Mount Saint Vincent University in Canada since 1980. Additionally, preschool teachers have attended courses at Mohawk and Mount Saint Vincent University and have returned to assume positions of leadership in the field of early childhood education.

University of West Indies and Mohawk College

In 1980, five graduates from the early childhood program at Mohawk College in Hamilton, Ontario, Canada, spent five weeks assisting in a number of preschools in Antigua. Although the trip was arranged by the college, the students paid for the cost of their travel to and accommodations in Antigua. Groups of five graduates continued to come for the next five years. Teachers from Mohawk College also visited and offered a number of workshops to preschool teachers during the summers. This has continued on an informal basis up to the present.

In 1989, Mohawk College and UWI's School of Continuing Studies entered into a formal agreement that enables teachers from the Sir Luther Wynter Preschool to attend Mohawk College for further training and to gain experience in preschools in Canada. Two women completed a year of training in 1988–89. Since then, two others have attended the college for a month's training and by the end of 1991, six staff members of the Sir Luther Wynter Preschool will have attended the college. This program is sponsored by the Association of Canadian Community Colleges through funds made available by the Canadian International Development Agency (CIDA).

University of West Indies and Mount Saint Vincent University

In cooperation with Mount Saint Vincent University, Halifax, Canada, the School of Continuing Studies has offered in-service training programs and university-level certificate courses for both preschool and primary grade teachers since 1987.

Vocational-Level Training in Early Childhood Education

Between 1987 and 1989, a comprehensive program was conducted to improve the care and education of young children in the country's preschools by improving the formal preparation of preschool personnel. The program was predicated on the assumption that because limited financial and other supports are available to preschool teachers, any attempt to improve child care must go beyond the traditional preservice or in-service training offered in the classroom. Merely improving the training of preschool teachers will not do much to improve the care of children without, at the same time, considering the other supports needed to offer high-quality group care for young children.

This program was funded by the universities and CIDA and had the support of local governmental and community organizations. Two university professors, one from Mount Saint Vincent University and the other from UWI, specializing in adult education and early childhood education, respectively, designed and directed the program. Two early childhood educators—one Canadian and the other Antiguan—coordinated the program.

The program offered workshops and courses as well as on-site training in the preschools. These were offered to all preschool and primary school teachers wishing to upgrade their qualifications. The courses and workshops were held after regular working hours throughout the year and during holiday periods. (In Antigua and Barbuda, preschools usually follow the school calendar.) Workshop and course content were decided in consultation with the coordinator of preschool services. Financial assistance was available to participants to cover transportation costs.

On-site training was offered throughout the country and was seen as a critical component of the program. Ideally, the training was coordinated with teachers and/or supervisors enrolled in courses to help to ensure that it related to the actual circumstances of the preschools. This on-site intervention was seen as one way to encourage those not more fully involved in the training program to become so. The emphasis was on working within the confines of each center and on designing programs appropriate to what was available in each district. The project personnel learned valuable information about using what was already readily available to preschool teachers and received feedback that could improve their effectiveness in the classroom and in other centers. This intervention usually took place over approximately six months.

Written evaluations were completed by participants after every workshop, course, and on-site intervention. These evaluations provided ongoing feedback on the effectiveness of teaching and suggestions of areas needing additional attention.

Registration and attrition rates provide an indirect measure of the extent to which the program met the participants' needs. Over 150 women enrolled in the workshops and courses. This number greatly exceeded the projected enrollment number of 50. Eighty-five women in 15 centers were involved in the on-site training program. Only one center terminated the intervention before the scheduled time.

Program participants compiled *Activities Book for Teachers of Young Children* and a book of local children's stories. The project also produced *Guidelines for Supervisor Handbook* to assist supervisors in becoming guides and facilitators for teachers and to help them organize and operate their centers more efficiently. These resources are made available to interested persons at little or no cost.

Model Center

A major component of the program was the development of the campus-based preschool into a model for the country. To facilitate this process, the program coordinators' offices were in the preschool and all preschools staff were heavily involved in the training courses. Currently, staff of the center is providing on-site preservice training and is involved in other training workshops offered by the coordinator of preschool services. One of the staff who attended a year's study at Mohawk College had been the project's Antiguan coordinator. She is continuing to develop and offer training programs in the larger preschool community as well as in the Sir Luther Wynter Preschool.

The preschool has established a toy and book lending library. The number of private donations resulted in quite an extensive collection of child development and early childhood education texts, which are made available to the general public through the university library. Most significantly, the important contribution of the model center to the improvement of child care has been recognized by the community. The coordinator of preschool services has received funding and assistance from UNICEF and SERVOL to develop another model preschool and training center in another area of the capital. This will, no doubt, make a significant contribution to improving services for preschool-aged children and their families.

University-Level Certificate in Early Childhood Education

In 1989, UWI's School of Continuing Studies and Mount Saint Vincent University, with additional support from CIDA, began offering a one-year certificate program in early childhood education for both preschool and infant school (primary) teachers wishing to pursue a university education. This program is offered on a part-time basis over a two-year period. In 1992, it will be taken over by the School of Continuing Studies and offered as part of its general program in Antigua.

During the initial cooperative training program, it became clear that there was increasingly more community support and recognition of the need for early childhood educators to be trained at the college level. Many trainers had or were receiving training in early childhood education and others interested in preschool expressed their desire to pursue training at the college level. Offering a one-year-equivalent university-level early education certificate in Antigua was seen as one way to increase participation of women at the university level. In addition, having completed a year of university will make completing a degree out of the country less difficult for women who have family responsibilities. For others, it may provide the encouragement needed to pursue university degrees.

Infant Education

Infant education (i.e., early primary grades in North America or education for children ages 5 and 6 in Antigua) is offered in government-spon-

sored and private schools in Antigua and Barbuda. Virtually all 5-year-olds are enrolled in infant school. The average number of children per teacher is 30. Enrollment in government-sponsored schools has been approximately 1,500 a year since 1980 (Ministry of Education, Culture and Youth Affairs, 1987). Since the country has a very stable and low birthrate of 1.7 children per woman, no significant change in enrollment is expected in the foreseeable future. This stability of population helps to facilitate both planning and program development.

Similar to the situation in preschools, the curriculum in infant classes traditionally has been structured and adult-centered. The main emphasis has been on teaching reading, writing, and arithmetic. Teaching has been by rote with little attention paid to involving children actively in their own learning. The classrooms generally continue to reflect a structured approach, although changes are emerging due to the concerted effort of the Department of Education. A more child-oriented approach to teaching young children is being taught in teacher-training programs, and materials and equipment now given to teachers are designed to encourage the more active participation of the children.

Infant Teacher Training

Antigua and Barbuda State College. Those hired to teach in the governmental schools must have completed at least four 0-level examinations (roughly equivalent to grade 11 in North America). They usually teach for two years under the supervision of a senior teacher before attending the State College. The college offers a two-year teacher training program. At present, it is estimated that 50 percent of infant teachers have completed this program. Those who successfully complete the two years receive the Certificate of the University of the West Indies School of Education, which gives them endorsement to enter the first year of the degree program in education offered at the UWI in Trinidad, Barbados, and Jamaica. A number of the graduates of the State College are now enrolled in the certificate program being offered by UWI and Mount Saint Vincent University described above.

In-Service Infant Teacher Training. Extensive in-service training is offered by the Department of Education of the government of Antigua and Barbuda through the Infant Pedagogical Centre established in 1987. The supervisor of infant education designed the centre to support teachers in developing a more child-oriented curriculum. The center provides workshops and lectures and offers the latest applications of research in early childhood education. It also assists teachers in making materials for their classes as well as by providing general support through interaction with other teachers. The center's supervisor, the director of infant education, has implemented an inter-island exchange visit program among infant schools to facilitate the modeling of practices of the more progressive classes. Although established primarily for teachers in government-sponsored schools, the center also welcomes private school teachers, preschool teachers, and college students.

Young Children With Special Needs

Preschool Education

Similar to the situation in many other countries, there are no mandated services for preschool-aged children with special needs. However, there is a growing interest in identifying young children with special needs and in providing services to them during the preschool years.

The preschool community generally supports the integration of special needs preschoolers into regular preschool centers. This is probably facilitated by the fact that there are no segregated preschools and many preschools have children with special needs, although not formally identified as such. In 1987, the Sir Luther Wynter Preschool, in developing into a center of high-quality care and model early childhood educational practices, began to accept children with identified special needs. Since that time, a number of children with identified special needs (e.g., pervasive developmental disorders, visual impairment, mental retardation, and severe emotional disturbance) have attended the preschool. Integration of these children has facilitated not only the modeling of appropriate preschool practices but also provided an excellent opportunity to model community and parental involvement in the preschool. Parents and professionals from the community (e.g., speech therapists, teachers of the visually impaired, pediatricians, and psychologists) were central figures in integrating special needs children into the center. Community service clubs were involved in contributing funds for special toys and equipment. Such professional and community involvement provides an excellent model for integration. Reports that other centers are also accepting children with identified special needs are most encouraging. It appears that preschools are ahead of the school system in integrating children with special needs into regular programs.

Special Education for School-Aged Children

Although the Education Act of Antigua (1973) confirms equal opportunity for each child's "capability, aptitude, skill, and strength" to be "identified, nurtured, and cultivated" to its maximum, the general educational system is not yet prepared to meet individual needs. There is no system in place for dealing with young children with special needs in the regular schools. There is, however, one school designed to educate children with special needs, the Adele School for Special Children. The Adele School for Special Children was initiated in 1970 by Dr. Adele and Bernard Savory. (The school was named Adele School in honor of Adele Savory shortly after her death in 1977.) It was initially sponsored by the Association for Retarded Citizens, a group of interested parents and community members. In 1978, it was established as a governmental school under the jurisdiction of the Ministry of Education. The school has an enrollment of 24 students ranging in age from 5 to 12 years and a staff of 10 (Strei, 1988). These 24 children represent a small percentage of school-aged children with special needs in Antigua and Barbuda.

Residential Care for Children With Special Needs

A small group home (eight to ten residents) primarily for school-aged children in need of out-of-home residential care is operated under the auspices of a community group of concerned citizens. There is growing general awareness of the increasing need to provide alternative care to children whose home circumstances are such that they are unable to remain there. At the time of writing, a plan for a system of foster care is being developed.

Child-Life Program for Hospitalized Children

The general hospital established a child-life program in the mid-1980s. Child-life workers have participated in the preschool training available from UWI and the coordinator of preschool services. There is a well-equipped child-life center in the pediatric ward and young school-aged children can receive help in continuing their school work while they are hospitalized.

Special Health Programs for Young Children

A program named the Follow-up of High Risk Newborns has been in operation at the country's only major hospital since 1988. Approximately 100 children are seen each year at three-month intervals. Children who appear to have abnormal or delayed development are referred to community resources, such as those provided by occupational and physical therapists. Unfortunately, such resources are not always available in the country and are often insufficient to meet all the children's and families' needs.

There is a proposal to establish a developmental screening program that will be managed by the Family Health Nurse Clinicians in the six regional health centers operating throughout the country, but no funds have been made available at time of writing.

Child Mental Health Services

The Child and Family Guidance Centre was established in 1987. Its purpose is to provide community-based outpatient diagnostic and treatment services to children up to age 18 who have emotional and behaviorial problems and to their families. It is governed by a volunteer nonprofit organization. The center has received considerable support from the Christian Children's Fund and the national government. The center's success depends to a great extent on the continued availability of appropriate professional staff and consultants, of whom there is often a shortage in the country.

Parent Support and Education

Parental support and education is a major component of training programs and is also strongly encouraged by the coordinator of preschool services. The Child Welfare League, established in Antigua in 1988, has as one of its mandates the support and education of parents. To this end, it has organized meetings and workshops addressing the needs and concerns of families. Part of the mandate of the Child and Family Guidance Centre is to serve as a resource center for public information and education. The center, in cooperation with UWI's School of Continuing Studies, is currently offering a training program for parents.

Conclusion

The importance of early childhood education has been recognized in Antigua and Barbuda. During the 1980s, the availability of preschool education increased substantially and significant improvements were made to preschools and infant schools and to teacher training programs. Other resources for children and families, such as a children's mental health facility and parental educational programs were established. In the early 1990s, there is an increasing recognition of the need to develop programs for the early identification and education of and services for children with special needs and their families. A problem in the foreseeable future is that current economic conditions may retard this progress.

References

Berk, L. (1985). Relationships of educational attainment, child-oriented attitudes, job satisfaction, and career commitment to caregiver behavior toward children. *Child Care Quarterly, 14*, 103–129.

Clarke-Stewart, K.A., & Gruber, C. (1984). Daycare forms and features. In R.C. Ainslie (Ed.), *Quality variations in daycare* (pp. 35–62). New York: Praeger.

Howes, C. (1983). Caregiver behavior in center and family day care. *Journal of Applied Developmental Psychology, 4*, 99–107.

International Planned Parenthood Federation. (1988). *Family planning in Latin America and the Caribbean.* New York: Author.

Ministry of Education, Culture & Youth Affairs. (1987). *Report on the education division 1985–1987.* Antigua: Antigua Printing & Publishing, Ltd.

Sinha, D.P. (1988). *Children of the Caribbean 1945–1984.* Kingston, Jamaica: Caribbean Food & Nutrition Institute.

Status of Women. (1986). *Report of the task force on child care.* Ottawa: Supply & Services Canada.

Strei, C. (1988, Dec.). A look into the past. *Adele School Newsletter,* pp. 2–3.

UNICEF (1990). *State of the World's Children.* Oxford: Oxford University Press.

PRESCHOOL EDUCATION IN ARGENTINA

• • • • • • • • • • ◆ • • • • • • • •

Carlos Héctor Hurtado
University of Córdoba
Córdoba, Argentina

Most Latin American systems of education have experienced difficulties that can be linked to economic underdevelopment as well as to political and social instability in the region. While Latin American countries are currently struggling to achieve economic growth and political stability, this is not an easy process and it clearly affects all aspects of life, including the educational system. Preschool education in Argentina has to be viewed in light of these conditions and struggles.

Any examination of preschool education in Argentina is hampered by a lack of information on this topic, which is only now being corrected. Historically, preschool education has played a minor role in the country's national educational programs, although that is now changing. This chapter discusses some of the conflicts that presently characterize the field of preschool education in Argentina. It describes significant events that have occurred in preschool education and addresses both normative and legislative issues.

Translated from the Spanish by J. Bernhard.

Recent History of Preschool Education

In Argentina, "preschool education" usually refers to the systematic education of 4- and 5-year-old children in kindergartens, although it is also beginning to be used to refer to the education of children between birth and age 3 in maternal schools. Maternal schools operate in private homes, enterprises, or municipal facilities and have varied schedules. Children attend kindergartens for either single shifts (three to four hours) or double shifts (six to seven hours). The kindergartens with a full-day or double shift (extended hours) arose as a response to the problems faced by certain groups. For this reason, the initiatives—either official or private—differ according to the group they are intended to serve and the provinces responsible for the administration of the kindergartens; that is, the kindergarten is structured according to their own needs and formulated objectives. Due to the decentralization process in effect since the 1970s, there are no national programs for full-day kindergartens. Rather, the provincial jurisdictions have administrative autonomy.

In 1972, prior to decentralization, the Ministry of Culture and Education, in its document entitled "Curriculum for the Preschool Level," under the title of "Basic Outline for the Daily Timetable," suggested similar activities for both types of kindergartens with the addition in the full-day centers of lunch, rest, snack, and group experiences (gardening, music, physical expression, manual arts, or recitations).

At the present time, other than a few exceptions, this scenario does not appear to have varied much since it is possible to observe a tendency to distribute the daily schedule in much the same way as the half-day programs. What is observable, however, is a different emphasis on certain activities—an emphasis according to the specific social group being served. For example, in centers oriented toward communities with few economic resources, there is a greater emphasis on providing assistance (nutritional information, preventative health practices), while at those centers oriented toward communities of middle or upper resources, there is a greater emphasis on socialization. While in school, they follow the current elementary school schedule, except where certain local conditions—such as climate or parental work schedules—require the set schedule to be modified.

Kindergartens and maternal schools have developed in quite different ways. For example, no formal certification is required to operate a maternal school; kindergarten teachers, however, must be certified. Also, while kindergartens have become widespread due to strong governmental support, maternal schools have not enjoyed the same favor. This chapter focuses on the education of 4- and 5-year-olds in kindergartens.

Educating children before they enter primary schools has historically been problematic for the Argentinean state. Formal interest in early childhood education dates back to 1884, with the passage of Law No. 1420 regarding common education. The first chapter of that law "General Principles Regarding Public Education in the Primary Schools," asserts: "In addition to the common schools mentioned, the following special primary schools will be established: One or more kindergartens, in the cities where it is possible to equip them adequately . . ." (art. 11).

This goal was not quickly realized. Because preschool education was not compulsory, those who benefited from any attempts to establish kindergartens were mostly upper-middle-class children living in urban areas. In the 1960s, this inequity became a concern, prompting one prominent educator to state: " considering the potentially large demand, if the state does not seriously address the problem, kindergartens will not be developed or will remain virtually in the private domain. . . ."[1]

Subsequently, the Argentinean government committed further resources to the development of kindergartens and over the years, has progressively increased the amount of funds available to meet a growing demand. According to the census for 1980, there were 605,187 5-year-olds in Argentina (289,819 girls and 306,368 boys). Of this group, 360,238 children (179,412 girls and 180,826 boys), comprising 59.5 percent of all 5-year-olds, attended some type of preschool.

As Table 1 shows, preschool enrollments increased significantly from 1974 to 1984. In this 11-year period, the 100 percent increase in preschool enrollments greatly surpassed the rate of increase of either the primary or secondary school level. The rate of expansion of preschool enrollments, however, did not take place uniformly. The rate was lower between 1978 and 1980, a time of nondemocratic government in Argentina.

TABLE 1

Preschool Education: Total Enrollment, 1974–84

Year	Enrollment
1974	327,303
1975	378,523
1977	430,916
1978	444,780
1979	455,745
1980	480,216
1981	526,964
1982	570,353
1983	602,226
1984	654,645

Source: Department of Statistics, Ministry of Education and Justice.

The capability of preschools to attract students differs significantly from province to province. According to the 1980 census, while 88.9 percent of all 5-year-olds living in the capital attended kindergarten, only 28.7 percent of all 5-year-olds living in Chaco were attending kindergarten. Provinces with low attendance rates include Misiones (37.32 percent), Formosa (44 percent), and Corrientes (47.7 percent). This indicates that areas with lower productive capacity, scarce resources, and low population density also have lower levels of kindergarten attendance. This leads to the conclusion that children living in marginal areas, where poor socio-economic conditions prevail, do not receive the education they need. There is clear discrimination (whether or not intended) against poorer sections of the country.

However, the fact that more than one-half of all Argentinean 5-year-olds can attend kindergarten is a hopeful sign because kindergarten education is not mandatory. In spite of the inequities and relative backwardness of the preschool educational system, there has been a solid record of expansion of services during the last several decades. While such progress is laudable, preschool education in Argentina is still far from obtaining its long-term goals.

The incorporation of women into the workforce cannot be analyzed separately from the context of social classes and their "geo-cultural" location. With this reference, one should note the following.

In rural zones, women traditionally had productive tasks such as caring for the vegetable garden, raising small animals, and other subsidiary activities. Due to the increase in the capitalist mode, however, the traditional family structure is forced to change to confront the new reality being developed. Therefore, the mobility—temporary or permanent—toward urban areas or other rural areas characterizes families presently living in the countryside.

In urban-marginal areas, the incorporation of women into the workforce also has a long history. The disintegration of the family that is evident in significant proportions (i.e., absence of parents) and the need to survive due to the difficult conditions of life forced women to perform tasks away from the family environment. In these cases, the younger children were usually left under the care of siblings or relatives when they are not induced into begging or other informal economies. In urban areas, the middle and upper classes also contribute to the changes in the female role. Because of socio-cultural reasons, not subsistence, the woman begins increasingly to develop productive activities.

In marginal sectors (urban and rural), the children are incorporated into either the productive structure or new family roles at an early age. In the middle- and upper-class urban sectors the lack of a female figure in the home—and consequently the loss of an important socializing agent—was solved or improved by the integration of children into institutions that offered this service (in our case, the kindergartens).

For this reason, one can affirm that the preschool level has been primarily an institutional response to the needs of urban middle- and upper-class sectors and has not adequately served marginal groups. This is the risk taken when announcing uniform educational policies for different groups. The state in this case has not generated adequate responses to the diverse social realities and has favored certain sectors over others. This discriminatory reality is not only limited to the preschool sphere but is also evident in basic instruction: although the average enrollment levels appear satisfactory, those with low attendance are primarily found in rural or urban-marginal areas.

Interpreting the Growth of the Preschool Educational System

The remarkable increase in enrollment levels in kindergarten programs over the last two decades has been due to several factors. These include changes in the structure of the Argentinean family and more positive actions carried out by state agencies in meeting the demands of parents.

Changes in the Argentinean Family Structure

Women's labor force participation rates have greatly increased over the last several decades. The mass movement of Argentinean women into the labor force began in the 1960s and gained momentum in the 1970s. Census figures for 1960 and 1970 indicate that the percentages of women between the ages of 25 and 29 in the labor force increased from 29.4 percent in 1960 to 36.24 percent in 1970. With this movement of women into the labor force, various processes associated with the socialization of the child, historically performed in the home, were " displaced toward the extra-familial institutional environment. . . ."[2]

Actions by State Agencies

During this same period, the Argentinean state devoted an increasing amount of resources to meet the new social demands resulting from women's entry into the labor force. Kindergartens, teachers, and equipment appeared on the scene, enabling many children whose mothers were employed outside of the home to enter the educational system by age 5.

In 1982, 5,301 government funded (official) kindergartens had been established, making up 72.2 percent of all the country's kindergartens and accommodating 69.1 percent of all kindergarten students. These official kindergartens also employed 67.3 percent of the country's kindergarten teachers. This percentage distribution has remained stable to date. In 1986, there were 719,928 kindergarten students (of which 495,285 attended official establishments) enrolled in 8,294 institutions (of which 5,922 were official), with a staff of 39,842 teachers (27,449 employed in official kindergartens). Unfortunately, published statistics provided by the Department of Statistics of the Ministry of Education and Justice cannot be properly interpreted due to the lack of data on the total number of school-age children nationwide. Nevertheless, actual provincial percentages indicate that there has been an increase in the number of 5-year-old children attending kindergarten since 1980.

The state, serving as the guarantor of primary education, has played a central role in the establishment and the growth of kindergarten education in Argentina. Its presence today is directly associated with work in democratizing education and in overseeing the expansion of preschool education into the more underdeveloped areas of the country. To promote this objective, however, compulsory school attendance must be required of 4- and 5-year-olds.

Women's increasing participation in the labor force has led to situations in which many children are no longer being supervised by their mothers. This raises the question: Why, in the poorer sectors, which have already experienced this change in family structure, have the children's educational needs not been adequately met? The question is not capricious, since it is these groups that have the lowest enrollment at the preschool level.

Whether the state was unable or unwilling to provide the poorest and neediest members of its population with adequate social welfare provisions, the fact remains that Argentineans must now rectify the consequences of previous inadequate social policies. Argentineans must create strategies that will provide economically disadvantaged children in both urban and rural areas with access to a kindergarten education.

Factors Contributing to the Quality of Preschool Education

Although the data show an increase in the numbers of children receiving preschool education over the last 15 years, the quality of that education is another matter. It has been noted that "in contrast with other levels of instruction preschool has not traditionally set specific cognitive goals; rather its objectives have been directly related to the socialization process . . . ."[3] In spite of this approach, preschool education is thought to be useful in helping students to overcome problems that they might face in primary grades, including poor marks, and inability to adapt to school.

As a result, there now exists in Argentina a movement to establish preschool education as part of the regular school curriculum and to substitute the term "initial level" for preschool, thus making kindergarten a part of the formal educational hierarchy. The idea of an initial level in a child's educational career is directly related to the new interpretation of the role of early childhood education, which is understood to be directed toward not just 4- and 5-year-olds, but also to include younger children (from birth to age 3) and even to include the parents themselves. Realizing this new and complex view of early childhood education, however, requires Argentinean educators to develop a new curriculum. Today, almost everyone agrees that preschool education is important to a child's socialization and psycho-emotional development. The approach now being promoted is to develop a curriculum for preschool educational programs that combines teaching life skills with traditional learning objectives.

The problems involved in developing such a curriculum have been discussed at educational conferences, meetings, and seminars. One problem concerns jurisdiction: to what extent should the federal government have control and to what extent should the provinces be able to influence administrative decisions? Should kindergartens depend directly on existing institutions of primary education?

At the same time, there is agreement that regional curricula need to be developed and adapted to local interests and needs. In situations where local conditions are not considered, instruction tends to become disconnected from the children's daily experiences.

Empowering teachers is another a major priority. The demand for a systematic and permanent professional development is rarely enunciated, and it is recognized that the major responsibility rests with the state in this matter. It is also recognized that the government must play a role in guaranteeing teachers rights, while at the same time individual instructors themselves must work for self-realization as professionals.

Another concern is research in preschool education, which has been almost completely neglected.[4] To resolve this situation, some instructors recommend that it would be helpful for the state to create "centers of investigation," and "centers of educational research" staffed by post-graduate specialists.

What Can Be Done?

In Argentina the problems inherent in providing preschool education are felt most acutely in the poorer rural areas. This is where the state can and should work to guarantee the provision of preschools. Such a goal is difficult to achieve, since both the ideal and actual structures of the educational system—preschool as well as primary—

have been established in response to needs of those in the cities. Moreover, those needs are specific to the interests of certain social sectors. The current educational model has clearly been designed to meet the needs of people living in areas of high population whose daily life is largely influenced by the demands of employment in commercial, industrial, or public sectors. The model fails in rural areas, where people's lives are not affected by the same concerns and rhythms as those of city dwellers.

Rural and urban areas differ in many ways. The rural population is migrant, following the itinerary of local production needs. The people are unevenly dispersed and children must travel long distances to reach the schools. Poverty is widespread and severe among peasant households, social services are almost nonexistent, and lines of communication are inadequate.

It is immediately apparent that in rural areas, the problem of providing preschool education cannot be resolved simply by opening preschool centers. By itself, this is not sufficient. If the primary schools that serve children between ages 6 and 14 function mostly with multiple grades, and 30 percent of rural schools have one or fewer teachers per grade because of low enrollment, what can be expected for the preschools? Faced with these conditions and inadequate funds, it is necessary to generate alternatives that surpass the rigid models of the past.

Local innovative strategies have been implemented as tentative answers to the rural preschool education. The origins of these strategies have been diverse, coming from the teachers, the communities, or the provincial governments. Despite some promising new strategies, however, the problems are far from being solved.

It is a common practice, for example, for rural teachers, especially those teaching multiple-grade classes, to incorporate 5-year-olds into grade 1. This practice, which goes against official policy, is an attempt to meet community needs. While the 5-year-olds do not gain the regular accreditation or even appear in official statistics, they do obtain some preparation for the following formal year. Teachers in these situations have noted good results from students with this kind of previous experience; such children already have experience of school and have shared group experiences when they finally enter grade 1. While opinions on this practice are divided, the fact is that these teachers are supplying a service that the state is not willing to provide and the children concerned are receiving an extra year of education.

There are various ways to analyze the effects of incorporating 5-year-olds into grade 1 classes in rural areas. On the one hand, because it is not required by legislation, many school supervisors do not support it. The situation is further complicated by the parents. When the parents of 5-year-olds allowed to informally attend grade 1 classes noted that their children had formed concepts and acquired abilities appropriate to grade 1, they argued for the recognition of these achievements and demanded that their children be promoted to grade 2. Thus, both the lack of support by supervisors and the inconvenient attitude of certain parents have been used to argue against this approach.

But the greatest objection to this approach is that it refuses to recognize the need for preschool education as such. Teachers who allow 5-year-olds to attend grade 1 classes do not intend to offer a preschool program to those children. They recognize both that they are not specialists in preschool education, and that they do not follow appropriate curricular guidelines for preschool in their grade 1 classes. Support for the continuation of the practice of allowing 5-year-olds to attend grade 1 classes, however, arises out of a sensitivity to the needs of parents and children.

In some instances, local initiatives have been undertaken, and the state has recognized those initiatives by supporting the preschool teachers. In some cases, itinerant preschool teachers have been designated to help the teachers accepting 5-year-olds in grade 1 classes. The visits of itinerant teachers are systematically planned. Their objectives are to aid in assessing and supervising of children and to cooperate with regular teachers in the "educational" task. Schools that have participated in this system of itinerant teacher assistance have been evaluated positively. However, one major drawback is that the personnel designated to provide the services are not trained as preschool specialists.

Critics of the use of itinerant teachers have questioned the advisability of emphasizing expansion over quality of teaching. In general, it is arguably discriminatory that children in urban areas have the advantage of exposure to certified preschool teachers, while children in less populated rural areas have only nonspecialists as supplemental teachers. Nonetheless, there has been some agreement that the overall experience is a positive one and that it is worth continuing support to improve offerings in areas where an interest is shown for this approach.

Another state initiative outside the conventional model of education has been to establish amalgamated schools. This initiative requires the children to go outside the service-area limits of the school that they will attend for their primary education. The strategy is simple, but requires a detailed knowledge of the area, as well as the social supports that ensure parental participation.

In the first test case, an area was selected that included both a rural population and an urban center to which the rural population already had commercial, economic, and cultural ties. The rural population chosen lived within a 15-kilometer radius of the urban center which had both a functioning preschool and accessible communication lines.

The rural primary school was a main element in this approach. Parents associated with this school had to trust in the new strategy and support the teachers. The rural children were transported three times each week from their homes to the urban center's primary school, where they attended kindergarten, and then back to their homes. Initially, there were many concerns about the project. It was feared that parents would not allow their children to be bused. It was also feared that the rural children might be discriminated against by the children already at the urban school. Finally, there were fears that once their children had experienced kindergarten education in the urban center, the parents would attempt to enroll them in the primary schools there.

An evaluation of the project, carried out in 1986, revealed the following:

• almost total attendance by eligible children (over 90 percent), in spite of the distances traveled;

• few problems for either rural or urban children in adapting to the new experience;

• general support by parents, who organized themselves independently in both urban and rural areas to participate in the activities of the kindergarten; and,

• subsequent enrollment of the children in the schools close to their homes, with no attempts by the parents of the rural children to enroll them in the urban schools after kindergarten.

The overall transportation logistics were laid out by the community and the state, with the details being worked out by parents and teachers. A relevant conclusion of this experience is that it might not work in all rural situations. Its successful application depends on certain conditions (e.g., geography, population, transportation, etc.). Clearly, to overcome the educational problems of the children living in rural areas, many different strategies are needed. This is certainly one of the responsibilities that presently faces the Argentinean state and its citizens: to systematically and continually harmonize the initiatives that under certain conditions have been demonstrably successful in overcoming educational inequities.

Expansion of Initial Level Education

The growth of the demand for initial level education has been a direct result of the increasing demands expressed by Argentineans and the government's response to those demands. In this respect, the state's activities as the agency principally responsible for education are visible and significant. Over time, the state has begun to prioritize goals and to structure the legal framework within which educational development can take place.

In Argentina, there has been a progressive movement toward decentralization, which—although incomplete—has resulted in the delegation of responsibility for education to the provinces. For this reason, primary schools, like preschools, depend administratively and technically—with minor exceptions—on the provincial states. Today, it is the provinces that are directly charged with dealing with the problems of kindergartens. Because of the relative independence of the provincial educational systems, once federal initiatives are established they are affected by the specific circumstances that exist in each province. Because

of this, the level of preschool education varies from province to province: from rudimentary, but promising, to satisfactory in terms of attracting and serving the children of a given area. Future progress will depend on the sharing of the results of local initiatives at a national level.

In 1986, a National Pedagogic Congress was held in Argentina. As a result of this meeting, public opinion was surveyed concerning the kind of educational system the country needed. The following section discusses the legislation passed by one of the provinces that established of obligatory attendance in kindergartens.

Rioja Province and Compulsory Preschool Attendance

Rioja province, in northeastern Argentina, was among the first provinces to legislate compulsory preschool education. The provincial parliament, following the desire of the community, passed Law No. 4554 on August 22, 1985, establishing obligatory attendance for 5-year-olds in kindergartens. The motives, for the law are stated in the *Fundamentos* and the *Despacho* of the Commission on Education, Justice, and Sports of the Camara de Diputadores.

From studying both documents, it appears that the following issues were discussed in the parliament:

• *Equality*: providing equality of opportunity for all children[5] and guaranteeing space for all children wishing to attend.

• *Labor Relations*: ensuring that preschool teachers who graduate from pedagogical institutes are able to find work within the school system.

• *Pedagogy*: preparing children in kindergartens not only to read and write but also to develop their physical, psychological, intellectual, and emotional capacities,[6] attention to the child using an effective-emotional perspective that allows the child to socialize and to gain self-affirmation as a human being,[7] and realizing that the integral formation during the early years of life is definitive for the development of the child's personality and in assuring a balanced adulthood.[8]

Certain functions of kindergartens with respect to admission and the passing of the child on to primary school are highlighted because it is assumed that an experience in kindergarten will eliminate or reduce the frustrations children might feel on entering school. It is also expected that attending kindergarten will reduce the need for grade repetitions. In this way it is expected that "the early detection of problems in language, behavior, emotional development, and learning abilities can be facilitated, and that problems can be treated before beginning primary school."[9] According to the authors of this report, the early detection of problems would allow for the establishment of special education classes at the primary level, staffed by specialized personnel. The topic of leveled grades is a subject of great debate in Argentina.

Because there are no entrance criteria applied to enter public schools, there is a wide variety of individual abilities. In other words, there are children who are quick to construct knowledge, develop skills, or incorporate information while there are other children who are slow to develop some of these processes. This naturally generates different learning rhythms.

A traditional conception, which is quickly becoming unpopular, was to label these slow children as "problems," which directly impacted on the rhythm of those most favored because the time and attention they required slowed them down. In this manner, the pedagogical option of "adjustment/levelling grades" was employed—classes formed of "slow" children who required special attention. Once children are "levelled" and they reach the expected rhythm—a rare occurrence—they are incorporated into the "fast" or supposedly normal track.

Another conception, which accepts diversity in learning rhythms, does not label slower children as problem children but rather integrates them with the faster children and allows them to progress at their level, thus creating a more heterogeneous group. There is a research-based conviction that the diversity of experiences, and the opportunity to observe various rhythms, stimulates the slower children and allows them to develop to their optimal capacity. This stance means that, inevitably, professionals will be challenged to change their methods to work with children who manifest different levels of progress in their achievements.

Conclusion

This chapter provides an overview of the initial, or preschool, level of education in Argentina. It describes and explains several alternative models for future educational possibilities. The facts, interpretations, and concepts discussed in this chapter are based on census data, published studies, and the author's experiences working in the field. From this information, it is possible to see that Argentina has experienced a growth in the provision of early childhood education over the last ten years. At the same time, certain difficulties are clearly apparent that need to be confronted.

It is the rural areas that are experiencing the most serious problems and limitations. But regardless of setting, problems have their roots in political, economic, and social factors.

Overall, the state has undertaken and sustained a relatively consistent effort in improving preschool education in Argentina. Yet, in spite of important accomplishments, these efforts have not been sufficient. New answers to Argentina's problems in the field of early childhood education will have to emerge out of a full consideration of all the difficulties and possibilities. The state needs to actively work to dismantle social injustices, while working at the same time to consolidate and expand advances. This task requires the support of all Argentineans, but especially of those who are knowledgeable about the problems inherent in providing early childhood education.

Notes

1. Cirigliano, Gustavo F.J. "Educación y Política—El paradojal sistema de la educación argentina." Librería del Colegio, Argentina, 1977, p. 22.

2. Tedesco, Juan C., et al. "El sistema educativo en América Latina." Editorial, Kapelasz-UNESCO-CEPAL-PNUD-Buenos Aires, Argentina, 1984, p. 43.

3. Ibid.

4. Braslavsky, Cecilia, et al. "El proyecto educativo autoritario—Argentina 1976/1982." FLACSO—Argentina, 1983, p. 97.

5. Documento de "Fundamentos del Ante-proyecto de Ley de Obligatoriedad del Jardín de Infantes de cinco años." Cámara de Diputados, Prov. de la Rioja, Argentina, 1985, Item 7.

6. Ibid., Item 4.

7. Ibid., Item 5.

8. Ibid., Item 6.

9. Ibid., Item 10.

References

Acuerrondo, Inés. (1988). *Una nueva educación para un nuevo país.* Buenos Aires: Centro Editor de América Latina S.A.

Bravo, Héctor Félix (comp.). (1985). *A cien años de la Ley 1420.* Buenos Aires: Centro Editor de América Latina S.A.

Braslavsky, Cecilia y Riquelme, Graciela (comp.). (1984). *Propueslas para el debate educativo en 1984.* Buenos Aires: Centro Editor de América Latina S.A.

Censo Nacional de Población y Vivienda. (1980). Serie B. Características Generales—Total del País—República Argentina.

Ciricliano, Gustavo, F.J. (1977). *Educación y Política—El paradojal sistema de la educación argentina* (4th ed.). Buenos Aires: Librería del Colegio.

Hurtado, Carlos. *La educación popular en zonas rurales—Apartes para un debate.* Buenos Aires: Centro Editor de América Latina S.A.

Materi, Lilia E.H. de, & Bähler, N. Ruth (eds.). (1987). *Administración y Organización de los sistemas escolares.* El Ateneo-Argentia.

Nassif, Ricardo, et al. (1984). *El sistema educativo en América Latina.* Editorial Kapelusz S.A.-UNESCO-CEPAL-PNUD, Argentina.

Oréal-UNESCO. (1982). *Guía para proyectos de educación preescolar de communidad.* Santiago de Chile.

Rodriguez, Soledad, & Haeussier, Isabel M. (eds.). (1985). *Manual de estimulación del niño preescolar-Guía para padres y educadores.* Galdoc Ltd., Chile.

Tedesco, Juan Carlos, et al. (1983). *El Proyecto Educativo Autoritario, Argentina 1976–1982.* FLACSO, Argentina.

AUSTRALIAN EARLY CHILDHOOD EDUCATION

S. Vianne McLean, Barbara Piscitelli,
Gail Halliwell, and Gerald F. Ashby
Queensland University of Technology
Brisbane, Australia

Over the last century, Australia has developed an extensive network of early childhood services to meet the needs of children under age 8 and their families. While many of these services are supported by governmental funds, there remains a strong community base to early childhood education in this country. In keeping with many other aspects of Australian life, educational provisions are organized on a state-by-state basis and there exists a plethora of terminology to describe early childhood services.

For example, there are differences in the uses of the terms "preschool" and "kindergarten." In New South Wales and the Australian Capital Territory, "kindergarten" refers to programs for children entering primary school. In other states "kindergarten" and "preschool" are both used to mean sessional educational programs for children under school age, though some states and agencies use one term more than the other. In recent years, there has been a tendency in some states to use "preschool" to refer to programs for 4-year-olds and "kindergarten" to refer to similar services for 3-year-olds. Other terms, such as the South Australian "parent child centers," and the Western Australian "pre-primary centers," are also used to describe sessional educational services for children under school age.

In this chapter, "preschool" and "kindergarten" are used interchangeably to refer to educational services provided on a sessional basis for children in the two years preceding primary school. "Child care" refers to services that aim to provide supplementary care while parents work outside the home. This may be full-day care or occasional care. If it is a formal, home-based care service, "family day care" is used. Private child care arrangements between individuals are identified as "informal" care.

Recent governmental initiatives at a national level have begun to address some of the discontinuities that create confusion between different state terminologies and practices. However, many Australians see such rationalizations as infringing on state rights and change is resisted. In the area of education, discussions about standardizing the age of school entry and introducing a national core curriculum have taken place, but as yet, they have had little impact on early childhood educational services.

History of Early Childhood Services in Australia

The development of early childhood education in Australia has paralleled that of Europe and North America despite Australia's geographic isolation from the West. Just as the final decade of the 19th century saw an increasing concern for the urban poor in the developed nations of the Northern Hemisphere, so these years saw a similar rise in the Australian social conscience.

Australian philanthropists of the late 19th century turned to Freidrich Froebel's kindergarten in hope of alleviating the plight of poor children, and in 1895, formed the Kindergarten Union of New South Wales. In 1896, this organization established the first Australian kindergarten in Wooloomooloo, Sydney. This innovation spread rapidly, and in less than 20 years volunteer early childhood organizations were established in all states of Australia (Kelly, 1982; Spearitt, 1979). (See Table 1.)

These volunteer organizations remained the primary providers of early childhood education for over 50 years, and their extensive network of services gave Australian early childhood education many of its distinctive characteristics. Despite recent criticisms of the philanthropic orientation of these early services, the volunteer organizations offered educationally sound programs and provided an exceptionally strong base for the development of early childhood education in Australia.

Before the start of governmental subsidies following World War II, volunteer agencies provided these services at little or no cost to families by raising money from the public sector. Many of those who volunteered were women from comparatively well-to-do families who later became involved in early childhood education in professional capacities.

Early Teacher Education

Australia's first kindergarten teacher had trained at the University of Chicago, but as the network of kindergartens expanded, the demand for local teacher training programs quickly escalated. By 1916, the volunteer organizations had established kindergarten teacher's colleges in Sydney (1900), Adelaide (1907), Brisbane (1911), Perth (1912), and Melbourne (1916) (see Table 1). In Australian society of the early 20th century, kindergarten teaching was one of the few professions open to young women. However, because kindergarten teacher's colleges charged tuition fees and salaries for kindergarten teachers were very low, access was limited to women of financially secure backgrounds.

TABLE 1

Volunteer Agencies and Kindergarten Teacher's Colleges

State	Year	Organization	Year	College
New South Wales	1896	Kindergarten of New South Wales	1900	Sydney Teachers College
New South Wales	1905	Sydney Day Nursery & Nursery Schools Association	1932	Nursery School Teacher's College
South Australia	1905	Kindergarten Union of South Australia	1907	Adelaide Kindergarten Teacher's College
Queensland	1906	Creche and Kindergarten Association of Queensland	1911	Brisbane Kindergarten Teachers College
Victoria	1908	Free Kindergarten Union of Victoria	1916	Melbourne Kindergarten Teacher's College
Tasmania	1910	Kindergarten Union of Tasmania		(No kindergarten teacher's college)
Western Australia Teacher's College	1912	Kindergarten Association of Western Australia	1912	Perth Kindergarten

Source: Fry, J. *et al*. 1973. Care and Education of Young Children. Report of the Australian Preschools Committee, p. 27.

In common with many fields in the newly established nation, locating persons with advanced levels of expertise was difficult. In early childhood teacher education, as elsewhere, the solution was to import staff from Great Britain and the United States. Australia had gained nationhood in 1901, but political, economic, and familial links to Great Britain remained strong. During this period, there were also extensive contracts with early childhood educators in the United States, a connection that was to become even stronger in later years.

During the interwar period in Australian kindergarten teacher's colleges, British and North American early childhood educators assumed academic leadership, assisted with the recruitment of academic staff, and helped Australian early childhood educators gain entry to advanced-level courses in both the United Kingdom and the United States. One influential figure was the British educator and psychologist Susan Isaacs. Although not on staff of any Australian college, her work was widely read in Australia, and when she toured the major Australian cities in 1937 (as part of an academic tour group organized by the Australian Council for Educational Research and the New Zealand Council for Educational Research), she made many personal contacts. The Advanced Course in Child Development, which she founded at the University of London Institute of Education, became a favored location for graduate studies for Australian early childhood educators. Isaacs's emphasis on child development as the basis for early education curriculum became the core of Australian early education.

Although Australian early childhood education gained much from the importation of overseas expertise, it made few contributions to early childhood education in other nations. An exception was Lillian De Lissa (Jones 1975) who, after becoming prominent in Australian early childhood education prior to 1917, took a senior academic post at the Gipsy Hill Training College in England. Some recent writers (Spodek, 1986:8) have criticized Australia's long-standing reliance on overseas experts, claiming it delayed the development of a unique identity for Australian early childhood education. This reluctance to recognize the existence of high-quality Australian programs and "home-grown" expertise is a problem common to

all areas of Australian life. Only in the last two decades has Australia overcome this "cultural insecurity" and begun to fully acknowledge the achievements of its own citizens.

State and National Initiatives Post-1930

One characteristic feature of Australian education is that while funding for education is derived from the federal government, the provision of public education is a state responsibility. This has led to a diverse range of public educational services. Early childhood organizations have maintained a strong state focus even within the volunteer sector. From 1930 to 1950, these organizations slowly expanded their networks and the kindergarten teacher's colleges continued to produce a relatively small number of teachers. During this period, the first governmental initiatives were seen in early childhood education as the states assumed some responsibility for monitoring and subsidizing kindergarten services.

There were also important national initiatives during this period. In 1938, the Australian Association for Preschool Child Development was formed. It was later renamed the Australian Preschool Association and is currently known as the Australian Early Childhood Association (AECA). Since its formation, this coalition of volunteer organizations (and later, governmental departments) has provided services for young children and their families and published a national journal for early childhood educators (currently titled the *Australian Journal of Early Childhood*). Although composed of professional early childhood educators and lay persons, the organization has been a strong voice for the professionalization of early childhood education. In 1974, it supported the establishment of a national professional organization, the Australian Association of Early Childhood Educators.

For many years the AECA focused largely on kindergarten services, while the child care and early primary sectors were underrepresented. This has been corrected over recent decades, with the most recent name change reflecting the desire to broaden the organization to incorporate all care and educational services for children from birth to age 8. In this expanded role, AECA has made a significant contribution to the improvement of child care standards in Australia.

A second major national initiative also occurred in 1938, when the federal government entered early childhood education for the first time, by establishing the Lady Gowrie Child Centres. Throughout Australia, the Depression of the 1930s had brought widespread malnutrition and health problems for families, and once again, attention turned to kindergarten programs as a means of alleviating these poverty-related problems. Acting on an initiative from the National Health and Research Council, the Commonwealth Health Department provided funds to establish a demonstration early childhood center in each state's capital city. These centers were named the Lady Gowrie Child Centres, honoring the strong support given by the wife of the governor-general to Australian early childhood organizations.

These centers became models for Australian early childhood educational practice. Their concern for good health was reflected in daily health checks and carefully planned nutrition programs. The physical environment was designed with great care, and many of the specifications for buildings, furniture, and equipment determined at that time remain in use today (Cumpston and Heinig, 1944). The quality of the physical environment has remained an important consideration in Australian services for children under school age, and exacting standards try to ensure the physical well-being of young children through provision of adequate space, fresh air, natural lighting, and appropriately scaled furniture and equipment.

Beginnings of Child Care in Australia

As in other countries, child care services in Australia have developed in two distinct streams. One stream—the volunteer organization child care networks that developed alongside the kindergarten movement—has been reasonably well documented (Mellor, 1990). Another stream—comprising private or "informal" child care arrangements—has continued with little acknowledgement or documented history. In the 1990s, Australian child care provisions continue to reflect both streams.

Statistics on the number of working mothers in the early 1900s are virtually nonexistent, but with over 6 percent of married women in paid work and with an average family size of five children (Spearitt, 1979), it is likely that many families needed supplemental child care. Kindergartens operated by the volunteer organizations were, for the most part, unable to meet this need, since they offered only part-day sessions and had a lower age limit of 2 years. Further, it was emphasized that kindergarten programs had serious educational intentions and were quite distinct from the lowly "child-minding" services (Brennan and O'Donnell, 1986:19).

The first volunteer organization to become involved in child care was the Sydney Day Nursery & Nursery Schools Association, formed in 1905. Initially, it was planned to provide a care service that would supplement the kindergarten programs offered by the Kindergarten Union of New South Wales, but this cooperative arrangement quickly broke down and the day nursery association extended its operations to provide free-standing full-day care programs for children up to age 6. This separation of child care and kindergarten services was further exacerbated in 1932, with the opening of a second early childhood teacher's college in Sydney, specifically to prepare teachers for work in day nurseries and nursery schools.

Only in Queensland was a single volunteer organization responsible for both child care and kindergarten services. From its inception in 1906, the Creche and Kindergarten Association of Queensland has had a dual focus, and many of the early purpose-designed buildings in the city of Brisbane reflect this. The architectural arrangements, in which one wing was devoted to the child care function and the other to the kindergarten, was indicative of the distinctiveness with which these two services were viewed. Staffing also was distinctive. The person in charge of the creche was a qualified nurse and carried the title "matron." The person responsible for the kindergarten was usually a qualified kindergarten teacher and carried the title "director," a term still in use in Queensland community kindergartens today.

Nonprofit child care services enjoyed modest growth through the 1920s and 1930s. During World War II, small grants were made through the federal Department of Labour and National Services to the kindergarten and day nursery organizations, so that expanded services might allow more mothers to reenter the workforce. Although Australian child care programs did not experience the massive expansion experienced during the war years by programs in the United Kingdom and the United States, the involvement of a federal labor department in early childhood education was noteworthy. This was probably the earliest acknowledgement of the link between employment and child care availability; a link that was to assume much greater importance in the 1970s and 1980s (Simons and Vella, 1984).

The Post-War Years to the 1960s

In the 1940s and 1950s, the focus of kindergartens changed, moving from philanthropically motivated services for disadvantaged families to educational programs for all children. With this change, responsibility for the establishment and management of kindergartens gradually shifted from the centralized volunteer agencies to localized community-based groups, with more parental representation. Although in most states, these decentralized groups retained affiliation with a central volunteer organization, the degree of autonomy of the local groups differed markedly among the states.

The funding levels also varied widely, and this quickly led to significant differences in the extent of the services provided in each state. Despite these differences, overall Australian early childhood education developed as a series of distinctive community networks characterized by parental involvement in decision-making, considerable autonomy in operation, and some recognition by governments in the form of subsidies. Allocation of governmental funds by the state volunteer agencies, however, enabled the agencies to maintain control over standards in their networks, and in each of the agencies, advisory and inspection services were established for this purpose. By the end of the 1960s, early childhood education began to assume a higher profile in educational circles and, increasingly, questions were asked about the appropriate role of government. In a report published in 1968, Fitzgerald concluded:

Though the importance of early childhood experience has yet to be understood fully, the kindergarten appears to be well placed to make a significant contribution to the child's educational development. Should this be so, then there is an urgent need for all governments in Australia to review their prospective roles in this field and to make explicit their policies in respect to future funding and organization for preschool facilities (p. 11).

Australian Social Policies 1970–90

The term "decade of turbulence" has been used by Brennan and O'Donnell (1986) to describe the sweeping changes that occurred in Australian child and family policies during the 1970s and 1980s in response to changing social patterns and shifts in social attitudes. As the Fitzgerald (1968) report foreshadowed, intense lobbying for increased and more equitable funding for early childhood education in the late 1960s helped place it on the national political agenda. In 1970, the federal government announced that it intended to establish a national network of early childhood centers to provide both child care and kindergarten services. Although the number of women in the paid workforce had been steadily growing throughout the 1960s, this was the first recognition of the need for expanded child care services.

At the same time, state governments were also taking initiatives. Because of the nature of community-based education, in which local groups took the lead in establishing kindergartens, coverage was historically uneven. Several state governments now saw a need to take a more direct role in providing access to preschool education for all children.

In 1968, the Tasmanian government became the first to fully fund kindergarten programs. It also adopted an integrated "3 to 8 [years of age]" curriculum policy that foreshadowed later nationwide developments. The two Australian territories (Australian Capital Territory and the Northern Territory) were also providing high levels of per-capita expenditure on preschool education as the new decade began.

In 1972, Queensland launched an ambitious program to provide access to one year of free preschool education for all young children. The size of this undertaking can be understood when one realizes that the population of 4-year-olds in Queensland in 1972 was 42,000, and only 8,500 were attending community kindergartens (Ashby, 1980:152).

The state initiatives were supported by the

new federal Labour government that was elected in late 1972. It quickly established the Australian Preschool Committee, chaired by Joan Fry, a former principal of the Sydney Nursery School Teacher's College. The membership of the committee reflected the mainstream of Australian early childhood education, with a heavy representation of educators, but no representatives of women's groups or trade unions.

Even as the committee was preparing its report, rapid changes were occurring in Australia's social attitudes and policies. For example, in the governing Labour party, the women's lobby group managed to change party policy to support child care, rather than short sessional preschool programs. Early childhood policy was broadening its area of concern from children's welfare to include mothers' welfare (Maas 1984).

The committee's report, *The Care and Education of Young Children* (1973), contained estimations of relative demand for short sessional preschool and long day care services. It recommended that by 1985 the federal government should provide preschool education for 70 percent of the national population of 4- to 5-year-old children, but estimated that only 10 percent of children would be needing funded child care places in the same period. The report was not well received by the federal Labour government and a new body was constituted under the auspices of the Social Welfare Commission. The chairperson of this group was Lenore Cox, who formerly had been the head of the Women's Bureau in the Department of Labour and National Service.

The commissioning of this group represented a major shift in early childhood education in Australia. The strong educational emphasis that had traditionally characterized all decisionmaking in early childhood educational services was replaced by a new focus on child care as a broadly interpreted social issue (Simons and Vella 1984). Cox's report, *Project Care* (1974), recommended governmental support not only for child care and preschool services, but also for a range of family services, playgroups, babysitting clubs, and private childminders. It recommended that services be based on local needs. Although these recommendations were supported in principle, there were problems in their implementation. As a re-

sult, a third review group—the Policies Review Staff—suggested instead that a national Children's Bureau, later conceptualized as the Children's Commission, be established.

The ill-fated Children's Commission held great promise as a force that would bring about the much awaited integration of care and educational programs for young children. However, the act to establish the commission was not proclaimed before the Labour government fell from power in November 1975. Brennan and O'Donnell (1986), in summarizing this period, suggest that

in spite of its failure to introduce new legislation or to move beyond the community submission model of funding new services, the Whitlam government made some significant advances in the child care field. It introduced, for the first time in Australia's history, the idea that the Federal government could become involved in a national program of providing child care (p. 38).

During the Labour party's term of office, the federal government had been making sizable grants to the states for early childhood programs, but approximately 80 percent of this money had been used by the states to support part-time sessional preschool programs. At their peak, these funds enabled the states to meet 100 percent of preschool teacher's salaries. Although the remaining funds had been used to establish child care services, the extent of this provision fell far short of what had been envisaged in the Social Welfare Commission's report. Under the Conservative government that followed, the distinction between child care and preschool education funding schemes was further strengthened, with child care funding being directed specifically toward "needy families" (Fraser in Coleman 1978, quoted in Brennan and O'Donnell, 1986:41).

From the mid-1970s and into the 1980s, state governments assumed increasing responsibility for providing preschool services, with the balance gradually shifting from the volunteer agencies to state governments and ever-increasing levels of provision. Federal early childhood funding failed to keep pace with the growth in this sector, however, so that states were required to provide an increasing proportion of the costs of preschool education from their general funds. In 1986, the federal government ceased funding preschool programs entirely, so that the states are once again characterized by very different levels of preschool/kindergarten services.

The federal government did maintain a commitment to child care services, however, and the late 1970s and 1980s saw a rapid increase in the number of federally supported child care spaces. This distinction between funding models for child care and preschool services has helped perpetuate the discontinuity that has characterized Australian early childhood services from their inception.

Patterns of Early Childhood Services in Contemporary Australia

In the 1980s, early childhood education professionals in Australia identified their area of concern as the provision of a range of care and educational services for children from birth to age 8. As has already been indicated, governmental funding arrangements tend to be separated into "education" and "care," and into services for under-school-age children and school-age children. In contemporary Australia, many types of education and care services are available, though not necessarily evenly spread throughout the nation.

According to the most recent statistics (Australian Bureau of Statistics, 1988) about one-third of Australian children ages 3 to 5 are enrolled in preschool or kindergarten programs. Just over 20 percent of the children in this age group are in child care centers while another 2 percent are in family day care schemes. This means that almost one-half of 3- to 5-year olds in Australia are served by formal education or care services.

In contrast, very few children under age 3 are enrolled in formal early childhood services, though long waiting lists are common in funded programs. About 10 percent are enrolled in formal child care, with a further 40 percent spending some time in informal care arrangements involving neighbors, friends, or other family members.

One of the most widespread services available for children under age 3 is the parent-sponsored playgroup. National statistics gathered by the Playgroup Association of the Northern Territory (Wyles, 1990) suggest that over 100,000 Australian children regularly participate in playgroups. While figures are not available on the ages of these children, general patterns of playgroup use suggest that most are under age 3. Other services for children under age 3 include toddler groups for parents and children and occasional care centers.

FIGURE 1
Use of Formal and Informal Early Childhood
Services by 3 to 5 years old

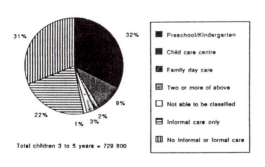

Source: Australian Bureau of Statistics (1988): Table 3

FIGURE 2
Use of Formal and Informal Early Childhood
Services by 0 to 3 years old

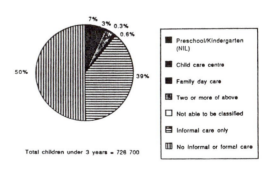

Source: Australian Bureau of Statistics (1988): Table 3

Funding of Early Childhood Services

Governmental funding policies in the 1990s reflect the strong community base of Australian early childhood services so that many Australians have a sense of ownership and involvement in the provision of services for young children. Federal governmental policy on child care funding allows state governments, local governments, voluntary agencies, community organizations, trade union, women's groups, and religious groups to apply for registration as approved child-care-sponsor organizations. Such registration provides access to both capital and recurring grants.

Federal Responsibilities. In the last decade, there has been considerable national debate over the extent to which governments should fund child care and the means of calculating and equitably distributing such funding. Some argue that child care should be on a user-pay basis and that governments should make no contribution to funding the service. At the other extreme, some desire universal, free child care sponsored by governments and community groups. Within the field of early childhood education, there is strong support for extending the level of governmental funding to child care, but debate continues on the means of allocating funds.

Earlier models made funds available only to nonprofit programs and calculated funding according to staffing qualifications and patterns. With the increased demand for child care spaces, however, there has been considerable growth in the number of commercial child care centers (i.e., where the owner/operator expects to make a profit from the service). This sector has become a strong lobby group in the debate over appropriate funding models and since 1991, commercial child care center users who meet eligibility requirements have been able to seek fee relief from the federal government in a manner similar to that for nonprofit service users. The provision of governmental support for commercial centers was a contentious issue in Australian early childhood education in the late 1980s. It characterizes the way in which concerns about individual family rights, governmental responsibilities, and child and parent needs are interrelated. It is similar to the debates taking place in other modern societies (Ward, 1986).

New services are funded under a needs-based model where state planning committees determine locations of greatest community need of child care of a particular type, such as occasional care or full-day day care. Once the program had been approved, it is given an establishment grant from the federal government. Other bodies—such as state governments, local governments, or interested parties—might make a contribution to capital expenditure. If the proposed program meets governmental guidelines, the federal government will contribute to operating costs, though it is expected that users should also contribute. Presently, these grants are calculated on the number of full-time child care spaces utilized in the services. This aspect of the funding policy (adopted in 1986) has attracted considerable comment, with some arguing that the former practice of calculating funding according to staffing patterns rather than by the number of full-time spaces, promoted higher quality care (Murray, 1986).

The federal government also provides fee relief for eligible families so that those on very low incomes receive a subsidy almost equivalent to the full cost of the service. While a sliding scale exists to provide a partial subsidy for other families, recent criticism has suggested that the level of support is insufficient to meet the ever-increasing cost of quality care. The current funding policy attempts to encourage a mix of income groups, single- and two-parent families, special needs children, and minority cultural groups in programs, thus ensuring that there will be no enclaves where different agencies serve different types of clients (Hurford, 1987).

Governmental policy in the 1980s was directed toward increasing the number of spaces available in approved facilities. More of these funded spaces were in family day cares than in center-based full-day or occasional care facilities, perhaps because of the lower establishment costs associated with home-based services. Out-of-school care for school-aged children also attracted considerable governmental funding. For the most part, families with special needs, such as recent immigrants or minority group members, were served within regular services.

Table 2 indicates the number of full-time equivalent spaces funded by the federal govern-

TABLE 2

Child Care Places in Federally Funded Programs, 1988

Full Day Day Care	Occasional Care	Family Day Care Care	Out of School	Aboriginal Families	Disabled Children	Migrant Families
35,085	1,712	39,414	29,912	248	49	40

Source: Department of Community Services and Health, June 1988.

ment in 1988. Although a center is funded for full-time equivalent spaces, not all children attend full time, thus the actual number of children using the service may be much higher than the full-time equivalent figures indicate.

In the 1980s, there was remarkable growth overall in the number of children enrolled in child care services. In 1982, only 5.8 percent of the nation's 1.1 million children under school age attended a child care center or participated in a family day care scheme (Brennan and O'Donnell, 1986:1). By 1987, the proportion had grown to 12.8 percent of the 1.3 million children under school age. There was also a significant number of children of school age enrolled in out-of-school care services. One-fifth of the total number of children who spent part of their week in a child care center in 1987 were of school age (ABS, 1988).

State Governmental Responsibilities. In most states, there are extensive preschool or kindergarten services for children in the year before they enter primary school, but the provision of services for 3-year-olds is much lower, since there has been

less governmental funding available for this age group.

In Queensland, Tasmania, Northern Territory, Western Australia, and the Australian Capital Territory, the Departments of Education sponsor many preschools. In other states, different governmental departments are responsible for preschool provision. For example, in New South Wales and Victoria, the major thrust has been to fund community-based kindergartens. The Department of Health is the authority in Victoria responsible for granting funds in this area. In New South Wales, the Department of Youth and Community Services has this responsibility, and in South Australia the Children's Services Office and the Education Department jointly supervise, support, and fund centers.

In all states, approved community-based early childhood groups receive governmental support for centers, but the level of funding and the extent of the overall provision of services vary across the states. Table 3 indicates the number of children

TABLE 3

Population of 3- to 4-Year-Olds by State and Total Preschool Enrollments of 3- to 4-Year-Olds in Preschool/Kindergarten (In Thousands)

	New South Wales	Victoria	Queensland	South Australia	Western Australia	Tasmania Territory	Northern Territory	Australian Capital Territory
3-year-olds	83.0	60.4	41.3	20.2	23.7	7.1	3.1	4.2
4-year-olds	84.2	60.8	43.0	19.8	32.8	7.1	3.3	4.4
In	167.2	121.2	84.6	40.0	47.4	14.2	6.4	8.6
Preschools	81.8	57.5	50.2	19.5	29.1	7.1	4.4	4.0
(3-to-4-year-olds)								

Source: ABS, June 1987.

ages 3 and 4 and the number of children who attend preschool or kindergarten in each state.[1]

State governments are responsible for the development and enforcement of regulations covering early childhood services, although local governmental officers may also visit centers to see that regulations are followed. All early childhood education and care services must be licensed annually by the relevant governmental authority. Regulations have traditionally focused on health and safety matters and the "suitability" of the physical plant. Attention has been given to staff-child ratios and the characteristics of staff, but little is specified about the quality of the experiences that children should have in a program registered under state regulations.

Currently, several states are undergoing extensive reviews of their regulations for early childhood services offered outside the state educational system. One of the most contentious issues in these regulations deals with appropriate levels of qualification for workers in child care services. This issue is discussed in more detail in the section on teacher education.

Kindergarten Programs

Sessional kindergarten was the fastest growing service for young children during the 1960s and the 1970s when public demand led to federal and state governmental involvement in sponsoring and funding sessional services. Growth continues but at a much slower rate than the provision of child care services.

Children attend kindergarten for part of the day and/or part of the week. Some programs may operate for two and one-half hours per day up to five days a week, offering morning and afternoon sessions. In other centers, sessions may be about five hours a day with children attending either two or three days per week. Kindergartens are usually open for the same number of weeks per year as primary schools.

A common group size in a kindergarten is 25 children ages 4 to 5, or 20 children ages 3 to 4, with a qualified teacher and a paid assistant (who may have taken a short training course). This pattern varies slightly in South Australia, where group size is commonly 30 children with two qualified teach-

ers and an assistant.

Preschools and kindergartens operated by state departments of education are usually free and most offer places to children only in the year before primary school (i.e., when children have turned age 4). Approved community kindergartens may have a larger proportion of 3-year-olds. State subsidies mean that parents in community centers pay only a portion of the cost of providing the services. Over 86 percent of those using kindergartens in 1988 paid less than $15 a week (ABS, 1988).

It is generally accepted that kindergarten programs in Australia provide services for both children and parents. It is the responsibility of the teachers to provide developmentally appropriate experiences for children and to ensure that parents receive information about the program and their child's developmental progress. Teachers are expected to have skill in working with parents, supporting the parenting role, involving parents in the children's program and working collaboratively with parents in determining program priorities and center needs.

Kindergarten Curriculum

The curriculum in a kindergarten is generally recognized as educational in the sense that it is planned with certain goals in mind for children and is implemented by qualified teachers. Educational goals tend to be stated in terms of aspects of development to be fostered or enhanced (AECA, 1987; Cohen and Schiller, 1988). Parents enroll their children in kindergarten because they believe it will benefit their children (Ebbeck, 1982). Of the 236,500 children attending kindergarten in the late 1980s, 222,600 were doing so because parents considered it was "good for children" and would "prepare them for school" (ABS, 1988, Table 9).

Knowledge about child development and behavior is the key to an early childhood educator's approach to setting goals and designing a curriculum for the kindergarten. At the same time, there are debates within the field about whether teacher decisionmaking relies primarily on knowledge about child development and child study or whether wider values also influence goals and practices. Some accept that curriculum practice is the application of developmental principles, while others argue that educational values shape perceptions about the type of development that ought to be nurtured and the developmental principles considered to be most relevant for guiding teachers' decisionmaking (Ashby, 1972). For example, Halliwell (1977) claimed that an educational program should help young children to become more autonomous, rational, sensitive, and socially competent than they might otherwise have become.

Whether justified in terms of developmental or educational values, most curriculum goals reflect concerns about children being physically, socially, and cognitively independent, and acting cooperatively in group situations. Emphasis is placed on children creatively expressing their thoughts and feelings, and in extending their understandings about self and the world. Developing oral language skills and related social competencies also figure in goal statements.

Two characteristics of kindergartens in Australia are the emphasis given (1) to planning learning environments and (2) to play as a basis for learning. How space and materials are organized to promote independent and cooperative behaviors is also considered. In addition, styles of adult-child interaction that encourage problem-solving through open-ended questioning are emphasized. Resources and activities are carefully designed to encourage children to engage in vigorous physical play, to use dramatic play to further develop their knowledge about their world, and to develop social skills associated with working competently in groups.

A distinctive feature of Australian preschools and kindergartens is the quality of the outdoor environment. Because the Australian climate is conducive to extensive use of outdoors in both winter and summer, centers are designed to ensure easy access to outdoors. Extensive landscaping provides shade, and equipment is flexible so that it can be adapted to meet changes in children's abilities and interests. The outdoor activities that take place on the patio space that is usually provided between indoor and outdoor areas—which helps guard against artificial distinctions between "indoor" and "outdoor" programs—are regarded as being just as educationally important as the indoor program.

Kindergarten teachers are more likely to be described as guides, facilitators, or directors of learning than as instructors. Teachers are expected to observe children and to make inferences about their interests and abilities. They are expected to nurture interests, challenge current understandings and competencies, and stimulate further learning. Large blocks of time are usually given to "free play," when children select their own activities with some guidance from the teachers, though children do assemble in groups to listen to a story or for a music session.

Variations on Center-Based Kindergartens

Variations on the sessional kindergarten model have developed in response to the specific needs of particular communities and children. Although these programs may be guided by principles similar to those described above, the services may differ from one location to another or in the means of delivery.

Distance Educational Programs. Geographic isolation is a feature of life for a small but assertive proportion of Australian families. For many years, state correspondence schools have provided educational opportunities for older children, using print material and shortwave radio links. More recently, audiotapes, videotapes, microcomputers, and satellite television links have been used to maintain contact between a teacher and a group of children. As state educational departments began to establish preschool educational services, it was necessary to include a component of distance education. For example, in Queensland about 800 children a year are enrolled in the State Preschool Correspondence Program. Teachers develop individual programs for children, working in close cooperation with parents. Families are loaned educational toys, story books, audio- and videotaped stories and songs, and other materials that introduce ideas for further exploration. Despite the huge distances involved, close relationships develop between the teachers and families. Although face-to-face meetings with the teachers are rare, efforts are made to bring children and parents together in small groups.[2]

Mobile Kindergartens. Several states provide mobile kindergarten services for clusters of families living out of reach of permanent preschool facilities. In some cases, it is a temporary service provided until permanent facilities can be established. In most mobile kindergartens, basic accommodation is provided in community buildings, with a small van of equipment moving to several different locations each week. Qualified teachers staff the programs, building up rapport with an extended cluster of clients. In New South Wales, a research project funded by the Van Leer Foundation is exploring the provision of mobile kindergarten and other support services for families living in mobile home parks (Schiller, 1987).

Programs for Special Cultural and Religious Needs. Cultural and religious groups desiring to establish preschools with a particular curriculum are able to apply for a subsidy from both state and federal departments of education. Early childhood centers with a higher level of enrollment of aboriginal and Torres Strait Islander children are eligible for funding from both state and federal governments. Centers with a high level of enrollment from different ethnic groups also are eligible for special support services. Such services include multicultural liaison officers and migrant resource centers. Centers that serve particular ethnic or religious groups have been established in most large cities.

Hospital Programs. A recent initiative of governments and volunteer agencies is the introduction of hospital programs for preschool children. These may be based on a preschool sessional model or be designed as play programs for wider age range. Staffing patterns and qualifications vary widely in these programs.

Maria Montessori and Rudolph Steiner Centres. The number of programs associated with the philosophies of Maria Montessori and Rudolph Steiner is small, though there has been growth in the last decade. Some have been approved by the volunteer agencies and receive subsidies, but others operate without governmental assistance.

Center-Based Child Care

The center-based sector of early childhood services grew rapidly in the 1980s and further growth is predicted. In 1987, there were 51,300 more children in child care than in 1984, accounting for approximately 10 percent of the under-school-age population in Australia (ABS, 1984, 1988). Terms commonly used for center-based child care include day nurseries, day-care centers,

neighborhood centers, and child care centers.

Most child care centers are open for a least eight hours per day, five days a week, and operate for 48 to 51 weeks of the year. A comparatively small number offer a 24-hour service for parents who work shifts (Brennan and O'Donnell, 1986: xii). Although centers are open for long hours, about one-third of the children attend less than five hours per day and 80 percent attend less than 20 hours per week (ABS, 1988:9).

In contrast to preschool services, where group size, facilities, and staffing are relatively uniform throughout Australia, child care center standards and sizes are diverse. Some centers serve up to 100 children in age-segregated groups; others are small, with 25 or 30 children of mixed ages. Some centers are in facilities constructed specifically for child care services; others may use converted homes or church halls. The balance between qualified and unqualified staff varies considerably from one center to another, as does the educational program for children and parents.

The extent of variation in standards and style of operation can be traced to differences in state regulations, levels of support, staffing patterns, and sponsorship. Sponsoring agencies hold different assumptions and values about what constitutes good care. Creative responses to identified needs include the work of some community child care groups that have established small centers in converted houses close to children's homes. They are a practical demonstration of a "family-group" philosophy, where it is believed that better care for children will result if total group numbers are small and age groups mixed.[3]

Centers operated by parental cooperatives tend to offer a range of services, such as occasional care when parents are engaged in leisure pursuits or part-time work, full-day care for working parents, drop-in morning coffee sessions where parents can meet, and playgroups where very young children can engage in group play under the care of their parents. These centers, which provide information on a range of parenting topics, are usually small, consisting of 25 of 30 children.

Child care centers sponsored by employers tend to be close to the parents' workplaces (e.g., in a hospital, university, or factory). Unions have also taken an interest in establishing centers and in contributing to the development of management policies for such centers. As the relationship between child care availability and women's career development becomes more widely understood, equal opportunity concerns are becoming influential in the expansion of work-based child care services.

In all states, the early childhood education and community child care networks sponsor a substantial number of child care centers. Because of their size and long-recognized expertise, these have been powerful lobby groups in advocating well-qualified staff and high-quality experiences for children and parents.

During the last five years, the federal government has funded many occasional care services, in which a proportion of children may attend for regular part-time care, with the remainder attending on a drop-in basis. In some cases, this form of care is provided in addition to full-day care. Other occasional care services are offered by the commercial sector.

Public companies operating chains of fully owned or franchised child care centers is a relatively new and controversial phenomenon in Australia. While there has been considerable growth in the commercial sector, most has been through small, owner-operated centers.

There is currently an unmet demand for child care centers in Australia. It is estimated that one-half of all children are in funded centers, which means that up to 70,000 may be in commercial centers where standards vary widely. In some states, a limited advisory and support scheme is available on a voluntary basis for those wanting help in designing programs for young children and an accreditation scheme is currently under consideration both at a national level and in some states (McCrea and Piscitelli, 1990).

Along with the increasing opportunity to use government-approved and -supported centers is a growing perception among parents that in addition to providing supplemental care for children, child care can and should nurture children's development and learning. While most parents surveyed in 1987 indicated that their main reason for using this service was as substitute care while they were at work, shopping, or engaged in recreation,

about one-third of the parents indicated their main reason for using the service was that the services would be good for the child or would help prepare the child for school (ABS, 1988).

Some centers now plan to integrate a range of services, such as sessional preschool for 3- to 5-year-olds, occasional care, full-day day care, and counseling services for families in need of additional support. These centers help to promote the idea that the care and education of young children need not be artificially separated.

Programming in Center-Based Child Care

Sebastian (1986:5) identified three basic orientations in center-based care: custodial, developmental, and comprehensive. Custodial care, in which the focus is simply ensuring the physical health and safety of the child, is generally accepted as being inadequate. In a developmental program, children are encouraged to actively explore their physical environment and social world, and interesting and challenging opportunities are provided. Creative strategies are devised to allow working parents to become meaningfully involved in the program. A fully comprehensive program also provides a developmental program for children, but goes beyond parental involvement to provide a wide range of family support services, such as counseling, crisis intervention, and parenting skills programs.

The interface between care and education in child care centers is addressed in a number of ways. In some centers, the "educational component" is provided by an early childhood teacher who operates a preschool-like program within the child care setting for a limited time each day. Similarly, some commercial centers arrange to transport preschool-age children to local kindergarten programs. In other child care centers, education is conceptualized as permeating the entire program. In this approach, qualified staff operate an integrated educational program that provides learning opportunities for children throughout the day. This is generally considered the optimal approach, but it is dependent on the presence of suitably qualified staff members.

Family Day Care Schemes

Registered home-based care is a relative new-comer in formal services for young children, though informal minding of children by neighbors, friends, and relatives remains a significant component of Australian early childhood care arrangements. Family day care schemes have qualified staff who register and monitor care providers and provide other forms of support. One of the major advantages of this form of care is its flexibility, which enables care providers to respond to the individual needs of families and to put them in touch with a network of support services.

Family day care caters to children from birth through primary-school age. Only a small proportion of children, 42,500, or 3.3 percent, of children under school age are enrolled in family day care. A higher proportion of children under age 3 than 3- to 5-year-olds are enrolled in this service, perhaps indicating that parents consider the services to be more "home-like" for very young children, though it may also reflect the scarcity of center-based spaces for this age group.

Regulations in most states limit the number of children cared for by a care provider to four or five, including the provider's own children. Families using the service pay fees to the care provider, with means tested fee relief (i.e., families with a sufficiently low income will receive a rebate on some of their child care fees) available in a similar way to the scheme operating for child care centers. Governments provide subsidies for the operation of approved family day care schemes.

Family day care is able to provide full-day day care, though only 25 percent of children using the services are with the care provider for more than 20 hours per week, suggesting that some families may be using more than one type of service. This is a cost-effective form of child care, but some groups argue that there are other compelling reasons for maintaining and expanding family day care schemes. Anne Gowers (1979: 275) argues that this service can provide "an opportunity for families within a community to become related to one another, thus fostering community interdependence and support." On the other hand, members of the Working Women Centre (Brennan and O'Donnell, 1986: 89) argue that family day care is providing an inexpensive service at the expense of the care providers who are paid quite low rates and whose contribution to society may therefore be undervalued.

Primary Schooling and Out-of-School Care

Schooling is compulsory for Australian children ages 6 to 15. Some 75 percent of 5- to 8-year-old children are enrolled in state governmental schools, attending for six hours per day, five days per week. Nongovernmental schools provide education for nearly 25 percent of Australian students. A high proportion of these schools have religious affiliations with either the Anglican or Catholic church.

State school systems make some provision for education before and after the compulsory years, providing 12 years of free state schooling. All states except Western Australia and Queensland provide a preprimary year within the primary school system and many nongovernmental schools also have preprimary school programs. There is a bewildering range of terms used for these preprimary classes—"reception" in South Australia, "transition" in the Northern Territory, "kindergarten" in New South Wales and the Australian Capital Territory, and "preparatory" in Victoria and Tasmania.

Despite similarities in the year structure of schooling in Australia, across the states variations in age of entry and progression policies result in different age compositions at each year level. Some states have a yearly intake, permitting children to commence school in the January after their fifth birthday, others permit entry at age 4 1/2 on the fifth birthday, or at the commencement of the term following the fifth birthday. The relative merits of *annual intake*, where children who have reached the required age begin school in January, *continuous intake* where children begin school on their birthday, and *staggered intake*, where groups who have reached the required age are enrolled at set times during the year, have been the subject of considerable debate in the 1980s among educators and policymakers (Ashby and Boulton-Lewis 1988; Murray, 1987).

The different starting ages and progression in the first years of schooling result in state differences in the age composition at each year level. For instance, 40 percent of children in grade 3 in Queensland are age 7 and only 1 percent of Victorian children in grade 3 are age 7. Nine-year-olds comprise 2 percent of the grade 3 group in Western Australia and 24 percent in the Australian Capital Territory (derived from ABS, 1988:39). These differences pose serious difficulties for families who move between states, since children may have to change grade level or be placed with children of a different age. This situation has strengthened demands for national standardization of schooling arrangements.

Most children in the first years of primary school are enrolled in age groups of about 25 children. Some classes are held in double teaching spaces with two teachers and 50 children. During the 1980s, there was increased interest at the school level in establishing multi-age grouping, where 5-, 6-, and 7-year-olds are taught using flexible, child-responsive curriculum practices.

In the past, most states referred to the first two or three years of primary school as the "junior school" or the "infant school." Despite the early childhood designation suggested by these terms, classroom practices in primary school reflecting early childhood education philosophies and practices varied considerably from state to state and even school to school. Specialist qualifications were required in a few states for teaching in the early years of primary school, though many teachers of 5- to 8-year-olds were generalist primary teachers.

Recently, state school systems are moving to develop curriculum resources that emphasize sequences in learning in school subjects, from the preprimary school level to grade 12. There is interest in creating national curriculum frameworks that may assist in resolving some of the transition problems for older children moving from one state to another. Some educators, however, fear that these moves may deemphasize the special curriculum needs of young children in schools.

Other initiatives have created closer links between kindergarten curriculum practices for 4- to 5-year-olds and those for 5- to 8-year-olds. One curriculum initiative sponsored by the federal government involved most teachers of children under age 8 in Australian state schools in an Early Literacy In-service Course. The course brought together recent thinking about appropriate curriculum practices for young children that would lead to enhanced literacy learning. The national First Years of School conferences of 1984, 1986, 1988, and 1991 have focused governmental attention on the similarities in thinking about curricula for young children among teachers in all states in Australia.

The extent to which closer links between preschool and primary school programs will lead to a move toward early childhood education practices or a move toward practices more suited to older children is a concern within the field of early childhood education. A number of studies have been undertaken to examine curriculum practices in preschool and primary school and the transition between the two (Cross, 1988; Cullen, 1988; Halliwell, 1989).

Early Education Classes

In Queensland, there are some 133 early education classes, involving 1,633 children aged 4, in small schools where the yearly intakes are too low to be able to form a viable state preschool group. In these schools, facilities are provided to enable teachers with approved early childhood education qualifications to teach a mixed group of 4- to 7-year-olds. The program is expected to be appropriate for the development of the children involved and the expectations of the primary school in which the class is situated (Ashby, 1986; Halliwell, 1984).

After-School Care

Most primary school children, approximately 65 percent, go home after school to primary caregivers, usually their mothers. Another 34 percent are cared for by neighbors, relatives, or look after themselves. About 2 percent of school-age children use formal out-of-school care services (ABS, 1988).

The number of spaces in government funded out-of-school care programs has increased dramatically in the last few years, as has the number of schools offering a formal program of out-of-school care. Many of these programs operate in primary school facilities and cater almost exclusively to primary school children. It is possible, though, to find groups offering out-of-school programs from other than school facilities. The Queensland Children's Activity Network, for instance, encourages programs with a focus on play and creative expression in a wide range of settings. Volunteer organizations and local councils maintain supervised playgrounds where children may spend time out of school. Out-of-school programs may offer care before school, after school, during vacations, or for just some of these times. They may be primarily recreation-oriented, provide supervision of children with homework, or offer a play-based educational program. In a study of out-of-school programs undertaken by Piscitelli and Mobbs (1986), few respondents reported that their aim was merely custodial.

Special Education Programs for Young Children

The historical development of educational provisions for children with special educational needs followed a pattern somewhat different from other sectors of schooling (Elkins, 1990). In spite of differences between the states in terms of the range and availability of services, provisions were invariably made by volunteer bodies with little or no governmental financial support. These provisions tended to relate to particular categories of identifiable needs. Blind persons and deaf persons represented the earliest groups to be served, with various other disability groups following. Provisions for intellectually disabled children were among the last to be made. Special programs for gifted children and particular cultural and ethnic groups are also very recent.

The large-scale involvement of public educational authorities in special education services has expanded rapidly since the mid-1970s. Public educational authorities have replaced many volunteer agencies in the provision of school services, allowing volunteer agencies to provide other types of services. However, including special education as an integral component of public education has led to many significant changes in the organization and delivery of services for special needs students. These are discussed below.

Two important objectives underscore contemporary developments in special education in Australia: decategorization and normalization. The first objective calls for categorically based assessments and services to be abandoned and replaced by functionally based assessments and generic services. Although the use of some labels to describe disabilities and consequential handicaps serves some uses, this also leads to stereotyping. Generic services alleviate stereotyping, and are generally provided within the local community, so that children and parents do not have to travel to receive more central segregated services. The second objective calls for replacing segregated special schooling with mainstreaming, (i.e., integrating disabled children into regular schools and classes).

It should be noted that even under previous arrangements, many handicapped children attended regular schools. For example, Andrews *et al.,* (1979) found in a national survey of special education in Australia, that only about one-half of the students with a declared disability were attending special schools and other services. The remainder were enrolled in regular schools.

The pursuit of these two objectives has caused a rethinking of the traditional organization of special education services based on segregated facilities and an infrastructure of specialized personnel. Current practices aim to provide support and resources to teachers in regular schools. This shift in the *modus operandi* of special education has been uneven in terms of implementation across Australia and has been unsettling, particularly for teachers and parents who have to adjust to quite new and sometimes difficult situations. Overall, special education in Australia is currently characterized by considerable experimentation and uncertainty.

The major principles driving this reconceptualization derive from Tomlinson's (1982) sociological critique of special education—the principle of "the least restrictive environment," which resulted in the mainstreaming principle of Public Law No. 94–142 (Education of All Handicapped Act) in the United States and the principle of a continuum of placement options as advocated by the Warnock Commission (1978) in Great Britain. These three principles, when combined with major objectives previously noted, give rise to a range of options from which students and their parents are able to select the services that can be flexibly adapted to meet their individual needs. The desire for such a range of options represents an alliance between professionals and parents. Ashman and Elkins (1990) have depicted this development in terms of a hierarchy of service provisions as set out in Figure 3.

Placement in mainstreamed classrooms, with varying levels of additional support, provides an important cluster of options. However, integration has resulted in considerable controversy among regular school teachers and parents (Gow, 1990). The central issue involves the extent to which guaranteed additional support can be provided to schools and classrooms serving disabled students. Teachers feel vulnerable because they lack training, and parents of both disabled and nondisabled children are concerned that students could be disadvantaged by integration arrangements.

The area of early childhood special education has followed a similar, if more recent, pattern of development to that of special schooling. Initial provisions made by volunteer organizations or through university-based demonstration projects were generally category-based in terms of client group. As parental demands for access to "early intervention" programs grew, however, the number and variety of programs expanded dramatically.

Such rapid expansion has its problems, as Bettison (1988) points out:

Early intervention is not a unitary concept, as the national review demonstrated. It has become a catch-all term often used to encompass almost every type of regular, non-medical contact with a child under school age which purports to influence the child's development. Programs range from group play once or twice a week in a preschool setting to highly structured intensive individual teaching directed at specific goals for each child. Most programs aim to enhance development by counteracting developmental delay or impairment. However, there has been no examination of where these, or any other outcomes, have in fact resulted from early intervention (p. 4).

A further problem has been an imbalance in the provision of services for children under and over age 3. The majority of services are available for children over age 3, although services differ in terms of sponsoring agency. In broad terms, services for children under age 3 cater to children with specific, identifiable disabilities and are provided only by volunteer agencies. Services for children over age 3 are provided by governmental authorities (e.g., education, health, or welfare) and a wide spectrum of community groups (Ashby, et al., 1990). Services for children over age 3 are usually of a sessional nature with part-time participation in a regular preschool program, while programs for children under age 3 are usually in the form of one playgroup session a week.

Several innovative projects have sought to meet a range of individual needs. For example, Hayes's (1988) description of the CAPS (Child and Parent Support) Project in a rural community

FIGURE 3
A special education services hierarchy

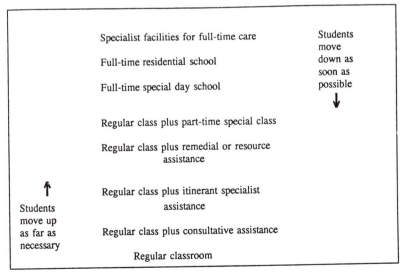

Source: Ashman and Elkins (1990: 17)

highlights the positive results when a strong community will develops and otherwise unavailable services become available. This project was developed in a community where parents had to travel about 200 kilometers (each way) to obtain specialist early childhood services. The services developed through CAPS included a home visiting program, a center-based program, an outreach program to regular preschools, parental training, coordination of therapy and related services, and the creation of small localized toy lending libraries. In several respects, CAPS was typical of an emerging type of flexible, local service. However, evaluative data concerning the efficacy of such programs are not yet available on a national basis.

An important gap in service provision for young children with disabilities, in addition to the need for programs for children under age 3, is the relative absence of coordinated approaches in the programs for the growing proportion of children below school age who participate in full-day child care programs (Ashby, et al., 1990). While there are moves to develop high-quality national standards for all child care services, at this time disabled children do not form part of the target population.

Early childhood special education in Australia is in a process of rapid expansion and experimentation. Its development has outpaced the theory and research necessary for such services to provide a coherent educational and social direction and to articulate with the schooling system to which children will progress.

Training Programs for Teachers of Young Children

The expanding early childhood services of the 1970s and 1980s have created a need for a range of qualified staff. The three key groups of qualified staff working in early childhood care and education have come from distinctly different preservice training programs. A final group providing early childhood services is fairly large but untrained.

Early childhood teachers traditionally have been trained in three-year courses in Kindergarten Teacher's Colleges in the capital cities. Since the early 1980s, these colleges have merged with larger, more diverse institutions and have maintained preservice training courses. The content of the courses varies from institution to institution.

A second group of early childhood personnel has completed certificate or associate diploma courses at Technical and Further Education (TAFE) Colleges or Colleges of Advanced Education. The courses for this group concentrate on practical issues related to child care and were initially established to prepare assistants to work with teachers in child care centers. As child care programs have proliferated in recent years, two-year diploma-trained staff are taking increasing responsibility for group leadership in the birth to 4-year-old age groups.

Nurses make up the third major professional group working in child care. The practice of employing nurses has been deeply entrenched in the child care field. Until 1986, federally funded programs were required under the federal Child Care Act to employ at least one nurse to care for children under age 3. Some nurses working in child care have undertaken short training programs known as "Mothercraft" courses but others have general nursing qualifications.

A fourth group of personnel in early childhood care is educational staff with no specific training for this work. Although nationwide statistics on such staff are limited, Queensland data indicate that at least one-third of all care providers in center-based programs are unqualified (ABS, 1988:19). Since all state regulations allow similar pattern of employment for unqualified staff, this situation is likely to be the same across Australia.

Teacher Training

Since the early part of this century, early childhood teacher education courses have offered specialized training for those intending to work with children under age 8. Between 1978 and 1984, major changes occurred in early childhood teacher education in Australia. Adverse economic conditions affecting higher education forced small specialist colleges to merge with larger, more economically viable tertiary institutions. By 1989, a new federal governmental initiative brought about a second wave of consolidations, which forced further reductions in the number of higher education settings. In some cases, early childhood teacher education retained a distinct identity within these larger universities by being granted "Institute" or

"School" status.

Currently, university preservice programs offer different orientations, course lengths, and end points. Students may focus on work with children birth to age 8, birth to age 5, or ages 5 to 8. Two main types of training courses exist. In specialist early childhood courses, students study human development, and curriculum theory and are given field experience. Students are prepared to teach in a range of early childhood settings.

A second type of early childhood teacher preparation program consists of a "generalist" teacher course with an early childhood education component. Such courses vary considerably in structure and organization. Graduates may be granted an early childhood specialization after completing some field experience in preschools and undertaking some curriculum and teaching strategies components with an early childhood emphasis. Many students complete human development subjects as part of an educational foundation course in common with students preparing for other levels of teaching. Typically, students in this type of program work with children ages 4 and older, and focus on preschool and lower primary settings.

Prospective students intending to undertake tertiary study in early childhood must pass rigorous entry requirements, and must have had a high level of achievement in secondary school. The demand for places in early childhood teacher preparation courses far outweighs the number of available places. A limited number of places for special entry and mature-age students is made available at most institutions. Since the 1980s, programs have been developed to encourage aboriginal peoples and Torres Strait Islanders to participate in early childhood teacher education courses.

As early childhood teacher education has faced the challenges of the 1980s, and now faces them in the 1990s, debate has continued about how best to maintain the distinctive early childhood identity of these courses. Issues of concern include length of course, age group specialization, balance of theory to practice, and models of teacher education programs. Recent surveys (Briggs, 1984; Spodek, 1986; Tayler, 1990) have examined the characteristics and components of early childhood teacher educa-

tion programs. The findings indicate that in this time of rapid change, student populations are becoming more diverse and represent an increasing number of men, racial and cultural groups, and mature-age persons. Course content has responded to changes in contemporary Australian society by placing an increasing emphasis on human relations, multiculturalism, and diversity of family structure, and has responded to the needs of the rapidly expanding child care sector. Several major reports on teacher education were commissioned in the early 1990s (Australian Schools Council, 1989; Ebbeck, 1990; Speedy, 1989) and are likely to have profound effects on the nature of early childhood teacher education programs.

Practicum arrangements vary widely across the early childhood teacher preparation courses. The range of age groups and settings reflects the broad diversity of early childhood programs. Students in most courses must demonstrate competence for teaching in preschools, kindergartens, and lower primary grades. Some teacher education courses require practicum in child care centers and with children under age 3. Because teacher educators recognize the need for students to observe and experience teacher contexts similar to prospective employment situations, some programs allow students to undertake teaching practice in small towns and on remote settlements. The supervision of such innovative practicums is costly however, so these programs are rare.

While some early childhood teacher preparation involves a three-year preservice course, some universities offer a four-year degree. Graduate diploma courses (one-year full-time equivalent courses) are also offered in several institutions. The nature of these courses varies. One institution offers a graduate diploma in early childhood for already qualified primary and secondary teachers who want to gain appropriate credentials to teach in early childhood settings. Other courses have been designed for liberal arts university graduates who want to obtain a first teaching credential. A further range of graduate diplomas has been developed in child development, program management and administration, and parental education. Master's degree courses with an early childhood specialization currently are offered or are under development in most states, yet at present the profession does not have a clearly articulated progression of courses in early childhood education.

In 1972, the Australian government adopted a policy of free tertiary education. This policy came into question in the mid-1980s with the introduction of an annual administration fee of $250 for all Australian tertiary education students. By 1991, under the Higher Education Contribution Scheme, annual fees had increased to approximately $2,000 for full-time students.

Compared with other nations, Australian early childhood teachers enjoy a very favorable working life. Their wages and working conditions parallel those of teachers in primary and secondary education. Equal status and wage parity across state, private, and community-based settings are protected by strong union support.

Child Care Training

Workers in child care enjoy a less settled existence than those in early childhood education. The working conditions for various categories of child care personnel are confused and indistinct. Many factors have contributed to this situation. Historically, child care has been a disparate collection of services—formal and informal, highly regulated and unregulated, employing many people or few, using qualifications from several disciplines or no qualifications.

During the past decade, the early childhood field has been increasingly concerned with disparities between child care and preschool programs. Concern has been expressed about the paucity of qualified staff, the lack of advanced qualifications, and the low pay and poor working conditions of some child care workers. (Brennan and O'Donnell, 1986; Clyde, 1981; Stonehouse, 1988). To address these problems several initiatives have been taken.

For example, a number of preservice courses have been designed for child care personnel. In 1985, existing postsecondary vocational courses were upgraded to two-year associate-diploma level and achieved standardization though the Technical and Further Education (TAFE) system National Core Curriculum. To enter a TAFE child care course, the student must be at least age 17 and have satisfactorily completed five years of secondary education. Some provision for special entry is also made. Applicants must possess basic academic skills and personal characteristics suitable for work with young children.

The TAFE associate diploma course stresses the acquisition of early childhood-related knowledge, skills, and attitudes through extensive practical experience in child care centers. Field placements provide students with opportunities to work in a range of settings, including center-based care, family day care, and after-school programs. Theoretical study emphasizes child development and includes studies in family and society and professional behavior. All students must meet standardized basic competencies in order to receive their diploma.

Some universities retain an interest in the preparation of child care personnel and currently offer (or have under consideration) degree courses with a specialization in child care. In New South Wales, for example, where state regulations require three-year trained early childhood teachers in child care centers with more than 30 children, a substantial number of graduates have child care experience.

For graduates of two-year courses, employment prospects are excellent, with graduates assuming positions as group leaders in infant and toddler care, program administrators in small child care centers, coordinators in family daycare programs, administrators in child care centers, assistants in kindergartens and preschools, and coordinators of after-school-care programs. Despite the expanding number of courses, there remains a shortage of qualified personnel in child care.

In child care centers, graduates from the associate diploma course work alongside teachers, nurses, and unqualified staff. This blend constitutes a unique working environment for child care personnel. It should be noted that the complement of staff differs in funded and commercial child care settings. Prior to the new state regulations, a child care census in New South Wales, suggested that approximately 40 percent of staff in commercial centers were qualified (NSW Department of Youth and Community Services, Planning and Research Unit 1982, in Brennan and O'Donnell, 1986:97). In government-funded centers nationwide, the balance is the reverse, with approximately 67 percent of staff holding some appropriate qualification (Office of Child Care Statistics on Funding, in Brennan and O'Donnell, 1986:97).

Union representation in the child care field reflects the diversity of staff backgrounds and qualification. Even in small centers, staff may be covered by three or four unions, though national restructuring is moving toward single-union coverage for each industry. Staff may be working different hours for various rates of pay and be entitled to vastly different holiday and sick leave allocations. Brennan and O'Donnell (1986:88) point to an important precedent in Perth where the Lady Gowrie Child Care Centre has negotiated a unified set of conditions. This may provide a model for more homogeneous working conditions for all child care personnel in Australia.

Training in Nursing

Nurses in child care generally enjoy favorable working conditions. This group includes those with certificates from short-term courses working in federally funded child care centers. Murray (1986) found that nursing staff comprised 17 percent of child care workers in such centers.

The position of nurses in Australian early childhood education is paradoxical. They have been present in child care centers since the turn of the century, and although the physical well-being of children has always been a major concern, nurses have rarely been acknowledged as partners in child care and have not spoken with a strong professional voice on early childhood issues. This situation is changing as nurses question the relevance of their preservice training for child care work.

Currently, there are many options in preservice nursing education. Hospitals provide opportunities for general nursing training and for Mothercraft nursing. Several Bachelor of Nursing programs are under consideration in colleges and universities. There is also a need for in-service training for nurses in child care (Stonehouse 1986:38) to provide supplementary information on child development and to afford opportunities for bridging communication gaps between nurses and other professionals working in child care.

Parental Support and Educational Programs

Throughout its development, Australian early childhood education has been mindful of the need to understand children in the context of their families and to work with families in addressing the needs of young children. For example, preservice teacher education programs have long emphasized the importance of good communication with parents, and students have been required to develop competencies in areas such as writing parent newsletters, leading parental discussion groups, and organizing parent-education programs.

Because of the importance of volunteer organizations in Australian early childhood education, where most centers until recent times have been essentially parent cooperatives, kindergarten teachers were required to work with parents on a daily basis to ensure the smooth running of the center. While the closeness of teachers and parents in these networks occasionally led to friction, it also led to long-lasting friendships and the meshing of professional and parental concerns for the education of young children.

Despite proclaiming the importance of parents, early childhood educators in the past have not always accorded parents equal status. While many early childhood teachers encouraged parents to help in the program, often by the use of parent rosters, the involvement of parents in collaborative decisionmaking about educational matters has been much less widespread. Recent Australian writers in the area (Henry, 1988) have emphasized the need to develop professional practices that empower parents in decisions about the educational activities of their young children. In keeping with this orientation, early childhood educators are now advised to play a more facilitative role, creating an environment where parents can provide mutual support, communicate freely with teachers, and feel free to identify the areas in which they would seek particular professional input.

While no national data are available on the extent and nature of parental programs in early childhood centers, it seems that most Australian early childhood programs incorporate some parental goals in their planning and provide a range of opportunities for parental development. For example, a child care center might offer a series of informal suppers for parents to meet, share experiences, and offer mutual support. At the parent's request, invited speakers also might be involved. Parental newsletters might be published regularly, to share information about events in the center, or to describe an educational issue or aspect of child development. Qualified early childhood staff also are expected to be knowledgeable about the range of family and child support resources that are available in their local area so they can refer parents to relevant services.

Parental programs are offered by all of the major early childhood networks. These include regular discussion groups and lecture services, seminars on management of community organizations, publications, lending libraries, phone-in advisory services, and programs for parents with young children. The most common form of these programs is the "toddler group" (sometimes called a "parent-child group") in which parents and their very young children meet, often with a qualified teacher, for a short program once or twice each week. There is both a play program for children and an educational component for parents—usually conducted in an informal way, with children present. The Lady Gowrie Child Care Centres play a large role in parental support work.

Australia has an extensive network of child health clinics. In some states, these are combined with kindergartens, so that new parents are aware of the early childhood facilities in their area and cooperation between health and educational services is made easier. In areas of needs, there are also health clinics set up to deal with the serious health problems of many aboriginal and Torres Strait Islander families.

Other sources of parental information include such self-help organizations as the Childbirth Education Association and the Nursing Mothers Association. In a similar way, the Playgroup Associations in each state provide many services to families, including advice on how to locate or establish a neighborhood playgroup, practical ideas for resources or activities and information on child development and parenting.

Other assistance for parents comes in the form of toy lending libraries, which provide a range of developmentally appropriate toys and are a source of information about children and their learning needs. Such services are often part of a large, multifaceted program and have some qualified staff. In some cases, postal services are available so that rural and isolated families can borrow packageable items, such as puzzles, children's books, and puppets.

Because of the geographical spread of the population, Australia has been a leader in the use of communications technology to create links with isolated families. The technology has been used for a range of purposes, including health, education, and community development. Educational radio and television programs have long been a feature of public broadcasting in Australia, for both rural and urban families. Many adults in Australia remember from their own childhood the songs and stories created for the long-running radio program "Kindergarten of the Air." There are some parental education programs on radio, such as the ABC program "Offspring," which broadcasts each weekday on an issue relating to the care and education of children.

Conclusion

As Australians approach the year 2000, this remains a comparatively "lucky country," though a harsh economic climate has created many uncertainties for early childhood education, as for all government-sponsored services. While early childhood education is an accepted part of Australian society, changes in the closing years of the century once again have created doubts in the minds of many early childhood educators, that the future of programs for young children and their families in this country is by no means assured.

Social change is occurring rapidly in Australia, as in other developed nations, so that services need to be under constant review and ever ready to make modifications to meet changing demands. But early educators are feeling the tension between the goals of social justice on the one hand and economic rationalism on the other. Legislators and professional early childhood educators must continue to address the issue of quality in programs and determine what can be done to best meet the needs of all young Australians and their families. As this becomes a more diverse society, the needs and preferences of families also diversify, creating difficult issues to be resolved in terms of appropriateness in the early childhood curriculum. What dimensions of the curriculum should remain constant and what should change in order to meet diverse community and family preferences? This issue needs far wider debate.

Australian early childhood education has developed in the humanist tradition, emphasizing the importance of human interactions among teachers, children and families. As increasing pressures are felt at all levels of education for teachers to assume more technocratic roles, as pressures mount for the standardization of education in the name of greater public accountability, early childhood educators will need to find new ways to convince others of the worth of their educational approach, with its breadth and depth of concern for young children and families.

In both the field and in teacher education, increasing pressures are being felt for more generic approaches. Generalist teachers and generic teacher education programs are believed by some to be more efficient in an economic sense and some would dispute that early childhood education is a distinctive approach that requires specialist expertise in its practitioners. If early childhood education is to be maintained and strengthened, early childhood educators themselves will need to speak out with a united, articulate voice. But despite some progress, the longstanding internal divisions remain within early childhood education; between the child care, kindergarten/preschool and early primary school sectors. They are maintained in the present day by a multitude of legislative, administrative, social, and industrial factors. One of the greatest challenges facing Australian early childhood educators as we enter the new century will be to strengthen unity in professional identification, commitment, and a sense of common purpose.

As this chapter has described, the succession of Australian government has explored several types of involvement in early childhood services. At this time, there remains little certainty about what the proper role of government should be. The debate continues about how responsibility for the welfare and education of the youngest members of our society should be shared among families, legislators, and professionals. This debate is likely to continue well into the next century.

Australia has a history for concern for all its citizens and Australians pay high taxes to support social welfare programs for all age groups. Even so, in the present economic climate, increasing numbers of Australians are asking if the nation can afford such programs. Further, as Australia's population grows older, re-evaluation of government spending priorities must occur. Should funds be withdrawn from early childhood services to support programs for older citizens? How will the government manage such a rebalancing of the budget in a equitable manner? How can we ensure that funds go where they are most needed, often to those with the least-heard, least-articulate voice?

Many of these issues can be integrated into a single area—advocacy for young children and their families. Into the 21st century, this may be where the greatest contribution is to be made by early childhood educators—both for the children themselves and for the future of our nation.

Notes

1. For a more detailed discussion of the various state provisions, see Brennan and O'Donnell (1986:61–76).

2. See Harley (1985) for further information about early childhood distance educational programs).

3. Sebastian (1986) provides further information about the types of center-based day care briefly described here.

References

Andrews, R.J., Elkins, J., Berry, P.B. & Burge, J.A. (1979) *A study of special education in Australia: Provisions, needs and priorities in the education of children with handicaps and learning difficulties*. St. Lucia, Queensland.: Fred & Elenor Schonnel Educational Research Centre.

Ashby, G. (1986). *Early education classes: Perceptions and issues*. Brisbane: BCAE, School of Early Childhood Studies.

———. (1980). Preschool education in Queensland, Australia—A systems approach. In L., Katz. (Ed.), *Current topics in early childhood education*, Vol. 3. Norwood, NJ: Ablex.

———. (1972). *Preschool theories and strategies*. Carlton, Victoria: Melbourne University Press.

Ashby, G., & Boulton-Lewis, G.M. (1988). Early schooling: What matters? *Australian Education and Developmental Psychologist, 5* (1).

Ashby, G.F., Robinson, N.M., & Taylor, A.J. (1990). *Early childhood special education: A review of the early special education element of the federal special education program*. Kelvin Grove, Queensland: Brisbane College of Advanced Education.

Ashman, A., & Elkins, J. (Eds.) (1990). *Educating children with special needs*. Sydney: Prentice Hall.

Australian Bureau of Statistics (ABS). (1986). *Child care arrangements: 1984*. Canberra: Government Printer.

————. (1988). *Child care arrangements: Preliminary, 1987*. Canberra: Government Printer.

————. (1989). *National schools statistic collection Australia: 1988*. Canberra: Government Printer.

————. (1988). *Preschools and child care centres—Queensland: 1987*. Brisbane: Government Printer.

Australian Early Childhood Association. (1987). *Policy statement*. Watson, ACT: AECA.

Australian Government Social Welfare Commission. (1974). *Project care: Children, parents, community*. Canberra: Government Printer.

Australian Schools Council. (1989). *Teacher quality: An issues paper*. Canberra: AGPS.

Bettison, S. (1979). Overview of Australian early intervention provisions. In M., Pieterse, S. Bouchner, & S. Bettison (Eds.), *Early intervention for children with disabilities: The Australian experience*. Ryde, New South Wales: MacQuarie University Special Education Centre.

Brennan, D., & O'Donnell, C. (1986). *Caring for Australia's children*. Sydney: Allen & Unwin.

Briggs, F. (1984). A survey of teacher education courses in Australia. *Australian Journal of Early Childhood*, 9, 5–13.

Clyde, M. (1988). Early childhood trends in the 80's: Forging ahead at a snail's pace. *Australian Journal of Early Childhood*, 6, 28–34.

Cohen, D., & Schiller, W. (1988). Curriculum in Early Childhood Centres. *Curriculum Perspective*, 8, 31–37.

Cross, T. (1988). The personal and interpersonal world of the young child—The communication imperative. Keynote address at the third National Australian and New Zealand Conference on the First Years of School, Melbourne.

Cullen, J. (1988). Are we creating dependent learners? The K-year one transition. Paper presented at the third National Australian and New Zealand Conference on the First Years of School, Melbourne.

Cumpston, J., & Heinig, C. (1944). *Preschool centres in Australia*. Canberra: Department of Health.

Department of Community Services and Health. (1988). Personal communication. Brisbane: Special Projects Branch.

Ebbeck, F.N. (1990). *Australian Education Commission Working Party of teacher education: Draft final report*. Canberra: Government Printer.

Ebbeck, M. (1982). Parents and early childhood teachers' expectations of preschool education. *Australian Journal of Early Childhood*, 7, 18–19.

Elkins, J. (1990). Introduction to exceptionality: Overview. In R. Butler (Ed.), *The exceptional child*. Marrickville, New South Wales: Harcourt Brace Jovanovich.

Fitzgerald, R.T. (1968). Facilities for preschooling in Australia. *Quarterly Review of Australian Education*, 1, 2–13.

Fry, J. (1973). *Care and education of young children*. Canberra: Australia Preschools Committee.

Gow, L. (1990). Integration in Australia. In R. Butler (Ed.), *The exceptional child*. Marrickville, New South Wales: Harcourt Brace Jovanovich.

Gowers, A. (1979) Family day care. In P. Langford and P. Sebastian (Eds.) *Early childhood education and care in Australia*. Kew VIC: Australian International Press and Publications

Halliwell, G. (1984). Implementing the curriculum in an EEC. *Links*, 6.

————. (1977). *An interactional model of early childhood education*. Brisbane: Department of Education.

————. (1989). *The Leafy Wood State School story*. Brisbane: CAE.

Harley, M. (1985). An alternative organizational model for early childhood distance educational programs. *Distance Education*, 6.

Hayes, A. (1988). The child and parent support project: Community initiative in a rural location. In M. Pieterse, S. Bochner, & S. Bettison, (Eds.), *Early intervention for children with disabilities: The Australian experience*. Sydney: NSW Special Education Centre, Macquarie University.

Henry, M. (1988). The dimensions of parental behaviour. Some implications for professionals. *Australian Journal of Early Childhood*, 13, 3–12.

Hurford, C. (1987). Child care since 1983—Priorities and achievements. *Australian Journal of Early Childhood*, 12, 3–8.

Jones, H. (1975). The acceptable crusader: Lillian de Lissa and preschool education in South Australia. *Melbourne Studies in Education*. Carlton, Victoria: Melbourne University Press.

Kelly, J. (1982). Child development and early childhood education in Australia: An historical perspective. Paper delivered at the second National Child Development Conference, Institute of Early Childhood Development, Melbourne.

Langford, P., & Sebastain, P. (Eds.). (1979). *Early childhood education and care in Australia*. Kew, Victoria: Australian Interaction Press.

Maas, F. (1984). *Should families be a focus for policies?* Melbourne: Institute of Family Studies.

McCrea, N., & Piscitelli, B. (1990). *Handbook of high quality criteria for early childhood programs*. Brisbane: Department of Family Services/BCAE.

Mellor, E. (1990). *Stepping stones: The development of early childhood services in Australia*. Sydney: Harcourt Brace Jovanovich.

Murray, S. (1986). *A review of research on primary school enrolment procedures*. Watson, ACT: AECA.

Pendred, G.E. (1962). Preschool centres in Australia. In *Review of education in Australia, 1955–1962*. Melbourne: ACER.

Piscitelli, B., & Mobbs, J. (1986). *The new extended family at school*. ERIC Document ED 2784.

Schiller, W. (1987). *The Hunter Valley Caravan Project*. Keynote Address at the AAECE Conference, "Family Perspective: Changes and Challenges."

Sebastian, P. (1986). *Handle with care: A guide to early childhood administration*. Melbourne: Australasian Educa Press.

Simons, J., & Vella, P. (1984). Why child care has become an industrial issue. *Australian Journal of Early Childhood*, 9, 17–20.

Spearitt, P. (1979). Child care and kindergartens in Australia, 1890–1975. In P. Langford, & P. Sebastian, (Eds.), *Early childhood education and care in Australia*, Kew: Australian International Press.

Speedy, G. (1989). *Discipline review of teacher education in mathematics and science*, 1. Canberra: Department of Employment, Education and Training.

Spodek, B. (1986). Australian programs that prepare early childhood teachers. *Australian Journal of Early Childhood*, 11 3–9.

Stonehouse, A. (1988). Changes in child care—for better, for worse, in sickness, in health, for richer for poorer. *Australian Journal of Early Childhood*, 13, 22–23.

———. (1986). *For us, for children*. Watons, ACT: AECA.

Tayler, C. (1990). *Summaries of early childhood courses*. Churchlands, Western Australia: Western Australian College of Advanced Education.

Tomlinson, S. (1982). *A sociology of special education*. London: Routledge & Keagan, Paul.

Ward, E. (1986). In Sound policies promote effective programs for young children. *Children are worth the effort: Today, tomorrow and beyond*. Canberra: AECA.

Warnock, M. (1987). *Special education needs*. Report of the Committee of Enquiry in the Education of Handicapped Children and Young People. London: H.M.S.O.

Wyles, M. (1990). *National playgroups statistics*. Personal communication.

EARLY CHILDHOOD EDUCATION IN AUSTRIA

• • • • • • • • • • ◆ • • • • • • • • •

Wilhelm Wolf
Oberrat University, Austria

To understand the Austrian system of early childhood education it is necessary to distinguish among day nurseries, which are for children from birth to age 3; preschools, which are kindergartens or nursery schools for children from ages 3 to 6, and primary school or primary education, which is the primary bracket (grades 1 to 4, plus the preschool stage). This chapter discusses day nurseries and the lower grades of the primary bracket.

It begins with a brief history of early childhood education from the introduction of compulsory education to the present. Social policies and parental support within the Austrian system of social services are briefly described. The chapter's final section outlines problems with the early childhood educational system and possible solutions to them.

Introduction of Compulsory Education

The public state primary school in Austria began in 1771, when a school reform took place during the reign of Maria Theresa. The main goal at that time was to teach—either at school or at home—religion, moral standards, reading, writing, and arithmetic to children between ages 5 and 12.

In 1869, the Imperial Education Act unified the entire system of compulsory education and increased its duration from six to eight years. The curriculum was extended to also include the study of the mother tongue, mathematics, natural history, geography, history, arts, singing, physical education, and needlework. The law was a decisive step in the progress of Austrian education and was based on liberal ideas.

After 1918, Otto Glöckel, the Under Secretary of State and later President of the Vienna Education Authority, introduced a reform of the school system that was finalized with a new curriculum in 1930. Glöckel's ideas still influence today's pedagogical thinking, particularly teaching methods that take into account practical reality and the child's mentality, democratic education, and education in the arts. Except for the period between 1938 and 1945, this curriculum was, with minor amendments, in force until 1963. In 1934, the government of the so-called *Slāndestaat* changed the curriculum of 1930 and abolished most of the innovations that had taken place.

During the rule of the National Socialists in Austria, the school system was adapted to the German one, although Austrian traditions were maintained. After World War II, the 1930 curriculum with some amendments was reintroduced and was not changed until the School Organization Act of 1962, primarily because during this period the conceptions of the two major political parties (the Conservatives and the Socialists) differed.

In 1962, Austria's educational system was reorganized by the School Organization Act. Compulsory education was extended from eight to nine years and compulsory secondary school took the place of the upper bracket of the *volksschule*. The reform did not include regulations for preschool or preprimary levels. In 1969, measures to promote the development of the child from birth to school age were emphasized in various educational pilot projects all over Austria. This development was envisaged as an emancipatory and compensatory form of education, which means that only children with learning deficits were attending preschools.

In 1983, preschool education, which had been a pilot project since the early 1970s, was made part of primary education, but only for pupils coming under compulsory education or pupils born between September 1 and December 31 of the current calender year. As a result, the emancipatory aspect of education was lost because of the inability of the political parties to arrive at a consensus. In connection with this reform, a curriculum was developed that in turn influenced the development of a new curriculum for primary school in 1986.

The new curriculum included the individualization of the teaching methods, learning through play, and strategies to compensate for deficits in language skills and social behavior in early childhood education. In 1986, the curriculum for the elementary school was reformed after a period of nationwide pilot projects in which more than one thousand teachers participated. The primary curriculum was guided by the following principles:

- elementary school should be child centered;

- learning is accomplished by doing;

- open education/open classrooms are preferred;

- education should be based on theories of compensation and emancipation;

- intercultural learning should be part of the educational experience;

- in addition to reading, writing, and arithmetic, primary education has to stimulate social, emotional, intellectual, and physical development; and

- the communicative approach in learning the mother tongue is the preferred approach.

This curriculum was viewed as "a steering instrument" that would provide children with a harmonious start at school. Primary school was conceived of as a school *of* children as well as *for* children, providing them with the basis for a lifelong learning process.

Many of the ideas proposed during the time of the educational reforms at the beginning of the 20th century are part of the current curriculum and the practical work in the classrooms.

Development of Kindergarten

Day nurseries (*Bewahranstalten*) were the first institutional arrangements in preschool education and date from the late 1820s. One of the main purposes of day nurseries was to protect the child. Guidelines and a program that included religion, spelling, mathematics, memory training, arts, and local and natural history were developed for day nurseries.

In 1832, it was decreed that the day nurseries did not have the legal status of schools. Rather their task was to guide the intellectual and physical development of the children as well as to offer moral education and prepare them for primary education. Most of these institutions were founded by private initiatives for children up to age 5, predominately for the poor. As a rule, a supervisor looked after about 60 children. For both day nurseries and primary education, the connection with the church was abandoned in 1869 with the Imperial Education Act.

Those who cared for the children were specially trained to do so. In the 1860s, more and more attention was given to day nurseries. Influenced by Friedrich Fröbel, new forms of preschool education were developed and the number of kindergartens grew. In addition, as the state became more interested in preschool education as a part of educating people, requirements were prescribed by the state for running a kindergarten. The Ministry of Education decreed that the kindergarten had to support the education of the children at home and to prepare them for school life. The existing day nurseries, predominantly for the working class, were changed into kindergartens, since the child could get a better preschool education there.

Kindergartens were open for all children from age 4 for three hours in the morning and two hours in the afternoon. The government decreed that one person should care for no more than 40 children, and, as in the day nurseries, there were to be no specific preparatory lessons for primary school. This decree also addressed the training of the "nurses" who teach in the kindergartens. Within a short time, two-year courses were established that emphasized practical training. Religion, language, arts, singing, and physical education were also taught. These courses, which were popular with young women throughout the monarchy, were only for women of high moral standards, who were in good health, and no younger than 16. After 1886, the teacher's training colleges could also maintain their own kindergarten.

In the 1920s, kindergarten was influenced by the ideas of Maria Montessori. At that time, of the world's capitals, Vienna had the most public kindergartens. In the early 1930s, some kindergartens were equipped with "corners" that had the character of a workshop. In these places, children could play with tools appropriate for their age. Courses in gymnastics and children's orchestras were also implemented. This development, however, was interrupted by the worldwide economic crisis in the 1930s.

Between 1938 and 1945, early childhood education was influenced by the educational philosophy of the Nazis' regime. Because obedience to the "führer" was required, all that strengthened authoritarian structure was stressed. Gymnastics was overemphasized and the "heroic man" became the ideal. Conflicts, difficulties in development, and the individuality of the child were denied. Approaches that emphasized the stereotype of the powerful, healthy, racially pure generation replaced the earlier approach. But because there was great variety in curricula in the Austrian nursery school system, it was not possible to quickly adapt it to the German requirements. After World War II, educational philosophies reassumed their prewar character.

It was not until 1962, when the School Organization Act was issued, that new philosophies about kindergarten emerged. This act entrusted each province with the nursery school system in both legislative and executive matters. In addition to the traditional tasks, a new concept was introduced: *preparing children for school but not by school methods* (i.e., preschoolers do not learn the 3 R's— the learning methods of preschool differ from those of primary school).

Focus on preschool education as a whole became predominant at the end of the 1960s. The School Reform Commission was established in 1969 as an advisory body to the Federal Ministry of Education, Arts, and Sports. It emphasized all measures concerning the development of the child form birth to school age. In the 1980s, attention was also given to children with special needs.

Educational Principles, Aims, and Objectives

The 1962 School Organization Act states that "entry into every school shall be common to all, without discrimination as to birth, sex, race, social background, class, language, or religion, with the proviso that schools and classes may be set up which are designed only for boys and only for girls." The aims of education in Austria as stated in the act are as follows:

[I]t shall be the task of the Austrian school to foster the development of the talents and potential abilities of young persons in accordance with ethical, religious, and social values and the appreciation of that which is true, good and beautiful, by giving them an education corresponding to their respective stages of development and to their respective courses of study. It shall give young people the knowledge and skills required for their futures lives and occupations and train them to acquire knowledge on their own initiative.

Young people shall be trained to become healthy, capable, conscientious, and responsible members of society and citizens of the democratic and federal Republic of Austria. They shall be encouraged to develop an independent judgment and social understanding, to be open-minded to the philosophy and political thinking of others, they shall be able to participate in the economic and cultural life of Austria, of Europe, and the world and to make their contribution, in love of freedom and peace, to the common tasks of mankind.

The act also states that "in addition to the exemption from school fees provided for under other enactments relating to public compulsory schools, the attendance at any other public schools now covered by those Federal Act shall also be free of charge."

In Austria, three types of compulsory schooling are stipulated by federal laws and their respective bylaws: (1) general schooling (first to ninth school years) by the Compulsory Schooling Act; (2) vocational schooling by the Compulsory Schooling Act; and (3) agricultural and forestry schooling by the Federal Act for Compulsory Schools of Agriculture and Forestry. The requirements of compulsory schooling are fulfilled by attending a *volksschule* (primary school), a *hauptschule* (compulsory secondary school), *polytechnisher lehrgang* (prevocational course), or a *sonderschule* (special school). Any of these schools can be either public schools or accredited private schools.

In compulsory schooling, the right to education is supplemented by measures to facilitate school entrance and by particular attention being given to children in need of special care. The principle of *equal educational opportunities* is ensured regionally by boarding schools and is ensured socially by student grants (e.g., school and boarding school allowances, lower annual fees).

In Austria, equality of opportunities and freedom of choice are inseparably connected with the right to education. However, this freedom of choice presupposes extensive information on the matter in question. Accordingly, to realize the right to education, an extensive system of educational counseling was created. This is to enable students to make the most and best use of the existing possibilities of the educational system and to choose responsibly the educational career appropriate for their talents, personality, and interests. In addition, the child is to be helped by promotion measures in the case of partial deficiencies and difficulties, or by altering socialization conditions in order to realize the child's right to education in the best possible way.

Preschool Education

Preschool education includes all measures that promote the development of the total personality of a child from birth to school entrance. These measures encompass both the family and facilities for assuring a good start in formal education (and hence the chances of success at school).

The primary aim in Austria is to maintain the child's family context (e.g., by the legally guaranteed right of working mothers to a subsidized leave of absence). Changes in the social situation and the concomitant changes in the family structure (divorce, for example), however, tend to produce cases where parents are not fully up to the tasks of child education and upbringing. This is why various activities to promote parents' educational capabilities are undertaken under the auspices of institutions of adult education and by the responsible provincial and federal authorities.

Facilities that complement education in the family include infant day care centers for children between ages 1 and 3. For children from ages 3 to 6, nursery schools are operated both as a complement to the family and a means to ensure a good start in formal education.

The Austrian nursery school system is entrusted to the provinces in both legislative and executive matters. There are nine Provincial Nursery School Acts, corresponding to the number of Austrian provinces, which are identical in their essential points. Under these legal provisions, attendance at nursery school is optional. Children who are at least age 3 can attend nursery schools until they are admitted to a school which is usually at age 6. A nurse is responsible for about 30 children. Nursery school activities are directed toward developing the child's total personality. Nursery schools are expected to meet this goal by having children work in small groups, by encouraging individual forms of activity and work, and by systematically offering a wide range of games and material. Above all, the child at nursery school should have the chance to gain experience through play without the pressure of time or achievement.

The facilities for assuring a good start in formal education, which are also expected to assure improved chances of success in primary education, include the nursery schools described above and preschool classes or groups. The most important goal of these preschool classes or groups is to help children who must attend school on the basis of their age, but who are not yet mature enough to attend school, overcome the often difficult transition from home to school. The child should be at a level that would allow the child to succeed in the first grade of primary education. For these children, attendance at a preschool class or group is compulsory. Preschool classes or groups may also be attended by children who are age 6 by December 31. The curriculum of these classes or groups provides for "compulsory exercise," that is, children have to attend instruction but are not graded at the end of the year, receiving only an attendance certificate. These compulsory exercises include religious instruction, reading, writing, speaking, the environment, arithmetic, music and singing, artistic education, physical education, and traffic education.

Nursery Teacher Training

The 1982 amendment to the School Organization Act extended the duration of nursery teacher education from four to five years. The final exams qualify the students to go to universities or other academic institutions. This education is provided for both men and women, although few men apply. Before attending a training institute for nursery school teachers, an aptitude test must be taken. It tests mathematics, mother tongue and English, music, handicraft and arts, and abilities in social learning and communication.

Normally, education at a training institute for nursery school teachers starts at age 14, but because of a shortage of qualified nursery teachers, graduates of a secondary school can attend courses during their working time and later pass an external examination. During this time they are employed and are paid a full salary.

At the training institutes, the following subjects are taught: religion, pedagogics (including pedagogical psychology, pedagogical sociology, philosophy), therapeutic pedagogy, didactics of the kindergarten and preschool, practical training in the kindergarten, mother tongue (including speech training and literature for children and youth), foreign language, history and social studies, geography and economics, law, mathematics, physics, chemistry, biology, health education, music, guitar or flute, rhythmical education, arts, handicrafts, and physical training. A course of practical training is also obligatory. Optional subjects are stenography; making musical instruments; specialization in early childhood education; and Slovene, Croatian, and Hungarian. Optional courses are choir singing, music, drama, speech training, literature, biological exercises, and the use of media. Finally remedial instruction is offered in the compulsory subjects of the mother tongue, mathematics, foreign language, and music.

Primary Education

Basic schooling comprises, in addition to the preschool stage (preschool groups, preschool class, etc.), the first four grades of primary school. There are also special schools for mentally or physically handicapped children that offer these children a basic and well-balanced education. Because the overall educational task of basic schooling is to recognize each child's individual needs, attention is paid to the educability of each pupil while at the same time ensuring a continuity of that pupil's learning development in all schools. In general, basic schooling should create the foundation for successful learning at the schools leading to higher forms of education.

The aim of primary school is to give all pupils a basic general education. Within the lower secondary cycle, the upper elementary school aims to build on the common education given to all pupils in the elementary school and to *give them an extended education beyond the 3 R's, possibly also a complementary education*. Thus the pupils are to be prepared for practical life as well as for continuing their education.

Primary School Curriculum

The curriculum for the primary school provides an overall framework for the teacher's pedagogical work, rather than a precisely defined codification of educational subject matter. While this permits the application of a nationwide curriculum, limited shifts of subject matter and additional content pertaining to the local conditions can also be included. The number of weekly periods assigned to individual compulsory subjects may be determined, within the limits given in the distribution of class periods, by the provincial school board depending on the local conditions. Moreover, there exists the possibility of offering optional subjects and exercises that cater to individual student talents and preferences. Remedial instruction can also be offered.

The grades are combined into two "cycles" covering grades 1 and 2, and grades 3 and 4, respectively. This subdivision is based on the different development characteristics of the age brackets and on an administrative desire for a cautious modification of the system of single-year classes.

Primary school covers the following compulsory subjects: German, reading, writing, factual instruction (grades 3 and 4), mathematics, music education, arts education (grades 1 and 2), handicrafts, and physical education. Starting with grade 3, a foreign language (English or French) is offered as a compulsory exercise (without achievement grading). In grades 1 and 3, there is also the compulsory exercise traffic education; optional exercises, such as choir singing, instrumental music, and physical training, are also offered in all four grades and drama is offered in grades 3 and 4.

The basis of assessment in primary education is the observation of pupils; oral examinations are not given at the elementary level. However, there are six written tests in the mother tongue and in mathematics in grade 4, and dictations are possible in the mother tongue as well and standardized tests (although they are few in number).

The primary curriculum was changed in 1986 to incorporate the guidelines of the Innovations in Primary Education Project of the Council of Europe. (See Project No. 8 of the CDCC, "Innovation in primary education," Final Report, Strasbourg 1988.)

Schedule of Primary Schools

As a rule, instruction must not start before 8 a.m. and may last no more than six periods in the morning, if it is a morning-only program. The total number of periods per week must be distributed by the school head as evenly as possible over the individual days of the week. The decision to operate schools from Monday to Friday or from Monday to Saturday is decided by the teachers and parents. There are different systems for decision-making in the federal provinces, but in general if more than 20 percent of the people want to change from a five-day week to a six-day week (or vice

versa), there has to be a vote. The number of periods during a week varies between 20 and 26; there is one additional hour of remedial instruction for pupils who have learning problems. A period lasts 50 minutes and between periods a sufficient number of breaks lasting between 5 and 20 minutes must be scheduled.

In the federal provinces of Hurgenland, Lower Austria, and Vienna, the school year starts on the first Monday, (in the other federal provinces on the second Monday) in September and lasts until the beginning of the following school year, the summer vacations (July and August) included. Students are in school for about 40 weeks a year.

Links Between Primary School, Parents, and the Community

In many primary schools there are parents' associations that have legal standing. In theory, they function mainly in an advisory capacity in certain educational matters (e.g., in the choice of textbooks); in practice, they also have a social function. Their fundamental aim is to enhance the cooperation between parents and school.

There are various forms of parent-teacher communication, including parents' associations, communication between the class teacher and the parents about educational issues concerning the child, and the "class-forum," which consists of the parents and the class teachers. This body decides such matters as school skiing courses and school country weeks, rules of the house, and topics for health education. It may also give advice on teaching and educational practices, school activities, dates of consulting hours for parents, and teaching materials.

Special Schools

The special schools in the primary bracket provide remedial instruction to physically and mentally handicapped children in a manner adapted to their handicaps, so as to give them an education corresponding to that of the primary school whenever possible. Whether a child is to attend a special school is decided by the district school board, either on application by the parents or by the head of the school on the board's own initiative. Before making such a decision, the district school board must obtain the expert opinion of the head of the special school in question and, if necessary, that of a school doctor or public health officer. An appeal of the decision of the district school board can be made to the provincial school board, which may also order the submission of a psycho-pedagogical expert opinion. If a child is physically or mentally handicapped to such a degree that he or she is unable to follow even special school instruction, the child is exempted from compulsory general schooling.

Austrian special schools are divided into categories so that specific services for the various handicaps of children can be offered. The categories are the *allegmeine sonderschule* (general-purpose special school for underachievers); special schools for children who are blind, deaf, and severely handicapped children, physically handicapped, hard of hearing, or visually handicapped; children with speech defects; reform schools; and hospital schools. Because of the low numbers of students per class (10 to 16, depending on the type of handicap), the specially trained teachers, and their specific methods of instruction (which are geared to the individual requirements of students), handicapped students receive a well-rounded general education. It helps them to cope with further technical and vocational training and enables them to attend schools leading to higher forms of education.

The general special school and the special school for deaf-mute, blind, and severely handicapped children have special curricula. At special schools for physically handicapped, hard of hearing, and visually handicapped children, the curricula of primary school or that of a different type of special school apply, depending on the age and educability of the pupils.

This is also true of the special hospital school with the exception that the distribution of weekly class periods in each subject is determined by the head of the school on the basis of the expert opinion of the physician in charge of treatment, taking into account the pupil's state of health. In addition, exercises (two to four periods per week) are provided adapted to the children's handicaps.

In several federal counties, projects have been undertaken to integrate handicapped children into normal classes. In these projects, the class teacher and the teacher of a special school work as a team, sometimes with the whole class and sometimes only with groups. Because these projects are in the beginning stages, only limited data are available on their effectiveness. However, these pilot projects are strongly demanded by parents.

Although Austria has a long tradition of special schooling, these projects cause many problems, including the fact that pupils from special schools have fewer chances to get a good job. Whether schooling in normal classes is the best way to help pupils with special needs is unclear. To some extent, it is not only a question of supplying specially trained teachers and special teaching materials, but a financial question as well. Beyond this, the issue is what integration really means.

It is not possible to give a precise definition, but overall it means that pupils of both groups should be able to work together for a longer phase of the lessons, to fulfill more or less the same tasks, to solve the same problems, to do the same work, and so on. Merely sitting together in the same classroom is not integration. Nor is it integration if the handicapped child serves only as a teaching device for other pupils.

Teacher Education

In Austria, teachers are trained at various locations depending on the qualifications required by the type of school and the disciplines of interest. Teachers can be trained at:

- intermediate teacher training schools (which are being phased out);

- higher level teacher training schools;

- teacher training academies;

- vocational teacher training academies;

- academies for the training of teachers of religion;

- teacher training institutes; and

- universities.

The teacher-training academies train teachers for primary school and for all other types of compulsory general schools.

The requirements for admission to a teacher

training academy are the matriculation examination of an academic secondary school and proof of physical health. The length of the training is six semesters according to the seventh amendment of the School Organization Act.

There are five distinct curriculum areas in teacher training:

- human sciences (25 percent of the time);

- teaching methods (47 percent);

- alternative studies (2.5 percent);

- practical training (17.5 percent); and

- supplementary studies (8 percent).

Social Policy and Legislation

Anyone who is a permanent resident in Austria and is legally responsible for the maintenance of children is entitled to receive a monthly family allowance whose amount depends on the age of children (birth to age 9 AS 1,300; from age 10, AS 1,550). The allowance may be claimed for all dependants up to age 19, for dependents undergoing vocational training up to age 25 (under certain circumstances up to 27), and for any handicapped dependents.

Every female resident in Austria receives maternity allowance: AS 5,000 on the birth of child, a further AS 5,000 on the child's first birthday, and AS 3,000 on the child's second birthday. To be eligible to receive this allowance requires the mother to present the "mother-child pass" (introduced in the 1970s to reduce the rate of infant mortality) certifying that both she and her child have had all required medical examinations.

Several legislative measures have been introduced to allow women to retain their jobs beyond the period of maternity. These measures include legal provisions safeguarding the health of expectant mothers, pre- and post-natal leave, maternity pay for one year after the birth, the inclusion of maternity leave in the overall years of insurance, and provision for continued social insurance at lower rates.

Couples receive AS 15,000 when they marry on the condition that it is their first marriage. Other family benefits include free tuition at all state-run schools, colleges, and universities; free school text-books; free travel for school children and students; and allowances for children of school age.

Since 1976, a law has been enforced providing for the advance payment of alimony when payments are not forthcoming. The state then takes over the legal process of enforcing payment. At present, the state advances maintenance sums for approximately 30,000 children. The scheme costs approximately AS 35.5 million, one-third of which is recouped.

Private Social Welfare Services

In many areas of social welfare in Austria, private organizations and services exist in addition to state welfare schemes. These are run by religious institutions, political parties, or nonpolitical organizations, and the facilities they provide include kindergartens, homes for the disabled, special educational institutions, old people's homes, and home nursing services. Many large companies also run social services for their employees. The SOS Children's Village Scheme, which began in Austria, has since spread throughout the world and is a widely acclaimed organization.

The family guidance counselors provide free counseling in all questions pertaining to family life and personal relationships. In larger town and cities, there are also social services that provide counseling for mothers, expectant mothers, children, those with drug or alcohol problems, the physically and mentally handicapped, patients suffering from certain diseases, and people experiencing severe depression.

In principle, anyone is entitled to use the facilities provided by Austria's health service. The costs are borne by the social insurance scheme or, in cases of hardship, by the social welfare scheme.

Changing Role of Women in Austria

According to the national census conducted in 1981, there are 3.58 million men and 3.97 million women living in Austria. The proportion of women in the total adult population is thus 52 percent, which is a result of the two world wars and the higher life expectancy of women. On average, Austrian men reach age 69, while Austrian women live to be 76. Although the Austrian constitution provides for complete equality between the sexes, men tend to dominate virtually every aspect of life. In general, women complete a lower level of education and gravitate toward the typical women's professions with lower incomes; they are markedly underrepresented in senior posts in industry, the civil service, cultural management, the media, and politics. In recent years, however, a change in attitude has led to a higher social status for women. Important legislative and administrative steps have been taken to bring about equality of rights and opportunities for them. This applies not only to education and professional life but also to the political sphere.

By enacting a new code of family law in 1975, Parliament created the basis for the establishment of genuine partnership within marriage. The centerpiece of this legislation is the law governing the legal effects of marriage on individual rights. This law abolishes the concept of superior and subordinate roles within the family and provides for equal responsibilities in running the household and raising children. The wife no longer automatically takes the name of her husband; the couple can choose by which name they want to be known. The underlying concept is that of marital partnership; the wife is no longer obliged to move to her husband's domicile, and the husband no longer has the right to forbid his wife to work. Both partners have equal obligations to contribute to the maintenance of the family. The reform of family law was completed with a revision of the legal provisions governing marital property and inheritance rights and with measures designed to bring divorce legislation into line with current social circumstances.

There are numerous regulations in force in Austria to protect working women, particularly mothers. These generally take the form of legal provisions but can also be included in the terms of collective labor agreements. For example, legislation exists to regulate conditions of night-shift work for women. Special legislation for working mothers includes a minimum term of notice, and during the 16 weeks of paid maternity leave women cannot be dismissed from their employment. In addition, expectant mothers may not be required to do any work that might endanger their lives or health or that of their unborn child.

Since 1990, one parent is permitted to stay home for a two-year period after the birth of a child. This period can be divided into two and used by the child's mother and father. In addition, families pay less taxes if only one parent is employed. There is also aid for single mothers.

Recommendations for Change

At present there is little interest in changing the overall nursery school system in Austria. Perhaps this is because the federal provinces are more interested in increasing the number of kindergartens or in reducing the number of children within the groups. Although efforts are being made to integrate pupils with special needs of the children of migrant workers or refugees into kindergartens, there is little innovation in methods.

In any case, there is little attention given to early childhood education despite the growing number of working mothers. At present, about 184,006 children attend kindergarten while about 44 percent of them have employed mothers. There are 6,604 children in day nurseries, which are provided for children from birth up to age 3. More than 80 percent of their mothers are working.

At the moment neither politicians nor educators intend to change the duration of compulsory education or to commence schooling earlier than age 6. The more important question is how to help children to have a good start to their schooling. Approximately 13 percent of children are deferred for one year and are required to attend a preschool while about 1 percent have to stay at home if the nearest preschool is too far from their homes. More than 1 percent of the pupils repeat grade 1 voluntarily, although every pupil is allowed to enter the second grade regardless of his or her achievement. At the end of grade 2, more than 2.5 percent are not able to pass to grade 3 and have to either repeat a year or attend a special school for slow learners. Therefore, it could be said that the Austrian school entrance phase is highly selective.

The so-called preschool groups (with fewer than ten children and instruction on two or three days per week only) is a type of preschool education system that should be offered in sparsely populated areas. But it leads to questions of what should happen with children on the days the preschool group is closed. This can be a problem for working mothers because in some cases it may not be possible for their children to attend a kindergarten on the other days.

School statistics reveal that the number of institutions for the preschool stage differs widely among the nine provinces; enrollments range from a low of 1.0 percent to 22 percent of eligible children. In this regard, it is important to remember that the communities are responsible for running compulsory schools and that kindergartens do not cost as much as preschools.

There is a strong need for change. But before making sweeping reforms, pilot projects must be undertaken. The projects may differ in some respects but overall the aim must be more or less the same: to give pupils three years for passing the lower cycle or primary education (at present, preschool stage and grades 1 and 2) if they need it.

To make these projects a regular part of the school system, a two-thirds majority in Parliament is necessary to change the School Organization Act. But because these projects have been conducted for only about three years, there is little experience with them. Therefore, it will take much more time to change the school system in the entrance phase.

Innovations have also been tried in the private preschool system as alternatives to the state schools (e.g., following the ideas of Rudolf Steiner, A.S. Neill, or others who advocate anti-authoritarian education or the so-called *kinderläden* in the Federal Republic of Western Germany in the late 1960s and early 1970s). There are also "day mother" projects, in which a woman provides day care for a few children in her home.

Considering the pedagogical problems and the fact that the provinces are in charge of a well-developed system of kindergartens on the one hand and a preschool on the other, Austria has to reconsider the early childhood education system as a whole.

Acknowledgment

I want to thank my colleagues Ministerialrat Dr. Walker Denscher, Ministerialrat Dr. Klaus Diemort, Dr. Peter Seitz, and Oberrat Mag. Johann Wimmer from the Federal Minis try of Education, Arts, and Sports for reading the drafts and for very helpful comments that have been incorporated into the final version of this chapter.

References

Austria—Facts and figures. (1983). Vienna: Federal Press Service.

Austria—Facts and figures, to the friends of Austria (1986). Vienna: Federal Press Service.

Baltuschrat, Ch. (1986). Zur Geschichte der Ausbildung von Kindergårtnerihenne. In Österreich, Pådagogischer Verlag Eugen Ketterl, Wien.

Buchberger, F., & Riedl, J. (Hrsg.). (1987). Lehrerbildung-heute; Kommentar zum Lehrplan der Pådagogischen Akademie/-Teil I; Bundesministerium für Unterricht, Kunst und Sport, Wien.

Burgstaller, F., & Leitner, L. (1987). Pådagogische Markierungen, Problems-Prozesse-Perspektiven. Österreichischer Bundesverlag, Wien.

Educational careers in Austria. (1985–86). Bundesministerium für Unterricht, Kunst und Sport.

Education at a glance. (1990). Basic data of first, second, and third level (nonuniversity) education in Austria; academic year 1989/90. Federal Ministry of Education Arts and Sports.

Eltern, Kinder. (1990). Partner-Familienförderung. In Österreich, *Eine information des bundesministeriums für umwelt, jugend, und familie*, Wien, Auflago.

Engelbrecht, H. (Band IV 1986, Band V 1988). Geschichte des österreichischen Bildungswesens, österreichischer Bundesverlag, Wien.

Federal Ministry of Education, Arts, and Sports. Austria: Development of education: 1986–1988. (1989). Vienna: Federal Ministry of Education, Arts and Sports, in cooperation with the Federal Ministry of Science and Research.

Primary education in Austria. (1990). Report by Austrian Authorities, Council of Europe, Project 8: "Innovation in primary education." DECS/EGT (84) 104 rev. Strasbourg.

Verordnung des Bundesministere für Unterricht, Kunst und Sport vom 20. Mårz 1985 über den Lehrplan der Bildungsanstalt für Kindergartenpådagogik. BGBl. Nr. 312/1985.

Wolf, W. (1990). Grundzüge der entwicklung der volksschullehrpläne. In K. Satzke & W. Wolf (Eds.), *Kommenter zum Lehrpan der Volksschule*. Österreichischer Bundesverlag, Jugend und Volk, Wien.

EARLY CHILDHOOD EDUCATION IN BAHRAIN

• • • • • • • • • • ◆ • • • • • • • • •

May Al-Arrayed Shirawi
College of Education
Arabian Gulf University, Bahrain

The Organization of Education

Bahrain, with a population of 400,000, is a small country of 33 islands located in a central position in the Gulf.[1] It has 26 systems of education. Though they differ widely, they all strive toward the same education goals in terms of conduct and acquisition of knowledge.[2]

In Bahrain, "primary education" refers to the education of children form ages 6 to 12. It is free and compulsory in all state schools. Parents who are aware of the importance of education send their children to school before age 6. This encourages the growth of private preprimary schools in Bahrain.

Preprimary education refers to the education of children from birth to age 6. Run wholly by the private sector, preprimary schools are fee-paying and outside the state educational system. It is more correct, therefore, to speak about preprimary education, since neither nurseries nor kindergartens are a part of the Bahraini educational system.

This chapter discusses the preprimary education offered by Bahraini nationals, either individuals or groups. The reason for this approach is that foreign private educational establishments (e.g., American, British, German, Japanese, Indian, and Persian) follow the system of education established in their country. For this discussion of early childhood education in Bahrain to be understood within a broad cultural, social, and economic context, the forces affecting the development of education in Bahrain are briefly discussed. A brief description of the overall Bahraini system of education is also necessary. This is because some issues in early childhood education are closely related to the economy of the country in general and to the system of education in particular.

Overview of Forces Affecting the Development of Bahraini Education

The development of education in the islands of Bahrain has been influenced by the country's geography, history, and people. Relating education to the country's economy is a high priority in Bahrain, since the government's policies and interests are directed toward that goal. Bahrain, unlike the neighboring countries in the Gulf, is currently a relatively oil-poor country, thus it has been forced to diversify in terms of both its economy and its education, especially in recent years.

From its first inception, education in Bahrain has reflected the country's economic conditions. Before the oil era of the 1920s and 1930s, Bahrain boasted a strong tradition in fishing and dhow building. In 1919, the first modern public local school was founded, named At Hidaya (the "Enlightenment").

Over the years, Hidaya school's for boys with one level of education evolved into multiple schools for both boys and girls with classes divided according to grade. During these pioneering years, attempts were made to relate education to the economic activities of the country. The study of mathematics, especially calculations related to diving and trading expeditions, was included in the curricula of the town schools. Subjects related to agriculture and farming were emphasized in the village schools. In addition to basic education, girls were taught basic first aid, hygiene, sewing, and embroidery. The chief objective of the boys' school was to train the boys to earn their own living, because at that time there was no employment for women except in the Education and Medical Departments. The aim of the girls' school was to teach the girls better methods of managing their homes and bringing up their children (Government of Bahrain, 1939).

These three separate curricula reflected the country's economy at that time. The values of hard work, of perseverance, and of enduring hardships and suffering to make a successful life pervaded all schools on the islands as a manifestation of the relationship between the livelihood of the people and education.

The discovery of oil in 1923 was one of Bahrain's silent revolutions. Its impact was a rapid economic transformation. The pace of this change increased appreciably following independence from Britain in 1971 and the 1974 rises in oil prices. Today, however, Bahrain is confronting the decline of its oil exploration and production, Bahrain is now among the first to experience output declines and to embark upon the diversification of its economy.

These are difficult times for Bahrain, and it is unclear whether the country can adjust easily to the impact of Western ideas and technology. The decline of the country's natural resources, coupled with the diversification of its economy (which has attracted a large immigrant labor force), points to the need for a rapid increase in educational facilities to educate not only native Bahrainians but also the large numbers of newcomers. Today, attempts are being made to relate education to a more diversified economy. In fact, linking education with the world of work is a major governmental policy for the 1990s.

Another factor profoundly affecting Bahrain's educational system is its relatively high growth rate, which is affecting the age structure of the population. The age pyramid in the country is extremely broad at the base, with around 42 percent of the population under age 15. Such a population structure is putting a heavy burden on the country's educational system.

A study of the historical development of education in Bahrain shows that for the past 80 years or so, education has gone through several difficult stages of development. By 1980, problems had arisen in relation to the school population, in the differentiation of secondary education, in pedagogy and methods of teaching, in teaching Bahrainian culture, and in the allocation of funds to train preprimary teachers. These problems have directly or indirectly influenced the development of all levels of education in Bahrain, but especially early childhood education.

Overall, however, the system of education in Bahrain has made impressive gains over the past seven decades. Bahrain was the first Gulf state to initiate modern formal education, to introduce female education, to develop technical education, to practice co-education, and in recent years to implement selected innovative educational projects. Within the Bahraini primary and secondary education, there are today noteworthy examples of large-scale responses to the reforms in various areas, which have accelerated throughout the 1970s and developed further in scale and scope during the 1980s. It has never been possible to build expensive schools or to employ large number of foreign teachers, but these limitations have not been a serious disadvantage. In fact, Bahrain today provides primary, intermediate, secondary, university, higher, technical, and medical education.

Organization of Education

Education in Bahrain is organized into preprimary (both the nursery and the kindergarten), primary (grades 1–6), intermediate (grades 1–3), secondary (grades 1–3), and higher. These five levels through which a student passes constitute the structure of education in Bahrain. Currently, all children ages 3, 4, and 5 are receiving education in classes outside the state schools on a fee-paying basis. In addition, many children attend informal school playgroups organized by parents and volunteer groups, and in a few areas there are separate nurseries. Such a system means that free education in state schools, in effect, begins at age 6.

The transition from one grade to another depends on daily performance and on the end-of-semester examinations, except for the first three grades of primary education, where automatic promotion is practiced because these grades are considered as preparatory only. At the end of each level (except for the primary), pupils who are not permitted to continue their studies because of their low academic performance, are eligible to learn a craft.

Following graduation from the secondary schools, students can continue their education at any of the specialized colleges of higher education in Bahrain. Those following the technical track are admitted to the Gulf Polytechnic; those following health services (e.g., nursing) are admitted into the College of Health Sciences; those following engineering, business studies, social sciences, and education are admitted to Bahrain University; and those following medicine are selected by their governments in one of the seven Gulf states to enter the Arabian Gulf University. Other vocational or technical courses are given in specialized institutions, such as the Hotel and Catering Centre.

Parallel to the system of education described above is a system of religious education, which combines general studies with religious education. Upon successful completion of the secondary stage, students may enter Al-Azhar University in Egypt. This branch of education in Bahrain is open only to male students.

In addition to the state schools, there are a number of private schools. There is also The Hope School, for mildly mentally handicapped children, and the Al Noor Institute for the Blind, serving blind pupils from the Gulf region.

For a number of years there has been a growing trend to provide education for handicapped children in ordinary schools where this is in the educational interests of the child and where the nature of his or her disability permits. The Ministry of the Interior, however, provides special education for children with emotional or behavioral disorders.

Education at all levels in the private schools and in the Bahraini colleges of higher education is co-educational and fee-paying. However, while the state schools are all single sex, both boys and girls are offered the same opportunities for learning.

Because of economic limitations, the development of education at all levels in Bahrain has, over the years, undergone several changes and reforms. Developing an educational system that equips students for a lifetime of work and provides them with the professional knowledge and skills required for the economic development of the country are major educational priorities in Bahrain.

Preschool Education

Preprimary education in Bahrain has never been viewed as a luxury. It has always been seen as necessary to meet the demands of working mothers with children under age 6.

The first modern school that offered kindergarten and primary education in Bahrain can be traced back to 1892 when the American Dutch Reformed Church established a missionary elementary school where Arabic, English, mathematics, and religion were taught. The Mission School gradually developed into a valuable institution. Although it was closed in 1933 for lack of funds, by that time governmental education had advanced to such an extent that the need for it was not as great as it had been (Government of Bahrain, 1956); the school was reopened some years later under a different administration. During the academic year 1956–57, it had two levels of education: kindergarten and primary classes 1 through 6. It also had a grade 7 specializing in elementary teacher training (Government of Bahrain, 1956). Recently, the school has changed its name from the American Mission School to Al-Raja to indicate the change in administration.

In spite of difficulties, past and present, the school still stands in the heart of the town of Monama as a testament to the rise of modern education in Bahrain nearly 100 years ago. In times of unprecedented change and the erosion of moral standards, this school has provided, since 1892, a constant element in the steady evolution of education and a beneficial influence on the traditional society which the Bahraini people endeavor to promote.

The first public statement concerning the establishment of a school for children of prestatutory age (i.e., before the age of 6) dates from 1943 when a primary school was founded by the Department of Education. But in those years, the stages of education were not clearly defined and the children of a wide age range attended the same school. Later, between 1946 and 1948, the three-year kindergarten was reduced to a two-year infant school called Al-Tahdiria (Al-Hamar, 1969). However, in 1960, due to financial cutbacks, the Bahrain government handed over responsibility for preprimary education to the private sector.

The interest of Bahraini women in preschool education is strong, partly because of the large numbers of women entering the workforce. Since 1961, several members of women's societies and many retired Bahraini teachers with long experience in dealing with young children have been establishing their own nurseries and kindergartens.

The first private nursery in Bahrain dates back to 1955 when an Egyptian woman, Mama Janette, founded a nursery in Manama for children from birth to age 3. It was then called Dar Al-Hanan (Al-Hamar, 1969).

By 1986, there were 76 preprimary educational establishments in Bahrain classified into the following three categories:

1. nurseries and kindergartens established and conducted by individual Bahraini or non-Bahraini citizens;

2. nurseries and kindergartens attached to private schools; and

3. nurseries and kindergartens established and run by women's associations.

Currently, nurseries and kindergartens in Bahrain are run and financed by private organizations or by individuals, both Bahraini and non-Bahraini. Although they are outside the direct control of the government, there is a directorate at the Ministry of Education responsible for the supervision of private education. However, the Ministry of Education involves itself only indirectly, (e.g., through supervision of curriculum materials and methods of teaching). In financial matters and financial aid, the Ministry of Labour and Social Affairs is responsible for both the nurseries and the kindergartens.

Like all private establishments on the islands, preschool education acquired an autonomous administrative structure with the establishment of the Private Education Inspectorate office in the Ministry of Education in 1961. Most kindergartens employ the class teacher system, where each teacher is responsible for a specific group of children, subdivided into several smaller groups according to age. The teacher supervises the class for the entire school day. In addition, each teacher has one or more assistants whenever possible. The informal atmosphere in nurseries and kindergartens makes it possible for children to move around freely under the guidance of teachers.

Kindergarten teachers follow no set syllabus, but versatility and flexibility are their requisites. The teachers evaluate the children in their care and watch for the children's responsiveness, imagination, and progress. Preschool education aims at recognizing children's talents and inborn skills, helping them to form acceptable behavioral patterns, instilling in them cultural and religious values, making them psychologically secure, aligning the foundations for them to develop a sound personality full of health and moral vigor, and preparing them for primary education.

Parents of children at nurseries and kindergartens pay fees, which vary from one establishment to another. In 1986, for instance, the Society for Mother and Child Care charged BD 22 per child per month, while Al-Majid Kindergarten charged BD 200 per child per term (Government of Bahrain, 1986). Such variations are due to the fact that some establishments offer more services than others, such as meals or longer hours.

Table 1 shows that the increase in the number of preschool children enrolling in nurseries and kindergartens has been gradual. This is partly because not all towns in Bahrain have preschool facilities and partly because most nonworking mothers prefer to look after their children themselves. It is significant that 90 percent of the total enrollment were Bahrainis.

TABLE 1

Children Enrolled in Private Preprimary Schools, 1977–78 to 1985–86

School Year	Male	Female	Total
1977–78	1,239	1,164	2,403
1978–79	1,353	1,268	2,621
1979–80	1,549	1,382	2,931
1980–81	1,962	1,768	3,730
1981–82	2,313	2,086	4,399
1982–83	2,636	2,417	5,053
1983–84	2,699	2,516	5,215
1984–85	3,576	3,155	6,731
1985–86	4,009	3,599	7,608

Source: Ministry of Education, *Statistical Summaries on Education in Bahrain, 1977–78 to 1985–86.*

Teacher Training

A survey conducted in 1980 by the High Council of Youth and Sports showed that 87.5 percent of preschool teachers had secondary education; 6.9 percent had intermediate; 4.2 percent had university degrees; and 1.4 percent had only primary education. Almost 34.7 percent of the kindergarten staff had not received any training in child care, while 55.6 percent had received a short training of 15–30 days in the methods of educating young children (Al-Mubayyed, 1980). The survey also showed that the levels of salaries for kindergarten teachers were not commensurate with their training and qualifications. The salaries reflected the level or prosperity of the organization or society financing the school. In addition, teachers in preschools are not eligible for the retirement pension received by employees in the state schools. As a result, most of them seize the first opportunity to leave their jobs as preprimary teachers for better ones in the state school system (*ibid.*).

Improving the Quality of Preschool Education

Leaving complete responsibility for preschool education to the private sector has had its disadvantages. A 1984 study showed that many buildings used as nurseries and kindergartens are old, rented, and not designed for educational purposes, and are therefore unsuitable for and incompatible with modern educational requirements. In addition 75 percent of the old rented buildings are situated by busy, crowded roads, which makes access to the schools hazardous. Similarly, a few are adjacent to factories or workshops where the children can be disturbed by noise and smoke (Hammoud, 1984).

Another disadvantage is that in such buildings, there are no rooms for film presentations, music, drawing, handiwork, libraries, and first aid. The administrative and teaching staff at the preprimary schools reported that there are insufficient educational equipment and aids. Individual games and outdoor playing facilities are also lacking (*ibid.*). It was also reported that only 51.2 percent of all nurseries and kindergartens had adequate facilities for preprimary education. In 48.8 percent of the facilities, there were approximately 47 children in each classroom, which is too high by modern standards (*ibid.*). Such crowded classrooms impede the achievement of educational objectives and reduce the standard of services provided. Combined with the lack of understanding of educational methods by parents, the lack of qualified assistants, and insufficient support from official sources, it is clear why these establishments have often been unable to achieve the objectives for which they were founded.

To accomplish the aims of nurseries and kindergartens, the preprimary schools must have a proper place in the educational system under the control of the Ministry of Education in cooperation with other concerned persons and agencies. The untrained members of women's societies, no matter how well-intentioned, lack the knowledge necessary for running preprimary schools. In addition, they must make a profit or at least make enough to meet their expenses. For these reasons, the government should have clear guidelines for establishing and running nurseries and kindergartens, and maintain firm supervision over every aspect of these schools.

The inadequacy of the teachers at this early stage of a child's education is mainly due to two factors. First, most do not have any solid background in the techniques and methods of teaching. Second, for those who have had some training, the 15-

to 30-day training course in the methods of educating young children is not adequate preparation. Unqualified teachers have been recruited to provide an immediate solution to the problem of teacher shortages. Moreover, highly qualified teachers demand high salaries, which most volunteer societies cannot afford. The following is a possible remedy for this situation.

First, the Ministry of Education should extend reforms in the state schools to the preprimary sphere by offering in-service training to kindergarten teachers, similar to the training given their colleagues in state primary schools, so that they may be qualified as teachers. If carefully implemented, such an approach based on the psychology of children at the early years will improve the quality of kindergarten education.

Second, fees for children from needy families should be subsidized by the government, either through the Ministry of Education or through the Ministry of Social Affairs.

Third, all forms of preschool education, including day care facilities, should be systematically expanded as a means of increasing educational opportunities for younger children.

In addition, the establishment and availability of nursery facilities will also have importance to Bahrain in the future, where the next generation of families will have both parents pursuing careers. The cost of providing these facilities would therefore be an investment for the future and a benefit to the educational system.

The Ministry of Education is currently collaborating with Bahrain University to set up special programs to improve the quality of early childhood education. Although it will take years for all teachers in Bahrain preprimary schools to be trained and for old buildings to be replaced, such innovations are introducing a new era in the history of early childhood education in Bahrain.

Conclusion

Bahrain has gone through a very difficult period in its history. Without the strong support of the government to diversify the country's economy and to reform education so that it relates to the economy, Bahrain could never overcome the problems resulting from limited and steadily declining oil reserves

The discussion in this chapter may contribute to a better understanding of how specific historical, social, religious, and economic factors affect the way educators view the objectives of the educative process. Alternatively, it may also suggest that irrespective of differences in the cultural environment and in social needs, educators striving to achieve similar goals for children tend to pursue similar policies and encounter similar problems.

Notes

1. The Persian Gulf (as it is called by the Iranians) or the Arabian Gulf (as it is called by the Arabs) is referred to in this chapter as "the Gulf."

2. This chapter is based on materials issued by the Ministry of Education and other governmental agencies in Bahrain. It is also based on information gathered from interviews conducted with teachers, headmasters and headmistresses, inspectors, senior staff in the Department of Private Education at the Ministry of Education (which supervised kindergarten education), and staff at other departments at the Ministry of Social Affairs (which supervises the nursery schools), as well as other people with relevant experience.

References

Al-Arrayed, M. (1989). *Education in Bahrain: Problems and progress*. London: Ithaca Press.

Al Fadhel, W. (1989). *Preprimary education in the state of Bahrain*. Bahrain: Directorate of Private Education, Ministry of Education.

Al-Hamar, A. M. (1969). *Development of education in Bahrain, 1940–1965*. Bahrain: Oriental Press.

Al-Hashimi, I. J. (1980). *A conceptual framework of the preparation of occupational education and training*. Bahrain: Gulf Polytechnic.

Al-Misnad, S. (1986). *The development of modern education in Bahrain, Kuwait, and Qatar with special references of the education of women*. London: Ithaca Press.

Al-Mubayyed, M. (1980). *A field study of children and their needs in Bahrain*. (In Arabic). Bahrain: Council of Youth and Sport, with the help of the Ministry of Health.

Bahrain. *The law of private education establishment*. Decrees No. 11, 12, for 1961, 1977, 1985 (In Arabic).

Children and Mothers' Welfare Society. (1953–56, 1959–60). *A Guide to the society's kindergartens, Bahrain*.

————. (1984). *The Hope Institute for handicapped children.* (In Arabic).

Government of Bahrain.(1926–37). *Administrative Reports.*

————.(1939–56) *Annual Reports.*

————. Education Department.(1953–56; 1959–60). *Annual reports.*

————. Ministry of Education. (1979) *Bahrain directory of education systems in various educational institutions in the state of Bahrain.*

————. Ministry of Education. (1983–84). *Bahrain guide to private schools, 1983–84.*

————. Ministry of Education. (1983–84). *Directory of private education establishments, 1983–4.* (In Arabic) Bahrain: Directorate of Private Education.

————. (1981) *Population census.*

————. Ministry of Education. (1986). *Directory of private education establishments, 1986.* Bahrain: Directorate of Private Education. (In Arabic).

————. Ministry of Labour and Social Affairs. (1983). *Condition and needs of Bahrain's working women.* Bahrain. (In Arabic).

Hammoud, R. (1984). *Child education in Bahrain.* University College of Arts, Science and Education, Bahrain. Seminar February 25–29, 1984. (In Arabic).

————. (1986) *Primary education in the state schools of Bahrain.* Paper presented at the second Annual Education Conference Regarding Primary School Curricula, April 8–10, 1986, Bahrain.

Jain, J. L. (1986). *A brief history of education in Bahrain.* Bahrain: Arabian Printing & Publishing House.

Nashif, H. (1986). *Preschool education in the Arab world.* London: Croom Helm.

UNESCO. (1982). *UNESCO report on education reform in Bahrain.* UNESCO Mission to Bahrain, May 22–June 4, 1982. Paris: UNESCO.

Winder, R.B. (1959) *Education in Al-Bahrain from the world of Islam.* London: Macmillan.

PRESCHOOL EDUCATION IN BELGIUM

• • • • • • • • • • ◆ • • • • • • • • •

Marc Depaepe and Ferre Laevers
Catholic University of Louvain
Leuven, Belgium

Countries differ widely in how their educational systems are organized. One particular feature of the Belgian system is its extensive educational facilities for children ages 2 1/2 to 6. Children within this age range attend preschools that are usually linked to elementary schools and are supervised by the same principal. As in elementary schools, there is one teacher per class of about 25 children.

Preschool education is organized on a full-day basis and is free. The content of preschool education, however, is totally different from the elementary school curriculum. Likewise, the training of preschool teachers differs from that of elementary school teachers (although the training for both takes place in the same institutions). While attendance is not compulsory, nearly 100 percent of five-year-olds attend a preschool program.

This chapter describes the origins of preschool education in Belgium, the main features of current practice, and the Experiential Preschool Education (EPE) model, an influential experimental project in Flanders.

Historical Background

As in most other European countries, preschool education in Belgium goes back to the so-called dame schools. The earliest such schools were in the Low Countries as early as the 13th century; they reached their greatest number at the end of the 18th and the beginning of the 19th centuries. Dame schools had few, if any, educational objectives apart from some religious training and tried to provide only basic child care.

The first "infant schools" were started in Brussels (Elsene) in 1827. They were modeled very closely on the English infant schools of Robert Owen and were co-founded by the Dutch *Maatschappij tot Nut van't Algmeen* (Society for Social Improvement), which tried to improve the welfare of the people within the limits of the existing order. Out of a kind of paternalistic philanthropy, the enlightened Dutch king William I encouraged such initiatives by giving subsidies to towns that wanted to establish an infant school.

After Belgium won its independence in 1830, the Catholic Church, which was the strongest power in the field of education in Belgium both institutionally and ideologically, contributed to the further spread of infant schools. Education, care of the poor, and charity all supported its mission: to convince as many people as possible to live a Christian life in the prospect of a later eternal life. In 1857, it was reported that there were 218 free (i.e., Catholic) nonsubsidized, 138 free subsidized, and 24 municipal (i.e., public) infant schools. Although the stress in all these institutions was on moral and religious education, reading, writing, and/or arithmetic were often also taught. Since there was no compulsory school attendance before 1914 and since child labor was unrestricted until 1889, the infant school could, theoretically, be the only school that the children of workers would ever attend.

Nevertheless, for the first half of the 19th century, there was no organized training for infant school teachers. In the best case, a woman who wished to start an infant school first went to learn from a colleague for a few weeks or months in order to become familiar with the customs and methods of infant school education. Moreover, the requirements placed on someone who ran an infant school were related primarily to moral qualities—such as religion, zeal, promptness, and docility—rather than to knowledge.

Influenced by Friedrich Froebel's concept of the kindergarten, Belgium gradually opened up to a more pedagogical approach to the education of preschool children starting in the middle of the 19th century. This type of school, introduced by a few enthusiastic women who were concerned mostly with the practical applications of Froebel's method, found supporters initially only in the liberal environment. The first Belgian kindergarten was opened with private initiative in 1857, again in Elsene. In 1858, also in Elsene, the first courses for "Froebel teachers" were organized, with the support of the government. It is difficult to determine whether this new form of preschool care was successful, since official statistics of that period use the terms kindergarten, Froebel school, Froebel division, and infant school interchangeably. Nevertheless, it is clear that many infant schools of the old style were started or still continued their activities after 1857.

In its general objectives, the kindergarten differed little from the infant school. In both cases,

the idea was to protect children from the evil influences that could endanger their physical, moral, or intellectual development and to accustom them to order, regularity, work, and hygiene. The difference between the two types was found in the amount of stress placed on the various elements. For example, in the new style kindergarten, the stress was explicitly on education, while the predominant concern in the infant school was traditionally on protection. Even though the changing global vision of preschool education gave rise to a more positive treatment of the child, still the educational practice in the kindergartens was very near that of the old infant school, where, it was said, the "teaching" was much too "mechanical."

When the Liberals were in control of the government between 1878 and 1884—the period of "school struggle" in Belgian primary education—they took several measures to activate Froebelian education. In 1880, the government not only introduced a model program for the official schools that was drawn up in the spirit of the Froebelian materials, the *Spielgaben*, but it also established courses for diplomas or certificates for infant school teachers. When the Catholics, who emerged strengthened from the school struggle, regained power, this program was immediately eliminated; Froebel, in the eyes of most Catholics, had given too little attention to religious education.

Nevertheless, this did not keep the Catholic government from establishing in 1890 a model program and regulation that, entirely in the spirit of Froebel, was intended to stimulate the self-activation of the child. In this program, the Froebel method was certainly not conceived of as an integral educational system, but rather as a series of valuable exercises (primarily folding and tearing) that were intended to promote eye-hand coordination, to develop endurance, and to improve individual taste. Such an interpretation, which was close to the actual implementation of Froebel's ideas in Belgium as elsewhere, left space for an integration with Catholic ideology. Apart from the emphasis on religion, the expectations of Catholics and Liberals from preschool education were not very different. As a whole, preschool education was seen to be a good way to promote moral development, and it was accepted unquestionably that many children from the working class had become better behaved, healthier, and more intelligent thanks to this institution.

After the turn of the century, discussion of the purpose of the kindergarten continued. Should one, in the spirit of Froebel, allow the children primarily to play, or must they be mostly taught? The program of 1890 gave no definitive answer to this question. One may, however, assume that systematic teaching did still often occur in the kindergarten, even though this institution was permeated above all with a moralizing and religious atmosphere. To begin with, the pedagogical press did not initially disapprove of teaching arithmetic, reading, and writing in preschool, and this was also the explicit wish of some parents. The unremitting demand for education for the preschool children fitted in with the general objective that was worked out in the first decades of this century for the preschool level. On the eve of World War I, the pedagogical opinion-makers pointed out that preschool education, although it might not be instruction, still provided the best transition from the family life to primary education. In this sense, it was regarded more and more as a necessity, even for children from the better-off classes. Indeed, between 1878 and 1914, the number of infants schools in Belgium almost tripled (from 1,129 to 3,231).

Influences of the "New Education" Movement

Almost immediately after World War I, the first signs of dissatisfaction with an exclusively Froebel-inspired pedagogy emerged. The "German" system was rejected by the Belgians as too rigid, too mechanical. More benefits were seen in, for example, of Maria Montessori's method, which was based on activity and the principle of individuality, and thus gave children greater freedom.

Nevertheless, the Montessori method, in spite of a few fervent supporters in Flanders and Wallonia, was also criticized. It was accused of a certain unrealness. More favored was the method espoused by Ovide Decroly, who met with considerable success, certainly in official education, with his concentration of teaching content around "central concepts" and/or "interest centers."

All these elements could be found in some form in the model program of 1927 introduced by the Socialist Minister C. Huysmans. This same minister also increased the length of the training of the infant school teacher from two to three years (after primary school). In general, the reforms were received quite well. The content of the new programs consisted of five components, in which the intellectual-sensory aspect occupied an important place, it is true, but still envisioned as part of a whole in the harmonious development of the child. In the accompanying model regulations, self-education and free activity of the preschool child were praised, even though one remained faithful to concepts and ideas that had proven their usefulness over the years. More particularly, the new emphasis on play meant that children, much more than their teachers—generally nuns in the free system—had to take greater part in activities (e.g., puppet shows). The objective was, in conformity with the principle of "guided freedom," to stress internal commandments rather than external prohibitions.

Nevertheless, the idea was not for the preschool education ever to operate without punishments or rewards, as certain forms of modernism would lead one to believe. There was certainly no question of unrestricted freedom. In any event, the teacher was expected to guide the various class activities with a "gentle hand." Moreover, it was regularly pointed out that the emphasis on free self-activity and play was difficult to combine with the requirements of discipline. Whether or not one wanted to, one was locked in the straitjacket of classroom education and the hoped for individualization was necessarily limited. The principle of self-education might be accepted theoretically, but in everyday practice it was seldom implemented. Moreover, the Catholic pedagogues of the interbellum period were frightened of a far-reaching ethic of freedom, which, like the cinema and other contemporary phenomena, was considered a sign of moral degeneracy. In Catholic preschool education, the Catholic mission must never be neglected, even if it means going against modern pedagogical trends.

After World War II, many found that preschool education, which was being attended by virtually all children, was due for a new orientation. In spite of its claims for total personality development, preschool education had not succeeded in achieving a real integration in the formation of children. The down-playing of physical development, certainly neglected in the free (i.e., Catholic) system, speaks volumes in this regard. Moreover, it was said that the Montessorian pedagogy, with its stress on systematic sensory exercises, had given rise to a coldly intellectual and analytical approach to the child. In the spirit of the Decroly-inspired curriculum of 1936 for the primary school, complementary plans were suggested for the preschool level. These came about in the 1950s.

The search for a renewed preschool didactic was crowned in 1951 by the publication of the *Werkplan voor opovedende activiteiten* (Work Plan for Educational Activities). According to the ministerial decree of October 2, 1950, this plan replaced the program and regulations of 1927. Although this plan had emerged under the Catholic minister, P. Harmel, the Catholic educational authorities issued their own program in 1952, as they had done in 1936 for primary education.

With few shifts in emphasis, the new plan was based on the same psycho-pedagogical principles as primary education. Both directives sought to "de-school" preschool education, for the infant schools teachers still admired the primary schools, which, it was said, involved a "masking" of childhood. Ironically, this was associated with an increasing professionalization of the training of the preschool teachers, which was increased, in 1957, to four years after the completion of lower secondary education.

The new psycho-pedagogical orientation was found in authorities like Decroly and Edouard Claparède. It was based on "functional psychology," which held that what was achieved in the school had to correspond to the true needs of the child. In other words, only what interested the child could be offered. Further, the new working plan, in an effort to promote integral education, eliminated the 1927 division of physical, moral, and intellectual teaching, which seemed to be artificial. The point of departure became the needs and drives of the child, which, under the influence of genetic psychology, were further differentiated as a function of age.

Nevertheless, the "metamorphosis" reported in the educational press primarily concerned the content and exterior form of the kindergarten (with, for example, little tables and stools that could be easily moved) and less the pedagogical mentality as such. Perusing the professional journals of the 1960s, one is struck by how much the fragments of the past persisted with respect to the view of the teacher, the child, and the interaction between them. Moreover, the increasing child-orientedness often degenerated into a kind of sentimentality, which seriously impeded true emancipation if not making it impossible.

In any event, it was clear that the ideal of preschool education without discipline remained unrealized. The advocated climate of freedom had nothing in common with "laissez faire" but was intended to form the foundation for inner discipline. In Catholic preschool education, regulation was conceived of as a form of "precatechesis." Thus, it was obvious that children should go to class in an orderly row and that, in this class, a more or less typical school atmosphere should prevail.

Punishment could not be completely ruled out. Withdrawal of affection, moreover, was presented as good remedy for undesirable behavior. It was advised that the negative feelings of the child be converted as much as possible into positive feelings.

Opposition to the contours of an all too rigidly organized preschool education arose again only at the end of the 1960s and the beginning of the 1970s. It is striking that this change occurred again at a time in which the training of preschool teachers was extended. In 1970, the training for preschool education was finally assigned to higher pedagogical education. Around the middle of the 1970s, the demand arose in Flanders for experience-oriented preschool education that would respond to the authentic feelings of the child and would impose itself as little as possible. Even though this renewal was not universally supported, it is indisputable that it had an effect on practice, even among preschool teachers who resolutely rejected the system.

Current Preschool Education

In spite of various daily routines, one can discern a basic pattern in Belgian preschool education. Most of the classes begin with "circle time," in which children are welcomed and invited, in turn, to present personal experiences or comments. After 15 to 30 minutes, depending on the age of the children, the first learning activity is started.

The content of learning activities can vary from an "exploration" (e.g., the teacher brings in an object that is observed and discussed), to more specific cognitive activities (e.g., sorting tasks, early mathematics, writing or reading skills, or learning spatial relation concepts). This takes about 25 minutes and is followed by group activities. Classes are usually divided into three groups (each with its own chosen group name) always sitting at their own set of tables. Every group has a task on which children work individually for about 25 minutes. Most of the tasks involve manual activity or expression (e.g., making models out of paper or fabric, (finger) painting, copying patterns on the pegboard, etc). The teacher accompanies one of the groups in an activity that involves more guidance (e.g., cutting vegetables to make soup or introducing a new cognitive game). After a short snack time, children leave for outdoor play.

During the second part of the morning, group activities are continued for about 30 minutes. Eventually the groups change tasks. Generally, the activities are programmed so that by the end of the week every child has preformed all the tasks. The morning session closes with a traditional playful activity: singing songs, dancing, all-around games (with such cognitive goals as exploring spatial relations, observing, and paying attention).

After a short gathering (circle time), most of the afternoon is dedicated to free play. After a break (outside time), children clean up and the day is closed with story telling. Table 1 is an example of a typical class day for 4-year olds.

Content and Goals of Preschool Education

The content of preschool activities affirms the basic assumptions of the educational policy makers: preschool education takes into account a wide variety of goals. There is attention to normal and religious education, socio-emotional development, exploration of the natural and cultural reality, language education, cognitive development, all forms of artistic expression, and stimulation of motor skills. Because there is no clear-cut curriculum for the preschool, the teacher can stress some elements and neglect others.

The general principles that make it possible to understand how the "average" preschool teacher functions in her classroom are discussed below. Five are identified.

TABLE 1

Example of One-day Classroom Activities for 4-Year-Olds

8:30 A.M.	Circle time: reception and conversation
8:50 A.M.	Classical activity: children sort objects (e.g., sitting in a circle, children take turns sorting a basket of carnival objects)
9:20 A.M.	Group activity: group 1 makes a paper carnival collage by cutting and pasting; group 2 decorates a picture of a clown; group 3 draws trumpets with a pencil
9:40 A.M.	Clean up and rehearsal of poems
9:55 A.M.	Snack time and outside time
10:25 A.M.	Group activities: continuation of the work in three groups; children who have finished can choose a quiet activity (after having cleaned up)
11:00 A.M.	Classical activity: attention game (one child takes an object, a carnival attribute, away while the others close their eyes; the class tells what is missing)
11:30 A.M.	End of the morning session
1:30 P.M.	Circle time: reception and short conversation
1:40 P.M.	Free play
2:20 P.M.	Clean-up time
2:30 P.M.	Folk dancing
2:45 P.M.	Outside time
3:10 P.M.	Story telling (e.g., *The Elf and the Giant*)
3:35 P.M.	End of the day

Centers of Interest

One of the most important features of pre-school practice is the thematic link among nearly all activities. Every week or two, the teacher introduces a new center of interest. The themes usually reflect seasonal evolutions and the feast calendar. But even when there is no intrinsic connection with the time of the year, the program tends to be theme-oriented. This is largely influenced by the planning guides for preschoolers that the teachers frequently use.

The center of interests must, in the first place, be regarded as a guideline for the teachers to program activities. It gives them a basis for selecting materials for guided exploration; games and tasks for manual expression; and songs, poems, and stories.

The Impression-Expression Cycle

A more implicit but no less influential principle is the use of a two-phase strategy in programming activities. The "impression" phase is realized through such activities as outside trips (e.g., visiting a bakery, a hospital, or the park), guest speakers, (e.g., the postman, a policeman, a fisherman) or, most often, a guided exploration of a "piece of reality", (e.g., a basket of apples, a bunch of asters, a nest of young chickens, a dead bird). The teacher stimulates sensory exploration, helps to elicit observations, and tries to expand vocabulary. In the second phase, the impressions or experiences are assimilated through expression activity (mostly in groups). Children work at specific representational tasks, often copying models given by the teacher or decorating printed representations of the observed objects.

Teacher Guidance

In current practice, the teacher takes a predominant role. She determines the centers of interest and program activities. In the agenda, one can find the type of activities, the time of execution, needed material, and the operational goals. Despite the emphasis on explorations, the school day has a rather predictable course.

Another way in which the teacher's impact on the children is felt is through what we have termed the "dosing principle". That is, teachers feel that children should get a regular "dose" of each activity which is deemed to be good for them. This is reflected in the scheduling of activities and in the teacher's regulatory interventions throughout the day. Teachers often move children on to the next activity not because the previous one is finished, but because the children must experience all the planned activities for the week. While this is often defended as a concern that the children be exposed to a broad spectrum of activities in order to foster a holistic and harmonious development of the child, the "doses" of specific activities which teachers plan are often not based on general developmental principles. For example, teachers will expect children to participate in a specific period of cutting and cleaning activities at least once a week, but they will generally not look for other possible ways to develop fine motor skills.

Child-Centeredness

Despite the predominance of the teacher, the overall impression of the average preschool is one of child-centeredness. A quick reference to the practice in elementary school (where children are enrolled in September of the year they turn 6) is enough to confirm that impression. The elements that contribute to the child-centeredness of preschool are the amount of free initiative (especially in the afternoon); the predominance of play-like activities, even in the cognitive areas; the room for artistic expression (e.g., in painting, drawing, construction, role-play, etc.); the fact that the preschool teachers, in contrast with their colleagues in elementary schools, often use group activities instead of traditional teacher-centered methods; and an informal atmosphere (e.g., within certain limits, children can talk freely while working).

Socialization

Many teacher interventions are motivated by the concern to promote adaptation to the basic social rules. Teachers emphasize politeness, the ability of listen to others, self-control and task persistence, independent behavior, and most of all, a pro-social attitude (e.g., being nice to one another).

Experiential Preschool Education

An overview of preschool education in Belgium must include a description of Experiential Preschool Education (EPE). This innovative project was initiated by members of the Department of Educational Sciences of the University of Louvain. Started in 1976, it is still expanding in terms of research, development, and dissemination. An important vehicle for the latter is the project's periodical *Kleuters & Ik*, and other publications that have influenced pre- and in-service teacher training in Flanders.

Basic Assumptions

The basic assumptions of the EPE project are rooted in the theories of the emancipatory movement that came to life at the end of the 1960s. The most important sources of inspiration were humanistic psychology (Rogers and Gendlin), the critical psycho-analytic movement, and later, Piagetian theory.

The project began when 12 preschool teachers were selected to join in a mutual effort to critically analyze current preschool practice. A main source of inspiration for this reflection was the experiential movement (Gendlin, 1964). The crucial angle of approach for the group sessions was the reconstruction of what children experience during a school day, especially in connection with teacher interventions. The main concern was to get a better insight into how children experience the many aspects of the educational context.

The (experiential) analysis of the classroom life confirmed and deepened the critical reflections on current education. These criticisms can be categorized into two lines of thoughts. First, attitudes, especially moral attitudes, develop dogmatically, moralistically, and artificially. Children are often moved to express feelings they do not have. In a gentle way, children are forced to show gratitude, admiration, and above all positive feelings toward others. In this atmosphere, genuine interaction between teacher and children is made difficult. Children are not helped to explore their real feelings and to cope with them. The whole approach leads to alienation.

Second, despite the child-centered look of preschool practice, it has many rigid and scholastic elements. Initiative of children is rather restricted. Even free play suffers in many cases from many constraints. In some classes, children may choose only from four activities and can change but once during free play time. Children who tend to make the same choice as the day(s) before are urged to do

something else. As to the use of "center of interests," one can observe some kind of inflation of the term: the themes do not always reflect the real interests of the children. Although the impression-expression cycle is a useful guide, in current preschool it is used rigidly. Teachers act as if they can predict which impressions children will have had and how and when these can or must be assimilated. During the phase of impression in the cycle, the stress on vocabulary is often an obstacle to a lively exploration. Further, the dosing principle does not take into account the many ways children can develop nor the fact that their development tends to occur in waves (i.e., children are active in the same activities for weeks before they choose new ones). Finally, the standard for judging the effectiveness of imposed learning activities is low as these activities are usually geared to the learning of whatever is seen as an "average" child.

The work with the group of selected teachers shifted gradually from describing the process to putting it into action. Through this an alternative approach to teaching preschool children was developed.

Conceptual Framework

The core of EPE is represented by the "temple scheme" (see Table 2). This scheme, developed in 1979, remains a point of reference for current project research and dissemination.

The foundation of the approach is the experiential attitude of the teacher. According to Gendlin, "experience" is part of reality; it is "the process of concrete, bodily feeling which is the basic matter of psychological and personality phenomena." According to this definition, experience is not what people "have" (and accumulate while living) but rather what people "are" at a particular moment and situation. It consists of "inwardly sensed, bodily felt events." The experiencing (the process of experience) is the source of human behavior, leading to actions and inspiring reactions. It involves not only feelings (which are the constant evaluation of situations according to human needs), but also felt meanings, which are the necessary inner referents of even the most abstract concepts: "without our 'feel' of the meaning, verbal symbols are only noises (or sound images of noises)."

Teachers who have this basic experiential attitude intentionally focus on the reality of "bodily

TABLE 2

BASIC CONCEPTS OF EXPERIENTIAL PRESCHOOL EDUCATION

	Emancipation		the general goal of education
	Developmental Processes		the processes in
	Therapeutic Processes		the child
EXPERIENTIAL DIALOGUE	FREE INITIATIVE	ENRICHMENT OF THE ENVIRONMENT	the means or principles
	EXPERIENTIAL ATTITUDE		the fundamental approach of the teacher

felt meanings" in the child. They try to get in touch with the inner process of experiencing. This approach is possible because humans can not only attend inwardly to their own experiences, but can also use the "inner stream" to understand others. This involves the concept of "reconstruction of experience." Researchers and educators can get in touch with their "inner stream", try to empathetically feel what this "inner stream" must be like for the observed person, and express these feelings in a process of symbolization (mostly verbal description). This process of reconstruction is not easy. It requires much sensitivity, a rich experience, a developed linguistic feeling, and a cautious attitude (the concern to take into account all the available facts).

Looking at current preschool practice from the experiential angle leads to the critical reflections described above. It also engenders ideas about a more emancipatory model of education for young children. The ingredients of this model are three principles or modes of intervention, two kinds of processes the teacher should have in mind, and the final goal of experimental education.

Means or principles. In the three columns of the temple scheme one finds the principles that guide all practical decisions the teacher has to make and all actions she has to take to encourage the two processes discussed further.

The first principle refers to the teacher's efforts to create a condition wherein every child can feel free to be himself or herself and to choose activities that meet his or her emotional, motor, social, and cognitive needs. The realization of this principle involves rules to guarantee a smoothly running class and the most freedom for every child (and not only for the "fittest"). Most of the rules in EPE classes have to do with cleaning up and respect for materials and for the well-being of others. Few limits are set on the choice, duration, or quality of activities. This open organizational system, in which self-selection of activity is promoted, has to be implemented gradually. It changes the implicit theories of teachers about learning and development. For some children, it takes thoughtful guidance to help them discover their own interests and to teach them to cope with a less structured environment.

The second principle is to provide a rich and interesting environment for the children. Free choice makes no sense in a drab and sterile setting. Therefore much teacher initiative should be directed toward the provision of materials and activities (even guided ones) that meet the developing needs of each individual child. Insofar as the enrichment of the environment is seen as an offer from the teacher, it does not contradict the first principle. This second principle, an indispensable complement for the first guideline, requires careful observation and inventiveness.

The third principle involves the teacher in dialogue or in sustaining activity by giving specific impulses. The importance of an experimental attitude is quite obvious in this most refined of the three principles. Teacher interventions that lack feeling for the emotional, motivational, or cognitive properties of children's minds turn education into a dull or even threatening endeavor.

Process and Final Goal. All efforts of the EPE teacher are directed toward two possible changes. First is sustaining therapeutic processes in children. This concern does not mean that teachers take the place of psychiatrists or play therapists. But 15 years of active research in the project has provided impressive documentation of the way the regular classroom can have a prophylactic function and can even play a decisive role in healing emotional problems. The general atmosphere of EPE classes helps the children to keep in touch with their own feelings. But specific intervention—in the form of materials (e.g., bed in the classroom, doctors' utensils), of information (verbally or through books), of thematic stories in which children can recognize their own problems, and of personal dialogue—has been shown to be powerful in helping children cope with difficult experiences.

Preschool education has another aspect that enhances emotional health and contributes to a positive self-image. In other words, after caring for the child-with-problems, it is necessary to help the child-with-possibilities. The focus here is on so-called developmental or creative processes. This particular form of learning—as opposed to superficial learning—is "creative" because it leads to the development of new basic structures in the child, which widen his or her possibilities to relate to the world (things and people). The influences of Piagetian theory are evident here, especially the principle that learning best takes place when there is "active involvement" of the child with the environment.

These two processes lead to the ideal of the emancipated person. This final goal of education consequently entails two basic qualities: freedom of emotional or irrational complexes, and a strong exploratory attitude.

Involvement as Criterion for Effective Education. One of the most crucial aspects of EPE is the selection of "involvement" as an indication of the so-called creative processes. The theoretical foundation for this criterion remains the conviction that behind every act there is a basic structure that explains human performance. When a toddler does not look for an object that has fallen out of sight, he shows a level of functioning that affects many situations in his life. Fundamental schemes determine the world we are living in. By them, we interpret new situations and we do, or do not, act competently. It is hypothesized that there are different sets of schemes for every basic dimension of reality, such as biological phenomena; human behavior; economic facts; technical and organizational problems; mathematical questions; body-movements; and forms of expression (e.g., language, music, painting, and sculpture). The unveiling of these basic schemes or fundamental representations of reality is an immense task. But lines of development can be seen as going from elementary, mechanistic, and gross images of reality to complex, dynamic, and differentiated structures. A reference to shifts on the level of paradigms might be helpful to understand what is meant.

Effective education should engender changes in the level of fundamental schemes and go beyond the learning of specific information, skills, or "tricks." The question is how this "deep level learning" can be stimulated.

First, the possibility of direct transmission of basic schemes, assuming these can be identified, has been rejected. Fundamental schemes are the residuum of countless concrete actions. This view gives strong support to the principle of exemplary teaching. But which concrete activities should be programmed? Here, the nature of developmental processes is helpful. In reflecting on the activities of young children as well as of adults, it can be established that people, as far as the circumstances are favorable, tend to show concentration, involvement, and even enthusiasm in activities that meet their (recently) acquired fundamental schemes. These are "motivation structures." They make people attentive to specific elements of their environment and determine what motivates them. This close relationship between aptitude or competence and (developmental) needs is the ultimate legitimation for "involvement" as a criterion for the quality of education.

Why involvement is such an important factor can be understood by depicting what goes on in an involved person. Referring to Gendlin, it can be said, first, that the full potential of experiencing is used. This high intensity of experience indicates that much of (mental) energy is mobilized and used most efficiently. Furthermore, the activities reflect the level of functioning attained by a particular person. He is at his best. One cannot get involved in activities that are either too easy or that require much more developed capabilities. This point is sustained by Csikszentmihayli (1979), who introduced the "state of flow" to describe a pattern experienced by people when they have engaged in activity that "went well."

Involved persons are highly motivated. But the source of this motivation is limited to the exploratory need, by eagerness to understand and learn, and by the drive to get a good grip on reality (in the literal and figurative sense of the word). Although other needs can intervene, involvement always implies intrinsic motivation.

One can hypothesize that this kind of activity leads (gradually or suddenly) to shifts in the fundamental schemes. These changes are predetermined and unidirectional. Persons act, after some time, on a higher level (i.e., in a more differentiated way). The grasp on reality becomes broader and more subtle.

The development process cannot be seen as an overall evolution. The fundamental changes occur only in the domains represented in the activities in which children are involved: hence the concern for a rich environment in terms of broadness (all important fields of development should be present) and in terms of complexity. So it is obvious that the predetermined character of developmental stages does not mean children can grow up by themselves. Maintaining a level of intense activity requires the highest educational competence of adults. This involvement has nothing to do with the state of arousal easily obtained by the "entertainer."

Preschool Practice and Involvement. Experiences accumulated in the EPE project support the conclusion that it is important to maximize involvement. In one research project, a five-point rating scale was developed for observing children from ages 3 to 6 in a preschool setting. The reliability of the scale (interscorer correlation) was .90, which is very satisfactory. The data in four classes (on the basis of a sample of ten children per class, observed three times during one school day) showed a variety of involvement levels of individual children and class averages.

Qualitative analysis of the data indicated that the class average, to a certain degree, reflected characteristics of the educational environment (e.g., teacher style). Further research is necessary to confirm if the levels of involvement of individual children and of classes tend to be rather constant.

In a second research project, children of families with low social economic status showed an average level of involvement of 3.06. Considering that a score of 4 represents only a minimal level of concentration and involvement, this is a low score. These data confirm the relevance of involvement as criterion of the quality of education.

Assessing the level of involvement is one step, taking initiatives to heighten this level is another. Experiences gathered in the counseling of preschool teachers implementing EPE led to an inventory of possible initiatives to improve the intensity of children's work and play. Ten points have been identified. They can be regarded as a further elaboration of the components of the temple scheme:

1.   Rearrange the classroom in appealing corners.

2.   Check the content of the corners and replace unattractive materials.

3.   Introduce new and uncommon materials and activities.

4.   Observe children, discover their interests, and find activities that stimulate these interests.

5.   Give more stimulating feedback in activities that require intervention.

6.   Widen the possibilities for free initiatives and support the children's choices through both boundaries and praise.

7.   Explore the relation with each of the children and try to improve it if needed.

8.   Introduce activities that help children to explore the world of feelings and behavior.

9.   Recognize children with emotional problems and work out helping interventions.

10.   Recognize children with developmental needs and work out interventions that address the problem.

Conclusion

Preschool education in Belgium is on the move. It always was. Looking at how the present generation always seems to criticize the one before, the historical evolution can be seen as a constant attempt to meet the developmental needs of children. In this endeavor, adults have had to constantly refine their definition of childhood and to remodel preschool practices according to their better understanding of the child. Experiential Preschool Education is a step in that process. The major contribution of this project is that it gives a scientific basis to the intuitions of traditional preschool and by doing so has strengthened the identity of early childhood education. Through the concept of involvement, it is possible to transcend the dilemma of "freedom of structure." One has to give children as much of both as needed to enhance the intensity of activities. The process in the child is the ultimate point of reference.

But, despite these new insights, the work is not finished. The implementation of the preschool that invests more in the natural energy of children requires ever more competence from the preschool teacher. This is the main challenge for the future, together with the need to show that the conceptual framework developed for preschool can also be fruitful for other educational contexts, such as elementary school, remedial teaching, special education, and teacher training. The work already started on this field indicates that involvement is a promising angle of approach. For once, the preschool system is in a position to inspire the whole educational system into following its lead.

References

Csikszentmihayli, M., (1979). The concept of flow. In B. Sutton-Smith (Ed.), *Play and learning.* New York: Gardner, 257–73.

Gendlin, E. (1964). A theory of personality change. In P. Worchel & D. Byrne. (Eds.) *Personality change.* New York: Wiley, 100–48.

ELEMENTARY SCHOOL EDUCATION FOR YOUNG CHILDREN IN BELGIUM

• • • • • • • • • ◆ • • • • • • •

George Meuris
Catholic University of Louvain
Louvain, Belgium

Three districts (*communautés*), based on French-, Flemish-, and German-speaking populations, were created in 1970 in the movement toward a new federalism in Belgium. Each district was given control over the cultural, social, and linguistic domains of life within its boundaries. The three districts may pass their own decrees, which have the same weight as national laws within their areas of jurisdiction. An appeals court was set up to settle any jurisdictional conflicts that might arise from this new arrangement.

Education, however, remained essentially the responsibility of the state until January 1, 1989, when the districts took over almost complete management of teaching in their areas. National authority is now used only for issues involving the beginning and end of compulsory school requirements, the minimal standards for the granting of diplomas, and the management of pensions.

To make these changes, Article 17 of the Belgium Constitution was modified on July 15, 1988. The Constitution states:

Teaching is free, anything to prevent this is forbidden; offenses are to be settled only through laws or decrees. The district ensures parents the freedom of choice. The district organizes teaching that is neutral, especially in regard to the philosophies, ideologies, or religion of parents and students. Everyone has the right to be educated in their fundamental rights and liberties. Access to education is free until the end of the compulsory schooling period (6 to 18 years old). All pupils under compulsory school age have the right, at the expense of the district, to a moral or religious education. All students, parents, staff, and educational establishments are equal before the law.

In Article 17, the term "teaching" is used in a broad sense; it includes university teaching and educational programs at child assessment centers (psycho-medical-social centers or CPMS). The Constitution recognizes the freedom of public bodies, other than the state and the districts, and of individuals to organize courses and to liberally define the characteristics and teaching methods of such courses. Private individuals, moreover, can freely determine the philosophical base of their teaching.

The districts, provinces, towns, and organizers of free education offer classes at all levels: prekindergarten, kindergarten, primary, secondary, and superior.

In Belgium, basic education is offered to children ages 3 to 12. It is carried out by preschool centers for children ages 3 to 6, and by primary schools (elementary education) for children

Translated from the French by Corinne Chénier.

ages 6 to 12. Although each has its specific aims, preschool centers and primary schools share a common objective: the personal development of cognitive, affective, and manual skills, and moral behaviors. The desire to change, or to adapt oneself is a major characteristic of our epoch. The school is the heart of change, at the center of moral, socio-economic, psychological, and pedagogical interactions.

In Belgium, at the turn of the century, basic education was considered an end in itself, given that most students quit school by age 12. It was viewed as providing both the intellectual and the moral training necessary to equip students for life, with teaching being the intermediary between a fixed knowledge and a receptive student. This kind of education responded well to the requirements of Belgium society at that time.

Today, the goals of basic education have changed due to the many demands made upon it, the many years of schooling required, and the progress made in the educational sciences. Differences in aptitudes and motivation to study, school failures, especially by socio-cultural disadvantaged (or emotionally disturbed) children, cultural inequalities among family environments, an increasing number of immigrant children, as well as changes that profoundly affect family life and parental control of children, all provoke a rethinking and a remaking of educational practices.

In Belgium, it is now understood that basic education must develop a curriculum that considers the individuality of each child and the totality of each as a person. Basic education must deal with life in its physical, biological, human, and moral dimensions. It must develop a climate that encourages harmony between family settings and the school. It must also maintain a continuity between kindergarten and primary school levels for both students and teachers. To give to each child the best chance of success, basic education must ensure the individualization of learning. This includes providing preventive and/or compensatory education in response to psychomotor, emotional, socio-cultural, and instrumental handicaps.

Prekindergarten Education—The "École Maternelle"

In general, children attend prekindergarten between the ages 3 and 6, although children as young as age 2 1/2 sometimes attend. While attendance is not compulsory, voluntary attendance is widespread. Prekindergarten education helps to assure the transition from family life, or its substitute, to the school. Preschool education in Belgium is discussed in detail in this volume in the chapter by Marc Depaepe and Ferre Laevers.

Elementary Education—The Primary School

In Belgium, primary schools enroll children between ages 6 and 12. Education in the primary schools is organized into three cycles (lower, middle, and upper) of two years each. Primary education continues the sensory and psychomotor education first undertaken in prekindergarten classes. It is intended both to reconfirm and maintain basic cognitive capacities and to provide the foundations of knowledge upon which all other learning can be built. It stimulates effective maturation, helps create a well-rounded personality, and prepares the child to take his or her place in society.

The Law of May 29, 1959, requires the program of studies in all primary schools in Belgium to include reading and writing; mathematics and systems of measurement; the basic elements of either the French, Dutch, or German language (based on locale); geography; Belgian history; the elements of drawing; hygiene; the natural sciences; singing; physical education; and road safety. In addition, it must include instruction in either religion or morality.

During the first three to four years of primary studies, teaching is concentrated on the mother tongue, reading and writing, elementary arithmetic, and geometry. During the final two years of primary school, children are also introduced to history, geography, and the natural sciences. Following the example of Ovide Decroly, Belgium's foremost educational scholar, the primary school system is geared toward being both a "school for life and a school through life."

In this way, primary school initiates children into adulthood by stimulating their interest in exploring their surroundings. The primary school system provides each child with the tools to make this exploration—tools that include the ability to observe, to express oneself both orally and in writing, and to synthesize acquired knowledge.

Two methods are used to teach children to read and to write. In the first method, children learn to read by identifying the sounds represented by a letter or a group of letters and by uniting them into a group of phonemes, forming first a word and then a sentence. Techniques of using associations of gestures or movements based on the emission of sounds are part of this method. The second method is the "global" ideo-visual method of teaching reading. Through this method, the child recognizes words and syllables first and then recognizes letters. Today, neither method is used alone, but rather the two approaches are combined by relying constantly on a group process with its auditory and visual elements, and by placing the young student in front of words that have significance for him or her.

Class time is often divided between two types of learning activities: (1) class lectures, and (2) individualized tasks or activities for smaller groups. The children are often asked to formulate their own individual or group projects as a way of involving them directly in their learning process. These group activities provide an opportunity to learn both cooperation and social responsibility. In these types of activities, the teacher acts more as a resource consultant than as the source of all knowledge and authority.

A concerted effort is made to make learning a pleasurable life-enhancing undertaking. Often areas of the classroom are organized to accommodate specific activities or workshop themes. Tables and chairs arranged in a circle or a square have replaced the parallel lines in which school benches were arranged in the past.

Educational games are used to increase the child's ability to reason and to think structurally, although manual work and outside activities are also important. Classes of children take walking tours or visits that bring them into direct contact with their environment. They are encouraged to observe their environment carefully and to discuss what they have observed when they return to the classroom. Often writings that the children produce while recording their learning experiences are used instead of regular school books.

Transition From Preschool to Primary School

Moving from preschool to primary school is a difficult step, one often fraught with academic difficulties. Moreover, early educational experiences are decisive for future academic success. A ministerial circular by educators representing the state, the provinces, the districts, and alternative educational institutions, dated March 15, 1977, gives a legal basis to the restructuring of schooling for 5- to 8-year-olds (Cycle 5–8).

Cycle 5–8 is a new educational structure that brings together children ages 5 to 8 for three years of study consisting of the third year of preschool education and the two first years of primary education. Cycle 5–8 replaces age-segregated classes consisting of children of identical ages with mixed-age learning groups, which are more flexible and dynamic. In this way, students are able to mature, according to their own rhythms and with assistance from a team of educators. The Cycle 5–8 program consists of the basic elements of physical education; manual and fine arts; introductory mathematics and natural science directed toward developing reasoning and logic; verbal communication skills, including reading and writing; and social skills and environmental awareness, as well as training in social responsibilities and morality.

The educational team of preschool and primary school teachers is placed in charge of a group of 5- to 8-year-olds. The former practice of a single teacher, responsible only for his or her own class, is replaced by a new practice in which a group of teachers shares responsibility for children who have been grouped into a "formation cycle." Participation in such cooperative educational projects will, hopefully, lead to a change in the teachers' attitudes toward students and the educational process. The diversity and complementarity of strengths and abilities of the teachers in each educational team should lead to a better understanding of each student, thereby allowing the specific needs of each student to be better met.

An evaluation of the Cycle 5–8 program shows that it facilitates the implementation of new modes of classroom organization and the diversification of didactic practices. These include the ability to give on-the-spot assistance to students who are working together in small groups and to develop strategies of individualization, thereby reducing the possibility that the education process proceeds along only one line of development

Cognitive-orientated activities generally remain organized for children working in same-age groups. Observations of students indicate that social activities—such as cooperation, mutual help, sharing, and negotiation—are the activities most often engaged in by children in mixed-age groups, while such behaviors as submission and imitation are more frequently found in the group activities of same-age children. The Cycle 5–8 model is expected to be extended to groups of older children.

In 1990, it was estimated that approximately 100 schools were using the Cycle 5–8 model, while an additional 40 were employing some form of 8–12 model of classroom organization. This innovation is especially popular in subsidized alternative schools and least used in community schools.

Special Education

The first special education classes in Belgium were organized at the end of the 19th century. Later, the Law of 1914 supported the establishment of special schools for mentally and physically handicapped children.

The objective of special education is to assure the physical and intellectual development, as well as the social and professional adjustment, of disabled children and teenagers. Special education is characterized by a combination of treatment modalities, including ortho-educational, medical, paramedical, psychological, and social. It also includes collaboration with an organization in charge of the student's welfare.

Today, special education is regulated by the Law of July 6, 1979, and by different royal proclamations, especially those of July 27, 1971, and June 28, 1978.

Children who receive special education are divided into eight categories, depending on the specific type and severity of the disability. Those categories are the following:

1. minimal mental retardation (IQ 80–50)

2. moderate or severe mental retardation (IQ under 50)

3. personality disorders

4. physical deformities

5. sickness

6. visual impairment

7. hearing impairment

8. instrumental deficiency (e.g., motor coordi nation, dyslexia, lateralization problems)

Preschool special education classes are available to children between ages 3 and 6, although exceptions are made to allow younger children to be admitted and to allow older children to remain in the preschool program. Primary school special education classes accept children between ages 6 and 13, although in some cases the upper age limit may be extended to 14 years. Some children who cannot attend special education classes because of the nature of their handicaps may receive training in their homes or through correspondence courses.

The prolongation of schooling, particularly observable after 1945, has been accompanied by an increase in both vocational and academic guidance. This guidance, which is offered not only to teenagers but also to younger children, is intended to help each child with his or her personal development and with developing a career. Guidance is made up of three parts: psychological, medical, and social. To provide both scholarly and professional counseling, Psycho-medical-social centers (CPMS) were established by the Law of April 1, 1960. According to this law, all levels of government, as well as private and public associations, are capable of establishing centers. Some centers, therefore, serve public schools, while others serve students attending private schools. The personnel of a CPMS includes, at a minimum, a psychologist as director, a psychoeducational counselor, a social worker, and a paramedical auxiliary. A doctor is available for each center.

The objectives of the centers are set out in the royal decree of August 24, 1981. A major objective of the centers is to contribute to bringing the psychological, educational, medical, paramedical, and social conditions of each student and his or her educational milieu to an optimal level for the child's development. Each student is to be provided with the best possible chance of developing his or her capacities. Each CPMS is charged with giving students, parents, and educators information and advice on each child's vocational and academic development. As well, the centers help provide teachers with a better knowledge of their students. They advise teachers on how to handle problems involving teacher-student relationships, student evaluations, remedial education, and admission to special education classes.

With regard to services provided at the primary school level, the CPMS centers help to orient children, teachers, and parents toward providing a coherent, integrated program of study. They do this by observing children's individual and classroom behaviors. Where necessary, an individual child is examined using tests and interviews to evaluate his or her sensory motor capacities, mental abilities, and personality. Health records are also updated periodically.

A disabled child is admitted into special education classes after a professional assessment has been made and a report written outlining the special teaching needs that the child requires. In some cases, the assessment is carried out in a CPMS or by a professional educational counseling service. In other cases, such as children with visual or auditory impairments or with children who have a long-term illness, the assessment is carried out by a qualified medical practitioner. Special advisory boards are asked to evaluate children for admission to special education programs or for transfer from one type of special education program to another, or to determine when a child might be able to be admitted to a regular education program.

The centers also provide on-going specialized counseling or guidance service for children receiving special education. This counseling service involves the student, parents, and the staff of the school in information exchange sessions. While study programs designed specifically for students with special needs are used, they are few in number. In most cases, teachers adapt the curriculum of regular schools to the specific needs and abilities of their learning disabled students. Experiments in integrated classrooms are also being carried out. Here the objective is to integrate handicapped children into the regular classroom and to provide them with an education that is adapted to their specific needs within the regular classroom setting. In addition, hospital schools offer children who are confined by long-term illness a variety of ways to help reduce the adverse effects of being away from regular schooling opportunities. They also help young patients deal with the emotional and psychological traumas of their illness.

Teacher Training

Teachers of both preschool and primary school are trained in postsecondary teacher training institutes. These institutes grant diplomas. By the Laws of July 7, 1979, and of July 19, 1971, the normal kindergarten and primary teacher training programs were provided through the high schools; they are now part of postsecondary teacher training institutes. In 1984, in a move to standardize with the rest of Europe, the duration of teacher training for the preschool and primary levels changed from two to three years and the course of study is being revised. The goals of this curriculum revision are to elevate the level of teacher training, to reinforce the scientific basis of pedagogy, and to develop professionalism for teachers.

No specific training exists for beginning teachers in the methods of special education. All teachers can teach in these types of classrooms. However, in 1981, a special diploma was offered on a trial basis to teachers who took further courses in special education.

EARLY CHILDHOOD EDUCATION IN BOTSWANA

• • • • • • • • • • • ◆ • • • • • • • • •

Ruth Monau
University of Botswana
Gaborone, Botswana

Little has been written about early childhood education in Botswana. The only literature that exists is in the form of workshop and consultancy reports, a UNICEF program plan, and a few research reports. The Ministry of Local Government and Lands also makes its own report occasionally on the activities of preschool education throughout the country. For the purpose of this chapter, day care centers, creches, and nursery schools are used interchangeably to mean preschool.

Historical Background

Traditionally, in Botswana, the rearing of young children was the responsibility of the family. The family unit, which included members of the extended family, was also responsible for other basic survival needs of the child (e.g., health, education, and socialization). Grandparents and older siblings were directly responsible for these services while parents were engaged in the agricultural and other related economic activities. This might have been a family of two or more families which are closely related. Overall, members of the same household associated together more intimately and shared more problems and responsibilities

than any other members of the tribe. Schapera (1971) states that, in Botswana, "They live, eat, work and play together, consult and help one another in all personal difficulties and share in one another's fortune of even bad luck. . . . Few couples ever live away from the immediate environment of their relatives" (p. 926).

The Republic of Botswana, which became independent in 1966, has experienced considerable economic and social changes. These changes have adversely affected the family structure. Rising costs of living and food shortages resulting from long spells of droughts have become more prevalent than before. These changes have primarily affected the lives of women and young children.

One change has been the migration from rural to urban areas. Younger men have moved into urban areas, leaving their families behind. Later, the wives and children follow, leaving the older family members behind. More women have also started working outside the home to supplement the little that their husbands bring into the family and to ensure the survival of their children. The number of women-headed households has also increased, meaning that more children are being left on their own or with unskilled helpers who

111

have no knowledge of child care, or who are themselves too young to care for other children. These arrangements still pose a risk to the health and welfare of the young child.

These difficulties and other pressures from interested groups have led to the creation of day care services in larger villages and towns. However, only a small percentage of preschool children (about 2.9 percent) have access to child care services. The reason for the inaccessibility of such services is either because of location or because parents do not have enough money to pay for their children's participation.

Day care programs in Botswana were started just after independence (Otaala, Njenga, and Monau, 1989). They were operated by voluntary organizations such as the churches, the Red Cross, women's groups (e.g., Botswana Council of Women and the Young Women's Christian Association), and private individuals (mostly wives of expatriate staff). When these groups started operating, there were no clear policy guidelines on how such programs should be run.

It was not until 1977 that a committee was formed that could look into the affairs of the day care program. This committee—composed of representatives from Ministries of Education, and Health, Local Government and Lands, voluntary organizations, and religious groups—decided that the day care program should have the Ministry of Local Government and Lands as its home base. A day care policy was enacted in 1980. The committee also recommended that a preschool advisory committee be formed. The committee, formed in 1985, is made up of representatives from the Ministry of Education, the Ministry of Health, the Ministry of Agriculture, nongovernmental organizations, the University of Botswana, and the day care associations.

In the Ministry of Local Government and Lands, the day care program is under the direct responsibility of the Social Welfare and Community Development unit. This unit is composed of (1) the senior officer, who heads the unit at the ministerial level; (2) the chief community development officer and social welfare officers at the town and district levels; and (3) day care teachers. The social welfare officers at the town and district levels are responsible for the coordination and supervision of day care centers in their region. Although social welfare officers are charged with this responsibility and other similar professional support and guidance, their training has not prepared them for early childhood education curriculum and methodology. The senior officers at the headquarters and at the town and district levels have had no training in either human growth and development or in early childhood education. Rather, their professional training has been in community development and social work.

Early childhood education is therefore supervised by personnel with no relevant training. Although these officers are keen to help day care teachers, problems arise when professional advice is needed by teachers and when they hold in-service workshops. They always rely on resource persons outside their department when related issues arise. This is not to say that social workers are not providing a good service to day care teachers, but rather that they lack the professional and technical expertise to deal with certain problems connected with day care teaching. Ideally, a specially trained officer needs to be appointed as a coordinator and to provide professional support for teachers and center owners.

Governmental Policy in Early Childhood Education

Licensing of child care programs and establishing other regulatory standards are done mostly to protect the health, safety, and welfare of the children who enroll in such programs (Sciarra and Dorsey, 1979). In Botswana, the national day care policy was formulated in 1980. In the policy, a "preschool" child refers to a person who has not reached age 7, the official age of starting a public school in Botswana. If an individual, organization, or group of persons proposes to open a center, they apply to the local authority in the area where the center is to be situated. (The local authority is the town clerk in the case of a city council of a township; for districts, one applies to the council secretary). A certificate of registration is given to any person who is granted permission to start a day care center. This certificate is to be renewed annually. The policy specifies the number of children in any age group who may be enrolled in a center, the required teacher-pupil ratio, and the required qualifications of teachers. It also specifies the resting and feeding schedules related to the number of hours children spend in the center.

Any authorized person (e.g., the locally based health inspector) may inspect the premises of any center and the records of the children. If the authority is unsatisfied with conditions, the authority can report to the magistrate, who in turn may order the center to be closed if necessary.

Although licensing is a national requirement and includes the educational qualification of staff, it does not address the educational quality of the program. Teachers are, however, expected to be able to read and write. Whereas licensing may be expected of all centers, certification is not always a prerequisite. There are some centers that are run by adults who have no certificate, although such people are encouraged by social welfare officers to enroll at the Lobatse Teacher Training Center.

As can be seen, the licensing system has many shortcomings which the responsible authorities are quite aware of. The standards of some centers are unsatisfactory and are a risk to the health of children. Some centers operate in a garage in the owner's residence. Although such centers provide a much needed service to the parents and children, some conditions to which children are exposed leave much to be desired.

Most of the houses that are used as day care centers have only one toilet facility to be used by 40 or so children, in addition to the owners of the house and the teachers or helpers. This can cause a very serious health problem, especially in the hot climate of Botswana where diarrheal diseases and other such related outbreaks are common. Some owners see the danger of operating under such conditions but cannot extend the facilities because the houses belong to the Housing Corporation and are only leased to those people who pay monthly rentals.

Children are also housed in garages, some of which are too small and poorly ventilated for the children, especially in the hot summer days. Some are open and pose a problem during rain and the winter. The licensing authorities, sometimes due to pressure from both parents and owners, and seeing the dire need for day care services, grant permission to owners to operate under such conditions, hoping that the situation will improve.

Some organizations, however (e.g., Botswana Council of Women, the Young Women's Christian Association, the Red Cross, and churches) have adequate buildings specifically designed for young children. Perhaps the time has come for the Botswana government to build day care facilities and rent them to individuals and other organizations. In this way, the safety and security of children can be ensured.

Integrated Day Care Services

As can be seen, day care programs in Botswana have considerable problems, some of which will not be remedied in the foreseeable future. The Community Development and Social Welfare Office feels that there is a need to have an integrated and community-based day care approach. The services that are being provided currently concentrate either on prereading and prewriting skills, while some solely provide custodial care and add very little to the total development of the child. Others are modeled after formal primary schools where children are expected to read and write and behave like primary school children.

The programs do not address the comprehensive view of child development, which includes social, emotional, cognitive, and physical needs. An integrated day care service is to be initiated by the Community Development and Social Welfare Office and run by the community, which will ensure that it is affordable even to children from very poor families. Children of families on welfare will attend free, and children will be offered nutritional meals. In the traditional services, health nurses do not have access to children. In the integrated model, health personnel will be able to work with the teacher in identifying underweight and at-risk children and to devise programs to help such children. This approach can help parents become aware of their role in the developments of their community or villages.

Experience has shown that projects that are initiated by the community last longer than those that are government or agency sponsored. The community looks at them as "ours" and not "theirs" and does not want to see their efforts fail. In addition, people are aware of what is happening in their community and to their children.

One such center was started in a district in western Botswana, which had a high number of malnourished children under age 5. The center is not fully functioning at this time because the officers in charge did not fully introduce and explain objectives of the center to the community and allow people to digest the ideas. A complete review needs to be made so that why the center failed can be understood. It appears that before such centers are to be implemented, a community survey has to be conducted to establish community needs, ambitions, and specifications. Botswana (i.e., people of Botswana) are known for their active participation in self-help projects. Many schools at the primary, secondary, and university levels have been built through self-help. The late president of Botswana, Sir Seretse Khama, had this to say about self-reliance among the people:

What are the roots of "Kagisano." It is not anything new. Everybody here knows what it means. Its application to our national policy is the logical outgrowth of our national principles. It has always been essential part of life. It has always been part of our custom that members of a family should help each other face and overcome the problems of life. The well known proverb "kgetse ya tsie e kgonwa ke go tshwaraganetwa" accurately sums up our approach to national policy and to life in general. What we are trying to do in the new Botswana is in fact nothing new. We are simply applying a well established value, applied in the family, the word, the tribe and to the wider concept of nationalhood. (Carter and Morgan, 1980: 145).

Types of Preschool Programs

Day care programs in Botswana can be classified into the following six:

Preprimary Units

Preprimary are attached to primary schools, mainly the so-called English medium schools, although there are some in the public primary schools. The units prepare the children under age 5 for a one-year period before they join the formal school program. Prenumber, prereading, and prewriting skills are developed using various approaches and teaching materials. Teachers in the English medium schools are trained to teach in the early classes of the primary grades, but this is not usually so in the ordinary public schools. Although these units are for younger children, they usually take the form of a formal primary school and usually lack the flexibility and freedom of a preschool.

Privately Owned Day Care Centers

In most big villages and urban areas, some day care centers are owned and managed by private individuals. The quality of such centers varied depending on the center's location, and on the training and experience of the owner as well as the teachers. There are two types of privately owned day care centers: high-cost day care centers and low-cost day care centers.

High-cost day care centers are normally utilized by children of expatriates and well-to-do local persons. In them at least the leading teacher is usually well trained and there is a good number of teacher aids so that the teacher-pupil ratio is usually good. Learning opportunities, including play material, are usually adequate. The fees charged are usually very high.

Low-cost centers are mainly used by the average Botswanan. The facilities including buildings are usually poor. The teacher-pupil ratio is high, and most teachers are not trained. Consequently, the learning environment is poor. The fees charged are usually low and affordable to most of the people, even those who may not be well to do.

In both these types of privately owned centers, the learning does not always take place in a specified environment. For instance, children are sometimes taught on the verandas of residential houses or in garages.

Church-owned and NGO Day Care Centers

Various churches (e.g., Assemblies of God, Anglican, Catholic etc.) own and run day care centers. Similarly, Nongovernment Organisations (NGOs) such as the BCW, YMCA, Red Cross and others also own and run day care centers. They usually meet in churches, church halls, or classrooms on the premises that have been purposely built.

VDC and Council-owned Day Care Centers

In most villages, both big and small, the affairs of the village are supervised by the village development committee (VDC). Its membership consists of the chief and/or headman and elected members (e.g., field officers, health nurses, agricultural officers, policemen, teachers, and any other active members of the community). In the district, town, and city councils, the affairs of the municipality are managed by the town or district councils. There are a number of day care centers that are owned and run by the VDCs or by the councils. These are of two types (1) those that are run wholly by the councils, which provide facilities including buildings and payment of teachers; (2) those that are run by both the council and the VDCs. In the latter case, the council provides grants and subventions to supplement the services of the VDC, which provides facilities and pays teachers.

In both these categories are schools that were previously owned by NGOs but were subsequently taken over by VDCs either for lack of funds or for other reasons. Teachers in these two types are paid differently. In the council-owned centers, teachers are included in the payment of structure of the council and they receive yearly or so increments and other benefits entitled to the council workers of the teachers' calibre. On the other hand, the teacher in the VDC-owned day care program is usually paid from the children's school fees. Both teachers might be trained but their salary structure differs considerably as do their conditions of service.

CHILD-to-Child Programs

In 1979, the CHILD-to-Child Program was launched in Botswana as a result of the International Year of the Child. The program, which is found mostly in rural areas, encourages older children to look after the health and welfare of their younger brothers and sisters as well as that of other younger children in the community. In its application in the primary schools, the program involves primary school children choosing younger children, sibling, relatives, or neighbors who are due to start school in the following year. The little teachers (i.e., the primary school children) receive instruction from the CHILD-to-Child teachers once a week, at the end of the normal school day. The little teachers then teach younger children (i.e., preschoolers) the knowledge, skills, behaviors, and concepts they have acquired. Preschoolers come to school twice a week to take part in the CHILD-to-Child sessions.

During these sessions, the preschoolers become acquainted with the school environment, school routine, the teacher figure, routines, and the rudiments of prewriting, prereading, and prenumber skills. There are currently over thirty primary schools in Botswana where the CHILD-to-Child program operates. Many more schools are calling for the program because they have realized its worth. The CHILD-to-Child report of 1989 says that children who participated in a CHILD-to-Child program are found to be socially and emotionally ready to participate in formal school activities. They are also reported to be more aware of basic health routines.

Training

The success of any program depends on its training program. During training, the teachers are expected to model and demonstrate the methodologies the trainees are expected to perform on completing the training course. If a participatory approach is to be used by teachers, the trainers are expected to demonstrate to the trainees. Furthermore, the trainers should be trained not only in teaching preschoolers but in training preschool teachers as well. They must be qualified trainers of teachers.

The training program in Lobatse (a town in the south of Botswana) has not been as successful as was expected. First, the trainers are underqualified in that they have had no formal education in training teachers. Rather, they have been trained as primary school teachers with a special concentration in infant methods. Second, besides the short courses that they have attended in Zambia and Mauritius, the trainers never attend in-service courses inside or outside the country to update them on the current developments in preschool and early childhood education. They receive no journals to keep them abreast of the current developments in childhood education. These problems need to be addressed if early childhood education is to improve in Botswana.

As already said in the above paragraph, the trainers in Lobatse training center were originally trained as infant primary school teachers and subsequently trained in Montessori approach in Nairobi, Kenya. Their original academic level considering the entry level into the teacher training college is rather low. The Montessori approach demands a high degree of competency from the teacher if it is to be used effectively, so the user must be of high calibre. The method needs someone who can adapt and adopt it to different and changing, geographical, economic and cultural situations and ages of children. As is the case at the Lobatse training center, it looks like the trainers did not meet these standards. Their graduates are failing to adapt to remote and rural conditions where they are posted after completing the course. The Otaala Njenga and Monau report (1989) has shown that the trainers can foresee the inadequacies of their training program but they do not know what changes to implement in order to remedy the situation.

The trainees also have problems. The entry qualifications are very low, like those of their trainers. This lack of a good education and the type of training they receive have resulted in teachers demonstrating a low morale and lack of initiative in the centers. They do not fully understand what is expected of a preschool teacher, nor do they fully understand the needs of young children. Their lack of creativity was shown in the way they religiously followed the Montessori approach without adapting it to the local environment and to the needs of the children. In addition, most of the teachers have failed to solicit help and information from the local community for the provision of play and learning materials.

Because some centers are run under very tight budgets, they depend solely on the money paid by the children, which is not enough to pay teachers, buy food for the children, and maintain the school. That is why the local community has to be exploited and utilized to provide play and learning materials. The Montessori kit on which most teachers rely is very expensive even for the high-cost centers. So the utilization of local material is very important, since such material can be produced free or cheaply.

The increase in the number of day care centers nationwide is a good indication that day care services are in demand, and the need is felt not only in the urban areas. The rural areas mostly need day care services that can be integrated with other services that are necessary for the survival of young children.

Botswana experienced six consecutive years of drought from 1981 to 1987. When such disasters strike, it is the remote areas that are most adversely affected, with women and young children suffering most. Women suffer because of lack of employment opportunities and literacy. Their suffering as mothers, household heads, farmers, and workers, in turn, affects the development and survival of their children (UNICEF, Play 1987–89).

Botswana's population is growing at the rate of about 3.4 percent a year (Republic of Botswana, 1985–91). This shows that population growth is accelerating significantly and the bulk of the population is in the range of 1–15 years of age. Since the number of day care centers is also increasing, there is a great need for more and better trained teachers who can competently handle the complicated needs of children in both urban and rural areas. This is impossible, however, because the only training center in Botswana produces very few teachers. From 1981, when it opened, to the end of 1988, the Lobatse Teacher Training Center has produced only 206 teachers (Otaala, Njenga, and Monau, 1989).

One factor that contributes to this low production rate of preschool teachers is the length of training. Trainees spend two years being trained. Of this period, nine months make up a residential component and another nine months are used as a field-based component in the form of internship. Normally, the center owners and managers are responsible for sending their staff for training. To be admitted into the training center, the trainee must, at the time of entry into training, (1) be working in a day care center; (2) be sponsored by the owner of the center; (3) be at least age 20; and (4) have a minimum of seven years of primary education or above (Otaala, Njenga, and Monau, 1989)

For some trainees enrolling in the training program means being separated from their family for that period, except for short visits during holidays. In cases where the woman is the sole breadwinner, training is not possible. Both trainers and trainees have accepted that the initial center-based training is too long. The trainers and consultants have recommended that the period be only six months, with a subsequent series of follow-up courses at the district level. This would make the course more flexible and participants would not be separated from their families for such a long time.

Training nearer to home would also give the trainee a chance to exploit the local environment for teaching and play materials and for resource people.

The certification of day care trainees is done by the Ministry of Local Government and Lands. It has been observed, however, that some privately owned day care managers and owners give these certificates little or no recognition, claiming that the Montessori approach is not suitable for the children and that it is irrelevant to their daily experience. This may be true in cases in which the practitioners are inflexible in their method.

The graduates of the Lobatse Training Center have a very low morale generally. Among the reasons for this situation is that day care teachers have no job security, no job descriptions, and no conditions of service. Some return to the centers and are paid a lower salary than untrained teachers in other centers. The jobs of some are terminated when the center closes due to lack of funds or because the owner was an expatriate who had to leave the country at the end of a contract. Some work for up to three months without a salary, because not enough money was collected from the children's school fees. Overall, there are many problems concerning the salaries and working conditions of day care teachers. Although the formation of an association of workers has been encouraged, to date nothing has been done. These problems contribute to the low morale of teachers and slow the progress of early childhood education in Botswana.

Curriculum

Realizing the inadequacies of the implementation of the Montessori approach, the Ministry of Local Government and Lands appealed to the Preschool Advisory Committee to revise the curriculum for the trainers. As a result, the curriculum was changed to a more general and integrated approach. One of the major criticisms of the Montessori curriculum was that its graduates teach difficult concepts to young children and expect too much from them. Some supervisors (social welfare officers) have reported that day care center teachers resort to ready-made materials and use formal methods of teaching, whereby children are placed in rows, are lectured to, and are made to recite words that do not make sense to them. They also observed that children are expected to read and write for long periods of time. These criticisms demonstrate that teachers have not had a good foundation in child growth and development and in the rudiments of how young children learn.

A new teacher training curriculum, completed in 1988, has not been implemented because the trainers find it difficult to teach. It draws heavily from the principles of child growth and development. The content and prescribed methods of teaching have been selected according to the developmental level of children. Topics are introduced in a thematic approach. The first is human growth and development, the development of language, and prosocial behavior. The trainees are also introduced to the needs of exceptional children in order to enable teachers to have a basic idea of how to identify and work with them. It is hoped that exceptional children can be identified early and integrated into ordinary day care centers.

Trainees also study health, safety, and nutritional needs of young children, and day care center teachers are expected to read and interpret the health card of the children under age 5. This aspect of the curriculum will help teachers to identify children who are underweight, as well as those children who need immunization. The trainees also study methods of community and parental involvement in order to help them to use the local environment for teaching and learning materials, and for additional human resources.

The above curriculum was designed to be relevant to the needs of all children in Botswana and encompass the "whole" development of the child. It is hoped that intensive workshops on implementing the curriculum will be held for teacher trainers or that a totally new cadre of better qualified teacher trainers will be employed to implement it. Its success will depend on the dedication and creativity of its users.

References

Botswana, Republic of. (1977) *Education for Kagisano*. Report of the National Commission on Education. Gaborone.

———. (1979). *National development plan, 1979–85*. Gaborone: Ministry of Finance and Development Planning.

———. (1985). *National development plan, 1985–91*. Gaborone: Ministry of Finance and Development Planning.

———. *Programme plan of operations and plans of action, 1987–1990*. Gaborone: Government of Botswana and UNICEF.

Carter, G., & Morgan, P., (Eds.). (1980). *From the frontline: Speeches of Sir Seretse Khama*. London: Rex Collings.

Kann, U., Mapolelo, D., & Nleya, P. (1989). *The missing children: Achieving universal basic education in Botswana*. Gaborone: National Institute for Research and Documentation.

Mangadi, T.R. (1986). *Government initiatives: Provision for the the preschool disabled child in Botswana*. Reading, UK: University of Newcastle upon Tyne.

Monau, R. (1984). *Guidelines for a preschool program in Botswana*. Athens, OH: Ohio University.

Otaala, B., Njenga, A., & Monau, R. (1989). *An evaluation of the day care program in Botswana: A consultancy report for the government of Botswana and UNICEF*. Gaborone.

Schapera, I. (1971). *Married life in an African tribe*. London: Pelican Books.

Sciarra, D., & Dorsey, A. (1979). *Developing and administering a child care centre*. Dallas, TX: Houghton Mifflin.

Townsend Coles, E. (1986). *Education in Botswana*. Gaborone: Macmillan.

PRIMARY EDUCATION IN BOTSWANA

• • • • • • • • • • • ◆ • • • • • • • • • •

John H. Yoder
University of Botswana
Gaborone, Botswana

Botswana is a sparsely populated country in southern Africa. Slightly more than one million persons live in an area of about 600,000 square kilometers, an area about the size of the state of Texas in the United States. Because much of Botswana is arid or semi-arid and only about 5 percent of the land is suitable for agricultural cultivation (Republic of Botswana, 1984), most of the population is clustered in a rough semi-circle extending along the southern, eastern, and northern borders of the country where there is more water. About 84 percent of the central part of the country is occupied by the Kalahari Desert.

The land is divided into eight areas representing the major ethnic groups found in the country (approximately 50 percent of the total area), government land (approximately 47 percent), and privately owned farms (approximately 3 percent) (Swedish International Development Agency, 1972). This distribution of land has changed little over the past few decades. Though there are now several urban areas within the country, most Batswana (i.e., people of Botswana) still have strong links to the villages and rural areas. Many people living in the major towns regard their residence there as temporary, necessitated because of their work, and maintain a primary allegiance elsewhere in the country.

The majority of Batswana are a traditionally agrarian, cattle-owning people. Historically, a Motswana (i.e., a citizen of Botswana) practices what has been referred to as "three-site farming" (Republic of Botswana, 1984). This means that the family is able to live together as a unit in the villages only during the winter months, from approximately June to November. The remainder of the time, the men and boys stay at the cattlepost while the women and girls stay at the "lands" (i.e., small farms). Predictably, attendance at primary school is adversely affected by this pattern of residence. Though this pattern is gradually changing, it is still widely practiced and, continues to affect school attendance in some areas. However, along with many other developing African countries, modern Botswana faces increasing problems of urbanization as rural persons move into the towns and the cities to seek employment.

The Kalahari Desert has been the traditional home of widely scattered family groups of the hunting and gathering San people, often referred to as "bushmen." Though the San can still be found in parts of the desert, it has been governmental

119

policy to encourage them to move into villages where boreholes (i.e., wells) are provided. This permits services such as schools and clinics to be more readily made available to them.

Formerly know as the Bechuanaland Protectorate, Botswana received its independence from Britain (and took its new name) in 1966. At that time, the population was about 550,000 and the country could be cited as a prime example of underdevelopment (UNESCO Report, cited in Townsend Coles, 1986). Since its independence, the population has more than doubled and phenomenal changes in the country's infrastructure have occurred as Botswana has moved from a pre-industrial, rural, agrarian society to become one of the most rapidly expanding economies in Africa. At the time of independence, Garborone, the country's capital, was only a small village of some 4,000 persons clustered around a siding on the railroad from South Africa to what was then Rhodesia. In the entire country, there were only approximately six kilometers of paved road. Economic activity was limited and industry virtually nonexistent.

Phenomenal changes have take place in Botswana since that time. Encouraged by political stability, spurred by the discovery of major deposits of high-grade diamonds, and propelled by large amounts of aid from international donors as well as foreign investment, tremendous resources have poured into the infrastructure of Botswana. Near the site of the original village, the modern city of Gaborone has risen, literally, from the ground. It is now a major center of government, industry, and commerce, serving not only Botswana but the entire southern Africa region. Its population has mushroomed to well over 100,000 persons, and the city continues to be one of the most rapidly growing urban centers in Africa. Industrial and commercial development have exploded, and the international airport at Gaborone serves as a hub for national and international air travel in the southern part of the continent. Paved roads now span the country and rush-hour traffic is a facet of everyday life in the city.

The pace and extent of educational development in Botswana since independence have paralleled the development of the other sectors of the country. A UNESCO report (Townsend Coles,

1986) indicates that in 1964 there were 239 primary schools in the country, with an enrollment of 54,845 pupils and a teaching staff of 1,310 (in 1957 there were an estimated 166 primary school with 29,000 students) (Republic of Botswana, 1984). Secondary schools were far fewer. In 1964, there were only two schools in the entire country that offered the full five-year cycle of secondary schooling. Thus, only a fraction of the number of primary school children were able to complete their secondary schooling. According to Townsend Coles (1986), the "total stock of Batswana degree holders [at the time of independence] was about 40."

By 1988, the number of primary schools had more than doubled to 559. Primary school enrollment, however, increased nearly fivefold to 261,352 students (Kann, Mampolelo, and Nleya, 1989) as did the teaching force, numbering, by 1989, 7,704 (Ministry of Education, 1989). Secondary education also underwent rapid expansion, and in 1988 it was reported that 93 secondary schools enrolled 40,865 students (*ibid.*).

Development of the Educational System

Traditional Education

"Education" in Botswana did not begin with the introduction of formal schooling by the missions. Traditionally, education was part of the totality of life, that is, "a whole system of belief, or religion, as well as a means of socializing children into the accepted norms of society" (Parsons, 1983). Education in the home, though informal, was of great importance and consisted mainly of interaction with parents and other adults, learning how to relate to parents and members of the extended family and siblings. There was a special emphasis on the aged as "repositories of wisdom." For young persons in their early to mid-teens, traditional education included the initiation schools of both females and males (known as *bojale* and *bogwera*). These schools were the responsibility of the chief, the village elders, and the "royal children" (*ibid.*).

Younger children of primary and preschool age were socialized and taught by the extended family, including, in particular, the maternal uncles and aunts. It is traditional in Botswana society that the teaching and discipline of young children are the shared responsibility of the family group. When a young child misbehaves, any adult present is responsible for disciplining that child. Formal schooling for young children was not known until the advent of the first mission schools, but even then it would have been unusual for a child of age 6 or 7 to enter school. Despite the rapid modernization in the country today, Botswana society remains strongly traditional in many ways and the modern, formal primary school should be understood, at least in part, as exercising something of the traditional role of the extended family in the teaching, socializing, and disciplining of young children.

Colonial and Mission Education

The first formal school in Botswana was established in 1847 by the missionary David Livingstone along with Batswana assistants who set up a Christian school at Kilobeng some 30 kilometers from present-day Gaborone. The foundations of the school can still be seen today. The curriculum consisted of study of the Christian scriptures, the New Testament having been translated into Setswana several years earlier. There was also an infant school, which enrolled as many as "60 to 80 pupils, though drought scattered the children to collect roots and locusts in 1848" (Parsons, 1983). This school was destroyed a few years later, but was revived by German Lutheran missionaries at a nearby site in 1857.

Numerous mission schools (all of which were primary schools) were established from the middle of the 19th century by different mission groups (notable among them the London Missionary Society, or LMS) in different areas of the country. Parsons (1983) describes one such school in which the "children were taught reading, writing, arithmetic, and scripture in Setswana, and older children were trained as monitors to drill younger children in groups of twelve" (p. 24). For some years, the mission schools comprised the only formal, that is, Western, education in the country. In time, however, there was increasing dissatisfaction with the education that was offered and controlled by the missions. By the turn of the century, some of the *merafe* (i.e., the traditional

African groups or nations within the Protectorate) were beginning to establish their own schools, known as self-help (*ipelegeng*) schools, financing them through a special education tax. These schools were under the control of the *dikgosi* (or chiefs) and were popular among many of the people (Tlou & Campbell, 1984).

Financing for mission schools came from the sponsoring mission organizations, while the independent national schools were financed by combinations of school fees and locally collected levees imposed by the *merafe*. Until 1904, no governmental funds were provided for education. At that time, following a recommendation by the British inspector of schools, the government began making nominal contributions to missionary bodies and to the *merafe* for the running of schools (*ibid.*). These grants, which were for equipment and materials only, were insufficient. Most of the costs continued to be carried by the missionary organizations and the *merafe*. In 1919, the administration adopted the concept of a national education tax applied to the whole country. The tax became the major means of paying for education in the Protectorate.

The administration of the jointly funded schools was, in most cases, carried out by local school committees, composed of representatives of the government, the mission, and the *merafe*. Beginning in the early 1930s, the overall administration of the schools was taken over by a Protectorate subcommittee body composed of the same representatives, and in 1935 by a newly established Education Department. In 1931, approval was received for the adoption of a more locally oriented syllabus in which it was stated that "the aim of Education and the purpose for which our schools exist is to equip the children with a training such as will enable them to live fully their lives." The document also instructs teachers to use "activity, creativeness, song, story, and dramatization as vehicles of instruction" (Parsons, 1983). Until 1940 there were no schools in the Protectorate that offered schooling beyond the primary level (Tlou & Campbell, 1984).

The quality of formal education under both the mission societies and the *merafe* of pre-independence Botswana often left much to be desired. Funds were limited, and most of the mission societies saw education as a means of conversion rather than as an end in itself (*ibid.*). Nevertheless, by the late 1800s nearly all the major villages in the country had schools. By that time, the curriculum generally consisted of reading, writing, arithmetic, Setswana (the major African language of the country), domestic science (sewing, baking, etc.), geography, history, and (in the mission schools) scripture. During the early years of mission education, only reading, writing, and scripture had been taught (*ibid.*).

The early schools did not always function smoothly. Often there were conflicts between parental needs or values and those of the schools. Frequently parents wished their children to work at home or to herd cattle during the time school was in session. Some schools experimented with allowing boys to take books to the cattle posts and to teach one another there; however, this system created its own problems and was abandoned (*ibid.*). There were also conflicts between the desires of the parents who wished their children to have a practical education and the desires of the students who rejected manual labor, feeling that it lowered their status as educated persons. In some cases parents, too, rejected practical education as lowering the dignity and aspirations of their children.

In the early days of formal education, only children of royalty or other high-status classes were permitted to attend school. This was partly because of the difficulty the poor would have paying the school fees, but also because the ruling groups felt that permitting the lower classes to become educated would mean that they would aspire to more or less the same social status as they held. They also feared that the Christian teaching about equality might cause the lower classes to revolt. These patterns were beginning to change by the early 20th century. Nevertheless, the quality of education remained low throughout the pre-independence period, in part because low salaries made it difficult to attract good teachers (*ibid.*).

Postindependence Development

From its beginning, the Botswana government placed high priority on education. During the period immediately following independence, this translated into an emphasis on secondary and higher education. At the time, primary education was viewed mainly as preparation for entry into secondary schools. Since the number of places available in the secondary schools was limited, it was thought that there was no need to produce large numbers of primary school leavers. The emphasis was on "quality rather than quantity" (Kann, Mampolelo, and Nleya, 1989) and primary school enrollments were restricted.

In the mid-1970s, partly as the result of an influential report by a national commission on education (Republic of Botswana, 1977), educational strategy changed to stress achievement of Botswana's national philosophy of *kagisano,* or social harmony, and emphasized the importance of equitable distribution of educational resources. This led to the universalization of primary school education and the end of tuition in 1980. The National Development Plan, which followed the commission's report, states:

> Government attaches the highest priority within education to the primary education sector. First, in the interests of equality of opportunity and of developing the potential of all children, the Government seeks to provide universal access to primary education. Secondly, since primary education lays the foundation for further education and training and for productive employment, the Government seeks to improve its quality and relevance (Republic of Botswana, 1979: 107).

It has been estimated that at the time of independence, approximately 54 percent of the primary-school-aged children were enrolled in school. This percentage was estimated to vary from around 85 percent (Kann, Mampolelo, and Nleya, 1989) to around 94 percent (90 percent for boys and 97 percent for girls) by the late 1980s (Central Statistics Office, 1989b).

Primary Education in Botswana Today

The primary education system in Botswana today comprises seven standards, or grades. (A small number of private, fee-charging English medium schools offer both a "reception class" and an eight-year sequence of classes.) There are three terms in the school year, which operates from late January to early December, with breaks of three to four weeks between each term. There are presently seven years of primary schooling. However, significant changes in the structure of schooling are underway and it is anticipated that the present 7-2-3 system (seven years of primary schooling followed by two years of junior secondary schooling and three years of senior secondary schooling) will change to 6-3-3 system by the middle of the 1990s. This change is intended to accompany universal access to school enrollment as far as the junior secondary level, whereas there are now selection points at the end of standard 7 and again at the end of the junior year secondary school.

Since 1968, governmental policy has been to automatically promote all children from one standard to the next regardless of a child's level of achievement. Although some repetition is permitted following standards 4 and 7, the policy has meant that many children are moved upward through the standards without having mastered the skills and content of the previous level. Government-prepared examinations are administered to all children at the end of standard 4 for diagnostic purposes, and at the end of standard 7 for selection into junior secondary school.

Setswana is the language of the majority in Botswana, while English is the "official" language and is used in government and business as well as in all postprimary education. Except for the English medium primary schools where English is the language of instruction, instruction during the first four years of primary school is in Setswana, with English taught as a second language. English becomes the medium of instruction in standard 5.

A typical school day begins at 7:30 A.M. and continues until 1:00 P.M., with a half-hour break at midmorning when, in most cases, food prepared by the school is provided. Unless children are boarding at the school, they normally go home for lunch and return at approximately 2:00 P.M. for the afternoon activities. Except in "double-session" classes (which are described later), the mornings are devoted to instruction and the afternoons are used for a variety of activities (e.g., sports, clubs, field trips, remedial activities, and supervised homework). During the past few years, the importance of maintaining a strict daily timetable in the primary schools has been deemphasized by the Ministry of Education in favor of specifying the number of hours per week that should be devoted to each subject. However, it is still common to see a daily timetable displayed prominently in primary schools. Where such a schedule is followed, the normal class period (the time devoted to one subject) is about 30 minutes.

Organization of Schools

There are three recognized types of primary schools in Botswana: government schools, private schools, and grant-aided schools. About 93 percent of the schools are local government schools. These schools are run by an education committee whose members are appointed from a locally elected council. About 5 percent are private schools, and about 3 percent are grant-aided schools (Central Statistics Office, 1989). Private schools receive no financial support from the government, while the grant-aided schools are privately owned or may be run by nongovernmental organizations, but receive limited government grants in support of special programs.

Administrative responsibility for primary education in Botswana is shared by two ministries. The Ministry of Education has responsibility for all matters pertaining to curriculum, instruction, and instructional personnel, while the Ministry of Local Government and Lands has broad responsibility for matters pertaining to supplies and physical plant. This includes responsibility for teaching materials such as textbooks, as well as classroom and office facilities and accommodation for staff.

School Finance

Since independence, schools have been supported by a combination of local levees, governmental subsidies, and fees charged to the parents of children attending. In an effort to equalize educational opportunities for all children, primary school fees were cut in half in 1973 and completely abolished in 1980. Abolition of school fees had the predictable effect of markedly increasing enrollment. However, parents still incur significant costs because they must pay for the required school uniform, a feeding fee (in many, if not all schools), sports fees, and other incidental fees. Added to these are the indirect cost (opportunity costs) of forgone labor in the home or in herding cattle, especially for boys.

Recurrent expenditures for primary education

are shared between the Ministry of Education and the Ministry of Local Government and Lands. Responsibility for most capital expenses has remained with local authorities (councils), but governmental subsidies have increased over the past few years. As of 1990, almost all the cost for primary school classroom buildings and teachers' houses, for example, were subsidized by the central government through the Ministry of Local Government and Lands. However, local communities may be involved in establishing the school itself as a private facility (Kann, Mampolelo, and Nleya, 1989).

In the 1987–88 fiscal year, the Ministry of Education reported a per-pupil recurrent expenditure of P200 (approximately U.S. $100) across the primary school standards (Ministry of Education, 1989). This figure includes funds administered by both the Ministry of Education and the Ministry of Local Government and Lands other than those for capital costs.

Facilities

Faced with long-term and rapid expansion in primary school enrollment, the government has struggled, with only partial success, to meet the demand. Teachers and classrooms have long been in short supply. The introduction of automatic promotion in 1968 was one step taken to reduce the number of students in a class by permitting no repeaters. Another step is the so-called double-shift system to more effectively use the existing classrooms. In this system, some classes are taught in the morning and others in the afternoon, usually with different teachers for each session. This has become accepted as normal practice in many schools. But because some teachers and students have opted to conduct classes outside rather than adopt the double-shift system, there now exist many open-air classrooms.

Another approach taken to alleviate the shortage of classrooms has been to combine two classes in the same classroom. Such an arrangement typically means that about 80 children are in the same classroom. Sometimes this involves one teacher "looking after" both classes. In other cases, there may be two teachers in the room, both teaching at the same time.

According to statistics for 1987 (Central Statistics Office, 1989b), there were 4,847 primary classrooms in Botswana accommodating 6,954 "streams," or classes. This means that there were more classes than classrooms—an overall shortage of 2,107 classrooms, or about 30 percent. Kann reports an overall shortage of 2,330 classrooms in the country in 1988, of which 2,110 were on double shift, leaving 220 classes that were apparently taught in the open air (Kann, Mampolelo, and Nleya, 1989).

Though there is some variation among different parts of the country, the average class size in primary schools in 1987 was 33.8 pupils (ibid.). This average appears to apply to both the early years of primary school and the later years.

Teachers

Primary teachers in Botswana do not specialize either by level or by subject. Previously, primary teachers were awarded a teaching certificate that designated a specialization in either upper or lower primary; the present qualification normally required for teaching in a primary school is a generic primary teachers certificate. A small number of primary teachers have also completed a two-year diploma course at the University of Botswana. Many of the diploma holders occupy positions of responsibility in the schools as head teachers, deputy heads, or senior teachers. Plans are presently underway to develop a three-year diploma program at the primary teacher training colleges in the near future (Leep, 1989).

As with classrooms, the rapid growth in numbers of primary school children has resulted in severe shortages of qualified primary school teachers. The government has addressed the problem by hiring untrained persons to teach in classrooms for which there are no trained teachers. Frequently these untrained teachers have completed no more than standard 7, though more recently an increasing number have completed up to the junior secondary level.

Another measure taken to alleviate the teacher shortage was the introduction of a "half-session" system in 1968. In this system, a teacher is assigned to teach two classes with each class attending school on alternate days. This system, which results in halving the number of instructional hours that each child receives (Kann, Mampolelo, and Nleya, 1989) is no longer widely practiced.

With a continued increase in trained teachers, it has been possible to steadily reduce both the number of untrained teachers and the number of half-session classes in the primary schools. In 1979, the proportion of untrained primary teachers was reported to be 36 percent; by 1984, this had decreased to 29 percent (Republic of Botswana, 1986). Kann reports that by 1988 the proportion of untrained teachers had shrunk to 18 percent (Kann, Mampolelo, and Nleya, 1989), and that half-session classes had likewise decreased from 348 in 1987 to a reported 118 in 1988 (*ibid.*). A recent study projecting future demands for primary teachers indicated a possible oversupply of qualified primary teachers by 1994 (Leep, 1989). However, in light of the historic teacher shortage these conclusions may be overly optimistic.

Students

As mentioned earlier, more than one-quarter million children were enrolled in 550 primary schools in 1988-89. According to the provisional statistics of the Botswana government for 1988, children in the first four years of primary school ranged in age from 5 to 17. Approximately equal numbers of girls and boys were in each of the first four years (grades), though in each year girls maintained a slight, but consistent advantage in numbers (Central Statistics Office, 1989a). Interestingly, this figure changes considerably by standard 7 when girls outnumber boys by nearly 4,000, or more than 20 percent (*ibid.*).

Botswana has long had a minimum age before which children were not permitted to enter school. In an effort to extend the opportunity for school attendance as widely as possible, but at the same time mindful of the limited educational facilities, the government has also established a maximum age beyond which children may not enter school for the first time. Though the official minimum and maximum ages for beginning school have shifted at various times since independence, currently the minimum age for initial entry to government primary schools is 6 years and the maximum is 9 years.

Governmental policy notwithstanding, not all children in Botswana start school at the same age. As indicated in Table 1, some children start before the minimum age while others start after the maximum entry age. However, Kann estimates that 95 percent of children who enter primary school do so when they are 6, 7, 8, or 9 years old (Kann, Mampolelo, and Nleya, 1989). Table 1 lists government statistics for 1987 for the median age and ranges of ages for children in the first four standards of primary school.

TABLE 1

Ages of Children in the First Four Standards of Primary School

Standard

Age	1	2	3	4
under 6	421	0	0	0
6	4,843	254	7	0
7	17,038	4,275	376	4
8	13,222	14,703	4,203	323
9	4,299	11,745	13,120	4,230
10	952	4,501	11,469	12,678
11	225	1,176	4,670	12,209
12	102	281	1,360	5,528
13	37	87	396	1,839
14	23	28	134	612
15	19	19	60	196
16	15	5	32	72
17 and over	26	28	57	86
Total	41,215	371,102	371,102	37,777
Median Age	7.5	8.5	9.6	10.8

Source: Central Statistics Office, 1986b.

Clearly, there is considerable variation of ages at which children begin and continue their schooling, which makes it difficult to generalize accurately about the standard (or year of schooling) in which children of specific ages are likely to be found. However, one is fairly safe in saying that the "typical" 7-year-old child is in standard 1, with the "typical" 8-and 9-year-olds in standards 2, 3, and 4 respectively. The major exceptions to the official age policy appears to be in the very remote areas of the country where children who, for a variety of reasons, may not have been able to begin school at the correct time and are nevertheless permitted to enroll.

School Attendance

The provision of a primary educational program is only the beginning. Which children, and how many, actually enroll in primary school is another matter. Because of the difficulty of obtaining reliable census figures for a given year, it is not possible to accurately present the numbers of children in school as a percentage of each age group. For some years, however, it has been estimated that approximately 85 percent of the children of primary school age attend (Kann, Mampolelo, and Nleya, 1989).

More recently, Kann and her colleagues have explored this issue and have reported extensively on it (Kann et al., 1989). While they cite considerable difficulties in obtaining reliable figures for making such estimates, they nevertheless conclude that in 1987 some 8 percent of primary-school-age children were not enrolled in school. Though this number suggests a significant improvement over the earlier estimates, it has not been accepted by all without reservation. Nevertheless, even if one accepts the more optimistic figure, it is still clear that there are significant numbers of children in Botswana who are not attending school. Kann and her colleagues have identified some 11 issues which, in their opinion, have contributed to the problem of nonschool attendance. Among these are the following:

1. *Poverty.* Though primary school fees have been abolished, parents must pay for school uniforms, fees for feeding children while at school, and other direct and indirect costs. In many cases of nonattendance, these fees cannot be met by the child's family and the child is thus prohibited from enrolling.

2. *Distance to the nearest school.* Though there has been a massive attempt by the government to increase the number of primary schools available, it has still not been possible to build schools in all villages. In addition, some villages are very small and do not justify establishing a school. Sometimes children are able to walk for some distance to the nearest school. However, often even this is not possible. For many remote area dwellers, the only option is to send their children to stay at a village where a school is located. Many parents, however, are understandably reluctant to do this. Most primary schools do not offer any type of boarding facilities and the parents who want their children to stay in the community must make their own arrangements.

3. *Children who are working at home or herding cattle.* Frequently such children will have passed the maximum age for entering primary school as a result of staying out and are now no longer eligible to enroll.

4. *Parents who do not value education or who have values that conflict with the school's.* Not all parents are convinced of the value of formal education for their children. Some cite religious or cultural beliefs, or school practices conflict with their own. In other cases, they fail to see the relevance of the school curriculum to their lives or those of their children. Related to this is the fact that there are no real employment opportunities for the vast majority of those who leave school at the end of the primary or even the junior secondary cycle.

Primary School Curriculum

The school curriculum reflects the basic value system of a society through the content of the subjects taught in the school, the way the educational experience is structured, and the methodology that it is chosen as the vehicle of delivery.

The standardized curriculum in the primary schools of Botswana, consists of Setswana, English, mathematics, integrated science, social studies, religious education, home economics, and agriculture in each of the standards 1 to 7. Except for the small number of private, English medium schools, the first four standards are taught in Setswana, the majority language of Botswana. (The subject "English" is an exception to this and receives about four to four and one-half hours of instruction per week in English.) The language of instruction changes to English, the official language of the country, at the beginning of the fifth year in standard 5. Reflecting the government's policy for enhancing national unity through a common language, there are no provisions in the school curriculum for those whose first language is one of the several minor languages spoken in different areas of the country.

Responsibility for development of the primary curriculum lies with the Curriculum Development Unit within the Department of Curriculum Development and Evaluation. Among the unit's tasks are the following: (1) coordinating the implementation of all curriculum development policies; (2) translating the government's educational goals into educational programs; (3) monitoring revision of syllabi; and (4) planning for the design and preparation of material to be used in learning and teaching. (Republic of Botswana, 1986: 5–3).

This unit produces all syllabi for primary education and distributes them throughout the country. Teacher representatives also assist in curriculum development by participating in national subject panels where programs are conceptualized and syllabus outlines are developed. Teachers are also requested to provide feedback on curriculum implementation. Curriculum revisions and materials are normally pilot tested in several "trial schools" before final production and national dissemination.

Traditionally, education in Botswana has been aimed at those expected to move toward increasingly higher levels of education. Very little attention was paid to those who might move into technical or vocational fields. Even less attention was given to those who might not complete the educational sequence. This orientation led, predictably, to a highly academic curriculum which ignored the needs of those moving in different directions. This led to such criticisms as those voiced by a 1972 report, which stated:

There is a consensus of opinion in Botswana . . . that the syllabi and curricula are in general unsuitable. They are often too advanced, they are to a great extent irrelevant and alien to the needs of the Botswana community, and they are very little related to the development problems of the country as a whole or to employment realities. Primary education is heavily academic in character. It is no more than a ladder leading up to secondary education (Swedish International Development Agency, 1972: 41).

The significance of the final statement in the above quotation can be understood only in the context of a country where (at the time) far less than one-half the primary school population was able to proceed to secondary school. It was in response to such criticisms that revised syllabi in several subjects were introduced into the primary schools in the early 1980s. The revision process is a long one, however, and is still continuing.

The official philosophy of education can be said to emphasize, among other things, the following:

1. a child-centered approach where learning and teaching strategies are responsive to the needs and interests of the child rather than to those of the teacher, and where the teacher is viewed as a facilitator and guide rather than as a reservoir of knowledge;

2. an understanding of child development and individual differences which recognizes that children learn at different rates and by different modalities;

3. that reinforcement and success are two of the best motivators in learning;

4. active learning (doing) is much more effective than passive learning (listening);

5. all children can be successful within their own limits; and

6. the progress of children should be continually evaluated (Republic of Botswana, 1986).

The official policy also includes a call for a "shift [of attention] from the most capable [students] to all students" (Republic of Botswana, 1986: 5-11).

Tradition dies slowly, however, and in spite of the official philosophy, many of the teaching methods in the primary school classrooms remain highly teacher-centered. Furthermore, the curriculum at the primary school level is strongly linked to the three external achievement examinations used in all schools to select students for the next higher level of study. The selection takes place at the end of standard 7, the end of form 2 (the final year of junior secondary school), and the end of form 5 (the final year of senior secondary school).

The content of the examinations, which is strongly academic and knowledge-based, influences the curriculum both directly and indirectly. The curriculum at the senior secondary level is determined directly by the syllabus and the examinations for the Cambridge Overseas School Certificate (COSC), which are prepared and graded in the United Kingdom. At the junior secondary level, the curriculum content is indirectly influenced by the COSC and indirectly by the syllabus and content of the Junior Certificate Examination (JCE), which is prepared and administered by the Ministry of Education. Given the critical importance of both the COSC and the JCE, it is inevitable that the Primary School Leaving Examination (PSLE), given at the end of standard 7, aims mainly at preparing students to pass through the system of assessment hurdles. Needless to say, the curriculum of the upper primary standards is directly influenced by the content of the PSLE (Republic of Botswana, 1984; 1986).

A standard examination is also used to assess

children at the end of standard 4. This examination is graded by the schools themselves and was intended to be used primarily for diagnostic purposes. However, it is frequently used to determine whether students should move on to standard 5. As a result, it also functions as a selection instrument.

Students who fail to perform successfully on the standard 4 examination are likely to be permitted to repeat the year (official policy notwithstanding).

Those who fail the PSLE (at the end of the standard 6) may also be permitted to repeat the year. However, it is more likely that they will leave school. Some may attempt to enroll in a remedial course and repeat the examination later. Although remedial courses are not widely available, they are increasing in number. In most cases, the remedial classes are private, fee-charging courses run by individuals or sometimes by a community organization. Little is known about their effectiveness.

References

Bäckman, D. (1983). *Special education in Botswana: Hints and directions for a policy on the education of handicapped children.* Unpublished paper prepared for the government of Botswana under the auspices of the Swedish International Development Authority.

Barr, J. & Jonnson, T. (1984) *Special education: A report prepared for the government of Botswana and UNESCO.*

Brodeur, D. (1988). *Manual to accompany the Botswana teaching competency instrument: Improving instruction in the primary schools.* Gaborone: Ohio University and the U.S. Agency for International Development.

Central Statistics Office. (1989a). *Provisional educational statistics for 1988.* Gaborone: Government of Botswana.

———. (1989b). *Education Statistics.* Gaborone: Government of Botswana.

Johnson, C., James, R., Capie, W., Ellet, C., & Adams, P. (1978). *Identifying and verifying generic teacher competencies.* Athens, Georgia: College of Education, University of Georgia.

Kann, U., Mampolelo, D., & Nleya, P. (1989). *The missing children: Achieving universal basic education in Botswana.* Gaborone: National Institute for Research and Documentation.

Leep, A. (1989). *A proposed plan for developing and phasing in a diploma programme for primary teachers. A consultancy report to the Botswana Primary Education Improvement Project, Phase II.* Gaborone: U.S. Agency for International Development.

LeGrande, R. (1985). *End of tour report.* Unpublished report submitted to the Primary Education Improvement Project. Gaborone: U.S. Agency for International Development.

———. (1984). *The Botswana teaching competency model.* Unpublished report for the U.S. Agency for International Development, Semi-Annual Report No. 6, Gaborone.

Ministry of Education. (1989). *Education for the future.* Second Biennial Report. Gaborone.

Navin, S. (1985). *Guidance and counselling programme development in the Botswana educational system.* Gaborone: Ministry of Education.

Parsons, Q. (1983). Education and development in precolonial and colonial Botswana to 1965. In M. Crowder (Ed.), *Education for development in Botswana.* Gaborone: Macmillan Botswana.

Republic of Botswana. (1977). *Education for Kagisano. Report of the National Commission on Education.* Gaborone.

———. (1979). *National Development Plan, 1979–85.* Ministry of Finance and Development Planning. Gaborone.

———. (1984). *Botswana education and human resources sector analysis, June 1984.* Coordinated by the Ministry of Finance and Development Planning. Gaborone.

———. (1986). *Botswana education and human resources sector update, March 1986.* Coordinated for the Government of Botswana by the Improving Efficiency of Educational Systems (IEES) Steering Committee. Gaborone.

Serpel, R. (1982). *Childhood disability in Botswana.* A report prepared for UNICEF and the government of Botswana.

Swedish International Development Agency. (1972). *Education and training in Botswana: A survey by a mission for the Swedish International Development Agency.*

Tlou, T., & Campbell, A. (1984). *History of Botswana.* Gaborone: Macmillan.

Townsend Coles, E.K. (1986). *Education in Botswana.* Gaborone: Macmillan.

United States Agency for International Development. (1981). *Botswana Primary Education Improvement Project.* Project Paper 633-0222.

Vanqa, T. (1989) *A history of education in Botswana from 1966–1986.* Unpublished paper.

Yoder, J., & Evans, M. (1988). Performance of three cohorts of mature age students enrolled in a degree programme in the Department of Primary Education at the University of Botswana. *Boleswa Educational Research Journal, 6.*

Yoder, J., & Kbria, K. (1987). Learning disabilities among primary school children in Botswana: A pilot study. *International Journal of Special Education, 2 (1).*

PRESCHOOL EDUCATION IN BRAZIL: HISTORICAL AND CRITICAL PERSPECTIVES

•••••••••◆•••••••••

Lucia Regina Goulart Vilarinho
Federal University of Rio de Janeiro
Rio de Janeiro, Brazil

Although specialized preschool service started later in Brazil than it did in France or the United States, it followed the same evolution as the preschool programs in those countries. It was first influenced by the pedagogical principles of educators such as Johann Heinrich Pestalozzi, Friedrich Froebel, Maria Montessori, Ovide Decroly, and Célestin Freinet. More recently, preschool services have evolved into a form of compensatory education (Campos, 1979; Souza, 1979).

Pioneer Period: 1896–1973

No federal agency was directly involved in preschool education from 1896 to 1940, however, Souza (1979) claims that the first continuously functioning kindergarten, modeled on Froebel's teachings, was opened in São Paulo in 1896. A teacher training program was established at the same time. Over the following 25 years, there were three major initiatives in preschool education and child welfare in Brazil, all in the city of Rio de Janeiro (Kramer, 1984):

1. The creation in 1899 of the *Instituto de Proteçao e Assistencia á Infância no Brazil* (Institute for the Protection and Assistance of Childhood in Brazil). The institute's mission included the legal aspects related to child protection and the creation and administration of maternity hospitals, day care centers, and kindergartens. Accomplishing its mission, however, was restricted by a lack of public resources, which led the institute to develop a very narrow scope of action;

2. The founding of the *Jardim de Infância Campos Sales* (Campos Sales Kindergarten) in 1909, considered the model school of its time; and

3. The creation of the privately funded *Departamento da Criança no Brazil* (Children's Department in Brazil) in 1919, established to distribute information about the situation of childhood in Brazil.

Until the beginning of widespread industrialization in Brazil in the 1930s, most children did not have access to any formal preschool education outside of the home. Souza (1979), for example, notes that in 1935, in the country's biggest city, São Paulo, there was an official network of only three children's centers, all located in working-class neighborhoods. A.S. Teixeira, a great Brazilian educator, who in 1932 was General Director of Public Instruction in Rio de Janeiro, did not include preschool services in a report about his administration.

In 1930, the Ministry of Education was created as a department of the federal government, and ten years later the *Departamento Nacional da Criança* (DNCr) (National Children's Department), was created under its authority. Through the DNCr, the coordination of activities related to preschool education became a public responsibility. Until its dissolution in 1973, the objective of the DNCr was to coordinate activities related to maternity, childhood, and adolescence. During its 33 years of existence, it developed programs mainly dedicated to promoting children's health through emergency care, nutrition, vaccination, and hygiene campaigns.

From 1940 to 1973, a number of agencies became responsible for preschool children; these included the Ministries of Labor, Health, and Education. Agencies connected to the presidency, such as LBA, were also involved in child welfare.

The *Legiao Brasileira de Assistência* (LBA) (Brazilian Legion of Assistance) was formed in 1942. It was dedicated exclusively to motherhood and childhood issues, creating and maintaining maternity hospitals, children's hospitals, and day care centers. LBA currently focuses on children from birth to age 3. In 1984, it attended to almost 1.555 million needy children through its day care *Projetco Casulo* (Cocoon Project) (Coutto, 1984).

In 1943, the federal government's Law No. 5452/1943 was enacted. It requires establishments employing more than 30 women over age 16 to provide an adequate place for the worker's children to be accommodated and cared for while they are being nursed. Although this law is still in effect, there are only a few establishments, either private and public, that sponsor day care.

Also in the 1940s, a specialized preschool service was created in the form of preschool classes (for children ages 3 to 4) modeled on the Frobelian kindergarten. In general, the schools were well planned. The well-known Brazilian educator Lourenço Filho (1950) notes:

In 1946, preschool education was represented by little more than one thousand preschool and kindergarten establishments, enrolling 60,000 students. The limited development of this branch of education can be explained by the family life conditions and by the nature of housing in small country towns. Only in the large urban centers, where women working outside the home was more frequent, could a larger number of kindergarten schools be found (p. 16).

In 1946, the population between birth and age 6 was approximately 10.2 million (*Instituto Brasileiro de Geografia e Estatistica* (IBGE), 1950) (Brazilian Institute of Geography and Statistics). Since the specialized service enrolled only 60,000 children, only 0.69 percent of the child population attended preschool.

The 1950s witnessed the expansion of international organizations devoted to child welfare and education, such as the World Organization for Preschool Education (OMEP) and United Nations International Children's Emergency Fund (UNICEF). During the same period in Brazil, a limited amount of research concerning preschool education was sponsored by the DNCr (1956).

In 1961 *Law No. 4024/1961* (Norbrega, 1972) was approved after lengthy debate. The law includes

two articles that define the guidelines and foundations of national education and deal with preelementary schools. Although the articles have not meant an increase in the numbers of preschool programs, they represented the first time that educational legislation for the entire country dealt with this topic. Some changes have been made to the law but none have affected preschool programs. This means that, from a legal point of view, the situation has remained unchanged since 1961. The new Brazilian constitution (1988), however, does give more attention to children's issues. Brazilians are currently awaiting the approval of educational legislation that will conform to the new constitution and address the social and economic realities of the country.

Reports published by the Ministry of Education in 1953 and 1961 offer an overview of preschool services in the years 1933, 1950, and 1957. They are summarized in Table 1.

TABLE 1
Growth of Preschool Education in Brazil

Year	1933	1950	1957
Schools	421	1,412	3,057
Teachers	837	2,704	6,144
Enrollment	25,582	83,844	181,312

According to data from IBGE (1950 and 1960), the population of children age 6 and younger was 4.7 million in 1933, 12.04 million in 1950, and 15 million in 1957. From 1933 to 1950, although the child population had grown by 156 percent, the percentage of programs remained almost unchanged (0.54 percent and 0.69 percent, respectively). The child population increased by 25 percent between 1950 and 1957, and although preschool service was kept to a minimum, it grew by almost 100 percent (from 0.69 to 1.2 percent, respectively).

According to official reports, preschool educational services in Brazil prior to 1974 were characterized by location and sponsorship. Most services were in the urban areas of four states in the southern and southeastern regions of the country—São Paulo, Rio de Janeiro, Pio Grande do Sui, and Minas Gerais—where the process of industrialization was greater and the standard of living was higher. Most of the preschool programs at this time were private, primarily serving the children of the Brazilian elite and middle classes.

The minimal assistance offered the poorest children (e.g., campaigns for milk, food, clothes, and vaccinations) was primarily provided in times of emergency. Examples of such emergencies are a drought in the northeastern region of the country that caused deaths or an epidemic or flood that left people homeless, forcing the government to respond temporary assistance for children and families.

"Child saving" was the dominant ideology of preschool education before 1973. The theme had been evident at the First Congress for Childhood Protection in 1922, and later at the First Inter-American Meeting for Childhood Protection in 1968. Both dealt with two aspects of "protection": (1) a concern for health, nutrition, and hygiene and (2) the provision of programs designed to "socialize" children through recreational activities, for example, games, art, music, theater, play, and stories. It was not until the mid-1970s that a broader approach to preschool education focusing on the "whole child" became popular.

In the late 1960s and early 1970s, several events advanced the development of preschool service in Brazil. In 1968, under the sponsorship of several agencies, including OMEP-Brazil, the ì *Econtro Interamericano de Proteca ao Pre-Escolar* (First Inter-American Meeting for Preschool Protection) took place. At the meeting, studies were presented by Carrazoni (1968) and others describing preschool education in Brazil. In addition, the participation of many Latin American educators in the meeting contributed to the spread of the "new" compensatory approach to preschool education. Overall, Latin American children were described as needy in many ways—a result primarily of the underdevelopment of the region.

From 1969 to 1972, three governmental bodies assumed responsibility for child welfare. The first, established in 1969, regulated workplace safety (*Departamento Nacional de Segurança e Higiene no Trabalho*) (DNSHT) (National Department of Safety and Hygiene at Work). The second, established in 1970, the *Materno-Infantil* (CPMI) (Coordination of Mother-Child Protection), under the Ministry of Health, was responsible for activities concerning maternity, childhood, and adolescence.

The CPMI replaced the DNCr. Established in 1972, the third, the *Instituto Nacional de Alimentaçao* (INAN) (National Institute of Feeding and Nutrition), had as its primary mission the provision of lunch programs for children registered in public schools. INAN's activities also included nutrition educational programs for pregnant women, nursing mothers, and preschool children in disadvantaged areas. Although all three agencies still exist, their effect is limited because of the overwhelming number of Brazilians living in abject poverty.

In summary, despite various governmental efforts, there was no significant improvement in preschool services by the end of 1973. At that time, the population between birth and age 6 was 19,000,4000, (IBGE, 1973), but only 2.4 percent received any special assistance or formal service.

Present Period: 1974–89

Ferrari and Gaspari (1980) point out that the origin of the government's interest in preschool education in the 1970s could be related to the popularity of theories in the United States related to cultural deprivation. Developed between 1955 and 1965, with the consequential articulation of compensatory programs, these theories spread throughout the United States and Western Europe.

The U.S. studies seem to have inspired Brazilian researchers. For example, Poppovic (1972) investigated cultural marginalization and Patto (1973) studied cultural deprivation. These studies and others in the area of nutrition probably influenced the public agencies, especially those related to the Ministry of Education. By the mid-1970s, pressured by international organizations such as UNESCO, these agencies gave priority to programs for preschool children.

As a result, there was a shift toward increased governmental involvement in preschool services after 1974. The involvement assumed several forms: the formulation of political definitions; official standards and recommendations for their implementation; proclamations by officials (educators) from the Ministry of Education; congresses and meetings supported by the federal government on preschool children; and projects and studies at federal universities implemented with the objective of expanding their services. Each of these factors is explained in detail below.

In 1975, preschool education was dealt with in the *Planos Setoriais de Educaçao* (PSE) (Educational Sector Plans), which are details of the federal government's national objectives. The second PSE (1975–79) emphasized preventive action directed at the performance of low-income children in elementary school. Preschool education served as a means of economic and social development, in other words, as a way of investing in human resources. The second PSE plan had six main points:

1. Inter-Ministry cooperation, integrating efforts in the fields of health, education, social assistance, and labor;

2. Creative expansion of services (e.g., informal programs, assistance offered by nonprofessionals, alternative methodologies);

3. Public assistance;

4. Incentives for new programs;

5. Integration of elementary and preelementary school; and

6. Development of a system to disperse information.

The third PSE (1980–85) contained a similar message, although it focused more on the impoverished areas of the country.

The Sarney administration (1986–90), which replaced the military government, was not concerned with elaborating sector plans. There was an obvious decrease in the interest of the federal, state, and municipal governments in preschool education. Instead, the focus turned to literacy training. The change can be attributed to the results of evaluations of programs such as Head Start (Organization for Economic Cooperation and Development (OECD), 1980), which became widely known throughout the Brazilian educational world. The studies presented evidence that the gains obtained by needy children in compensatory programs were lost within a few years.

With governmental interest now focused on this area, the Preschool Coordination Authority (COEPRE) was created under the Ministry of Education in 1975. The elaboration of a national plan for preschool service was the primary objective. In conjunction with another sector of this same ministry, *Conselho Federal de Educaçao* (CFE) (Federal Education Council), legislation was created to set standards for the implementation of this service.

The CFE focused its attention on making politicians and educators more aware of the importance of preschool services and on developing pedagogies relevant to the Brazilian context. It also stimulated the creation of undergraduate-level courses offering various opportunities for study in the field.

COEPRE produced reports and other written materials on topics ranging from theoretical perspectives in preschool education (1976–80) to practical information on preschool practice (1981–85). COEPRE was terminated in 1988, reflecting the government's diminishing interest in preschool education.

Several important developments, originating from the Ministry of Education during the period of preschool education's priority status in the government (1975–79), have also affected the field. Ministry initiatives between 1975 and 1986 stressed the need to develop a multidisciplinary approach to service development, utilizing nonconventional models and targeting poor children as the primary client group (Vilarinho, 1987). There have been no ministry proclamations on preschool education since 1987.

Between 1974 and 1986, many official reports on Brazilian preschool education were produced. In addition, teaching experiences and research about preschool education were stimulated through financial or technical-pedagogical support of the federal government. Other important initiatives during the late 1970s and early 1980s were the coordination of the Brazilian Congress of Preschool Education (held every three years) and the founding of a Preschool Educational Center by the Bernard Leer Foundation in northeastern Brazil.

Prior to 1973, there was virtually no research on preschool education being conducted in Brazil. However, during the peak of governmental support for preschools, a number of projects related to education, teacher training, health, and nutrition were undertaken by the federal system's 34 universities (Vilarinho, 1987). In addition, from 1975 to 1986 as a product of various graduate programs, at least 42 theses and dissertations were written focusing on early childhood issues. Research was also conducted in graduate programs in the private universities in Brazil. Despite the official and academic interest in preschool education, however, the number of children served increased only slightly. In 1984, only 8.3 percent of the 27 million Brazilian children under age six were enrolled in day care centers or kindergarten (Ministry of Education, 1985).

Critics of official policy have focused on the quality of education offered by the compensatory programs for poor children (Abramovay and Kramer, 1984; Abrantes, 1984; Jobim and Sousa, 1984; Rodrigues, 1983). These children, it is argued, have an even greater need for a high-quality preschool education.

In fact, the preschool movement started by the federal government was superficial and hollow. It represented a dependency on the pedagogical thought of the various international organizations involved in Brazilian education. This dependency leads to an inhibition of autonomous educational thinking and to the incorporation, without criticism, of ideas irrelevant to the Brazilian situation. More-over, it promotes a romantic view of preschool education, perceived as the solution to all problems, with the miraculous power of diminishing significantly the high drop-out and repeat levels (50 percent or more) in grade 1 of Brazil's public school system. In addition, because the cost of services was seen as the primary consideration, they can be seen as perpetuating social inequalities. The preschool movement is viewed as essentially a political movement that will have no lasting effect on the lives of Brazilian children. Current governmental efforts in preschool education are mainly directed to literacy classes.

The valorization of the preschool between 1974 and 1986 did result in an increase in Brazilian literature and research in this area and called attention to the importance of offering quality services to working-class children. It is hoped that in the future Brazil's response to the need for preschool education will be founded on good pedagogy and not offered solely as a stopgap emergency assistance program.

References

Abramovay, M., & Kramer, S. (1984). O rei est á nú: debate sobre as funçðes da préescola. *Cadernos CEDES*, (9): 27–38.

Abrantes, P.R. (1984). P pre e a parábolla da pobreza. *Caderno CEDES*, (9)L 8–26.

Brazil, Governo Federal. (1943). Decreto Lei o 5452. *Consolida cao das Leis do Trabalho*.

Campos, M.M.M. (1979). Asistência ao pré-escolar: uma abordagem cirtica. *Cadernos de Pesquisa*, (28): 53–59.

Carrazoni, M.E. (1968). O ensino pré-escolar no Brazil. In *Anais do io Encontro Interanericano de Protecã o ao Pré Escolar*. Rio de Janeiro: OMEP/DNCr.

Coutto, P. (1984). Nota sobre a LaBA. Rio de Janeiro: *Jornal O Globo*.

Departamento Nacional da Criança (DNCr). (1980). *Centro de Porietaçao Junveile 1946–1956*. Rio de Janeiro.

Ferrari, A.R., & Gaspari, L.B.B. (1980). Distribuicao de Oportunidades de educaçao préescolar no Brazil. *Educaçao e Sociedade*, 2(5): 62–79.

Insitutti Brasileiro de Geografia e Estatistica (IBGE) (1950, 1960, 1973). *Anuário Estatistico do Brazil*. Rio de Janeiro.

———. (1988). *Anuario Estatistico do Brazil*. Rio de Janeiro.

Jobim, & Souza, S. (1984). Tendencieas e fatos na politica de educaçao pré-escolar no Brazil. *Cadernos de Pesiqisa*, (51): 47–53.

Kramer, S. (1984). *A politica de pra'e-escolar no Brazil—a arte e o disfarce*. Rio de Janeiro: Achiame.

Lourenço Filho, M.B. (1950). *La educatión en el Brazil*. Rio de Janeiro: Ministerio das Relaçan Exteriores—Divisào Cultural.

Marcilio de Souza, M.T.O. (1980). Comparaçao entre educaçao pre-escolar no Brazil e nos Estados Unidos. *Educaçao*, 9(33): 49–55.

Ministèrio da Educaçao—Secretaria Geral. (1980). *II Plano Sentoial de Educaço e Cultura—1975/1979*. Brasilia: Departamento de Documentaço e Divulgacao.

Ministèrio da Educaçao—Servico de Estatistica da Educaçao. (1985). *Daos prè-escolar, lo e 2o graus*. Brasilia.

———. (1961). *O ensino no Brazil—o ensino primario geral—1957*. Rio de Janeiro.

Ministèrio da Educaçao—Servuci de Estatistica da Educaçao. (1953). *Principais Aspectos do ensino no Brazil*. Rio de Janeiro: Departamento de Impressa Nacional.

Nobrega, V.L. (1972). *Enciclopèdia Legislaçao do Ensing*. Vol. 1, Parts 1 and 2. Rio de Janeiro: Romanitas Livraria Editora.

Organization for Economic Cooperation and Development (OECD). (1979). Vers une politique pour les enfants en age prescholaire. *The OECD Observer*, (103): 305–6.

Patto, M.H.S. (1973). *Privaçao cultural e educaçao pré-escolar*. Rio de Janeiro: José Olympio.

Poppovic, A.M. (1972). Atitudes e cogniçao do marginalizado cultural. *Rivista Brisileira de Estutos Pedagogicios*, 57(126): 244–54.

Rodrigues, N.A. (1983). A realidade sócio econômica educacional brasileira—reflexaes sobre a educaçao pré-ecolar. *AMAE-Educando*, 16(158): 10–13.

Souza, P.M.P. (1979). *Pré-ecolar—uma nova fronteira educacional.* São Paulo: Biblioteca Pioneira de Ciecias Sociai.

Teixeira, A.S. (1932). O sistema escolar do Rio de Janeiro—relató rio de um ano de administraçao. *Boletim de Educacan Publica.*

Vilarinho, L.R.G. (1987). *A educaçao pré-escolar no Brasil e no mundo ocidental—prespectivas histórica e critico-pedagogica.* Doctoral Dissertation. Rio de Janeiro: Universidade Federal do Rio de Janeiro.

PRIMARY AND PRESCHOOL EDUCATION IN BULGARIA

• • • • • • • • • ◆ • • • • • • • •

Plamen Radev
University of Plovdiv
Plovdiv, Bulgaria

Bulgaria was established as a state in 681 A.D. Orthodox Christianity was adopted in 865. After 870, Saint Ciril and Saint Methodius began spreading Slavonic writing and literature throughout the state of Bulgaria. The first Bulgarian kingdom lasted until 1018, when it was conquered by Byzantium. The second Bulgarian kingdom existed from 1187 to 1396. For the next five centuries Bulgaria was under Turkish domination as part of the Ottoman Empire. As a result of the war between Russia and Turkey in 1878, the independence of the country was restored. In the same year, as a consequence of the Berlin Treaty, Bulgaria was divided in two: the Principality of Bulgaria, with the capital city of Sofia; and Eastern Roumelia, with the capital city of Plovdiv. In 1885, the unity of the country was restored, marking what is considered the start of the modern Bulgarian state. On September 9, 1944, the so-called Socialist Revolution was carried out. From 1943, after the death of King Boris III, to 1946 Bulgaria was governed by a council of regency, after which it became a republic. After 1947, a totalitarian communist regime was entrenched in Bulgaria. On October 10, 1989, a new chapter in the history of Bulgaria began, and today the country is on the brink of democracy. These radical changes will inevitably influence education and its institutions in Bulgaria.

Early Ideas of Preschool Education

The first article on preschool education in Bulgaria, an authorized translation from French sources, was published in the periodical *Bulgarski knizhitsi* in 1861. It was edited by the Bulgarian Literary Association (the initial form of the Bulgarian Academy of Science in the Ottoman Empire). The article was entitled *Gardens for Children* and was unsigned. It acquainted Bulgarian readers with the practice of Friedrich Froebel's kindergartens in Western Europe and the United States. Admittedly, this article appeared nine years after Froebel's death when there were few preschool educational institutions in Bulgaria.

A more widely influential publication in Bulgaria on public preschool education appeared in 1874 in the pedagogical section called "A guide to Primary Education," in the periodical *Chitalishte*. The author of the articles, under the common title of "Nursery School or School for Children From 5

135

to 7 Years Old," was Dragan Tsankov (1828–1911), a prominent Bulgarian intellectual and politician. He was educated in Odessa, Kiev, Vienna, and Istanbul. Prior to 1878, he was a leader in a political movement for an autonomous Bulgarian church under the rule of the Pope in Rome. A Catholic by faith, he later gave up the idea of a union, since it was not accepted by the Bulgarian people. After 1878, he was a deputy to the National Assembly of Bulgaria and a leader of the Liberal party.

In his articles, Tsankov pointed to the need to open kindergartens and nursery schools, and outlined a set of regulations, methods, and means of administration. Organized preschool education was to be the first stage of a school system modeled on that of Bell and Lancaster (see Chapter 1), and was to include children from ages 2 to 7. The purpose of the nursery school was to promote moral inspirations, religious impressions, and useful training. Nursery schools were to be, in the author's words, "cheerful resorts" in which a "judicious and methodical" management and control was effected.

The moral and physical development of children was ensured by religious education, reading, writing, oral arithmetic, line drawing, handiwork, singing of psalms, and physical exercises. Tsankov pointed out that the nursery school building should be separate from the school, spacious and well lit, providing two cubic meters of space for each child.

Nursery schools were opened only under specific conditions by the municipalities and school boards. They were sponsored by the local women's associations, which also were responsible for controlling the nursery school work. The associations were headed by a director, and if the number of children exceeded 80, there was also an assistant director. Teachers were appointed only after passing a practical and theoretical examination. The children were to be admitted after a medical examination. The nursery schools were free and intended to be universally accessible.

The model regulations specified the house rules and the curriculum. The nursery school was to include a study hall, a dining room with lockers and coatracks, a washroom, a shed, and a spacious yard. In the study hall, there were two rows of desks with space between them as well as beds and cradles. Instructional aids included a blackboard, chalk, beads for arithmetic, drawing models, slates, slate pencils, bells, and pipes.

The order of the day was identical to Bell and Lancaster's monitorial system. Everything was accomplished through commands and instructions. The classes, called Principles of Knowledge, lasted 15 minutes. These were followed by 30 minutes of handiwork, 15 minutes of practical arithmetic, and 30 minutes of religious singing. In the afternoon, there was 15 minutes of handiwork, 30 minutes of listening to stories, 15 minutes of singing, and games till the end of the day.

Topics studied in the Principles of Knowledge included time, the seasons, colors, shapes, animals, plants, the earth, earth surfaces, and major countries and cities. Handiwork included sewing, knotting, and embroidery. Elementary mathematics included an introduction to numbers, Arabic figures, addition, subtraction, and multiplication.

The goals for reading included a familiarity with vowels and consonants, letters, syllables, and words of two and three syllables. Physical exercises, performed in a group, included running and gymnastics. Unfortunately, Tsankov's system was based on an academic school that would suppress to a considerable degree the activity and personal initiative of children.

Again in 1874, and in the same magazine, Tsankov published "The System of Education in Froebel's Nursery School," which informed Bulgarian readers about the views of this great German educator. Tsankov, however, drew more widely from the work of Johann Heinrich Pestalozzi, Jean Jacques Rousseau, and Herbert Spencer. Although his ideas were never applied, they provided the theoretical basis and stimulus for Bulgarian preschool education.

Also in 1874, in the magazine *Guide to Primary Education*, V. Radoslavov pointed to the nursery schools in Czechoslovakia as a potential model, while the need for public preschool education was supported by Dr. M. Spassovich in the private Bulgarian magazine *School* in 1875.

A more practical attempt at kindergarten education was made by Nikola Zhivkov (1847–1901), a Bulgarian intellectual, teacher, school inspector, and deputy to the National Assembly after 1878. When a teacher in the town of Veles in 1874, he gathered 20 children ages 4 and 5 who were trained for about three months at the local school. Though a follower of Tsankov, Zhivkov advocated a more orthodox Froebelian method. He objected to the schools being called nursery schools or kindergartens, and suggested instead the name "child's wisdom."

It is evident from this brief history of preschool ideas in Bulgaria that despite the Turkish feudal domination over Bulgarian lands, the kindergarten movement evolved in specific forms, and there were even modest attempts at its realization.

In 1882, Zhivkov founded a child's wisdom school in his native town of Svishtov. Fifty-three children were enrolled (25 girls and 28 boys) ages 4 to 7. There were two teachers, Zhivkov and his wife, and two "field mothers." The syllabus included physical exercise, listening to rhymes and stories, Froebel's gifts, pasting, folding, needlework, drawing, writing, reading, and counting. In 1883, N. Zhivkov moved the school into the local community center, and later opened a second school in Svishtov. In 1884, a kindergarten was opened in Varna.

The major town in Eastern Roumelia in the late 19th century was Plovdiv. In 1884, the women's association called Mother's Care opened the first Bulgarian preschool in the town and in the region. Fifty-five children were enrolled under the tutelage of Ekaterian Dessimirova. Fees were paid only by the children of wealthy parents while the poor were schooled at no cost. After being housed in a private building for a short time, the women's association nursery school moved to a specially renovated house.

By 1886, Dessimirova had an assistant. In the same year, another Bulgarian kindergarten was opened. There were also Greek kindergartens in Eastern Roumelia in the towns of Plovdiv, Pazardjik, Stanimaka, and Assenovgrad. In Plovdiv, there were also an Armenian and two Jewish kindergartens.

In 1888, the Ministry of Public Education opened a public nursery school and a course for kindergarten mistresses at the Sofia public girls' grammar school. The director of the training course and nursery school was Henrieta Moteux, specially brought in from Geneva. She followed Froebel's method, using gifts and occupations, materials for drawing, modeling, cutting, sticking, working with cardboard, needlework, stringing (needles, threads, and beads), garden tools, and play materials (e.g., skipping ropes, drums, carts, and hobbyhorses). During the first year of the course, Moteux trained 15 kindergarten mistresses.

A new Law of Public Education was passed in 1881 by the Minister of Education Georgi Zhivkov, brother of Nikola Zhivkov. This law regularized for the first time the existence of infant schools. They were divided into a lower level (children ages 3 and 4) and an upper level (children ages 5 and 6). The curriculum in the lower course included games, singing, object training, natural history, and handiwork. The second level emphasized drawing and elementary mathematics. Although the public infant schools were free of charge, they were few in number and therefore did not serve many children.

A new Law of Public Education was passed in 1909, which shifted the age range to 4 to 7. After 1909, these schools developed erratically. Their numbers tended to increase in periods of economic stability (1894–99 and 1906–08) and decrease during economic crises and war (1901–03 and 1918–19). Infant schools were almost exclusively found in the towns. After 1900, there also appeared French, German, and U.S. missionary infant schools. After 1905, the Greek schools were closed, leaving only a few U.S. and Jewish infant schools.

From 1920 to 1923, the government of the Bulgarian Agrarian Union was in power, headed by Alexander Stambolijski. The Minister of Education, Stoyan Omarchevski, drew up a new Law of Public Education, which was passed in 1921. The law did not make infant schools compulsory, but it did narrow the age range to 5 to 7 years. According to the law, the main purpose of these schools was "to contribute to the development of the senses and stimulate children's activity by instruction and observation, games, and appropriate studies." The infant schools were supported by the municipalities and were to be opened in towns of over 20,000 inhabitants, a condition that was in force until 1934. From 1920 to 1923, most infant schools and kindergartens operated on a half-day basis and were modeled on a loose interpretation of Froebel. The infant schools determined their own curriculums, which generally included talks on various topics, rhythmic exercises accompanied by music, studies with Froebel's gifts, and handiwork. On Saturdays, there were concerts for the parents organized to display the individual talents of the children.

On July 9, 1923, the democratic government of the Bulgarian Agrarian Union was removed by a *coup d'état* and a fascist government, headed by Alexander Tsankov, who was also a Minister of Education, came into power. He drew up and enforced a Law of Public Education in 1924. The law, largely a return to the conditions of the law of 1909, resulted in few changes for infant schools. Under the new law, the aim of infant schools was the development of children ages 5 to 7, by suitable talks, games, songs, and handiwork.

After the *coup d'état* on May 19, 1934, the government of Kimon Georgiev abolished all political parties and ruled the country without the Parliament, by decrees. A decree on preschool education was issued in 1934 by the Minister of Education Yanaki Mollov. In fact, this was the first independent normative act on preschool education in the country up to that time. The decree graded two kinds of preschool education institutions: (1) "children's hearths" for children up to age 5 and (2) kindergartens for children ages 5 to 7. The hearths—intended to serve homeless children, orphans, and foundlings—were day and boarding schools. Fully developed children's hearths had two stages: (1) children's cradles for babies and (2) creches for children up to age 5.

The decree enlarged the system of educational institutions for children. The old infant schools and nursery schools were never referred to again. According to the regulations, each kindergarten teacher was responsible for 20 children. A doctor and a nurse took care of the children's health. According to the decree, preschool education was aimed at the overall development of children. However, official education became permeated with politics and the ideology of national socialism. By 1937, there were 219 in Bulgaria serving 10,548 children.

After 1934, industrial enterprises and charity organizations also opened kindergartens. Summer kindergartens had begun to open as well, the first in 1933 founded by a U.S. missionary group headed by Edward Haskon in the village of Pordim in the Pleven district. A few Greek and Armenian kindergartens were also registered. The number of German and Italian kindergartens increased, while in some towns there were Czechoslovak, Romanian, and Russian kindergartens. In 1944, there were 197 town and 46 village kindergartens employing 239 and 55 teachers, respectively.

Theories of Preschool Education, 1878–1944

In the first years after the liberation of Bulgaria from Turkish domination, some magazines published articles in support of kindergartens. Actually, there were already social and economic conditions and factors to support these children's institutions. The greatest contribution to the theory of preschool education before 1900 was made by Zhivkov. He was the author of the first Bulgarian book on preschool education, *Child's Wisdom*, published in 1887 in Varna. It follows the methodical instructions of Froebel with the addition of some innovations of the Russian pedagogue E. Vodovozova. Its four chapters describe the education of children ages 3 to 7 using games, songs, talks, and riddles in the Bulgarian spirit. The particular contribution of Zhivkov to Froebel's methods is the avoidance of the original rigidity; for example, the classes with Froebel's gifts are accompanied by songs, chats, and verses. In his book, Zhivkov recommends "scientific observations" of natural phenomena, combined with elementary experiments. At the end of the book, he suggests how to furnish the study halls (mainly with desks and lockers).

An analysis of Zhivkov's work shows that the author expertly introduces the Bulgarian principle in educative work while avoiding the obscure orthodox Christian symbolism, mysticism, and typical German interpretation of the gifts. For many years *Child's Wisdom* remained the only book—except for a few Russian sources—available to Bulgarian kindergarten teachers. Zhivkov was also the first to train kindergarten mistresses. The first two graduates worked in his kindergarten in Varna and later, in 1888, managed the kindergarten in Sofia. In the same year, Moteux trained, with the help of these two kindergarten mistresses,

15 other teachers by Froebel's methods, who in turn began work at various kindergartens in Bulgaria. Froebel's methods were also disseminated through Moteux's course, articles, and teacher's conferences (e.g., the Svishtov conference in 1890). Other major promoters of Froebel's method and kindergartens were Zhivkov's sister Vela Zhivkova, Ivan D. Shishmanov, later Minister of Education, and various contributors to the magazines *Pedagogy*, *School Review,* and *Teacher.*

In 1892, the Ministry of Education sent three young women to Dresden to study at the Froebel Institute, which was headed by the Baroness Von Bynlov, Froebel's niece. In 1893, another nine scholarship students were sent to Dresden for the two-year program, the most eminent among them was Eugenia Milkova, substitute for Moteux. Attempts at training kindergarten mistresses were also made at some girls' grammar schools in Bulgaria that had a pedagogical department.

In 1905, a special course for kindergarten mistresses, regulated by a statute, was organized, but it existed for only two years. From 1907 to 1942, kindergarten mistresses were trained primarily in private courses. The subject matter of the 1905 two-year course included Bulgarian, natural science, hygiene, general pedagogy, Froebel's educative method, and gymnastics. The course in general pedagogy included infant psychology, didactic principles, methods of teaching at primary school, and problems in pedagogical history. There was a nursery school attached to the program for practical training.

In 1911, the regulations concerning the state final certification examination for full-time teachers in children's schools were issued. Only those who had taken the course for teachers in children's schools, also called the "Froebel Department" of the six-year grammar schools, were admitted to the examination. The examination consisted of a talk on Froebel's gifts and occupations, following which the candidate had to write a test lesson and demonstrate a practical lesson in the presence of a board of examiners.

The U.S. missionary Elizabeth Clark (1867–1942) also contributed to the training of teachers for infant schools. The daughter of a U.S. missionary, she was born in Bulgaria, spending her childhood in Plovdiv and Samokov. She graduated from a Chicago college for kindergarten mistresses based on Froebel's method, returned to Bulgaria, and in 1897 opened a U.S. kindergarten in Samokov. In 1900, she moved the kindergarten to Sofia and organized a course for kindergarten mistresses. The course was private, had few students, and was conducted in English. From 1900 to 1911, Clark's course had 17 graduates. Clark continued the course until 1932.

In 1920, a second private course for training infant school teachers was established in Sofia; this one headed by Eugenia Milkova. In a dispute reminiscent of that between Susan Blow and Patty Smith Hill in the United States, Clark and Milkova disagreed as to the interpretation of Froebel's method. While Milkova adhered strictly to Froebel's philosophy, Clark interpreted his method more democratically and freely. Clark's ideas were much more popular at the time.

In 1934, Professor Dimitar Katsarov, the famous Bulgarian educator, opened another private course for infant school teachers. Katsarov's course combined theory with practical training in various kindergartens in the capital city. The subjects studied were general pedagogics, including didactics and methods; school organization and legislation; history of pedagogy and education in Bulgaria; pedagogical psychology; infant psychology; infant psychopathology and deficiencies; methods of Maria Montessori, Ovide Decroly, and Froebel; maternal and children's diseases and hygiene; a foreign language of the student's choice; drawing; modeling; handiwork; singing and music; hospitalization of children; and teaching practice. The course as a whole was held in the spirit of Katsarov's theory of free education.

Clark's "American" course did not remain static during its years of operation. When in 1925 Clark returned for a visit to the United States, her director, Haskel, began working with the students using the project method. In 1929, the graduate student Penka Kassabova returned from the United States having mastered the method of projects in Chicago, which she applied in the course. In 1932, Kassabova took charge of the course, the major subjects of which were child nature, applied infant psychology, keeping children's diaries, making of dolls, learning games, cardboard articles, woodwork, drawing and modeling, gymnastics, rhythmics and harmony, mother's games, intelligence tests, children's hygiene, literature for children, sociology, general psychology, pedagogy, singing, elementary mathematics, and practice at a model kindergarten.

In 1939, Clark's course became subject to special regulations approved by the Ministry of Education. In 1942, a state institute offering a two year course for infant school teachers was founded in Sofia. All private courses were closed and the teachers became lecturers at the institute.

Theoretical views of preschool education were presented mainly in specialized magazines, such as *Children's Life* (also called *Kindergarten*), which began publication in 1922 under Clark's editorship. Later, the magazine was edited by Clark's student, Dobra Pelasheva. It presented mainly the orthodox method of Froebel; however, after 1925 it also began to support Montessori's system. The method of projects based on the ideas of John Dewey, William Kilpatrick, and E. Callings was promoted by the book *Life in the American Kindergarten,* published in 1931 and translated by A. Cheshmedjiev, and in L. Schleger's book *Practical Work in the Kindergarten,* published in 1933. *Kindergarten* magazine was succeeded in 1934 by the *First Steps*, which contributed to the popularization of the project method in Bulgarian kindergartens. There were no centralized curriculums and plans and the teachers were guided in their work mainly by the ideas, views, themes, and practical elaborations of classes presented on the pages of this magazine. An examination of the history of the kindergarten in the interwar period in Bulgaria reveals that after 1930 Froebel's method began to lose significance in Bulgaria, giving way instead to interpreted and borrowed elements from the systems of Montessori, Decroly, and the American progressives.

Preschool After 1944

The Department of Preschool Education was established at the Ministry of Education on September 9, 1944, and existed until 1946. From 1946 to 1949, preschool education was under the management of Social Affairs, and later by the Ministry of Labor and Social Welfare. A Law of Social Care and Child Education was passed in 1946, establishing the Central Council for social care and children's education. Local councils with similar functions were formed in the district towns. In 1948, by a Law of Public Education, the aims of kindergartens were declared to be the total intellectual and physical development of children ages 3 to 7 in the spirit of socialism, and the preparation of these children for the primary school. According to the law, there were three types of kindergartens: half-day, weekly, and seasonal. The same law required the training of kindergarten teachers to be conducted at colleges in two-year programs of study.

The first Statute of Kindergartens was issued in 1949. This occurred at the time when the totalitarian system of the communist administration came into operation, which resulted in a new policy for public preschool education. The updated Regulation of Kindergartens of 1952 stated for the first time that the kindergarten was to be where the foundations of communist education were laid. Until 1950, teachers in kindergartens still followed the project methods or the systems of Ovide Decroly and Montessori. Later, however, educational pluralism was replaced by Soviet kindergarten theory. After 1948, work in kindergartens began to be planned. Kindergartens were to include physical training, games, acquaintance with nature and the environment, development of speech, elementary arithmetic, drawing, modeling, handiwork, musical education, and principles of socialist ideology. Compulsory classes in which socialism and its "advantages" were propagandized were introduced in 1949. From the early 1950s, the practice of strict planning and accountability, drawing on a rigid syllabus, took the upper hand. All elements of free education were eliminated. At the same time, Soviet ideas of preschool education—mainly those of A.P. Ussova, E. Tiheeva, E. Flyorina, and V.V. Manuilenko—penetrated Bulgaria on a massive scale. As a result of the Soviet *Guide to the Teacher's Work in the Kindergarten*, translated in 1954, a program of studies was introduced that reformed the curriculum to resemble that of the primary school. Thus, the scholasticism of totalitarian education became even stronger.

Until 1950, infant school teachers were educated at the Sofia Institute and the institute for infant school teachers in Rousse, which opened in

1948. After 1950, the independent institutes were closed and one-year courses for infant school teachers were organized at the pedagogical schools and secondary schools in Rousse and Sofia, while in the primary teacher training schools in the towns of Bourgas, Varna, and Blagoevgrad there were departments for infant school teachers. Evidently the education acquired there was insufficient, and thus, in 1960, a number of colleges were founded in Sofia, Haskovo, Bourgas, and Rousse. In 1953, the Department of Pedagogics of the Sofia University established a specialization in preschool education.

A special decree of the Central Committee of the BCP and the Council of Ministers of 1957 envisaged the expansion of the kindergarten network, the establishment of continuity between kindergartens and primary schools, and an emphasis on children's habituation to work—work at home, in the carpenters, and in nature's nooks. The goal was to have 53 percent of Bulgarian children of kindergarten age in programs by the beginning of the 1960s.

In 1951, management of kindergartens was the responsibility of a "kindergarten manager," who was in charge of several kindergartens. The provisions after 1951 were for each kindergarten to have its own director. A kindergarten for "oligophrenic" children from ages 5 to 8 was opened in 1955 in Sofia. By the late 1950s, the general picture of kindergartens in the country was a system of 289 day kindergartens and 952 half-day kindergartens (in 1948 there were 523 day and 1,632 half-day kindergartens).

A new program of educative work in kindergartens was drawn up in 1963. The kindergarten was viewed as a public and educational institution, the aim of which was (1) to ensure the versatile development of children of preschool age, including physical intellectual, moral, aesthetic education, and habituation to work, by taking into account the individual and age peculiarities of children; and (2) to lay the foundations of the communist society.

This versatile development had to be accomplished through various types of games, studies, and work. According to the program, the children were organized into four groups by age (3 to 4, 4 to 5, 5 to 6, and 6 to 7). The play in the kindergarten included role play, construction, dramatic plays, active games, and deductive games. Studies in the kindergarten used natural experiences to promote language, including observation, talks, plays, puppet shows, stories, dialogues, and rhymes learned by ear. Physical training included running, rolling a ball, climbing, throwing, jumping, and active games. Visual arts activities included drawing lines, spheres, and rectangular forms; mastering various colors; modeling with clay; elementary application and construction, folding paper sheets, and formatting angles. Musical education involved listening to music and movements accompanied by music.

Tasks became more complex in each succeeding group, but no explicit aim of psychological and physical preparation for school education was set, though it was implied. According to the program, the timetable for the kindergarten was the following: inspection of children and gymnastics at 7:00 A.M., breakfast at 8:00 A.M., studies from 8:45 A.M. to 9:50 A.M., walks and games from 9:50 A.M. to noon, lunch at noon, a rest in the afternoon from 12:00 to 3:00 P.M., and a snack at 4:00 P.M. The kindergarten day ended at 7:00 P.M.

A new program of educative work in kindergartens was adopted in 1971. The curriculum is outlined in Table 1.

TABLE 1

Kindergarten Curriculum

Type of Study	Weekly Number of Study Periods Per Group			
	1st Group	2nd Group	3rd Group	4th Group
Native Language and the Environment	2	3	4	4
Physical Training	2	2	2	2
Reckoning	1	1	2	2
Drawing	1	1	2	2
Modeling	25	25	5	1
Application	25	25	25	1
Construction	50	50	1	1
Musical Education	2	2	2	2

The present curriculum is based on the 1984 regulations and program. A part of this Program (Petrova, 1985), which reveals the state of kindergarten education in Bulgaria today, is quoted below.

The Philosophy of the Integrated Program

In the conditions of public preschool education, children at the age of 3 to 6 years develop aspirations and abilities, intellectual, and behavioral mechanisms that are of major importance for the versatile development of their personalities, and are determinants for the program and the pedagogical process.

Children's institutions provide conditions for the harmonious psychophysical development and upbringing of children. In accordance with the needs of society and the age peculiarities of children, the various activities, forms, and methods of work continue to protect the health and increase the efficiency of the children's organism, to improve the coordination of movements, the quickness of reactions, and self-regulation of moral activity and of conduct.

By a theoretically substantiated regime, the children acquire cultural and hygienic habits, learn to dress and wash in the right way, to keep clean, and be orderly. Rational feeding and organized medical control activate the physiological functions of the child's organism, ensuring its proper physical development.

Contemporary kindergartens for children of up to 6 years of age provide conditions for active mental and cognitive activity, for the formation of cognitive needs.

A major task in educative work in kindergartens is to develop elements of school activities promoting mental development and learning abilities of children. By mastering the system of knowledge and skill and on the basis of total intellectual maturing, the child gets ready for conscientious solving of school problems and for actions that will be controlled and regulated; he learns to use models—symbolic means in solving the set problems. By knowledge systematization and the integrative approach, children assimilate sensory standards, elementary relations between objects and phenomena, get ready for the perception and comprehension of some natural and social phenomena. A specified, though original, system of knowledge is acquired in the entire pedagogical process; the speech activities, which are directly connected with determinants for the mental development, are also promoted. The development of cognitive processes and oral speech condition the manifestation of a cognitive and social activity.

The kindergarten provides the necessary condition for social and moral education of children. Qualities of moral content and social purpose are formed in collective games, studies, and work. Play, as a vital necessity at this stage of children's development, provides a possibility for the formation of universal features in the child's character that help to regulate interactions between children. Moral norms of responsiveness and friendships are inculcated.

Children are taught to be purposive in solving general problems, to keep the rules, to feel satisfied with their achievements. In labor activities, they join together to achieve a beneficial result. They are brought up to be industrious, organized, to have a positive attitude to the work of those around them, to be interested in the products of their labor and in modern technology. Some more specific problems are solved through labor and constructive-technical activities. The first skills of planning and activity are cultivated. Children come to know various materials and techniques, their sensory processes are developed, initial labor, and constructive-technical skills are formed.

Habituation to work is accomplished by various kinds of labor effected in the nature's corner when eating, cleaning the study hall or making self-made toys. Children acquire organizational skills, habits of making effort in their work, skills at maintaining order at their work place and skills for a constructive-technical activity.

Educative work in kindergartens involves a number of issues concerning aesthetic formation. The series of artistic and aesthetic activities develops at an early age the aesthetic perceptivity and attitude to the world, and a complex of abilities characterizing the creative personality is being formed.

Being in touch with art, the child begins to acquire a sense of the beautiful in nature and the environment, and a desire for creative work. The child's conscious needs, feelings, imagination are thus simultaneously stimulated. Emotional responsiveness to colors, sounds, intonation, and rhythm is cultivated in dramatic games, by literature, by making toys, and by observations. Qualities needed in creative and practical work are formed on the basis of the aesthetic experience gained.

The purpose and goals of preschool education, consistent with the age characteristics of children of 3 to 6 years, define the specificity of principles and approaches and the structuring of the syllabus contents. The systematic and integrated approach at preschool age is objectively conditioned by the level of a child's psychological development. The complex stimulation of mental, aesthetic, moral, and physical development of the child is considered when selecting the contents of the program of studies.

Integration is effected at several levels:

1. By the choice of global topics in the section on "Acquaintance With the Realities Around." The methodological grounds of the integrated functions in this section are to be found in the realities of children's "life as experienced" as a source of subject matter for all sections of the syllabus. Syllabus content is integrated by several complex themes intended to acquaint children with the social and natural environment, such as "My Home," "The Kindergarten," "Our Residential District," "Our Town/Village," "Homeland," "Autumn," "Winter," "Spring," "Summer."

Children up to 6 years cannot assimilate the logical system of concepts in certain fields of science. Instead, specific systems, skills, and habits in speech development, formation of elementary mathematical notions and concepts, physical culture, visual and plastic art activities, musical activities, etc., have a direct connection with the syllabus material on "Acquaintance With the Realities Around" and the "Development of Speech."

2. Integration of tasks in each section with all other sections of the program of educative work.

3. Integration of tasks from notions and concepts in the children. For example: the integration of tasks from the sections "Development of Speech" and "Acquaintance With the Realities Around" is a precondition for the unity of thoughts and speech, for acquiring knowledge and developing the mental faculties; integration of pictorial and plastic arts activity with labor and constructive technical activity; pictorial and plastic arts, music and literature; musical and physical culture.

4. Integration of tasks and syllabus subject matter within the same section. For instance: Native Language—relation and system of speech components; pictorial and plastic art activities—drawing applications, modeling; music—singing, listening, movement, playing an instrument; physical culture—exercises for total development, drill and preparatory exercises in the morning gymnastics system, active games, sports studies.

Integration at four levels ensures complete perception of objects and phenomena and facilitates the adoption of skills for practical orientation and creative work. Integration is accomplished by the thematic principle. The themes on "Acquaintance With the Realities Around" and "Natural and Social Environment," enrich the vocabulary and bring into unity the word and the idea and facilitate the communicative function of speech.

Thematic integration of the program contents covers knowledge, skills, and habits determining the child's development in each age period. This amount of knowledge, skills, and habits is reflected in the educational contents of various sections and its developing nature.

The specific feature of the integrated approach in the entire system of education work in kindergartens is determined by the dominance of play activities. It integrates program tasks and contents of other section of the program and brings about a unity between the basic activities.

Integration does not place all educative work within strictly defined themes. Integration is not at variance with the specificity of educational contents of the separate activities, for example, the play as an activity that reflects life takes its plots and models from the themes on "Acquaintance With the Realities Around" and fulfills integration and organization functions. But the play is also a wider reflection of the theme. It covers in a rather original way the children's experience gained from literature and life in general. Themes in play are more generalized and rich since the transformation is performed in an imaginary situation.

Arts and musical activities involve issues in the thematic areas, while at the same time an emotional purpose is pursued, and the aesthetic experience with speech activity of children is stimulated.

The ensuring of a certain amount of knowledge, skills, and habits for the versatile and harmonious development of children by thematic integration is a major approach to the structure of program and its pedagogical process.

The Educative Nature of the Program

The program contains both basic and complex knowledge reflecting elementary objective laws and relations that a child of up to 6 years can perceive and make sense of. This knowledge is the basis for developing conditions and for ensuring the development of intellectual and social qualities that facilitate the process of learning at school.

The development of general mental faculties, such as synthetic perception, inquisitiveness, keenness of observation, visual and figurative thinking, and constructive imagination, also has its place in the program. Educational contents for the last age group includes the acquiring of knowledge on elementary relations between objects and phenomena in the natural and social environment, which help with the formation of generalized problem solving, intellectual activity and cognitive needs, and also for mastering various modes of action and thought. Assimilation of the program contents in the various age periods brings about new physical formation and qualitative development of abilities, changes in the cognitive activity, to develop the cognitive process of thinking, memory, and imagination. The material related to "Acquaintance With the Realities Around" is grouped in several themes, one of which is basic to the others. Themes on nature cover knowledge of animate and inanimate nature and of people's work. Grouped by seasons, the program tasks for the separate groups of children contain introductory knowledge in botany, zoology, geography, and physics.

The Structure and Content of the Program

The program material is determined by a new approach to the major Marxist formulation concerning the formation of personality in the process of work. The program reflects the relation between the main goals of education and development of the socialist personality, between public needs at the stage of mature socialism and the abilities of children at preschool age. The realization of this preceptive goal brings forward the educative tasks as a determinative feature of program contents, its volume, and degree of complication. The various types of play, study, and labor activities envisage the mastering of knowledge skills, modes of action, and thought. The unity of these activities guarantees development in the intellectual, moral and motivational, and emotional and social spheres. This formulation is reflected in a new way in the program structure. The forms of education are being enlarged by including some of the play types. Didactic, constructive, and dramatic play is used as a means of mastering program tasks without infringing on the play situation and psychological essence of the play as a specific activity. On the contrary, the play in all its varieties remains separate as an independent children's practice. On the other hand, play and labor activities relate closely with the studies as a form of education. The main integrative function of these in, for example, "Acquaintance With the Realities Around" presupposes a relation between thinking and speech. Hence comes the connection between the sections "Acquaintance with the Realities Around" and "Development of Speech."

Labor and constructive-technical activities are part of the program contents and structure, but they remain relatively independent as productive activities. The ideas of the "Banner of Peace" movement are rendered more concrete. In the section on "Acquaintance With the Realities Around," thoughts focus on tasks concerning education in the spirit of patriotism and internationalism. They are related to aesthetic education and the early development of abilities. Aesthetic perceptiveness and attitude to the world as components of aesthetic culture are formed by means of a series of artistic and aesthetic activities. This series in the program includes acquaintance with works of fine arts, music, and literature. The formulation that aesthetic education, along with the intellectual, moral, and physical one, directly determines the specificity of the pedagogical process is realized. At the same time, the emotiveness called into being stimulates the child's intellectual activity, behavior, creative work, and ability to enjoy life.

The Organization and Content of the Pedagogical Process

A typical feature of the organization and content of the pedagogical process is the integrative function of play. It takes a central place as an independent

TABLE 2
Plan of the Educative Work in Kindergartens

Age groups	1st	1st "A"	2nd	3rd
Educational Sections and Activities Weekly Number of Classes				
Acquaintance With the Realities Around Development of Speech	1	1	1.5	2
Formation of Elementary Mathematical Notions and Concepts	—	—	1	1
Visual and Plastic Arts Activities	2	2	2	2
Musical Activities	2	2	2	2
Labor and Constructive-Technical Activities	—	—	1	1
Physical Culture	2	2	2	2
Optional Education: Russian	—	—	—	1

child's practice. In the Bulgarian preschool, play serves both as a means of self-expression for children, as a way of teaching important aesthetic and moral lessons. These functions of play permit the use of additional forms of education and assimilation of knowledge, skills, and habits in the afternoon. The timetable covers the major moments of the pedagogical process. Its content and organization ensures motivation and varied activities so as to prevent the neuropsychological overburdening of children and to create conditions for a creative approach and a well-balanced rhythm of the pedagogical process. Unpremeditated effect is achieved also by the special feature "Optional Work." Before the morning exercises and after snack in the afternoon the children are encouraged to take up various activities of their own choice, such as pictorial, musical, speech, play, labor, constructive or sports, which stimulates self-dependence in settling problems and in assimilating various modes of action and thought. The organization and contents of the pedagogical process reflect the system of educational tasks and the contents and structure of the program and provide conditions for the teacher's creative work. [See Table 2.]

Formation of Groups

Three age groups are differentiated in the kindergartens. Children born from January 1 to June 30 enter kindergarten on July 1 together with the children born from July 1 to December 31 of the preceding year to form group one. The children born from July 1 to December 31 form variant "A" of the first group. Where there are not enough children to form a separate "A" group, a mixed first group is formed. The second group is formed of children who have turned age 4 years by June 30. The third group includes children who are age 5 by June. All other older children who are to become first grade pupils but have not gone to school for medical reasons or for lack of material equipment for the education of 6-year-old first graders are included in this third group.

In 1989, there were 4,666 preschool programs of all kinds in Bulgaria, serving 339,000 children. Service also extends to work with the parents, such as enlightening lectures on various problems related to child development, parent-teacher meetings, and individual consultation with parents by psychologists and educators. The specialty magazine *Family and School* contributes greatly in this respect. Since November 10, 1989, processes aimed at transforming the country into a democratic and constitutional state and at demolishing the totalitarian administration have taken place in Bulgaria. This will inevitably lead to a change in the system of preschool education—in its forms, methods, and means—that will promote humanistic and democratic principles.

References

Chakarov, N., & Nacheva, v. (1961). Petkova, Istoria na preduchilishtnoto vazpitanie v Bulgaria. [History of Preschool Education in Bulgaria.] Sofia.

Programa za vazpitatelnata rabota v detskite gradini. [Programme of education work in kindergartens.] (1963). Sofia.

Programa za uchebno-vazpitatelnata rabota v detskite gradini. [Programme of educative work in kindergartens.] (1971). Sofia.

Programa za vazpitatelnata rabota v detskata gradina. [Programme of educational work in the kindergartens.] (1977). Sofia.

Programa za vazpitatelnata rabota v detskata gradina. E. Petrova, ed. [Programme of educational work in the kindergarten.] (1985). Sofia.

EARLY CHILDHOOD EDUCATION IN CANADA

Andrew Biemiller
University of Toronto
Ellen M. Regan
Ontario Institute for Studies in Education
Donna Lero
University of Guelph

Early childhood education in Canada is concerned with the care and education of children from birth through age 8, and older children in "school-age" day care programs. The traditional focus on day care, nursery, and kindergarten programs has expanded in several ways. First, public education has incorporated traditional "early childhood" objectives and methods into primary programs (through grade 3). Second, the rapid growth of women's employment has been accompanied by an increased need for school-age day care. This involves children in at least two different care/educational settings. Third, during the past two decades, there has been considerable interest in infant day care. However, as in other countries, the use of formal, or center-based, infant care has not increased as much as care and educational programs for toddlers, preschoolers, and school-age children.

Early Childhood Settings in Canada

In Canada, young children are served by a variety of center-based and home-based programs. Most day care and nursery school programs are licensed. This means that they conform to standards set by the provinces and are often eligible for direct subsidies or are eligible to accept children who are subsidized. Some "family day care" (i.e., care provided in the caregiver's home) is also licensed and eligible for subsidies. Kindergartens are run by and paid for by local boards of education, often with provincial assistance. Provinces differ in the degree of support for kindergarten. Three (Ontario, Quebec, and Manitoba) offer funding for 4-year-old as well as 5-year-old kindergarten. One (Prince Edward Island) offers no provincial support for kindergarten. The rest support kindergarten for 5-year-olds.

In addition to the "formal" types of care and education provided for young children, many children experience "informal" care through private arrangements between parents and caregivers, and informal and unlicensed after-school programs in elementary schools.

Use of Early Childhood Programs

Children Under Age 5

In 1989 (the last year for which detailed census data and day care and school enrollment data are available), 5 percent of infants and toddlers (children under age 3) were enrolled in licensed group or supervised family day care. Among 3- and 4-year-olds, an average of 19 percent of children were in licensed day care or nursery programs. By age 5, the percentage dropped to 11, as more children attended kindergarten. Thus, although the number of licensed spaces almost tripled between 1980 and 1989, only a small fraction of the total population was served.

Publicly supported kindergarten is available to 98 percent of Canada's 5-year-old children. In September 1991, New Brunswick began supporting kindergarten on a provincewide basis for the first time. Furthermore, the New Brunswick kindergartens are full day (i.e., 9:00 A.M. to 2:30 P.M.). Several provinces also support kindergarten for some 4-year-old children with almost one-half of the 4-year-olds in Canada reported to be enrolled in kindergarten (see Table 1). Statistics from provinces and territories report kindergarten attendance to exceed the population of 5-year-old children.[1] While this seems unlikely, it can be assumed that most children attend kindergarten at age 5.

Table 1 shows percentages of children from birth through age 5 in centers (day care and nursery school), licensed private home care, and kindergarten. (Some children may attend more than one type of institution.)

In addition to formal day care and educational programs, a substantial number of children receive nonparental care in their own and others' homes. Analyzing data from a 1981 survey of 18,000 families with 9,000 children under age 15, Biemller, Regan, and Lero (1987) found that 36 to 40 percent of children from birth to age 5 received in-home (19 percent) or private-home (18 percent) day care. While most children attended kindergarten for half-days at age 5, 36 percent still received informal care. More recent figures are not yet available,[2] but it is safe to assume that these percentages have not declined. Thus, more preschool children receive informal care than formal care.

Many young children receive both formal and informal care. The 1981 survey indicated that over 30 percent of Canadian 5-year-olds were attending kindergarten and receiving some other form of nonparental care. Again, it can be assumed that even more children are doing so now.

Children Age 6 and Over

The number of licensed school-age day care spaces has increased significantly during the 1980s. However, by 1989, the number of spaces represented less than 3 percent of children ages 6 to 12. This contrasts with 41 percent of children with mothers who were in the labor force or full-time students (National Day Care Information Centre,

TABLE 1

Canadian Children Ages 1 to 5 Receiving Licensed Child Care and Public Education (1989)

Age	Total[a]	% in Center Care[b]	% in Family Care[b]	% in Kindergarten[c]
0.0–1.4	545,000	2	1	na
1.5–2.9	543,000	5	2	na
3.0–3.9	362,000	1	1	na
4.0–4.9	362,000	3	1	45
5.0–5.9	362,000	0	1	95

[a] Population estimated on basis of 1986 census (Statistics Canada, 1987). This census indicated stable population growth for children from birth to age 5.

[b] National Day Care Information Centre (1990).

[c] Estimates based on Statistics Canada (1989). These estimates must be considered very rough enrollment figures and are not consistent with population estimates. Four-year-old kindergarten estimates are based on subtracting the population aged 5 from the enrollment figure for "5 and under." Note that some children attend both licensed care facilities and kindergarten.

1990). What did the remaining 39 percent who needed care do? The 1981 survey suggests that about 7 percent of elementary school children "cared for themselves," while another 6 percent were cared for by siblings. (It is expected that the 1988 survey will show larger percentages of elementary school children in self and sibling care.) The remainder were cared for by others in their home or in others' homes.

Jurisdictions

As in other countries, young children's programs in Canada fall under many different jurisdictions. Day care centers, nursery schools, and licensed after-school programs are under the jurisdiction of provincial ministries of social services or human resources. These are responsible for establishing standards, licensing programs, and ensuring that standards are met. Funding comes from provinces, federal matching funds, and municipalities (i.e., property taxes), as well as from fees.

Public schools, including kindergartens, are in all cases under different ministries in each province. Funding of public schools rests largely on local property taxes. Standards (regarding space and child-staff ratios) are often less demanding than those applying to licensed day care and are generally left to the local board to enforce. Partly because of complications arising from federal funding (which is channeled through social service ministries), many children "serve two masters"— their public or separate[3] school for three to six hours a day, and their day care for three to six hours a day. Mathien (1989) suggests that coordination between schools and child care centers is often less than perfect.

Program

Typical Day Care and Nursery School Programming

The content and structure of "typical" day care and nursery school programs in Canada do not differ markedly from those in the United States. Fairly traditional "child-centered" programs are common, incorporating a variety of activity centers plus some large-group, teacher-directed activity (mainly songs, games, and story reading). While there was some experimentation with "compensatory" programs during the 1970s (Fowler, 1978; Wright, 1983), there has been little during the 1980s. Most of the focus of attention has been on the supply of service rather than on the quality or effects of that service.

Family Day Care

In the day care field, Canada has been a leader in the development of licensed private home or "family" day care. Following the development of several services by nonprofit groups in the Toronto area, mechanisms for licensing and providing funding[4] were developed in the 1970s in many provinces. As of 1990, licensed family day care represented about 14 percent of the total number of day care spaces, including 45 percent of infant spaces and 25 percent of toddler spaces (National Day Care Information Centre, 1990). Despite Canada's role in implementing licensed family day care, the authors are not aware of any formal studies of the advantages or disadvantages of licensed family day care in comparison to center care.

Kindergarten for 4-Year-Olds

In public education there has been some experimentation with "junior" or 4-year-old kindergarten. In Ontario, about one-half of 4-year-olds were enrolled in junior kindergarten in 1986. At that time, local boards had the option of providing junior kindergarten with some provincial support. In 1989, the provincial government announced that junior kindergarten would be provided by all boards for all children by 1992. This appears to have been primarily a political decision—there have been no studies to support (or refute) this decision in terms of criteria involving the quality of education or care.

Full-Day Kindergarten

In public education, there has also been experimentation with full-day kindergarten programs. At least three boards in Ontario have used full-day (i.e., 9:00 A.M.–3:00 P.M.) kindergarten programs with a view to improving educational outcomes during the 1970s and 1980s. Two rural boards applied this approach to all kindergartens. A longitudinal evaluation showed no measurable effects with regard to achievement or behavior ratings by teachers in comparison to half-day and alternate full-day programs, either at the time of the program or up to four years later (Biemiller, 1983, 1985). The Toronto Board of Education has implemented full-day kindergarten for children from inner city (disadvantaged) environments. A complex formal study of the effects was conducted (Bates, et. al., 1982). Again, no meaningful effects were found with regard to achievement or observed behavior in comparable children attending half-day programs.[5]

Despite these outcomes, the province of Ontario announced in 1989 that it would extend funding for full-day kindergarten programs to all boards of education on an optional basis. In making this announcement, the Premier cited day care needs as the main motivation for the decision. This trend is discussed later in this chapter.

Language

Another area of program variation in Canada concerns language. As a bilingual country—(68 percent officially anglophone, the remaining 32 percent francophone (Statistics Canada, 1983))—Canada has been interested in promoting bilingualism. This has included the development of "immersion" programs in which English-speaking children attend school in either French-only kindergartens or in half-day English and half-day French programs.

In reality, there are many other languages as well. More than one-half of the children entering the Toronto and Vancouver school systems (major immigrant reception areas) come from families whose native language is neither English nor French. Thus, day care and kindergarten programs must be prepared to deal with children and parents from many linguistic backgrounds.

Trends in Early Education and Care in Canada

Day Care Expansion

As in many western countries, the continued trend toward higher percentages of working mothers implies a continued increase in children requiring various forms of extra-parental care (Lero, 1989). While the 1992 economic downturn may slow this process, it seems likely that the percentage of children with both parents (or a single parent) working will continue to rise. At the same time, this trend reduces the pool of women available as family day care workers. Combined, these trends will increase pressure for provision of group day care and demand for salaries and working conditions that will attract and keep day care personnel.

Use of Schools to House Day Care[6]

The combination of declining enrollment[7] and increasing pressures for day care in the latter half of the 1970s, led many school boards to embrace in-school day care. Priority was given to day care centers (for both in-school and preschool children) as space in schools became available. Funds were made available to assist programs in renovating space and with start-up costs. In Ontario, the number of schools housing day care operations increased from 25 to 800 between 1975 and 1989. Thus, over 30 percent of all public and Catholic elementary schools housed some form of day care. As of 1989, almost one-half of all licensed group day care spaces in Ontario were in public schools. In addition, a large but unknown number of children receive partial after-school care in unlicensed after-school programs, which offer a variety of hobby, sports, and other activities to children for one to five days a week. Comparable figures are not available for other provinces, but it is likely that similar trends have occurred. In Quebec, about 40 percent of all day care spaces are operated by the Department of Education. It is assumed that most of these are operated in school buildings.

Licensed Family Day Care

Licensed family day care has been a growing Canadian approach to supplying more day care, especially to infants, toddlers, and school-age children. Licensed care offers caregivers the opportunity to benefit from day care subsidies and input from a support team. It offers parents some security about the quality of care provided. As with other forms of child care, the future growth and quality of licensed family day care probably depend more on the nature of funding that will be available than anything else.

Issues in Early Education and Care in Canada

Need for Services

The need for child care services continues to grow. In 1989, the National Day Care Information Centre (1990) estimated for children of full-time working mothers and students, 10 percent of infants, 20 percent of toddlers (i.e., 18–35 months), 48 percent of 3–5-year-olds, and 7 percent of children over age 6 were served by licensed day care services. The percentage of mothers of young children who find it necessary or desirable to work has continued to grow (Lero, 1989). The need for child care services continues to grow correspondingly.

Who Pays

North Americans remain ambivalent about child care in general and paying for it in particular. Having seen personal income decline to the point where two incomes are necessary to maintain the housing and food conditions that one income would formerly support, while house prices have increased out of proportion to the cost of living, many more families require two incomes.

During the 1980s, Canadians were moving toward increased federal financial support for day care. However, recent budgetary problems and other political crises have returned child care to its usual low priority, and additional federal money now seems unlikely. Some provinces are continuing to increase day care funding. The federal government has promised a strategy on child care by 1992, but the thrust of this strategy is not known.

Staff

Child care wages remain extremely low (below wages for supermarket clerks, for example). Low wages result in high staff turnover and recruitment of relatively low-level staff. Recent efforts by the province of Ontario to supplement day care wages in licensed centers represent one attempt to help.[8]

The problem of attracting and keeping quality staff has been made more difficult by the fact that the educational system, having hired very few teachers for a number of years, is now hiring many as older staff retire. In the early 1970s, when the gap between pay in public education and public day care was small, a number of high-quality, selective training programs for day care workers (i.e., early childhood educators) were established in community colleges and universities in Ontario and elsewhere. The pay gap has widened markedly, while the demand for qualified day care staff has increased tenfold since the early 1970s. The result is that early childhood education programs no longer attract the able students they once did, and that programs can no longer afford to be "choosy" about whom they select. Conversely, few graduates now view early childhood education as a lifetime career, as indicated by high turnover rates.

Multiple Settings

More and more children are attending two or more nonparental care/educational settings. In 1981, over 30 percent of 5-year-olds were in two or more settings (Biemiller, et al., 1987). Most typically, multiple settings involved kindergarten plus in-home or private-home care. That figure is surely higher today, and includes many more cases where children participate in kindergarten and in-school day care. Anecdotal evidence suggests that there is relatively little communication between the school and other care settings. Surprisingly, the authors have found no research focusing on the issue of multiple settings, despite the prevalence of this situation in Canada.[9]

Private Enterprise

There has been a continuing debate concerning the role of private enterprise as a day care provider. In 1989, commercial operations provided 35 percent of all licensed day care spaces. This percentage declined from 50 percent of spaces in the past decade. However, the absolute number of commercial spaces more than doubled during the decade. Day care advocacy groups have argued before provincial and federal parliamentary committees that commercial operations provide less adequate care. Little research evidence has been developed demonstrating that children in commercial centers develop less adequately. An unpublished study for the Ontario government has indicated that private day care centers are more likely to fail provincial licensing standards. The effect of this on children could be extrapolated by applying findings from a large study by Ruopp *et al.* (1979) on the effects of group size and staff qualification on children to conditions maintained in some commercial centers. Possibly the most serious problem with commercial centers has been the consequences of low pay: high staff turnover and less adequate staff (the "rejects" from higher paying nonprofit and municipal operations).[10] The fact is that people "cannot afford" to pay what good day care costs. The question is whether child care should be subsidized like schooling, as part of a "social cost." If so, should commercial operations be subsidized?

Transitions Between Kindergarten and Elementary Programs

In at least two provinces (Ontario and Alberta), there has been an explicit attempt to blur or smooth the "transition" from kindergarten to grades 1 and 2.[11] However, the only research conducted has used teacher opinions of what should happen, rather than assessments of the effects of different models of transition on children's skills and behavior.

Implications of Increased Use of Schools for Day Care

While schools have always in effect served as child care centers during their normal hours of operation and are the best-equipped facilities for extended-day group care in most communities, the addition of care functions to schools has raised a number of issues.

1. *"Coordination" of Program and Children's Welfare.* Under both provincial and federal rules, schools are not allowed to operate child care programs. The usual solution has been to create a separate legal entity in each school responsible for running the day care program. As children move from one jurisdiction (school) to the other (day care), it is often difficult to ensure an appropriately balanced program over the course of the child's entire day. It is also sometimes difficult to ensure effective communication between the two settings about an individual child's problems and needs; the same holds true for communication between parents and the school or day care center (often it is only the day care staff who see the parents, rather than the school teachers).

2. *Staff Relations.* Day care staff are typically paid at much lower rates than teachers. In some cases, this leads to problems of status and creates other differences. The existence of two separate jurisdictions sometimes creates a "we/they" mentality on both sides. Closely related are problems of attracting qualified staff to a growing school day care system. With most positions low-paid and part-time, there may be serious difficulties in attracting staff who are able to provide an appropriate program. Paradoxically, the move to full-day kindergarten may exacerbate this problem. (Some full-time positions could be maintained when care for kindergartners was provided for five or six hours a day.)

3. *Sharing of Space.* With few exceptions, regular classroom space has not been "shared." Special facilities, such as gymnasia and libraries, are sometimes used by day care programs, as are outdoor facilities.

4. *"Curriculum."* As noted above, creating an appropriately balanced program can be difficult. This may particularly become a problem in full-day kindergartens. How a full-day kindergarten program might differ from a half-day program has not been much explored.

5. *Competition for Space.* In areas where school populations are growing, providing day care in the school may mean operating "regular" classes in portable classrooms located in the school yard. This may lead to further conflicts between school and day care personnel, and among parents using or not using day care.

6. *Funding.* When schools used "surplus space" for day care, relatively little additional cost was incurred as a result of the presence of day care. (Of course, savings from closing schools were missed.) Now that many schools and boards are operating at or over capacity, the true cost of adding day care services will be considerably more noticeable. In effect, by having schools provide facilities for day care services, some day care costs are carried by local property taxes rather than by provincial income taxes. In addition, federal capital subsidies for child care are not available to schools. This may result in shifting the burden of day care costs in "unfair" ways.

The move toward using schools to meet growing day care needs is in some ways very logical—schools have extensive facilities for appropriate child care activities and the children are there anyway. However, as the use of schools for child care grows, issues of "coordination," program, staffing, space, and funding will have to be resolved. One hopes that this "resolution" will place the interests of children's care first and institutional conflicts over territory and money second.

Summary

In recent decades, the significant changes in early childhood education in Canada have involved changes in the quantity of care available, and in where and how that care is provided to children. The clear trends have been toward increased use of school sites for day care (both for children attending school and for younger children) and increased use of licensed family day care. While these changes have had implications for the nature of the programs offered to children, little research has yet been published on this issue. (The only major "program" focus has concerned the transition from kindergarten to grades 1 and 2.) Focus on program issues has been lost in the scramble to provide more spaces as the demand for day care services grows.

Notes

1. An anomaly best explained by per capita financing of school programs.

2. The Canadian National Child Care Study is currently being undertaken by a team of researchers (including Donna Lero, Allen Pence, Hillel Goelman, and Lois Brockman) in collaboration with Statistics Canada. Detailed research reports are in preparation as of this writing (expected late 1991).

3. In Canada, "separate" or Roman Catholic schools are constitutionally required in Manitoba, Ontario, and Quebec.

4. Much provincial funding for day care is on a "per diem" basis. An individual parent who "qualifies" for complete or partial day care subsidy (based on income, family size, and other considerations) enrolls his or her child in a center. The center may then collect the partial or complete fee (up to some provincially fixed limit) from the province for each day the child is present.

5. This may not be surprising, since no systematic effort was made to modify the nature or content of the kindergarten programs.

6. This section is mainly based on information from Julie Mathien's paper, "Initiatives in School Age Child Care," presented at the annual meeting of the Canadian Association for Teacher Education, Quebec City, Quebec, June 1989.

7. Canada experienced a 20-percent decline in births between 1961 and 1981. Since then there has been a modest (2 percent) recovery and the current birthrate is stable. All of this resulted in a period of declining school enrollments.

8. Note that if the system moves to greater public financial support for day care personnel, the alternative of "subsidizing parents to stay home," or otherwise removing disincentives (e.g., loss of pension and social insurance coverage) may become more economically attractive.

9. Julie Mathien is currently conducting such a study for the government of Ontario. Another study is under way in Quebec by M. Baillargeon, R. Presser, E. Jacobs, and D. White.

10. Licensing could be used as means of keeping track of staff turnover, pay, etc. in commercial and noncommercial centers. The basic issue may not be "commercialism," but rather what the necessary conditions for quality care are and how to maintain them.

11. See Pain (1984) and the Early Primary Education Project (1985).

References

Bates, J., Death, M., Wright, E., & Vernon, J. (1982). *The full-day kindergarten study*. Toronto: Ministry of Education, Ontario.

Biemiller, A. (1985). *From kindergarten to grade four: a longitudinal study of thriving, average, and non-thriving children*. Toronto: Ministry of Education, Ontario.

————. (1983). *A longitudinal study of thriving, average, and non-thriving children from kindergarten to grade two*. Toronto: Ministry of Education, Ontario.

Biemiller, A., Regan, E., & Lero, D. (1987). Early childhood programs in Canada. In L. Katz, (Ed.), *Current topics in early childhood education*. Vol. 7. Norwood, NJ: Ablex Publishing Corp. (pp. 32–58).

Early Primary Education Project. (1985). *Report of the Early Primary Education Project*. Toronto: Ministry of Education, Ontario.

Fowler, W. (1978). *Day care and its effects on early development*. Toronto: O.I.S.E. Press.

Lero, D. (1989). *Child care needs and use patterns*. Paper presented at the National Symposium on Social Supports, Ottawa, Canada, March 1989.

Mathien, J. (1989). *Initiatives in school age child care*. Paper presented at the annual meeting of the Canadian Association for Teacher Education, Quebec City, Quebec, June 1989.

National Day Care Information Centre (1990). *Status of daycare in Canada, 1989*. Ottawa: Minister of Supply and Services, Canada.

Pain, K. (1984). *Articulation linkages: Children and parents in early basic education*. Edmonton: Planning Services, Alberta Education.

Ruopp, R., Travers, J., Glantz, F., & Coelen, C. (1979). *Children at the center*. ERIC document ED 168733. Cambridge, MA: Abt Associates.

Statistics Canada (1983). *1981 Census of Canada: Population, mother tongue, official language, and home language*. Cat. 92-910. Ottawa: Ministry of Supply and Services, Canada.

————. (1987). *The Nation: Age, sex, and marital status*. Cat. 93-101. Ottawa: Minister of Supply and Services, Canada.

————. (1990). *Elementary and secondary school enrollment, 1989–1990*. Cat. 81-210 annual. Ottawa: Minister of Supply and Services, Canada.

Wright, M. (1983). *Compensatory education: A Canadian approach*. Ypsilanti, MI: High Scope Press.

PRESCHOOL EDUCATION IN CHILE

• • • • • • • • • • ◆ • • • • • • • • •

Selma Simonstein Fuentes and
Maria Cristina Varas Aceituno
School of Education, Central University
San Bernardo, Chile

Historical Evolution of Preschool Education

Preschool centers were established in Chile as a result of the initiatives of German residents during the second half of the 19th century. Following his visit to Berlin, the Chilean educator Valentin Letelier recommended the creation of "kindergartens," while another educator, Jose Abelardo Nunez, translated Friedrich Froebel's *The Education of Man* into Spanish. But it was Leopoldina Maluschka, who worked for Nunez in his school, who made some of the most important contributions to the early development of preschool centers in Chile.

Maluschka was born in Austria and emigrated to Chile with her family in 1899. She began her teaching career in Valdivia and by 1902 had become a teacher of music and physical education in the town of Maule. In 1906, she officially took charge of Chilean preschool education when she became director of normal kindergarten education, a position that had been created for her in the normal school run by Nunez. In this position, Maluschka disseminated the fundamentals of Froebelian pedagogy and introduced the kindergarten to the Chilean educational system.

Maluschka was responsible for consolidating and systematizing the startup of various individual private nursery schools, adapting the Froebelian method to the Chilean setting, and training the first kindergarten teachers. She also published texts on preschool education and the monthly journal *The National Kindergarten in Chile*.

The teaching method developed by Maria Montessori was introduced in Chile in 1925 through articles published by don Guillermo Labarca and his wife Amanda Labarca. These articles were the beginning of a widespread interest in the Montessori method by Chilean educators, who were particularly impressed by the emphasis placed on observation and experimentation by the educator, the expression of children's individuality, and the development of children's autonomy. They were also interested in the Montessori method because it focused on the importance of children's direct contact with nature and on the development of their senses. The Montessori movement in Chile reached its peak between 1927 and 1952 when many educators attempted to apply the new methodology to their own teaching practices. In its time, it was an important milestone in preschool education because it approached children's education from a scientific perspective.

The first institutions for preschool education were established in Chile as a result of the initiatives of foreign communities living in Chile. In 1900, two preschools were created and given governmental support. The first popular kindergarten operated only one year, between 1910 and 1911, due to its funding structure (private donations) and the criticism kindergarten education in general was receiving. While there were 101 state-supported kindergartens in 1913, many were subsequently closed due to a withdrawal of governmental support for the education of preschool teachers. Following this withdrawal of funding, various individual and private efforts were made to establish preschool education centers.

By 1948, there was a significant increase in preschool enrollments—a 48.8 percent increase compared with the previous year. This pattern continued between 1948 and 1958. Enrollments increased by 55.08 percent between 1952 and 1958. But in 1960, the actions of the Ministry of Education resulted in the closing of many centers. Between 1964 and 1970, the government's attention to preschool education increased, culminating with the passing of Law No. 1730, in April 1970, creating the *Junta Nacional de Jardines Infantiles*. As soon as this legal body was created, there was a positive quantitative development in preschool education.

Educating Preschool Educators

Due to the efforts of Matilde Huici Navas from Spain, the School of Preschool Educators in the *Universidad de Chile* was created in 1944. This school initially had an experimental character and depended directly on the support of the Rectory headed by don Juvenal Hernandez.

Thanks to the innovative position taken by Huici regarding what should constitute a preschool teacher's education, the school was oriented toward the following objectives: giving children security through an appropriate affective environment, balancing the deficiencies of the home environment, assessing the effect of teachers' activities on the child, and selecting the activities that best fulfilled educational goals. To achieve these objectives, it was necessary to strengthen

teachers' training in physiology, psychology, ethics, and nutrition, among other areas. The result was that Huici emphasized a multidisciplinary approach to the training of preschool teachers. This approach included emphasis on both theoretical and practical issues. Preschool teachers were taught that their role was to protect the child, facilitate the child's overall development, motivate the development of positive values in the child, and provide a liaison between the home and the educational institution.

In 1945, due to demand for preschool teachers, normal schools were also established in the cities of Serena, Angol, and Santiago. With the passing of time, however, the normal schools were closed and preschool teacher training was assumed exclusively by the universities. In 1981, a law regarding the universities was passed that affected, among other areas, teacher training. Teacher training is now no longer exclusively undertaken in the universities but can also be undertaken in private or fiscal academies or institutes. As a consequence of this law, beginning in 1982, there are now private institutions that train preschool teachers, including the *Universidad Central* and *Universidad de Gabriela Mistral*. These two universities have specialities in training preschool educators. Nevertheless, many of the universities that receive state support continue to teach preschool education throughout the country, although it is expected that their programs will eventually be eliminated by those in the private universities.

Educational Objectives of Preschool Programs

The first program for the preschool level was established in 1948 to promote objectives that merely reflected the general objectives of Chile's primary education program. The goals of the preschool level were to promote physiological development and the formation of habits regarding hygiene and personal security; and to increase observation skills, spontaneity, and receptiveness to learning.

In 1958, this program was revised and directed specifically toward children ages 4 to 6. This new program emphasized a greater independence of learning for preschool-level children in relation to the objectives set for primary education. It also focused on the setting of objectives based on the specific characteristics of children at this earlier stage of development, centering the education around the child, with the educator in the role of facilitator, and harmonizing the learning skills taught in the preschool center with those of the home. The new program was further concerned with the organization of teaching units and the establishment of a systematic means whereby the program could be evaluated. Several programs were established under these guidelines, including: transition (1974); infant care (1980); and middle and primary level of transition (1981). The three programs are similar in their concepts of early childhood education and curriculum. The three programs are similar in their concepts of early childhood education, the role of the educator, and curriculum. They differ in a number of ways, including structure, their position regarding teacher training and professional development, the formulation of objectives, the educational level of instructors, the freedom given to teachers to plan their own programs, and in the extent to which they use formal evaluation.

Institutions Serving Preschoolers

Law No. 17,301 passed on April 4, 1970, created the National Junta of Preschool Centres (JUNJI). The JUNJI is an institution of major influence because of the numerous children attending its centers: in 1989, enrollment reached 59,000 children. In the same year, the provision of preschool education in other governmental agencies was as follows: National Foundation of Help to the Community, 47,000; CAEDL, 10,500 (CAEDL is an agency set up to stimulate and support new pedagogy for preschool centers); and the National Committee of Preschool Centres, 4,000. There are also Chilean preschool centers that are dependent on the Ministry of Education and that function as part of the primary schools, and there are preschools in private centers. These nongovernmental institutions accommodated approximately 8,000 children in 1989.

Chilean Preschool Education in the International Environment

Since 1956, Chile has been represented in the World Organization for Preschool Education (*Organizacion Mundial para la Educacion* or OMEP). The year 1956 was also the year that the *Comite Nacional Chileno* was formed. This committee is the Chilean branch of the international organization. Since its inception, this committee has participated in various OMEP efforts by disseminating specialized texts on preschool education; organizing events (e.g., seminars, meetings); participating in conferences and national and international seminars; and in general, participating in all initiatives that help children and improve preschool teachers' education.

PRIMARY, OR BASIC, EDUCATION IN CHILE

• • • • • • • • • • ◆ • • • • • • • •

Mario Zambrano Bobadilla
School of Education, Central University
San Bernardo, Chile

Before 1965, basic education in Chile was called primary education. Its development in Chile is similar to that of other countries in that it is affected by the political, socio-cultural, and economic conditions of the country. This chapter discusses the evolution of basic education in Chile in light of these factors. This overview is incomplete due to the limited space available and the large amount of information available on this topic. In addition, the framework used to present the available facts may be criticized by some.

Evolution of Basic Education in Chile

The first schools were established by the Spaniards at the time of the Conquest and were run by religious communities (the Franciscans in 1533, Dominicans in 1591, and Jesuits in 1593). Beginning in 1811, Chile, as an independent state, began to restructure its educational services. Accordingly, the Republic, in the political constitution of 1833, included education as a service provided by the state.

But it was not until 1842 that a real effort to construct a national system of education began, with the foundation of the first *Escuela Normal de Preceptores*, the first normal school in Latin America, begun with the effort of the Argentine Domingo Faustino Sarmineto. In 1854, the first normal school for girls was founded under the direction of the religious order of nuns, *Sagrado Corazon de Jesus*. These nuns contributed to raising teaching to the level of a scientific discipline. Before that, teachers knew little more than reading and writing and taught because they had no other career opportunities.

In July 1856, the Society of Primary Instruction was founded by altruistic people of the era as a result of the poor state of primary instruction. This contributed to the expansion of the teaching profession by creating new schools.

Before 1860, the school-age population was neglected. There was a strong division among the social classes between those in power and the popular masses. The higher classes attended the private schools, and the public schools were attended by children of artisans or laborers. In 1833, there were no more than 20 public school buildings. By 1860, the public schools were nationally funded and increased to 486. In 1852, the children who attended school numbered almost 9,000; by

1860, this had increased to more than 23,000.

The law of 1861 declared public education as free and mandated that separate schools for boys and girls be established in each district with more than 2,000 inhabitants. The curriculum was traditional Christian doctrine, reading, writing, arithmetic, drawing, geography, history of Chile, and the constitution of the state. For girls, the two latter subjects were replaced by home economics (e.g., sewing, needlepoint). Between 1880 and 1912, primary instruction prospered due to the increased interest of the community and various distinguished educators.

This was a period of modernization of the teaching profession. Chilean teachers traveled to Germany and perfected their skills and learned systematic pedagogy with an emphasis on didactic techniques. The German inspiration contributed to the professionalization of teaching but also reinforced the authoritarianism and formalism that existed in the schools.

Between 1912 and 1938, the middle classes aspired to obtain control of the educational system and favored a democratic process of national development, which had many difficulties and setbacks. These changes contributed to the enactment in 1920 of the first law of compulsory primary instruction, which also reaffirmed the control of the school system by the state.

Despite the economic crisis of the time, the educational system continued to expand, although a low priority was assigned to it. In 1915, 306,000 children were registered in primary public schools; in 1926, 436,000; and in 1928 registration reached 525,000. Nevertheless, in 1933 it decreased to 397,000. The level of registration for 1928 was only reached again in 1940.

From this era came the financial support of the *Juntas de Auxilio Escolar* (school boards) at the municipal level. In 1936, the Society for Educational Establishment was created. Until 1927, 15 normal public schools and some private schools graduated approximately 300 primary teachers per year.

In 1923, the first significant union for teachers was formed: the General Association of Primary Teachers. It fought for the integral reconstruction of education under the influence of libertarian and social ideals. It envisioned a new pedagogy and fought for a school climate that was permissive and open to nature and to the surrounding community; programs based on the interests of the children and their functional needs; and active and cooperative methods of learning. These ideals were not accomplished given the authoritarian context of the government at the time.

Nevertheless, there were concessions allowing the creation of experimental schools in order to test new methods. Between 1938 and 1961, with gains on the popular front, the middle-class groups consolidated the control of the educational system and the sectors of urban laborers began to gain an easier access to the school system. As in previous times, developing and improving education were the responsibilities of the state.

In 1953, the Superintendency of Public Education was created. Its goal was to give an integral and technical foundation to educational development. This expanded the level of participation, since representatives included governmental authorities, professional organizations of teachers, parents, private educators, and the business community. The organization of professors coordinated by the Federation of Educators of Chile lobbied for the democratization and modernization of teaching. Private education was favored by the system of state subsidies but served only a small proportion of the population.

Between 1940 and 1957, primary education increased from 554,00 to 880,000 children. At this time there was an expansion of the number of schools in the countryside and in the communities surrounding the cities. This educational expansion brought with it the creation of new normal schools, and the universities expanded their teacher training. There was a growth in financial resources earmarked for education but they were not sufficient to guarantee that the expansion would improve the quality of the teaching.

Because the expansion of the system was not planned, it generated discontent and created the conditions that introduced techniques of planning for the future. Between 1961 and 1970, with the purpose of planning, there was a delay in the educational development in relation to the other demands of Chilean society and a resurrection of a technological option to confront the educational problems. There was also evidence of an effort toward expansion and modernization in all levels of education, which culminated with the educational reform of 1965 to 1970.

In this reform, the traditional school system's structure of six years of basic education was replaced by eight grades of general basic education. Between 1961 and 1970, registration of basic education increased from 1.371 million to 2.044 million children. In 1961, 83.6 percent of children between ages 8 and 14 were registered in these schools and in 1970 more than 96 percent of children were registered. The expansion of the system made access to the system universal and incorporated into the first grades children from urban and rural areas, as well as working and other classes. In 1964, a national system of scholarships and grants was created which enabled equal educational opportunities, improving the quality of education and subsidies given to the school-age population. To increase the registration, special programs were developed to train teachers.

In 1967, teacher training became more rigorous and scientific. The reform initiated in 1965 did not only alter the organization of the educational system but also introduced a new curricular concept based on the theories of Benjamin Bloom and Ralph Tyler, adding some views and applications of the modern educational technology. To materialize the pedagogical reform the Center of Experimentation and Pedagogical Investigation was created in 1967. This was aimed at massive in-service training of teachers and the development of educational research. The period between 1970 and 1973 was characterized by the inauguration of the Allende's government of the Unidad Popular.

In some ways the educational reforms that occurred during Allende's regime had continuity with the previous period. The process of expansion that had begun earlier reached a maximum. It spread widely with the participation of the popular sectors in the infrastructure and the control of the education. New projects were started to change the way in which young children were introduced to school, and to improve the content of the primary curriculum.

During this period, the bureaucratic educational administration of the earlier period was replaced with one that allowed the educational system to advance through equalitarian efforts and new educational politics. The educational authorities tried to increase the aspirations of the working masses and developed with them an educational plan that conformed to the general program which aimed at creating a noncapitalist society. These efforts were thwarted by the traditional administration and the political opposition, which resulted in the fall of this regime.

During this three-year period, the educational system reached its maximum expression. It was possible to gain full enrollment for children between ages 6 and 14, increasing the registration of basic education from 2.044 million to 2.316 million. There was an increase in the hiring of teachers who were legally recognized in their union organizations. They were given fundamental teaching in educational issues, their salaries were increased, and their professional development possibilities were widened.

At the end of 1972 a project was developed for the *Escuela Nacional Unificada*, which proposed a profound restructuring of the educational system in order to overcome the traditional segmentation of social classes in the educational system. In the educational realm specifically, it was proposed that the personality of the students be developed through general and polytechnical education. It was hoped that students would develop skills, concepts, attitudes, and values favorable to productive labor, democratic cohabitation, and social compromises.

The project's goal was the formation of a national conscience to be promoted through a scientific conception of man and nature and a view of consumption as being productive and characterized by solidarity. The presentation of the report about the project's results given by the *Escuela Nacional Unificada* in January 1973 generated severe criticisms focusing on ideological and political factors. The government was accused of taking away the freedom of teaching and making the school an instrument of manipulation. This criticism forced the government to terminate the project.

The military government of 1973 to 1989 was oriented toward the establishment of a new social order where the market is postulated as the basic regulatory mechanism of the social community. Not being elected voluntarily by a majority, it was induced politically and militarily with force. The previous compromise of democratic and participatory character supported by the popular masses was replaced by an authoritarian state of repressive character supported by military force. The government took possession of the educational system and began the process of ideological purification through which it expelled many teachers who were involved with the government of the Unidad Popular. The programs of study were revised and the texts considered ideologically dangerous were eliminated from the libraries. The foundations of the educational politics can be summarized as follows:

• The military government maintains authority regarding the content of what is taught and it is prescribed that education be politicized with the objective of forming good workers, good citizens, and good patriots.

• The government restricts its social responsibilities regarding ensuring that all have access to basic education. Those who want to attend basic and secondary schools must pay, since it is a privilege to do so (this was contrary to the principle of equity of opportunity which had been established in the past).

• It is decided that the state's role in education be transferred to the private sector. This does not impede the government from maintaining its normative and fiscal functions requiring authoritarian methods of education. The subordination of education to the market is to be reinforced.

In June 1980, the initiative was taken to transfer the administration of public education, centralized in the Ministry of Education, to the municipalities. At the same time, a more accentuated role for the private initiatives in educational tasks was promoted. Due to the lack of existing democratic mechanisms for the municipal authorities, the municipalities faced great obstacles in attempting to efficiently administer education and meet the needs of the users. There were no channels for effective participation between the community and the municipal administration. These circumstances, instead of promoting the participation of the community in education, tended to reinforce the mechanisms of authoritarian control above them. On the other hand, the mechanisms for giving greater control to the municipalities caused the danger of accentuating the inequities that existed in conditions of the population and the resources that different municipalities had. During the military government, there was a significant decrease in the growth of educational funding that

had been maintained in the past. The private educational sector increased its relative weight and public education suffered.

Presently, there are three subsystems of basic education: the fiscal municipal, the private sector which is subsidized, and the private sector which is not subsidized. These subsystems have significant differences in the quality of teaching they provide, resulting in the best education being provided to those who are not subsidized (i.e., the smaller proportion of registration within the system and those from families with great economic resources).

With respect to the modalities of basic education, in addition to the regular system of eight grades to which the majority of the children attend, there are other modalities to satisfy special sectors of the population. Among these are the following:

• multi-grade schools in which the same teacher teaches children of various grade levels (this type of school exists where there are not enough children to justify a second teacher or one classroom per grade);

• basic accelerated education which allows children over age 15 to cover two grades of material in one year;

• education of native children, which assumes the existence of bilingual teachers;

• education for groups of children with learning problems;

• special education schools for children with various disabilities; and

• schools with free examinations for children who have received private education and have not attended regular schools.

The efficiency and efficacy of the basic educational system seem to be at a low level. Only 70 percent of children finish grade 4 and barely 50 percent complete grade 8. Further it is calculated that one-third of the children never learn to read and write, add and subtract, thus remaining illiterate throughout their lives. The educational practices have not been sufficiently modernized, methods that insist on routine activities (e.g., copying and dictation) persist, and very often children are forced to memorize and repeat without comprehending. Children are rarely urged to use their imaginations or to ask about or find solutions to their own problems.

This leads to the need to review teacher training. Beginning in 1965 post-secondary institutions with courses lasting for two years were reviewed and now they have been increased to three years and more.

At the end of the 1960s, the remuneration of teachers was increased. This encouraged those finishing high school with good grades to opt for this career. Recently, however, the level of remuneration has deteriorated and many of those who apply do so not because of vocation but because their grades do not allow them to opt for other opportunities of professional training. This is reminiscent of the former *Escuelas Normales,* which stressed vocational aspects and had an ambience of a boarding school that guaranteed extensive contact between students and teachers. As a result, students were inspired with a mystical attitude toward their work, which positively influenced the children and their communities. The evidence of the efficacy of these schools is that following the sudden closure of the *Escuelas* in 1917, the *Escuela Normal de Ancud* was reopened in 1985 as an experimental school in order to train teachers for children in rural areas. This experience will likely provide a vehicle for correcting the errors that should never have occurred. If this experiment is successful, it could lead to the reopening of other normal schools. In any case, the correction of errors committed in teacher training presents the need to examine the foundations on which it is based, including the political and economic factors involved.

SPECIAL EDUCATION IN CHILE

● ● ● ● ● ● ● ● ● ● ◆ ● ● ● ● ● ● ● ● ●

Hernan Ahumada Aldoney and Shelma Soto Sanchez
School of Education, Central University
San Bernardo, Chile

Special education in Chile is an educational sub-system that ranges from regular levels or courses at the preschool level to workshops for adolescents and young adults. It is guided by the philosophical principles that characterize the entire educational system. One principle is that all individuals have a right to education. As stated in the *Compen dio de Normas*, "Each citizen must have the opportunity to develop themselves integrally as a person and as an active member of a progressive society oriented toward the common benefit. . . ."

Special, or differential, education is aimed at children and youngsters with auditory or language deficits; visual or motor disabilities; mental retardation; specific learning disabilities; behavioral problems; or multiple disabilities. Its general objective in Chile is to enable children who have difficulties to participate in the normal educational process so that they can be successfully integrated into society.

Historical Background

From the mid-1800s until the beginning of the 20th century, the education of the disabled was not systematic. Disabled individuals were attended to in hospitals or, in some cases, by people who attended to their educational needs as a form of charity or goodwill. During this period, systematic special education in Chile focused on only those who had the more obvious disabilities (e.g., the deaf or the blind). It was not until 1920, when the obligatory primary instructional law was enacted, that the principles of obligatory and free education for all were emphasized. But because the infra-structure was not equipped with the necessary human resources to effectively implement the law, it was difficult or almost impossible to integrate normal children into the educational system, let alone children with disabilities.

To alleviate this situation, special instruction was given to "normal" children with major learning difficulties. For others, "special classes" were created, which, according to some critics, caused significant disciplinary problems and much school absenteeism. As of 1925, special schools were created specifically for the educational needs of children with deficits.

But meeting the educational needs of children with deficits was a process that continued very slowly. Until 1946, in addition to the special school for development and the school for the blind and

Translated from Spanish by J. Bernhard.

deaf mute, there were only two special schools in the entire country. Between 1947 and 1959, psychoeducational groups focusing on education and health were created. In 1953 a course for the deaf was established in the city of Valparaiso at the Van Buren Hospital. A school for children with mild mental retardation had been created in Santiago in 1928—one of the first such schools in Latin America. Most of these initiatives were developed in collaboration with the Ministries of Health.

Until the 1970s, an era that witnessed a significant increase in special education, special education was essentially based on a medical model rather than a pedagogical model. Children with mental and physical differences were mainly seen as patients rather than students, in spite of the fact that these differences were permanent rather than temporary as is the case with sickness. This situation came into question, however, with publication of the Review of Education by the Ministry of Education in 1974. The highlights of this document are summarized below:

1.   There are indications that approximately 4 percent of the total school-age population has some mental handicaps; about 1 percent has physical disabilities; and about 0.2 percent audio-visual handicaps. The schools that specifically deal with these conditions today are only 1.6 percent of the total schools.

2.   Because it was shown that special education lacks official plans and programs specific to each handicap, a new decree of education (No. 1358) was enacted on March 6, 1967.

3.   To date, there are 50 schools for mental conditions, serving about 50 percent of those with these conditions.

4.   There are nine schools for those with auditory or language retardation, serving 8.7 percent of these handicaps.

5.   There are three schools for those with visual handicaps, serving about 3.6 percent of those with these conditions.

6.   There are two schools for those with motor handicaps, serving about 8.6 percent of those with these handicaps.

Toward the end of the 1970s and the beginning of the 1980s, the Ministry of Education became much more involved with the issues concerning special education. Plans and programs for each disability were made official: for mental handi-

caps, according to Decree No.310 of 1976; for oral language, according to Supreme Decree No. 148 of 1980; for visual handicaps, according to Supreme Decree No. 175 of 1980; for auditory handicaps, according to Supreme Decree No. 15 of 1981; and for specific reading-, writing-, and arithmetic-related disabilities, according to Supreme Decree No. 143 of 1980. In 1984, the Ministry of Education published a set of norms for special education according to Resolution No. 3323 of December 27, 1983. This document contains specific plans and programs, technical and pedagogical structures, and outlines their relation to general basic education.

From this short history, it is possible to appreciate how quickly special education in Chile has grown as a service and in the quality of the options currently available. The goal is to bring special education into line with the regular educational politics, so that the number of people being served will increase. It is also hoped that attention will be given to improving the pedagogical practices involved in integrating with a view toward normalization. Particular attention should be paid to the means and specialized resources available for those who are disabled and who will be attended to in the regular educational system. Through various initiatives, it is hoped that educators will be able to attend to their needs, respecting the feelings and needs of students, parents, teachers, and the community.

Training for Special Education Teachers

The first course for specialized teachers for the disabled was created in 1964. This two-year course was aimed at professionals in education (i.e., teachers of basic education and early childhood educators). The entrance examination was developed by the Institute of Psychology of the *Universidad de Chile,* which allowed the course. The teachers and students accepted received a commission of service from the Ministry of Education so that they could pursue their studies full-time.

This first course was formed out of the dissatisfaction of Professors Don Abelardo Iturriaga and Jean Cizaltti. Don Lepoldo Donnenbaum, who provided special education in a private school, joined the team of professors. In 1967, and with the same basis, a course for instructors of the deaf was created. In 1970, the course for instructors of the blind was also added.

The diversification in instruction, the increase in the number of students, and the increased preoccupation regarding special education led to these courses becoming independent of the Institute of Psychology. The new autonomous center, which was formed in 1971, depended on the faculties of both philosophy and education at the university. Beginning in 1971, two types of students were admitted: students under scholarship from the Ministry of Education (post-graduate) and undergraduate university students. As a result, the courses were transformed into a university undergraduate career. As of 1974, the course was extended to four years of full-time study, with a progressive system of credits, thereby leading to the title of state teacher of special education. At the same time, a fourth special was created relating to learning disabilities.

Beginning in the 1970s, other Chilean universities have also begun to offer this course of training. Among them are the *Universidad Catolica de Chile*, which has a master's in learning disabilities (LD); *Universidad Austral de Chile* in Valdivia, with an undergraduate degree in mental disabilities; *Universidad Catolica de Valparaiso,* which has an undergraduate degree in LD; *Universidad de Tarapaca* in Arica with an undergraduate degree in mental disabilities; *Universidad de Talca,* with specialty in LD; and the *Universidad de Concepcion* with a specialization in mental disabilities since 1985.

As of the 1980s, teacher training for students with learning disabilities and the mentally disabled is also being offered at the universities above as well as at the *Professional Institute Blas Canas; Instituto Profesional Educares; Instituto Profesional de Providencia;* and others.

EARLY CHILDHOOD EDUCATION IN THE PEOPLE'S REPUBLIC OF CHINA

• • • • • • • • • •◆• • • • • • • • •

Zihixin Laing and Lijuan Pang
Department of Education
Beijing Normal University
Beijing, China

History of Chinese Early Childhood Education, 1949–90

The development of early childhood education in China in the 20th century corresponds to China's political history. It can therefore be divided into four stages: (1) "the steadily advancing stage," (2) "the unplanned growth and consolidation stage," (3) "the seriously damaged stage," and (4) "the stage of restoration and vigorous growth."

The First Stage

"The steadily advancing stage" (1949–57) corresponds with the eight years immediately following the establishment of the People's Republic of China. The years include the three-year economic restoration period (1949–52) and the first five-year-plan period (1952–57). Early childhood education progressed rapidly during these years.

An important first step was the formation of policies for developing Chinese early childhood education. In December 1950, the Cultural and Educational Commission of the Government Administration Council of China approved a report by the Ministry of Education that suggested that the two kinds of preschool institutions in China, the nursery school and kindergarten, be under the administration of the Ministry of Health and the Ministry of Education, respectively. The nursery school was responsible for children under age 3, while the kindergarten admitted children ages 3 to 7.

Guidelines for kindergartens, elementary schools, and normal schools were established at the First National Conference on Elementary Education and Teacher Education convened by the Ministry of Education in 1951. The aims of the kindergarten were to both educate and provide child care. As a result, it was decided that kindergartens should be full-time, that summer and winter vacations would be cancelled, and that entrance examinations would be discontinued.

The conference also established two general developmental principles for early childhood education. The first was that early childhood education should be developed according to a plan that takes into account the needs of different regions and the diversity of urban and rural areas. According to this principle, known as "consolidating, improving, and developing," development occurs first in the factories and other enterprises and second in the schools, suburbs, and countryside.

The second principle stressed the need to rely on the support of local authorities and various mass units—such as trade unions, women's federations, and relief unions—to facilitate the development of early childhood education. Thus, early childhood education was guided by local interests and the state in a principle known as "walking on two legs" (Liang, 1985).

In October 1951, the Ministry of Education conducted the first reform of the Chinese educational system. As a result, early childhood education was made a part of the educational system as the first level. Early childhood education was mainly provided in kindergartens, which admitted children from ages 3 to 7. Children were grouped into three classes according to age (3- to 4-year-olds, 4- to 5-year-olds, and 5- to 7-year-olds). This enabled all children to develop both body and mind before they entered the primary school. It also reaffirmed that kindergartens should be established gradually, first in the cities under the right conditions, and then in other areas.

Under the guidance of these policies and the Ministry of Education, the number of kindergartens gradually increased over the next decade. For example, in 1957 there were 16,420 kindergartens in China, an increase of 12.6 percent over the maximum before liberation (Liang, 1985).

Chinese Kindergarten Reform. Shortly after the founding of the People's Republic of China, the Chinese government began to reform the old early childhood education, which was based strongly on semifeudal and semicolonial styles. At that time, the Soviet Union was helping China to conduct social and economic reconstruction. Beginning in 1950, China started to learn from Soviet preschool educational theories and experience and to develop a new Chinese preschool education.

In September 1950, the Ministry of Education called on preschool educators throughout the country to learn from the Soviet preschool educational guidebook and curriculum. In 1950 and 1956, the Ministry of Education invited two Soviet early childhood experts to China to introduce the Soviet's then current preschool educational theories and practices by giving lectures and direct guidance to several experimental kindergartens. In 1956, the Department of Education at Beijing Normal University, under the auspices of the Ministry of Education and under the guidance of Soviet experts, drafted *The Guidebook for Kindergarten Education.* It elaborated on the goals, tasks, curriculum, teaching methods, and organization of early childhood education in China. The book integrated Soviet educational theories and experience with Chinese preschool educational practice. It represented a major shift in the practice of kindergarten education in China.

Kindergarten Administration and Teacher Training. At the end of 1949, the Early Childhood Education Division was formed as a department of the Ministry of Education. It became the central administrative institution for the management of early childhood education in China. At the same time, corresponding early childhood educational sections, consisting of a group or an individual, were set up in provincial, municipal, regional, and rural areas as the bureaus responsible for early childhood education at various levels (Liang, 1985).

In 1956, the Ministries of Education and Health further clarified the administrative principle of combining centralized unified administration with diversified administration by local governments. It was stipulated that the state was responsible for nursery schools and kindergartens, and for their educational policies, rules, regulations, plans, standards, curriculum, and child health care. The local health and educational departments, authorities, enterprises, and various mass units were responsible for funding, personnel, buildings, equipment, and hands-on executive administration. In addition, the local health and educational departments were required to regularly observe and supervise their local preschool educational institutions and to provide them with help and guidance.

At the same time, the Chinese government developed an early childhood staff training system. From 1952 to 1955, preschool educational specialities were established at higher normal universities as well as at preschool normal schools. Various educational departments of government and different regions developed diversified forms of in-service training programs, (e.g., teaching and research groups, teacher networks, lectures on special topics, and observations of model teachers).

In sum, between 1949 and 1957, Chinese

early childhood education developed in both quantity and quality. Moreover, this early period provided a base for continued development of Chinese early childhood education by making available large numbers of preschool teachers, administrators, and researchers.

The Second Stage

The second period in the development of early childhood education is referred to as the "Unplanned growing and consolidating stage (1958–65)." Beginning in 1958, through the influence of the extreme left, there was unchecked growth of preschool education in China. This growth was due to the unrealistic aim of "popularizing nursery schools and kindergartens within 35 years." As Liang (1985) indicates, by 1958 there were 695,297 kindergartens in China, 42 times more than in 1957. By 1960, kindergartens numbered 784,905. Kindergarten expansion was so rapid during this period that funding was strained to the limit. As a result, equipment, facilities, and materials in most kindergartens at this time were quite simple and crude, and teachers were untrained in early childhood education.

Political thought during this period in China's history was critical of traditional preschool educational techniques and philosophy. For example, stressing developmental characteristics was criticized as having a "children's focus"; attention to nutrition and hygiene as adopting a "capitalist's life style"; recognition of nature, art, and music as assuming a "capitalist's mood"; using materials and toys was termed "using objects instead of people," thereby demonstrating a "lack of basic feeling and respect"; and emphasizing play was referred to as an "interest focus." As a result, curricula for preschool education became arbitrary and adult-oriented and the quality of early childhood education suffered.

The Chinese government was aware of the repercussions of leftist principles on early education. In 1961, the Ministry of Education proposed that the focus of kindergartens be on quality and not on quantity. It urged putting the main focus of developing preschool education on improving the quality of kindergarten and on consolidating low-grade kindergartens. It insisted that kindergartens follow developmental principles and sound edu-

cational practice. After a period of hard consolidation and improvement, preschool education began a new normal development.

The Third Stage

The third period in the development of early education in China, corresponding with the beginning of the Cultural Revolution, is the "seriously damaged stage" (1966–76). The Cultural Revolution shifted the focus of preschool education to promoting "revolutionary thoughts" in children. As noted by Sidel (1982), from the late 1960s to the mid 1970s "the values and attitudes taught in preschool facilities in China . . . were some of the clearest expression of the policies and politics of the decade dominated by the Cultural Revolution." During the Cultural Revolution, the goal of preschool education was to involve children in "revolutionary criticism" and military training (Liang, 1985; Gentry, 1981). The teaching of elementary knowledge and the developing of children's intelligence were replaced by reciting and memorizing poems and quotations from Chairman Mao. Physical education stressing hygiene and the development of motor skills was replaced with giant gymnastic exhibitions and organized sports.

At the same time, the existing system of preschool administration was dismantled. Preschool normal schools were closed and in-service training was stopped. A number of kindergartens were either closed or had parts of their buildings and spaces occupied by other agencies. Many experienced teachers and directors were not permitted to teach and were reassigned to new jobs. There were prohibitions against producing educational materials. During this period, Chinese early childhood education was devastated. The number of kindergartens was greatly reduced, and the quality was seriously affected.

The Fourth Stage

During the "restoring and vigorously developing stage" (1976–present), the political focus has shifted to developing and modernizing China's economy (i.e., structure). Education, and in particular early education, has become an important part of this goal.

In 1979 in Beijing, the Ministries of Education and Health, the State Labor Bureau, the All-China

Federation of Trade Unions, and the All-China Women's Federation sponsored a national conference on nursery school and kindergarten work. Administrators, early childhood educators, and other experts discussed the future of preschool education in China. The widely distributed *Summary of the National Conference on Nursery School and Kindergarten Work* identified six key issues: (1) strengthening leadership and administration, (2) securing adequate funding, (3) reaffirming the principle of "walking on two legs," (4) restoring nursery and kindergarten organizations, (5) rebuilding teacher training programs, and (6) emphasizing the quality in health care and education for nursery and kindergarten children.

The goals of the 1979 National Conference were endorsed by the Chinese government, the Ministry of Education, and later, the State Education Commission. More recently, the State Education Commission established Management Regulations for Kindergartens (1989) and Work Rules for Kindergartens (draft version, 1989).

A number of achievements have been made in early education in the past decade. The Early Childhood Education Division of the Ministry of Education has been reestablished. A new kindergarten curriculum based on developmental principles has been introduced on a trial basis. Teacher training institutions at all levels have been restored. Since 1978, normal colleges and universities systematically revived and set up preschool educational specialities to train normal school teachers, early childhood researchers, and administrators. In addition, the provinces, municipalities, and autonomous regions have all gradually restored normal schools to train preschool teachers. Secondary-level health schools have reopened their maternity and child care specialities.

In 1984, there were 47 preschool normal schools in China; in 1985, there were 57. In several large cities, provinces, and municipalities (e.g., Beijing, Shanghai, Tianjing, Jiangshu, and Shichuan), there are two to four preschool normal schools. The enormous efforts to develop a workforce of professional preschool teachers have been a major contributor to the renewed growth and quality in early education in China in recent years.

Preschool research institutions and organiza-tions have also been established. In 1979, the National Preschool Education Research Association was founded as the first nationwide organization devoted to preschool research. By 1985, 26 provinces, municipalities, and autonomous regions in China established their own preschool educational research associations.

Also contributing to preschool educational research in China is the Early Childhood Education Research Division of the Chinese Central Education Research Institute, which was founded in 1978. Research sections also exist in regional education research institutes.

These tremendous efforts have brought about concrete results. In 1984, there were 66,000 kindergartens. Three years later, in 1987, there were 176,000 (Liang, 1988).

Current State of Early Education in China

The goals of early education in China are consistent with the goals of Chinese education in a more general sense. That is, the task of early childhood education is to provide children with an education in physical, intellectual, moral, and aesthetic domains, to enable them to develop healthy bodies and minds, and to prepare them for primary school.

In conforming with these goals, early childhood education in China provides children with comprehensive educational content in eight areas: (1) habits of hygienic living, (2) physical activities, (3) morality, (4) language, (5) natural and social common sense, (6) mathematics, (7) music, and (8) art. The areas can be further categorized into four groups: habits of hygienic living and physical activities; morality; language, mathematics and natural and social common sense; and music and art. Morality and language are described below in detail.

Morality

Morality includes teaching children to love the motherland, its people, and their families. Children are also taught to love their kindergarten, teacher, and classmates. Morality also includes teaching children to love work, and more specifically, working within the collective. Another aspect of moral education is the development of respect for public property. In the kindergarten, this is demonstrated through the responsible use of materials. Morality also includes the development of altruism, sharing, modesty, the ability to accept criticism, honesty, respect for adults, the use of social manners, hospitality, and a sense of optimism and confidence.

Language

Language is part of a larger area, which includes mathematics and natural and social common sense. This area of the curriculum emphasizes intellectual development, while at the same time, children are also educated in important aspects of morality and beauty.

Language instruction consists of six main aspects. The first is to teach children to pronounce clearly and correctly and to learn to speak the standard language (*potonghua*). Children of national minorities learn to speak the language of their nationality. The second is to enrich children's vocabulary. The third is to develop expressive language, that is, to educate children to give clear expression to their own wishes and thoughts and to speak without inhibitions. The fourth is to develop descriptive language (e.g., teaching children to describe the content of a picture). The fifth is to foster enjoyment in listening to stories, and in singing songs, to learn to understand the main content of a task, to learn the essential plot of texts, and to recite 25–30 simple poems and to retell 8–10 simple stories. The sixth involves the development of a love of books as well as listening to children's programs on the radio. Children are required to be able to relate part of the content of the books and radio programs.

Educational Activities and Methods

Chinese preschools only partly resemble primary schools. Until recent years preschools were organized around six main lessons: gymnastics, language, mathematics, common sense, music, and art. Lessons were taught in a formal manner, with teachers standing in front of the children, the children sitting below or around the teacher, and discipline being stressed. However, formal pre-

school lessons are not the only activity of children in China. Children also observe, play, and work as part of their daily lives. In addition, in more recent times, lessons take the form of play, especially for younger children.

In both the youngest and middle classes, children's interest is maintained through a variety of methods, including the use of audiovisual materials and games. Even with the older children, who are being prepared for primary school, play is still the most important form of lesson. This view of play as the basic educational activity for young children is consistent with the Ministry of Education's document Work Rules for Kindergartens (1989). An example of this principle at work is the use of dramatic role playing in language and mathematics lessons. Playing "marketing," "zoo," or "farm," children develop their language ability and number concepts.

Although most kindergarten activities in China take place with all children at the same time, it is becoming more common to use the small-group method. Play, therefore, has an extremely important place in Chinese early childhood education.

In addition to formal lessons and play, observation is a commonly used educational experience. It is an important way for children to acquire and understand direct experience of nature and society, and to develop their attention, observation, and cognition skills. It is the foundation of the teaching of various subjects. For example, in art education, teachers encourage children to draw, paint, or model based on their careful observation of the forms, colors, structures, and relationships of objects and phenomena, in order to express the most important features of them.

Work and daily life are two other common methods of educating children in Chinese kindergartens. The goal of "work" is to foster good morals and habits in the children so that they love and can be proud of work, are willing to serve others and the collective, and to develop their capacity to be independent and to carry on simple manual operations.

"Daily life" includes the routines of the children's day. The morning greeting, cleaning activities, outdoor play, lunch, nap, snack, field trips, supper, and departure provide teachers with educational opportunities. In Chinese kindergartens, there is an "on-duty system" during daily life which, beginning from the middle class up, organizes all children in one class into several (usually six) groups. Each group is on duty one day per week (Chinese kindergartens are open Monday to Saturday). On-duty children are responsible for a variety of daily tasks (e.g., cleaning tables, watering plants, feeding birds, cleaning up toys, setting tables at meals, and distributing teaching materials).

The "duty" system is designed to rear moral and disciplined children. Children generally enjoy their duty days to the extent that if they are absent on "their" day, they often ask to participate with another group.

Current Issues in Chinese Early Childhood Education

Although great progress has been made in Chinese early childhood during the past three decades, there are still problems to confront. Partly because of the vastness of the country and partly due to the diversity of teachers' professional levels, the quality of programs is inconsistent. In different programs some aspects of the curriculum may be emphasized while others are largely ignored. Moreover, some teachers maintain a more traditional focus. For example, in mathematics, some teachers focus on teaching children to count to very high numbers and to master addition and subtraction, rather than fostering flexible, divergent, or creative thinking skills.

Similarly, many Chinese kindergartens are highly structured with activities initiated, regu-lated, and terminated by teachers. Even in play, the topics, themes, roles, and procedures are arranged by teachers. The children simply follow the teacher's lead and obey the teacher's requirements and the regulations. Many parts of the children's daily lives (e.g., morning free activity, walks, games, field trips, group lessons, and observations) are under much of the teacher's direction and control, which goes far beyond suggestion and guidance.

Collective activities, rather than individual or free activities, are consistently stressed. Children in a class tend to engage in the activities simultaneously in most of the kindergarten day. For instance, all children may be engaged in painting the same picture, singing the same song, folding the same shape, or creating the same block structure.

The typical model of teaching is for teachers to speak and children to listen, teachers to demonstrate while children watch, and teachers to ask while children answer. If children can listen quietly so that the teacher can carry on the lesson smoothly, and if children can correctly recite a rehearsed answer, some teachers consider themselves successful.

However, as has been stressed throughout this chapter, Chinese early childhood education is undergoing slow reform. For example, program time spent in collective activities is gradually decreasing. Play and the active exploration of materials are increasingly viewed as the primary source of children's learning. There is also an attempt to build a more process-oriented, integrated curriculum, in which "multi-educational projects" (Chao, 1986; Song, 1984) provide the focus for student learning.

References

Chao, Q. (1986). My opinions about multi-education. *Early Childhood Education*, 1, 2–5.

Gentry, J. M. (1981). Early childhood education in the People's Republic of China. *Childhood Education*, 58, 92–100.

Liang, Z. (1985). Early childhood education after the founding of the People's Republic of China. *Early Childhood Education*, 6, 42–48.

———. (1988). *Early Childhood Education*. Beijing Normal University Press.

Shun, A. (1985). Current reforming in early childhood education. *Early Childhood Education*, 4, 2–5.

Sidel, R. (1982). Early childhood education in China: The impact of political change. *Comparative Education Review*, 26, 78–87.

Song, Y. (1984). Early childhood education reforms in China. *Early Childhood Education*, 5, 10–13.

Zhen, M. (1986). Promoting reforms in early childhood education. *Early Childhood Education*, 2, 2–4.

PRESCHOOL EDUCATION IN COSTA RICA

• • • • • • • • • • • ◆ • • • • • • • •

Irma Zúñiga Leon
National University
Heredia, Costa Rica

Background to Costa Rican Preschool Education

Preschool education began in Costa Rica in 1878 with the schools for preschoolers. These schools, which were fundamentally religious in nature, were not government administered. In 1916 the director of the Normal School of Costa Rica , don Omar Dengo, made the government aware of the lack of official attention being paid to preschool-aged children. Subsequently, in 1919–20, three teachers were sent to study in France, England, and Spain: Lillia Gonzalez, Matilde Carranza, and Maria Isabel Carvajal (Carmen Lyra). They returned to Costa Rica with a great wealth of materials and extensive knowledge regarding the methods of Maria Montessori and Frederich Froebel on active approaches to early childhood education.

They had serious difficulty, however, in implementing their ideas, since the government, for ideological reasons, did not support them. After many attempts, Lyra was successful in persuading don Jorge Urena, senior official of the Ministry of Development, to find funds for furnishing a preschool. Unfortunately, Professor Miguel Obregon Loria, the Secretary of Education at the time, ordered the furnishings to be given to a school of

a religious order. It was not until 1924, that Lyra finally succeeded in obtaining authorization for the opening of the first secular preschool, *La Escuela Maternal Montessoriana*.

In keeping with her philosophy, Lyra visited the poorest subdivisions and counted the children who were under age 6, with the goal of forming the first group of students for her preschool center. The next government, headed by Ricardo Jimenez Oreamuno, lent substantial support to this new school. With the enthusiastic help of don Ruben Coto, an official at the Ministry of Development, the building was repaired and furnished.

The Escuela Maternal Montessoriana opened on April 20, 1925, with two groups of children. The school staff included Carvajal, director and teacher; Luisa Gonzalez, teacher; Margarita Castro, music teacher; and Consuelo Alvarez, concierge.

In addition to developing the educational, artistic, and health programs for the children, the staff spent some afternoons with the Mothers' Club in such activities as health and nutrition seminars, sewing lessons, and medical conferences. Doctors Antonio Pena Chavarria and Julio Ovares provided the children with free medical attention.

In 1928, don Ramiro Aguilar, Inspector of

Translated from Spanish by J. Bernhard.

Schools, attempted to close the institution, since he considered the budget to be inadequate to cover the necessary costs. Closing was prevented by don Ricardo Jimenez, President of the Republic, and Professor Luis Dobles Segreda, of the Ministry of Education.

A committee was formed in 1930 to erect a new building by a system of selling shares; various distinguished citizens and journalists participated. The initiative, however, was endangered when Lyra, the director of the school, was accused of being a communist. (Years later, she was ordered to leave the country for this reason; she later died in Mexico).

Some years later, Arturo Urien, another preschool center, was formed in honor of the Argentinean ambassador of that name. Urien had provided great support to the Montessori school, which adjoined the school Garcia Flamenco. The next preschool to be built was Jardin de Ninos Omar Dengo. Luisa Gonzales, its director, had written a work of social criticism and was removed for political reasons. In 1935, other preschools were formed that functioned in connection with specific primary schools. There also existed certain semi-official preschool centers that charged a monthly fee.

In 1966, the Universidad de Costa Rica assumed direction of preschool teachers' education. The first preschool teachers graduated in 1970 from a program that combined preschool and primary education. Due to the initiatives of the National Preschool Board of the Ministry of Education, courses were offered in 1967 in the methods and arts in the kindergarten. On its own initiative, the Escuela Normal of Costa Rica, at about the same time, began to offer short training courses for primary teachers who were working with preschool children.

The Law of Education in the Costa Rican Political Constitution (dated September 24, 1957) outlined the following objectives of preschool education:

- to protect children's health and stimulate their harmonious physical development;
- to promote the development of good habits;
- to stimulate and guide childhood experiences;
- to cultivate aesthetic feelings;

- to develop attitudes of sharing and cooperation;
- to facilitate the expression of the child's internal world; and
- to stimulate the development of observation abilities.

In 1967, the Assembly of Preschool Education was created. At the same time, the National Plan of Educational Development declared preschool education a priority and proposed the progressive expansion of services in rural areas. The goal was to serve 33 percent of the population by 1980. This prioritization gave major importance to small children and enriched preschool education by creating Nutrition Centers. The nutrition centers were transformed into nutrition and education centers, which operated in close cooperation with the Ministries of Health and Education. The latter committed itself to providing the necessary human resources and to creating 20 new positions each year. The children were to be fed by the Ministry of Health. The main objective of the expansion of services was to complement nutritional and educational aspects and eventually to extend this to the community at large.

In 1971, as a result of completion of the diagnostic plan for national education, as well as general attempts to qualitatively improve education, it was discovered that there were no official educational programs at the preschool level. The only available help was the teacher's guide prepared by the National Preschool Assembly in 1965. Faced with this situation, cognitive and effective objectives were specified for each level in the educational system so that children could be measured and evaluated. According to these objectives, each level was to be completed according to the psychological and social developmental stages of the students being educated.

In 1972, the first year of the program, 525 children attended nine centers. In 1979, there were 244 centers nationwide, staffed by 244 teachers and an enrollment of 6,000 children. This was a considerable growth which significantly fulfilled the educational needs of preschool children. In fact, these programs have become the most important in the nation, benefitting children in both urban and rural areas.

In spite of these valuable initiatives, the work was not sufficiently coordinated, and the political aspects sufficiently defined, to avoid duplication of efforts, to regulate private initiatives, and to encourage parent participation in preschool centers. For this reason, in 1973, a law was passed to clarify terms and to develop a national plan for educational development. In the same year, the following was established through the *Proyecto de Ley General*:

Article 17: Preprimary education is the first step in the formal educational system. It consists of a systematic education aimed at initiating the child into social interactions that are broader than that of the family and placing the child in conditions favorable to embark on later studies.

Article 18: The aims of preprimary education are

a. To help children in their physical and mental development, helping them to form balanced and harmonious personalities.

b. To augment children's experiences and to initiate them in the development of dexterity and basic skills through play, cooperative work, observation of nature, and contact with their environment.

c. To develop the natural abilities of children in order to enhance the free expression of their personalities.

d. To socialize children toward generosity and voluntary cooperation.

e. To augment the children's formation of habits, attitudes, and values that allow positive adjustment to the social environment.

Article 19: To attain the above goals, preprimary education shall attempt:

a. To allow children of disadvantaged backgrounds to reach an adequate level of verbal abilities in order to compensate for their cultural deprivation.

b. To detect the accidental physical, psychological, and social deficiencies of the children to allow for early correction through therapeutic actions.

Article 20: Preprimary education is to attend, normally, to children between ages 5 and 6. It is not mandatory, but the state will attempt to make it available to all families, particularly those in rural and marginal areas.

Article 21: . . . the Ministry of Public Education, in coordination with other competent ministries and organizations, will enhance parents' abilities, in this decisive period of education ranging form birth until the first level of formal education (Gamez, 1981).

In 1975, the Regional Advisory of San Jose (Asesoria Regional de San Jose) was created. The positive acceptance of the previous programs and the preoccupation with children who had to remain alone due to their mothers' absence during the day, led to increased attention on providing formal education to 6-year-olds. This led to the creation of Infant Centers for Nutrition and Integral Attention (CINAIs). The first 12 centers opened in 1975, and were attended by approximately 200 children. Since the preparation and education of the personnel working at these centers were undertaken by the universities, it was possible to count on adequately trained personnel. Although the beneficiaries, community members, and various political figures stressed the importance of preschool education, the work was problematic due to insufficient resources.

The Centers of Education and Nutrition (CENs) were established for Costa Rican children under the Ministry of Health and the Ministry of Education. Their goals were to provide food and psychological and social stimulation to enhance the children's overall development. These centers serve a dual function: as educational centers and as providers of social services. They are situated in rural and urban areas throughout the country. The children going to these centers must meet the following four requirements: (1) be between 6 months and age 6, (2) live within one kilometer of the center and have transportation to and from it, (3) be within the economic conditions specified by the Ministries concerned, and (4) be under medical supervision.

The members of the Nutrition Committee are democratically appointed in a community meeting. This committee is in charge of administering the money that the Ministry of Health provides to the center, buying food, repairing the buildings, purchasing educational materials, and paying personnel. In addition, the committee undertakes various fund-raising initiatives.

CINAIs are part of a program run by the Ministry of Nutrition and the Ministry of Health. They have greater financial support than the CENs since they have a larger staff who provide care throughout the day. The CINAIs have three general objectives. The first is to promote the socioeconomic, educational, and physical well-being of the children in an integrated manner. The second is to promote family and community participation in the activities that enhance health, education, and nutrition. And the third is to promote the development of policies that integrally protect

Costa Rican preschool children.

The specific objectives of the CINAIs are as follows:

1.   to provide the opportunity for overall development to malnourished children, those at risk of being malnourished, or those suffering from maternal deprivation;

2.   to offer initial education to the children in the program;

3.   to offer education as a substitute for family education to children of women and families who work during the day;

4.   to offer education as a substitute for family education to children whose families have severe socio-economic problems;

5.   to organize and educate families regarding health in order to promote their well-being; and

6.   to offer nutritional loans to families at risk.

In general, the CINAIs offer preschool education for the 5-year-olds enrolled in the program and provide overall attention for 2- to 4-year-olds. In addition, they encourage social promotion of the family and the community and promote cultural, social, and work-related issues in collaboration with corresponding programs. Education in health and nutrition through short courses is also offered. The centers also provide complimentary meals, including, breakfast, snack, and lunch.

To qualify for the services provided by the CINAIs children have to meet the following requirements:

1.   be abandoned by the mother due to her work, medical treatment, alcoholism, drug addiction, prostitution, delinquency, or other socio-economic or physical problems;

2.   belong to a large, low-income family, or one with various preschool age children;

3.   have some physical or mental defect that requires specialized attention; and

4.   be between ages 2 and 6.

As with the CENs, the committee of the CINAIs is appointed by the community and is in charge of all financial activities from fund-raising to administering funds.

Present Functioning of the CENs and CINAIs

The CENs and the CINAIs have gradually evolved in various areas which are described below.

Physical Plant. There are standards for the physical plant that are established by the Ministry of Health, depending on the type of center. Nevertheless, in some communities where centers have not yet been built, they are in different buildings, depending on the available resources. Not all the communities have equal economic resources and therefore, not all the CENs and CINAIs are structured the same way. The minimal prerequisites that must be met when opening a CEN or a CINAI are a garden where children can play freely, a classroom, an eating area, a kitchen, two storage areas (one for food, the other for materials), offices for the staff, washrooms and sanitary services, and, above all, a great deal of light and ventilation.

Financing. The CENs and CINAIs are presently funded by family allowances, a portion of the taxes, and donations from the Ministry of Education, which consist of milk and various foods.

Committee of Nutrition. The Committee of Nutrition is in charge of finding funds for the functioning of the center in order to purchase foods, educational materials, and materials and labor for renovation of the premises.

Other Preschool Programs

Day care centers were established by the Ministry of Labor and Social Security in 1959. This service is free to the working family for children who have no adults to care for them during the day. These centers are in industrial sectors where the necessity for this type of service has been proven. This allows laborers to work without being preoccupied, is beneficial to employers in reducing absenteeism, and is stimulating for the children in that they participate in activities relating to recreation, art, language, concept acquisition, games, dance, and music. The day care centers operate from 6:30 A.M. and 6:00 P.M. There is a sliding fee, which is determined by a social worker, based on the economic situation of the home. The enrollment in 1989–90 was around 43,527 children in the kindergartens, 12,000 in the CENs and CINAIs, and 9,015 in day care centers.

Philosophy and Guidelines

In 1965, the first efforts for an official teacher training program were initiated. Up until that time, guidelines were developed yearly by the personnel in each institution. The first teachers' guide entitled "Teaching in the Preschool," appeared in 1967. The goal was to promote the growth of a democratic society through children's participation in games, tasks, and communication, and by allowing children to collaborate with each other and with adults who provided gratifying and significant experiences. Such experiences could include the resolution of conflicts, experimentation, search for information, and creative expression of thought and feelings as a basis for learning. In addition, there were attempts to attend to physical, emotional, intellectual, and social needs as a way of helping children to achieve their potential. There were also directions regarding the combination of short active periods, alternated with periods of rest.

In 1972, a new teachers' manual was published; it was entitled "Preschool Education." Although many of the previous guidelines were included, this guideline was organized with a view toward children's abilities, skills, habits, and attitudes.

In 1982, the manual still in effect today was published. It reflects a view of development as a continuous process that must be attended to by the educator in order to help children develop their potential and form their personalities. Activity is the method and motivation of the system. The proposed objectives are aimed at helping children feel secure and acquire experience that will allow them to incorporate themselves into the systematic process of education and acquire specific skills and basic knowledge. Enhancing the children's emotional, social, physical, and psychological development is also emphasized. Ultimately, the goal is for children to arrive at primary school with better training. This program suggests an organization around centers of interest. In 1988, an alternative plan was proposed in order to include the new curricular ideas of this area and the emphasis was on the "process" of learning as opposed to the accumulation and transmission of knowledge. Unfortunately, this plan has not been formally implemented due to a change in government.

In summary, the preschool programs in Costa Rica reveal the influence of the most notable educational theorists: Jean Jacques Rousseau, Heinrich Pestalozzi, Froebel, Montessori, Ovide Decroly, Rosa Agazzi, and Rachel and Margaret MacMillan. More recently, the work of Jean Piaget has been a notable influence at all levels of the educational system.

Teacher Training

As previously mentioned, in 1966 the Universidad de Costa Rica combined courses in primary and preschool education to train preschool educators. In 1977, a new study plan was implemented whose content was specific to the preschool level.

Another initiative in the preparation of preschool teachers was begun in 1968 in the old Normal School of Costa Rica. This involved an in-service course for primary school teachers who worked with preschoolers. This course offered a B.A. in preschool education in 1973, the same year in which the career of preschool educator was officialized. To meet the needs of the CENs and the CINAIs, the teachers were trained to assess children's developmental levels, to plan and evaluate programs of early stimulation, and to develop activities that would extend into the community. This plan of study was revised in 1978 with specific requirements for entry into the program, course prerequisites, and co-requisites.

Since 1987, there has also been another plan of study, entitled "Science of Education," with an emphasis on early childhood education. After obtaining the 66 credits required for the diploma under this plan, graduates are able to work in private or public centers. To obtain a bachelor's degree, 65 additional credits must be earned for a supervisory position. For a graduate degree, 36 more credits must be earned to do research work. To be accepted into the program, the applicant must pass a series of tests (e.g., proof of knowledge, personality, ability, reading, spelling, and composition tests) and be interviewed. There are about 200 applications annually of which 35 are accepted.

Another program is that of the University of Distance Education in Administration of Children's Social Services. It offers technician, diploma, bachelor's, and graduate degrees. This program combines studies in administration, community services, and the elaboration and execution of projects. Due to the nature of this university, it is possible to reach many isolated areas of the country where other institutions of higher learning are not available.

More recently, private initiatives have centered around the Autonomous University of Central America. These plans of study are characterized by the speed with which it is possible to obtain a degree. The academic degree is granted once the student has accumulated a minimum residency of 72 academic units and has successfully completed comprehensive exams.

PREPRIMARY AND PRIMARY EDUCATION IN CYPRUS

• • • • • • • • • • ◆ • • • • • • • •

Antonis Papadopoulos
Ministry of Education
Nicosia, Cyprus

Preschool education in Cyprus started with the English colonization of the island in 1878. The colonial government financed and organized nursery schools in cooperation with local educational authorities. By 1932, there were 44 nursery schools in Cyprus. In 1933, the colonial government decided to exclude preschool education from the state educational system, leaving it entirely to private initiative and enterprise. The responsibility of the government was then limited to supervising the existing nursery schools. The result was a decrease in the number of nursery schools to 15 in 1934. From 1933 to 1960, the existence of preprimary education relied entirely on private initiatives. Nursery schools and some day nurseries for children of the poor were established by voluntary or charity organizations, or in some cases public institutions such as municipalities or mining companies.

From Independence to the Turkish Invasion (1960–74)

In 1960, the British ceased occupation of Cyprus. The recognition of the importance of the first educational experiences in the subsequent life of the individual and the growing concern about the quality of preschool provision were significant issues from the very beginning of the Cyprus Republic.

According to an official investigation of early education at the time of independence, 48 preschool units were in operation, some at nursery schools and others at day nurseries or children's centers. The units were staffed by 73 teachers and provided care and education for 2,373 children ages 3 to 4 1/2. The majority of teachers were unqualified.

The curriculum consisted mostly of sedentary, manipulative, and repetitive activities; group games; songs; poetry; reading; writing; and arithmetic for the purpose of helping children bypass the first grade of the primary school.

On the basis of the committee's recommendations for the improvement of preprimary education, the first official Regulations for the Operation of Private Nursery Schools, known as Regulations 5/61, were approved. For the first time, standards were set for the physical plant, materials and equipment, staff qualifications, and teacher-pupil ratios. The educational program was described in terms of principles, activities, and teacher responsibilities.

Nursery schools were placed under the educational authorities of the state, while day nurseries or day care centers became the responsibility of the Department of Welfare Services of the Ministry of Labor and Social Insurances. Primary school inspectors began to visit nursery schools for inspection and guidance. In 1960, only 14 of the existing preschool units met the new standards for teacher qualifications.

The government's concern for the preprimary education in the 1960s focused on developing a systematic model of supervision and guidance and organizing in-service training courses. The first public nursery school was established in 1961 in collaboration with a charity organization in Nicosia, the capital of Cyprus. Due to budgetary restrictions, the planned expansion of public nursery schools was subsequently limited to one nursery school in each of the six towns and three large rural communities. During the same period, schools in the private sector continued to increase in number (see Table 1).

TABLE 1
Post independence Growth in Preschool Services

Year	Government Nursery Schools	Private Nursery Schools	Day Nurseries (under the auspices of the Department of Welfare Services)
1961–62	1	14	NA
1962–63	6	15	NA
1963–64	6	—	NA
1964–65	9	—	NA
1965–66	9	—	NA
1966–67	9	26	20
1967–68	9	31	35
1968–69	9	33	35
1969–70	9	29	38
1970–71	9	37	56
1971–72	9	30	51
1972–73	9	31	71
1973–74	13	37	67

NA = Not available

The Private Schools Law of 1971 established standards for private nursery schools. It required that the establishment and operation of private nursery schools be approved by the Minister of Education. Centers had to meet standards for buildings, equipment, staff qualifications, pupil-teacher ratio, and program quality. In general, the years from 1961 to 1973 were characterized by slow but steady development of nursery education. A major contribution to improved quality was the introduction of nursery education as one of the third-year electives for elementary school teachers at the Pedagogical Academy of Cyprus, the island's teacher education institution.

Nursery Education From 1974 to the Present

In 1974, the Turkish invasion divided the island and brought its northern section, amounting to 40 percent of the total, under Turkish occupation, a situation that remains to this day. Following the invasion, 200,000 refugees fled to the south. The shift of peoples from their ancestral homes changed the socio-economic conditions of the country and increased the demands on the government to relieve refugees; parents and children were particularly vulnerable.

As a result, the government established public nursery schools in refugee camps between 1974–76. The schools were an attempt to compensate for the agony and horror of the invasion, to provide the refugees with security, to relieve the deprivation of refugee camps, and to provide support, as well as child care, for overburdened mothers.

The early refugee nursery schools operated in tents and prefabricated huts in the camps. Their role was educational as well as humanitarian in the sense that they offered care, education, and companionship to children and at the same time they offered relief and encouragement to refugee parents. The refugee camps were gradually closed as families were relocated, and the nursery schools were transferred to refugee housing estates where the families were living.

The immediate post-invasion period saw several important achievements in preprimary education:

• the establishment at the Pedagogical Academy of a separate branch for the education of nursery school teachers in 1975;

• the approval of a plan for the expansion of public preprimary education by the Council of Ministers in 1979;

• the development of a nursery school curriculum of nursery schools in 1981;

• the appointment of two inspectors for preschool education in 1977 and 1980;

• the secondment of teachers to act as advisers in nursery schools; and

• the establishment of community nursery schools in addition to the public and private schools.

These developments are discussed below.

Teacher Education

Until 1974, most teachers employed in public nursery schools and as directors of private nursery schools were diploma holders of Kallithea College for nursery school teachers in Athens or primary school teachers trained at the Pedagogical Academy of Cyprus. Graduates of the latter attended special courses in preprimary education during 1961–63 and 1972–75.

Following a decision of the Council of Ministers, a two-year course for nursery school teachers was instituted at the Pedagogical Academy in September 1975. The program was later extended to three years, thereby equalizing the status of primary and preprimary school teachers.

Expansion of Public Nursery Schools

According to the 1979 expansion plan for public preprimary education, 300 public nursery school classes were to be established over a four-year period. The classes would serve 7,000 children ages 4 1/2 to 5 1/2. The expansion was deemed necessary for a number of factors:

1. the new role of the mother in society, her need for self-actualization, and the need for her to contribute to the family budget;

2. the consequences of the new socio-economic conditions imposed by the Turkish invasion;

3. the urbanization of many agricultural families and their housing conditions in flats as well as the limited experience of children during a crucial period of their life;

4. new theories in educational psychology that demonstrated the importance of early experience;

5. the need for equality of educational opportunities for all children, with special concern for refugee children and children from deprived homes; and

6. the importance of early diagnosis and provision for children with special needs.

To achieve the intended expansion within the economic possibilities of the state, the government decided to pay the salaries of nursery school personnel and a small subsidy for educational equipment (U.S. $180 annually), while the communities would provide the building, maintenance, and basic equipment.

Nursery School Curriculum

Throughout the decade, private nursery schools were operated according to the 1961 regulations. Because many teachers in Cyprus were trained in Greece during this period, the curriculum was heavily influenced by the very structured and rigid Greek public nursery school curriculum. The regulations of 1961 also needed adjustment and modification in the light of new trends and theories concerning the development and education of young children.

In 1979, a new curriculum for preprimary education was developed. The technical committee included inspectors on behalf of the Ministry of Education and representatives from the Pedagogical Academy, the Pedagogical Institute, and the Teachers' Union. The curriculum was published in 1981 and is currently being evaluated and revised. (The curriculum is described later in this chapter.)

Inspection of Nursery Schools

According to the 1961 regulations, nursery schools were to be supervised and inspected by primary school inspectors. The expansion of preprimary education increased the need for guidance of teachers, in-service training programs, and teacher evaluation. As a result, two inspectors with special qualifications in preprimary education were appointed to oversee standards in nursery schools, one in 1977 and one in 1980.

Preprimary Education Advisers

To assist the inspectors, a number of experienced teachers act as advisers for preprimary education. Their services are particularly needed by teachers who work in single-teacher schools or schools in remote rural areas.

Present State of Preprimary Education

Today there are nursery schools operating throughout Cyprus, all under the jurisdiction of the Ministry of Education. There are three categories of nursery schools: public nursery schools, community nursery schools, and private nursery schools.

Public nursery schools are established by the Ministry of Education in collaboration with parents' associations and community authorities. The Ministry of Education appoints the teaching staff and subsidizes the equipment. The parents' associations or community authorities are responsible for the physical facility and the basic equipment. They also employ the school janitor, who acts as a teacher's aid. While teachers are all qualified, school janitors/teacher's aids are high school graduates.

Community nursery schools are established and operated by parents' associations or community authorities. They are registered with and subsidized and supervised by the Ministry of Education. They are staffed by qualified nursery teachers.

Private nursery schools are established and operated by individuals with the approval of the Ministry of Education. They operate according to the Private Schools Law No. 5/1971.

All three categories of nursery schools develop

TABLE 2
Nursery School Expansion in the 1980s

Year	Number of Schools
Before 1979	50
1979	120
1980	180
1981	210
1982	220
1983	230
1984	239
1987–89	269

their educational programs according to the officially approved curriculum. As of 1990, there are 184 public (with 269 classes), 97 community (125 classes), and 169 private nursery schools (221 classes). The expansion of the public sector planned for in 1979 is still underway (see Table 2).

The most recent development has been the government's decision to raise the subsidy for community nursery schools. The intent is to offer immediate support to small, rural communities to establish their own nursery schools and to slow the expansion of the public sector.

Nursery Schools and Public Day Care Centers

Nursery schools are seen as educational institutions. There is continuity in terms of philosophy, goals, and practice between their educational program and that of the primary schools.

Day care centers are separate institutions for preschool children. Their primary aim is to offer care and protection to children beginning at age 6 weeks through age 5 1/2, at which time they enter the primary school. Centers are registered and inspected by the Department of Social and Welfare Services of the Ministry of Labor and Social Insurance.

Nursery School Curriculum

The nursery school curriculum was published in 1981 by the Ministry of Education in the same volume as that of primary schools. Both preprimary and primary education are governed by the Director of Primary Education. Thus, there is a continuity between the two programs.

The 1981 curriculum for primary education was a revision of the old curriculum on the basis of new information in the areas of education, psychology, and technology. However, the 1981 nursery school curriculum was the first curriculum developed in Cyprus for preschool children. The nursery and primary school curricula are organized according to the objectives discussed below.

The general aim of education is set by the state on the basis of the national, religious, and cultural heritage; socio-economic conditions; and international, scientific, cultural, and educational achievements. Its purpose is to create free, democratic, self-actualized citizens, who have developed spiritually, are cultivated morally, and are industrious and creative. They are expected to contribute to the social, scientific, economic, and cultural development of the country and to international understanding, cooperation, freedom, justice, and peace among the nations.

More specifically, the basic objectives of primary education are the following:

• to develop the full mental, physical, and emotional potentials of the pupils by helping them acquire the knowledge, skills, and attitudes necessary for contemporary life;

• to allow pupils to develop a proper understanding of the world through the systematic observation and study of the surrounding natural and social phenomena;

• to teach pupils history, particularly national history, and the achievements of civilization;

• to train pupils to use language correctly and to develop their ability to express themselves clearly and precisely;

• to encourage pupils to develop (1) love for their country, humanitarian ideals, and democratic attitudes; (2) respect for work, social conscience, and responsibility; (3) conscious discipline and ability to safeguard and exercise their rights; (4) understanding and respect for other people's ideas, initiative, cooperation, and friendship; and (5) their interests, talents, and inclinations;

• to help preserve and develop the pupil's health and the necessary skills and attitudes to maintain their health;

• to provide pupils with an aesthetic education and systematic acquaintance with national and international art works.

As mentioned above, preprimary education in Cyprus is part of general education. The importance of early experiences justifies the need for a well-organized preprimary school education offered in the nursery school. Thus, formal early childhood education supplements the work of the primary socialization agent, that is, the family. Such early formal education is of particular importance to children with special needs.

Preprimary education is also considered a measure of social justice and a possible remedy for social or cognitive impoverishment. To this end, the nursery school is geared to satisfy the educational needs of children through a wealth of activities. Preprimary education is considered a right and not an obligation of the child. It is therefore open to all but not compulsory.

The aim of preprimary education, as defined in the curriculum, is to facilitate the children's adjustment to school and to contribute to their socialization and all-around development. Goals and objectives for children are listed in a general manner, as discussed below.

The teacher is expected to translate the general objectives into instructional ones, expressing them, when possible in behavioral terms. In doing so, the age and abilities of children are taken into account, as well as the background and experience of the particular groups of the children concerned.

Through continuous supervision and in-service training courses organized by the inspectorate and/or the Pedagogical Institute, nursery school teachers engage in workshops to become efficient in forming the scope and sequence of the curriculum. It was considered important to employ all teachers in curriculum development, thus stimulating a two-way development (program and staff development). In applying this process for program development, it is also intended to help teachers acquire the necessary knowledge and skill in developing and applying integrated learning in an activity/problem-centered curriculum.

The physical environment presents a constant challenge for learning. Children have frequent outings to take advantage of this. When outings are not possible, children study, for example, living plants and animals in the classroom. The social environment also has infinite opportunities for learning. Outings are supplemented by visits from parents and others, who are invited by the teacher to present a topic related to their expertise.

Furniture and Equipment

Furnishings and equipment are specially designed by the Technical Services division of the Ministry of Education. They are manufactured according to standards for proper quality and required dimensions. Nursery school teachers know that the arrangement of furniture and equipment is their responsibility and that it creates the learning environment. In the curriculum, there are several suggestions to help teachers arrange effective environments.

The educational means and materials needed are numerous. They cover all aspects of the program, ranging from primary materials (water, sand, clay) to technological equipment, didactic and scientific materials, and everyday materials.

Learning Activities

The educational program of the nursery school is activity-centered. It capitalizes on the child's physical way of learning through play. Many activities are available to children to satisfy their needs and interests. These activities also serve children's different levels of development.

The school atmosphere is home-like. Children need warmth, security, and acceptance. The development of a strong bond between the teacher and the children is a prerequisite for a good adjustment to school and for the teacher being accepted by the child as a guide and support in learning. To develop a positive self-image requires that the child succeed in his or her endeavors. The child's self-respect, uniqueness, and dignity are all encouraged. Discipline is primarily gained through the encouragement of self-control. Guidance and advice are preferable to threat and punishment.

Learning is adjusted to the child's stage of development. Not only the child's maturation, but also his or her experience, social influence, and creative abilities are taken into account. The teacher capitalizes on the child's interests as indicative of the child's readiness to follow a learning task. The principle of individual differences and respect for each child's uniqueness is of primary importance in the educational program of the nursery school.

There is a balance between freedom of choice and structure. The teacher takes into account the developmental stage of the child but also organizes the school environment to offer challenges for motivating the child and speeding up readiness for learning.

There is a direct relation between the child and the learning task. Concrete tangible materials are always available. Gaining experience from well-organized activities, the child is guided toward more abstract thinking (with reference to Jerome Bruner's enactive, iconic, and symbolic levels). There is emphasis on sense perception combined with language development and conceptualization.

Lecturing, didacticism, and rote learning have no place in the nursery school. The child is actively seeking learning though investigatory activities, experimentation, and problem-solving. The process-product dilemma is resolved in favor of process.

The child's creative thinking is cultivated alongside cognitive objectives. The production of ideas is encouraged as well as production of creative constructions and improvisations in music, movement, language, and drama.

Drawing from gestalt psychology, learning in the nursery school is integrated, with opportunities for production of ideas and the creative solution of problems. But mostly, learning is the result of interaction between the child and the social and physical school environment.

Daily Program

The daily program of the nursery school is a flexible succession of activity periods, decided by the teachers on the basis of program planning with consideration of children's needs, abilities, and interests. The day begins with 60 minutes of indoor free activities. This is followed by 15 to 20 minutes of class work, which includes discussion of a selected or incidental topic while the class is actively engaged in learning initiated by a problem situation. Thirty minutes of washing, toileting, and breakfast precede a 50-minute free outdoor play session, which may include 15 to 20 minutes of physical education, gardening, and study of the physical environment. After returning to the classroom, there is a period of 25 to 30 minutes of storytelling, including poetry, creative drama, and mime, followed by 30 minutes of music.

Evaluation

Long-term as well as short-term program planning is based on formative and summative evaluation. General diagnostic evaluation at the beginning of the child's school life helps the teacher gather as much information on the child as possible. Personal records are available for completion by the teachers who are expected to develop their own evaluation instruments and evaluation records. The curriculum provides guidelines for evaluation.

Primary School Programs

Organization of Primary Education

Education in Cyprus is centralized. The Ministry of Education forms educational policy in all areas (e.g., administration, curricula, and books). The system, however, allows interested parties (e.g., teachers and parents' associations) to participate in policy formation.

According to the Education Acts for Primary Education, primary schools are financed and administrated by the government. Primary education, consisting of six years of schooling, is free and compulsory. All children at age 5 1/2 are obliged to enroll in the first grade of a primary school. At the end of their six-year schooling, primary school pupils receive a learning certificate.

The Head of the Department of Primary Education is responsible for the smooth running of primary schools and the implementation of the government's educational policy. He is assisted by the Inspector-General and the inspectors of general and special subjects.

Every town and village with more than 15 children has a primary school. Area schools serve neighboring communities with less than 15 pupils. During the school year 1989–90, there were 364 primary schools in Cyprus, with a total pupil population of 58,051 and 2,622 teachers.

The six-year primary education is offered in one-teacher schools (15–25 pupils), two-teacher schools (26–50), and three-teacher schools (more than 51 pupils) as well as in schools with more than three teachers. The maximum number of pupils in a class with one teacher is 34. At the national level, the official pupil-teacher ratio is 21. Most of the big schools in urban and rural areas are divided into cycles A (grades 1 to 3) and B (grades 4 to 6).

Every school has a school committee, whose members are elected by the local citizens. The committee is responsible for the building and the maintenance of the school.

Every school also has a parents' association, whose committee is elected by the parents of the pupils. Although it concentrates on the welfare of the pupils, it demonstrates a keen interest in the whole school program as well.

The primary school term starts on September 15 each year and finishes on June 28. There are two weeks of vacation for Christmas and another two for Easter. There are approximately 120 school days; each day lasts from 8:00 a.m. to 12:30 p.m. There are six school days a week.

Table 3 shows the weekly distribution of the subjects taught in primary schools.

TABLE 3

Cyprus Primary School Program

40-minute periods per week

Subjects	Class I	Class II	Class III	Class IV	Class V	Class VI
Religious Education	2	2	2	2	2	2
Greek	12	12	12	12	12	12
Mathematics	5	5	6	6	6	6
History	—	—	2	2	2	2
Geography	—	—	2	2	2	2
Science	—	—	2	2	2	2
Environmental Studies	3	3	—	—	—	—
English	—	—	—	—	2	2
Art	2	2	2	2	2	2
Music	2	2	2	2	2	2
Physical Education	2	2	2	2	2	2
Practical Activities	—	—	—	—	2	2
Free Activities	—	—	—	—	2	2
TOTAL	28	28	32	32	36	36

Note: The above program varies slightly according to the type of school. There are schools with one teacher, two, three, four, five and six teachers and over.

Contemporary Curriculum for Primary Education

A contemporary curriculum was developed for all subjects of primary education by the inspectorate in cooperation with the Teachers' Union, the Pedagogical Academy, and the Pedagogical Institute. As discussed below, the curriculum shifts the emphasis in many areas of primary education.

Democratization. Democracy is emphasized. It is manifested through respect for each person's dignity and individuality, respect for majority opinion, opportunities to participate in decisionmaking, encouragement of cooperation and responsibility, and equality of opportunity in all aspects of social life.

The Teacher's Role. The teacher is no longer the only authority and the only dominant figure in the classroom, rather the teacher cooperates with the pupils to organize educational activities. In essence, the teacher becomes the child's guide, animator, and collaborator.

Children's Active Participation. The active participation of children in all aspects of the school life is emphasized. This is encouraged because it is believed that this participation leads to real learning and develops responsibility, self-esteem, self-dependence, and creativity.

Environmental Study. Studying the environment is given primary importance. The children are helped to "experience" the environment, thus becoming able to understand, describe, and love it. This awareness and positive attitude will hopefully help the children proceed to the understanding of other places and the world in general.

Integration of Subjects. Teachers are encouraged not to compartmentalize subjects. Instead, they are to integrate activities, concentrating their attention on topics that interest children rather than topics prescribed by a textbook or syllabus.

Affective Domain. The new curriculum has a long reference to the affective domain, underlining the importance of values, interests, and attitudes for the developing personality of the child.

Individualization of Instruction. The steadily decreasing pupil-teacher ratios and the construction of new school rooms have allowed individual instruction and remedial teaching to be given more emphasis.

Evaluation. The new curriculum emphasizes the importance of children's self-evaluation and of the evaluation by the teacher on a systematic basis (formative-summative).

Continuously Developing Curriculum. The new curriculum is fluid; there is no "fixed" or "stable" curriculum for every school. Teachers are encouraged to modify and adjust the curriculum, according to their environment and the needs of their children.

Education About Occupied Cyprus. Children have many opportunities to learn about the geography and history of the area of Cyprus that is under Turkish occupation. These are to help them remember their homeland. They also remind students of the need to demand and struggle for freedom, justice, and the reunification of Cyprus.

Special Education Programs for Young Children

By law, the Cyprus government is responsible for educating children between the ages 5 and 18 who are moderately mentally retarded, mildly mentally retarded, slow learners, emotionally disturbed, deaf, blind, or physically handicapped.

The Council of Ministers is empowered through a 1979 law to organize schools and programs throughout Cyprus for children categorized by the above disabilities. This legislation also requires that a committee representing the handicapped in each district be established. The committees must include a psychiatrist, a clinical psychologist, an educational psychologist, and representatives of the Ministry of Education and the Welfare Office.

Any child between the ages 5 and 18 suspected of having learning or behavioral problems may be referred to the proper authorities for possible special education placement. Before such placement can occur, the child must have had complete medical and psychological examinations. An assessment is a multidisciplinary process that includes a variety of professional disciplines.

The policy of the government is not to segregate children with special needs but rather to give them the opportunity to grow and to learn with normal children. They are encouraged to learn as much as their abilities and potential permit in the normal environment. The children whose physical, mental, social, or emotional problems are so severe that they are unable to benefit from the ordinary school curriculum are placed in a special environment where they can be guided by specially trained staff. They receive instruction in schools that are equipped to deal with their particular handicap.

In general, Cyprus has adopted modern international trends and concepts advocating equal education of all children. Children with special needs are being integrated into society, where they naturally belong and where they are expected to live as equal citizens. Special schools are established only for children with moderate mental retardation (trainable), children with severe affective or psychological problems, and children with severe sensory handicaps (deaf and blind). All other special classes have been abolished. Deaf and blind children are also being integrated into normal schools (e.g., the gymnasium and lyceum for the blind no longer functions and many deaf children have been integrated in primary schools). This practice is to be further extended. Speech therapy is offered in the primary schools to those who need it.

Present Status of Special Education in Cyprus

As of 1990, five special schools for mentally retarded children, attended by 245 children and staffed by 40 teachers, existed. There is one school for children with severe affective or psychological problems; it has 87 children and 16 teachers. There is also one school for the deaf, attended by 52 children and staffed by 16 teachers. The one school for the blind has 23 registered children and 11 teaching staff. The one school for physically handicapped children has 27 children and 4 teachers.

In addition, 26 teachers for special education are posted in 56 elementary schools. They offer individualized programs to 465 children with learning difficulties. Four special teachers for the deaf and four speech therapists are in the primary schools, where they offer educational programs to 32 deaf children. Meeting the educational needs of children who receive treatment in the district hospitals of Nicosia, Larnaca, and Limassol is the responsibility of three teachers. Individualized instruction is offered by ten teachers to children with

special needs attending the following institutions: Center for Spastic Children, Center for the Rehabilitation of the Disabled, Children's Psychiatric Institutions, Nea Eleousa Institution (Institution of Severely Mentally Handicapped Children), and the Red Cross Convalescent Home.

As of 1990, there are several projects underway relating to children with special needs. Curricula are being prepared for children who are mentally retarded, have severe affective and psychological problems, and are deaf and blind. In addition, a handbook for teachers who work in special education is soon to be published. Research to establish the number of children with special needs nationwide is being conducted. The Pedagogical Academy of Cyprus offers classes in special education, as well as in-service training for teachers who work in special education as well as for teachers who work in ordinary primary schools. There is also a biannual educational journal on special education.

Training Programs for Nursery School Teachers

Until 1975 nursery school teachers were trained at Kallithea College for kindergarten teachers in Athens or at the Pedagogical Academy, where students could take several specialized courses. In 1975, the government established a two-year nursery education course at Pedagogical Academy. It was later extended to three years. The teacher training curriculum was revised in 1980. One change was the introduction of the study of Cypriot literature as a means of preserving the cultural and national heritage.

Nursery school teacher training follows the same principles as primary teacher training. Most subjects, especially general education and psychology, are common to both groups of teachers, except for the emphasis on older or younger age groups. Approximately one-quarter of the program is devoted to general education and three-quarters to professional studies.

To educate teachers adequately, theoretical knowledge of what to teach and how to teach it is not sufficient. Teachers must develop their competencies through school visits, observation, demonstrations, and teaching practice in nursery schools and classes. To accomplish this, demonstration lessons are conducted by master teachers, tutors, and advanced students of the Pedagogical Academy. Teaching practice lasts for 14 weeks and is divided into five periods. Various types of nursery schools and classes are used in both urban and rural areas to help students acquire rich experiences and to link theory and practice. Students discuss emerging problems with their tutors, who visit them for the purpose of guidance and evaluation.

Many students also join special interest clubs during their training program. The clubs offer them the opportunity to develop a specialization and contribute to their initiative, responsibility, and creativity. Clubs relating to the following subjects operate for this purpose: religion-social, literature-philosophy, science, folklore, history, music, photography, art, international understanding, recitation, athletics, nature, theater, and dance.

Extra curricular activities offer students the necessary knowledge and skills to undertake varied social roles in the school and the community. Examples of such activities are Girl Guide training, infant care, and Sunday School teaching.

Looking to the future, the government of Cyprus has decided to establish a university. Preliminary plans suggest that a school of education and humanities will be one of the first faculties to operate. When this happens, nursery school teacher

TABLE 4

Time Allocation of Subjects in Nursery School Teacher Education At the Pedagogical Academy of Cyprus

	Number of periods per semester						Percentage of time allotted per semester						Percentage of time allotted to each sector
	A	B	C	D	E	F	A	B	C	D	E	F	
1. General Education	6	8	8	11	7	6	17.14	23.52	22.85	31.42	20.58	18.18	22.33
2. Education and Psychology	9	9	9	6	12	12	25.71	26.47	25.71	17.14	35.29	36.36	27.66
3. Lessons of subject matter	7	4	5	5	—	—	20.00	11.76	14.28	14.28	—	—	10.19
4. Technical lessons	13	13	13	13	7	7	37.14	38.23	37.14	37.34	20.28	21.21	32.03
5. Specializations	—	—	—	—	8	8	—	—	—	—	23.52	24.24	34.76
	35	34	35	35	34	33	99.99	99.98	99.98	100.18	100.17	99.99	99.97

education will be upgraded from three to four years, leading to a university degree. The content of the new program is being studied.

Training Programs for Primary School Teachers

All primary school teachers are graduates of the Pedagogical Academy (Teacher's Training College) of Cyprus, an institution of tertiary education with a three-year program of study located in Nicosia, the capital of the country.

The students are selected through entrance examinations. To participate in the entrance examinations, candidates must be Cypriot citizens and hold a certificate from a six-year secondary school recognized by the Ministry of Education. The number of students admitted each year to the Pedagogical Academy is decided by the Council of Ministers on the basis of anticipated needs of primary education in teaching staff.

The students of the Pedagogical Academy do not pay tuition. They also receive their textbooks free. In return, graduates are bound by contract to work in the public primary school system in Cyprus for five years.

The aim of the Pedagogical Academy is to provide the Greek primary and nursery teachers with initial preparation and training both in theory and practice. The Academy attaches particular importance to the practical preparation of its students. Teaching practice totals 14 weeks and is divided into five periods. Students work in different classes and schools for each period in order to acquire as wide an experience as possible.

All teaching practice is in primary schools. In the course of the teaching practice each student teaches at least three different lessons daily and spends the remaining time observing lessons in her class or in other classes. In the final week of the fifth period of teaching practice, the student assumes full responsibility for the class.

The responsibility for student guidance and evaluation during teaching practice rests mainly with the teachers of the Academy, who visit the students regularly at the schools. The heads of the primary and nursery schools in which the students teach also submit a report on the student's work to the principal of the Pedagogical Academy. During the course of their studies, the students have the opportunity to attend many demonstration lessons, which are given by primary and nursery teachers as well as by teachers and students of the Academy.

The teachers of the Academy use various methods for training (e.g., lectures, seminars, tutorials, independent studies, micro-research, and cultural visits). Students are expected to make extensive use of the library and to select their own bibliography of resources.

As a rule, student academic achievement is measured through continuous assessment. This is done by using different methods, such as oral and written tests, the active involvement seminars, the writing of essays, the carrying out of micro-research, and the construction of teaching aids.

Because the program attaches equal importance to the development of the overall personality of the student, and in order to provide the student with individual guidance, the Academy also assesses the student's personality. This assessment is based on observations of the student by the teaching staff. Students are assessed on such qualities as maturity, perseverance, responsibility, and keenness.

Parental Support and Education

The Pancyprian School for Parents was established in 1968 to serve as the primary agency of parental education in Cyprus. Many specialists, including pediatricians, gynecologists, psychiatrists, psychologists, educators, and sociologists cooperate with the school. The school sponsors a series of classes for parents at various locations in the country. Topics are typically related to marriage, child development, women and the home, first aid, and educational issues.

The school receives support from the Ministry of Education, which has helped it to extend its activities into urban and rural areas. It offers a unique service in the field of adult education, in particular on issues of child rearing. The school is a member of the International Federation of Schools for Parents. It works in close cooperation with the other educational organizations of the island, in particular the parents' associations, the Cyprus

Family Planning Association, the School Radio Department of the Ministry of Education, and, the Ministry in general. It also publishes the magazine *Family and School,* which is distributed to parents throughout Cyprus.

Note

The following inspectors contributed to the writing of this article: Leto Papachristophorou, Christos Kombos, and Argyros Constantinou.

EARLY CHILDHOOD EDUCATION IN FINLAND

• • • • • • • • • • ◆ • • • • • • • •

Mikko Ojala
University of Joensuu
Joensuu, Finland
Martti T. Kuikka
University of Helsinki
Helsinki, Finland

The development of early childhood education is a fascinating part of the history of education in Finland. Early childhood education has progressed in two distinct ways. First, the education of children under age 6 is part of the history of day care, that is, the history of kindergarten and nursery schools. Second, the education of 6- to 8-year-old children is part of the history of primary schools. This chapter follows both of these paths and describes the current situation.

Historical Background

Finland was the first Scandinavian country to offer day care services. A significant historical factor affecting the development of the training, care, and education of preschool-age children in Finland, as in other Scandinavian countries, has been the ideals of the Froebelian kindergarten expounded in Prussia in the first half of the 19th century (Ojala 1984, 1985, 1989).

Friedrich Froebel's ideas were very quickly brought from Prussia to Finland through the auspices of the founder of the Finnish public educational system, Uno Cygnaeus. Cygnaeus became acquainted with kindergarten operations and teacher training while in Prussia in the mid-19th century. When Finland's first teacher training college was established in 1863, a kindergarten and creche were founded along with the public school, as Cygnaeus had proposed. The creche cared for children under age 4 and the kindergarten enrolled 4- to 10-year-olds.

In the early developmental stages of kindergartens, the German and Finnish systems were similar. Both Froebel and Cygnaeus saw the task of the kindergarten, first and foremost, from the point of view of enlightenment. Both viewed the existing institutions as providing a social service but lacking a pedagogical foundation. Each believed that an intellectual and practical reform of education was imperative. Each also believed that a child's education had to begin before the child reached school age. Only in this way could the national level of education be raised. Mothers and nursemaids also had to be schooled in training tasks. Both Froebel and Cygnaeus stressed the need to develop and institute new operational methods and equipment that were pedagogically appropriate to the education of small children.

Following the deaths of Froebel and Cygnaeus, a change occurred in the development of the kindergarten ideal in Finland as well as in Germany (Ojala, 1984, 1985). The Finnish successor to the kindergarten development work inaugurated by Cygnaeus, Hanna Rothman, shifted the development of kindergarten in the direction of the German model, particularly in regard to its social service aspects. The model was adopted from existing social welfare institutions. Public kindergartens, serving a child care function, were first established in 1888 to serve "children of poor families who were left to walk the streets uncared for" (Committee Report, 1974:15).

Administratively, the kindergartens were at first placed under the jurisdiction of the school authorities (Nurmi, 1981). Since 1924, the kindergartens have been governed by the social welfare authorities. Until the enactment of the 1973 Day Care Act, kindergartens were meant for children ages 3 to 7. Kindergartens in Finland have been either private or municipal; and from their inception, the greatest number have been public. Both public and private kindergartens have been eligible for state subsidies since 1913. (Hänninen and Valli, 1986).

Creches have existed in Finland since the 18th century. Unlike kindergartens, creches were not eligible for state aid prior to the enactment of the 1973 Act.

The playground (outdoor) movement in Finland started in the 1910s while day club (indoor) activities for children began in the 1940s. Special care and education started in the 1920s, when kindergarten programs were adapted for use with children in hospitals (Hänninen and Valli, 1986).

Since the beginning of Finland's independence, great attention was paid to children and their development. First, education for 7- and 8-year-olds was reformed when specific teacher training seminars were established. During the period 1917–21, four two-year training seminars, open only to women, were implemented. Woman were seen as the proper teachers of young children because they were viewed as the mothers of the classroom "family." The second step was the Compulsory Education Act of 1921, which resulted in separate schools for 7- and 8-year-olds. These schools, called "under primary schools," have a very important significance in Finland. (The development of under primary schools was very slow

and problematic. The law of 1921 guaranteed its development both economically and pedagogically.)

At the same time, the number of kindergartens in the towns increased. Initiative for their development came from communes, industries, societies, organizations, and various associations. Until 1927, most of these private kindergartens did not receive assistance from the state. The programs were financed by the operators and the parents and guardians of children, who paid a small sum. The Parliament ratified the Act on State Aid in 1927, permitting kindergartens and nursery schools to receive a grant equal to 30 percent of their operating costs. There were no state controls regarding curriculum. One result of the act was an increase in communal kindergarten activity.

Most preschools in the 1920s were of two types: (1) nursery schools for children under age 3, with 5 to 15 children per group, and (2) kindergartens for children ages 3 to 7, with no more than 25 children per group.

The main goal of kindergarten was to support children's development while taking into consideration their individual differences. Kindergarten activity was based on the Christian ethic, while pedagogical ideas came directly from Froebel and his supporters. In this century, both child-centered pedagogy and developmental psychology have also had a role in teacher training and the development of the kindergarten.

In 1926, there were 79 kindergartens receiving state aid. The 1930s saw a greater increase in communal kindergartens, and by 1944, 61 percent of kindergartens were communal. The 1936 Child Welfare Act stimulated much of this growth by mandating that communes establish their own kindergartens or support others established by private organizations or persons. Communal kindergartens also supported family education.

World War II disrupted educational reform and development in Finland. Although the Finnish Parliament proposed changes in the school system in the 1940s, the various political parties were not united. One significant development in post-war Finland was the creation of a committee by the government in 1948 to plan a system of child care. The committee proposed that kindergartens support and complete children's home education by furthering the child's physical, intellectual, and moral development. A system consisting of nursery schools and three types of kindergartens, (i.e., part-time, full-time, and one serving school children) was proposed. However, the proposal was not realized until the 1970s. Because of the belief that young children are best cared for in the home by their mothers and the anti-institutional movement represented by John Bowlby and others, there was widespread opposition to nursery school and creche care of children under age 3 (Munter, Kuvaja, and Viitanen, 1977).

Children's Day Care Act

Rapid change in the social and occupational structure occurred in Finland in the 1950s and 1960s, changing the nation from an agrarian, rural-based society into an industrial urban one (Ojala, 1985, 1989). One dramatic change was the significant number of women who joined the workforce. Until the end of World War II, the proportion of women who worked outside the home had remained about 10 percent. In 1950, the number rose to 34 percent, in 1960 to 48 percent, in 1970 to 58 percent, in 1980 to 64 percent. By the mid-1980s about 80% of women having preschool children were employed outside the home. Consequently, there was a need for a dramatic increase in day care services.

The reorganization of day care culminated in the enactment of a Children's Day Care Act in 1973. The act requires each municipality to provide publicly organized or supervised day care to such an extent and in such forms as the need demands. Prime consideration must be given to families requiring day care for educational and social reasons. Private individuals or groups may also engage in day care activities under the supervision of the municipal social service authorities.

It was only after the enactment of the act that the goals and content of day care programs were discussed to any extent. The result was a 1980 report on the educational goals of day care. In 1983, the following educational goals became part of the Day Care Act:

• to support the homes of children in day care in their educational functions and, together with the home, to further the balanced development of the child's personality;

• to offer the child ongoing, safe, and warm human relations; activities supporting the child's total development; and a favorable growth environment;

• according to the needs of the child while considering the general cultural tradition, to further the child's physical, social, and emotional development and to support the child's aesthetic, intellectual, ethical, and religious growth (in supporting religious growth, the conviction of the child's parents or guardians must be respected); and

• to support the child's growth in responsibility, peace, and caring for their environment.

Educational activities support the general goals outlined in the act, within specific content areas (Committee Report, 1980: 31). As a result, there are separate goals for physical, social, emotional, intellectual, aesthetic, ethical, and religious growth. Activities focus on basic care situations, games, small tasks, crafts, teaching periods, contact with the environment, celebrations, and excursions (Ojala, 1985).

The act guarantees a state subsidy for child care. The costs are distributed as follows: state, 42 percent; communities (and private organizations), 42 percent; and parents, 16 percent. State subsidies to communes vary from 31 percent to 64 percent of operating costs. Parental fees vary according to income, with some parents paying no fees.

The result of the act was a large increase in child care spaces (Children in Finland, 1988). From 51,000 in 1973, the number of spaces reached 200,000 by 1988, 54 percent of which were in public day cares. The 2,400 communal kindergartens served over 100,000 preschool children (Children in Finland, 1988), with 70 percent attending full-time. The number of private kindergartens in 1988 was about 300.

Day Care Centers

Day care centers (called kindergartens in the past) offer full-day day care (8 to 10 hours) or part-day care (4 to 5 hours). Full-day day care is primarily intended for children whose parents work outside the home; 24-hour care is available for parents who work irregular shifts. Day care centers serve from 5 to 100 children, although in exceptional circumstances the number of spaces can slightly exceed 100. There are five major types of groupings of children:

1. 1- to 2-year-olds (12 per group)
2. 3- to 6-year-olds (20 per group)
3. 6-year-olds (25 per group)
4. "sister and brother" groups for children ages 1 to 5 (15 children per group)
5. after school care for 7- and 8-year-olds

Since the 1980s, there has been a preference to form groups that ensure the best possible care and educational conditions and increase the child's feelings of security. This means that the same groups can contain both full- and part-time children, children of different ages (from ages one to six), and children with special needs.

Mobile kindergartens offer preschool activity for 6-year-olds in sparsely populated areas. The mobile centers operate on a part-time basis and offer a four-hour program. The intent is to expose all children in Finland to preschool (Ojala, 1983).

The number and training of the staff depend on the composition of the group. Since 1981 staff requirements have been as follows:

• one preschool teacher/social pedagogue and two child nurses: 12 children ages 1 to 2 (full-time care);

• two preschool teachers/social pedagogues and one child nurse: 20 children ages 3 and above (full-time care); and

• one preschool teacher/social pedagogue and one child nurse: 20 children ages 3 and above (part-time care).

Since 1983, preschool teachers have received three years of training at either a teacher training college (university) or a preschool teacher institute (vocational school). Both options require a high school diploma for admission. Social pedagogue training consists of four years of professional training. Child nurses are trained at intermediate-level institutions, which have one-year programs for students with a high school diploma and two to five year programs for those completing junior high school.

Day care centers also have auxiliary staff for the kitchen, cleaning, or laundry and to assist teachers. A new training scheme was instituted at intermediate-level institutions for day care nurses. The intent is that in the future day care nurses will replace child nurses in day care work.

Special Care

One aim of day care is to detect developmental problems as early as possible. Children requiring special care and training are usually cared for in the same groups as other children, with the group size reduced by two with the presence of each special needs child. Separate day care facilities for special needs children also exist in which the group size is reduced by 50 percent.

Family Day Care

Family day care in Finland is also subject to Day Care Act (Ojala, 1989). Family day care, which can be public or private, is defined as care in private homes or other family-like conditions. Public care is in nature and content a part of public day care and is directed in municipalities by a separate supervisor. Private care is based on an agreement between the care person and the child's guardian. In 1988, there were nearly 40,000 municipal family day care homes, used by 90,000 children (Children in Finland, 1988).

Family day care may be full- or part-time and is used for children of all ages. Its major clients, however, are children under age 3. Providers can care for a maximum of four children, including their own, under age 7.

Providers are trained in courses approved by the National Board of Vocational Education. In selecting providers, consideration is given to their personal suitability and work experience. The provider's home is carefully assessed for its suitability for child care.

Normally, care takes place in the provider's home. However, a variation is the "three-family" day care system, in which two or three families employ a provider from the municipality (maximum of four preschoolers). Care occurs on a rotating basis in each family's home. A recently developed model is "group-family" care, in which two or three providers each care for a small group of children in facilities arranged by the municipality.

Play Activity

The act defines play activity as indoor or outdoor children's games or activities guided and supervised in a place or area designed for this purpose. It is the primary recommended activity for children in all forms of child care. There are three types of play activity—play clubs, playgrounds, and toy libraries—which can exist separately or in any combination. Play activity can be either public or private.

The "play club" activity is mainly organized by the Lutheran Church. In 1988, there were 6,000 play clubs used by nearly 100,000 children and 2,000 playgrounds used by 30,000 children.

Preschool Education

The term "preschool education" can be understood in a narrow and broad sense in Finland. In the narrow sense, preschool means school-like activity for children under age 6 that is designed to promote school readiness. In the broad sense, preschool means all systematic and organized education and teaching for children under school age.

An essential task of preprimary schools is to provide preschool experiences. Generally, preschool is the name given to educational and teaching activity for 6-year-old children. It occurs in both day care centers and in comprehensive schools.

Preschool Education in Comprehensive Schools

In comprehensive schools in the 1970s, preschool education was experimental. It occurred in separate preschool classes and in mixed-age groups. Experimental preschool curriculums changed continually in the 1970s. A starting point was the identification of 18 centers of interest, each with its own goals and content. To teach all of the interest areas, the curriculum includes detailed instructions describing the form of the activity and learning materials. The results of this experimental curriculum were positive, with young pupils developing in many areas. They learned to work in groups and follow the daily program.

According to the Comprehensive School Act of 1983, preschools can be organized for children who are not yet of compulsory school age. The length of time is one school year. This means that municipalities can decide on developing preschools in their area in the future.

Preschool Curriculum in the Day Care

The preschool curriculum follows the educational objectives of day care. Objectives are divided into seven areas: physical, social, emotional, aesthetic, intellectual, ethical, and religious education. For 6-year-old pupils, a specific curriculum was formulated in 1984. This curriculum was developed in view of centers of interest, which included a so-called year plan. In planning a year-long program, many factors must be considered, including the individual developmental needs of every child, prior day care experiences, special talents, the number of children, and local and home conditions. In daily planning, current events and children's ideas are considered. The aim is to create a positive enjoyable experience and to develop children's thinking skills.

Because all 6-year-old Finns are not in day care, the school system also engages in preschool training for 6-year-olds (Ojala, 1989). According to the 1983 School Act, Finnish elementary schools can organize, with the consent of the Ministry of Education, a maximum of one year's training for children not yet required to attend school. Preschool training in the schools can be provided only for 6-year-olds and only on a voluntary basis.

Preschools can function either in conjunction with teaching at the lowest grade in the primary school or as separate classes. In combined grade 1 and preschool classes, the maximum number of 6- and 7-year-olds is 25. In 1985–86, 950 pupils participated in preschool training in conjunction with the schools (National Board of Education, 1986).

Organization and Structure of the Comprehensive School

There are three levels in the Finnish comprehensive school. Basic compulsory schooling is provided by nine-year comprehensive schools. It is divided into a lower (primary) stage and an upper (lower secondary) stage. Finnish children begin comprehensive school in the year they turn age 7. Preschool education is also given at comprehensive schools.

While day care is administrated by the Ministry of Social Affairs and Health and the National Board of Social Welfare, preschool education and comprehensive school are generally administered by the Ministry of Education and the National Board of General Education. The Finnish government has reformed the educational administration and made the National Board of General Education and the National Board of Vocational Education part of the same agency.

Educational administration traditionally has three levels. The first level is national, consisting of the central government which is led by the Finnish Parliament. The Ministry of Education prepares educational bills and drafts decisions of education made by the government or the Ministry itself. The National Board of General Education (after 1992, the Education Department of the Ministry of Education) is responsible for practical school administration as well as educational planning and implementation in its respective sectors. For example, the Ministry of Education has the overall responsibility for planning reforms, whereas the National Board plans and develops national curriculum and syllabi (Development of Education 1986–88: 15–16).

Second is the provincial level. Finland is divided into 12 administrative regions called provinces, each consisting of provincial offices and headed by a governor. Each provincial office also has a school department. While previously these departments mainly dealt with general education, since 1987 they have also handled matters pertaining to vocational training and have acted as regional authorities. This means that decisionmaking is transferred from the central government to the provincial level. Finnish regional administrations do not have representative bodies with decision-making powers. Such bodies were set up to assist the regional authorities in implementing the extensive school reforms launched in the 1970s.

The third level, local administration, is the responsibility of the self-governing municipalities. In practice, the municipalities, which have the right to levy taxes, have independent powers of decision. The supreme powers of decision are wielded by municipal councils, which consist of 17 to 85 members elected by the residents of the municipality by direct and secret ballot. The municipal council nominates the municipal board, which prepares matters to be discussed by the council and implements the decisions it makes. The municipal council elects 7 to 13 members to the school board for a four-year term. Of these, at least two must be teachers working in local schools. The school board guides and supervises instruction in municipal schools and issues instructions for the curriculum.

All comprehensive and upper secondary schools are locally operated. They have governing boards representing parents, teachers, and other school staff, and at the upper level of comprehensive and upper-secondary schools, the students. The governing board executes tasks relating to the development of school work and cooperation between the school and the families.

Primary School Curriculum

The objectives for primary education are laid down in the Comprehensive School Act of 1968. Under this act, basic general education in Finland is given in unified comprehensive schools, which were gradually introduced between 1972 and 1977. The goal of comprehensive school instruction is to encourage children's growth in becoming balanced, fit, responsible, independent, creative, cooperative, and peace-loving human beings and citizens. Another important objective is to establish good relationships between the school and children's families in order to support parents in the rearing of their children. The main task of the school is to stimulate the development of a unique personality in the pupil.

The curriculum of the comprehensive school is defined in legislation. In 1985, the government approved the hourly distribution of the school subjects (see Table 1). Based on distribution, the National Board of General Education defined the basic principles underlying the curriculum of the comprehensive school. Local authorities design the curricula, which consist of the compulsory core curriculum and a locally designed optional part.

TABLE 1
Instruction Given on the Lower Stage of Comprehensive School and the Number of Lesson Hours Per Week

Grade Subject	1	2	3	4	5	6	Total
Mother tongue	7	7	5–6	5–6	4–6	4–6	32–38
Foreign language or second national	—	—	2	2	2	2	8
Environment studies, biology, and geography	2	2	2–3	2–3	3–4	3–4	14–18
Civics and citizenship[1]	—	—	0–1	0–1	0–1	0–1	2–3
Religion or philosophy of life	2	2	2	2	1	1	10
History	—	—	—	—	1–3	1–3	3–4
Mathematics	3	3	4	4	4	3	21
Music[2]	1–2	1–2	1–4	1–4	1–4	1–4	6–18
Arts[2]	1–2	1–2	1–4	1–4	1–4	1–4	6–8
Handicraft[2]	1–2	1–2	2–4	2–4	2–4	2–4	10–18
Physical Education[2,3]	1–2	1–2	2–3	2–3	2–3	2–3	15–16
Total[4]	19–21	19–21	23–25	23–25	24–26	24–26	134–144

[1] The civic and citizenship lessons also include student counseling according to the instructions of the National Board of General Education.
[2] The total of music, arts, handicraft, and physical education is a minimum of 44 hours.
[3] If there are 16–18 hours of music, arts, or handicraft, the total hours devoted to physical education can vary between 10 and 16 hours.
[4] If an optimal subject (as stipulated in the Comprehensive School Act, chapter 27, section 4) is taught at the lower level of comprehensive school, the total number of hours can be increased according to chapter 21, section 2, of the Act.

The total class hours per week in grades 1 and 2 is 19 to 21. The largest allocation of time for a single subject is language instruction, which receives seven hours. In the first two grades, pupils study their mother tongue. Other subjects are environmental studies, religion or philosophy of life, mathematics, music, arts, handicrafts, and physical education. Most pupils receive instruction in the religion of their parents. Religion textbooks are examined by the Bishop's Council. Most Finns are members of the Lutheran Church (90 percent).

Following the Act of 1968, grades 1 and 2 of comprehensive school were called "beginning learning." Schooling is compulsory from ages 7 to 17, unless comprehensive school is completed early. Each child is required by law to be educated in the knowledge and skills taught in the comprehensive school. Comprehensive school provides all of its services free of charge (e.g., instruction, books and other educational materials, and health services). A noon meal is provided for children in grades 1 and 2 who live a distance from the school.

Special Education Programs for Young Children

One of the goals of Finland's child care system is to screen children for developmental delays or other problems that may require intervention. If a child requires special care, child care experts, together with the child's parents and day care staff, prepare a rehabilitation plan for the child.

The first special day cares were established in Helsinki in the 1950s. In 1952, a kindergarten for deaf children was established. The next few years saw the establishment of the following: the first kindergarten for children with cerebral palsy (1954), a kindergarten for children with emotional disturbances (1956); and a kindergarten for children with speech problems (1957). The city of Helsinki was responsible for all costs associated with these day cares, because of the absence of any state funding. Today, special needs children are not educated in segregated groups, but join regular programs in smaller groups.

The Day Care Act of 1973 improved the situation of handicapped children. The development of special needs day care has continued in two forms, integrated and segregated. According to general principal, children who need special care and education are able to take part in normal day care activity. In family day care, the child caregiver employed by the municipality receives higher wages for caring for handicapped children. In larger towns, a variety of services are available for special needs children (e.g., speech therapists, remedial gymnastics instructors, psychologists, and resource teachers).

The family day care homes cooperate with a number of agencies. Among them are local health centers with full-time social workers and psychologists and child guidance clinics for children with emotional disturbances. In addition, many volunteer organizations perform valuable services, especially for children under school age.

The second form of care involves specialized kindergartens. As of 1990, such kindergartens exist for children with social-emotional disturbances, cerebral palsy, muscular dystrophy, hearing-impairments, intellectual handicaps, and speech impairments.

Special Education in the Primary School

In 1959, Finland passed a declaration of child's rights that supported the principle of equal educational opportunity for all children. This principle was entrenched in the school reforms in the 1968 Education Act. The act specified that schools and special classes were to be developed for children who cannot follow normal class teaching because of physical or psychological illness, defect, or injury. In the 1970s, the emphasis shifted to educating all children, handicapped and nonhandicapped, in the same group. The general principle is that a child can be exempted from compulsory education only because of very serious learning disabilities.

A very general form of special teaching in comprehensive schools is remedial teaching. Remedial work can commence only with the permission of the child's parent or guardian. The service is also available for pupils who are absent from school for a prolonged period of time. Remedial teaching in reading and writing is very general. If the difficulty is not great, the pupil often improves without intervention through regular class teaching and maturation. Many schools employ special education teachers who are able to assess learning difficulties and offer educational programs.

Teaching Training for Teachers of Young Children

There are two categories of teachers for young children: kindergarten teachers, who work with 3- to 6-year-olds, and primary teachers, who teach 7- to 8-year-old children.

Teacher training for public schools began in Jyväskylä in 1863. Women candidates in the teacher training college worked in nursery schools and kindergartens. They generally taught at the lower level in public schools, and especially 8- to 10-year-old pupils. Later, colleges were founded: in Tammisaara (1871) and in East Finland (1880) (for Finnish-speaking teachers).

Teacher training for kindergarten began in Helsinki in 1892 through the initiative of Hanna Rothman. She had visited training colleges in Germany and aimed to establish one in her own country. At the beginning, training was one year in duration, later it was extended to two years. Training was given in Swedish until 1905, when one course started in Finnish. For a long time, this college was the only school for kindergarten teachers.

With the arrival of independence in 1917, Finland took steps to reform the public schools. The first step was to establish new colleges for elementary school teachers for 7- to 8-year-olds. The first college opened in 1917, and later three other colleges were founded. The school reforms also brought a new curriculum, which stressed child activity and learning by doing, according to John Dewey and the advocates of progressive education. A new act on compulsory schooling divided public schools into two levels: (1) 7- to 8-year-old pupils (lower level) and (2) 9- to 13-year-old pupils (upper level).

The four training colleges for teachers of 7- to 8-year-olds continued until the passing of the 1957 Act. In the new legislation, both levels were joined in the same structure at a comprehensive school. As a result, some of these colleges were reoriented to train teachers for 7– to 15-year-old children, and others ceased operation.

The establishment of a new system of colleges for kindergarten teachers began after World War II. A kindergarten seminary was founded in Jyväskylä in 1947, and in Tampere in 1956. The first college conducted in Swedish opened in Pietarsaari in 1958. Earlier, Swedish-speaking teachers had received their education in Helsinki, and only in separate courses. Training lasted two years and included a large amount of practice teaching. Admission requirements were good health and graduation from middle school, meaning five grades of secondary school. Admission to Jyväskylä was more demanding, and required a matriculation examination.

At the same time as the 1960 school reforms were taking place, plans were being made for a new curriculum for teacher training. The first change, in 1968, was to increase admission requirements so that all applicants had to pass the matriculation examination. The program was also extended in length to three years.

The present system for training comprehensive and upper-secondary school teachers is based on the 1971 Teaching Training Act. In 1975, all training of primary and secondary teachers was incorporated into eight universities, which have faculties of education functioning as teacher training units, and two art academies. A faculty of education consists of at least two departments: a department of teacher training and a department of educational or behavioral sciences. Four faculties of education have two institutes of teacher training, one of which is situated outside the university. Thus, the teacher training institutes are situated in different parts of the country. Some faculties have a third department devoted to some closely related sciences.

Apart from teacher training, the faculties of education give other instruction and carry out research in education and related sciences. The teaching staffs are composed of professors, associate professors, lecturers, and assistants. In addition to other qualifications, lecturers in charge of practice teaching are required to be competent comprehensive or upper-secondary school teachers and to

have practical teaching experience.

The teacher training network includes 13 state-maintained practice schools. These schools provide facilities for both practice teaching and educational research. The practice schools are subordinate to the faculties of education. The teacher trainees do their teaching practice in a training school at the level they intend to teach.

Students who aim to become classroom teachers can select two subjects of specialization. Many of them, including male candidates, take a course in teaching beginning pupils. This course provides the competence to teach young children in preschools and the first classes of comprehensive school.

Although one function of the Teacher Training Act of 1971 was to unify all teacher training, it did not have as direct an effect on kindergarten training as on other kinds of training. In the 1970s, there were two ways to become a kindergarten teacher. One way was to continue the earlier practice and to attend a private but state-supported kindergarten seminary (college). In 1977, the seminaries became operated by the state and administered by the National Board of General Education. Today, there are five such institutions, four Finnish and one Swedish. Kindergarten teacher institutes also train other personnel working either within children's day care or in allied fields.

Since 1974, a second way to become a kindergarten teacher has been to study at a faculty of education. Kindergarten teacher training has been developed through decisions by the government and the Ministry of Education. In the early 1980s, the study time was extended to three years. The curriculum for kindergarten teacher training at an institute (seminary) or university is the same and leads to the same diploma.

There are several recent initiatives in kindergarten training. Credit can now be received for the kindergarten teacher diploma for subsequent degree studies, thereby enlarging a graduate's career prospects. Training programs for child care personnel, private children's caregivers, and day care center assistants are being developed. Efforts will be made to ensure that all personnel working in the field of children's day care have the necessary basic competence in the care and guidance of children. In planning the curricula, efforts will be made to design the components so as to reduce redundancy for students who wish to proceed toward the university basic degree. The training of people working in child care will be offered through a form of continuing education. In addition, institutes for this training will be changed into vocational colleges. The aim is to make the training more scientific, to raise the status of this training, and to ensure the cooperation with universities.

Parental Support and Educational Programs

The churches have been very active in supporting family education. Since the 1840s, the Lutheran Church has held Sunday schools for 3- to 6-year-old children. After the World War II, the church began to establish play clubs in the towns. In the 1960s, this activity spread to the countryside. Children came to the clubs for three hours, two days per week, and later every day (Seppälä, 1988: 69–72). In the 1970s, the church planned a large educational program that included educational goals for each age group of parish members, from 3- to 6-year-olds to adults over age 65. The church established the Church Education Center to be responsible for all Christian education. The Orthodox Church has organized activities for young children and their parents, and has emphasized association within the parish.

Besides the churches there are many organizations that support parents through education. For example, Mannerheim's Child Welfare Union, established by General C.G. Mannerheim in 1920, has organized many courses and seminars for parents and has cooperated in research with universities.

An important goal defined in the Day Care Act is to support the educational function of the family and to cooperate with families in contributing to optimal development of children. One way centers attempt to meet this goal is to hold regular meetings for parents.

Research in Early Childhood Education

The effects of the care, training, and teaching provided by day care centers vary. In general, it seems that the readiness and development of children in day care in Finland are comparable to that of children in home care. Day care centers do not disrupt or further in any substantial way the child's development (Ojala, 1985).

According to some studies, day care centers have promoted children's creativity or mental and motor development (Heikkilä, 1973; Ruoppila and Korkiakangas, 1975). On the other hand, particularly children under age 3, have problems in adapting to the routines of day care centers and have a shorter attention span or are more disruptive when they enter school (Kamppinen, 1979; Lahikainen and Sundquist, 1979). In the opinion of parents, large groups and the possibility of the child becoming ill are negative aspects of institutional day care centers. However, Finnish parents are generally confident in the care provided at day care centers and see as positive the increased social contacts of children in group care (Munter, 1984).

Research on family day care has shown the benefits of small group size, the home-like environment, and the operational flexibility (Ojala, Lius, and Pättänon, 1981). The care by family providers is seen to be in greater harmony with the home than that of group care (Huttunen, 1984). In addition, the family day care center is considered a suitable form of day care for small children at risk of infections. Major drawbacks are seen to be the low education level of care providers, the short duration of vocational training, and the turnover in day care staff.

According to evaluations by teachers, preschool training (for 6- year-olds), while promoting development in all areas, has had a particular influence on socio-emotional development (National Board of Education, 1982).

Recent Developments in Family Policy

The Finnish government decided that as of 1990 all children under age 3 should either be able to attend a kindergarten or have the option of home-care support. The latter offers incentives for parents to care for their children at home, (e.g., a parent-leave program that ensures they will not lose their employment during this three-year period).

About 80 percent of Finnish mothers work outside the home, most in full-time jobs. According to recent legislation, parents of children under age 5 and in grade 1 can reduce their workday to six hours. Parents may also have flexible work hours and a statutory three-day leave to care for sick children at home.

There is an obvious need in Finland to be more concerned with the qualitative development of day care. Finnish early childhood education needs to consider new alternatives based on research. Day care in Finland has met its social tasks, that is, there are enough day care spaces to meet the demand and most parents are satisfied with day care arrangements. The pedagogical task, however, is far from complete.

References

Act 296/1927, The act on state-aid for kindergarten (in Finnish).

Act 80/1936, The act on state-aid for kindergarten (in Finnish).

Act 36/1973, The act on children's day care (in Finnish).

Act 467/1968, The act on the basics of school system (in Finnish).

Act 476/1983, Comprehensive school act (in Finnish).

Children in Finland. 1988. Central Union for Child Welfare in Finland. (February).

Circular A3/1984/pe. Children's day care (in Finnish). Helsinki: National Board of Social Welfare.

Committee Report. (1974). Report of the Committee on Training Early Childhood Education Personnel (in Finnish). Helsinki: National Publication Center.

Committee Report. (1980). Report of the Commission on the Educational Goals of Day Care (in Finnish). Helsinki: National Publication Center.

Development of Education. (1986–88). Reference Publications 14. Helsinki. Ministry of Education.

Hänninen, S.-L., & Valli, S. (1986). The history of Finnish kindergarten work and early childhood education (in Finnish). Helsinki: Otava.

Heikkilä, J. (1973). Differences in creative thinking in first- and second-graders who have or have not attended kindergartens. (in Finnish). Research Reports in Education No. A:22. Turku, Finland: University of Turku.

Huttenen, E. (1984). Family and day care co-operation as a supporting factor of Education and the child's development (in Finnish). Research Reports in Education No.2. Joensuu, Finland: University of Joensuu.

Kamppinen, V. (1979). On the connections between development environments and the child's behavior at school (in Finnish). Unpublished master's thesis. University of Helsinki.

Kuikka, M. (1981). Society and development of an elementary school system in Finland, 1866–1968. Scandinavian Journal of History, 6(1): 7–28.

———. (1982). The development of pre–school objectives in Finland 1966–1978. Conference paper for the 4th Session of the International Conference for the History of Education. Budapest, September 7–10, 1982. (pp. 222–32).

Lahikainen, R., & Sundquist, S. (1979). Reactions of children three years old and younger to day care. (in Finnish) Research Reports from the Department of the Social Psychology No. 1. Helsinki: University of Helsinki.

Munter, H. (1984). Psychophysical strain on small children (in Finnish). Social Magazine (Sosiaaliviesti), 3 43–8.

Munter, H., Kuvaja, T., & Viitanen, H. (1977). Education in under three-year-old children's day care centers (in Finnish). Report from the Department of Psychology. University of Helsinki.

National Board of Education. (1982). Ten years of preschool activity (in Finnish). Bulletins on School Trial Programs and Research No. 2 Helsinki: Author.

Nurmi, V. (1981). The Finnish school system (in Finnish). Helsinki: Werner Söderström.

Ojala, M., (1983). Education for children living in sparsely populated areas in Finland. Seminar paper presented at the International Standing Conference for History of Education. Seminar group 6: Science, technology and society since 1954 (pp. 79–82). Westminister College, Oxford, England, September 5–8, 1983.

———. (1984). Friedrich Froebel and the kindergarten movement in Finland. Informationen fur Erziehungs—und Bildungshistorische Forshung (Heft 25, pp. 202–12). Universität Hannover.

———. (1985). Fundamentals of early childhood education (in Finnish). Helsinki: Kirjaythymä.

———. (1989). Early childhood training, care, and education in Finland. In P.P. Olmsted & D.P. Weikart (Eds)., How nations serve young children: Profiles of child care and education in 14 countries. (pp. 87–118). Ypsilanti, MI: High Scope Education Research Foundation.

Ojala, M., Lius, E., & Pättönen, P. (1981). Family day care as a part of day care and early childhood education. (in Finnish). Publications of the National Board of Social Welfare No. 4. Helsinki: National Publication Center.

Rouppila, I., & Korkiakangas, M. (1975). Effects of preschool, kindergarten, and the home on children's development 2. Results concerning the effects (in Finnish). Publication of the Department of Psychology No. 17. Jyväskylä, Finland: University of Jyväskylä.

Seppälä, J. (1988). Opettava ja kasvattava kirkko. Helsinki: University of Helsinki.

Vihamaa, L., & Vuorento, R. (1989). A survey concerning day care and support of home care. Situations 31.12 1988 and 1.1 1990 (in Finnish). Report from National Board of Social Welfare No. 12/1989.

EARLY CHILDHOOD EDUCATION IN FRANCE

● ● ● ● ● ● ● ● ● ● ◆ ● ● ● ● ● ● ● ●

Marie-Thérèse Le Normand
Salpêtrière Hospital
Paris, France

Until the end of the 18th century, French society provided inadequate care for many of its young children (Ariés, 1970; Rollet, 1982, 1983). As a consequence, infant mortality rates were high. These high rates and the conditions that produced them were denounced by both philosophers and physicians. To a certain extent, their concerns helped to bring about major changes in child care practices in France. The particular concern was with the lot of foster children, and certain health and security measures to ameliorate the poor conditions for them were proposed. These measures, which were put into practice during the late 19th century, applied to the regulation of "nurses," the term used to designate women who cared for the children of others (Roussel, 1874). However, nurses employed in the child's own home did not come under this legislation.

From the "Knitting Schools" to the Ecole Maternelle

Influenced by the social conditions of poor children in his parish, the Alsatian pastor Jean-Frédéric Oberlin created in 1770, in the Vosges area, the first small "knitting schools" to take care of and to educate preschool children ages 4 to 7. The preschool teachers trained these children using the following curriculum: spinning, knitting, shredding, linen making, paper and picture cutting, alphabet reading, calligraphy, songs, recitation, mental counting, color naming, natural history, and Bible study. Teaching was first given in *patois* (local dialect) and then in French. The class started and finished with a prayer. After each one and one-half hour class, there was a five-minute break.

Following the English model of monitorial education, large day care centers opened in France, the first in Paris in 1826. Denys Cochin, mayor of 12th arrondissement, created the first Parisian day care center, which admitted 2- to 6-year-old children "still too young to attend the primary schools and whose parents were too poor or busy to keep them at home."(Norvez, 1990). The curriculum of the first day care center was ambitious. It included basic principles of religious instruction, reading, writing, linear drawing, manual work, songs, and physical exercises.

In 1829, the Director of Paris Hospices decided to take all Parisian day care centers under his

205

guardianship. Following that, Adolphe Theirs, in an 1833 order, directed prefects throughout France to create day care centers, assigning to them an educative role. By 1836, there were 100, with over 4,000 children, under the jurisdiction of the Ministry of Public Instruction. These figures quickly increased so that by 1843 there were 1,500 day care centers with over 100,000 children.

In a typical day care center, many children gathered together in the same room, sitting quietly in long rows. The emphasis had changed from teaching children to controlling and disciplining them. In 1845, Victor Duruy requested Madame Pape-Carpantier to organize a better system of management for the day care centers. For the first time, the issue of appropriate training for the staff was raised, since Madame Pape-Carpantier was appalled at the quality of education in these settings. Pauline Kergomard, who is considered the pioneer of a new type of preschool institution, the "maternal school" (école maternelle), held the same views of the day care centers.

The decree of the August 2, 1881 provided for the recruitment of trained professionals already teaching in primary schools to work in the maternal schools. The 1881 order and other official decrees resulted in a unique model of early childhood education. The goal of the maternal school became "respect for the young child; avoidance of exercises which are too academic; play as natural form of learning for the child; knowledge of the psychology of the child in planning learning activities which would maximize his or her development."(Norvez, 1990).

In 1885, the maternal schools came under the jurisdiction of individual townships for capital costs and equipment, while the national government continued to pay teachers' salaries. The number of schools grew considerably, until all communities of more than 2,000 inhabitants had at least one maternal school. By the end of the 19th century, children from ages 2 to 6 were allowed to attend these early educational settings. Teacher qualifications gradually increased. By 1940, teachers at the maternal schools were required to have a bachelor's degree.

In 1948, the World Organization for Pre-school Education (l'Organisation mondiale pour l'éducation préscholaire (OMEP)) was created under

France's initiative. One of the goals of OMEP was to "allow the entire world to know about the French école maternelle and how preschool education can be of assistance to the young child" (Norvez, 1990).

Creches

For children under age 3, the first infant day care centers, or creches, appear in the nineteenth century, founded by F. Marbeau. At first, the creches had a sanitary goal—to improve the poor conditions for a growing population. Children were admitted from 15 days old to age 3. The government provided financial support under the authority of the local prefect. Some of the first creches were also developed in factories as a result of the initiatives of certain managers. At the beginning, creches were open 12 hours a day, but since 1921 the hours have decreased to eight hours.

After World War II, the Social Security System (Law of October 4, 1945), and the provisions for the Protection of Mothers and Children (Order of November 2, 1945) have regulated the creches. Since the war, female labor has been encouraged and new national associations have taken over the running of creches from the charitable associations; now the government, as well as the Caisses Nationales d'allocations familiales (CNAF), intervenes in early childhood politics.

Starting in 1960, specialized temporary child care centers, family creches, and parent-run creches have been implemented, regulated, and administered by the CNAF and the Ministry of Health. A 1974 decree regulating such creches specified their role in fostering children's cognitive and physical development. The increase in French women in the labor force, the shortage of day care centers, and the increasing costs have gradually led the authorities to develop and regulate "maternal assistants," and to encourage unofficial creches to meet regulations. This law also created parental leave without financial aid.

Primary Schools

For many centuries, teaching was undertaken exclusively by the clergy (monks and priests, and then nuns). This changed with the Order of February 29, 1816, promulgated during Louis XVIII's reign. The order defined the conditions under which primary schools should be set up throughout France, under the joint authority of the town council and the priest.

In June 28, 1833, during Louis-Philippe's monarchy, Francois Guizot began trying to equip each township with a public primary school, although they were not totally free, compulsory, or secular. Such public schools could even, under certain conditions, be confessional (i.e., run by the church).

The passionate struggle between public schools and private schools, still alive today, started on May 15, 1850, with a Law of the Second Republic ("Loi Falloux"), named after the minister of this period. It assured the freedom of teaching, freedom of which private schools especially took advantage.

In the Second Empire, the Duruy Law (April 10, 1867), created teaching for girls in each town over 500 inhabitants. In the Third Republic, primary schools became compulsory until children reached age 13, free (parents only paying for supplies), secular (Thursday is saved for religious instruction) by laws initiated by Jules Ferry on June 16, 1881, and March 28, 1882. Primary school organization has been more precisely defined in numerous orders and decrees since that time. Compulsory school was prolonged until age 14 in 1936, and to age 16 in 1956. A complete reform of the educational system was started by the Law of July 11, 1975, and later by a law on education passed on July 10, 1989.

Special Education

Precursors of Special Education

France has a long history of organizations and institutions created for the express purpose of caring for and controlling segments of the population deemed to be outside the norms of French society. In the 5th century, the first special institution for problem children was founded at Angers (Capul, 1984). In the 7th century, Saint Bertrand created the first charitable establishment for blind persons in the West at Le Mans (Fougeray and Couëtoux, 1896). Charlemagne issued an ordinance in 789 A.D. protecting charitable establish-

ments, including orphanages (Capul, 1974), and an edict in 805 A.D. threatened severe penalties for those who mistreated the blind (Fougeray and Couëtoux, 1896). A hospice for the blind was started in Normandy in the 11th century (Gauthier, 1984). Perhaps the most famous institution for disabled people in the Middle Ages was the hospice of the Quinze-Vingts in Paris, founded in the 13th century by Louis IX (St. Louis) for 300 blind poor persons in Paris. The blind children of the Quinze-Vingts, according to the rules of 1522, were to learn the beliefs necessary for their salvation. They were also taught to sing and recite the psalms in church and to have an "honest countenance." At the beginning of the 17th century, the Charity of Lyon taught the violin to blind orphans (Capul, 1983).

Care of Abandoned and "Difficult" Children. In the 12th century, F. Guy founded a hospice for abandoned children in Montpellier in the south of France. By the 13th century, there were more than 20 such hospices run by the Order of Saint-Esprit (founded around 1178–79) throughout Western Europe. This order also opened one of the first hospitals to receive the insane in Europe at Montpellier (Capul, 1974).

The first welfare office in France was opened in 1531 in Lyon, followed by one in Paris in 1546. In 1533 in Lyon, an establishment was created by the city to receive "little children crying and sobbing from hunger" (Capul, 1974). In 1632, Vincent de Paul was given the Parisian priory of Saint-Lazare, which had historically been a leprosarium. He gathered the mad, the abandoned children, the poor, and the disabled into Saint-Lazare, but there is little evidence that much else was done for them besides provision of the most meager necessities.

Deaf Children and Blind Children. Public awareness of the needs of blind persons and deaf persons was raised in Europe with Diderot's publication of his *Letter on the Blind* in 1747 (for which he served a prison term for being subversive) and his *Letter on the Deaf* in 1751.

Education of disabled children in France first began for children who were deaf, with Jacob Peireire and l'Abbé de l'Epée (1784), and with blind children, with Valentin Haüy (1786). The National Institute for Deaf Children opened in Paris in 1760, followed by the National Institute for Blind Children in 1782.

Mentally Handicapped Children. Special education with children who were mentally handicapped began with the work of Jean Itard in France with Victor, the "Wild boy of Aveyron." Itard, who worked at the Deaf and Dumb Institute in Paris, first saw Victor in 1799. He and Madame Guerin tried to teach Victor to speak and to read. They were only partly successful, but their methods, along with those of Itard's successor, Edouard Seguin, started a tradition that drew attention to the importance of sense training and stimulation in the development of the child's cognitive abilities.

In 1828, Pierre Ferrus, along with the superintendent Felix Voisin, organized the first "school for idiots" at the Bicêtre, an institution for mentally handicapped women. It was Voisin, in fact, who seems to have coined the term "special education" when in 1830 he published a report entitled "Application of the physiology of the Brain to the Study of Children Needing Special Education."

In 1831, Jules Falret created a school at the Salpêtrière for 24 "idiots, imbeciles, and chronic slow learners." In 1834, Voisin opened an "orthophrenic" establishment, which the Academy of Sciences later ordered to close. In 1837, Seguin, a teacher, undertook his first attempt at educating "idiots" and created the "medical-pedagogic" method of education. He published his results under the direction of his superiors Itard and Jean Esquirol in 1838.

The 1866 founding of the Société pour l'Instruction et la Protection des Enfants Sourds-Muets ou Arriérés (SIPSA) by Augustin Grosselin marked the beginning of the growth of many nonprofit private organizations that both lobbied the government and set up service systems of their own for adults and children with various disabilities.

First Special Education Classes in the School System

Preceding the initiation of special classes in the school system, Dr. Désiré-Magloire Bourneville created the first special sections for teaching mentally handicapped children at the Bicêtre Hospital (Gateaux-Mennecier, 1989). In 1896, Fougeray and Couëtoux wrote one of the first manuals for special education teachers—*Manuel pratique des méthodes d'enseignement aux anormaux* (Practical Manual of Methods for Teaching the Abnormal), which was published under the general editorship of Bourneville.

The first special education class for mentally handicapped children in France began in Paris on February 4, 1907 (Vial, 1986), but the law that formally provided for such classes was passed on April 15, 1909. This same law provided for a Certificate of Aptitude for teaching abnormal children for teachers in the national educational system. With this shift to educating mentally handicapped children in regular schools, the "asylum school" at the Bicêtre closed in 1920.

Other types of special classes and special schools began early in the 20th century as various groups became identified as needing special settings for education. The first "fresh air school" began in Mulhouse in 1906, followed by one in Lyon the following year (Martinez, 1985). In Bordeaux in 1907, the first classes for emotionally disturbed children were formed (Martinez, 1977). In Strasbourg, Professor Redslob created the first class in a regular school for visually impaired children in Europe (Nougaret, 1975). Hellen Poidatz founded an institute for physically disabled children at Saint-Fargeau (Pas-de-Calais) in 1919.

An order of January 22, 1964, created the Centres régionaux pour l'enfance et l'adolescence inadaptée (CREAI). These organizations were designed to play a coordinating role in the provision of special education services, to supply expert advice to local authorities, and to carry out research at the local level. At the national level, the coordination of information and research on special populations was given to the Centre Technique National de l'enfance et de l'adolescence inadaptée (CTNEAI), also founded in 1964. It became, in 1975, the Centre Technique National d'études et de recherches sur les handicaps et les inadaptations (CTNERHI).

Child Care and Primary Schooling in France Today

Child Care

As of 1990, there are more than 800,000 births every year in France; it is estimated that there are

4.5 million children from birth to age 6 (Bumel, 1990). Of these, it is thought that approximately 770,000 children under age 3 need care. If the 200,000 children with private day care providers are excluded, only 173,000 are in supervised group care. Of this number, 100,750 spaces are in regular creches, 52,700 are in family creches, 7,300 are in associative or parental creches, and 12,200 are in nursery schools (Thiémé, 1990).

In France, attitudes concerning child care are generally of the two types discussed below.

Child is Cared for at Home by Parents. Support for this option includes maternity leaves, which vary according to the employment status of the mother, and since 1977, postnatal leaves and educational parental leaves. Family allowances provisions have traditionally favored two categories of families: recently established families and large families. However, the Social Security budget for family allowances has decreased in relative terms from 1946 to 1982, while health expenditures have risen correspondingly.

Child is Entrusted to Private Caregiver in Her Own Home or to Child Care Institution. The May 1977 law protects caregivers and sets up a specific legal status for their profession. Legal structures of such institutions as creches are flexible, but requirements concerning the medical aspects and the general functioning of these institutions are very precise.

In France, nearly 50 percent of children under age 3 years of age whose mothers are working are cared for outside their home. About 25 percent of them are entrusted to private day care providers who may or may not have a license. Barely 8 percent go to creches, while 10 to 12 percent attend nursery schools. Having a child cared for outside the home creates difficult problems not only for the child, who has to internalize both the image of the mother and of the caregiver(s), but for the parents as well.

A young child should be gradually introduced to life outside the home to learn peer relations and to enjoy socialization (Stambak, 1984). The child should be provided with an environment that has a continuity both in terms of physical surroundings and of staff. It is important for the staff to encourage parents to visit the center where their child is cared for.

In France, it is considered that education ideally takes place both in the home and in child care centers. To reach such a goal, much is done to prepare parents not only to take part directly in their children's education, particularly by improving the situation of low-income families, but also to cooperate with the educational authorities.

Parental participation develops in the institutional framework of school associations and councils, where the parents' elected representatives are able to participate directly in the educational life. The evolution of parental participation has been influenced by the dramatic increase in women in the labor force; from 1975 to 1984, the percentage of women working outside the home went from 41.9 percent to 45.4 percent. The percentage for women between the ages of 20 and 44 went from 31 to 70 percent (Bumel, 1990).

The School System

Schools are managed by townships or municipalities. The school council includes the director, teachers, and parents' representatives. In 1972, specific inspectors for the maternal schools were replaced by regional inspectors for elementary schools and maternal schools or for elementary schools and special education.

Schooling is divided into cycles which are defined by national goals and an official national curriculum. This includes procedures for annual promotion as well as assessment criteria. However, in 1989, the notion of a learning cycle replaced the notion of a class, allowing teachers to better account for each child's psychological and physiological evolution. The learning cycle is a pedagogical reality, as distinct from the notion of chronological age and school grades.

Schooling, from the maternal school to the end of elementary school, a six-year period, includes three cycles:

1.   the pretraining cycle from ages 2 to 5, which is divided into small children, middle children, and other children of the maternal school;

2.   the cycle of fundamental learning, from ages 5 to 7, which is divided into the preparatory course (CP) and the elementary course (CE1); and

3.   the cycle of further learning, from ages 7 to 9, which is divided into the middle course, first and second years (CM1 and CM2).

Generally, children belonging to the same chronological age group attend the same program in the same classroom, with a maximum of 35 students per class, and the mean being 25. However, there are some classes with mixed programs, with children at two or more different levels.

Since 1989, a child cannot be forced to repeat a year within a cycle, as the goals have been set for each cycle. At the time of change from maternal school to primary school, it is particularly important that students be followed up in order to check for educational continuity.

This is the ideal pattern, but as Wresinsky (1987) has noted, schools for culturally and economically disadvantaged children often appear to be "a strange world because its unfamiliar way of life and sophisticated language or code used in manuals." Because of this, there are many school failures in these groups of children. The year before the 1989 reform, at the national level, the percentage of children who were repeating a year, at least twice, during primary school was 9 percent. Most of these children belonged to the lower socioeconomic classes (unskilled workers, 26.1 percent; salaried employees, 22.3 percent; unemployed, 19.5 percent; skilled workers, 14.4 percent). In contrast, the proportion of children belonging to upper class who failed did not exceed .4 percent.

Early schooling in the maternal school attempts to compensate for sociocultural handicaps. Positive effects and school success by the end of primary school are noticeable for children of the lower socioeconomic classes. One study showed that while the percentage of school success increase 11 points for upper class children, the gains for lower class children were between 18 and 22 points. These figures have to be tempered by taking into account other factors, such as family's ambition level, older children's schooling, and birth order, which can mask results that are coached only in terms of the work statuses of the parents.

Mainstreaming of Handicapped Children

The decrees of April 22, 1988, and October 27, 1989, set new technical conditions of agreement for private institutions of care and prevention funded by Social Security. The main goals were to change from the notion of custody to the notions of welcome and development of capacities. This official report introduced school mainstreaming and partnerships between schools and special institutions, affirming a role for parents in the planning of any future programming for their handicapped children.

However, school mainstreaming, although favored by many parents, is still resisted by physicians and teachers. In general, school mainstreaming has been delayed by the lack of resources, especially a shortage of specially trained teachers.

The Ministry of Education stresses the importance of the following measures for the development of special education:

• the opening of special schools or classes within ordinary nursery or primary schools (based on the belief that the problems of handicapped children are on the whole ameliorated by contact with normal children);

• an increase in the number of social services offices;

• an increase in the number of special schools;

• easier access to training for special education teachers; and

• the improvement of the technological and educational equipment in special schools.

The identification of children needing special education involves the collaboration of teachers, the school medical officer and, in some cases, an educational psychologist. Children who do not appear to be making satisfactory progress are usually referred by their teachers for examination by a school medical officer, who carries out a thorough examination to see whether the child has learning disabilities. School medical officers who examine children thought to be educationally subnormal have special training for this work.

The child's abilities are tested by an educational psychologist. The report of the school medical officer is then sent to the local educational authority. After considering it in relation to the reports on information from the child's head teacher and other persons, this authority decides whether the child needs special educational treatment, and, if so, of what kind.

Special Classes

Special classes in the French public schools can be presented as three types of structures: (1)

opportunity classes, (2) adjustment classes, and (3) integrated classes.

Opportunity Classes. The opportunity classes, created in 1909, receive children ages 8 to 12 (in exceptional cases up to age 14), with an IQ between 50 and 80. A special commission examines different psychological, social, and medical reports for each child. These classes are usually annexed to elementary schools. The number of students in each class is reduced to 15 or 16. Specific curriculum materials have been developed and appropriate teaching involves interpersonal skills, problem-solving, empathy, self-awareness, communication skills, and skills for coping with stress. Child-centered programs are enhanced, here, involving parents and connecting them with two sets of children's services: (1) psycho-educational support teams and (2) child guidance centers.

There are over 3,600 psycho-educational support teams in France (one for every 1,140 primary school students). They were created by the Ministry of National Education in February 1970 to reduce and prevent school failures. The team includes an educational psychologist, a teacher trained in pedagogical methods of special education and a specialist in psychomotor training. Although only 84 percent of the psycho-educational support teams include all three professionals, 95 percent have an educational psychologist. The role of the teams is to apply the concept of prevention not in terms of exclusion but in terms of integration. The child guidance centers include a multidisciplinary team (i.e., child psychiatrist, speech pathologist, social workers, and psychomotor specialist) and provide direct services to schools and parents.

Adjustment Classes. The educational purpose of the adjustment classes, created in February 1970, is to work with children who have learning difficulties, emotional and/or behavioral disorders, or who are suffering from cultural disadvantages. The main goal is to integrate them, as soon as possible, usually within a year, into regular primary schools.

Integrated Classes. Integrated classes were created to allow some handicapped children from medical educational facilities to go to regular schools. Such integration is educational for both disabled and nondisabled children, but for the disabled children, their education is not disconnected from their medical care. Integrated classes

are supported by both the Ministry of Health, Solidarity, and Social Affairs and the Ministry of National Education. The boundaries of their jurisdictions are not stringent: difficulties that arise can be handled either by educational staff or by medical staff.

Data reported by the Ministry of National Education show that handicapped children (i.e., those with sensory deficits, motor handicaps, behavioral problems, or intellectual deficits) represented 10 to 12 percent of all students. From 1982 to 1988, the number of children admitted to integrated classes remained relatively the same (between 1,500 and 5,000 students), but the number of students admitted to opportunity classes decreased by 25 percent (from 78,000 to 62,000). During the same period, the number of handicapped children in regular schools decreased by 3 percent. Despite the efforts made to mainstream handicapped children, the chances for their integration remain very low (in each year, only 5 percent of students in an opportunity class leave for a regular class) (Ravaud, 1991).

The School Day

In public schools, the day is organized according to governmental guidelines. School begins at 8:30 a.m. and ends at 4:30 p.m. The 26-hour school week is divided into nine half-days. Wednesday and Saturday afternoons are free so that parents who wish to can give their children religious instruction. In several townships, after 4:30 p.m., supplementary time is given to let students do their assignments or to allow qualified teachers help them. The purpose of *"études surveillées ou dirigées"* (supervised study) is twofold; they are a type of after-school day care and also allow the student to do his or her homework. For example, the city of Paris is responsible for after-school care in the primary system for about 14,000 students. At Angers, teachers personally take responsibility for 80 percent of all after-school supervision.

An academic calendar is set up each year by the Ministry of National Education. Revisions are possible, under conditions set down by the decree, to take into account local conditions. The academic year includes 36 weeks divided into five school periods and four holiday periods: the week of All Saints Day, two weeks at Christmas, a two-week spring break, and two and one-half months of summer holidays. An extra day can be given by the local inspector on the request of the mayor of the town or city. There is no school on Sundays.

Teaching Staff

Data from National Education statistics indicate that 307, 098 teachers practiced in public schools during the 1988–89 academic year: 73,795 (24 percent) in preschools, including directors, teachers, and assistant teachers, an increase of 0.6 percent from the previous year. A total of 198,922 (64.8 percent) teachers were in primary schools, a decrease of 0.6 percent from the previous year. The number of teachers and allied professionals in special education was 22,860 (7.4 percent) in special schools, an increase of 3.1 percent over the last two years.

Preschool and primary school teachers are recruited on the basis of a competitive examination. Before taking it, applicants are required to get a college degree. Training and supervision are given in the normal schools and last two years. The directors of the normal schools are responsible for these two years of theoretical curriculum (i.e., philosophy, history, psychology, paedagogy, didactics of curricula, education science, and legislation) and practical training. This compulsory teacher training is done mainly by professors of the normal schools, but other professionals also collaborate. During this training, the students are considered government-employed teachers and are paid. They are required to work ten years for the government but are guaranteed a position after their degree. Beginning in fall 1990, the French government began a gradual phasing out of the normal schools, replacing them with University Institutes for Teacher Training (Instituts Universitaires de Formation des Maîtres (IUFM)).

Special education teachers receive training in a separate division of the normal schools. This training takes three years and leads to a diploma that gives the immediate right to an appointment in a special education establishment. This degree is required in order to be a special education teacher or a psychomotor specialist.

Curriculum in the French School System

In the French school system, the curriculum is defined by the national government, which publishes *Programs and Official Instructions* (Babin and Pierre, 1986; Pierre, Terrieux, and Babin, 1991). The Order of August 1, 1990, divided the school week into 26 hours for both the maternal schools and the elementary schools. Given that compulsory schooling lasts until age 16, the elementary school deals primarily with development of cognitive skills and intellectual performances in order to prepare the child for the secondary level. The maternal school covers a broader spectrum of activities, which are designed to foster social behavior as well as intellectual learning.

Preschool Curriculum

At the maternal school, the goals of the curriculum are to develop children's physical, social, behavioral, and intellectual skills in order to provide them with the ability to cope with the wide variety of situations that a complex environment imposes. The curriculum is therefore to be holistic because children's emotional, social, and intellectual needs are intricately entwined with their family and community. The teacher helps the child develop skills and attitudes needed to cope with the demands and challenges of everyday life. Children are expected to learn behavioral controls of self-care, to try new tasks, to share and yield, and to stand up for their rights when these are unfairly challenged. This learning is to occur in a wide variety of situations over a period of time rather than deliberately "taught." For example, youngsters, who, because of a multicultural background, appear to be disorganized and deficient in language and concepts, usually can benefit from short periods of child-initiated activities. The teacher leans more toward different activities or particular interests and needs of the children in the group (often identified as an *experience*) rather than towards a set curriculum. The artful teacher observes the progress of the children in problem-solving, concept formation, memory, judgment, perception, and logical thinking, through communication and interaction with peers. In short, the main goals of the pretraining cycle during the maternal school are to develop children's skills in motor abilities, communication and written expression, arts, sciences, and technical activities (Pierre, Terrieux, and Babin, 1991).

Motor Abilities. The didactics of physical education are to be functional, child-centered and developmentally appropriate in order to help the child reveal his or her aptitudes, enjoy socialization, and overcome weaknesses or handicaps.

Communication and Written Expression. Official documents suggest that the maternal school should let the child acquire an orientation to reading through exploring written language.

In the first pretraining cycle for children ages 2 to 5, the teacher uses various materials to teach children to pay attention to pictures, stories, games, and other activities that foster visual, auditory, and kinesthetic discrimination and familiarize them with simple concepts appropriate to their level of understanding. Although acquisitions are different from child to child, the emphasis is on the development of the learning skills and their use in everyday life rather than on their application in symbolic practice of formalized learning experience. For example, titles in picture books are distinctly read by the teacher in order to facilitate discrimination and to develop memory processes. Nursery rhymes, songs, and ritual formulas are used to let the child acquire syntactic structures from rote learning or from repetition, as well as for the sheer pleasure derived from making sounds.

In the next cycle, such experiences are more developed. It is important to make the children familiar with the diversity of written language and to use a variety of props: signs showing the name of the streets, game boxes, wrapping paper, business cards, etc.

In the final cycle, work in written language is further intensified. The teacher focuses the activity on spatial organization to help the child first to find landmarks and to make hypotheses. The texts are further expanded, providing the child with the opportunity to analyze not only calligraphic letters, but also to expand syntactic structures and lexicon.

Painting and Arts. Painting and arts are valued as contributing to learning. Supervision is supportive rather than directive in order for children to test their skills, ideas, perception, knowledge, initiative, and control. By providing a large variety of materials, the teacher lets the child blossom through manipulative activities that permit the child to become aware of his or her creativity; to control his or her gestures and motor activities; and to develop manual skills, coordination, and balance. Different types of activities are suggested to children to develop free expression; to acquaint them with materials, tools, and supports; to find solutions to problems; and to teach them to think about materials, thereby allowing the child to gradually enrich his or her knowledge.

Science and Technical Activities. According to a Ministry circular dated January 30, 1986: "Scientific and technical activities lead the child to explore, to discover and to build. The child observes, uses material, selects techniques." The teacher should facilitate—through observation, action, and direct contact—the elaboration of concepts concerning life and scientific techniques. The teacher's role is to encourage children to ask questions, to try out answers, and to develop a critical mind in order to understand the world.

The approach to numbers at the maternal school consists of associating names, figures, and collections. (Daurat-Meljac and Verba-Raid, 1975; Piaget and Szeminska, 1941; Pire, 1959). Two representations play an important role: (1) numerical series (i.e., orderly lists that allow counting to become a prelude to a mental image of graduation) and (2) the constellations of numbers (e.g., those found on playing dice, dominos, or cards).

Primary School Curriculum

The priority in primary school, according to the Ministry of Education, is to be ready to cope with secondary school. About 65 percent of French students eventually receive their the baccalaureate degree (Babin and Pierre, 1986). Obviously, it is necessary to master reading, writing, and counting, but that is not sufficient.

In 1989, the French educational system revised the curricula in the primary schools. The increasing complexity of the knowledge to be taught makes it necessary for the students to have real contact with the notions to be studied. To learn about the environment in theory, for example, is less desirable than to gain experience in controlling it. Likewise, becoming a participant in town life is better than studying dogmatic notions from manuals of civic education. Such examples indicate that evolution of society makes primary school knowledge multidimensional: *savoir* ("to know"), *savoir-faire* ("to know how to do something"), *savoir-être* ("to know how to live"), and *savoir-devenir* ("to know how to change") are key terms in the philosophy of the new primary curriculum (Cruchet, Férot, and Leroy, 1989).

French Lessons. Teachers are guided by four goals in preparing and conducting a French lesson in the primary school; they seek to teach children to: (1) master the oral language, (2) learn to read and write, (3) learn grammar rules and word formation so that the children can write from dictation, and (4) discover and enjoy national and international nursery rhymes and poetry.

In the preparatory course, the aims of the curricula are: (1) to learn basic pronunciation and writing rules (e.g., letter segmentation, space identification, correct punctuation, and accentuation) and (2) to write in good style stories, legends, or posters using appropriate vocabulary and syntax. In the elementary course, the teacher focuses more and more on the way to write a script organizing different paragraphs. In the middle course, the emphasis is on expressing ideas using narrative sequences and argumentative statements. At this level, the children give talks to other students, expressing and organizing their personal thoughts.

Mathematics. In the preparatory course, attention is paid to mastering the following mathematical strategies: (1) classification and sequencing of objects, (2) writing and identifying numbers from zero to 100, (3) ordering numbers in increasing or decreasing series, (4) comparing two numbers, and the concepts of equal, greater than, and less than, (5) problem-solving using addition, and (6) measuring such things as length and mass. In the elementary course, students increase their skill at writing numbers (zero to 10,000); learn to solve problems using more complex formulas; identify symmetrical patterns using rulers, compasses, gauges, and squares; and learn the metric system. In the middle course, students study the decimal system and learn to solve problems using the rule

of three, fractions, and percentages, and to use mathematical formulas to measure length, surface, volume, angle, and duration.

Science and Technology. In the preparatory course, knowledge of the properties of common materials and how to use basic equipment, such as tape recorders and cameras, is required. Students also study biology, with such topics as growth of the human body and the development of vegetal and animal life. In the elementary course, biology is studied in more depth, and students are introduced to physical and earth sciences. Students also learn the properties of matter and its transformations (e.g., solids, liquids, gas) and the properties of air, water, and minerals. Technological projects are conceived, organized, and realized (e.g., the notion of electrical circuits, levers, and balances). In the middle course, students learn to solve problems of space and time, formulate hypotheses concerning astronomy and geographical phenomena, and experiment to find solutions to problems (e.g., electrical wiring). As students begin to understand the consistency and the social dimension of their discoveries, they become familiar with the elements of technological culture (e.g., computer, robots, and automatons).

Civics Education. In the preparatory course, ethical notions and fundamental rules for social life are presented (e.g., concepts concerning hygiene, security, effort, work value, self-respect, respect of equipment, and human rights). Some national symbols are also taught (e.g., the statue of Marianne, the French flag, the national anthem, "Marseillaise," and Bastille Day). In the elementary course, society's common rules and expectations, with a clear awareness of their justification (e.g., the concepts of person, property, contract, homeland, and the Republic principles of liberty, equality, and fraternity) are explained. The framework of institutions is also outlined (e.g., townships and schools). In the middle course, students focus more on French society through an analysis of the main institutions. They learn important dates, (e.g., 1789—Declaration of human rights; 1948—Universal Declaration of human rights), the main institutions, regulations of social life, and the role of France in the world.

History and Geography. In the preparatory course, students learn to organize time (e.g., day, night, seasons, calendar, hours) and space. They use some precise and simple words to locate and describe human beings, events, and phenomena (e.g., birthdays, feasts, holidays, and commemorations). They become aware of the past and learn basic chronology. In the elementary course, students examine the chronology of the main events in French history and learn to place themselves in history and in geographical space. At this level, they begin to master some methodology and tools of representation. In the middle course, students systematically investigate French history and geography. They improve their methods of working, and vocabulary and pay critical attention to school documents and to audiovisual information.

Arts. In the preparatory course, students listen attentively to folk songs, nursery rhymes, and cradles songs; they also learn the pitch of their voices and the words and melodies of a number of songs. In the elementary course, students learn to discriminate noises and sounds, to analyze short excerpts of musical masterpieces, and to try to create and to improvise. In the middle course, students learn and interpret a repertoire of 30 to 50 songs, and learn how to accompany these songs with an instrument. They also develop improvisation resources and critical judgment on different types of music. French students must all know a specified national list of 28 songs, as well as regional songs and songs of their own choice.

Recreational Activities and Sports. During the preparatory course, students begin to explore recreational and athletic resources. In the elementary course, individual and group activities are offered (e.g., track and field, swimming, outdoor activities, gymnastics, dance and body expression, games, and collective sports). In the middle course, different types of activities are suggested. For outdoor play, horseback riding, ice skating, canoeing or kayaking, sailing, rock climbing, skiing, and sledding are offered. Gymnastics includes balance, tumbling, apparatus, beam, parallel bar, and fixed bars activities. Dancing includes rondos and indi-

vidual and group dances (modern and jazz). Athletics games and sports are also among the suggested activities for students.

Future Directions in Preschool and Primary School in France

Much more research must be done and radical changes have to be made for schools to better meet individual children's needs. This means making the school system less centralized, more adaptive, culturally more open, and attractive, while maintaining high academic standards. Some of the future directions in preschool and primary school are summarized below:

• Multicultural curricula in early childhood education must be developed.

• The idea that social interaction plays an important role in the development of communicative and cognitive competencies must be emphasized in the curricula. The notion that cooperation, constructive confrontation, and exchanges between students enhance the development of knowledge should be emphasized.

• Research into learning by computers should be conducted so that the learning process can be better understood and used to develop potentialities in the young child and to prevent school failure.

• Research in family education should be conducted in order to examine social determinants and to describe and analyze parents' attitudes, practices, language, educative behavior, expectations, roles, needs, motivation, and projects.

• Families should be supported on an everyday basis to enrich parents' capacities and to improve the cultural and family environment in which the child lives.

• The mainstreaming of handicapped children should be improved to allow better collaboration and communication among all institutions involved with children (i.e., family, school, medical structures, and social institutions).

References

Abbé de l'Épée, C.M. (1784). *La véritable manière d'instruire les sourds et muets confirmée par une longue expérience.* Corpus des oeuvres de philosophie en langue français, 1984. Paris: Fayard.

Ariés, P. (1960). *L'enfant et la vie familiale sous l'ancien régime.* Paris: Plon.

Aymé, M. (1939). *Les contes du chat perché.* Paris: Gallimard.

Babin, N., & Pierre, M. (1986). *Programmes, instruction, conseils pour l'école élémentaire.* Paris: Hachette.

Binet, A. (1905). *Rapport au nom de la Sous-Commission pédagogique des anormaux.* Paris: Commission pour l'éducation des enfants anormaux.

Binet, A., & Simon T. (1907). *Les enfants anormaux.* Paris: Cité.

Bumel, R. (1990). L'accueil de l'enfant, élément essentiel d'une politique familiale globale, 14, Réalités Familiales. *Revue de l'Union Nationale des Associations Familiales,* 1.

Capul, Maurice. (1974). *Les groupes éducatifs.* Paris: Presses Universitaires de France.

———. (1983). *Internat et internement sous l'ancien regime.* Vol. 1 and 2. *Les enfants placés.* Paris: CTNERHI.

———. (1984). *Internat et internement sous l'ancien regime.* Vol. 3 and 4. *La pédagogie des maisons d'assistance.* Paris: CTNERHI.

Chevrie-Muller, C. (1987). *Provision and management for children with language disorders, the situation in France.* First International Symposium on Child Speech and Language Disorders, Reading, U.K. March 29–April 3, 1987.

Cochin, D. (1834). *Manuel des fondateurs et des directeurs des première écoles de l'enfance connues sous le nom de salles d'asile.* 2d, ed. Paris.

Dany, E., Durand, C., Elsen, P., & Renaudeau, S. (1990). *L'école maternelle, première école, formation des enseignants.* Paris: Armanud Colin.

Daurat-Meljac, C., & Verba-Raid, M. (1975). Evolution de l'utilisation du nombre dans la discription d'une collection chez les enfants de 4 à 7 ans. *Revue de Psychologie appliquée,* 25, 67–90.

Ducoing, J.L. (1965). Les rééducateurs de l'éducation Nationale. *Les cahiers d'enfance inadaptée,* 6.

Fougeray, H., & Couêtoux, L. (1896). *Manuel pratique des méthodes d'enseignement spéciales. Sourds-muets, aveugles, idiots, bègues, etc. Méthodes—statistique—institutions—legislation, etc.* Paris: Alcan.

Gateaux-Mennecier, J. (1989). *Bourneville et l'enfance aliénée.* Paris: Centurion.

Gauthier (1984) as cited in Le Disert, D. (1987). Entre la peur et la pitié: quel ques aspects socio-historiques de l'infirmité. *International Journal of Rehabilitation Research,* 10 3: 253–65.

Georges, J. (1986). *Les comptines, classique juniors.* Paris: Larousse.

Haüy, V. (1786). *Essai sur l'éducation des aveugles.* Reprinted by Editions des Archives Contemporaines, Paris, 1985.

Jospin, L. (1989). La rénovation est une affaire de volonté, de conviction et de temps. *Cahiers de l'Education Nationale,* 74, (September–October.)

Martinez, M. (1977). Histoire de l'enseignement spécial: 1° mai 1907: Les classes de perfectionnement de Bordeaux. *Cahiers de l'enfance inadaptée,* 216, 26–29.

———. (1985) La création de l'école de plein air de Nîmes (Gard), 1922. *Cahiers de l'enfance inadaptée,* 277 (February): 16–20.

Norvez, A. (1990). *De la naissance à l'école: Santé, modes de garde et préscolarité dans la France Comtemporanien.* Travaux et Documents, Cahier No. 126, PUF. Paris: Institut National d'études démographiques.

Nougaret, H. (1975). *L'Action médico-sociale en faveur des enfants handicapés physiques.* Thèse, Doctorat en médecine, Université de Montpellier.

Piaget, J., & Szeminska, A. (1941). *La genèse du nombre chez l'enfant.* Neuchâtel: Delachaux & Niestlé.

Pierre, M., Terrieux, J., & Babin, N. (1990). *Orientation-projects—Activités pour l'école maternelle, la classe au quotidien.* Paris: Hachette.

Pire, G. (1959). Sur le chemin du nombre. *Enfance,* 6, 473–92.

Ravaud, J.F. (1991). La scolarisation des enfants handicapés en France. In *Les personnes handicapés, données sociales, France 1990.* Paris: Cahiers du CTNERHI.

Raynaud, P. (1982). L'éducation spécialisée en France 1882–1982. *Esprit,* 65, 75–126.

Rollet, C. (1983). Naissance et développment d'une politique de la petite enfance (1870–1940). *Revue de Comité National de l'enfance.*

———. (1982). Nourrices et nourrissons dans le départment de la Seine et en France de 1880 à 1940. *Population,* 3.

———. (1988). *La politique à l'égard de la petite enfance, sous la IIIème République, Thèse d'état.* Université de René Descartes, Paris V.

Roussel, T. (1874). Rapport concernant l'application de la loi du 23 décembre 1874. *Journal Officiel,* 2 Février 1882, 596.

Stambak, M. (1984). Children under two years of age in daycare center: the importance of peer-relations. In N. Kobayaski & T.B. Brazelton (Eds.), *Child growth in family and society.* Tokyo: Tokyo University Press.

Thiemé, G. (1990) Realités familials, *Revue de L'Union Nationale des Associations Familiales, L'Accueil de la Petite Enfance.* No. 14, March-April.

Velche, D. (in press). Les instituts médico-educatifs: Repères historiques. *Cahiers de L'Education—Pédagogie et Informatique.*

Vial, M. (1986). *Les origines de l'enseignement spécial en France.* Paris: INRP.

Vildrac, C. (1975). Recueil de six chansons. In G. Jean (Ed.), *Le premier livre d'or des poètes.* Paris: Seghers.

Woodill, G. (1988). *Bibliographie signalétique, Histoire des handicaps et inadaptations.* Vanves, France: Editions du CTNERHI.

Wresinky, J. (1987). Grande pauvreté et précarité économique et sociale. *Rapport au conseil économique et sociale,* (Février).

PRESCHOOL EDUCATION IN GERMANY

●●●●●●●●●◆●●●●●●●●

Arnulf Hopf
Oldenburg University
Oldenburg, Germany

In the second half of the 19th century increasing industrialization and urbanization resulted in the founding of the first "guarding nurseries" by Fölising (1818–12) and Fleidner (1800–64). In Prussia alone there were 400 institutions of this kind by 1850. The aim of the nurseries was to prevent children from being morally and physically neglected as well as to teach them to become diligent, pious, and orderly citizens.

At the same time, beginning in 1840, nursery schools were being started by Friedrich Froebel for the German bourgeoisie. As the lowest level of a uniform system of education still under the influences of the democratic demands made by the French Revolution, the kindergarten also served to teach cognitive educational concepts (discussed below).

The need for nursery schools and the demand for regulations for the existing system of care privately organized for Christian and charitable motives became particularly obvious during and after World War I when more and more mothers were gainfully employed. With the Youth Welfare Law of 1924, it was finally decided not to include nursery schools in the national system of education, but rather to entrust them to the independent associations of private youth welfare. This meant that denominational associations and, therefore, the subsidiary principle (i.e., the priority of private initiatives over those of the state), which is still valid today, were asserted against governmental and socialist desires.

Moreover, from this time, the priority of parental rights was established, consequently interpreting all preschool facilities as supporting family education. This means that while, on the one hand, attending nursery school is optional even today, children have no legal claim to preschool education (in a nursery school or in a creche). After the breaking up of the Third Reich, during which child education was oriented toward Nazi ideology (i.e., instilling obedience, following the Führer, and making boys accept the role of a future soldier and girls a future mother), the nursery school system in East and West Germany followed different lines of development. The nursery school system in East Germany was integrated into the unified school system, thus becoming part of the public educational system. In West Germany, the social welfare aspects of nursery school education were emphasized, denying the nursery schools an independent educational task until 1970. Only since the critical incentives given by the *Kinderladen* movement of 1968 and the German *bildungsgesamtplan* (1970) has the nursery school been clearly subsumed in the educational system as part of elementary education.

Although more nursery school places have been created since then, the overall situation has not been improved significantly. As of 1990, it was particularly precarious, since an increase in the growth of population is expected.

In general, the nursery schools in the Federal Republic of Germany are half-day facilities; only about 12 percent are all-day nurseries. The provisions for children up to age 1—the creches—and for children between ages 1 and 3—toddler centers—are even less satisfying. In 1986, only 1.7 percent of children in these age groups were served in such programs. Cities with the two largest numbers of children in nursery schools are Berlin (22 percent) and Hamburg (10 percent).

In contrast to the nursery school system, there is less emphasis on education in the creche system. Moreover, a conservative family policy has resulted in a shortage of child care spaces and an overrepresentation of children from low-income families in the spaces that do exist. This, in turn, has added to the social stigma of creche education.

The general increase in the employment of mothers of young children, the increasingly difficult housing situation, and the changing family structures must result in an improvement in the system of care for children under age 3. Because of a lack of public facilities, many parents have organized private self-help groups (this is discussed below). These parent-child groups, however, have developed differently from the anti-authoritarian playgroups organized by parents in the late 1960s. Thus far, the preschool initiatives have not been able to compensate for the loss of significance of the nursery school and its place in educational policy.

Preschool Programs

Because of the many directions taken by the German kindergarten, there is no standard educational program. However, it is still possible to find nursery schools using the approach and materials of Froebel and Maria Montessori, together, the two most important influences on Germany nursery education. "Froebel education" views the child as an integrated person. Through play, the child presents his or her inner world. The play things (e.g., a ball, bowl, cube, or pyramid), once explained metaphysically by Froebel, as well as the materials he offered for "occupations," are still important in preschool education in Germany. The most popular materials, however, are being used in rather unorthodox ways (e.g., weaving paper strips, playing with wooden sticks and pearls, or building with wooden bricks).

Similarly, deprived of the former anthropological meaning, Montessori materials are used strictly as "didactic" materials. As learning games, they are part of the basic equipment of every nursery school to train independent activity as well as the senses. There are only a few Montessori nursery schools ("children's houses") that use the material in the original manner. Another traditional educational program is the anthroposophical concept developed by Rudolf Steiner (1861–1925) and used in the Waldorf-Kindergarten (Grunelius, 1975).

Since the 1970s, two interconnected programmatic approaches, the function-oriented and situation-oriented, have joined these traditional methods and philosophies. Influenced by a socioscientific pedagogy and German educational reform (Deutscher Bildungsrat, 1975), training programs were developed aimed at improving children's level of achievement and development. Didactic learning and teaching material, training files, and exercise material for individual psychological functions and skills, such as early reading, are now mainly used in the West German nursery schools where achievement-oriented parents expect their child to be prepared for school. On the whole, however, the function-oriented approach has not been accepted. The main criticism of the approach is that it is short-sighted. The long-term results of working with children from deprived families did not meet the expectations. In addition, initial improvements in intelligence and achievement were quickly lost. Finally, children's need for free play and self-determined learning were not sufficiently considered.

The situation-oriented approach, on the other hand, was more popular. Originally derived from a very broad model project (Deutsches

Jugendinstitut, 1971–76), the aim is to enable children from different social backgrounds and with different learning histories to act as autonomously and competently as possible in present and future situations. The advantages of the approach are its flexibility in terms of the curriculum; the ability for children of different ages and stages of development to learn and play in heterogenous groups; its focus on the involvement of parents, neighbors, and other adults who are connected with the nursery school; and the use of social situations from the everyday life of the children.

In the situation-oriented approach, stimulating learning processes, rather than determining them, is part of the nursery teacher's task. Teachers function less as experts for the learning process and possessors of knowledge, and more as providers of the framework in which the children are to learn the social and instrumental abilities as independently as possible. In summary, although most German nursery schools are following the tradition based on Froebel, they are attempting to extend its possibilities. In this context, the situational approach is of enormous significance.

Play is the focus and main characteristic of today's nursery schools. In the course of a morning, in a relatively steady rhythm, there is self-determined free play (e.g., table games, building games, and role playing) from about 8:00 a.m. to 10:00 a.m., outdoor or indoor activities (e.g., movement games, handicrafts, drawing, or looking at picture books) until about 11:00 a.m., and going for walks and free play until the parents pick the children up between noon and 12:20 p.m. In general, the same pattern is repeated in the afternoon.

Special Educational Programs for Young Children

There are only a few models for remedial education for preschool children at home in West Germany. The Munich *kinderzentrum* is a system based on multidimensional therapy and integration in nursery schools (Hellbrügge, 1981). Early integration in nonfamily institutions is aimed at providing an alternative to permanent residential care. Special nursery schools and kindergartens in

particular have tried in the past to provide programs for the different kinds of handicaps (e.g., learning disability, behavioral disorders, and physical handicaps). However, only about 1 percent of all nursery schools are special nursery schools, while the relative proportion of handicapped children of the same year amounts to about 10 percent (Topsch and Kiel, 1978). Some handicaps, such as learning disabilities, speech impediments, and behavioral disorders, are often recognized only when the child reaches elementary school. This is one reason why preschool programs for handicapped children have not been more satisfactory.

However, integrated public nursery schools are becoming more common. There are two kinds of integrated groups: (1) handicapped and nonhandicapped children are grouped together for a few hours each day or (2) about 12 nonhandicapped and 3 handicapped children are permanently grouped together. In both cases, a specially trained staff is required but not often available.

While these groups are formed mainly to improve the childrens' ability to play, they have a more general influence on the children's development of other abilities and skills. Above all, in mixed-age groups it has become apparent that children who have difficulties are not excluded but rather are integrated into a broader context of abilities and dispositions. Children generally accept individual differences. Many people see the long-term goal of this integration as amalgamating the socio-integrative potential and the curative educational-therapeutical potential into one system.

A common facility is the nursery school in an elementary school where children of school age who are not ready for school are given special attention in order to prevent them from being placed in a special school. On the whole, there are increased efforts at prevention through early diagnosis. In this context, cooperation with the parents through socio-educational family care, family counseling, and parental education have become more important. Parental self-help groups have also formed in connection with certain childhood handicaps and early disorders.

Training Programs for Teachers of Young Children

The qualifications for preschool education teaching differ with regard to the level of training—training college (*berufsfachschule*), technical college (*fachschule*) or university. They often also differ with regard to the content and design of the training among the individual federal states. Consequently, there are many different qualifications in the area of elementary education in the Federal Republic of Germany (see Table 1).

TABLE 1

Qualifications of Staff in Preschool Education (1982)

Qualifications	Percentage (%)
University (*Diplompädagogen*)	1.6
Technical College (*Erzieher*)	51.0
Training College (*Kinderpfleger*)	15.5
Other Academic Training	.5
Nursing Training	.5
Other Noneducational Training	4.5
Still Being Trained	15.2
No Qualification	11.3
	100.0

As shown in Table 1, both skilled and unskilled staff with many different qualifications are working in the same jobs. This causes fragmentation and creates a hierarchy in preschool education. The different regulations are also due to different training interests on the part of financing and governing agencies, (e.g., churches, charities, communes, or the state). The different training courses are summarized below.[1]

University

A small proportion of the skilled staff working in preschool education are "Sozialpädagogen" or "Diplomapägogen" with a focus on social education. Training is either at "Fachhochschulen" in a four-year course including a one-year field placement, or at universities in a four-year course (without a placement). In either case, the program is very academic and divided into a basic and a main course of studies and a thesis. The qualification required is the "Abitur" or another academic standard qualifying for university entrance. The majority of these graduates work in leading positions in larger day nurseries or institutions.

Technical College

Since 1973, the qualification for a technical college degree has been based on a three-year training program at "Fachschulen für Sozialpädagogik," which as a rule are affiliated with other technical colleges. About 50 percent of these technical colleges are privately maintained, mostly by the churches. A certificate from a vocational school or any other secondary school is generally required for admission, as well as a one-year preliminary placement in any social or socio-education institution.

The training is divided into a two-year phase of mainly theoretical orientation with approximately 15 different subjects, and a subsequent one-year placement supervised by the technical college. The subjects taught (on average two lessons per week) are (using the example of Lower Saxony): German, social studies, religious education, psychology, youth assistance, education, didactics and methodology, literature for children and young people, art, handicrafts, music, rhythmics, playing, sports, and other compulsory subjects. For many years this training, which resembles school education in so far as it allows the students little independence, has been under discussion and a more satisfying interconnection of theory and practice is being sought.

Training College

The general admission requirement for the training college is completion of "Hauptschule." The training takes between one and three years, varying from one federal state to the other. Training institutions are the "Berufsfachschulen für Kinderpflegerinnen."

Originally, this qualification was aimed solely at family assistance. However, socio-education training has been added to the domestic and nursing skills in recent years. There is still general agreement that the training college graduate is to be employed as assistant helper in the nursery school. Demands have been make to raise this training to the level of that of the technical college, since responsible educational work is the same for each category of staff.

In addition to these three groups, a considerable proportion of untrained staff work in preschools. These include parent helpers, persons from other professions, as well as students in training. Part of this group are childminders participating in short training courses.

Parental Support and Educational Programs

The necessity of support programs for parents or families in order to safeguard the educational capacity of the parents is the undisputed object of all family legislation. The system of parental and family programs is very diverse.

Parental and family education is a special field of adult education aimed at preparing parents for family life and at helping them cope with their educational tasks. One focus is on developing skills to cope with problems and conflicts. In general, parental and family education is organized by independent institutions (*freie Träger*, for example, the churches) and organizations.

Socio-educational family aid is a specific assistance program for families with children in difficult situations. This aid, which is free of charge for the user, consists of practical and educational support given in the homes of families with small children. It is financed by charitable organizations or communal youth welfare departments. This program is staffed by professional social workers with specialized training. They work with a family for about one or two years, five to ten hours per week. The aim is to help the family to help themselves.

Supplementary aid takes the form of individual assistance with educational problems to overcome developmental risks and disorders. The program is an essential part of youth welfare work. The main focus is on counseling parents and single parents by the youth welfare departments on social or educational problems. Mothers of illegitimate children are also assisted under this program in determining paternity and securing maintenance claims.

Throughout the Federal Republic of Germany there is an almost unbroken network of centers for educational and family counseling. However, due to the great demand for the service there often is a waiting period.

The family relief measures financed by the federal government between 1985 and 1990 included a child allowance. It consists of 50 DM per month for the first child, 100 DM for the second child, 220 DM for the third child, and 240 DM for the fourth and every additional child if the net annual income of the married couple does not exceed 26,600 DM. Otherwise, the parents receive only 70 DM for the second child and 140 DM for every additional child. The government also provides an educational allowance. Starting in 1990, an educational allowance is paid for 12 months; in the first six months a fixed sum of 600 DM is paid to everybody, after that the sum depends on the parents' income. In 1988, 94 percent of all gainfully employed women who had a baby received an educational allowance; 1.3 percent of the persons receiving the allowance were men. Educational leave is extended to 18 months for children born after July 1990. Mothers receiving an educational allowance or who are on educational leave may be gainfully employed for up to 19 hours per week.

"Families Helping Families" is a model project started in certain regions and cities of the Federal Republic in 1987. The family-oriented programs are aimed at self-help and self-organization as related to all issues that impact on the family. As of 1990, a network of contacts was being established all over the Federal Republic involving different groups (e.g., single-parent groups, parent-and-child play groups, toddler centers, child-minding emergency service and parent-child houses).[2]

"Childminders" was a nationwide model project carried out in the 1970s to secure paid home-based care for children of working mothers. Since there are not enough places for children in nursery schools and creches, this kind of facility still exists. An association called "Arbeitsgemeinschaft Tagesmütter" e.V.[3] has the following aims: (1) governmental recognition of childminders through further education and assistance; (2) the promotion of exchange of experience between childminders; and (3) an increase in remuneration and legal securities for childminders. There is no standardized system of payment for childminders. In general, the remuneration is negotiated privately (ranging between 200 DM and 500 DM per month). The child-minding system is of benefit to infants and toddlers because of the homelike surroundings and the attention of a single caregiver.

Parent-child initiatives, in the area of infant and toddler care, are the result of both financial problems and the growth of the self-help movement. Under different names and in varying forms they can be found throughout West Germany. Often these playgroups, mini-clubs, and parent-child associations have developed in connection with family educational centers and universities and/or adult education classes.

Once a parent-child initiative becomes an association it is able to apply for financial assistance from the youth welfare department. Concerns expressed go beyond the lack of child care spaces to include a desire to make contact with other parents, to have a say in the content and practice of education and to provide their (only) child the opportunity to make social contact with other children.

The movement is particularly strong in West Berlin, which has approximately 8,000 places in more than 450 parent-child initiatives. This means that in the context of early education, self-help groups are as important as communal facilities and institutions run by charitable organizations. Most of the parent-child initiatives are now affiliated with the Deutscher Paritätischer Wholfahrtsverband (a charitable organization), thus receiving further assistance.

Notes

1. For a detailed description, see Bundesanstalt für Arbeit (Ed.), Blätter für Berufskunde, Bertelsmannverlag Bielefeld.

2. For further information contact, Bundesverband Neue Erziehung e.V., Oppelnerstr. 130, 5300 Bonn, West Germany.

3. Registered in 300 Hannover, An der Lister Kirche 1, West Germany.

References

Grunelius, E. (1975). *Der Waldorfschulkindergarten*.

Hellbrügge, T. (1981). *Fortschrifte der Sozialpürdiatrie*. München.

Statistisches Bundesamt, Fachserie 13, Reihe 6,1, S. 40, Wiesbaden 1983

PRIMARY EDUCATION IN GERMANY

• • • • • • • • • ◆ • • • • • • • • •

Hans A. Horn
Johann Wolfgang Goethe University
Frankfurt, Germany

A distinct and separate system of primary education began in Germany following World War I. Until that time, the first four years of schooling, which began at age 6, represented the lower stage of the eight years of common public school. The special needs of 6- to 10-year-old students were generally not considered. The program was limited to basic knowledge in reading, writing and arithmetic, moral education, and concrete subject matters. The goal was to teach facts in a rather formal mode of instruction that was determined by the teacher's questioning guidance. This style of teaching had its roots in the late 19th-century philosophy of the Herbartianer, whose formal pattern strictly dominated the elementary school. The Herbartianer focused on applying the educational theory of Johann Friedrich Herbart (1776–1841) to teaching, specifically his concept of mental processing. In this way the Herbartianer devised a quite rigid system for lesson planning and implementing that was not a correct interpretation of Herbart's genuine intention.

In addition to the four years of common public education, there were private and even public classes with only a three-year program. These schools, for 7- to 10-year-old students, operated as part of middle and high schools and charged tuition. Wealthy parents, making up approximately 10 percent of the population, welcomed the chance to send their children to these classes because they included three years of basic instruction within the system of higher education. However, the constitution of the German parliamentary republic of 1919 (i.e., the Weimar Constitution) provided a compulsory, free primary education for all children from the age of 6. After the constitution went into effect, the special three-year classes, which represented a social separation, no longer existed. Although three German states opted for a six-year organization, all others adopted a four-year program. The kindergarten was not integrated into primary education despite a discussion of the issue in 1920. As a result, the kindergarten has remained within the realm of welfare in Germany up to the present.

A new curriculum was developed in 1921 for the primary school. It was influenced by the educational reform movement that had started in Europe at the beginning of the 20th century. Reformers railed against the old, teacher-centered school and demanded that the school become child-oriented, activity-centered, and based on life as lived. The reformers viewed the newly created primary school as the best opportunity for integrating their child-centered education and curriculum. This was particularly true of grades 1 and 2, since child psychology also sought to demonstrate that the young child had need for adequate education. Although private primary schools have always been possible, and today a small number exist, primary education in Germany has been predominantly public from its beginning.

The primary educational system continued to develop until 1933. With Hitler's rise to power, all schools became a tool for political indoctrination. During World War II (1939–45), development in primary schools stopped. Following the war and Germany's division into East and West, the process of recovery in education was completely different in the two parts of the country. In West Germany, where a democratic society was established, the reconstruction of primary education was characterized by efforts to return to the innovations of the pre-Hitler years. On the one hand, this return to the principles of the early reform movement was perhaps the most effective way to reconstruct a system of education. On the other hand, it precluded a critical evaluation of the changes in society and science that had occurred since 1933, which may have affected new curricula.

Development of a Modern Primary School

Although significant changes had been initiated in secondary schools in the 1950s, it was not until 1965 that there was public discussion related to reforms in preschool and primary education in West Germany. The research of U.S. psychologists Benjamin Bloom and Jerome Bruner, stressing the importance of the early years in education, were adapted to education, psychology, sociology, and other sciences in Germany. This new thrust contributed to a completely new concept of preschool and primary education. The necessity for educational reform was more apparent than ever before. The principle aims were to make learning as effective as possible for every child and, in this way, to ensure equality of opportunity from the very beginning of organized instruction. In other words, the compensatory effect of education became a

leading function.

Reforming the primary school involved (1) a renewal of the emphasis on child-centered instruction and (2) a revision of the curriculum to be consistent with new objectives and modern subjects. The next decade (1965–75) was filled with passionate and controversial debate over the extent and direction of educational reform. Experiments with purely cognitive programs (e.g., early reading, and language training) did not meet their early promises.

The focus of development in new primary school curricula in West Germany during the 1970s was on scientific correctness, particularly through the adoption of U.S. elementary school programs (e.g., Science Curriculum Improvement Study, Science-as-Process Approach). However, many of these programs and innovations lost sight of the children's needs and experiences as the key to primary school curriculum planning and were thus rejected. The view of primary science curricula as a simple reduction from secondary level instruction was finally laid to rest. Similar tendencies were evident in the new primary teacher training programs that existed during this period.

By the end of the 1970s, then, children's needs were again accepted as the priority in primary education. In this spirit, another revision of the curricula is now taking place in an attempt to determine the necessary balance between a child-orientation and scientific precision.

Recent curriculum developments are based on subjects representative of the life conditions of today's children, combined with child-centered methods of learning. The curricula in all German states emphasize open forms of learning and the student's active role in instruction. The tradition of the early 20th-century reformers is obvious. Current practice involves individualized learning following weekly assignments, group activities in project learning, discussions, parental involvement, and the use of other experts in the community. Modern primary education attempts to provide a learning environment with varied experiences that will support the development of the whole child.

Progressive education also requires a progressive method of assessing students' achievement. Primary education has to be concerned with encouraging students instead of selecting them for future school and career paths. Throughout West Germany grade 1 and some grade 2 teachers provide only verbal reports. Traditional reports are used starting in grade 3.

Multiculturalism is another new focus of primary and preschool education, especially in urban areas. The presence of many cultures in contemporary West Germany presents problems for students, teachers, and parents. Many of the 4.5 million foreign workers who have come to West Germany during the last 25 years are from Greece, Italy, Portugal, Spain, and Turkey. In addition, huge numbers of people seeking asylum have arrived from Asia, Africa, and South America, as well as from Poland, Romania, and other countries. Added to these groups were thousands of East Germans in 1989, and others of German descent from Poland, Hungary, Romania, and Russia. The problem is more critical in highly industrialized areas, where there have frequently been enrollments in first grades of up to 90 percent foreign-born students. Attempts to implement multicultural educational practice have been based on the need to make school beneficial for students and teachers, while at the same time being aware of the possibility of remigration. In this context, bilingual education is difficult to put into practice.

Since the mid-1960s, the focus of special needs education has been on integrating children into the regular school system. Today, integrated kindergartens are common, and integration is also beginning to be introduced in many primary schools.

English and French instruction has existed in a few model primary classrooms (starting with grade 3) for several years. Spurred by the 1991 arrival of the European Economic Community, there is a trend in many German states to provide early instruction in French and English. This important event will unquestionably lead to a nationwide understanding that foreign languages represent an indispensable element of modern primary education.

The transition from kindergarten to primary school or from primary to secondary has always been a crucial component of German primary education. Initiatives aimed at easing the transition from kindergarten to school were started in all states in the 1970s. Cooperation among educators at all levels is encouraged. The link between primary and secondary educators is, however, less difficult because teachers in both groups are in the same system. The focus on transition is consistent with the fundamental educational goal of supporting continuity in the process of learning and educating in preschool and school.

Following this goal the Federal Republic's Council of Education (Deutscher Bildungstrat) developed a new structure of education in 1970 (Strukturplan für das Bildungswesen) which provided a transitional class in primary school for all five-year-old children (either with a two years' program or a one-year program, called Eingangsstufe). This class, related to the English infant school, was considered to avoid problems of transition from kindergarten to school and to lead to a more child-centered education at the beginning of school as well. Yet there has not been any chance to realize this concept as a compulsory program all over the country as intended. Today we find this "Eingangsstufe" as an alternative form of public education for five-year-old children in three states (Berlin, Hamburg, and Hesse) where parents can choose either kindergarten or Eingangsstufe).

For those students who have reached the age of six and are thus due compulsory education but do not yet seem to be able to follow the lessons successfully, all states have established special classes based on a one-year course (Schulkindergarten, in Hesse Vorklasse). These classes have a long tradition (beginning in 1906), and can be found in every state, mainly in towns and cities.

A good relationship with parents is considered a basic part of primary education. In general, parents have the right to share in all school-related matters. Teachers, however, are responsible for maintaining productive contact with parents. This includes creating opportunities for parental participation in classroom and other program activities (e.g., trips and special events) and as observers and volunteers. At this time, only one state has developed an effective arrangement for parental participation in classroom activities. With the exception of the efforts of a few highly engaged teachers, the reality in the remaining states is a rather formal parent-teacher relationship.

Students admitted to primary teacher training institutions in West Germany have generally completed a three-year program at a college or university following high school (two states have four-year programs). The final teaching degree is granted only after an additional in-service training period of 18 months of teaching and a final examination. Programs in all states follow the same basic pattern (general and primary education, psychology, social science, major subject, minor subjects), yet differ in some details.

The reunification of West and East Germany in 1990 included the difficult process of integrating two educational systems. Although sharing the same origin, they have grown differently since 1945. Intense discussion and debate should focus on retaining the principles of child-centered education in the new united Germany.

PRESCHOOL AND PRIMARY EDUCATION IN GHANA

• • • • • • • • • • ◆ • • • • • • • • • •

George O. Collison
University of Cape Coast
Cape Coast, Ghana

Formal efforts to provide for the education of young children in Ghana date from 1843, when the Basel missionaries established a kindergarten in the country. However, governmental participation in early education dates only from 1951, when it was realized that child care needed to be provided for the children of women working in the markets. As a result, the central government, through the Department of Social Welfare and Community Development, established six day nurseries in 1954. These "pioneer institutions" were located near markets in the large urban centers at Cape Coast, Accra, and Sekondi. Private individuals and voluntary organizations were responsible for the financing and day-to-day operation of the day nurseries. However, the government assumed a supervisory role, exercising minimal control with regard to physical structures, staffing, and programs.

In the early 1960s, the Education Department became the professional unit of the Ministry of Education. The Education Act of 1961 legalized and streamlined both central and local governmental responsibilities in the administration and organization of education. In 1965, nursery education became the responsibility of the Ministry of Education. As a result, the Department of Social Welfare continued its supervisory role in the running of creches and day care centers, while the Ministry of Education focused on nursery education.

Educational reforms in the 1970s also had an impact on preschool services and primary education. In 1974, a new educational plan, contained in the document *The New Structure and Content of Education for Ghana*, was approved by the government. This document outlined an elaborate program for education from the kindergarten and primary levels to the junior and senior secondary school. A critical reform in the legislation, in terms of preschool development in Ghana, was the ruling that 18 to 24 months of nursery school education was now compulsory for admission to grade 1 of the primary school system (the official school starting age is 6).

A second reform changed the Education Division of the Ministry of Education to the Ghana Education Services (GES) in 1974. The GES was to ensure the effective implementation of *The New Structure and Content of Education*. In general, the GES is responsible for the provision, administration, and supervision of public pre-university education, and for registering and regulating the operations of private schools.

Part of this system is the Basic Education Directorate, which is responsible for the first level of education. The Directorate has a Nursery Education Unit, which has established "model nursery schools" at regional Centers in the southern portion of the country. These Model Nursery schools were designed to function as resource centers for private day nursery operators. The aim was to improve the overall quality of programs for young children. Unfortunately, this objective has not fully been achieved due to uncooperative proprietors and the absence of stringent legislation.

The two legal instruments that set minimum standards for day nurseries are the Supreme Military Council Decree (1978) and the Day Care Regulation (1979). The main provisions of the decree and regulations are the following:

1. a proprietor or proprietress must apply to the Director of Social Welfare for inspection of premises and approval three months before a day care center begins operation; and

2. to encourage parents to immunize their children, children will not be admitted into a day care center until they have been immunized for smallpox, diphtheria, whooping cough, tetanus, tuberculosis, and measles.

Thus, by 1979, the legal basis for organizing and operating preschool education was established in Ghana. The development of a bureaucracy to coordinate the activities of the various agencies followed.

In addition to efforts by the central government, private individuals, local communities, and voluntary organizations (e.g., the 31st of December Women's Movement, various churches, and the World Vision International of Ghana Mission) have all contributed to preschool education in Ghana. They have assisted in the construction of physical facilities and in the provision of materials for creches and preschool services, especially in the rural areas. International organizations, such as UNICEF and UNESCO, have provided support through grants, funds, food, and equipment. At the national level, the National Commission of Children coordinates all child-related activities, including preschool programs. The Ministry of Health operates pre- and postnatal clinics in hospitals, in health centers, and in the community. Services

include immunization programs for children from birth to age 2 and health inspections of children in creches, day care centers, and nursery and kindergartens.

In addition to its responsibility for creches and day care centers, the Department of Social Welfare administers an orphanage called The Children's Home, in Osu, Accra. It also provides hospital welfare and family counseling. As mentioned above, the GES has responsibility for preschool education, that is, kindergarten for children ages 4 to 6, through a Preschool Unit within the Basic Education Directorate.

Teacher Training Programs

The GES and the Department of Social Welfare are the two main training agencies. The GES operates a nursery teacher's training school in Accra. It also organizes in-service and refresher courses to update and improve the performance of teachers in preschools. The programs last from one to six weeks. The Department of Social Welfare operates a national day care training and demonstration center, and a model day care center to train center supervisors and attendants (teachers). The centers also offer professional development courses for working teachers.

Recruitment of teachers is a major problem in Ghana preschools. Most prospective attendants and teachers are former elementary school teachers who have no preservice training. It is these teachers who are the principal target of the in-service courses. Day care supervisors are often retired elementary school teachers. In nursery schools, teachers are graduates of the GES-sponsored training colleges.

Parental Support and Education

The Ministry of Health and the Department of Social Welfare operate some parental education programs. A chronic problem with such programs and similar intervention is that child rearing practices of families in rural areas and in urban slums clash with current ideas regarding child care and development. Moreover, income and wage levels make providing even basic needs for children difficult. The indirect impact is an increasing rate of adolescent childbearing and abortion and childhood malnutrition.

References

Ministry of Education. (1976). Ghana Official Handbook. Accra, Ghana.

EARLY CHILDHOOD EDUCATION IN GREAT BRITAIN

•••••••••◆••••••••

Audrey Curtis
University of London
London, Great Britain

Compared with many countries, Great Britain has a long tradition of infant and nursery education. For more than a century, education has been compulsory from the term after the child's fifth birthday, a year or more earlier than many other countries. This early start has naturally affected the way educational provision has developed and is even now affecting what is offered to young children.

Although the three countries (England, Scotland, and Wales) that make up Great Britain have many characteristics in common, there is a separate educational system in Scotland and not all changes occur in each of the three countries. Many of the innovations and ideas discussed in this chapter concerning the preschool field are to be found throughout Great Britain, but the changes discussed relating to the primary sector do not affect Scotland.

Background—Historical and Current

The ideas of infant education for children from ages 2 to 7 developed early in the 19th century. The most famous innovator of that time was Robert Owen, whose school at New Lanark, Scotland, was the first infant school in Britain. Unlike many of his fellow philanthropists, Owen viewed education for the poor not as moral training but rather as an instrument for social change. There was widespread interest in the New Lanark School, which encouraged people like Samuel Wilderspin to open other infant schools, particularly in the London area. However, there were too few infant schools. Many poor children found themselves in baby classes in elementary schools alongside their older brothers and sisters, where, according to the inspectors of the time, the presence of children under age 7 hindered the learning of the older children.

While the children of the poor were being given an education to fit them for their place in society, middle-class parents were seeking new ways to educate their young children. The influence of Friedrich Froebel was being felt, and by late Victorian times, upper and middle-class parents were sending their children to Froebelian kindergartens or employed Froebel-trained governesses.

Until 1870, it was generally accepted that children would not begin their elementary schooling until age 7. However, at the time the Education

Act of 1870 was introduced, there were many arguments concerning the age at which children should begin school. Eventually it was agreed that compulsory attendance would begin at age 5. This decision was based on the arguments prevailing that "it was never too early to inculcate habits of decency, cleanliness, and order" (NEU, 1870). So in spite of the original practice of the Voluntary Society Schools, which had regarded seven as the starting age, the 1870 Education Act formally included the infant stage of education within elementary education. It was at this point that Britain's policy differed from the rest of Europe and America. Even today, Britain is one of the few countries that commences compulsory schooling in the term after the child's fifth birthday.

Early childhood education for the masses during this period was strictly utilitarian in approach. In the late 19th century, large numbers of 2-, 3-, and 4-year-olds were in classes in the elementary schools because of the lack of public nurseries. Attention was drawn to the plight of these children by the report of the Women Inspectors in 1905, which makes some of the most depressing reading in the history of British education. As a result of their recommendations, children under age 5 were excluded from elementary school classes. Many of these excluded children were farmed out to childminders or looked after during the day by older siblings while their parents worked.

Rise of Nursery Education

The state of nursery education in the 20th century has been closely related to the economic position of the country. The removal of children under age 5 from the elementary school classes encouraged recognition that a social need for nursery education existed. But progress was slow, since its provision depended largely on the efforts of volunteer pioneers. "The nuisance who wrought miracles" (Ballard, 1937) was how Margaret McMillan, one of the leading exponents of nursery education, was described, and there is no doubt that the modern nursery school today owes a great deal to her efforts. She argued that if children are to develop their full potential, they must be physically healthy and have full stomachs; the role of the nursery school was therefore to further the physical, emotional, and mental well-being of children.

McMillan's influence on the training of teachers and the ways in which professionals should work with parents and other agencies is still felt today, since there are many teachers who were trained in her approach to early childhood education.

While McMillan was working in Bradford and later in Deptford, Esther Lawrence was claiming that the Froebel movement was active in working class districts and that they were providing the first example of free nursery schools in Britain. In setting up these kindergartens for the working class children, rather than the middle-class children for whom the Froebelian tradition had been strong, Lawrence commented on how much more capable of looking after themselves were the children from the poor rather than the children from the middle classes.

With its own training institutions and colleges, like that established by Maria Grey, the Froebelian movement gained considerable influence, particularly as their teachers were given a three rather than the usual two-year course of training. During the 1920s and 1930s, the influence of Maria Montessori spread to England, but her ideas and materials never had the strong impact there that they did in other parts of the world. In fact, the Froebelians reacted to both her theory and practice with closed minds. They were particularly scornful of her apparent mistrust of teacher's abilities and her insistence that imaginative play and stories must be firmly based in reality. At this time, the Froebelians were firmly entrenched in the English educational world, acknowledged alike by government, training colleges, and public opinion.

Nursery education received a boost during World War I, when women were needed in the factories. As soon as the war was over, however, the nurseries were closed and except for parents who could afford to pay, children under age 5 were expected to stay at home with their mothers. Working parents were forced to find somewhere to leave their children while they were working—either with a minder or a relative of a friend. The prevailing philosophy was that women should not work and therefore no provision should be made for their children. So although local health authorities were empowered by law in 1918 to provide day nurseries or to assist voluntary nurseries, this enabling power was ineffective in expanding provision.

The beginning of World War II once again led to the expansion of nursery provision so that women could be released to work outside the home. But once again the cessation of hostilities saw the dismantling of many nurseries. It was assumed that mothers would stay at home until their children reached school age, even though the Education Act of 1944 had given local educational authorities the power to plan for provision for children under age 5. The work of John Bowlby, Anna Freud, and other psychoanalysts, who emphasized the effects of separation on young children, did much to influence the attitudes of the time; where the nursery education was provided, it was on a part-time, rather than a full-time, basis. This situation still exists today.

The nadir of nursery education in Britain came with the introduction of the Ministry of Education Circular 8/60, which specifically prohibited the expansion of facilities for nursery education and introduced a two-shift system of part-time attendance as a means of accommodating more children under age 5 at no additional cost. It is from this low point in the history of child care sponsorship, which lasted for over a decade, that the country is still recovering.

In spite of the embargo of Circular 8/60, the Central Advisory Council for Education (the Plowden Report, 1967) recommended a large expansion of nursery education on a mainly part-time basis, suggesting that by the late 1980s there should be nursery provision for 90 percent of all 4-year-olds and 50 percent of 3-year-olds whose parents so wished it. Like all recommendations, the effects of this report were felt only slowly. In 1972, however, a governmental White Paper entitled "Framework for Expansion" advocated that the Plowden Report be implemented as soon as possible, fostering hopes for an improvement in the provision (DES, 1972).

There were some signs of change with the introduction of the Urban Aid Program in the 1970s. It was funded to provide nursery school places for children in areas of social need. As in the United States and other Western countries, programs were established to help disadvantaged children (Curtis and Blatchford, 1980; Woodhead, 1976). Nursery education was seen as a form of compensation for the ills of society. Only gradually has it come to be accepted that nursery education is a valuable experience for all children irrespective of their backgrounds.

More and more parents are demanding some form of educational provision for their children before the commencement of statutory schooling and all political parties are pledged to provide increased places. The goal has partly been met by early admission policies into primary schools, with children entering the first class of school at age 4. As of 1990, 76 percent of all 4-year-olds are attending some form of state educational provision, most of them in infant classes in primary schools.

The Present Position. The attitude of government today is still that mothers with young children under school age should stay at home. However, an increasing number of young women with small children are working outside the home and the demand for all-day day care is increasing. The state educational system provides for 44 percent of the 3- and 4-year-olds, but mothers need care for their children for longer periods of time. The state day nurseries, under the aegis of the social service departments, provide for only 1.8 percent of the children from birth to age 5.

There is an increasing demand for private day nurseries, some of which are subsidized by employers. The need for women to return or remain in the labor force is essential to the country's economy, and in 1990, for the first time, tax allowances were given to parents who use private nurseries. As is to be expected, there are wide variations in these nurseries, some are superb while others are much less desirable, and meeting only the minimum safety and staffing requirements. For most mothers who work, however, childminding is the most common form of day care.

Progress in Infant Schools

While the nursery schools were laying down a pattern of developing the full potential of the child predominantly within a play setting, the infant departments of the elementary school were developing progressive ideas that were to be influential in many parts of the world. Since 1905, when the inspectors condemned formal instruction and fixed the standard of attainment in the basic skills at age

7, it has been advocated that the general aim of education for young children under age 7 was to encourage mental and physical growth and the development of good habits.

The new infant teachers leaving training college were being trained in the reinterpretation of Froebel's principles in the light of the writings of John Dewey. The period leading up to World War I saw a number of eminent educators, such as Edwin Holmes, displaying extreme dissatisfaction with many aspects of education in both the private and public sectors. He and others, including Homer Lane, came together to discuss and develop what has now come to be called the "Progressive Movement of Infant Education." The concept of the child-centered infant school was nurtured and developed in Great Britain during this period. The Hadow Reports of 1931 and 1933 reflected the marked change that had taken place in the early years of education in this country. The 1933 report recommended the setting up of separate infant and junior schools and recognized that, since age 5 marked no significant developmental stage, infant teachers should follow the principles advocated for nursery schools. This child-centered approach, which was encouraged and developed by such eminent British educators as Dorothy Gardner and Christian Schiller, is still a basic tenet of teachers of young children today. However, there is a danger that the introduction of the new "national curriculum," even though it does not lay down established patterns of working, may mean that a degree of formality will creep into the infant schools.

The trend over the last few years has been for the infant and junior schools to merge. This has advantages administratively, but there is a fear that the greater formality of the junior school will be adopted by the infant school departments. At present, however, the infant school is still a place where children are seen as individuals with unique needs and interests.

Provision for Children Under Age 5

The diversity of the provision for children under statutory school age is both a strength and a weakness. Few countries give parents so much choice, although the geographical distribution of the various kinds of provision is uneven. Provision for children under statutory school age is the responsibility of two ministerial departments: (1) the Departments of Education and Science are responsible for all the educational provision, and (2) the Social Services departments in local authorities are responsible for day nurseries, both public and private, and for registering playgroups and childminders.

However, recent developments have resulted in a more coordinated approach to services for children under age 5. In some local authorities (e.g., Strathclyde in Scotland and Leeds and Sheffield in Yorkshire) the education department has taken over the responsibility for all provision for children under statutory school age. This approach is being adopted by an increasing number of other local authorities. A recent survey carried out by the National Children's Bureau (Pugh and De'Ath, 1989) has shown that more and more local authorities are planning and managing their services for young children and their families in a coordinated way, with education, social services, and health authorities working alongside the voluntary organizations. A coherent national approach is still lacking, however.

Nursery Education

The state provides free nursery education in nursery schools or nursery classes attached to primary schools. As of 1990, 26 percent of the children were attending this form of educational provision. Admission is open to anyone living within the catchment area, but some institutions have waiting lists and a policy of selective admission may operate. For example, single parents or a family that has been referred by the social services department may be given preferential treatment.

Nursery schools are separate institutions. They have a head teacher who is responsible for the administration and for liaison with parents, outside agencies, and the schools to which the children will proceed. The adult-child ratio is approximately 1:10, the staff being either trained nursery teachers or nursery nurses. In recent years, the trend has been for new provisions to be in nursery classes attached to primary schools. The arguments for this are both educational and economic. The educational argument is that children attending a nursery class attached to the primary school that they will later attend experience less transition trauma than those who have to transfer from a separate school at age 4 or 5. The economic argument is that nursery education is more expensive if carried out in separate facilities.

In this situation, the head teacher of the primary school has the overall responsibility for the nursery class, normally with a teacher in charge and nursery nurses employed as the remaining staff. The adult-child ratio in these nursery classes is 1:13 or better. Both the nursery schools and classes serve 3- and 4-year-olds although there may be a few 2-years-olds attending in some parts of the country. Attendance may be full- or part-time. Ideally, children receive two years of nursery education. However, the current trend of encouraging 4-year-olds to enter the first year of infant school is affecting the age of children in nursery classes and school. In many instances, the children receive nursery education for only a year before moving into the primary school.

Most children attend part-time sessions, either from 9:00 a.m. to 1:30 p.m., or from 1:00 p.m. to 3:30 p.m. Children who attend full-time normally stay for lunch. In some nurseries, there are both full-time and part-time children, a situation that poses a challenge to the teaching staff.

In some nursery classes attached to primary schools, nurseries vary in size, from 120 places (60 children in the morning and 60 in the afternoon) to 40 place units (20–20). Both nursery schools and classes are open for the same length of time as the primary schools. They offer a secure relaxed environment for young children, with a curriculum based on the needs of 3- to 5-year-olds.

Day Nurseries

All day nurseries, public or private, must be registered by the social services department of the local authority that inspects the premises regularly and ensures that the staffing, sanitary arrangements, and other requirements are met. Normally, day nurseries are open year round (closing for only two weeks for cleaning) from 8:00 a.m. to 6:00 p.m. Children from approximately 8 to 10 weeks old to age 5, may attend these nurseries, although less than 10 percent are under the age 1. The adult-child ratio varies, but normally it is 1:3 for small

babies, rising to 1:4 or 1:5 for the older children. Staff are generally qualified nursery nurses, and the officers-in-charge may also have social work and/or nursing qualifications. However, the shortage of trained nursery personnel is resulting in many nurseries being forced to employ untrained staff. The children are organized into small groups, the maximum group size for children ages 3 to 5 is ten, and six for children from birth to age 3. Each groups has a responsible head teacher.

Within the public sector, the paucity of places has resulted in each nursery adopting strict criteria for admission. This has come to mean an increase in the number of "children at risk." The Ministry of Health Circular 37/68 recommended that priority be given to children with only one parent. But with the increasing numbers of single parent families, this has come to be defined as "children in special need of care." Fees are payable in the public nurseries, but for most parents they are either totally or partially reduced. Very few parents pay the true economic cost of child care.

As a result of this admission policy, the primary function of the public day nurseries can no longer be regarded as providing day care for children. Rather, the role of the staff in these institutions can be defined as addressing the broader needs of socially disadvantaged families. For this reason, many of the former public day nurseries are turning into family centers, where the entire family can come for help, advice, and support. This is because, in many cases, the admission of the child into the day nursery may not be due to the mother working, but rather because the family needs support. Such family centers have qualified counselors on their staff to help both parents and their children.

Since there are so few public day nurseries, and those that exist are more concerned with families with special needs, working mothers must turn to the private day nurseries. However, child care provided by the private and voluntary sector has not been expanding. (Between 1975 and 1985, the number of private and voluntary nurseries fell, from 1,065 to 999.) During the last two or three years, there has been an increase in the number of private nurseries, and currently industrial and commercial organizations (e.g., the Midland Bank) have established nurseries in town centers for their employees. Fees may be paid entirely by the parent, or in the case of many employers, subsidized according to the income of the employee.

A further development has been the establishment of community nurseries, often set up by parents themselves to meet their needs. These have developed particularly among black and other ethnic minorities, and in some cases have attracted public funding through local authority and urban aid. More recently, funding has come through a governmental initiative for children under age 5 (set up in 1983), which provides funds to voluntary agencies working with preschool children and their families.

Traditionally, the day nurseries have emphasized care rather than the education of children. More recently, however, there have been changes in approach, with teachers seconded from the educational services working alongside the staff. It was believed that many day nurseries were not giving appropriate and challenging experiences to the young children in their care (Bain and Barnett, 1980; Bryant, Harris, and Newton, 1980). The increase in the amount of private provision and concern about many aspects of day nurseries has led to the formation of a consortium organized by the National Children's Bureau. It is currently working on guidelines for good practice in day care settings (Cowley, 1990).

Combined Nursery Centers

Concern about the distinction between care and education led to attempts to combine these two aspects into a comprehensive form of provision in the shape of nursery centers. First established about 15 years ago, the initial attempts were disappointing, since a sharp line between day care and education lingered in staff attitudes toward parents and children (Ferri, et al., 1981). Nevertheless, as a result of efforts by dedicated staff, many of these combined centers are now working effectively. As of 1990, there are more than 50 centers in existence.

The centers provide all-day day care and education throughout the year for children from birth to age 5 (closing only for public holidays and two weeks for cleaning). Children move from a day nursery environment at around age 3 into a nursery school milieu, where they remain until they enter primary school. The opening hours are long but flexible (8:00 a.m. to 6:00 p.m.). Parents are encouraged to bring children in late or to take them home early if their work routines permit. Parents are also urged to become involved in the activities of the center. This involvement has been shown to be beneficial to the parents, children, and the staff of the centers. Many have "parent rooms," where not only parents, but grandparents and minders can meet socially.

A crucial issue arising from the establishment of these combined centers is the need to reconsider the training and preparation of all who work with young children and their families. This is currently challenging those concerned with this aspect of care and education.

Childminders

Childminding is the oldest form of child care outside the home. It has been the traditional form used by working mothers. The reduction in the number of day nurseries in the post-war years and the increase in the number of working mothers have led to an expansion in childminding. Provision for the regulation of childminders was first established in the Nurseries and Childminders Act of 1948, and modified 20 years later. A childminder, as defined by the Nurseries and Childminders Act of 1968, is anyone who "for reward takes any child to whom they are not related into their home and cares for him for two hours or more during the day." Childminders, who are usually women, are required to register with the social services department of the local authority. The authority is responsible for inspecting homes and ensuring that they meet the statutory health and safety regulations. Childminders are permitted to care for a maximum of three children under age 5 (including the minder's own children), although when the new Children's Act comes into force the age limit will be raised to 8. Childminders provide full-day care throughout the year. Although there are many thousands of registered minders (144,908 places in 1985), the majority are nonregistered, payment being made directly to the minder by the parents. The childminders are also the chief group of people who look after school-aged children before and after school hours.

During the late 1960s and the 1970s, there

was considerable criticism of the childminding service (Clark, 1988). Attitudes toward childminding have changed over the last few years, as it has generally become recognized that the childminder offers the nearest alternative to a child's own home and is particularly beneficial for those needing care for children under age 3.

The acceptance by the state that good childminders have a significant part to play in the total day care provision for children under age 5 has resulted in the National Childminder Association receiving substantial governmental funding for "new initiatives" by voluntary organizations in the preschool field. Much of this money has been spent on training courses for minders. One imaginative approach to supporting childminders is the Soho Family Centre in London, where the minders are registered in the normal way, but use the center as their "home." However, there are still too many nonregistered childminders whose practice causes concern.

Nannies

Another type of child minding that is increasing in Great Britain is the employment of nannies, (i.e., childminders who care for children in the employer's home). Traditionally the prerogative of the rich, many young professional women are now employing childminders in their home or are joining with another mother to employ one nanny. In some instances, these nannies are trained nursery nurses, but normally they are unqualified childminders. Since the Children's Act of 1989, nannies have to be registered. There are no reliable figures as to the numbers of minders, but it is probably in excess of 30,000, which means that they provide more care than the public day nurseries.

Preschool Playgroups

The Preschool Play Groups Association (PPA), a national voluntary organization, was formed almost 30 years ago to support parents, generally mothers, who wanted to establish playgroups to provide their young children with playmates, play space, and playtime. The idea came at a time when state nursery provision was minimal. This movement involving parents, especially mothers, in their children's early play has been of great advantage to many thousands of young mothers. Through

regular participation in their child's play, they have been able to strengthen their roles as parents and raise their self-esteem in their own contribution to the upbringing of their families.

Although the movement has middle-class origins, the groups have gradually spread. Now many children are referred by social services from families experiencing difficulties. There are also opportunity groups for children with special educational needs. As of 1990, there were some 18,000 registered playgroups in Great Britain.

The playgroups are required to register their premises with the local authorities and they are regularly inspected for safety and sanitary facilities. Preschool playgroups are normally open only in school terms and make provision for children for two to three hours in the morning for three to four days a week. Most children attend only two or three sessions. The minimum staff ratio is 1:8, and the age range of the children is generally 2 1/2 to 4 years, although increasingly the 4-year-olds are leaving to attend infant classes in school. This may be because state school provision is free, whereas parents have to pay on a sessional basis for their children attending playgroups, or it may be that most parents prefer their children to receive a more professional input by the time they are age 4.

The average playgroup serves around 20 to 24 children, who come together under the care and leadership of three to five adults. There is normally a playleader, who has some form of playleader's training, present at every session to provide continuity for the children, as well as other assistants, who assist on a rotating basis. The playleaders and assistants are paid a nominal wage and are often mothers themselves with small children. Teachers or nursery nurses with young children often run playgroups while their children are below school age, returning to their original employment once their youngest child enters school (Clark and Cheyne, 1979; Clark, 1988).

Playgroups seldom have exclusive use of premises. This means that the workers have to set up and clear away all the equipment before and after each session, which places a strain on both them and the children. The majority of playgroups have to be self-funding and balance their expenditures, augmenting their income with fund-raising in order to pay for rent, equipment, and the low salaries of the regular staff. Playgroups are not spread evenly across the country and are often concentrated in rural areas and parts of the country where there are few nursery schools or classes (Davie, *et al.*, 1984; Haystead, Howorth, and Strachen, 1980).

Playgroups provide opportunities for all types of play, encouraging children to explore, discover, and converse. Although parents are encouraged to stay and participate in the activities (it is one of the stated aims of the organization), probably only 70 percent at most really involve the parents. In recent years, the PPA has extended its interest and established several day care centers to serve the needs of working mothers. It has also set up a consultancy on good day care practice. Parents who wish to work in playgroups are given ample opportunity for training and development. The courses run from short, informal sessions, to the 120-hours foundation courses, and to further training for tutors and experienced playleaders.

Originally, playgroups arose from the needs of parents to find somewhere for their children to meet and play together. Now they are an important part in preschool provision in Great Britain. They offer low-cost, flexible conditions side by side with the state provision, enabling parents to have true choice.

Parent and Toddler Groups

Throughout the British Isles parents with young children under age 3 are meeting in "parent and toddler groups." These groups may also include mothers expecting their first babies, childminders, grandparents, and anyone interested in helping. Originally termed "mother and toddler groups," the name was changed because lone fathers were joining. An essential feature of a parent and toddler group is that the children's parents or caretaker must remain in charge of the children. Most groups meet once a week for about two hours. Generally, their express aims are to give parents and minders an opportunity to meet to share problems and pleasures of parenthood and to make friends while their children play nearby.

Many parents and toddler groups operate in indifferent or nearly impossible premises, but their popularity (as many as 80 parents and their young children at a session is not uncommon) demon-strate the need of parents of young children to meet. Meetings are held in all parts of the country, although the public remains largely unaware of the existence of this movement. Like playgroups, parents and toddler groups have provided a lifeline for those caught up in limitations of the mobile nuclear family and the low esteem in which parenting is held. Help from the local authorities is patchy. In some areas there is an initial grant of money to help with equipment and rent. Sometimes facilities or rooms are provided by clinics, health centers, or school classrooms. And in some parts of the country, a specialist on children under age 5 is involved in helping to set up and organize the groups. Governmental reports and circulars, (e.g., the DES/DHSS Circular (1987) of the Select Committee on Violence in the Family) have urged local authorities to make premises available free or at nominal charges, although market rents are charged in some instances.

Primary Education

The statutory age for commencing school is age 5, but most children enter school before then. Some children may enter an infant school for children up to age 7, while others may go to a full-range primary school where there are children up to age 11. In such cases, the school is divided into an infant and a junior department, with a nursery class or classes attached. There is no fixed date of entry. In some parts of the country, children may enter at the beginning of the school year in which they will be age 5, in others it will be in the term in which they are 5, while in other areas of the country children will not start until they are 5. Parents have the right to keep their children at home until after they are 5, but few exercise this right, believing that early entry into school is desirable. It is recommended that children who enter the primary school under statutory school age should be in classrooms with a staffing ratio, equipment, and curriculum appropriate to their age range, that is, they should be placed in conditions similar to those in the nursery classes (Select Committee, 1989). However, the reality of the situation is that many 4-year-olds are placed in classrooms with older children without the appropriate staffing arrangements or other conditions.

Attendance is normally full-time, from 9:00 a.m. to 3:30 p.m. with a break of one to one and one-half hours for lunch, which is usually eaten at school. The school year, which commences in September, is divided into three terms, with approximately two weeks holiday at Christmas and Easter and six weeks holiday in the summer months, usually from mid-July to the end of August.

On entering primary school, children are placed in a classroom with a teacher and about 25 children. In some schools, the teachers of the youngest children have help for a few hours a day. If there are many children under age 5, there is often a nursery assistant as well as a teacher in the classroom.

Most children in primary schools are grouped according to age, although some headteachers and their staff prefer to arrange the children vertically so that there are children of three different ages in the class (e.g., children ages 5, 6, and 7). Although children in vertically grouped classes may have the same teacher for three years, children in chronologically grouped classes have a different teacher each year as they move up through the school. Children do not repeat a school year except under exceptional circumstances.

Curriculum in the Primary School

Education history was made in England and Wales when the national curriculum was introduced in September 1990. The Education Act of 1988 ruled that every pupil in state-maintained schools is entitled to a balanced, broadly based curriculum that promotes spiritual, moral, cultural, physical, and mental development and that prepares pupils for the opportunities, responsibilities, and experiences of adult life. For the first time, children entering school were to follow a national program of study.

The national curriculum has three main elements: attainment targets, programs of study, and assessment arrangements. For primary-aged children (5–11 years), the curriculum comprises three core subjects (i.e., English, science, and mathematics), technology, art, music, history, geography, physical education, and religious education. It is intended that all children will be assessed nationally at age 7 in the three core subjects (the first assessment will take place in 1992), but at the time of writing this chapter it is still unclear what form the assessment will take.

Although described in terms of subjects, it is not envisaged that the curriculum should be delivered in this way. A cross-curricular approach to learning has long been considered desirable within the English primary system, and the organization of teaching and learning is a professional matter for the head teachers and their staffs; it is not intended that the introduction of the national curriculum will affect this freedom.

Many schools organize learning experiences for the children within themes or topics. There is ample opportunity for children to follow the national programs of study and to reach the appropriate attainment targets through this approach. Schools have been told that they must devote a "reasonable amount of time" to each of the core and other foundation subjects, but the act does not define "a reasonable time." It is left to the school to demonstrate that their schemes of work enable each pupil to develop the appropriate knowledge, skills, and understanding required in each of the subjects.

Classroom Organization

Whether children are vertically or chronologically grouped, a typical school day in an early years classroom finds children engaged in small-group activities, painting, carrying out assignments related to the core curriculum, and playing in the home corner. For the youngest children in the groups, most teachers believe that there should be opportunities for play, especially imaginative play, within the classroom setting. Both boys and girls use building blocks and construction toys.

Whole-class activities with the teacher giving direct instruction are infrequent. This is because the philosophy of the early years educators is based on the principle that young children learn by doing, and sound classroom practice involves an organization that encourages children to collaborate with others and manage their own learning. Teachers are encouraged to develop an interactive, rather than a didactic, teaching style. Naturally children come together for class teaching at story time, and during music and movement lessons or for school assembly. When children work together, there are occasions when the teacher decides on the composition of the group.

For the younger children, the school day is broken up as little as possible and there are few scheduled lesson times. Children are encouraged to become deeply involved in an activity and to spend time finishing the task. For this reason, a school day is normally blocked into four main periods: from the beginning of the school day until the mid-morning break, and from the break until lunch time; a similar pattern occurs during the afternoon.

Even within the national curriculum, it is expected that children will have opportunities to work at their own interests and levels. Integrated work is carried out in a number of schools, although the term can have different meanings in different contexts. Integrated can mean several different tasks are undertaken simultaneously in a single classroom. Alternatively, it can mean individuals or groups of children engaging in a study of various aspects of a common theme.

In spite of the many changes that are taking place within the English and Welsh educational systems, much of the philosophy that permeated the Plowden Report still prevails. Most early childhood education teachers are convinced of the need to have the child as a central focus in the learning process.

Preschool Programs in Great Britain

The curriculum for preschool children is concerned with the child, the context in which the learning takes place, and the content of the learning. Most early childhood educators agree that their practice is guided by the following principles as expressed by the Early Years Curriculum Groups (1989):

1. Early childhood education is valid in itself; it is part of life, not simply a preparation for work or for the next stage of education.

2. The whole child is considered to be important. Because the child's social, emotional, physical, intellectual, and moral development are interrelated, learning is holistic. For the young child, it is not compartmentalized under subject headings.

3. Intrinsic motivation is valuable because it results in child-initiated learning.

4. Autonomy and self-discipline are emphasized. In the early years, children learn best through first-hand experience.

5. What children can do (not what they cannot do) is the starting point in children's education.

6. There is potential in all children that emerges powerfully under favorable conditions.

7. The adults and other children to whom the child relates are of central importance.

8. The child's education is seen as an interaction between the child and the environment, which includes people as well as materials and knowledge.

In whatever setting, the curriculum for young children is seen as complementary to the learning of the home. Children are offered a wide range of materials and experiences to stimulate their curiosity and to enable them to learn through planned, worthwhile play activities. These encourage them to explore their environments, to be imaginative and creative, and to plan and reflect upon their experiences. Educators aim to develop in children such skills and competencies as self-awareness, social and cultural skills, perceptual and motor abilities, communication skills, analytical and problem-solving skills, and aesthetic and creative awareness (Curtis, 1986).

Much of this learning is based on purposeful play. This is not free and wholly unstructured activity; but rather through the selection of material and equipment provided, teachers ensure that during play children encounter the learning experiences that they intend. The staff, by their involvement, comments, and questions, encourage children to learn from their activities.

A well-organized nursery school or class has a program based mainly on play, but the opportunities offered to the children are part of a carefully discussed program which will ensure that all children are stimulated and challenged in all areas of development (Sylva, Roy, and Painter, 1980; Tizard and Hughes, 1984). Since the primary school children rarely come together in large groups, most of the time is spent in either small-group activities or free play with or without adults or other children.

Although the programs in the nursery schools and classes lay down the foundations for children to later learn the national curriculum, and many of the activities in the preschool year are similar to those offered in the infant schools, many educators are concerned that the preschool staff will introduce the programs of study of the national curriculum. If this happens, 3- and 4-year-old children will be deprived of valuable, appropriate learning experiences.

In the private nurseries, it is likely that the programs will be different. In some, children from age 3 are expected to sit in rows and to begin formal learning. Play is an activity for home, and workbooks, more appropriate for 7-year-old children, are used daily. In other private nurseries, play is totally unstructured and there is little purpose to the program. Both of these extremes cause concern, since neither develops the true potential of the child.

In recent years, some nurseries in the state, voluntary, and private sectors have introduced the High/Scope program from the United States. Since its approach is more structured than is normally considered desirable in British early years tradition, it has caused much controversy. It has been found to be particularly effective in settings where staff are not highly trained (e.g., nurseries run by voluntary organizations). Some British educational authorities have encouraged its use, believing that it is having a positive effect on the children. However, close examination of the schools that have introduced the program suggests that it has been modified by the teachers to meet the needs of their children.

In addition to the High/Scope program, there has been a revival of interest in Montessori education. Many parents are seeing the carefully structured program as ideal for their children. However, as with the High/Scope program, despite the use of Montessori equipment and the presence of Montessori-trained staff, many schools do not adhere rigidly to the orthodox method.

The principles and traditions of early childhood education are firmly established. The best provisions for children under age 5 take into account the need for continuity and progression in relation to the teaching and learning of the next stage of education. In the not too distant future, there may be a similar entitlement curriculum for children under age 5 as there is for children ages 5 to 16.

Educating the Early Childhood Educator

In the United Kingdom, there are two main groups of professionals working with young children: teachers and nursery nurses. Their training and legal qualifications are different but their roles are complementary.

Teachers

Students wishing to become teachers in the early years of schooling receive their training in either polytechnics or institutes of higher education or a university department of education (UDE). The majority of early years teachers train in the former, where they study for four years, receiving a B. Ed. degree on completing their course of study. However, an increasing number of teachers in primary schools are achieving professional status through university training. This involves obtaining a first degree, either a B.A. or a B. Sc., and then studying for the postgraduate certificate of education (PGCE). The PGCE course runs for 36 weeks. For primary teaching, many involved in teaching training believe that this is insufficient time to train a person to become a competent classroom teacher. The PGCE route has been the main way to train for secondary teaching for many years, but the current trend is for many young people to defer their decision to become primary teachers until a later stage in their studies and to follow a degree course first.

Whichever route is selected, the entry requirements are the same and involve showing proficiency in mathematics and English language, as well as the standard entry levels required by all who wish to proceed to higher education. Mature applicants without these formal academic qualifications may be admitted as special entrants, but these are relatively few in number.

Most students wishing to train as early years teachers follow a primary B. Ed. course, specializing in the age range 3 to 9 years, although a number of institutions offer courses covering the age range 3 to 11 or 5 to 11 years. When they have completed their formal training, all teachers are required to teach for a year as probationers and do not receive qualified teacher status (QTS) until this has been successfully completed.

Although there is no uniform program for teacher training institutions to follow, the Secretary of State for Education has laid down strict guidelines, which are closely monitored by the Council for the Accreditation of Teaching Education (CATE). This governmental committee was set up in 1985, for five years initially, to ensure that all courses involving the training of teachers meet the stated criteria. Institutions have to fulfill the criteria before receiving approval to continue to prepare teachers to work in any sector of the school system. A new council was reconstituted to take effect from 1990. The members are appointed by the Secretaries of State in England, Wales, and Northern Ireland and drawn from teacher trainers, other teachers in higher education and in schools, local education authorities, and the business community.

The council is assisted by 23 local committees, which play a critical role in monitoring and scrutinizing courses before they come to council for recommendation or amendment to the Secretaries of State.[1]

During their training, all primary student teachers spend at least 1,000 days in school gaining teaching experience during a four-year course and 75 days on a PGCE course. In reality, most students have much more than the minimum school experience. All primary phase students must devote at least 100 hours to the teaching of mathematics, 100 hours to the teaching of science, and 100 hours to the teaching of English.

All primary courses are expected to prepare students to teach at the level of the national curriculum in all the foundation subjects (i.e., technology, art, music, physical education, history, geography, and religion). Students also follow a course of professional and educational studies that enables them to evaluate children's performance, cope with children, and provide equal opportunities for all children. Courses also prepare students to work with parents and other external agencies.

An important factor in the training of teachers in England and Wales related to the CATE ruling requires all tutors involved in the professional training of students to have had recent and relevant experience within the age phase in which they are tutoring.

The training of teachers in the early years of schooling is as rigorous and demanding as that for teachers preparing to work in the secondary sector. Unlike some countries, pay and status of the teachers are the same as those for teachers working with older children.

In 1989, the government introduced two new schemes for the training of teachers: the Articled Teacher Scheme and the Licensed Teacher Scheme. The Articled Teacher Scheme is a two-year school based PGCE where students are expected to spend four-fifths of their time in schools where they receive most of their formal training. The remaining part of their training takes place in an institute of higher education. Articled teachers are paid a bursary that reflects the contribution they are making to the work of the school. The Licensed Teacher Scheme is an attempt to get more mature students into the profession. Entrants must be at least age 26, have relevant background experience, and a minimum of two years successful higher education, but need not necessarily be graduates. Their training is the responsibility of the schools and the local authorities, not the institutes of higher education.

Nursery Nurses

The other groups of professionals working in the field of early childhood are the nursery nurses. The majority of nursery nurses take the examinations of the Nursery Nurse Examination Board leading to a diploma in nursery nursing. This is a two-year course open to students over age 16, although most are 17 or over and study in colleges or continuing education. The board does not prescribe entry qualifications or conditions to start the course of study, although many colleges have their own entrance requirements. It is a popular course and is generally oversubscribed. Students are prepared to work with children from birth to age 8 in a variety of settings, including hospitals, day nurseries, family centers and educational settings as well as in the home. The course emphasizes the practical aspects of training and students spend 40 percent of the time in a variety of placements. Although much of the students' time is concerned with the physical care of children, in recent years there has been a stronger emphasis placed on teaching about social and intellectual development.

Another route for training to become a nursery nurse is through the B. Tech Courses. Students following this diploma in business and technical studies spend slightly less time in placements, but are expected to achieve a higher level of academic rigor in their courses.

Nursery nurses are to be found in positions of responsibility in the health and social services, although in the education service their role is always subsidiary to that of the teachers. Since there is a limited career structure for nursery nurses, many take further training to become teachers.

National Council for Vocational Qualifications

Although the National Council for Vocational Qualifications (NCVQ) was created to set standards for professional training in all areas, its scope has been extended to look at the training of workers with children under age 7. The Working With Under 7s Project was set up in 1989 to identify the competencies required for all types of work involving young children and their families, up to but not including graduate professional levels of qualification. It is new in that it is the first project that cuts across the boundaries of the care sector by including such workers as nursery nurses, playgroup leaders, home visitors, and others who work in education and health settings as well as social services and the voluntary sector. The first set of draft standards of competence is currently under discussion.

Involving Parents in Their Children's Education

The first official recognition of the positive contribution that parents make to their children's education came with the publication of the Plowden Report (1967), which had unequivocally called for a "closer partnership between the two parties in every child's education" (ibid, p. 37). But it was not until the late 1970s that it was accepted that parents have the right to be involved in the management of schools. The Taylor Report (1977), the Warnock Report (1978) on special educational needs, and the various legislation culminating in the 1988 Education Act ensured a greater involvement of parents in the management of schools and in their children's learning. It is now mandatory to have parental representation on each school's governing body and each local education authority has offered training courses for parent governors.

The influence of parents is not limited to the school governing bodies. Much research has demonstrated that collaboration between schools and home can have a highly beneficial effect on children's learning. At the primary school level, such studies as the Belfield Community Project (1981) and the Haringay Project (Hewison and Tizard, 1980) have demonstrated that involving parents in the classroom and encouraging them to listen to their children read at home can have a positive effect on children's reading progress. Projects in London have also shown that parental involvement in the mathematics that children learn at school can also be highly beneficial (Voss and Gittins, 1990). During the 1980s several studies highlighted the possible effects of parental participation in their children's learning (Donachy, 1979; Tizard and Hughes, 1984; Tizard, Mortimore, and Birchell, 1981; Tizard, et al., 1988).

Most teachers accept that parental involvement is a "good thing," but as Jowett (1990) comments, there is often no plan of action or real understanding of what parent involvement means. To clarify the issue, a project funded by the National Foundation for Educational Research investigated how parents can best be involved in their children's education.

At present, involvement ranges from being a school governor and therefore being involved in the administration of the school, to helping make coffee and tea during social functions, to working in the classroom with the teachers, hearing children read or helping in cooking or craft activities.

Several researchers (Pugh, et al., (1988), Smith (1980), and Van der Eyken (1982, 1984)) have looked at the meaning of parental involvement at the preschool level. They have concluded that for some families their involvement is solely for the benefit of the adults. For example, parents may come to the parents' room at the facility to make a cup of coffee, to chat with other parents, or to use the sewing or other facilities at the center.

The most widespread form of parent involvement in Great Britain at the preschool level is through the preschool playgroups movement. Started as a response to the lack of nursery education, playgroups have provided both education and support for hundreds of thousands of parents and their children. Involvement in playgroups has helped many parents to better understand the needs of their own children and how to provide for them. It has also been a starting point for many women to a new life-style and career, since the skills they learned in organizing the playgroups are transferable to the workforce when their children have grown up.

Parental Education Programs

Parental education, as opposed to involving parents in schools, gained momentum during the late 1970s and the 1980s. Much of that momentum stemmed from the ideas of Mia Kelmer Pringle, the first director of the National Children's Bureau. She argued that parenthood, and particularly motherhood, has been undervalued for too long, and that it should be a deliberately chosen role in which the community as a whole should invest resources (Pringle, 1975, 1980).

The first governmental initiatives to look at how to raise the standard of parenting in the country came in 1980, when the Department of Health and Social Security (DHSS) funded a three-year project whose goal was to find out what was happening in both the statutory and voluntary fields in different parts of the country and to promote discussion of some of the key issues.

The parental education programs that are examined in this section use the definition put forward by Pugh and De'Ath (1984). They define it as "a wide range of educational and supportive measure which help parents and prospective parents to understand themselves and their children and enhance the relationships between them. (p. 8). " There are many self-help groups and small local initiatives, but this chapter discusses only a few in order to give a general understanding of parental education in Great Britain.

Structured programs—such as the Parent Effectiveness Training which is popular in the United States (Gordon, 1969)—have never caught on in Britain. In Britain, parental education has mushroomed informally. Early groups aimed at helping parents suffered from a dearth of good resource materials for guiding discussion. Over the last few years, the Open University Parent Education courses have provided useful resource materials, covering childhood from birth to adolescence in four courses. These courses aim to foster the "process approach" of helping people to review their own experiences,

values, and attitudes toward child rearing and to make and implement decisions. The accompanying video programs have been instrumental in encouraging viewers to reflect on their own experiences.

Other organizations, such as the National Marriage Guidance Council, have established educational projects at different stages in the life cycle. Three of these projects have dealt with groups of mothers with preschool children (Pugh, Kidd, and Torkington, 1982), and most large cities have adult education centers that are involved in parental education schemes.

Scope

Scope, an organization that began in Southampton in 1976 to help families help themselves, has spread to several parts of Hampshire. The aim of Scope is to offer a supportive network of care at times when families are in difficulty. The main focus of the work has been to establish a network of neighborhood self-help groups for families with preschoolers. The groups, which are led by local mothers with training and support from a coordinator, encourage mothers to meet weekly to share experiences and anxieties and to provide mutual support. The children are cared for in a creche while the mothers meet.

The chief function of Scope is to help parents gain a greater sense of power and control over their lives. The importance and success of this model are that it offers a service that does not create dependency, but builds on existing strengths and resources within the local community. Scope also operates a home visiting scheme for those who find it difficult to join groups. It has opened a family center where any group member may stay for up to four nights, with or without his or her family, at times of particular stress .

Cope

Cope was set up in 1951 as an "experimental home advice center" to teach basic home-making skills to women whose families were "at risk" and who themselves had low educational achievements. There are now more than 40 groups in the London area, in addition to neighborhood-based groups, meeting regularly for mutual support and enjoyment. The network has grown and Cope now acts as a national consultancy and training agency to promote this particular approach to family groups.

Home-Based Programs

Educational home visiting schemes were first introduced in the 1970s (Donachy, 1979; Feeley, Rennie, and Robinson, 1980; Raven, 1980). Although they have apparently been effective, most have been discontinued due to economic cutbacks. However, one of the most successful is the Leicester Home-Start project set up by Margaret Harrison in 1974. As of 1990, there were more than 125 schemes throughout the country and many more were at the planning stage or awaiting funding. The Home Start volunteers are parents. They receive an initial training before they become linked with other families; their role is to offer support and friendship and practical assistance to families with children under age 5 who are experiencing difficulties. To the families, the volunteer is someone to whom they can relate and who cares about the family and its problems.

All the parental education programs concentrate on building the parents' self-confidence and encouraging them to feel that they have an important part to play in their children's development. The approach in Great Britain is to encourage the parents to help their children rather than to introduce educational home-based programs that focus on the concept of compensation and aim to raise the levels of children's academic performance.

Special Educational Needs

Under the 1988 Education Act, all pupils, including those with special educational needs, are entitled to a broad and balanced curriculum. Until the passing of the Education (Handicapped Children) Act of 1970, when it was argued that no "child is ineducable," children with severe learning difficulties had no legal right to education in Great Britain. The Warnock Report (1978) recommended that wherever possible, children with special needs should be educated in ordinary schools. Furthermore, this report called for a reconceptualizing of handicaps in an educational context, arguing that the concept of special educational need should be "seen not in terms of a particular disability which a child may be judged to have, but in relation to everything abut him, his abilities as well as his disabilities" (Warnock, 1978). This stance reflects a shift away from a medical model in which special needs are seen as within the child, to an interactive model in which special educational needs are regarded as a result of the interaction of the child, home, and school.

The report also called for a partnership with parents in assessment and educational programming. The legal changes arising from the Warnock Report are manifested in the Education Act (1981), which obligates local educational authorities to ensure that adequate provision is made for all children with special educational needs, who must be educated, where possible, within ordinary schools. However, resources and other economic factors have meant that integration has not progressed as quickly as some wish. The act also lays down specific procedures for the assessment of such children, which stress that assessment is a partnership venture between professionals and the child's parents. For the first time, parents are involved at every stage of the assessment process.

Although the national curriculum is seen as a legal entitlement for all children, it is possible for it to be modified for individual children. It is also possible, if it is considered advisable, to exclude a subject or subjects from the individual child's curriculum. However, the national curriculum documentation states that virtually all children should be able to participate in the programs of study, although some children may take longer to move from one level to another.

It has been argued that the national curriculum will foster integration for children with special educational needs, particularly for children with mild or moderate learning difficulties, since it provides for the first time a common curriculum for all children. In the realm of early childhood education, integration has existed for many decades and similar educational experiences have been offered to all children. However, for older children, research has shown that there are wide differences in provision within mainstream schools, and between classroom and withdrawal groups provision (Gipps, Gross, and Goldstein, 1987).

The Warnock Report (1978) cited the preschool years as being a priority area within special needs. This has led to important changes and developments in provision, programs, and staffing. The 1981 Education Act placed a duty on local authorities to provide appropriate services for children from birth to age 5, a responsibility that has involved close cooperation with the voluntary organizations that have a long-established tradition in this field. Children with special educational needs can be admitted into nursery education from age 2, but a study by Chazan (1980) indicated that children received little help geared to their particular needs, since the staff thought that normal nursery activities would be adequate. Further studies based on work carried out at the Hester Adrian Research Institute (Mittler and Mittler, 1982), suggest that given generous professional resources and opportunities to develop and adapt practice to meet individual children's needs, it is possible for children to benefit from involvement in normal nursery programs.

Over the last 15 years there has been a steady growth in the development of home-based programs in which parents have participated in multidisciplinary teams to help in the assessment and teaching of their children (Mittler and Mittler, 1982; Wolfendale, 1983). Probably the most comprehensive early learning program is the Portage Scheme, first introduced into Great Britain in 1976. It was originally devised as a home visiting service in which, with weekly guidance from trained workers, parents helped their children to learn new and specific skills. More recently it has been introduced into a range of different settings, including nurseries and playgroups, and in some instances has been used with children other than those with specific learning difficulties. The scheme is regularly monitored by all the groups involved.

Parents are now recognized as key workers with children with special needs. The most successful projects have been those that have given structure and informed support to parents to enable them to overcome negative feelings about their children's development and their own ability to help (Mittler and Mittler, 1982).

Throughout the country, there are neighborhood schemes, such as those at St. Lukes, Cambridge, and the Lawrence Weston Community Development Project at Bristol (Elfer and Gatiss,

1990), where a team of multidisciplinary professionals and volunteers work together to support caregivers and parents of children under age 5. In spite of the high profile given to the importance of the early years for all children, and for children with special needs in particular, there is still considerable unevenness of provision. However, an increasing number of parents have formed self-help groups that have not only been effective in providing mutual support and assistance, but have also functioned as lobby groups to remind local authorities and government of the needs of their children.

In considering the concept of special education, it is also necessary to look at the needs of gifted children. There is little state recognition of young children with outstanding talents and abilities. However, some local authorities have an adviser to help teachers plan special programs. In some areas, there are special Saturday schools, although these normally cater to older children. There is also a national association, the National Association for Gifted Children, that advises parents who believe their children to be highly gifted.

Looking to the Future

During the next few years statutory education will be watched with keen interest by educators, politicians, parents, and all who are concerned with young children and their families. The 1988 Education Act has brought about sweeping changes to the British educational system. Not only has there been the introduction of the national curriculum with its programs of study, attainment targets, and assessments, but the act has placed much of the management of schools in the hands of the governing bodies. The effects of these changes will naturally be carefully monitored, but it is hoped that they will benefit all children.

Changes are also taking place within the area of preschool as more and more parents are seeking extended day care provision for their young children. In 1989, a committee—chaired by Angela Rumbold, who was then Minister of State for Education with responsibility for children under age 5—was set up to look into the current position and to make recommendations regarding quality care and education for young children and their families. The trend is toward coordinated services, with health, social services, and education working together in partnership with parents, in the best interests of the child. The needs of children and their parents are diverse and the majority of people working in this field would like to see services that offer flexible, quality care, so that there is real choice of provision in all parts of Great Britain.

Note

1. See Circular 24/89 and 59/89 (Welsh) from the Department of Education and Science for further information on CATE.

References

Bain, A., & Barnett, L. (1980). *The design of a day care system in a nursery setting of children under five.* London: Tavistock.

Ballard, P. (1937). *Things I cannot corget.* London: University of London Press.

Birchall, D. (1982). Family Centre. *Concern, 43,* 16–20.

Board of Education. (1905). *Report on children under five years of age by women inspectors.*

Bradley, M. (1982). *The Co-ordination of services for children under five.* Windsor: NFER Nelson.

Brayborn, G. & Summerfield, P. (1987). *Women's experiences in two world wars.* London: Pandora.

Bryant, B., Harris, M., & Newton, D. (1980). *Children and minders.* London: Grant McIntyre.

Central Advisory Council for England. (1967). *Children and their primary schools (Plowden Report).* London: HMSO.

Chazan, M., (1980). *Some of our children.* England: Open Books.

Children's Act, 1989. London: HMSO.

Clark, M.M. (Ed.). (1983) *Special needs and children under 5.* Education Review Occasional Publications No. 9. University of Birmingham.

——. (1987). Early education and children with special needs. *Journal of Child Psychology & Psychiatry, 28* (3), 417–25.

——. (1988). *Children under five.* London: Gordon Breach.

Clark, M.M., & Cheyne, W.M. (Eds.). (1979). *Studies in pre-school education.* Sevenoaks: Hodder & Stoughton.

Committee on Child Health Services. (1976). *Fit for the future.* (Court Report). London: HMSO.

Community Education Development Centre (1982a). *Parents in the primary school.* (Coventry CEDC).

——. (1982b). *Parents in the classroom.* (Coventry CEDC).

Consultative Committee (Hadow). (1931). *Report on the primary school.* London: HMSO.

——. (Hadow). (1933). *Report on infant and nursery schools.* London: HMSO.

Cowley, L. (1990). *Young children in group day care.* London: National Children's Bureau.

Curtis, A. (1986). *A Curriculum for the pre-school child.* Windsor: NFER-Nelson.

Curtis, A., & Blatchford, P. (1981). *Meeting the needs of socially handicapped children.* Windsor: NFER Nelson.

Davie, C.E., Hutt, S.J., Vincent, E., & Mason, M. (1984). *The young child at home.* Windsor: NFER Nelson.

DES. (1972). *Education: A framework for expansion.*

——. (1977). *A new partnership for our schools* (Taylor Report).

——. (1988). *Circular 59/88.* (Welsh Office).

——. (1989). *Initial Teacher Training: Approval of Courses.* Circular 24/89.

DES/DHSS. (1987). *Violence in the family.* Circular, January.

Donachy, W. (1979). Parental participation in pre-school education. In M.M. Clark & W. Cheyne (Eds.), *Studies in pre-school education.* Sevenoaks: Hodder & Stoughton.

Early Years Curriculum Group (1989). *Early years curriculum and the national curriculum.* Stoke-on-Trent: Trenthem Books.

Elfer P., & Gatiss, S. (1990). *Charting child health services.* London: NCB.

Feeley, G., Rennie, J., and Robinson, F. (1980). *Education visiting.* Community Education in Action, 3. Coventry Education Committee.

Ferri, E., Birchall, D., Gingell, V., & Gipps, C. (1981). *Combined nursery centres.* London: Macmillan.

Gipps, C., Gross, H., & Goldstein, H. (1987). *Warnock's 18 per cent: Children with special needs in primary schools.* London: Falmer Press.

Gordon, I.J. (1969). Developing parent power. In E.H. Grotberg (Ed.), *Critical issues in research related to disadvantaged children.* Princeton, NJ: Educational Testing Service.

Hagarty, S. (1987). *Meeting special needs in ordinary schools.* London: Cassell.

Halsey, A.H. (Ed.) (1972). *Educational priority: EPA problems and policies.* Vol. 1. London: HMSO.

Haystead, H., Howarth, V., & Strachen, A. (1980). *Pre-school education and care.* Sevenoaks: Hodder & Stoughton.

Hevey, D. (1986). *The continuing under-fives muddle.* London: VOLCUF.

Hewison, J., & Tizard, J. (1980). Parental involvement and reading attainment. *British Journal of Educational Psychology, 50:* 209–15.

HMSO. (1944). *Education act 1944*.

———. (1948). *Nurseries and childminders act 1948*.

———. (1968). *Health services and public health act 1968*.

———. (1981). *Education act 1981*.

———. (1988). *Education act 1988*.

Hughes, M., Mayall, B., & Moss, P., et al. (1980). *Nurseries now*. London: Penguin.

House of Commons. (1986). *Report from the education, science & arts committee. Achievement in primary schools*.

———. (1989). *Report from select committee on under 5's*.

Jackson, A., & Harmon, P.W. (1981). *The Belfield Reading Project*. Rochdale: Belfield Community Council.

Jowett, S. (1990). Parental involvement in the early years. In *The voice of the child*. Proceedings of XIXth World Assembly & Congress, OMEP, London.

Lawrence, E.E. (1912). *Types of schools for young children*. London: Froebel Society.

Mayall, B., & Petrie, P. (1977). *Mother, minder & child*. London: Institute of Education.

McMillan, M. (1919). *The nursery school*. London: Dent.

Ministry of Education. (1960/61). *Circular 8/60 Nursery Education and Addendum No. 1 (1961)*.

Ministry of Health. (1988). *Circular 37/88*.

Mittler, P., & Mittler, H. (1982). *Partnership with parents*. London: National Council for Special Education.

Moss, P. (1987). *A review of child minding research*. Working Paper 6. London: Thomas Coram Research Unit.

Mottershead, P. (1988). *An evaluation of recent child care institutions*. London: HMSO.

National Curriculum Council. (1989a). *Science: Non-statutory guidance*. York: NCC.

———. (1989b). *Mathematics: Non-statutory guidance*. York: NCC.

———. (1989c). *English key stage 1: Non-statutory guidance*. York: NCC.

———. (1989d). *Curriculum guidance 1. A framework for the primary curriculum*. York: NCC.

———. (1989e). *Circular number 5. Implementing the national curriculum—participation by pupils with special educational needs*. York: NCC.

National Education Union. (1870). *Report on the debate in Parliament during progress of the education bill 1870: 442*.

OPCS. (1988). *General Household Survey 1988*. London: HMSO.

Osborn, A.F., Butler, N.R., & Morris, A.C. (1984). *The social life of Britain's five year olds. A report of the child health & education study*. London: Routledge & Kegan Paul.

Osborn, A.F., & Milbank, J.E. (1987). *The effects of early education*. Oxford: Oxford University Press.

Poulton, G.A., & Couzens, H. (1981). *SCOPE of parents & children*. Southampton: Scope.

Pre-School Playgroups Association. (1989a). *Guidelines, good practice for full day care playgroups*. London: PPA.

———. (1989b). *Guidelines, good practice for sessional playgroups*. London: PPA.

Pringle, M.K. (1980). *A fairer future for children*. London: Macmillan.

———. (1975). *The needs of children*. London: Hutchinson.

Pugh, G. (1988). *Services for the under-fives*. London: National Children's Bureau.

Pugh, G., and De'Ath, E. (1989). *Working towards partnership in the early years*. London: National Children's Bureau.

Pugh, G., & De'Ath. (1984). *The needs of parents: Practice and policy in education*. London: Macmillan.

Pugh, G., Kidd, J., and Torkington, K. (1982). *A job for life*. London: National Marriage Council.

Raven, J. (1980). *Parents, teachers and children*. London: Hodder & Stoughton.

Shinman, S.M. (1981). *A chance for every child*. London: Tavistock.

Smith, T. (1980). *Parents and pre-school*. London: Grant McIntyre.

Sylva, K., Roy, C., & Painter, M. (1980). *Child watching at play group and nursery school*. London: Grant McIntyre.

Tizard, B., & Blatchford, P. (1988). *Young children in the inner city*. London: Lawrence Erlbaum Associates.

Tizard, B., & Hughes, M. (1984). *Young children learning: Talking and thinking at home and at school*. London: Fontana.

Tizard, B., Mortimer, J., & Birchell, B. (1981). *Involving parents in nursery and infant schools*. London: Grand McIntyre.

Under 5's Unit. (1990). *Young children in group day care: A consultation document*. London: National Children's Bureau.

Van der Eyken, W. (1984). *Day nurseries in action*. Bristol: Child Health Research Unit.

———. (1982). *Home start: A four year evaluation*. Bristol: Leicester Home Start Consultancy.

Wedell, K. (1988). The new act: Special need for vigilance. *British Journal of Special Education*, 15 (3), 98–101.

Whitbread, N. (1972). *The evolution of the nursery–infant school*. London: Routledge & Kegan Paul.

Wolfendale, S. (1983). *Parental participation in children's development and education*. New York: Gordon & Breach.

———. (1987). *Primary schools and special needs: Policy planning and provision*. London: Cassell.

Wolfendale, S., & Topping, K. (1987). *Parental involvement in children's reading*. London: Croom Helm.

Woodhead, M. (1976). *An experiment in nursery education*. Windsor: NFER Nelson.

———. (1978). *Intervening in disadvantage*. Windsor: NFER Nelson.

Warnock, M., et al. (1978). *Report of the Committee of Enquiry into the Education of Handicapped Children & Young People*. London: HMSO.

PRESCHOOL EDUCATION AND CARE IN HONG KONG

•••••••••◆•••••••••

Silvia Opper
University of Hong Kong
Hong Kong

The education and care of preschool children in Hong Kong are the responsibility of two executive governmental branches: Education and Manpower, administered by the Education Department: and Health and Welfare, administered by the Social Welfare Department. Kindergartens are regulated by the Education Department and provide a three-year educational program for children ages 3 to 6. Nurseries and playgroups, also called child care centers, are regulated by the Social Welfare Department and provide care, supervision, and education for children ages 2 to 5.

History

Preschool education and care have become widely available only since the post-World War II years. During the early part of this century, a few private kindergartens and primary schools with kindergarten classes offered a small number of places to preschool children, mostly middle class. Child care centers were practically nonexistent, since most mothers remained at home to take care of their children during their first years of life. The rapid expansion of preschool came about as a result of the tremendous population boom that occurred in Hong Kong between 1950 and 1970.

According to government figures in 1946, the estimated population of Hong Kong was 1.6 million (Annual Report, 1947); by 1957, it had increased to 2.67 million (ibid., 1968), and in 1970 it was 4,127,800 (ibid. 1971). Today it is approximately 5,736,100 (ibid. 1989). The rapid increase between 1946 and 1970 was due to many factors but of particular importance was the influx of Chinese refugees seeking to escape the war and turmoil in mainland China. Many of the newly arrived immigrants needed work, thus creating a demand for the care of young children. This led to the establishment of child care centers. At the same time, a shortage of primary school places resulted in stiff competition for those that were available. Consequently, entrance examinations were introduced to select the "better" students. Parents turned to kindergartens as a way to prepare their children for these primary school examinations.

During the period 1950–70, there was an explosion in kindergarten education, with an increase in the numbers of both kindergartens and children. According to figures of the Education Department, by the mid-1970s there were 172,410 children enrolled in 806 preschools (Annual Survey, 1967–77). (See Table 1.) Most of these preschools offered half-day programs. All of the kindergartens were private and many were set up as profit-making commercial enterprises. The rapid proliferation of kindergartens resulted in an increase in class size and child-teacher ratio and a decrease in classroom space. In addition, reports of the Director of Education recorded a decline in the percentage of trained teachers from 60 percent in 1962, to 20 percent in 1972, and 13 percent in 1982 (Annual Departmental Reports, 1961–62, 1971–72, 1981–82). Program quality inevitably suffered, although no specific evaluation of this aspect seems to have been made at that time. The number of child care centers also increased during this period, although not as dramatically as the number of kindergartens. These establishments were set up by mostly voluntary organizations to meet the needs of working mothers. Overall, by the end of the 1970s, a great many children were attending preschool, the majority in kindergarten and many in programs that would be considered inappropriate for children of this age group.

During the 1970s, two major governmental initiatives were taken pertaining to early education and care in Hong Kong. The first is relevant to kindergartens and the second to child care centers. In 1971, the government adopted an Education Ordinance and Regulation, (i.e., legislation that regulates all schools, including kindergartens, on matters such as registration, inspection, premises, and staff) targeted at primary and secondary schools. Many of its measures are not directly relevant to kindergarten education and some are even unsuitable, such as a recommended teacher-child ratio of 1:45.

In 1975–76, the government adopted legislation more directly related to young children, the Child Care Centers Ordinance and Regulation. This legislation details the standards to be adopted by child care centers regarding registration, operation, safety, sanitation, and staff training. In particular, it requires that all child care staff complete a recognized course of training within one year of entering service. During the years immediately following the adoption of this ordinance, an extensive training program was set up to ensure that child care workers had been trained. According to figures of the Education Department, only 16 percent of kindergarten teachers were trained in 1979 (Annual Summary, 1978–79).

More recent initiatives related to early education and care, and more specifically to kindergarten education, include the publication of three documents: a government White Paper on Primary Education and Preprimary Services in 1981, the Lewellyn Report in 1982, and the Education Commission Report No. 2 in 1986.

The 1981 White Paper, the first publicly available document to set out governmental policy on

TABLE 1

Preschool Education in Hong Kong, 1950–70

Year	Number of Kindergartens	Number of Kindergarten Children	Number of Child Care Centers	Number of Child Care Center Children
1952	156	13,415	n/a	n/a
1959	221	19,547	8	920
1962	341	35,735	22	3,258
1968	564	86,421	79	11,042
1971	875	140,960	n/a	n/a
1977	806	172,410	125	13,026
1979	801	198,351	194	14,666

Sources: Annual Reports by Director of Education, 1952–53, 1958–59, 1961–62, 1967–68, 1970–71; Education Department Annual Summary, 1976–77, 1978–79; Annual Reports of Director of Social Welfare, 1958–59, 1961–62, 1967–68, 1976–77, 1978–79.

preprimary education, highlights the need to improve kindergarten teacher training and to increase the number of trained teachers in kindergartens. It proposes a fee-assistance scheme for low-income families, and a governmental refund of rent and property taxes, as well as a 5-percent subsidy on the school fees for nonprofit kindergartens. It makes recommendations on minimum space, materials, and equipment for kindergartens, and suggests improvements to the curriculum. Finally, it explicitly states the government's intention to set up a joint training institute to coordinate training courses for child care and kindergarten staff and to introduce preservice kindergarten teacher training similar to that for primary school teachers.

The White Paper was closely followed by the visit of a panel of internationally recognized educators to evaluate the entire educational system. The report of this panel, known as the Lewellyn Report, recommended that the training of kindergarten staff be a high priority and proposed that kindergartens should, in the long term, become part of the regular educational system and thus become subsidized by the government.

In 1986, the Education Commission, a body of eminent persons of the community, published its second report. It includes recommendations for preprimary education, particularly a restructured fee-assistance scheme, salary scales for kindergarten staff, expansion of kindergarten teacher training, a 1:15 teacher-child ratio, the unification of standards for kindergartens and nurseries, and the establishment of a joint committee to implement this unification, as well as suggestions for research into Hong Kong preschool.

Apart from the above, there is little legislation in Hong Kong directly related to young children. Schooling is compulsory and free for nine years, from primary levels 1 to 6, and from secondary 1 to 3 levels. In fact most children spend at least 11 years in school and continue until completion of the secondary 5 level.

Preschool Programs

Preschools are located throughout the territory, with the largest number in the New Territories, where many new towns with young families are found. All children in Hong Kong, almost without exception, go to preschool from age 3 on, often starting as early as age 2. Almost 89 percent (Education Commission, 1986) go to a kindergarten, generally to a half-day session lasting approximately three hours. The remainder go to a half-day nursery or playgroup or to a full-day child care center. About 15 percent of the preschool children are in full-day programs (Opper, 1990). Although most kindergartens offer half-day programs and 63 percent of the children attend the more popular morning session, full-day kindergartens are becoming increasingly available.

All kindergartens are private, some are profit-making, others are nonprofit. The nonprofit kindergartens, which are often located on the public housing estates, can apply to the Education Department for a refund on rent, utilities, and property taxes. In 1986, according to Education Department figures, the government paid HK$25,627,000 for the refund of kindergarten rents and rates (Annual Summary, 1985–86).

With the exception of one demonstration nursery run by the Social Welfare Department Training Section, all nurseries are also private. Half-day nurseries are either profit or nonprofit. Full-day nurseries, often operated by charitable organizations called voluntary agencies, are usually subsidized by the government and offer programs for children of working parents. A few nurseries cater to English-speaking children.

Kindergarten and nursery fees must be approved by the Education and Social Welfare Departments, respectively, before operating permission is granted. Subsequently, they must be approved each year. Kindergarten fees average HK$223 for half-day programs, and HK$648 for full-day programs and range from HK$130 to HK$1,945 (HK$7.80 = approximately US$1.00). Nurseries charge on average HK$710 for a half-day program and HK$918 for a full-day program, and the latter receive substantial subsidies from the government (Opper, 1991).

Every three years nurseries are inspected by staff from the Public Works or Housing Departments to ensure that buildings are structurally sound. Before entering a nursery program, all children must have had a physical examination and the appropriate immunizations, which can be obtained free from the Maternal and Child Health

Clinics of the Medical and Health Department. Health records are maintained by the nursery staff for each child. Kindergarten staff also keep health records for each child. These records include immunization data and monthly weight and six-month height measurements.

Children are eligible to enter primary school at age 5 years and 8 months. The Education Department assigns children during their fifth year to a primary school in their neighborhood. This is done by the Primary One Admissions System, which was introduced in 1981 in an attempt to remove the existing primary entrance examinations.

Kindergarten Curriculum and Methods

The Education Department has published two documents as guides to the kindergarten curriculum: the *Manual of Kindergarten Practices* and the *Guide to the Kindergarten Curriculum* (1984). These contain recommendations for kindergarten principals and teachers in the areas of curriculum aims, teaching principles, program planning, organization and content, space, basic furniture, and teaching equipment.

Suggested curriculum aims are very general. They emphasize social, emotional, intellectual, and physical development; linguistic competence; and aesthetic awareness and appreciation. The teaching principles suggested encourage teachers to create a safe, happy, and stimulating environment that will help children to develop their potential through their own interests and needs. The thematic approach and the use of activity centers are recommended as the framework for teaching, with Cantonese as the language of instruction. Homework, examinations, and tests are discouraged. The recommended program includes a balance between periods for welcome, self-selected activities, physical play, creative activities, language, number, social studies, music, and a snack.

The guide proposes a half-day schedule, which allocates approximately one-half hour for welcome and snack, one hour for theme teaching and group work, and the remaining one and one-half hours for outdoor play, interest activities, art, crafts, music, and movement.

Space specifications are 1.2 square meters for

each child and 2.4 square meters for the teacher in a half-day program for 4- and 5-year-olds, and 1.8 square meters for each child in a full-day program or for a half-day program for 3-year-olds.

The manual and guide give recommended height and width specifications for desks and seats; suggest basic teaching equipment and materials for specific curriculum areas; and include sections on food, health, and sanitation. Supervisors are required to submit their program of activities to the Education Department for approval.

In practice, kindergarten classes are large, ranging from 14 to 80 children, with an average teacher-child ratio of 1:32. Teaching methods often consist of whole-group, teacher-led activities interspersed with small-group activities. The initial welcome, music and movement activities, and snack are generally whole-class activities. For the remainder of the time, small groups of 6 to 12 children rotate among different activities. Some of these activities are academic (e.g., writing Chinese characters or English words or doing number work); others may involve art, crafts, table games, and so on.

Since the recommendations of the manual and guide are not compulsory, many kindergarten staff offer a program that incorporates some of the recommendations with a more formal didactic teaching approach similar to that of the primary and secondary schools in Hong Kong.

Nursery Curriculum and Methods

The Child Care Center Inspectorate of the Social Welfare Department has also prepared a curriculum guideline for nurseries entitled *Activity Guideline for Day Nursery* (1988). In addition, a chapter in the Child Care Centers Advisory Inspectorate Code of Practice entitled "Program of Activities" provides general principles on content and method, suggests the use of activity centers and play for learning, and makes recommendations of appropriate learning materials for groups, and suggests a full-day schedule that includes slightly over two hours for indoor learning activities.

In practice, half-day nurseries generally adopt a curriculum similar to that of kindergartens, although their lower child-teacher ratio allows for more adult-child interaction. Full-day child care centers tend to devote more time to learning through play and have a less intense curriculum than half-day programs, since children are in the center for a longer time.

Teacher Training

Kindergartens have three categories of staff: permitted teacher, registered teacher, and principal. Permitted teachers should have completed the Hong Kong Certificate of Education, which is equivalent to nine years of schooling. Registered teachers need to have completed the Hong Kong Certificate of Education and have ten years' experience, or have a university degree with either three years' experience or a teaching certificate. Permitted teachers have the same qualifications as registered teachers but lack the ten years' experience. No specific qualifications are given for kindergarten principals.

Nurseries and child care centers also have three categories of staff: trainee, child care worker, and supervisor. Trainees need to have successfully completed Form 3 or nine years of schooling, be 18 years of age, and intend to take a course of training within one year of entering service, which will entitle them to become qualified child care workers. Child care workers need to have completed Form 3 and have completed approved training. Supervisors of child care centers must be at least 25 years old; have passed at least two subjects in the Hong Kong School Certificate, which is equivalent to eleven years of schooling; have completed an approved training course; and have had at least three years' experience working in child care. (See Table 2.)

Training for Kindergarten Staff

Before 1950, no formal training scheme existed in Hong Kong for kindergarten teachers. Persons interested in working in the field went abroad for training (e.g., to Taiwan, Macau, the United Kingdom, or mainland China). The first systematic training for kindergarten teacher training was introduced in 1950 in the form of a two-year, part-time course at a primary teacher training institute. After the first 25 students graduated in 1952, this course was discontinued because its director was transferred to the Education Depart-

ment. In 1956, the Kindergarten Section of the Education Department started a similar course, enrolling 50 students every two years. However, such training was insufficient to meet the demand for kindergarten teachers that resulted from the rapid expansion of kindergartens during this period. Consequently, the percentage of trained kindergarten teachers dropped steadily from 60 percent in 1962 to 13 percent as of 1981.

In 1981, the government in its White Paper attempted to remedy this alarming situation. It is stated that it intended to require that kindergartens employ a substantial number of trained staff and set target dates for increases in the proportion of trained teachers. By 1986, 45 percent of the staff of each kindergarten were expected to be trained, by 1988, 60 percent; and by 1990, 75 percent. The White Paper also recommended an urgent expansion of kindergarten teacher training programs to meet these targets.

These recommendations resulted in two training programs: (1) a 12-week, part-time course offered by the Kindergarten Inspectorate of the Education Department for teachers with the equivalent of nine years of education and (2) a two-year, part-time course offered by a teacher training college for persons with a higher education level. The first leads to the title of Qualified Assistant Kindergarten Teacher and the second to Qualified Kindergarten Teacher, which entitles the person to become a registered kindergarten teacher.

By 1986, only 28 percent of teachers, rather than the proposed 45 percent, had been trained. Consequently, the Education Commission in its second report (1986) again highlighted the need to expand kindergarten training. In view of the increasing urgency of the situation, it recommended a further expansion of the 12-week course.

Training for Nursery Staff

Two courses are available for nursery staff or child care workers: (1) an eight-week, part-time course offered by the Hong Kong Polytechnic under the auspices of the Social Welfare Department and (2) a one-year, full-time course, or equivalent, offered by a technical institute. Persons completing training in either of these courses are deemed qualified; those who complete the longer course receive a Certificate in Child Care. A two-year, part-time advanced course leading to a Higher Certificate in Child Care is also offered by the Hong Kong Polytechnic for certified child care workers with an additional two years of experience.

In 1989, the Hong Kong Polytechnic introduced the first distance learning course in Hong Kong in early education and care. This is intended for both kindergarten teachers and child care workers and leads to a Certificate in Preprimary Education.

Training for Key Personnel

A two-year, part-time Master's in Education program is offered by the University of Hong Kong for university graduates working in the field of early childhood education, usually in leadership positions (e.g., teacher trainers, curriculum developers, researchers, coordinators, etc.).

In addition to the various recognized training programs some adult learning institutions offer courses in the field of early education and care.

Status of Early Childhood Educators

Preschool educators, particularly kindergarten teachers, have low salaries and low status. A government pay scale exists for child care workers, with monthly salaries ranging from HK$3,720 to HK$6,970 and for center supervisors from HK$7,390 to HK$11,585. In 1990, the Education Department proposed a pay scale for kindergarten teachers that ranges from HK$3,570 for Form 3 graduates with no recognized training to HK$9,970 per month for qualified teachers with considerable experience. Head teachers receive an extra HK$500 monthly allowance. Increases in teacher salaries are to be covered by increases in the fees charged to parents.

Primary School Programs

Starting at age 6, children receive six years of primary education in Hong Kong. According to Education Department figures, in 1988, 535,037 children were enrolled in 689 primary schools, of which 558 were government subsidized, 50 were government operated, in 81 were private (Enrollment Summary, 1988). Since 1971, primary edu-

cation has been free in all government-operated and subsidized primary schools. Private schools, however, charge fees.

Most primary schools have two sessions, with children attending either the morning or afternoon session. However, in order to have a less crowded timetable and provide more time for teacher-student conduct and extracurricular activities, the government plans to convert all programs to full-day sessions by the year 2000 (Education Commission, 1990).

All children are assigned to a primary school during their fifth year by means of the Primary One Admissions System. Efforts are made as far as possible to assign incoming pupils to a school chosen by their parents or, failing this, within the family's district of residence.

After six years of primary education, children at the primary 6 level are assigned to a junior secondary school by means of the Secondary School Places Assignment System. This system is based on the results of three internal school assessments covering all school subjects, with the exception of physical education, and an academic aptitude test administered during the primary 6 year. The results are scaled by a centrally administered academic aptitude testing service and are used, together with parents' preferences, to assign pupils to an appropriate secondary school.

Primary Curriculum

Since 1972, the Education Department has recommended that primary classes adopt an activity approach, which emphasizes a child-centered approach. As of 1990, 251 primary classes have adopted this approach. The remainder of schools and classes follow the traditional didactic and teacher-directed approach to curriculum.

Training for Primary Teachers

Primary teachers are trained at three government colleges of education. They offer a variety of programs depending on entry qualifications: two of three years full-time preservice and two or three years part-time in-service. Upon completion of the program, students become certified primary teachers.

TABLE 2

Early Childhood Education Training Courses in Hong Kong

Course	Offered by	Degree Earned or Status Attained
For Kindergarten Staff		
12-week, part-time, in-service course	Kindergarten Inspectorate, Education Department or Grantham College of Education	Qualified Assistant Kindergarten Teacher
2-year, part-time, in-service course	Grantham College of Education	Qualified Kindergarten Teacher
For Nursery Staff		
8-week, part-time, in-service course	Hong Kong Polytechnic	Trained Child Care Worker
2-year, full-time course for Form 3 graduates	Lee Wai Lee Technical Institute	Certificate in Child Care (CCC)
1-year, full-time course for Form 5 graduates	Lee Wai Lee Technical Institute	Certificate in Child Care (CCC)
2-year, part-time course for Form 5 graduates	Lee Wai Lee Technical Institute	Certificate in Child Care (CCC)
2-year, part-time course for holders of CCC and 2 years' experience	Hong Kong Polytechnic	Higher Certificate in Child Care
Distance learning course for kindergarten teachers and child care workers	Hong Kong Polytechnic	Certificate in Preprimary Education
For Special Education Staff		
9-month, part-time course for holders of CCC or qualified kindergarten teachers working with children with special needs	Hong Kong Polytechnic	Certificate of Attendance
For Leadership Staff		
2-year, part-time course for university graduates working in early childhood education	University of Hong Kong	Master's of Education

Special Education Programs for Young Children

Several types of regular programs are available for preschool children with special needs (WOPSCET Report, 1984). These include the following:

• early education and training centers, which cater to children from birth to age 6 who have a range of handicaps or developmental delays or are deemed to be at risk;

• special child care centers, which provide specialist training for children ages 2 to 6 who have moderate to severe handicaps;

• integrated nurseries of child care centers, which accept preschool children ages 2 to 6 who have mild handicaps, particularly children with mild mental retardation;

• integrated kindergartens, which accept preschool children ages 3 to 6 who have mild handicaps;

• preparatory classes for preschoolers ages 4 to 6 in schools that cater to children with specific handicaps (e.g., schools for the deaf, blind, and physically handicapped children), although there are no preparatory classes for mentally handicapped preschool children; and

• the Special Education section of the Education Department, which provides speech and auditory training for preschool children with mild to profound hearing impairments.

A screening system, the Comprehensive Observation Scheme, is available in 43 Maternal and Child Health Clinics to help identify various developmental delays in young children from birth to age 5. Every child is entitled to three developmental screening tests during this period.

Children who have been screened as having potential delays are sent to one of four child assessment centers for diagnostic purposes. A Coordinated Referral System, operated by the Social Welfare Department, then assigns children diagnosed as handicapped to an appropriate program within their neighborhood. Three government Special Education Services Centers also help with diagnosis and provide early remedial measures.

Training in Special Education

Training for the staff of special education programs varies depending on whether the program is regulated by the Education Department or the Social Welfare Department. Staff in preschool services come under the Social Welfare Department. They must first become qualified child care workers, after which they follow a nine-month, part-time, in-service course for staff working with disabled children offered by the Hong Kong Polytechnic.

Special education staff working with school children come under the Education Department. Teachers of integrated kindergartens are regular kindergarten teachers who, after completion of the normal kindergarten training, are eligible for the above nine-month course at the Hong Kong Polytechnic. Teachers in the preparatory classes are primary school teachers with a specialization in special education whose training includes an element of working with preschool children with special needs. Staff of the Special Education Section of the Education Department are generally either clinical psychologists with a university degree, often at the graduate level, in psychology or special education.

Parental Support and Education Programs

Two types of support are available for parents of young children: (1) financial assistance, and (2) educational and psychological support programs.

Financial Assistance

The Hong Kong government provides a fee assistance scheme, which partially refunds preschool fees of low-income parents of preschool children. The amount of refund is shown in Table 3. If preschool fees are greater than the allowance, parents pay the difference. A family of four with a monthly income of less than HK$2,500 (which is very low by present standards) would receive only HK$142 in fee assistance (Annual Summary 1985–86). No figures are available for families with children in nurseries.

Educational and Psychological Support Programs

There are a variety of parental education and support programs available for families of handicapped and nonhandicapped children. The government Maternal and Child Health Clinics (which

TABLE 3

Monthly Maximum Fee Assistance

Net Household Income (per month) (4 persons)	Full-Day Nursery	Full-Day Kindergarten	Half-Day Kindergarten
HK$1,500	$700	$287	$156
HK$1,500–2,500	$555	$142	$ 11

are being renamed to Family Health Centers to reflect the changing role of catering also to fathers and other family members) provide programs, information, and publications. Many social service agencies involved with child care run parental education programs for their clients and often also have an attached resource center. Regular and occasional courses related to children and child rearing are also offered by adult education institutes, such as extra-mural studies departments of the universities.

References

Education Commission. (1986). *Report No. 2.* Hong Kong: Government Printer.

Hong Kong Government. (1947a). *Annual report on Hong Kong for the year 1945.* Hong Kong: Government Printer.

———. (1947b). *Annual report on Hong Kong for the year 1958.* Hong Kong: Government Printer.

———. (1971a). *Annual report on Hong Kong for the year 1971.* Hong Kong: Government Printer.

———. (1971b). *Education Ordinance.* Hong Kong: Government Printer.

———. (1971c). *Education Regulations.* Hong Kong: Government Printer.

———. (1975). *Child Care Centers Ordinance.* Hong Kong: Government Printer.

———. (1976). *Child Care Centers Regulations.* Hong Kong: Government Printer.

———. (1981). *White Paper on Primary Education and Preprimary Services.* Hong Kong: Government Printer.

———. (1989). *Annual Report.* Hong Kong: Government Printer.

———. Education Commission. (1990). *Report no. 4.* Hong Kong: Government Printer.

———. Education Department. (1953). *Annual Report by Director of Education 1952–53.* Hong Kong: Government Printer.

———. Education Department. (1959). *Annual Report by Directory of Education 1958–59.* Hong Kong: Government Printer.

———. Education Department. (1968). *Annual Report by Directory of Education 1967–68.* Hong Kong: Government Printer.

———. Education Department. (1971). *Annual Report by Directory of Education 1970–71.* Hong Kong: Government Printer.

———. Education Department. (1972). *Annual Report by Directory of Education 1971–72.* Hong Kong: Government Printer.

———. Education Department. (1977). *Annual Summary 1976–77.* Hong Kong: Government Printer.

———. Education Department. (1979). *Annual Summary 1978–79.* Hong Kong: Government Printer.

———. Education Department. (1982). *Annual Summary 1981–82.* Hong Kong: Government Printer.

———. Education Department. (1984a). *Manual of kindergarten practice.* Hong Kong: Government Printer.

———. Education Department. (1984b). *Guide to the kindergarten curriculum.* Hong Kong: Government Printer.

———. Education Department. (1986). *Annual Summary 1985–86.* Hong Kong: Government Printer.

———. Education and Manpower Branch. (1984). *Report of the working party on preschool care, education, and training of disabled children (WOPSCET Report).* Hong Kong: Government Printer.

———. Social Welfare Department. (1959). *Annual Report by Director of Social Welfare 1958–59.* Hong Kong: Government Printer.

———. Social Welfare Department. (1962). *Annual Report by Director of Social Welfare 1961–62.* Hong Kong: Government Printer.

———. Social Welfare Department. (1968). *Annual Report by Director of Social Welfare 1967–68.* Hong Kong: Government Printer.

———. Social Welfare Department. (1977). *Annual Report by Director of Social Welfare 1976–77*. Hong Kong: Government Printer.

———. Social Welfare Department. (1979). *Annual Report by Director of Social Welfare 1978–79*. Hong Kong: Government Printer.

———. Social Welfare Department. (1984). *Code of practice for child care centers*. Hong Kong: Government Printer.

———. Social Welfare Department. (1988). *Activity guidelines for day nursery*. Hong Kong: Government Printer.

Lewellyn, Sir John. (1982). *A perspective on education in Hong Kong: Report by a visiting panel*. Hong Kong: Government Printer.

Opper, S. (1990). *Hong Kong's young children: Their families and preschools*. Paper presented at the 7th Asian Christian Conference on Early Childhood Education, Hong Kong.

Opper, S. (1991). *The Education and care of Hong Kong's preschool children*. Ypsilanti, Michigan: High/Scope Press.

PRESCHOOL INSTITUTIONAL EDUCATION IN HUNGARY

••••••••••◆••••••••

Eva Knoll Pereszlényi
Budapest Teachers Training College
Budapest, Hungary

Early History of Nursery Schools in Hungary

The first nursery school in Hungary was established in the city of Buda in 1828 by Brunszvik Teréz, a member of the noble family. Inspired by Heinrich Pestalozzi, Teréz championed the cause of early education in Hungary. At the beginning, however, the "infant schools" cared for the children ages 2 to 7 of working parents. The Association of Infant Schools had a considerable role in collecting donations and gaining the support of wealthy patrons. The first teachers in the schools were male. Women were not admitted to kindergarten teacher training until the 1850s. In this early period, the teachers spoke in German with the children. In fact, the first teacher in the original nursery school in Buda could not speak Hungarian.

The curriculum incorporated play and used methods from the primary level. The dominant focus, however, was on formal academic work even for the youngest children. Children were taught religion, reading, mathematics, geography, and singing. This curriculum evolved with the influence of Hungarian educators and drew more attention to the physical and spiritual development of children.

I. Varga, an influential headmaster in this early period, viewed the task of kindergarten education as essentially physical training. He organized the curriculum into four sections: (1) "heart development," (2) "mental development," (3) "development of patriotism," and (4) the formation of manual skills through handiwork, gardening, etc. Games and self-directed play as the basic activities of small children were missing from nursery school life for a long time. There are several reasons for this omission. First, children were cared for in groups as large as 150 children. Academic instruction was therefore tied to the need for strict child management. This was coupled with the popular notion of the child as essentially no different from an adult except in size.

The academic focus was also indicative of a moral philosophy. It was recognized that children must be made to work, that is, moved to do activities because it is important for a child to do something useful and good. That is why children were very often forced to make an effort that was beyond their physical and mental abilities.

259

The nursery school movement developed mainly through donations and individual philanthropic initiatives until 1848. For this reason, although many nursery schools were established in this early period, most survived only a short time.

The influence of pedagogical endeavors directed toward "fundamental education" was strengthened with the organization of preschool education and the first nursery school Educational Act in 1891. Although the act made nursery school compulsory, it did not make it universally available. Its real achievement was the recognition and support of the nursery school by the state.

At the turn of the 20th century, the most important influences were the educational theories of Friedrich Froebel and later, the system of Maria Montessori. Nursery schools were maintained by state, denominational, and private institutions or organizations. The structure and organization of nursery schools reflected their source of funding and sponsorship.

Development of the Socialist Nursery School

With few exceptions, the development of nursery education was stagnant until 1948 when nursery schools became nationalized and centrally directed. At that time, a unified Hungarian nursery school system was formed. In the post-World War II period, a child-centered nursery school has emerged, dominated by the recognition of the value of children's play.

After the war, the reconstruction of the country and industrialization mobilized masses of workers. Because of this, a creche and nursery school network was formed nationwide, but mainly in big cities, to allow mothers to return to work after their six-week maternity leave had expired. It was recognized, however, that infant institutional education causes socialization problems because of early separation from the mother. For this reason, since 1971, the maternity allowance has been paid for three years following the birth of the child. As a result, creches which were once overcrowded, are now in little demand. For example, in the 1950s, a creche worker cared for 16 infants; today a creche worker is responsible for three to four.

The creches that do exist operate 12 hours each working day, caring for children from infancy to kindergarten age. The optimal development of the children is followed through continuous and strict health care and reports on their progress. Teachers are trained in methodology with a focus on music education, which is based on the national music curriculum of Zoltán Kodály, who devised a method for teaching the fundamentals of music theory.

In the years following nursery school nationalization, important changes occurred that affected nursery school structure and focus. Its administration, for example, became the responsibility of the Ministry of Religion and Public Education instead of the Ministry of Welfare. In this way, the basic pedagogical function of nursery schools was determined. The new nursery education act of 1953 unified and regulated nursery education and stressed the aims of the socialist nursery school. In 1958, the periodical *Children's Education* began disseminating ideas regarding nursery school pedagogy. In 1985, a new Education Act integrated the Preschool Education Act and declared the kindergarten an organic part of public education.

From its very beginning, Hungarian nursery schools had both a social and pedagogical function.

Contemporary Hungarian Nursery School

The modern nursery school aims to promote the harmonious development of children ages 3 to 7. Preschool education occurs in an intimate, cheerful atmosphere to provide a diversified educational experience. On one hand, it continues familiar nursery education ideas; on the other, it supplements and completes their influence. The task of the nursery school is to ensure healthy emotional, social, and intellectual development. A successful preschool education results in a mentally and physically sound child qualified to attend primary school. The compulsory curriculum is laid down in Nursery School Pedagogy (1971).

Children are admitted to Hungarian nursery schools at the age of 2 1/2 or 3. They are free of charge for every child. Parents pay only for meals on the basis of their income. Regional nursery schools greatly differ from each other in size and structure. Teachers always take into account local and regional needs. The schools range from an institution with two groups of children to the so-called mammoth nursery schools that have 16 integrated groups. A group generally consists of 25 children. The composition of the groups varies annually and locally. Two types are typical: (1) a homogeneous group divided according to age (e.g., infant, middle, or preschool) and (2) heterogeneous group of different aged children.

In each group, two kindergarten teachers work in two shifts from 6 a.m. to 6 p.m. An assistant performs housekeeping duties and helps the teachers care for the children. Assistants are generally semiskilled women who have good pedagogical sense but have no qualification or formal training.

The headmistress, who holds a degree in kindergarten education, administers the nursery school. She is also responsible for creating a link between the nursery school and family life, decisions are made jointly with the teachers and parents. A pediatrician and a welfare officer also contribute to the integrated development of children. Children with speech defects or other minor handicaps are provided with special programs within the nursery school. Although the nursery schools have no staff psychologists, regional educational counselors provide guidance to individual schools and teachers regarding the children's readiness for school.

Each group of children is assigned a self-contained room of approximately 50 square meters in which they spend their day. The room is arranged according to need. In modern nursery schools, there is a spacious terrace and almost all have a playing field and a gymnasium.

Nursery schools are generally very popular with parents. Even mothers, who are at home on maternity care with a younger child enroll their elder children. This is supported by statistics, which reveal that 91 percent of children nationwide attend nursery schools. In Budapest, the capital city, the attendance is 98 percent.

Until 1990, all nursery schools were operated by the state. However, recent political changes have affected nursery education. As a result nursery schools could be sponsored and maintained either by the state or by various institutions, factories, or other enterprises. Regardless of the sponsorship, all nursery schools are subject to the same regulations and curriculum requirements. In Hungary, changes in the regime have affected nursery education. As a result, the trend is toward educational pluralism in nursery schools; this is discussed below.

Nursery School Curriculum

Tasks of preschool education are far-reaching and interdependent. They include the basic "frames" of education (i.e., caretaking, education for a healthy way of life, and communal education) and children's activities (i.e., games, work, and learning tasks), which are the means of preschool education. The various educational fields serve as the subject matter of children's activities. The most important is vernacular education, which incorporates literary, musical and visual education, and environmental studies, as well as mathematical and physical education. It is believed that none of this is possible unless family, creche, public educational institutions, and schools work together.

Children attend lessons according to a weekly timetable. Lessons are both formal and informal and led by kindergarten teachers. Physical education is compulsory for children ages 3 to 4, with all other lessons being informal in this age group. For 4- to 7-year-old children, literary study is informal and other lessons are compulsory, didactically constructed learning situations directly guided by the kindergarten teacher.

The teacher initiates informal activities or lessons for the children, but their participation is optional. Depending on the children's age, the lessons can last from 10 to 35 minutes. Currently, there is a debate over the relevance of formal learning activities in the nursery school, which may make the nursery school school-like and product-oriented. It should be emphasized, however, that most of the children's day is occupied in free play. The teacher is to be a facilitator and a resource for the children.

Nursery School Admission Requirements

Prior to 1985, the Compulsory Education Act determined school entry by the age of children: all those who had their sixth birthday by August 31 of the current year could attend. However, experience demonstrated that the youngest children, that is, those who had been born during the summer, had difficulties in adapting to school. Their poor accomplishment seemed to indicate that they began their grade 1 studies too early and were at a disadvantage because of their undeveloped skills. In 1985, the new Education Act moved the time limit to the May 31. Those turning age 6 after this date are admitted only if they demonstrate school readiness.

Information on a child's school readiness is provided by the kindergarten teacher, while the nursery school doctor provides a health verification. Various specialists may also be consulted. While the nursery school makes a decision, the parents decide the child's fate. As a result of good cooperation in most cases, decisions are made without conflict. When the child is in fact school age and neither the parents nor the kindergarten teacher suggests that the child be enrolled, the headmaster of the school can exempt the child from attending the school for one year.

The revised entry age seems to be a success. Nursery school children pass through a relatively simple procedure before enrollment. The small number of children who do not attend a nursery school participate in preparatory courses organized by a nursery or primary school.

Current Development and Renewal in Hungarian Nursery Education

Recent rapid changes in the Hungarian political and social life exert an influence on the development of preschool education. Moreover, the changes alter the various disciplines that feed Hungarian preschool education. For example, emphasis is put on broadening the rights of maintaining nursery schools. In addition, the state's monopoly over institutional education has been terminated. Sponsorship was never private because nursery schools belonging to factories and companies were state-owned. Modifications to the Education Act in 1990 allowed churches, denominational schools, and even individuals the right to organize and maintain nursery schools. The resultant possibility of "multiple" maintenance will obviously cause conceptional changes as well as a wider choice in the future.

Another important factor is that structural changes in the national economy and privatization raise the responsibility of the state to finance large-scale optional preschool preparatory institutional systems. However, it is questionable whether such schools can do more than make basic provisions. If it cannot, the institution will lose its character as a unique, social achievement.

If the current demographic pattern persists, the number of children in nursery schools will decrease. The number of children in nursery groups is still not optimal, considering the fact that factory or company nursery-schools are closed down. The decrease in the number of nursery schools is a fact, the irreversible process has begun.

Seeming to contradict this pattern is that the importance of early development of skills is being emphasized. The result is that the pedagogical function of the nursery school is gaining strength while the social caretaker role is overshadowed. When a nursery-school fee is introduced, there will no doubt be a growing demand for half-day nursery schools. This could lead to several, unfavorable actions that could affect the future and quality of nursery education in Hungary. In the view of the author, Hungarian families need preschool education because of its proven value in children's development as well as its social function of aiding families in times of economic crisis. For these reasons, it is hoped that the state will continue to support and even expand the nursery school network.

Whereas the influence of some factors on nursery schools is hypothetical, some changes are physically evident. Renewal is a fact in Hungarian nursery-schools. After years of outmoded practice and theory in Hungarian nursery education, the system is currently being reformed. An example of this change is the decline of the subject system. As a result, the curriculum is more adaptable to a younger enrollment. Parents and experts need to create more play opportunities and allow children to have their "own" time by using a less tense timetable and by focusing on individual needs all of which were inconsistent with the goals of communal education promoted by a socialist Hungary. There is further a need to create the image of the nursery school as a place in which sports, foreign languages, and religious education can be supported.

The new pluralistic society cannot be achieved without alternative pedagogical programs. For some time, the nursery school has been making changes in the national curriculum. However, it has been recognized that this is not enough. The current trend is to look to educational history as well as modern foreign preschool education for ideas and inspiration, while adapting them to the Hungarian context. For example, Waldorf's and Freinet's pedagogies are very popular. At the same time, there are experiments with an alternative national nursery educational curriculum.

References

Programme for preschool education. (1971). Budapest: Tankönyvkiadó.

Programme for preschool education. (1989). Budapest: National Institute of Pedagogy.

Vág, O. (1979). *Nursery schools and preschool education.* Budapest: Tankönyvkiadó.

PRIMARY EDUCATION IN HUNGARY

••••••••••◆••••••••

Agnes Szilágyi
Budapest Teachers Training College
Budapest, Hungary

In Hungary, the centrally organized education of pupils of the lower grades began in the 18th century when the state made significant efforts to seize control of educational affairs. Prior to this time, all schools were operated by religious organizations.

In 1806, a revised Ratio Educationis,[1] elaborating on the earlier one of 1777, systematized public education in Hungary. It was at this time that elementary schools for teaching the basics of mathematics, reading, and writing became the foundation of the educational system. This period of schooling lasted for three years and was aimed at making children literate and teaching them ethical and religious knowledge. It also prepared them for secondary school. The curriculum was later expanded to include mathematics, geometry, history, geography, and environmental studies. In the lower grades, teaching was carried out in the mother tongue of the children and supervised by the "ludi magister" (head master).

In 1845, elementary schools were restructured into four grades with the final grade to be completed within two years. In this way, the elementary school had in effect five grades. The subject matter became more varied and included drawing, geology, architecture, literature, and German grammar.

Economic and social changes in the mid-19th century increased the importance of each Hungarian having at least a basic education. József Eötvös, an eminent Hungarian statesman, elaborated its framework. On the grounds of his proposals, the Public Education Act was passed in 1868, making education compulsory for all children ages 6 to 12. In this way, elementary schools became public, with six grades. The implementation of the act required considerable effort and development of universal education was slow. In 1868, 48 percent of eligible children attended school, 55 percent in 1872, and 95 percent in 1913. As a result, 30 percent of the population remained illiterate at the turn of the 20th century. However, Eötvös' vision for educational and social reform was a true turning point in the history of primary education.

According to his concept, a public elementary school prepared children for a higher elementary school or secondary school with eight grades. It was also designed to teach various skills. Although with the 1968 act the state was obliged to establish public schools, parish and private schools continued to exist.

In 1945, a new type of school was created by amalgamating public elementary schools with the higher elementary grades and the initial four grades of secondary schools. The reformed elementary school consisted of eight grades and was fully implemented in September 1949.

Each Hungarian citizen from the age 6 to 16 has the right and obligation to a public education. The goal is to provide pupils with a general education and to prepare them for further education. The lower grades of elementary schools consist of grades 1 to 4. In 1948, a law was passed to nationalize schools. Since that time, all elementary schools have operated according to a uniform curriculum and under state supervision. The operation of the educational system is regulated by laws, which are renewed or modified according to need.

The Education Act was last modified in 1990. Recent changes permit churches, private organizations, and individuals to establish schools provided they meet the requirements of the law. Both the subject matter and the structure of the present educational system will be changed by the modified act. It promises more varied and diverse educational programs that are more attuned to local and regional needs. The act reinforces the theory that the primary level is the foundation of the educational system.

Characteristics of the Primary School System

Children are able to attend school if they are age 6 before May 31. In practice, however, children who are mature and whose birthday falls before December 31 of the school year may attend grade 1. Completion of the subject matter of the primary level usually takes four, but not more than six, academic years. The Education Act permits pupils to advance at a faster rate to concentrate their schooling.

The first two years of the primary system are regarded as a developing stage. Advancement of pupils in this stage is based on biannual oral reports from the classroom teacher. Marks are given beginning in grade 3. A five-mark system is used with 5 the best and 1 the worst.

Pupils have four to five lessons a day and attend school from 8 A.M. to 12:30 P.M., lessons last 45 minutes and are separated by 10- to 15-minute breaks. The school week is five days and the school year is 33 weeks, with holidays in the winter and spring. The number of compulsory lessons increases with the progression of grades. There are 20 compulsory subjects in grade 1, 22 in grade 2, 24 in grade 3, and 25 in grade 4. Pupils are ranked into classes according to grades. A class usually consists of 25 to 30 children. In villages and rural areas, grades may be combined.

While the subject content is identical in each grade, the proportion of time allotted for each subject varies. The subjects for the first four grades are Hungarian grammar and literature, mathematics, environmental science, music and singing, drawing, crafts, physical education, and a foreign language.

Children whose parents are unable to take care of them in the afternoon take part in all-day education. There are two options for children of working parents: day homes and all-day schools. In both, children are provided with lessons related to their morning work. All services of the system are free of charge with the exception of meals, which are paid for by parents on a sliding scale according to their income.

In day homes, pupils are able to complete their lessons with the aid of a teacher. After they have completed their lessons, they may relax, take part in outdoor games, organize activities, or do minor chores. In all-day schools, a group of pupils has two teachers who share the teaching task. The advantage of all-day schools is that the children's lessons are extended over the entire day, providing a better proportion of free-time activities, games, and work. Because the "homework" is completed in the classroom, the teacher can better follow and help in the educational process. All-day education forms the proper habits of a healthy, educated way of life; develops the ability of learning individually; and organizes the social life of children. Children are required to prepare for the lesson of the following day in the course of all-day education. Ideally, lessons are taken home only on the weekend.

Extracurricular activities are promoted by groups organized to share interests in subjects that include foreign languages, sports, stamp collecting, chess, mathematics, and folk dancing. These meet once or twice a week in the afternoon and are available to all pupils.

The Primary Curriculum

The educational work of the primary grades builds on the foundation began by the kindergartens and the family. Its goal is to create favorable conditions for children's physical, mental, and spiritual development and to prepare pupils for the next educational level.

The main pedagogical task is to lead young children from the play-centered system of kindergarten activities to the learning-centered school activities. It preserves and develops the openness and motivation to learn, which generally characterizes preschool children. It develops the sensitivity of pupils to the social, natural and spiritual values that correspond to their age. It organizes the process of acquiring the rudiments of knowledge and a moral and aesthetic education. It aids the favorable development of the child's relationship with the environment, the departure from dependency on adults, and the growing prominence of peers.

Within the framework of multitask learning activities, it lays the foundation for the abilities, skills, and knowledge that can be developed during the child's lifetime. Beyond these activities, it develops will power, persistence, and responsibility. The major orientating principle in the primary grades is that education must consider both developmental processes and individual needs.

At the primary level, the aim is not to acquire knowledge itself but to develop the abilities that are fundamental for further skill development. As children attain higher skill levels, they become more independent. Abilities and skills are regarded partly as conditions of learning and partly as the product of learning. Development, however, is not subject-centered. While development of fundamental skills, such as reading, writing, and counting, is mainly related to a subject, their interrelatedness with other subjects is stressed. The following section provides a more detailed description of two subject or skill areas.

Language and Social Sciences

Languages. The study of the Hungarian language is a high priority in the primary grades. The main aim is to promote the heritage of the Hungarian language by laying the foundation for its proper oral and written use. It prepares pupils to cope with basic communicative situations and starts the process of forming the abilities necessary for individual learning and education. It also provides the proper foundation for learning foreign languages.

In language development, diverse and regular activities and play, as well as individual experience and emotions, are more important than verbal acquisition. Conscious development of language use is not restricted to grammar lessons, but is always present in the classroom and is a continuous task of a teacher.

The study of literature consists of reading valuable literary works, tales, and poems, as well as work written specifically for children. Through the study of literature, children not only study structural and linguistic content, but also develop a love for Hungarian and the aesthetics of language.

Social Sciences. The study of social science includes learning about human and social relationships; the community, nation, and world; and religion. Studying social science helps children to orient themselves to the larger society and favorably influences their socialization and identity. There are various sources of knowledge in social science, (e.g., personal observation, literature, museological materials, photographs, and television). Realistic situations play a major role in social science in the primary grades. Analyzing such situations allows children to gradually acquire a stable system of norms with which to guide their behavior. Emphasis is put on forming a moral sense, developing social sensitivity, strengthening patriotism, acknowledging an individual's personal interest, and appreciating and respecting the point of view of others.

Current Trends in Hungarian Primary Education

With the goal of modernizing primary teaching and education, a variety of approaches have been developed. The diversity in methodology is evident in the area of teaching reading. All methods aim to develop a system that better follows the peculiarities and development of young children. There have been experiments with the adaptation of foreign education trends, for example, schools based on the ideas of Carl Rogers, Célestin Freinet, and Waldorf.

For many years public opinion has encouraged the identification and educational support of gifted children. Schools that do so include Iván Markó's school of dance, F. Sapszon choir following Kodály's traditions, and L. Polgár chess school.

This brief review of current trends indicates the diversity of pedagogical thought in Hungary. However, all share a desire to make primary education more responsive to the needs of young children, and to make the school experience enjoyable and worthwhile.

Note

1. The Ratio Educationis of 1777 was a curriculum written in Latin that developed out of the first educational reforms in Hungary. It describes a comprehensive, state-run educational system and a curriculum for a five-grade secondary school. The Ratio Educationis of 1806 extended the curriculum to primary public elementary schools and the university.

KINDERGARTEN AND PRIMARY TEACHER TRAINING IN HUNGARY

• • • • • • • • • • ◆ • • • • • • • • •

Suzanne Hunyady
Budapest Teachers Training College
Budapest, Hungary

Training for teachers of 3- to 10-year-old children has historically been closely related to educational and teaching practice in Hungary. As a result, until the mid-18th century there were no institutions for training primary school teachers. The pedagogue was not expected to have any special qualifications beyond secondary school. Professional knowledge was achieved only through practice. The institutionalization of teacher training began in 1775 with the founding of normal schools. Similarly, in the nursery schools of the early 19th century, teachers were unqualified. Although Theresa Brunswick employed 11 girls in the nursery school she founded in 1828 so that they could learn how to teach young children, a systematic training program began much later.

Because institutions founded to train kindergarten and primary school teachers developed differently the following description deals with each separately.

Kindergarten Teacher Training

The first institutionalized kindergarten teacher training in Hungary was begun in 1837 in Tolna by Istvan Wargha. From its original country settlement, the school was later moved to Pest. Students, who were all men, were expected to have completed secondary school. The course was expanded from one to two years in 1874. Successful graduation depended on passing a final examination. For decades, the school graduated mature, educated, and highly qualified teachers. Judged by the standards of the time, the school developed a high-quality pedagogical and psychological training program, which attained its zenith at the end of the 19th century.

This first stage of kindergarten teacher training was disrupted in a certain sense by the Education Act of 1891, which qualified kindergarten teachers at the secondary level. One criterion for admission was that applicants be at least age 14 while the program was left at two years in duration. It was not until 35 years later that the duration of secondary-level training was extended to four years. In the final year, students completed practicums and at the end they wrote a qualifying examination.

No real changes occurred in the years immediately following World War II. Kindergarten teacher training was left at the secondary level. The conversion into a pedagogical grammar school proved to be a failure. The consequences were twofold. First, the duration of the training was reduced to three years, with the result that 17-year-olds were responsible for the care and education of the nation's preschool children. Second, nursery education evening and correspondence courses were started on a large scale.

Evening courses had been available for some time, mostly to provide kindergarten teacher candidates with basic knowledge in theory and in practice. Unfortunately, correspondence training survived for many years. As recently as 1987, approximately 35 percent of kindergarten teacher graduates took their degree in this way.

Experts in preschool education continually fought for a more academic training program. The first institutions of this kind began in September 1959 when a special college-level training was implemented. It included lectures, seminars, and examinations designed to raise kindergarten education to a higher level. At the same time, the positive traditions of secondary schools were preserved. These included intensive, practical training in small groups, considerable opportunities for practice teaching, and informal relationships between teachers and students. Before long, however, it was realized that the number of subjects relevant to general education, intending to raise the educational level of kindergarten teachers, did not allow students to pursue any particular subject in depth. A new national curriculum only partially addressed the problems. The Education Act of 1985 fixed the final date of the issuance of certificates, and determined the pace of converting training institutions into colleges (completed in 1990).

The new kindergarten teacher training institutions are colleges with three-year programs. At present, kindergarten teacher training is carried out in various forms. There are three independent colleges, a kindergarten teacher specialty in ten teacher training colleges, and one college of education (Nyiregyhaza) designed to train both kindergarten teachers and teachers of 10- to 14-year-olds. Because recent legislation has resulted in the abolishment of a national curriculum, the College Senate of each autonomous institute compiles the curriculum on the basis of Curricular Directives containing the requirements for a degree.

When deciding the content of kindergarten teacher training, experts consider two factors. First, higher educational qualifications must be guaranteed so that young kindergarten teachers can acquire the education necessary for an intellectual course of life, general social and science knowledge, the ability to communicate in the mother tongue and foreign languages, and skills in physical education. Second, they must be given professional education in the development and education of young children.

Part of the curriculum is presented in educational blocks focusing on philosophical, sociological, ethical, economical, or historical knowledge. Such blocks make up 7 percent of the curriculum. Unfortunately, there is hardly any more time devoted to learning foreign languages (7.4 percent).

The study of teaching methods is the second part of the program. A special complex subject is puppetry and its methodology, which involves dramatic, musical, and visual education. Teaching methods comprise the bulk of training, a total of 52 percent. The practical and theoretical subjects are viewed as inseparable. To develop their skills, students are involved in practicums from the beginning of their training. They visit nursery schools, join in lessons and, after the first year, participate in practical training during the summer. Practical teaching experience under the guidance of an experienced kindergarten teacher and their own teachers makes up 13 percent of the training program. Practical training in the third year is supplemented with a six-week practicum in nursery schools.

Psychological and pedagogical subjects in kindergarten teacher training have an integrative role. Realizing the importance of age in personality development, the founding of right morality, the unfolding of the intellect, and the forming of the ideal habits in the course of life, enormous emphasis is placed on child development and educational psychology. Training is completed with the writing of a thesis and a state examination.

Although the first students graduated from this new three-year training program as recently as 1990, observations can already be made. It seems necessary to increase practical training, to pay more attention to alternative nursery-school programs, to promote the communicative and creative abilities of students, and to offer more optional subjects in the rather rigid educational program. In the future, it is expected that this will be the trend of Hungarian kindergarten teacher training.

Primary School Teacher Training

As noted earlier, organized teacher training started in Hungary in the last quarter of the 18th century. At the same time, in the struggle over the Hungarian language and the dominance of German, the great thinkers of the reform period at the close of the 18th century envisioned changes in the fundamental role for teacher training. The first Hungarian teacher training institute was founded by János Pyrker, archbishop in Eger in 1828. Based on grammar school education, the two-year course also trained students to perform some ecclesiastical duties. Those who did not want to take this opportunity could also teach after the first year.

Protestant teacher training was to some extent different. In Protestant teacher training, programs ran parallel with grammar school education for those who wanted to be teachers after completing the rhetorical or practical courses. Five teacher training institutions founded by the King's order in 1840 followed this model. At the time of the revolution for independence against the Hapsburghs in 1848-49, there were several important proposals that were not to be implemented until the compromise of 1867. At the time of Baron József Eötvös, an opportunity presented itself to send experts abroad, first to Swiss and German institutions.

The Eötvös' Public Education Act marked the beginning of state-directed teacher training. According to the act, 20 state teacher training institutions were to be founded, each with a training school and garden of 20 hectares. Training was to last for three years after the four lower grades of the grammar school or that of the higher elementary school. The subjects were religious and moral education, educational methodology, general and Hungarian geography, world and Hungarian history, mother tongue, German, natural sciences, economics and economical practice, gardening, mathematics, geometry, singing, calligraphy, draw-

ing, physical exercise, and teaching practice in the training school.

By 1881, training had been extended to four years. As is evident from the above list of subjects, general training was intense; but there was no special methodology, students were taught only general educational knowledge. The contemporary view of the ideal teacher was a country schoolmaster whose education was characteristically Hungarian and whose prestige as an educated man made him a "light" in the Hungarian village. Due perhaps to the latter consideration, basic elements of domestic industry were included in training, (e.g., apple and vine growing, beekeeping and silkworm breeding). However, in time the training standards were lowered and several subjects were eliminated.

Educational reforms in 1903 and 1911 could not ease the intensity of the training program. Hungarian experts, following foreign examples, worked out several variations of curricula for a two-year academic training program. The government, however, accepted only one, which was based on the shortness of time. It dropped the principle of the academy and simultaneously founded a teacher training secondary school. Following World War II, a new type of school for secondary level teacher training was founded: a pedagogical grammar school that was to last for only one year.

The basic problem of teacher training institutions was characterized by Imre (1937) as being rooted in the practice of admitting students for teacher training from age 15 and training them separately from the candidates for all other professions. As a result, they were removed from the spiritual community of other graduates from the secondary school. Imre was correct in that teachers who had not themselves completed secondary or grammar school could not be expected to promote the good of higher education.

In 1959, when teacher training became part of higher education, the Ministry of Education finally met a professional educational need. Instead of the former 40 secondary schools, 11 institutes of higher education were organized. Some time later, another three started teacher training. In 1975-76, the institutions became colleges. Following a successful professional entrance examination and aptitude test, training courses are three years long. The frequent changes to the curriculum—in 1959, 1964, 1970, 1973, 1976, 1980—indicated that the problems accumulated during the last century could not be coped with immediately. Historically, there have always been two viewpoints influencing the content of the curricula. They concern the need for the so-called basic subjects and special teaching methodology and practical training. One argument is that the secondary school offers general education to students and therefore methodological, pedagogical, and psychological education should be emphasized as the special task in teacher training. The other argument is that the weak knowledge is attained in the secondary school and the depth and volume of professional training decided the higher educational character of the institution. In addition to these arguments, professional relations were also decisive in forming the content of a curriculum.

The focus of the other argument was the tension between general and specialized professional training. Traditionally, teacher training prepared students for teaching all the subjects and to perform every educational task in primary schools. Undoubtedly, the risk was shallowness or at least stingy practicism. At the time when teacher training institutes were converted into colleges, the idea of training teachers to become "specialized teachers"—who would teach only certain subjects and teach them very well—became stronger. That was when the system of specialized courses came into being. The main point was to train the teacher-candidates thoroughly in Hungarian, mathematics, environmental science, and one optional subject so that they could teach these subjects later. There was a relatively large number of lessons in the special field and the students' learnedness was proved by an additional certificate attached to their degree.

Undoubtedly, the oppressive nature of training was eased a bit, although the numbers of lessons were unbearably large, but the problems were again raised. First, there was a gap between job opportunities and qualifications, that is, the schools' needs were different from the students' specialties. Schools would rather employ pedagogues who were able to teach any or all subjects. Specialization did not become a firm opportunity

of professional advancement either, since such studies were not accepted or recognized as a foundation course by other universities or colleges that trained students for upper grades. This led to the fact that from 1988, students were not compelled to choose a specialty. However, optional subjects that allowed the students to deepen their professional knowledge continued.

Essentially, since 1986 there has been no national curriculum as a directing document at this level of higher education either. As was the case with kindergarten teacher training, the Ministry of Education published only curricular directives, which referred to the goal of training, its duration, subject groups, and examination syllabus. The colleges were commissioned to prepare the local educational programs. In 1990, the Ministry abolished the curricular directives as well. In the future, it could insist only on meeting the training requirements, while in other respects the autonomous institutions of higher education would be able to form curriculum. That is why it is difficult if not impossible to introduce the curriculum of Hungarian teacher training. A description of what is similar in all institutions is all that is allowed.

Students are oriented toward the outside world through a block of social sciences. These include the study of philosophy, ethics, history, history of arts, and politics. In every college, students learn foreign languages. Theoretical training focuses on psychology, pedagogy, and the so-called professional subjects of Hungarian language and literature, mathematics, environmental science, physical education, visual education, music and singing, and crafts. Methodology is closely related to both subject groups. Finally, the optional subjects are included to meet individual interests and to allow an in-depth study of various subjects. In each institution, a thesis is required and the state examination must be taken.

Teacher training is currently undergoing immense changes. The recent governmental changes are evidently affecting the teaching institutions. But the changes have professional effects as well. The current problem has historical roots, that is, what relationship should exist between teacher training and the teaching that occurs in primary schools. This problem was addressed in many ways during the history of Hungarian teacher training. But essentially, it was addressed two ways. One solution was to organize teacher training according to a so-called preliminary picture theory, that is, in accordance with subjects. Under this approach, training would teach only what is taught and needed in primary schools. Underlying this solution, there are essential differences, but all agree that the school subjects must appear in higher education as well.

A second solution is based on the theory that while the needs of public education must be taken into consideration, the logic, tradition, and requirements of intellectual training must prevail. That is why there is no need to follow the structure of initial training in a mechanical way. More importance must be given to general subjects that are indispensable for training independent, creative

experts. Scientific criteria must also be met in the course of training.

The reform of 1986 consciously aimed at reconciling the different viewpoints. In the past few years in certain teacher training colleges, academic freedom is gradually taking place. In fact, only methodological subjects and training practices are strictly determined. Concerning the other professional subjects, there are wider choices. There are compulsory subjects that are necessary to earn a degree, but they can be taken at any time in the course of training. The students can choose from among several programs among several program options and therefore individualize their training program to suit their needs and interests. The result is a stronger, higher quality teacher training program.

References

Imre, A. (1937). Teachers' training and university. *Hungarian Teacher*, 1, 17.

EARLY CHILDHOOD EDUCATION IN INDIA

● ● ● ● ● ● ● ● ● ● ◆ ● ● ● ● ● ● ● ● ●

Venita Kaul
National Council of Educational Research and Training
New Delhi, India

Educational needs, resources, and services are largely a function of the social, economic, and geographic realities of a country. Any study of the status of education in India must, therefore, consider the context within which the country's educational system operates.

India is a vast country with a population of approximately 800 million. It is predominately rural (75.7 percent). The agro-climatic conditions across the country are widely diverse and influence the socioeconomic and cultural characteristics of the people. Wide regional disparities exist in terms of indicators of development (e.g., roads, irrigational facilities, agricultural production, cattle wealth, and health and educational facilities). In the area of education, there are districts whose literacy rate is as low as 7.15 percent, with female literacy going down to 3.7 percent. At the other extreme, there is a district in the southern state of Kerala in which 100 percent literacy has been achieved.

Wide disparities also exist between urban and rural areas in the availability of facilities for health, education, communication, and entertainment. While the urban populace is, by and large, vocal and organized, the rural districts are fairly unorganized and not very articulate in voicing their grievances and demands. This creates a need for special attention to education in rural areas.

The tribal communities in India constitute 7.8 percent of the population, with as many as 450 different tribes distributed throughout the country. These communities have their own distinct traditions, social organization, pattern of economic activities, customs, codes of conduct, and value systems. Despite deliberate, planned efforts and several programs with huge financial outlays for their development, a large section of this population continues to remain deprived and exploited. The challenges in molding educational efforts for this target group lies in speeding up their place within modern India, while, at the same time, preserving their distinctive cultural heritage.

India is also a land of numerous languages and dialects. Of the many languages in the country, 15 are mentioned in the Constitution as a national language. The issue of languages is important from the point of view of both education and fair competition in social and economic opportunities for the people. Further, the division of the country into states based on linguistic considerations has combined traditions and given it a complex emotional dimension.

Economic deprivation is another serious issue. It is estimated that more than one third of India's population lives below the poverty line (UNICEF, 1988). Children of these poor families join the work force at a very early age in order to supplement the income of the family. The problem of child labor, therefore, is immense. There are an estimated 40 million child laborers in the India. While child labor for wages is common among the poor, it also exists in the form of girls who are required to do a variety of household chores, (e.g., looking after younger siblings, and fetching water, fuel, and fodder). The families below the poverty line and the working children pose a serious challenge to the educational planners, since they are not in a position to use the educational opportunities offered to them.

Gender disparity is another significant characteristic of Indian society. Even though women have important roles in agriculture, handicrafts, and many other economic activities, they have an unequal status in the family as well as in the society. While several deprived sections exist in the Indian society, within these groups women are doubly disadvantaged. Despite equal facilities for education available for boys and girls, school attendance by girls (41.16 percent) is much lower than boys (93.6 percent).

The rapid population growth witnessed since the 1950s has compounded the complexities of socioeconomic planning in the country. Even modest projections indicate that the size of the population will be about one billion by 2000. Consequently, the number of school-aged children will also increase. The country is therefore faced with the challenge of providing education for all, while the population is expanding.

The wide variety and diversity in language, religion, culture, and regional differences have created a cultural richness in India. At the same time, the many disparities offer serious challenges to the educational planner. If they are not handled carefully, they may lead to social tensions and conflicts and, in the process, retard the pace of modernization and development.

Significance of Early Childhood Education in India

Against this backdrop of the Indian reality, this chapter analyzes the educational provisions for children between birth and age 8. Among the groups identified for early education are some who remain outside the mainstream of formal education. These include the following:

- very poor, urban slum communities;
- ecologically deprived areas where children are required to participate in agricultural and household chores;
- rural areas and artisan households;
- working children in the unorganized sector;
- itinerant, or seasonal laborers, who have transient life-style (e.g., as road workers);
- construction workers in urban and rural areas;
- landless agricultural laborers;
- nomadic communities and pastoralists;
- forest dwellers and tribes in remote areas; and
- residents of remote isolated hamlets.

In the total spectrum of human development, the early childhood years are critical for the development of cognitive, socio-emotional, language, and physical competencies. In the Indian context, early education has a dual significance. First, it has a direct influence on the total development of the child. Second, it has the potential to contribute to the goal of universal elementary education, which is presently an outstanding educational priority. The latter factor has two functional aspects. One aspect is that while the young child receives care in an early education center, its caregiver, usually a girl, is freed to attend school. This outcome helps to remove one basic cause of school dropout among girls. The other aspect is that the child, in addition to improved health and nutrition, also has a chance to become familiar with ideas of constructive play and to develop desirable competencies and behavioral patterns. Preschool education, therefore, becomes an important adjunct to preparation for primary school. This is expected to reduce subsequent possibilities of waste and stagnation in the early primary grades.

A Brief History of Early Education in India

Organized preschool education was unknown in India until the end of the 19th century. It was at this time that the European missionaries first introduced the concept of kindergarten education. In the 1920s, an organization known as Nutan Bal Shikshan Sangh was set up in Maharashtra to work for the cause of child education. Maria Montessori's visits to the country in the late 1930s provided a further boost to this movement, and soon several Montessori schools were founded in various part of India, particularly in Madras, Maharashtra, and Qujrat. Jijubhai Badheka and Tarabai Modak in Western India and the Arundales in the South were some of the pioneers who took up this cause in earnest.

At approximately the same time, Mahatma Gandhi's philosophy of basic education for the primary level also began to gather momentum. The Aryanayakams and their colleagues in Gandhi's Wardha Ashram extended this philosophy of basic education to the preschool years and termed it prebasic education. Some disciples of Gandhi, notably Jagatram Dace and Nanabhai Bhatt, worked extensively on this system. These experiments led to the establishment of the Kasturba Gandhi National Memorial Trust, which set up many centers to train women to work in the rural early education centers known as *balwadis*.

In 1945, Tarabai Modak, inspired by Montessori, started a preschool teacher training institute at Bordi in Maharashtra. Later she moved it to Kosbad Hills, in the same state, to work with the tribal children of that area. Modak conceived the idea of an *anganwadi* (courtyard center) as an early education center, which preschool education was literally taken to the doorsteps of tribal children. The nomenclature of *anganwadi* is today the accepted term for all early education centers operated by one of the largest government-sponsored early education programs in India, the Integrated Child Development Services (ICDS).

Since India gained independence in 1947, there has been a growing awareness of the significance of the early childhood years. In the 1950s, the Central Social Welfare Board was set up to initiate two types of programs for preschool education: (1) the Board-sponsored programs and (2) the grant-in-aid scheme for voluntary organizations. This step led to considerable expansion of preschool education in the rural areas. In 1959, a subgroup of Child Welfare, set up by the working group on Social Welfare, recommended that a new cadre of child welfare workers be trained in the new integrated approach to preschool education, preventive health, nutrition, recreation, and social work. This was the beginning of the holistic concept of early education. To achieve this objective, the Indian Council of Child Welfare was given the necessary financial assistance to start the Child Welfare Worker's (*Balsevika's*) training program. The first experimental training program took place in 1962.

In 1975, the ICDS became a centrally sponsored program of the Ministry of Social Welfare. It started with 33 projects and by 1987–88 had expanded to serve approximately 4.65 million children in 88,400 centers in rural, urban, and tribal areas. The program offers services catering to the health, nutrition, and developmental needs of children below age 6 and their mothers. The program is aimed at improving both the social and educational options of the people. Among the services it provides are health checkups, immunizations, referral services, supplementary nutrition, informal preschool education, health and nutrition education, and community participation programs. It is the largest program today in India in the area of early education.

Expert Committees, Policies, and Programs

Several committees, composed of experts, have been formed in the last several years in India. Their thinking and recommendations have led to the introduction of related policies and programs.

Viewed in historical perspective, the Sargent Committee was the first significant expert group.

Formed in the pre-independence era in 1944 by the Central Advisory Board of India, the committee emphasized the importance of the first five years of life and the need for providing education for all-around development of the child. As early as 1944, it highlighted relevant issues, such as the need for informal, experimental methods of imparting preschool education and the need to develop readiness for primary school through the establishment of nursery classes. It also indicated the need for special teacher training for the preprimary stage and suggested separate preschools for urban and rural children.

In the early 1960s, the Committee on Child Care (1963–64), set up by the Central Social Welfare Board, recommended considering the preschool education philosophy and principles in the Indian context and suggested the introduction of the mid-day meal program in preschools.

The Kothari Education Commission (1964–66) made a significant contribution to the cause of early childhood education. It recommended expansion of preschool education facilities, particularly for children from disadvantaged areas, and set a target of 5 percent enrollment of the total population of 3-to-5-year age group by 1986. It also stressed the need for state-level expansion of preschool education through a grant-in-aid program to private enterprises. It also recognized the need to reinforce the link between preschool and primary education.

The Department of Social Welfare, through the Canga Saran Sinha Committee (1968), made special reference to nutrition and health, and reiterated the need for expansion of preschool educational facilities, particularly for children from disadvantaged areas. In 1971, the Ministry of Education set up a study group to prepare a program of action for expansion of preschool facilities. Its report detailed different models of preschool programs that would be required to meet specified target populations.

The National Policy for Children (1974) was a landmark in that it served as a statement of governmental recognition of children as valuable human resources, and the state's acceptance of responsibility for their nurture and solicitude. This policy led to the formation of the National Children's Board.

The National Policy on Education (1986) is the most recent statement of governmental effort and thinking in the area of education. This policy extended the concept of preschool education to the holistic concept of "early childhood care and education" for the first time. It also brought it under the umbrella of Ministry of Education. It clearly outlined the need to invest in the development of the young child with an integrated program aimed at the whole child. The policy emphasized the importance of play in early care and education and cautioned against the dangers of using formal methods of teaching and of introducing reading, writing, and arithmetic to young children. Early education and care were viewed in the policy as a feeder service to primary education as well as a human resource development program. It also made a commitment that "day care" centers would be provided to enable girls taking care of siblings to attend school, and also to provide support for working women belonging to the poverty groups.

Despite the political will, in the absence of any constitutional or legal directives, early childhood education (ECE) remains a concern rather than a total responsibility of the government. The Constitution, at present, specifically directs the government to provide free, universal, and compulsory primary education within a stipulated period of time, but does not make any reference to early education and care. The government has not, as yet, been able to meet this conditional directive for primary education. In this context, the question of taking on the added responsibility for preschool children does not arise. As a result, the government has to depend considerably on the involvement of the voluntary sector. The emphasis on volunteerism is consistent with the government's view that social problems and social issues require active participation of the community, and they can only be resolved through the combined efforts of the government and voluntary organizations.

Existing Programs in ECE

The age group covered under ECE is birth to age 8. While the birth-to-age 3 age group is either in the home or day care/creche facilities, the 3-to-6 age group is in the ECE center or preschool. Between ages 5 and 6, the child enters grade 1 of primary school. This chapter therefore provides separate descriptions of day care/creche programs, ECE centers and preschools, primary schools, and special education facilities for young children.

Creche and Preschool Programs

There is a great variety of programs for children from birth to age 6. They can be broadly categorized as one of four main types:

• integrated child development services;

• ECE centers, *balwadis*, and day care centers run by voluntary agencies with governmental assistance;

• preprimary schools run by the state governments, municipal corporations, and other agencies (as adjuncts to primary schools); and

• commercial, fee-charging preschools run by private individuals or agencies.

Table 1 gives a detailed picture of the various state-supported schemes in ECE and the coverage under each.

The various state-sponsored and voluntary programs in India currently serve approximately 6,224,000 children. This number, though impressive, is a small proportion of those requiring services, and represents less that 12 percent of the corresponding age group.

For the youngest children—those up to age 3—the major program is for children of working and ailing mothers (see Table 1), providing grants to voluntary agencies to operate creches. While it does provide financial support for workers and materials, there is presently no provision for staff training. Under the Labor Regulation and Abolition Act (1970), there is also provision for maintenance of creches. The act stipulates that a creche is to be located within 50 meters of every establishment where 20 or more women are ordinarily employed as contract labor. Although the contractor is responsible for setting up the creche, the contractor is generally able to find a loophole in the law. For instance, the contractor may show that less than 20 women are in its employ. In addition, there is no network of specialized supervision to ensure that such creches are functioning.

A major voluntary organization serving children under age 3 is the Mobile Creche, started in 1969 for the children of migrant construction workers in Delhi. The program offered by these centers consists of health care, supplementary feeding, and creative and educational activities for children from birth to age 12. These centers are set up on large construction sites and operate until the construction is completed, after which they are moved to other sites. The staff of the Mobile Creche receive on-the-job training by a team of trainer-supervisors. The organizers believe that due to the special nature of the problems such a community presents, worksite training is more desirable than any kind of preservice institutional model. This Mobile Creches operate mainly in the large urban centers of Delhi, Pune, and Bombay.

The above programs are essentially state-supported or sponsored by voluntary organizations. There is also a commercial private sector which has grown enormously. It caters to the needs of the middle class, who see preschool education as the first level of primary education. There are no known data on the number of private nursery schools in operation. ECE programs therefore exist for preschool children in two different "universes." The existence of this dual system has profound consequences for the content and quality of ECE in India. In the absence of any kind of licensing, legislation, monitoring, or control, preschool education has become in most cases a downward extension of primary schools.

The Preschool Curricula

The objectives of preschool education, which emphasize a child-centered approach, were established by the National Council of Educational Research and Training (NCERT) and later approved and incorporated in the Report of the Education Commission. The eight objectives are as follows:

1. to develop in the child a good physique, adequate muscular coordination, and basic motor skills;

2. to develop in the child good health habits and to build up basic skills necessary for personal adjustment (e.g., dressing, toileting, eating, washing, and cleaning);

3. to develop desirable social attitudes and manners, to encourage healthy group participation, and to make the child sensitive to the rights and privileges of others;

TABLE 1
Existing pre-school education programs

S. No.	Program	Objective	Services	Beneficiaries	Present	Sponsoring	Budget
1.	2.	3.	4.	5.	6.	7.	8.
1.	Integrated Child Development Services 0–6 years	i) To improve the nutrition and health status of children in the age group of mothers ii) Lay the foundation proper physical and social development iii) Reduce the incidence of mortality, malnutrition iv) Achieve effective coordination of policy and implementation among various departments to promote child development vii) Enhance the capability of the mothers to look after the normal health and nutritional needs of child through proper health and nutrition education	i) Supplementary nutrition ii) Immunisation iii) Health check-up iv) Referral services v) Treatment of minor illness vi) Nutrition and health education vii) Pre-school education (children age group 3–6 years) viii) Convergence of other supportive services like water supply sanitation etc.	i) Pregnant mothers ii) Lactating 87.78 lakhs iii) Children below the age group 0–6 years iv) Women in the age group 15–45	i) 1,659 projects children covered by supplementary nutrition ii) Children covered by pre-school education iii) Pregnant and nursing mothers	Central Government Department of Women and Child Development	135.00 crores
2.	Scheme of Assistance to Voluntary agencies-early childhood education	i) to promote overall development of children ii) to improve school enrollment and retention and reduce dropout	i) Non-formal pre-school education to children between 3–6 years of age	children in the age group of 3–6 years	4,365 centres	Department of Women and Child Development	(1977–88) in Rs. 2,46,25,000
3.	Scheme of creches	envisages day care	i) health care	children in the	10,500	Central	(1986–87)

	Project	Objectives	Services	Age group	Coverage	Agency	Budget
	for children of working and ailing mothers	services for children in the age group 0–5 years	ii) Supplementary nutrition iii) Sleeping	age group of 0–5 years	creches 2,62,500 (children) iv) Play and recreation facilities	Socia Board	2,999,90,000
4.a)	Welfare extension Project original pattern	i) To provide basic minimum services for rural women and and children and to create awareness among rural people of the needs of children and basic services for them.	i) Salwadi and creches ii) Infant health iii) Supplementary nutrition for iv) Pre-natal and post natal services v) Art and craft classes for women recreation and cultural activity	Infants, pre-school children and Women in rural, border and urban slums	a) 3 projects 20 centres	State and Central Social Welfare Board	(1986–87) a) 1,800,000 b) 34,000,000 c) 58,736,000
b)	Welfare Extension Project (coordinated) pattern, 1958				b) 44 projects 33 centres		
c)	Welfare Extension Projects urban, 1958	ii) Balwadi Services and comprise a creche and pre-primary school, supplementary feeding, nutrition and health services for children.			c) 8 Institutions 92 Projects		
d)	Welfare Extension Projects in Border Areas	iii) Pre-natal and Post natal services, arts and craft training and elementary medical aid services iv) recreational and cultural activities					
5.	Balwadis in the erstwhile Integrated Child Welfare demonstration Projects (1964)	i) To offer integrated service for child ii) To coordinate the services of medical public health, education social welfare and other department	i) Recreational activities ii) Nutrition and health education	Children 3–6 years	11 projects 24 centres		(1986–87) 36,43,000

Source: i) Annual Report, Part IV, Department of Women and Child Development , Ministry of Human Resource Development, 1987–88.
          ii) Annual Report of Centre Social Welfare Board 1987–88.

4.   to develop emotional maturity by guiding the child to express, understand, accept, and control his feelings and emotions;

5.   to encourage aesthetic appreciation;

6.   to stimulate intellectual curiosity and to help the child understand the world in which he or she lives, and to encourage new interests by providing opportunities to explore, investigate, and experiment;

7.   to encourage independence and creativity by providing the child with sufficient opportunities for self-expression; and

8.   to develop the child's ability to express thoughts and feelings in fluent, correct, clear speech.

The curriculum is supposed to be framed or developed in such a way that it fulfills these objectives. The preferred approach is the "playway" method, which emphasizes children learning through active exploration. This approach is also recommended for the early primary grades.

While this method is recommended, most programs are in practice teacher-directed. The focus is on formal instruction at the preprimary level, which is inconsistent with the dictates of child development. The nursery schools in the private sector are mainly feeder schools to the large primary and secondary schools. Therefore, their priority is to prepare children for the demands of formal primary education system. In addition, there is generally a corresponding pressure for formal teaching of reading, writing, and arithmetic from the parents and community, to which the schools, for various reasons, succumb. With the commercial private sector being the trendsetter, the government-sponsored early education tends to follow suit unless closely monitored.

Major Agencies Involved in ECE

The major organizations working for the improvement of ECE in India are the NCERT, the National Institute of Public Cooperation and Child Development (NIPCCD), the Home Science Colleges and Indian Association for Preschool Education (IAPE). In addition to these, voluntary organizations such as

- the Indian Council for Child Welfare

- Gram Bal Shiksha Kendra at Kosbad (Maharashtra)

- Bal Niketan Sangh

- Gandhi Gram

- Tamil Nadu

- Mobile Creches at Delhi, Bombay and Pune

have also made significant contributions to ECE. UNICEF has also played a key role in supporting governmental and voluntary efforts in this direction. The specific contribution of each of these organizations is briefly described below.

NCERT. With the financial aid from UNICEF, NCERT has launched the Early Childhood Education and Children's Media Laboratory Project (ECE/CML) in ten states of India. The objectives of this project are (1) to develop prototypes of inexpensive material of educational and entertainment value for children; (2) to develop expertise at the state level in early childhood education; and (3) to serve as a clearinghouse for the latest developments in ECE, both national and international.

The Children's Media Laboratory has published a great variety of teaching and teacher training materials (e.g., picturebooks, pictures, posters, audiotapes, and slides) in several Indian languages. These materials are distributed free of cost to all organizations working in the area of ECE in India.

Under the ECE/CML Project, innovative experiments have also been initiated in the area of exploring alternative models in ECE. Some of these experiments are described below.

- *Home-Based Program.* Since the existing institution-based programs in ECE have not been able to meet India's needs, a community/home-based model was tried on an experimental basis in the tribal and urban slum areas of Orissa. It was found to be feasible. The program involves developing skills in mothers to empower them to function better as educators of their own children. The training of mothers is done by the community workers.

- *Child-to-Child Program.* This experiment involved strengthening the skills of older children in caring for their younger siblings. In the majority of disadvantaged homes, since both the parents must go out to work, child rearing is often left to the older siblings. In this program, the older children are taught basic skills in health, hygiene, nutrition, and child stimulation though games, songs etc. They are subsequently encouraged to practice these skills with the younger children.

- *Providing ECE Experience Through Radio.* This project was undertaken in collaboration with All India Radio and Department of ICDS and Education,

Rajasthan. Under this project, a 15-minute program called *Khilte Phool* (Blooming Flowers) is broadcast for preschool and early primary school children from the All India Radio, Kota (Rajasthan). The ICDS centers and primary schools are provided with radio sets. The workers/teachers are given guidebooks that describe the pre- and postbroadcast activities to be done with the children. The mid-project evaluation indicated a favorable impact not only on the development of children but also on the teaching style of teachers.

• *School-Readiness Program.* This program is specifically for areas where no preschool educational facilities are available. The six-to-eight-week program includes activities to be conducted at the commencement of grade 1 either in the first term of school or in the summer months preceding grade 1 for children of about age 5. The activities come in the form of a "School Readiness Kit."

NIPCCD. NIPCCD undertakes training and monitoring of the ECE component of the ICDS program. It plans and develops curricula and support materials for the training of personnel of the ICDS at all levels.

Home Science Colleges. These institutions have contributed significantly toward improving the quality of ECE through personnel training. They have also been involved in evaluation of ECE training programs.

IAPE. IAPE is a professional body of ECE workers at all levels, with branches throughout India. Each branch association organizes regular in-service training workshops. The aim of IAPE is to improve the quality of ECE.

Voluntary Organizations. The voluntary organizations work primarily at the grassroots level with field workers. The major voluntary efforts have been with specific groups, (e.g., tribal peoples, migrant laborers, and rural children). Their programs are characterized by a contextual, experiential approach to ECE. While these innovative programs work very successfully with the small groups, they have proved difficult to implement on a larger scale.

Primary School Programs

Provisions and Coverage

The Indian Constitution directs the government to "endeavour to provide free and compulsory education up to the age of 14 years." Determined efforts have been made since independence to achieving this goal. From 1950 to 1988, primary-level institutions in India have grown from 209,000 to about 543,000. In terms of accessibility, the data for 1986 (Fifth All India Educational Survey) show that about 51 percent of the population (including 80 percent of the rural population) has a primary school or section within the settlement. However, if one considers the accessibility to a school within a distance of one kilometer, the coverage increases to about 94 percent of the population. Since some people do not have access to a formal school, other forms of imparting education—such as the nonformal and open school systems—are being pursued. The number of nonformal centers in 1988–89 was 241,000. Each nonformal center serves children ages 9 to 14 and enrolls about 20 children.

The gross enrollment rate in primary schools has also increased in the past four decades. Whereas in 1951 only 37.8 percent of 6-to-11-year-olds were enrolled, in 1987–88 the total was 97.86 percent. The enrollment rate of girls has also increased by 5.1 percent at the primary level.

Despite these increases, the Indian educational system is characterized by a high dropout rate. This not only erodes the gains from extended coverage but also leads to a waste of scarce resources. Dropping out of school creates a sense of detachment from education among these children and some of them become cynical about the value of education. Due to their resistance to education, it becomes very difficult to bring them back into the fold of education, through either formal or nonformal programs.

A detailed analysis shows that the highest dropout rate occurs in the first two years of schooling. The Fifth All Indian Educational Survey (1986) indicates that by grade 5, one-half of all students will have left school.

The high dropout rate is a result of both the inadequacies of the educational system and the cultural, social, and economic constraints of individual families. The challenge for Indian educators and planners is to ensure that along with increased accessibility, children also receive instruction for a sufficiently long period so that their basic skills can be retained. Therefore, the goal of primary education becomes not only to provide equal opportunities for schooling, but also to ensure that children remain in school for at least five years so that they are able to acquire a minimum level of education. ECE and care programs can potentially make a contribution to this end.

Content and Process

In view of wide disparities in the structure and content of elementary education in different Indian states, the National Policy on Education (1986) has emphasized the concept of a National System of Education. This national system, which is not being translated into practice, envisages the following:

• A common structure of elementary education consisting of 5 years of lower primary and 3 years of upper primary.

• A national curriculum framework through which primary education will provide knowledge, skills, attitudes, and values necessary for survival, important in the quality of life, and for continuing education is to be established. Consistent with these goals, the areas of learning emphasized at the primary level are (1) functional skills in literacy and numeracy; (2) basic and practical knowledge of the self and environment (i.e., health education and environmental studies); (3) creativity, problem-solving, and application of knowledge; and (4) a concern for the proper development of the character of the child, which includes appropriate values and attitudes governing behavior. These four broad groups have been adopted by the NCERT as a basic framework of learning at the elementary stage.

• Minimum levels of learning common to all learners at different stages of elementary education also are to be established. The objective to ensure that all children undergoing primary education, or its equivalent through the nonformal system, will achieve at least these minimum levels.

The approach to curriculum development, however, is being decentralized so that the local environment and the needs of the community are properly reflected. Textbooks, supplementary reading material, and learning aids will be prepared by local teachers and the community to reflect local needs and concerns.

It is increasingly evident to educators that the old approach to teaching, which emphasizes attendance and rote learning, does not serve the needs of modern India and its children. Rather, the teacher is seen as a leader in an activity-based and child-centered approach to curriculum transaction. The emphasis is on creating a learning center around interesting, joyful activities that will provide the opportunity for every child to be actively involved in his or her education. Particularly in grades 1 and 2, when children are still in the concrete operational stage of cognitive development, the "playway" method is strongly advocated. NCERT and some voluntary organizations have worked extensively and intensively in training teachers and in implementing this methodology in the classroom. However, more financial support and staff training are required to make it a regular practice in the schools.

Education of Children With Special Needs

As mentioned earlier, universalization of primary education is a major priority for educators, planners, and policymakers in India. To achieve this goal, facilities have been expanded extensively in the postindependence period. However, the benefits of these expanded facilities have not reached some special groups of children. As indicated in the National Policy on Education (1986), not more than 1 percent of the mentally retarded and 5 percent of the deaf and blind children are estimated to be in school at present. The national policy has therefore laid special emphasis on the removal of disparities by attending to the specific needs of those who have so far been denied equal opportunity. The policy states that the objective should be to "integrate the physically and mentally handicapped with the general community as equal partners, to prepare them for normal growth and to enable them to face life with courage and confidence."

There are an estimated 12 million disabled persons in India, 4.3 million of whom are in the primary age group, and 1.4 million in the birth-to-age-4 group (these figures do not include learning disabled children). The youngest group will particularly benefit from identification, diagnosis, assessment, early stimulation, and preparation for education.

A Brief History and Description of Special Education in India

The history of organized special education in India can be traced to the end of the 19th century when institutions for the disabled were established by voluntary enterprises. These institutions were transplanted models of British institutions. The first school for the deaf was established in Bombay in 1885, and two years later, the first school for the blind was founded in Amritsar. Facilities for the mentally retarded were established in the form of a psychomedical retardation center at Ranchi in 1934. In 1941, the first home for the mentally deficient was founded in Bombay.

The constitutional commitment to universalization of elementary education and a concept of a welfare state led to the expansion of education for the disabled in the postindependence period. The government of India increased funding of programs for the prevention, education, and rehabilitation of the disabled from 15 million rupees in 1951 to 1,450 million in 1986. This amount was in addition to expenditures by individual states and funds raised by voluntary agencies. In fact, the major work in this area has been done through voluntary agencies.

A status analysis of the provisions for special education indicated that the number of special schools for the deaf, blind and mentally retarded has increased to 140, 200, and 200, respectively. There are only three schools for the physically handicapped, since the majority of these children attend general schools.

The Integrated Education plan for the disabled, which is currently being implemented, involves placing children with other disabilities in ordinary schools. The plan is coordinated by NCERT. National-level institutes have also been established for visually handicapped, hearing impaired, mentally retarded, and orthopedically handicapped to provide leadership in research, development, and training. NCERT have also been established at six university teacher training programs to develop courses in special education. In addition, about 80 to 100 district rehabilitation centers have been established to develop infrastructural facilities for the assessment, support, and rehabilitation of the disabled.

The inadequate number of facilities, however, is highlighted by the fact that only about 5 percent of disabled children are in either integrated or special schools. The exception is children with locomotor disabilities, who are able to manage in ordinary schools. Estimates of disabled persons are available from the National Sample Survey organization. They indicate that approximately 154,000 children ages 5 to 14 in rural areas and 25,000 in urban areas are visually handicapped. For the birth-to-age-4 groups, the corresponding figures are 96,000 and 16,000. In the case of hearing disability, figures are not available, but it is reported that the trend is similar. Regarding speech disability, about 80,000 and 28,000 children fall into the age group 5-to-14 years in rural and urban areas, respectively, while in the birth-to-age-4 group, the corresponding figures are 74,000 and 5,000 respectively. According to one estimate, there are about 3.98 million mentally retarded children in India.

Although these previous figures seem large, in terms of percentages of the total population they may not be very high. The major challenge appears to be to provide for these children in the rural areas, where the majority are located.

There are also large numbers of mildly handicapped children who enter general schools but fail to achieve the normal academic standards. Their failure has an adverse effect on their self-image and they tend to drop out of school. Such children, who may be having academic problems due to a disability, are often not identified and consequently they do not get corrective or supportive help. Another group of children are those who do not enter schools either because of their parents' reluctance due to the social stigma attached to the disability or because of the school's reluctance to admit them since teachers do not feel able to meet their educational needs. Special schools are generally not available in the rural areas.

The target groups in the area of special education in India at present are therefore:

• disabled children who are already in general schools and whose retention can be ensured through special support;

• children with mild disabilities who are out of school and can be brought within the general school system; and

• children who need education in special institutions because of severe disabilities.

Table 2 gives the hierarchical interdepartmental network of agencies and institutions involved in the implementation of programs in the area of special education.

To ensure the policy directive of equal educational opportunity for the disabled and their integration with the general community, the following specific measures have been set by the government:

• wherever it is feasible, the education of children with motor handicaps and other mild handicaps will be the same as that of others;

• special schools with hostels will be provided, as far as possible, at district headquarters for severely handicapped children;

• adequate arrangements will be made to give vocational training to the disabled;

• teacher training programs will be reoriented, in particular for teachers of primary classes and ECE centers, to enable them to identify and work with the special difficulties of handicapped children; and

• voluntary efforts directed at the education of the disabled will be encouraged in every possible way.

Teacher Training

The success of a program depends to a considerable extent on the competencies, motivation, and experience of those who are responsible for its planning and implementation. Teacher training, or preparation, is therefore a crucial component in early childhood education and care. (Table 3 gives a brief profile of the various training programs in ECE in India.)

Most of the teacher training schemes are program-specific, and consequently, the content and curriculum is determined by the job responsibilities of the worker/teachers in that particular program.

Major Teacher Training Programs

Anganwadi Worker's Training. Anganwadi workers are the ECE teachers in the ICDS program described above. Their major responsibilities are to conduct a survey of the community, to organize nonformal preschool education for the 3-to-6-year-old groups, to monitor development of program, and to organize supplementary nutrition program. In addition, the workers provide support to primary health centers, establish community contacts, and educate the community.

The course of study is geared to the job responsibilities described above. Table 4 outlines the relative weighting and content of the training.

At the end of the three-month training program, the trainees are assessed on the basis of their performance in seven areas: (1) assessment during the course, (2) classroom practical, (3) fieldwork, (4) written test, (5) preparation/maintenance of records/diary work done during training, (6) preparation of kit material, and (7) oral examination.

The trainees are awarded certificates for satisfactory completion of the course. The curriculum and support material are prepared by the National Institute of Public Cooperation and Child Development. This organization is also responsible for developing curricula for the training of personnel in the ICDS project, specifically the middle-level supervisors and the block-level Child Development Project Officers.

Integrated Two-Year Course in Preschool and Early Primary Teacher Education. In 1973, the Ministry of Education for India established the National Council for Teacher Education (NCTE). The council appointed a Preschool Teacher Education Committee, which recommended an integrated two-year course in preschool and primary teacher education for teachers of children in the 3-to-8-year age group. The rationale for the course was the need to view this period in childhood as developmentally distinct. The characteristics of children at this stage indicate that the preschool methodology, (i.e., the "playway" activity approach) be continued into grades 1 and 2. The result will be a smoother transition and better adjustment of the child in the primary grades, as well as more meaningful learning and sustained motivation. (Table 5 (a) and (b) outlines the training, including the relative weights given to theory and practice.)

While the curriculum is followed mainly in the training institutes of Delhi, it has been used as a basis for planning programs in other organizations. The training program for primary school teachers (i.e., for teachers of grades 1 to 5), is independent of this course and is generally offered by most of the training institutions. This is a recognized course leading to the B. Ed. degree (Bachelor of Education). The NCTE has recommended the inclusion of the playway activity approach for grades 1 and 2 as an important aspect of

TABLE 2

Departments and Agencies Involved in Special Education Program

CENTER			
Ministry of Health and Family Welfare	Ministry of Human Resource Development	Ministry of Welfare	Voluntary Organizations
All India Institute of Speech and Hearing Mysore	National Council of Educational Research and Training	Central Social Welfare Board; National Institute of Public Cooperation and Child Development	National Association for the Blind Blind Relief Association
All India Institute of Physical Handicap, Bombay for Handicap	University Grants Commission	National Council for the Handicapped; National Institute(s) for the Handicapped	Federation for Welfare of Mentally Retarded National Association of Equal Opportunities
National Institute of Educational Planning and Administration	National Children's Board Special Institutes like: — Model School for the Mentally Deficient, Delhi —Training Center for the Adult —School for Partially Deaf, Deaf, Hyderabad. Hyderabad		The Association for the Physically, Handicapped etc.
REGION			
Regional Colleges of Education		Regional Center for the Training of Blind	
STATES			
Medical Colleges Centers	Directorate of Education State Councils for Educational Research and Training, State Institute of Education	Department of Social Welfare; Middle Level Training Centres Balsevika Training Centres	State Chapters
DISTRICT			
District Hospitals	Boards of Secondary Education; University Department of Education District Education Office	District Social Welfare Offices	Local Branches
VILLAGE			
Primary Health Center	Block Education Office	Block Development Office Subdivision Welfare Office	
INSTITUTION			
Dispensaries	Secondary Schools Special Education Center Middle Schools Primary Schools Nursery Early Childhood Center	Anganwadi, Balwadi, Gram Sevika, Social Welfare Organizations	Parent Groups

TABLE 3

Training Schemes in Existence

	Training Scheme	Qualifications	Duration
1)	Anganwadi Workers Training	No prescribed qualifications (mostly eighth class pass)	3 months
2)	Nursery Teachers Training	10th class	1 year
3)	Integrated Two Years' Course in Preschool and Early Primary Teacher Education	12th class	2 years
4)	Nursery Teachers Training Vocationalisation Scheme of CBSE	10th Class	2 years
5)	Balsevika Training of Indian Council for Child Welfare	10th Class	11 months
6)	Montessori Training of Association Montessori International	10th Class	1 year
7)	Postgraduate Diploma in Graduation Early Childhood Education		1 year

TABLE 4

Contents of AWW's Training Under ICDS Project

S. No.	Subject	Classroom Instructions	Field work	Library and Audio Visual	Total Hours
1.	General Orientation	13½	19½	3	36
2.	Preschool Education	15	66½	1½	83
3.	Nutrition and Health	34	54	5½	93½
4.	Community Participation, Community education and communication	56	67½	4	127½
5.	Population Education	9	3	—	12
6.	Management	12½	35½	—	59
7.	Holistic approach to child and wrap up	12	—	—	12
8.	Evaluation	9	—	—	9
		172	246	14	432

TABLE 5(A)

Contents of Integrated Two Years' Training

	First Year	Paper	Marks		Total
			Ext.	Int.	
A.	Paper I	Child Development & Educational Activities	75	25	100
	Paper II	Early Childhood Education in Emerging India	35	15	50
	Paper III	Program Planning for Preschool	35	15	50
	Paper IV	Health and Nutrition	75	25	100
B.	Practice Teaching	(36 working days)	200	100	200
C.	Practical Activities	(See Table (5B))	175	50	224
				G. Total	825
	Second Year				
A.	Paper I	Child Development	75	25	100
	Paper II	Working with Parents & Community	35	15	50
	Paper III	Program Planning for Class 1 and 2	75	25	100
	Paper IV	School Organization	35	15	50
B.	Practice Teaching:				
	i) 36 working days		200	100	300
	ii) Summer Vacation Assignment (15 days)		100		100
C.	Practical Activities (see Table (5B))		175	50	225
				G. Total	925

TABLE 5(B)

Break Up for Evaluation of Practical Activities

First Year

S. No.	Activity	Internal Assessment	External Assessment	Total
1.	Preparation of teaching learning material	—	50	50
2.	a)Skill development music, drama, puppetry, creative activities	25	—	25
	b)Art and craft	—	25	25
	c)Use of apparatus/	—	25	25
	material	—	25	25
	d)Skills in communication	—	25	25
3.	Observation of Children, maintenance of cumulative record cards	15	—	15
4.	Health and Nutrition			
	a)First aid	—	20	—
	b)Cooking	—	30	50
5.	Field visits (Reports)	10	—	10
	G. Total	50	175	225

Second Year

S. No.	Activity	Internal Assessment	External Assessment	Total
1.	Preparation of teaching learning material	—	50	50
2.a)	Art and Craft	—	25	25
b)	Skill in Communication	—	25	25
3.	Project work based on environmental studies	—	50	50
4.	Case Study	—	25	25
5.	Parents and Community Activities			
a)	Home Visits	15	—	15
b)	Organization of parents programs—health, hygiene, and nutrition	20	—	20
c)	Organization of Children's programs for parents	15	—	15
	G. Total	50	175	225

this training.

Bal Sevika Training Program. The Bal Sevika program was the initiative of the Indian Council for Child Welfare in 1961. The council has a training center where the field-level workers are trained in all Indian states. The workers are local girls who can identify with the children and community and have an understanding of their cultural norms and values.

The main responsibilities of the Bal Sevika, or the ECE worker, in this program are (1) to coordinate the service in the area of health, education, and social welfare at the field level and to support the total development of the preschool child. In addition, workers maintain contact with parents, especially mothers, to provide them with basic health, nutrition, and child development information. Workers also ensure maximum community participation in the program. (Table 6 outlines the course content and time allocations for the different subject areas in the training.)

TABLE 6

Contents of Training and Time Allocation
in Bal Sevika Training

	Subject	Theory	Practical	Total Hours
1.	Orientation	18	—	18 hrs.
2.	Child Development	79	30	109 hrs.
3.	Preschool Education	108	88	196 hrs.
4.	Health	117	96	213 hrs.
5.	Nutrition	110	118	228 hrs.
6.	Social Welfare	106	210	316 hrs.
Total		538	542	1080 hrs.

Training for Integrated Day Care at Mobile Creches. This training program is exclusive to the Mobile Creches. It is characterized by an on-the-job apprenticeship for a minimum of two years. The training is competency- and skill-based and the worker is judged by standards of practical performance, which reflect both skills and attitudes.   The major areas of study are: (1) infant care; (2) preschool education; (3) nonformal education; (4) health, hygiene, and nutrition; (5) administration and community work; and (6) adult education. The training methodology is pragmatic, inductive, and participatory. Teaching is through demonstration, role modeling, and personal guidance, while learning is by observation, imitation, and practice.

The evaluation is done by a committee that includes external specialists and supervisors/trainers. The rating is on a five-point scale and consists of 50 marks for observation of work in the field, 20 marks for internal assessment, and 15 marks for the oral examination. Internal assessment includes self-evaluation in the course of the year; informal evaluation by peers, children, and parents; and systematic evaluation by trainers and supervisors.

Conclusion

While a variety of training programs exist, most aim to develop certain common areas. For example, the importance of including field placement under close supervision is being increasingly realized. This is imperative for providing practical training and experience that is specific to early childhood. Most programs also stress competency and skill development. As a result, the training methodology is also expected to become more participatory and activity-oriented. Refresher training for all levels of personnel is also emphasized as a necessary component of the training structure. Finally, training of day care/creche workers and special education staff are two areas that demand urgent attention. These are some of the focal points that are likely to influence planning for teacher training in the future.

References

ICCW Bulletin on Early Childhood Education , 38 (1), Jan.–Mar. 1990.

Jangira, N., & Mukhopadhyaya, S. (1987). Planning and management of I.E.D. Program. NCERT.

National Council of Educational Research and Training. (1989). Fifth all India educational survey: Selected statistics

———. Integrated two-year course in preschool and early primary teacher education.

National Institute of Education Planners and Administrators. (1990). Education for all by 2000—Indian Perspective.

National Institute of Public Cooperation and Child Development. (1989). Syllabus for job training of Anganwadi worker of ICDS programme.

UNICEF. (1988). *The state of the world's children.* Oxford: Oxford University Press.

PREACADEMIC AND ACADEMIC EDUCATION IN IRAN

•••••••••◆•••••••••

Mohamad Yamani Douzi Sorkhabi
University of Tehran
Tehran, Iran

The history of education in Iran dates back to the 5th century B.C., but it has been only in the last 100 years that it has been carried out within the framework of a state institution. It was during the Hakhamanechites dynasty (550 B.C.) that education was first seen as a way to bring up good citizens for the state. At that time, only a small privileged minority were educated. Xenophon (430–355 B.C.) in writing Education and Rights in Iran, compared the structure and the objectives of education in Iran with the those of ancient Greece. Xenophon distinguished between the education of children before age 16 and their education after age 16. He also noted that it is only after passing a 50th birthday that any individual had the right to teacher's status (Hekmat, 1971).

It was in the era of Sassanites (236–651 B.C.) that primary school was created for pupils from ages 7 to 15. Teachers enjoyed a very high social standing. Programs of studies included religious and moral education; physical education; reading, writing, and math; science; and practical courses in agriculture and botany. This was an oral tradition, and learning was based on memorization.

During this period, education occurred in three phases: (1) family education, which lasted until age of 7; general education, from age 7 to ages of 14–15; and (3) specialized education, up to age 25. During the last stage, students received specialized instruction, depending on their aptitudes. While the first two periods of study were equally open to boys and girls, the third period of study was reserved exclusively for boys (Hekmat, 1971).

At this time, the objectives of education were (1) religious and moral, (2) power and health, (3) military, (4) economic, and (5) political (Report of the Council for Reforming Iranian Teacher Education, 1987). After the introduction of Islam in 626 A.D., the content of the religious and moral goals changed and the belief in God and the Sharia became essential elements of education.

The most important aspect of the education, after the introduction of Islam, was uniting school and mosque, to a point that "these two ideas were seen as synonyms" (Ravardi, 1985). This union of school and mosque was the basis of the well-known schools called *nezamieh*.

Elementary education in Islamic Iran took place in the *makab-khane*, which were reserved exclusively for boys. Education there consisted of learning the Persian alphabet and reading the Koran. The only condition for entry was that the child be able to keep himself clean. This meant that

Translated from French by Corinne Chénier

children were generally admitted between ages 4 and 6. The length of schooling was not precisely set, but depended on family needs and the student's aptitude for study. In general, however, studies ended at age 15.

After the invasion of the Mongolians (580 B.C.), education in Iran received little attention (Safa, 1984). The first effort to establish public and generalized schooling was made during the empire of the Taherites (around 847–48 B.C.).

It was around 1886 that a Ministry of Sciences was created. Its major mission consisted in introducing the elements of European education into Iran. About 18 years later, the first school of foreign languages was opened in Tehran.

In 1890, there were 18 primary schools in Iran. Students learned through memorization and corporal punishment was widespread. Classes were organized around teachers who stood in front of the class. By 1914, primary education, which began at age 6, was made one of cycles in the Iranian educational system. That system was made up of a primary cycle of six years, followed by two more cycles of three years each. In 1967, the current structure was introduced. It consists of a cycle of five years followed by two more cycles of three years each.

Although the law of 1944 made primary school attendance mandatory, that law was not put into practice. According to the census of 1986, 18 percent of all eligible children do not attend primary school.

Goals of the Iranian Educational System

An educational reform in 1967 established six general goals, which were modified by the *Islamic revolution*. The goals of the 1967 reform are presented in Table 1.

Preschool Education in Iran Today

Preschool education is not officially part of Iran's existing educational system. Outside of the family, preschool education is confined to day care centers run by the Ministry of Health and Medical Education. Consequently, preschool education is not controlled by the Ministry of National Education.

Daycare

Day care centers in Iran were established shortly after the Islamic Revolution in 1979. There are two types: public and private. Public day care centers are few in number and have been created largely to provide care for children whose parents work. These day care centers are financed in part by the state and in part by fees paid by parents (roughly 7 percent of the parents' salary). They are not well equipped and are poorly organized. Because the organizational principles and official programs of public day care centers differ little from private day care centers, only private day cares are discussed below.

Private Day Care. Private day cares were established according to principles and approved laws and with the permission of the Ministry of Health and the practices of Medical Education. They were established to look after and to provide preschool education for healthy children between three months and 6 years old. These children are divided in three levels: (1) children three months to 18 months; (2) children aged 1 1/2 years to 3 years; and (3) children ages 3 to 6

The monthly payments for day care are fixed by the Ministry. In reality, the costs of day care vary widely depending on the area. Access to some day care centers is possible only for parents who are able to pay very high fees.

According to the law, each day care cannot accept more than 100 children and only women are granted permission to open centers. A proprietor of a day care center must also be Muslim and of Iranian descent.

Non-Muslims whose religions are accepted by the Iranian Constitution (i.e., Christians, Jews, Zoroastrians) can ask permission to open day care centers if those centers will serve only the children of the same religious community and if the centers are located near those children's homes. Prospective day care operators must believe in the Islamic Republic and its principles and may not belong to illegal parties or groups. They must also be at least age 22 and in good mental and physical health. (Physically handicapped women, whose handicap would not interfere with the administration of a day care are allowed to apply to operate a day care center. Applicants must be licensed in preschool education, educational sciences, psychology, or sociology, and have at least one year of practical experience. (Applicants may hold a certificate in secondary education if they have three to seven years of practical experience in day care.)

The responsibilities of the director in charge of a day care include supervising the correct application of ideological programs and seeing that regulations are followed. Directors also recruit personnel; present reports and statistics regarding the day care to the Ministry; and establish relations with similar organizations in order to exchange information. Teacher's responsibilities are for receiving the children at the beginning of the day and for preparing them to return home at the end of the day. They put education programs into practice and supervise the religious and emotional growth of the children and their learning of social skills. In addition, the teachers care for the physical well-being of the children and keep evaluative records of their educational progress. Finally, teachers separate sick children from the healthy ones.

Day Care Educational Programs

Day care educational programs must contain certain elements. The religious, social, cognitive, affective, and physical development of each child must be taken into consideration. Creativity is to be encouraged, as is the learning of language skills. Day care programs must provide guidance to the child, helping him or her to think, analyze, distinguish, resolve problems, and understand the Islamic religion. Day care programs must also prepare the child to enter primary school.

To realize these objectives, the Ministry recommends the following methods:

- presenting the content in a simple way;

- teaching through use of games, stories, poems in order to enhance the child's curiosity;

- motivating children by using pictures and lively colors;

- encouraging children to work in groups; and

- using a wide range of activities.

In addition, the day care must be well-equipped and the security of the children guaranteed. The name of the day care is decided by the director with the approval of the Ministry. In choosing a name, there are specific rules to be followed. The name must reflect a belief in Islam or denote days specific to Islamic nationalism (e.g., The Islamic Revolution, Liberty, or Autonomy). Foreign names or names that do not reflect Islamic culture or the Revolution are not permitted.

It should be noted that there are no major differences between the programs offered to children of different ages in the day care program. For example, the program for the 6-year-old in day care is essentially based on preparing the children for primary school by introducing them to writing, reading, and mathematics. At the 6-year-old level, there are some day cares controlled by the Ministry of the National Education, with monthly payments which are less high.

Preschool Education and the New Educational Reform

This chapter describes preschool education in Iran according to established laws and rules. It is unclear, however, how well these rules are actually followed. There are no studies on the operation of day care centers in Iran. What is easily observable is the effect of parents' income on how day care centers are run. Private day care centers aim to be more luxurious than educative.

There has been little attention given to preschool education in the new proposals for educational reform. The new educational reform has concentrated on a preparatory course given prior to entry into the primary school system. The age of admission to such a preparatory course would be 5 1/2 years of age, while the education of younger children would remain outside of the purview of the national educational system. This means that there will be few, if any, changes in the existing program of preschool education.

TABLE 1

The Goals of Teaching in Iran

After the Reform of 1967	After the Islamic Revolution
1. *Social Goals*: On the principles of the "White Revolution (1963), the teaching must be mandatory and free for all children of 6 to 14 years old. The education of the children must be to the service of the king.	1. *Social Goals:* *Respect and continuity of familial relations according to the first Islamic rights and morals. * Establish a social equality as well as economical and cultural. * Respect of the law. * Inform the people of the importance and of the the value of education and of its goals.
2. *Economic Goals:* Educate qualified personnel necessary to the administration of the growing economy of the country. The educational system must be sufficiently flexible to be able to adapt the studies of the students, to meet the changing needs of the economy of the country.	2. *Economic Goals:* To create the ability to cooperate in the development in land and industry, and to enable Iran to be autonomous as a nation.
3. *Cultural Goals:* Educate artistic and cultural attitudes as well as cultural of the young so they can eventually contribute to development of the cultural patrimony of the country. Art & Cultural courses will be the essential elements of school programs. — Learn Persian as well as Arabic to understand the Koran and Islamic knowledge. — Create a spirit of active participation in the permanent education.	3. *Scientific and Cultural Goals:* — Know the mysteries of the world and the laws of nature to contribute to knowledge and the progress of science.
4. *Political Goals:* Active participation in the political and social life; respect for the law; a sense of belonging to a free society which is progressing.	4. *Political Goals:* Accept the absolute sovereignty of God on the World and man; know the means on how to get in action this sovereignty in the society according to the principles of the constitution. — Reinforce the defense of Iran through education (military) in the schools to keep the autonomy and integrity of the territory and the system of the Islamic Republic and to be attentionate to physical education.
5. *Spiritual Goals:* Belief in a social and moral philosophy positive based on the principles of the King's People's Revolution, reinforcement of the verto and knowledge of the morals based on the religious principles and instructions.	5. *Spiritual and Educational Goals:* — Know the principles, the knowledge; the laws of Islam and the *schite* religion, according to the Koron and *Sinnat*; —Reinforcement of the studying spirit, of research, of innovation, in all the science framework, of technic and of Islamic culture. (There are no goals for physical education. This latter is mentioned in the framework of political goals).
6. *Physical Education Goals*: — Education of the body; good hygiene, happiness, development of cooperative spirit.	

References

Hekmat, A. (1971). *Education in old Iran.* Tehran: Institute for Research and Planning in Education and the Sciences. (text in Persian).

Principles of programming and administration for private child care centres. Ministry of Health: Behsisti Office of Public Relations and Information.

Ravandi, M. (1985). *Patterns in culture and the history of education in Iran and Europe.* Tehran: Gouya. (text in Persian).

Report of the Council for Reforming Iranian Teacher Education. (1987). Tehran: Ministry of Education.

Safa, Z. (1984). *Education in Iran.* Tehran: Touss. (text in Persian).

KINDERGARTEN AND PRIMARY SCHOOL EDUCATION IN IRAN

• • • • • • • • • • ◆ • • • • • • • •

Zahra Sabbaghian
Shahid Beheshti University
Tehran, Iran

The formal educational system of the Islamic Republic of Iran includes a one-year kindergarten, a five-year primary school, a three-year guidance school, and a four-year high school. This chapter discusses the first two levels.

Centralization

In Iran, the structure and administration of the educational system are centralized. The Ministry of Education in Tehran is responsible for providing the educational programs, materials, and books, as well as for making the final decisions regarding the recruitment of teachers and other educational personnel, the enrollment rules, and evaluation standards. As a result, primary education is uniform throughout the country in terms of its hours of operation, physical facilities, materials, methods, and content.

All schools are divided according to gender. The principals in girl's schools are female, and in boy's schools, male. The school year is nine months, running from mid-September to mid-June. In a few southern provinces where the weather is extremely hot, the year starts and ends earlier. In either case, schools operate six days per week, and

in public primary schools, students usually attend four hours per day. Children may enroll in grade 1 of the primary system if they are age 6 as of September 20, the first day of school. The maximum age to enroll in grade 1 is 10 in cities and 12 in villages. However, older children who have not attended school because of educational, economic, social, or cultural limitations, or family problems, can attend adult literacy programs and receive a primary education in adult classes. In such cases, their primary education is shorter and more condensed.

Education in Iranian schools is not optional. Even in primary schools, students must pass all the subjects set by the Ministry of Education for each grade level. Students who do not succeed in one or more subjects at the final examination in June may study the subject in summer and write a second examination in September. Failure of this examination results in a repeat of all subjects at that grade level.

Kindergarten

Kindergarten begins the year before primary school. The minimum age requirement for Sep-

299

tember enrollment is 5 (on or before September 20). The major objective is to prepare children for school. In regions and provinces in which the Persian language is not the children's mother tongue, an important objective is to acquaint them with the national language. Other goals are to develop the children's physical, emotional, social, and mental abilities, with an emphasis on moral and Islamic traditions.

However, the growth of kindergartens has been limited in Iran due to a lack of facilities and teachers. Approximately 250,000 6-year-olds currently attend kindergartens. Kindergarten attendance makes up about 3 percent of all students at different educational levels (Statistical Report of Education, 1986: 5). Most pupils are the children of working mothers. For these families, the kindergarten is viewed as a child care option.

There are two kinds of kindergartens. The first are public kindergartens, affiliated with the Ministry of Education and open from 8:00 A.M. to 11:00 A.M. The second is a range of kindergartens that function as child care centers. They are sponsored by different ministries, organizations, and factories to serve the children of employees. These kinder-gartens are open during the hours of employment, usually from 7:00 a.m to 4:00 p.m. While the workplace kindergarten is better equipped than the public program, both are financed by the government and parents.

The Primary School

Unlike kindergartens and nursery schools (or even high schools and colleges), all young Iranians are required to attend primary schools, which comprise the third educational level, but the first formal and compulsory one. There are four types of primary schools. The *public primary schools* are managed and funded by the Ministry of Education. *Private nonprofit primary schools* are managed by the parent-teacher association of each school and financed by parents. *Martyrs' primary schools* are managed and funded by the Ministry of Education, the Martyrs' Foundation, and the parent-teacher association of each school. These schools are for students whose fathers have been martyred during the Revolution and afterwards. However, 60 percent of students in these schools are selected from

TABLE 1

Anticipation of Development in Five Year Development Program of the Islamic Republic of Iran

Age	School Year					
13–18	13	Economy 3 years	Culture & Letters 3 years	Sci. Exp. 3 years	Mat. & Phys. 3 years	Agric. Service Industry
16–17	12 1 year	Humanities 1 year	Experimental Science			
15–16	11	Sec. Teaching Theoretical			Sec. Teaching Technical	
14–15	10			Secondary Teaching 4 years		
13–14	9			Cycle of Academic		
12–13	8			Orientation		
11–12	7			3 years		
10–11	6					
9–10	5					
8–9	4			Primary Study		
7–8	3			5 years		
6–7	2					
5–6	1			Preparatory Course 1 year		

among ordinary students who have excellent grades. The second and third types of primary schools are more active in terms of educational and extra-curricular activities. *Exceptional primary schools*, administered and funded by the Ministry of Education, are discussed later.

According to the Ministry of Education, the major goals of primary education are to promote moral, spiritual, physical, and mental growth; to build general skills and develop creativity; and to help children acquire skills in reading, writing and arithmetic and the proper social behavior and hygiene. (See Table 1.).

The constitution of Iran states that the government should provide free and compulsory primary education for all children of appropriate age. However, because of different social, cultural, and economic problems, the government has not been able to provide primary education for all children. Each year, about 400,000 children age 6 years old (approximately 18 percent of all 6-year-olds in Iran) are deprived of primary education and fail to attend schools (Etelaat, 1987). (See Table 2.)

TABLE 3

Number of Students in Primary Level From 1976 to 1992

Year	Number of Students
1976	4,764,486
1977	5,020,686
1978	5,009,325
1979	5,019,325
1980	5,180,032
1981	5,283,377
1982	5,586,071
1983	5,994,403
1984	6,336,116
1985	6,788,323
1986	7,242,820
1987	7,760,230
1988	8,218,291
1990	9,185,392
1991	9,666,640
1992 (projected)	10,173,102

Source: Educational Documents, Ministry of Education, Islamic Republic of Iran, 1987.

TABLE 2

Percentages of Children Ages 6 to 9 Attending Primary Schools in 1986

Total		Cities		Villages	
Male	Female	Male	Female	Male	Female
88.2	77.3	93.6	90.3	82.8	64.2

Source: Selected Statistical Matters, No. 17, Iranian Statistical Center, 1986, p.7.

Social Class in Early Education

In Iran, as in other societies, a distinct class system exists. Children from the wealthiest families usually attend private nonprofit primary schools. Although the Ministry of Education has had several plans and made conscious attempts to provide equal educational opportunities for all children following the Islamic Revolution of Iran, a few elite schools remain.

These private nonprofit primary schools, funded by parents, usually have modern equipment and facilities, including libraries, laboratories, and swimming pools. Classes are generally smaller, with approximately 30 students in each class. The school day lasts from 7:30 a.m. to 3 p.m. to permit for additional educational or extra-curricular activities. Such activities are important aspects of the schools.

The principal and instructors usually adhere to modern, scientific educational principles. They offer extensive recreation-based summer programs for their students. Schools are located in Tehran and in a few other large cities. Children in these schools often have tutors at home and may attend various private classes after school.

The middle class in Iran consists of families in which the men work in professional or service sectors. Women who work outside the home are generally from this group. Children of the middle class attend public primary schools. The school day in the public schools lasts from 8:00 a.m. to 11:30 a.m. However, in Teheran and some other large cities, a second shift operates from noon to 4:00 p.m.

The poorest groups in Iran include unskilled workers and peasants. These parents tend to see education as a way of learning skills. Dropping out of school early, to work at home or in the fields, is common among the poor. There are few schools in the crowded areas where many of the poor live. For this reason, the primary schools there usually have three shifts: 7:00 a.m. to 10:30 a.m., 10:30 a.m. to 2:30 p.m., and 3:00 p.m. to 5:30 p.m. Despite the shift system, many classes are overcrowded. It is not uncommon to have classes as large as 50 children.

Special Needs Education

The Bureau for Exceptional Children in the Ministry of Education is responsible for planning, conducting, and evaluating special educational programs. In Iran, there are special schools for exceptional children; of these, 66 (16.4 percent) are in the Teheran area, while 337 (83.6 percent) are in other provinces.

Five groups of children are identified as needing special education by the Bureau. These groups are as follows:

• *Visually impaired children*, who are taught by braille and magnified letters.

• *Hearing impaired children*, who are taught by oral methods, using their existing hearing and sign language, with emphasis on the structure of speech, grammar, and oral conversation. Although the educational curriculum for these children is the same as the regular primary program, the methods of teaching are different.

• *Mentally handicapped children* are children in the school system who have IQs between 50 and 75. The curriculum is adapted to their needs and schooling is usually limited to the kindergarten and primary levels. The educational program focuses on the basics of literacy and mathematics. In addition, self-help skills and independence are promoted. Children are also provided with instruction in handicrafts.

• *Children with behavior disorders* are provided with schooling that focuses on the development of appropriate behaviors. Special programs exist only at the primary level, after which these children rejoin the normal school system.

• *Physically handicapped children* are children who are unable to use ordinary educational facilities. They attend educational-rehabilitation centers jointly administered and funded by the Bureau of Exceptional Children education and the welfare organization.

Unlike normal children, kindergarten is compulsory for exceptional children. However, the duration and starting age differs according to the type of handicap. The duration of the kindergarten program for blind children, ages 5 to 9, is one year. Deaf children ages 4 to 8 may attend kindergarten for two years. Mentally retarded children ages 6 to 10 attend kindergarten for three years.

Blind or deaf children can enroll in grade 1 of primary school until age 10; while the maximum age for mentally handicapped children is 12. There were 25,738 exceptional students in primary grades in 1989, an increase of 11.3 percent over the previous year (Executive Regulation of Exceptional Children's Overall Education, 1989). (See Table 4.)

TABLE 4

Distribution of Exceptional Students According to Educational Grouping and Sex in 1989

Sex	Mentally Handicapped	Deaf	Blind	Behavioral Disordered	Total	%
Female	5,387	3,434	565	28	9,414	36.6
Male	10,768	4,323	953	280	16,324	63.4
Total	16,155	7,757	1,518	308	25,738	100
Percentage	62.8	30.1	1.2	5.9	100	

Source: Executive Regulation of Exceptional Children's Overall Education, 1989.

TABLE 5

Main Subjects and Weekly Number of Hours Allocated to Each in Two-Year Teacher Training Colleges

Subjects	Hours Per Week	
	First Term	Second Term
General Psychology	3	—
Educational Psychology	—	3
Methods of Teaching	2	2
Islamic Ideology	4	2
Islamic Morals	2	2
Persian Literature	2	2
Hygiene	—	2
Physical Education	2	—
Research Methods	2	2
Methods of Teaching Math/Science	4	4
Methods of Teaching Math & Studying of Math Books	4	4
Methods of Teaching Farsi	2	2
Methods of Teaching Social Science	2	2
Arabic Language	2	2
Physical Education	—	2
	Third Term	Fourth Term
Islamic Ideology	3	3
Islamic Education	2	2
Educational Technology	2	—
Guidance and Counseling	—	2
Methods of Evaluation	2	—
Educational Administration	—	2
Analysis of Islamic Revolution	—	2
Physical Education	2	—
Persian Literature	2	—
Practicum	6	6
Children's Literature	—	2
Exceptional Children	2	—
Methods of Teaching in Multigrade Classes	—	1
Methods of Teaching Science	4	4
Methods of Teaching Math	4	4
Methods of Teaching Farsi	2	2
Methods of Teaching Religious Studies	2	2
Methods of Teaching Arts	2	2
Methods of Teaching Physical Education	—	2

Training Programs for Teachers of Young Children

Training colleges for primary school teachers are affiliated with the Ministry of Education. Each summer, applicants who have completed their high school education take a comprehensive exam. Successful students attend a two-year teacher training college leading to a primary teaching certificate. The three areas of study relevant to primary school teaching in the training colleges are primary education, the education of exceptional children, and physical education. Table 5 shows the main subjects and the number of hours allocated to each subject in two-year teacher training colleges.

In recent years, teacher training high schools have been established to train teachers for primary schools in villages and rural areas. Applicants must have finished their three-year guidance school. After finishing the four-year training program, graduates work in rural areas as primary school teachers. A few primary school teachers also have Bachelor of Education degrees from universities affiliated with the Ministry of Culture and Higher Education.

In addition to the three types of preservice programs described above, a system of in-service training exists for upgrading teachers' knowledge and skills.

Kindergarten and primary school teachers have relatively low social and economic status in Iran. This is reflected in teachers' views of themselves. A recent survey indicated that 71 percent of teachers sampled felt that their job had low social prestige and an insufficient salary (Sabbaghian, 1990). Because of their low pay and the fact that full-time primary school teachers only work four days or 28 hours a week at school, many take on second jobs. This is especially true for male teachers, who are often the sole wage earner in their families. Teachers also work at various jobs during the summer months. Typical second jobs are in the areas of sales, teaching or tutoring outside of one's own school system, agriculture, or taxi driving. However, the frequent and substantial vacations are an advantage and inducement in the career of teaching, especially for female teachers who usually have more family responsibilities or small children at home.

Because the administration of education is centralized in Iran, there are similar regulations regarding teachers and their recruitment throughout the country. Work benefits (e.g., health insurance, income protection during disability, group life insurance, sick leave, retirement pay, and leave with pay) are the same for all teachers. There is gender equity in terms of salaries.

While payment is largely related to experience and education, teachers who work in deprived provinces and in schools for exceptional children have higher salaries. Despite this, teachers usually prefer to teach in cities, because there are usually better social welfare facilities and job possibilities. As a result, there is usually a shortage of primary school teachers in rural areas, small towns, and the suburbs of large cities. In 1987, for example, the teacher-student ratio in rural areas was 1:30, and in cities 1:33 (Report of the Evaluation of Educational Division Action, 1988: 30). The Soldier Teacher Plan, recently passed in the Consultative Assembly of Iran, is designed to correct this problem. Through the plan, young soldiers can complete their military service as teachers in primary schools in rural areas. Such a plan also existed in the years prior to the Islamic Revolution.

Parental Education

Educational programs for parents are mostly informal. Radio and television have several programs to provide information and to upgrade and develop the knowledge and understanding of parents in various subjects relating to child rearing and education (e.g., child psychology, educational psychology, and child and youth problems). Some programs are designed in response to parents' questions.

School is another source of parental education. There are usually monthly meetings at schools, arranged by the school principal, in which parents are invited to discuss their children's problems or to listen to the lectures of a specialist or child psychologist.

The third type of parental education is conducted by the Parent-Teacher Association (PTA) of the Islamic Republic of Iran. Affiliated with the Ministry of Education, it offers various programs to support parents, including an annual week-long seminar on various topics related to children and education. In recent years, the PTA has organized formal classes for parents. The duration of these classes is 45 days (two days each week) and university professors and instructors teach interested parents a variety of subjects related to childhood and education. At the end of the term, those who successfully pass an examination receive a certificate.

The Islamic Free University of Iran also has some educational programs for parents. The content and duration vary according to the needs of the applicants. Another source of parental education is publications.

References

Educational documents, Ministry of Education, Islamic Republic of Iran, 1987. *Etelaat*, Sept, 22, 1987.

Persian sign language collection of the deaf, education and research office. Rehabilitation Research Group, 1989.

Report of the evaluation of Educational Division Action. (1989). Ministry of Budget and Planning.

Sabbaghian, Z. (1990). Job motivation among school teachers: An Iranian survey. Paper presented at the 22nd International Congress of Applied Psychology, Kyoto, Japan, 1990.

Selected Statistical Matters, No. 17. (1986). Iranian Statistical Center.

Sewards, W. (1969). Elementary Education in *Encyclopedia of educational research*, 4th ed. New York: Macmillian.

Statistical Report on Education. (1986) Islamic Republic of Iran: Ministry of Education.

Statistical Yearbook. (1989). Ministry of Education: Bureau of Exceptional Children and Students Education.

THE PRESCHOOL EDUCATIONAL NETWORK IN ISRAEL

Rina Micholwitz
Ministry of Education
Tel Aviv, Israel

The investment of resources in preschool education addresses several national and social needs in Israel. It enables women to join the labor force, thereby addressing a national need. For children whose families do not provide an environment conducive to their optimal development, early educational settings have the potential to give them opportunities equal to those of children who are not so deprived. Above all, an early education lays the foundation for the healthy intellectual, emotional, and social development of children.

Kindergartens and day cares, as part of the preschool educational system in Israel, are multifunctional. They inculcate in children basic habits in health and daily living, improve their social and intellectual skills, develop their language and cognition, improve their ability to learn and to be creative, and help them to form their character and personality. Moreover, kindergartens and day care centers provide the primary settings for transmitting the cultural and national heritages and the social messages of humankind as a whole, which the educational system seeks to impart.

The early childhood educational network encompasses the education of children from birth to age 6. Within this network, the Ministry of Education is responsible for children from ages 3 to 6, who can be divided into the following two groups.

• *Precompulsory Kindergarten.* Precompulsory kindergartens, for 3- to 5-year-olds, are organized by local authorities, women's organizations (precompulsory kindergarten groups in day care centers), and private kindergartens. The kindergartens organized by the local authorities charge graded fees according to the income of the parents.

• *Compulsory Kindergarten.* Compulsory kindergarten is for children ages 5 to 6 in accordance with the law on compulsory education. The largest proportion of the outlay (salaries of the kindergarten teachers and about 90 percent of the salaries of the aides) is undertaken by the Ministry of Education in conjunction with the local authorities.

The Ministry supervises both types of kindergarten according to the law governing supervision of preschool settings.

The Ministry is involved with the education of the children from birth to age 3, mainly through programs intended to improve parenting skills and thereby to advance the development of the infants and toddlers. The Ministry is involved in preparing educational programs for these age groups by organizing training of the educators. However, although 64 percent of the nation's 2-year-olds are brought to day care centers, the Ministry does not supervise these centers.

The percentage of children in Israel attending kindergartens is shown in Table 1.

TABLE 1

Children Attending Kindergartens (in %)		
	Age	Percentage
Jewish Group		
	3-year-olds	90
	4-year-olds	96
	5-year-olds	98
Non-Jewish Groups		
	3-year-olds	20
	4-year-olds	30
	5-year-olds	95

It is clear from the figures in Table 1 that the percentages of attendance in kindergartens are high, even among the youngest Jewish children. Attendance has risen steadily since 1984.

In recent years, the educational system has developed and implemented pedagogic programs in the areas of education for health, road safety, verbal expression, visual thinking, reading readiness, arithmetic readiness, understanding democracy, and living together. In addition, some programs are being formulated, such as science and technology for compulsory education age groups and an integrated program for three-year-olds.

The rationale for the policy of early childhood educational enrichment stems from the assumption that learning habits, motivation, intellectual skills, and cognitive abilities should be fostered at an early age. It is also believed that children from an early age should be encouraged to broaden their experiences and to enrich their knowledge of the physical and social worlds.

Accordingly, the network has adopted three modes of enrichment. The first is concerned with individual intellectual enrichment. The second focuses on enrichment programs for groups of children and their parents; the third mode is intended to help parents advance their own children. By following up on some of these programs, it was found that the gap has been considerably narrowed and in some cases bridged, between recent immigrants and the more established populations.

One can deduce from the findings what the possibilities from the enrichment during early childhood are likely to be both in directing children toward normal development and in elevating children from a weaker population to that of the stronger group.

In recent years, the quality of teachers in the network has consistently risen. Most of the kindergarten teachers are qualified and many are studying to earn academic degrees in pedagogy, encouraged by the facilities for in-service training provided by the Ministry. The educational level of the supervisors and counselors is also continually rising. This is even though the population of children has grown annually while the number of kindergartens and the network of supervision and counselling have not grown. The creation and implementation of various models of supervision have only partly solved the problem of an overburdened system.

In recent years, the interest of parents in their children's education has increased. Parents are aware of how important the first years of life are on their children's future and as a result are more involved in what happens in the kindergarten and its programs. This involvement is expressed in a wide spectrum of activities, from parent's readiness to offer their time and talents, to organizing various study and enrichment groups. However, organizing groups—for which parents pay—raises the serious issue of accessibility. It should be noted that such activities of complementary and additional programs are permitted by law.

Problems

There are problems in the early childhood educational network that are inherent in the structure. Although the Ministry is responsible for the education of 3- to 6-year-olds, the division of responsibility for implementing the programs among the different authorities, public versus private, creates difficulties in the uniformity of the settings from the pedagogic point of view. In addition, since the supervision law includes only the 3- to 6-year-olds, the educational network cannot assume responsibility for the education of children under age 3. This is a critical issue, considering that 64 percent of the 2-year-olds in care are in private educational settings that have no supervision at all.

The current trend is to give pedagogic supervision and training to day care personnel in charge of children who are below age 3. This proposal has been generally accepted but is not yet enforced by law. Although not compulsory, day care personnel often volunteer to participate in training sessions and request the assistance of the department.

In-service programs for staff and continual guidance are planned by the department for children from birth to age 3, under the auspices of the Division for Preschool Education at the Ministry of Culture and Education. In recent years, many 3-year-olds in precompulsory settings, for which parents pay, are withdrawing due to the cost. Although parents pay on a graded scale, most of these children are from the underprivileged population.

Allocation of Resources

Government resources allocated to preschool education are for basic needs only, that is, for the continuous functioning of the kindergartens. The national educational system has no resources for educational initiatives, experimentation, or innovations. It does not have the tools or the funds for organized monitoring and evaluations of its activi-

ties. As a result, it is not always possible to carry out program evaluations. Besides the problem of the growing workload on the counseling and supervision network and the increased ratio of kindergarten children to staff, kindergarten teachers need much more counseling due to the practice of combining two or three age levels in each class. As a result, there is a need to use suitable strategies and programs.

There are several important challenges facing the early childhood educational network. The findings of recent research demand a renewed look at young children and their abilities. Educational programs and teaching strategies need to be reevaluated. The technological innovation of the 20th century, the computer, has been placed in classrooms without proper teacher education and support. This also demands reevaluation. In an attempt to respond to various parent needs, different solutions are being set up in the community. Examples are half-day child care and activity groups for preschoolers, and family day care homes and infant day care for children under 3 years of age.

It is important to ensure that these are educational settings where foundations for normal growth are laid for the optimal physical and mental development of the young child. To do this, the early childhood educational network will have to broaden its activities to include compulsory education for children ages 3 to 6 and to encompass the network for children from birth to age 3.

THE ITALIAN PRESCHOOL AND COMPULSORY SCHOOL SYSTEM

••••••••••◆••••••••••

Caterina Cicogna
Italian Consulate
Toronto, Canada

This chapter on the Italian preschool and compulsory school system describes how the system is organized and administered, recent legislation, and teacher training and responsibilities. Recent innovations in the education of young handicapped children are also discussed.

Historical Background

Since the industrial revolution in Italy, various religious groups and institutions, as well as some municipalities, have provided preschool facilities for Italian children, especially children of working class parents. Early examples of the care and teaching of young children in Italy include the *asili* (asylums) of Ferrante Aporti, and the maternal school (*scuola materna*) of the Agazzi sisters, which began at the end of the 19th century. The *Casa dei Bambini* (children's home), founded in 1906 by Maria Montessori for 60 poor preschool children in the San Lorenzo district of Rome, is well-known (Standing, 1957).

The government, however, did not begin supervising early childhood care and education until the passage of Bill 444 in 1968. This legislation provided for governmental control and management of preschool settings, which were not part of the compulsory education system. The spirit of Bill 444 focuses more on the educational process and the psychological development of the child than on the care of children in a protective environment. It establishes the minimum age for enrollment in a maternal school (the child must turn age 3 before December 31 of the year of enrollment), sets standards for teacher qualifications, and requires teachers to participate in a national pension plan.

The approval of Bill 444, which followed a long and fractious debate in the Italian national parliament, resulted in a governmental crisis. This initiative was seen as a deliberate attempt to destroy the mainly religious private institutions that offered preschool programs. Now, to be listed, to obtain a license to operate, and to receive governmental subsidies, every early childhood center in Italy must comply with the above legislation.

As a result of Bill 444, there was a proliferation of new types of preschool settings in the late 1960s. These included semiprivate preschools run by municipalities and new day care centers (*asilo-nido*) for younger children administered by local authorities, municipalities, or regional governments, to meet the needs of children under age 3. Private preschool settings run by the religious groups continued to grow as well. All three systems continue to prosper and the competition among them has resulted in a general improvement of the services offered.

Organization of Education for Young Children

The Italian school system consists of two levels: an optional preschool level and a compulsory grade school. Within each of these levels, there are two distinct divisions. (See Table 1.) The youngest children at the preschool level (from 6 months to age 3) may attend an *asilo-nido*, which is equivalent to an infant day care center in North America or to a creche in France. These are organized and financially supported by the local authorities.

The program operates in either the morning or the afternoon. Fees are commonly calculated on the basis of family income, and primarily cover the costs of meals. The staff are trained as "infant caretakers" or *asilo-nido* assistants. Both diplomas are granted after five years (after grade 8) in the secondary school special program, which also provides access to university. In addition to the *asilo-nido*, which are managed by municipalities, there are day care centers operated by private and religious institutions. These facilities must be licensed.

From ages 3 to 6, children might be sent to a maternal school, a setting comparable to kindergartens in North America. A maternal school, is controlled by the state through the Ministry of Public Instruction. As with the *asilo-nido*, the program is offered in the morning or in the afternoon.

Teachers in the maternal schools obtain a basic diploma after the secondary school special program (three years after grade 8). Some teachers seek a higher level of education (five years). A maternal school can also be managed by local authorities and/or private and religious institutions provided they follow the educational guidelines issued by the Ministry of Public Instruction and hire qualified personnel. Control of the physical facilities rests with the health department of the local city hall, while pedagogical control is the responsibility of the public school principal or superintendent.

At the compulsory grade school level, there are also two distinct organizational patterns. The elementary school (*scuola elementare*) is for children ages 6 to 10. Children remain with the classroom teacher for all instruction. The middle school (*scuola media*), for 11 to 14 year olds, utilizes subject teaching with individual teachers responsible for a subject. The middle school is comparable to junior high school in North America.

Children are still widely considered an "unfinished product" until they reach the "age of logic" (about age 7). This may be the reason why many Italian parents send their children to day care or kindergarten for the whole day. While a service to parents, they also believe that the social interaction is beneficial for children. Parents generally do not consider the influences of multiple caretakers on their children to have any negative consequence.

With the start of elementary school, parents expect serious academic instruction for their chil-

TABLE 1

Structure of the Preschool and Public School Systems in Italy

Service Provided	Timetable
Asilo-Nido (noncompulsory)	Six months–3 years
	9:00 a.m.–12:00 p.m.
	or
	9:00 a.m.–4:00 p.m.
Maternal School (noncompulsory)	3–6 years
	8:30 a.m.–12:30 p.m.
	or
	8:30 a.m.–4:30 p.m.
Elementary School (compulsory)	
1st cycle	from 6 to 8 years
grades 1 to 2	
2nd cycle	from 8 to 11 years
grades 3 to 4	
Middle School (compulsory)	
grade 6 (I)	from 11 to 14 years
grade 7 (II)	
grade 8 (III)	

dren. At the same time, parents fear that if their children spend more than half a day at school, they might lose control of their children's moral education and their values. This fear may be part of the reason that the majority of compulsory schools in Italy still operate from 8:30 a.m. to 12:30 p.m. (including Saturdays), even though the number of working parents has increased dramatically over the last 20 years. In an attempt to meet the needs of working parents, some schools offer instruction over the whole day or child care in the afternoon. Full-time schools (*scuole a tempo pieno*) were introduced in 1971 through Bill 820 as a result of lobbying by political parties, unions, and working parents. The bill was part of a larger effort to break up the monolithic centralized nature of the Italian school system. Although these schools have spread all over Italy, they are still considered experimental by the Italian government, and even today pupils attend in the afternoon only with parental consent.

Issues in the Italian School System

Teacher Training and Hiring

The Italian school system is highly centralized. The curriculum, the hiring of teachers, and the overall administration are directly managed by the Ministry of Public Instruction in Rome. Teachers can be hired only through a public examination. After being hired, they can apply for a transfer at the end of each year and can "claim" a new teaching assignment based on their relative position on the Provincial and National Official List. Their "score" on the list is calculated by considering teaching diplomas, years of service in the public administration, and "family reasons." The result of this system is that principals or superintendents cannot choose their own staff or even dismiss a teacher (although local authorities can initiate dismissal). Local school authorities merely maintain school buildings and provide free textbooks and transportation. (See Table 2.)

Paradoxically, while the system makes it easy for teachers to transfer between schools, there is a

TABLE 2

Teacher Training by Educational Structure

Level	Type of Teacher	Minimum Qualifications(*)
Asilo-Nido	Infant Caretaker Assistant Caretaker	High School Diploma (Special Program)
		5 years of study
Maternal School	Maternal School Teacher	High School Diploma (Special Program)
		(3 years of study)
Elementary School		Elementary School Teacher High School Diploma
		(Special Program)
		(4 years of study)
Middle School	Middle School Professor	High School Diploma
		(plus 4 years of study to earn a university or college diploma equivalent in specific subject area)

*Because of a lack of teaching positions, many teachers take additional college diploma or university degree courses in their subject area in order to become more marketable.

strong belief in the importance of "didactical continuity" in Italy. That is, as children are promoted from grade 1 through grade 5, they ideally keep the same teacher. If a child's teacher transfers to another school or retires, parents consider it harmful to the child.

This situation encourages a close and dependent relationship between teacher and pupils. Students often have difficulty at the beginning of the middle school (grade 6) when they suddenly have to deal with many teachers during the day. This situation is changing, however, as discussed later in this chapter.

Integration of Handicapped Children in the Primary Grades

In 1977, the Italian government introduced total integration of handicapped children into the Italian compulsory school system. Since total integration of handicapped children has been proposed but rarely implemented in the educational systems of the world, it is instructive to observe the impact this legislation had on the Italian school system. Because the process of implementing total integration has been described in detail elsewhere (Cicogna, 1987), the following is a brief overview of the legislation and its impact.

Pressure from unions, newly elected committees, political parties, and the public resulted in the passage of Bill 517 in 1977. This bill introduced total integration of handicapped children into the Italian compulsory school system. The act requires the teachers' staff committees to plan programs for each child, including special recommendations, teaching strategies, and activities in relation to the specific environment of their own school. The law also abolished the traditional report card with a mark in every subject.

Making such dramatic changes was not easy and there were many problems. Handicapped and nonhandicapped pupils, for example, were suddenly obliged to interact with one another in a stressful environment. Many teachers had spent their entire careers in a system where they remained with one group of children from grade 1 to grade 5, and then started with a new group at grade 1 again. Their main concern had been whether they would complete the Ministry program before the end of June. These regular teachers had no special training, no technical support, and no psychological preparation for the total integration of handicapped children into their schools.

It is no surprise that some teachers had nervous breakdowns and a few requested early retirement. Many others developed a paranoid behavior, seeing "special" children everywhere from the very first day of school and immediately applying for the medical assessment that would provide a support teacher (who they hoped would withdraw the pupils with problems as soon and as long as possible).

The situation slowly improved. Handicapped pupils were achieving unexpected progress in the more challenging and stimulating environment, particularly in the kindergarten and primary divisions. The teachers responded positively and were motivated to find new teaching strategies, to share experiences with their colleagues, and to organize special group activities in order to give more opportunities to handicapped children.

Meanwhile, an interesting phenomenon occurred in the former private special schools, which were obliged to enroll nondisabled children in order to be legally recognized and partially financed by the Ministry. These former institutions became leaders in suggesting new methodologies, improved school organization, and innovative teacher training strategies. The teachers in these schools discovered that "special" methods also worked well with nondisabled pupils.

For example, the Montessori method, which was designed specifically for teaching handicapped children, was part of the training of many of the special school teachers in Italy. Unfortunately, the Montessori-structured materials were extremely expensive, and therefore the method had not been widely used in practice. Because they lacked the materials, many special school teachers interpreted the method in their own way, sometimes creating materials themselves. In addition, because special school teachers were better trained professionally (two years beyond regular teacher training), they were generally better informed regarding the psychology of early childhood. As a result, many of the regular teachers changed their teaching methods to fit the new reality.

Support teachers are allocated to schools based on the ratio of one support teacher for every four medically certified handicapped children in the school. This is a problem in that it involves identifying and labelling children as handicapped in order to justify an increase in school staffing. This seems to work against the philosophy of total integration. A more appropriate method would be to assign an extra teacher to every 50 or 100 or 150 pupils (according to the budget), based on the national statistics on the ratio of handicapped to nonhandicapped children in the school system. There would then be no need to label the "special" students, and all children could benefit from the increase in the number of teachers in the school system. There are indications that this will be the policy of the Ministry in the near future, since medical certification is often difficult to obtain. In addition, there are many children with "special needs" who do not have medical problems.

In any case, all children may have specific needs that can be met using similar strategies, regardless of whether the child is classified as handicapped. There is now a strong movement of principals and superintendents and inspectors fighting for "enrichment centers," which will gather all children with the same pedagogical needs. It is easy to understand that integration, especially in a small village, has a very high cost for a relatively short period of time. But it is also true that the spirit of the act is integration in the child's own environment. This introduces another important question: What happens to handicapped children when the compulsory school ends? Unfortunately, integration in schools does not automatically result in integration in the larger social context, especially in Italy, which has a very complex and rigorous academic program in the high school and a physical environment with many architectural barriers.

Recent Reforms

The reform of the Italian school system is far from complete. As part of the reform, the Ministry of the Public Instruction introduced a new curriculum, *New Programs for the Elementary Grades* (1985), which began to be implemented in 1987, starting in grade 1, and moving up through the next four grades.

The main objective of the elementary school is to provide all children with equal opportunities by removing the economic and social obstacles that could limit their development as persons and citizens. Consistent with this goal, the final phase of the new programs curricula was introduced in the spring of 1990. The emphasis in the new programs is more on methodologies and teaching strategies rather than on the achievements and skills as before.

The last phase of implementation of the new programs in the Spring of 1990 also formalized that the teaching time for curriculum subjects in grades 1 and 2 (first cycle) should not exceed 27 hours per week, and that the teaching time from curriculum subjects in grades 3, 4, and 5 (second cycle) should not exceed 30 hours per week. In addition, in the 2nd cycle, there will be a new emphasis on linguistic education, including learning a second language, logic and math education, social studies, arts, etc. As a consequence, every two classes, starting at grade 3, will have three teachers with specialized professional skills who will rotate through the classes.

Junior high schools (grades 6, 7, and 8) will soon have a new type of teacher—a "social facilitator,"—to assist with integration of handicapped children in the schools. These new teachers will be drawn from industrial arts teachers (now in over supply), who have been attending, in the last two years, the course for special teachers in order to learn about this new assignment.

The next step will be to add two years to compulsory education, as required in the new law approved by the European Community to standardize education. Italian legislators are discussing whether these two years of school should be the two last years of the maternal school, the last year of the maternal school and the first year of the secondary school, or the two first years of the secondary school. As well, according to the European Community legislation, the school year in Italy has to include 200 days of school, but the start and finish, as well as the holidays, are flexible, and planned by each region according to local economies, and traditional and cultural expectations of the residents of each region.

The reforms outlined in this chapter are particularly remarkable in a country such as Italy, which has a very high population of students at the elementary level (more than 7 million) and limited financial resources.

References

Cicogna, C. (1987). Special educational needs in the Italian compulsory school system: a personal account. *International Journal of Early Childhood, 19* (2).

Government of Italy. (1968). *Orientamenti Scuola Materna.* Rome.

————. (1985). *Nuovi programmi della scuola elementare.* Rome.

Standing, E. (1957). *Maria Montessori, her life and work.* New York: Hollis & Carter.

EARLY EDUCATION IN JAPAN: FROM ANCIENT TIMES TO THE PRESENT

●●●●●●●●●●◆●●●●●●●●●●

Isaaki Noguchi,
Sumie Ogawa,
Tomoyoshi Yoshikawa, and
Santaro Hashimoto
Hirosaki University
Hirosaki, Japan

In primitive times in Japan, children were regarded as precious and were reared within the protection of the tribe. In the period of dynasties from the Yamato to the Nara (Heian Era to 794 A.D.–1185A.D.), children of the nobility were reared from early childhood to be cultured men and women. At the beginning of the Middle Ages (during the Kamakura and Muromachi Eras), when the Samuri (warriors) took charge of state affairs, boys were trained, in a severe manner, to become strong warriors, while girls were reared to become more "womanly" for the sake of the family. This persisted well into the Edo period (1603–1867, Japan's "feudal" era) when Confucianists, such as Nobuhiro Sato (1769–1850), began to preach the necessity for early education.

Meiji (1868–1912) and Taisho Periods (1912–26)

The founding of the American Women's Educational Facilities in Yokohama in 1871 for the children of poor women (*Amerika-fujin-kyojusho*) by three missionaries, Mary Pruyn, Julia Crosby, and Louise Pierson, marks the beginning of the modern preschool movement in Japan. The beginning of creches (or nursery schools, called *takujisho*) for the children of female factory workers is linked to the industrialization of Japan. The creche at Dai Nihon Boseki Company in Tokyo, established in 1894, is believed to be the first in Japan.

The early creches did not receive popular support in Japan. They were organized by the Department of the Interior and were seen as a type of welfare or relief work. Compared with the remarkable growth of kindergartens, few creches existed by the end of the Meiji period. However, early in the Taisho period, social welfare work thrived within a new respect for children, a movement referred to as Taisho democracy. In this context, there were 196 creches by the end of the Taisho Era.

In 1876, the first Froebelian kindergarten in Japan was opened by the Tokyo Women's Normal School at Yushima Hongo in Tokyo. The focus on children's self-activity, characteristic of the Froebelian kindergarten, is still a feature of modern Japanese kindergartens.

In 1882, the Ministry of Education, Science, and Culture opened special kindergartens, called *kan-i yochien* (handy kindergartens) for children of the poor. As a result, the number of kindergartens in Japan increased from 30 in 1885 to 222 by 1897. A consequence of this tremendous growth was the creation of national standards, the Official Regulations for Kindergarten Education and Facilities (1900). The passing of this regulation brought the kindergarten closer to the elementary school system. The 1926 Imperial Edict of Kindergartens (the Kindergarten Law) further popularized the kindergarten by providing for kindergartens within creches. As a consequence, there was a small increase in the numbers of kindergartens (from 957 in 1925, to 1,066 in 1926).

Early Childhood Education: 1926–Present

Although the Imperial Edict of 1926 establishing kindergartens included a place for nursery schools, it was not until the Ministry of Health and Welfare enacted the Law of Social Undertaking in 1938 that the nursery school had legal status. With the intensification of World War II, the number of wartime nursery schools increased to provide child care for women in war work, and kindergartens were incorporated into the wartime nursery school system in 1943. By 1944, there were 21,184 such nursery schools in Japan. But, because of the danger of air raids, many of these facilities were temporarily or permanently closed that same year. Nursery schools designed to serve a specific need are still part of the preschool movement in Japan. During the peak of the growing seasons, in spring and fall, 50,000 nursery school facilities operate for the children of farm workers.

The most dramatic increase in the years prior to World War II, however, was in kindergartens. From 1,066 kindergartens with an enrollment of 9,442 children in 1926, kindergarten enrollment swelled to 174,629 children in 2,046 by 1935.

Following the war, the child care and kindergarten systems were once again separated. In 1946, the United States Education Mission (representing the General Headquarters of the Allied Powers) oversaw the incorporation of nursery schools and kindergartens into the elementary school system. This was part of the postwar school reform in Japan. As a result, in 1947 kindergartens were defined as the first step in the school system under the new School Education Law. This legis-

lation also led to reform in the elementary schools, lower and upper secondary schools, universities, technical colleges, and schools for the blind, deaf, and mentally and physically handicapped.

At the same time, under the Child Welfare Law, nursery schools were renamed as day care centers and minimum standards were set, making day care a part of child welfare and not education. Since the mid-1950s, the demand for day care facilities has increased tremendously, so that today, there are centers nationwide. By 1965, there were 11,214 centers (6,856 were public and 4,358 private) caring for 829,296 children.

Throughout the 1960s, day care center staff became more and more interested in integrating kindergarten curricula into their centers in order to increase the "educational content" of their programs. In 1963, the Ministry of Education, Science, and Culture and the Ministry of Health and Welfare jointly prepared a document entitled *The Relation Between Kindergartens and Day Care Centers*. Efforts were also made to increase the numbers of spaces for children in day care centers. In 1966, a *Five-Year Plan of Urgent Improvement in Day Care Centers* called for the creation of 300,000 additional spaces.

Changes in Japan in the 1980s—smaller families, urbanization, and a broadening of the Women Worker's Act—resulted in an updated *Guide for Nurture in Day Care Centers* (first published in 1965). The new guide, which became law in 1990, provided for the unification of nursing and education in child care and placed a new emphasis on community-based "family day care." The program is broadly divided into a focus on life, play, and health for children under age 3 and health, human relations, environment, language, and expression for those age 3 and older.

Following its inclusion in the educational system in 1947, the kindergarten underwent significant changes. The Ministry of Education, Science, and Culture changed the focus from a compensatory to a normal program. As in the day care, the focus was on play, health education, and life (significant curriculum changes were made in 1956 and 1964).

Enrollment steadily increased in the five years following the war. In 1946, 6.5 percent of 5-year-olds attended kindergartens; in 1950 this percentage had increased to 20.1 percent. The greatest increases, however, occurred following the 1972 announcement by the Ministry of the Ten-Year Program for Promotion of Kindergarten Education." Intended to respond to the national need for early education, the slogan of the program was "All 4- and 5-year-olds can be admitted to a kindergarten if they desire." At the end of this ten-year initiative, the percentage of 5-year-olds in kindergarten had increased to 64.4 percent, 4-year-olds to 50 percent, and 3-year-olds to 10.6 percent.

According to the new curriculum standards for kindergartens, issued by the Ministry of Education, Science, and Culture in 1989, the modern Japanese kindergarten is expected to help children cultivate good social relations with adults and children, a respect for nature, healthy habits for living, and desirable social attributes.

Current Problems in Early Childhood Education in Japan

Currently, over 90 percent of Japanese children are in some type of preschool program in the year before they enter the primary school. From 1977–87 kindergartens represented 63–64 percent of the total number of children in preschool programs, while day care made up 25–27 percent. According to governmental objectives, however, kindergarten enrollment is still too low. There is also a regional imbalance in the numbers of day care centers and kindergartens. Some regions—like the Nagano, Kouchi, Ishikawa, and Tottori Prefectures—open more day care centers than kindergartens. Others—such as the Okinawa, Hyogo, Tokushima, Kagawa, Ooita, Kanagawa, and Saitama Prefectures—have the reverse pattern. This is a problem in that although day care and kindergarten are both part of early education in Japan, there are differences among them in terms of educational opportunity, quality, facilities, and user's fees.

In practice, the distinction between day care centers and kindergartens is not always clear. Many day care centers resemble kindergartens and many kindergartens are similar to day care centers. However, because almost all Japanese children are in some type of preschool program, a high standard of care is a major concern.

Preschool Programs in Japan

In Japan, preschool education is largely center-based. This is primarily because of the profile of the modern Japanese family: the majority of modern families have only one or two children, and very often both spouses are wage earners. As well, the passing of the Equal Employment Opportunity Law of 1986 has resulted in an increase in the number of women in the work force. The demand for out-of-home care has therefore increased. In addition, the proliferation of expert advice on child rearing has caused a crisis of confidence, even among mothers not working outside the home. Messages such as "Are you spoiling your children?" or "Is your child able to associate with other children?" make placing a child in a day care center easier than struggling at home without family or community support.

The influence of child psychology and other related fields, and the increased competitiveness in modern society, has lowered the age at which some type of formal training or schooling begins. The present trend of the Ministry of Education to promote learning throughout the life span, has resulted in a renewed interest in both adult and early childhood education.

Some of these programs are supplements to kindergarten or day care centers (e.g., swimming or gymnastics clubs). Others attempt to prepare children for life in school. *Juku* (i.e., private schools) aim to prepare children for prestigious private elementary schools. Since the elementary schools are usually attached to universities or colleges, children are more certain of higher education once they are accepted at the primary level. Because of the very difficult university entrance examinations, many parents want to send their children to elementary schools linked to a university.

Other programs attempt to train children in a special ability, (e.g, English, music, dance, or art). However, disparity in wealth, as well as regional differences, is producing unequal access to such programs.

The dominant forms of preschool programs, however, are the center-based kindergarten or the day care center. There are significant differences between the two (see Tables 1 and 2). Teachers in both types of preschool centers are expected to participate in many special programs in addition to their everyday responsibilities. There are a variety of yearly and monthly events: entrance, opening, and closing ceremonies; graduation exercises; guidance for road safety; training for disaster prevention; excursions; athletic meetings; literary exercises; swimming; camping for the oldest children; and celebration of children's birthdays.

There are many other traditional, seasonal and national events. They include the *Shichi-go-san* (November 15), a festival day for children ages 3, 5 and 7; *Tanabata* (July 7), the Star Festival; *Otsumkimi*, the autumn lunar festival; *Mame-maki* (around February 3), a bean-throwing ceremony; *Hina-matsuri* (March 3), the Girls' Festival; Christmas (December 25) (even at non-Christian facilities); Children's Day (May 5); *Tang-no-Sekku*, traditionally the Boys' Festival; Mother's and Father's Day; Day to Respect the Aged (September 15); Thanksgiving Day (November 23). Gathering vegetables on a farm is also a popular event.

Many institutions rehearse children in practicing the drum and fife for marching festivals. They also drill children in numbers and Japanese cursive *knan* characters, preparing them, at their parents' request, for the elementary school education.

The falling birth rate has meant greater competition for children in preschool centers, especially private institutions. The competition for children can be severe. Teachers are constantly urged to provide more and better programs to gain a good reputation and attract parents.

The most recent day care curriculum guidelines, however, stress that the primary aim of centers is to nurture and not to educate children. However, since all children do not have equal access to a kindergarten (or day care), and since they both provide a child care function, it is imperative that efforts be made to unify the two institutions.

TABLE 1

Comparison of Kindergartens and Day Care Centers in Japan

	Kindergartens	Day Care Centers
Jurisdiction	Ministry of Education, Science, and Culture	Ministry of Health and Welfare
Basic role	Academic instruction	Welfare facility for working parents
Children to be admitted	Preschoolers over age 3	Infants and preschoolers in need of nursery care
Hours per day	4 hours a day is standard	8 hours a day in principle
Admission criteria	Private contract with parents or guardian; sometimes there are entrance examinations	Placement by municipalities through the assessment of parents'/guardians' income
Curricular control	Course of Study for Kindergartens (1989)	Guidelines for Day Care for Day Care Centers (1990)
Curricular content	Promoting children's health, social relations, care of the environment, language, and expression	Basic care, emotional stability, health, social relations, environment, language, and expression
Personnel	Teachers	Nursery teachers

Source: Ministry of Welfare. " Statistics of Social Welfare," Ministry of Education. "Basic Research of Schools." Both are in *A White Paper on Childcare 1989* (nongovernmental) edited by National Liaison Association of Groups Engaged in Childcare, and the Childcare Research Institute.

TABLE 2

Statistics on Early Childhood Education in Japan

	Kindergartens	Day Care Centers
Number of children admitted	2,041,820 (May 1988) National: 6,606 Municipal: 467,611 Private: 1,567,603	1,784,193 (Oct. 1987) Public: 1,004,417 Private: 779,776
Number of facilities	15,115 (May 1988) National: 48 Municipal: 6,251 Private: 8,816	22,780 (Oct. 1987) Public: 13,462 Private: 9,318
Number of teachers	100,420 (May 1988) National: 272 Municipal: 25,500 Private: 74,648	178,072 (Oct. 1987) Public: 99,293 Private: 78,779
Number of children per facility	Average: 135.1 National: 137.6 Municipal: 74.8 Private: 135.1	Average: 75.1 Public: 71.4 Private: 80.3
Number of children per teacher	Average: 20.3 National: 24.3 Municipal: 18.3 Private: 21.0	Average: 10.0 Public: 10.1 Private: 9.9

Source: Ministry of Welfare. " Statistics of Social Welfare," Ministry of Education. "Basic Research of Schools." Both are in *A White Paper on Childcare 1989* (nongovernmental) edited by National Liaison Association of Groups Engaged in Childcare, and the Childcare Research Institute.

Primary Education in Japan

School enrollment in the elementary grades is nearly 100 percent as a result of compulsory schooling. The average number of children per class in the primary system was 30.3 in 1989. All elementary school children receive the same general or common education throughout the country. Classroom teachers assume responsibility for all subjects in the lower grades. (See Table 3.)

Special Education for Young Children in Japan

In Japan, special education for young children is carried out in special schools for handicapped children and special classes attached to ordinary elementary schools within the jurisdiction of the Ministry of Education, Science, and Culture. The institutions of child welfare under the control of the Ministry of Health and Welfare also carry out early intervention programs for disabled children.

There are three types of special schools: schools for blind children, schools for deaf children, and schools for physically handicapped and mentally retarded children. The latter also include provision for health-impaired children. Each type of school has its own course of study.

The criteria for entrance to one of these schools are specified in the School Education Law. If the degree of disability is severe and the child is difficult to place, there is provision for teachers to visit homes and hospitals.

TABLE 3
Subjects and Hours of Class Time for Elementary Schools Per Year

Grade	1	2	3	4	5	6
Subject				Hours		
Japanese Language	306	315	280	280	210	210
Social Studies	—	—	105	105	105	105
Arithmetic	136	175	175	175	175	175
Life	102	105	—	—	—	—
Music	68	70	70	70	70	70
Art and Handicraft	68	70	70	70	70	70
Homemaking	—	—	—	—	70	70
Physical Education	102	105	105	105	105	105
Moral Education	34	35	35	35	35	35
Special Activities	35	35	35	70	70	70
Total	851	910	875	910	910	910

Special education for young children is provided by the kindergarten and elementary departments of the special schools, with the standards being the same as those for regular kindergartens and elementary schools. It is compulsory for all severely handicapped or disabled children in Japan to attend one of these elementary classes, although kindergarten class is not compulsory. The standard class size for the special schools for handicapped children is seven pupils. The schools for handicapped children usually have a dormitory.

Special classes have been established in ordinary elementary school for mildly handicapped children. The standard class size of these classes is ten pupils. Special classes for children receiving medical treatment have been established in the hospitals, or teachers can be temporarily assigned to visit children who cannot attend school.

Starting in 1972, the Ministry of Education, Science, and Culture implemented a ten-year plan to create kindergarten departments in special schools and in 1974 began to provide private special education assistance for private kindergartens with over ten handicapped children in order to detect, educate, and train handicapped children in their early years.

Because of these policies, there have been many recent experiments on admitting handicapped children to regular programs in order to promote their development. The practice of integration allows nonhandicapped children to understand their handicapped peers, and attempts to remove the stigma attached to handicapped children, while drawing out their development possibilities.

Attending only special schools and classes makes it difficult for handicapped children to make friends with other children in their neighborhood. Through integration and interaction with regular classes and the local community, special schools or classes can assist in the education of all children. Because of this, integrated classes are actively being promoted at the present, together with exchanges between regular elementary schools and the special schools.

Other measures have been taken to assist disabled children outside the school system, through Institutions of Child Welfare. In 1970, the Fundamental Law for Mentally and Physically Disabled Persons was enacted to promote holistically the well-being of physically and mentally disabled persons. These measures included the provision of day care for mentally and physically disabled children started in 1972, a "treatment passbook" system developed in 1973, the provision of day nursing centers for disabled children in 1974, and new standards and centers for hard-of-hearing infants in 1975. Mentally and physically disabled children who, because of their handicaps, are restricted from a normal life, are given rehabilitation at institutes so that their handicaps can be dealt with as soon as possible. Programs for disabled children in Child Welfare Institutions do not have an educational focus.

Teacher Training Programs: Preschool and Primary

There are great differences in the training of nursery school and day care center teachers, and teachers in kindergartens and elementary schools. Certification is granted by the Ministry of Health and Welfare and the Ministry of Education, Science, and Culture, respectively.

Teachers in day care centers, maternity homes, baby homes, and mother and child homes must obtain a nursery teacher's license. Training is available in universities, junior colleges, special vocational schools, and other centers authorized by the Ministry of Health and Welfare. As of 1991, the total number of training institutions for nursery teachers was 339. Included are 20 universities, 221 junior colleges, 58 special training schools, 1 miscellaneous school, and 39 training facilities for nursery teachers.

A nursery teacher's certification is also granted to upper secondary school graduates (or the equivalent) who have passed the nursery teacher's examination offered by the local prefecture. The current criteria for certification have been in place since March 1977. Recently, a number of males have been entering the nursery teacher's profession.

Kindergarten and elementary school teachers are trained in universities or junior colleges approved by the Minister of Education, Science, and Culture. There are three categories of teacher certificates: regular, special, and temporary. Regular certificates are further divided into three classes.

First-class certificates for kindergarten and elementary school teachers are granted to university graduates (or the equivalent) holding a bachelor's degree (a "major" certificate is granted to candidates with a master's degree). Second-class certificates are granted to those who have studied

for at least two years in a university or junior college (or the equivalent) and have acquired at least 62 credits. The special certificates for elementary school teachers, with the exception of kindergarten, are given in four subjects: music, art and handicrafts, homemaking, and physical education. Special certificates are issued for a period ranging from three to ten years as set by local boards of education.

The temporary certificate for kindergarten and elementary school teachers is granted—only in cases of teacher shortages—to upper secondary school graduates (or the equivalent) who have passed an examination set by the Prefectural Board of Education. The temporary certificate is valid for three years and only in the prefecture in which it is issued. A regular teacher certificate is valid for a lifetime in all prefectures. Economic or legal distinctions among teachers holding major, first-, or second-class certificates are not significant. Nursery teacher's certificates are granted to those who have passed the examination for nursery teachers covering eight compulsory subjects: (1) general social welfare work; (2) an introduction to child welfare work; (3) child psychology and mental hygiene; (4) hygiene, sanitation, and physiology; (5) nursing science and practice; (6) nutrition and nutrition practice; (7) the theory of child rearing; and (8) nursery teaching practices.

In kindergarten and elementary-level teacher training, programs vary in content and length according to the type of certification. All programs include general and professional subjects. In addition, students have practice lessons and extracurricular activities under the instruction of the training school faculty.

Parental Support and Educational Programs

Under the supervision of the Ministry of Health and Welfare, each prefecture or designated city must have a certain number of public health centers, child guidance centers, and welfare offices to offer direct support to parents in various ways. Public health centers are concerned with child health in general. Principle services include the publication of the *Maternal and Child Health Book*, home visits by nurses within a month after the birth of a baby, and routine health examinations. The public health center is obligated to provide monthly health examinations to all children from ages 1.5 to 3. However, many centers offer examinations to infants before their first birthday. Examinations include a check of physical and mental development, and professionals advise parents on caring for and educating children at home.

Child guidance centers provide assistance to parents incapable of caring for children for various reasons, and to parents whose children have physical, intellectual, emotional, or behavioral problems. The welfare office provides similar services, although with more emphasis on financial support and social protection of children.

The Ministry of Education, Science, and Culture is also involved in parental education. Under the auspices of a Board of Education, many communities give lectures on home education (usually once a week for one year). Parents acquire a basic knowledge of child development and the role of home education.

In the Aomori Prefecture, for example, the Aomori Board offers services in home education. Several specialists in home education make up a consulting team that visits communities to talk with parents who are seeking advice on child rearing and education. The service is also available by mail. The Board of Education in the Aomori Prefecture produces a series of television programs on home education (presented twice a week for six months). The project, financed by the Ministry, has been in operation for the past 16 years. A publication service disseminates pamphlets and booklets for parents on the topic of home education.

The Aomori Board also operates education centers for research and consultation in each prefecture. The staff are usually experienced school teachers. They advise parents with children who have difficulty adjusting to school or who have a behavioral problem.

In addition to governmental organizations, private institutions offer support to young parents.

Because many pediatricians are beginning to realize the importance of educating parents, it is a common practice for doctors to have special office hours to provide consultation on the medical and psychological aspects of child rearing.

Schools, including nursery schools (day care centers), are important social resources for parental education. They provide parents with many opportunities to study about education through the daily activities of the schools. Parents can attend teacher-parent conferences, lectures on education, and various programs planned by the Parent Teacher Association.

Television and radio programs also offer programming for parents. NHK, a Japanese public broadcasting station, has several educational programs for parents each year. There are both informative programs in the form of lectures and consultative ones that respond to individual questions.

Summary

Primary education is available for almost all children in Japan. As well, special educational programs have been developed throughout the country and serve all those who need this type of education. At the preschool level, over 90 percent of the preschool children attend either day care centers or kindergartens for at least one year before entering the primary grades.

However, there are regional differences in the level, balance, and quality of preschool services throughout Japan. There is still a great deal of confusion concerning the aims and functions of day care centers and kindergartens. To solve this problem, new standards have been set up for all preschool programs in Japan, and in the future, there should be fewer differences among the various types of early childhood education in Japan.

References

Ashi Almanac. 1990.

Association and International Education, Japan. (Ed.). (1985). *Japanese colleges and universities 1985.* (Nihon no Diagaku 1985). Tokyo: Maruzen.

Bulletin of National Childcare Conference (No. 33). 1990.

Childcare Research Institute (Ed.). (1990). *How to evaluate the new guidelines for day care centers.*

Children and Families Bureau, Ministry of Health and Welfare. (Ed.). (1988, 1989). *Me de miru Jido-Fukushi.* (*Graphs and charts on Japan's child welfare services*). Tokyo: The Japan Research Institute on Child Welfare.

Crayonhouse Composite Institute on Culture (Ed.). (1986). *Monthly Periodical: A Child.* (newspaper clipping).

Hattatsu (Development), *11*(42), 1990.

Hosoi, F., Noguchi, I., & Fukushi, T. (Eds.). (1985). *Shoshisha no tameno Hoiku Genri.* (The principles of early childhood education and care for beginners). Tokyo: Gakujutsu-tosho.

International Children Institute (Ed.). (1990). *A commentary on the guideline for day care centers.* (revised).

Japan Childcare Association (Ed.). *A World of Childcare,* No. 188, 1990.

Japanese Association for Protecting Children (Ed.). (1989). *A white paper on children 1989.* (non-governmental).

Japanese University Accreditation Association. (1975). *Japanese universities and colleges.* Tokyo: Japanese University Accreditation Association.

Ministry of Education, Science, and Culture. (1989). *Gakko-Kihon-Chosa-Hokokusho.* (*A report of fundamental investigations into educational institutions in Japan*). Tokyo: Minister's Secretariat.

———. (1983). *Gakko-Kyoin-Tokei-Chosa-Hokokusho.* (*A report of statistical research on Japanese school teachers*). Tokyo: Minister's Secretariat.

———. (1989). (*Outline of education in Japan, 1989*). *Nihon no Kyo-ku, 1989.* Tokyo: The Asian Cultural Center of UNESCO.

———. (1979, 1989). *Education in Japan.* Tokyo: Gyosei Pub.

Ministry of Education, Association for the Study of Curriculum. (Ed.). (1989). *A commentary on the new course of study for kindergartens.*

Takakura, S., & Murata, Y. (Ed.). (1989). *Education in Japan.* (Nihon no Kyo-iku). Tsukuba: Association of International Education.

Teshima, N., Noguchi, I., & Hosoi, F. (1983). *Principles of childcare.* Tokyo: Kenpakusha.

Teshima, N., Noguchi, I., Sekiguchi, H., & Oyama, N. (Eds.). (1990). *Shinpan Hoiku Genri.* (The principles of early childhood education and care). Tokyo: Kenpakusha.

Teshima, N., Noguchi, I., & Hosoi, F. (Eds.). (1983). *Hoiku Genri.* (*The Principles of Early Childhood Education and Care*). Tokyo: Kenpakusha.

PRESCHOOL AND PRIMARY EDUCATION IN KENYA

George Godia
Moi University
Eldoret, Kenya

In traditional Kenyan society, most activities associated with early education were carried out by the family. The family provided children with the necessary emotional support that formed the foundation of their life. The family ensured that children were provided with adequate love, care, and security during the early years. It was within the family that children's physical, social, emotional, and intellectual needs were met.

Preschool Education

With recent social and economic changes leading to rapid modernization and urbanization, the family's role in early education has been supplemented by organized preschools. Formal preschools have existed in Kenya since the 1940s. The first were in urban areas and catered to European, and later, Asian families. With the independence of Kenya from colonial rule in 1963, there was a massive increase in the number of preschools. This was partly a response to the Kenyan President's call for *harambee* (uniting to build the nation). *Harambee* embodies ideas of mutual assistance, joint effort, mutual social responsibility, and community self-reliance. Participation of individuals in harambee projects is guided by the principles of collective good rather than individual gain.

Today, various terms are used to refer to the preschool. In rural areas, they are referred to as preschools, day nurseries, day care centers and kindergartens. While the programs primarily provide socialization and custodial roles, many parents also believe that preschools give children a head start in formal schooling. This view is likely related to the fact that the Kenyan educational system is competitive and examination-oriented.

Statistics demonstrate the dramatic expansion of preschools in Kenya. By 1972, there were about 5,000 preschools with some 6,000 teachers and an enrollment of about 300,000 children. In 1987, there were 12,192 preprimary schools with an enrollment of 662,045 children and 16,551 preprimary teachers. In the same year, there were 2.4 million children ages 3 to 5 in Kenya, of whom about 27 percent were enrolled in preprimary schools. As Table 1 indicates, there will be 3.6 million children of this age requiring preprimary education by the year 2000.

However, the expansion of the programs has not necessarily meant that the quality of programs has been improved. A major limitation has been the lack of trained preschool teachers. In addition, the curriculum has largely been irrelevant to the children's culture and background.

TABLE 1

Preprimary Education Enrollment to the Year 2000

Year	Estimated Number of 3- to 5-year olds
1987	2,441,208
1988	2,512,416
1989	2,588,579
1990	2,686,688
1991	2,764,991
1992	2,848,809
1993	2,937,055
1994	3,027,793
1995	3,114,742
1996	3,212,047
1997	3,310,279
1998	3,409,294
1999	3,509,070
2000	3,610,231

Source: Ministry of Planning and National Development.

The goals of preschool education in Kenya include:

1. providing an informal education aimed at developing mental capabilities and physical growth;

2. providing opportunities for living and learning through play;

3. encouraging the formation of habits for effective living as an individual and as a member of a group;

4. developing appreciation for cultural background and customs;

5. fostering spiritual and moral growth; and

6. developing the imagination and self-reliance.

A variety of governmental and nongovernmental agencies work to support these goals. The largest number of preschools, over 70 percent, were founded and continue to be operated by local parent's associations. These associations are responsible for providing and maintaining physical facilities. This includes provision of land, construction of buildings, provision of furnishings and materials, training of teachers, teacher's salaries, and administration.

Some churches have also established preschools within their compounds. These include the Church Province of Kenya, the Catholic Church, and the Presbyterian Church of East Africa. In addition, firms, cooperatives, state corporations, and women's organizations (e.g., the "Maendeleo Ya Wanawake" and the Young Women's Christian Association) have established preschools and day nurseries. Most private institutions are found in urban areas. In most cases, these preschools exist as businesses. The quality of education provided in these preschools varies greatly depending on the sponsor, teachers, and resources.

Both local and central governments are involved in preschool education in Kenya. Many local authorities assist communities in providing preschool services by providing some materials and employing teachers and sponsoring teachers for training. At the national level, prior to 1980 preschool education activities were coordinated by the Ministry of Culture and Social Services. However, a decade ago responsibility for preschool education was shifted to the Ministry of Education. The Ministry of Education is responsible for teacher training; curriculum development; the registration, inspection, and supervision of preschools; and the provision of policy guidelines to all program sponsors.

The headquarters of the preschool section of the Ministry of Education deals with all administrative matters (e.g., the registration of preschools, coordination of government grants and funds from external donors, and provision of policy guidelines for the preschool program). The Ministry's inspectorate monitors professional standards of the program. It coordinates inspection and supervision of schools as well as the teacher training program. This section is also responsible for the administration of the teacher's examinations.

The National Center for Early Childhood Education (NCECE), established in 1984, deals with such professional matters as teacher training, curriculum development, and research, as well as the provision of professional services to preschool sponsors. The center offers preservice and in-service training sessions ranging from nine months to a few weeks or days to the various personnel involved in early childhood education. The founding of the center is significant in that it makes early childhood education an official part of Kenya's National Development Program.

District centers for early childhood education were established to facilitate the decentralization of preschool services at the district level, in an attempt to meet the current governmental policy of making every district the focus of rural development. The first nine centers were established in 1985. These centers are responsible for training preschool teachers, developing and disseminating the local curriculum, conducting and coordinating relevant research, and mobilizing the community to provide quality services for young children.

At the district level, preschools are managed by a wide variety of sponsors, such as parents, community groups, churches, local authorities, and private individuals. They are supervised by the district education officers and a team of field officers from the Ministry of Education and local authority supervisors.

Curriculum Development

A shortage of suitable and culturally relevant teaching materials is a major problem facing preschool education in Kenya. Due to the cultural and geographical diversity of the country, a combined centralized/decentralized model of curriculum development has been adopted. The decentralized aspect of the model enables the preschool program to address various cultural, linguistic, and geographical needs. The centralized dimension provides the general framework to ensure that standards are maintained and national aspirations acknowledged.

In the decentralized approach, children, teachers, trainers, and the community are involved in curriculum development. They are assisted in developing a conceptual framework, in deciding on the appropriate curriculum materials, and in collecting and collating the relevant materials. Through this exercise, the participants acquire positive attitudes toward materials and their own role in human learning and development.

Some materials have been developed through this process. The first category of materials are those that are "collected and constructed" by parents and teachers. The environment around both the home and the school provides a wide range of materials and objects for children to manipulate. Basic materials, such as water, sand, wood, and clay found in the environment, are useful in preschool learning and play activities. Through discrimination and classification of materials, children start to develop their concepts of color, shape, size, and texture. The materials also encourage children to interact freely and unconsciously with other children and teachers, thereby helping them acquire language and social skills.

During training, teachers are exposed to skills and techniques of collecting and making low-cost materials from the environment. The teachers are also helped to acquire techniques for mobilizing parents, members of the community, and the children to participate in material collection and development from the environment.

A second major type of curriculum materials is termed "concrete manipulative." Concrete materials, especially those made from wood, are very popular among preschool children. The materials include jigsaw puzzles, building blocks, geometric and animal puzzles, toy cars, and wooden letters and numbers.

"Graphics materials" are the third major category. They are particularly important because they play a crucial role in the development of basic literacy skills and in preparing young children to learn to read and write. The materials include charts, workcards, card games, drawing books, coloring books, and story books.

The fourth category of curriculum materials consists of those related to Kenyan folklore and oral tradition. Over the years, NCECE and the district centers for early childhood education have continued to develop books of stories, poems, and riddles in various languages. A participatory model, involving preschool teachers, parents, children, and field officers, is used in the collection and development of these materials.

The fifth category of materials—"manuals, guidelines, and syllabi"—serves as the framework for the various consumers, schools, and training institutions. These materials help to ensure that with the decentralized approach of development in the other materials, a certain level of acceptable standards is maintained. Materials developed in this category include *The Guidelines for Preschool Education in Kenya* (1984), *Guidelines for Training of Trainers* (1984), *Preschool Teachers In-service Education Syllabus* (1987), and *Manuals for Preschool Teachers and the Development of Materials.*

The final category includes "audio-visual materials," such as films, videos, slide tapes, cassettes, cassette recorders, and photographs. These materials are available to preschools as curriculum packages. They are also useful for recording, preserving, and popularizing Kenyan songs, poems, games and rhymes.

Primary Education

The minimum age of entry into primary school is six years. After eight years of primary education, pupils sit for a national examination, the Kenya Certificate of Primary Education (KCPE). The present curriculum of the primary cycle is broad and has been designed to ensure functional and practical education aimed at meeting the needs of a large number of children whose formal education terminates at the completion of this level. At the same time, the primary education program prepares those who continue to the secondary level of education.

Objectives of Primary Education

The objective of the primary cycle is to provide learning opportunities that will enable pupils to:

1. acquire literacy, numeracy, and manipulative skills;

2. develop self-expression, self-discipline, self-reliance, and full utilization of senses;

3. develop ability for clear logical thought and critical judgment;

4. experience a meaningful course of study that will lead to enjoyment and successful learning and a desire to continue learning;

5. acquire a suitable basic foundation for the world of work in the context of economic and manpower needs of the nation;

6. appreciate and respect the dignity of labor;

7. develop desirable social standards and attitudes;

8. grow into a strong and healthy person;

9. develop a constructive and adaptive attitude to life based on moral and religious values and responsibilities to the community and the nation;

10. appreciate one's own as well as other peoples' cultural heritage, develop aesthetic values, and make good use of leisure time; and

11. grow toward maturity and self-fulfillment as useful and well-adjusted members of the society.

Primary Education Curriculum

The primary education curriculum aims to provide children with adequate intellectual and practical skills useful for living in both urban and rural areas. The primary curriculum is based on three broad principles. The first is improving the quality, content, and relevance of the curriculum so that it meets the needs of the majority of the children who receive no education beyond primary school. The second is making the eight years of primary education available to all primary school-age children. The third is diversifying primary education in order to enhance competence in a variety of development tasks.

The subjects taught in the primary curriculum are business, the creative arts (i.e., art and craft, music, and physical education), languages (i.e., English, Kiswahili, and mother tongue), mathematics, religion (Christian and Islamic), agriculture, general science, home science and health science, and social studies (i.e., civics, geography, and history).

The KCPE

At the end of the eight years of education, pupils sit for a national terminal examination. There are three principle objectives for the examination. First, it ranks candidates according to attainment of knowledge, skills, and attitudes as specified in various syllabi. Second, it provides an opportunity to improve primary schools by giving the schools constant feedback on candidates' performances. Finally, it can be used as the basis for selecting pupils for secondary and postprimary technical training institutes. The candidates for the KCPE are tested in six papers, covering all subjects in the primary curriculum.

Categories of Primary Schools

The majority of primary schools in Kenya are day primary schools. The schools are maintained by the government in that the government provides teachers and subsidizes parents' efforts to provide teaching and learning materials.

Another type of school is the three-tiered system of boarding schools. First, there are low-cost primary boarding schools. Presently, the Ministry of Education maintains 145 of these schools in 21 arid and semi-arid districts through grants and grants-in-aid administered by the district education boards. Another type of boarding school is the medium cost boarding primary school. These schools were established to provide boarding services where needed. Fees are supplemented by grants from the government. Finally, there are five high cost primary schools maintained by the Kenyan government. These schools have such facilities as swimming pools and libraries. To maintain such facilities, the schools have a statutory fee of K.shs. 1,800 per boarder per annum. Tuition in these schools is free as it is in all other government-maintained primary schools.

A separate system of boarding schools are the arid zone primary schools. These schools were established to implement the government policy on universal basic education for children of Kenya. Presently, the government has set up six arid zone boarding primary schools with the help of the World Bank.

TABLE 2
Primary Education: Growth of Schools, Pupils and Teachers, 1963–1986

Year	Schools	Pupils	Trained	Untrained	Total	% of Trained Teachers	Teacher-Pupil Ratio
1963	6,058	891,553	17,682	5,045	22,727	77.8	39.2
1964	5,150*	1,014,719	19,179	8,649	27,828	68.9	36.5
1965	5,078	1,020,889	20,112	10,480	30,592	65.7	33.4
1966	5,699	1,043,416	23,305	10,217	33,522	69.5	31.1
1967	5,959	1,133,179	25,050	10,622	35,672	70.2	31.8
1968	6,135	1,209,680	27,485	10,438	37,923	72.5	32.0
1969	6,111	1,282,297	30,001	8,311	38,312	78.8	33.5
1970	6,123	1,427,589	32,929	8,550	41,479	79.4	34.4
1971	6,372	1,525,498	37,617	11,779	49,396	76.2	30.9
1972	6,657	1,675,919	41,599	11,937	53,536	77.7	31.3
1973	6,932	1,816,017	43,990	12,553	56,543	77.8	32.1
1974	7,668	2,705,878	52,132	26,208	78,340	66.5	34.5
1975	8,161	2,881,155	54,823	31,284	86,107	63.7	33.5
1976	8,554	2,894,617	56,154	32,929	89,074	63.0	32.5
1977	8,896	2,974,849	59,640	30,124	89,764	66.4	33.1
1978	9,243	2,994,892	63,912	28,134	92,046	69.4	32.5
1979	9,622	3,698,196	68,361	28,401	97,762	69.9	37.8
1980	10,268	3,936,629	72,029	30,460	102,489	70.3	38.3
1981	11,127	3,980,763	76,499	34,412	110,921	70.0	35.9
1982	11,479	4,184,602	80,664	34,440	115,094	70.1	36.4
1983	11,856	4,323,921	84,036	35,673	119,776	80.2	36.1
1984	12,539	4,380,232	86,135	36,641	122,763	70.2	35.7
1986	13,392	4,843,423	99,680	43,127	142,807	69.8	33.9

*Number of schools dropped due to the amalgamation of Primary and Intermediate Schools.

Source: Ministry of Education

Growth and Development

There has been a tremendous growth in primary education since independence in Kenya (as represented in Table 2). Between 1963 and 1986, the number of primary schools rose from 6,058 to 13,392. Pupil enrollment increased from 891,553 to 4,885,925, while the number of teachers grew from 22,772 to 142,807.

There were two major increases in pupil enrollment during the 1970s. The first was in 1974 when payment of tuition fees was abolished, resulting in a 49-percent increase (from 1,816,017 in 1973 to 2,705,878 in 1974). The second was in 1979, following the introduction of free school milk, when enrollment rose by 23.3 percent (from 2,994,911 in 1978 to 3,698,246 in 1979). This expansion of primary enrollment has been accompanied by a commensurate increase in the number of teachers (see Table 2).

Special Education

Special education is for various types of exceptional persons whose educational needs deviate

TABLE 3

Special Education: Enrollment in Each Area of Handicap, 1985–1987

	Type of Handicap	1985	1986	1987
1.	*Visually handicapped*			
	(a) Special primary schools	1035	1110	1196
	(b) Secondary schools	140	158	158
	(c) Vocational training	130	160	170
	(d) Integrated programs, Hadley Correspondence Schools	186	190	190
	Total	1551	1701	1804
2.	*Hearing Impaired*			
	(a) Special primary schools	1740	2091	2190
	(b) Vocational training	215	229	245
	(c) Integrated programs	32	40	40
	Total	2187	2360	2475
3.	*Physically handicapped*			
	(a) Special primary schools	1311	1371	1402
	(b) Secondary schools	117	167	220
	(c) Integrated programs	30	40	40
	Total	1458	1578	1662
4.	*Mentally handicapped*			
	(a) Special schools	1107	1187	1220
	(b) Integrated programs	201	276	294
	Total	1308	1463	1574
	Grand Total	6504	7102	8525

from the norm due to being impaired, disabled, handicapped, or gifted and talented. In Kenya, special education caters to those with hearing, visual, mental, physical, and multiple handicaps. Special education programs, which are an integral part of each cycle of formal education, have the following additional objectives:

• to provide skills and attitude aimed at rehabilitation;

• to identify, assess, and provide early intervention for correction and rehabilitation;

• to promote awareness of the needs of the disabled and the methods of alleviating the effects of the various disabilities;

• to promote integration of the handicapped in formal education and training;

• to promote the provision and use of specialized facilities and equipment; and

• to promote measures to prevent impairment in order to limit the incidence of disabilities.

The government provides various services to the disabled through the Ministries of Education, Health, and Culture and Social Services. In 1987, special education programs within the Ministry of Education served about 8,000 children in 56 special schools and 46 integrated programs. The Ministry of Culture and Social Services also provides training in ten vocational rehabilitation centers.

Special Education Programs

Education for Visually Handicapped Children. This type of education aims to assist children in using any remaining visual abilities or to use other senses to compensate for the loss of vision. There are six special residential primary schools and one secondary school for blind children, which include both totally blind and partially sighted pupils.

Vocational training for the visually handicapped is provided at Machakos Trade Training Center and also in centers run by voluntary agencies. While in school, the visually handicapped are provided such equipment as Braille and standard typewriters, magnifying glasses, Braille protractors, compasses, and triangles.

Education for Hearing-Impaired Children. The category of the hearing impaired includes persons with various degrees of hearing loss and includes children who are unable to hear within normal limits due to physical impairment or dysfunction of the auditory mechanism distinguished by deafness. Some are unable to use speech to communicate, while others are hard of hearing.

Education for the hearing impaired is provided in 22 residential schools, two units in regular primary schools and two vocational training institutions. The existing services care for 2,190 children in special schools, 245 under vocational training and 40 in integrated regular schools as shown in Table 3.

Education for Physically Handicapped Children. Education for the physically handicapped serves persons with difficulties of movement caused by various factors (e.g., polio myelitis, cerebral palsy, accidents, and drug abuse). They may also have other disabilities (e.g., speech difficulties, hearing or visual impairments, and mental retardation), but to be classified as physically handicapped their primary disability must relate to a physical condition.

The majority of the physically handicapped children attend integrated schools from home, while the severely handicapped attend special primary and secondary schools. Some of the severely handicapped children attend regular schools while residing in small homes built by voluntary communities and large homes built by the government and voluntary agencies.

Education for Mentally Handicapped Children. Education for the mentally handicapped aims to serve children who, because of retarded intellectual development, are incapable of being educated effectively through ordinary classroom instruction. Most of the mentally handicapped children have no obvious physical disabilities that can easily be identified, and as a result their handicap is usually identified late.

There are 16 special schools for the mentally handicapped and 32 special units attached to regular primary schools, while preprimary education is offered in very few schools.

Education for Multiply Handicapped Children. This service is offered to children with more than one identifiable handicap. The children who are both physically and mentally handicapped are educated in special units within special schools while the deaf and blind are educated in a special school at Kabaranet in the Rift Valley Province of Kenya.

Education for Maladjusted Children. Maladjusted children are those who are either emotionally disturbed or socially handicapped. Children who are emotionally disturbed have behaviors inappropriate in normal educational settings as shown by inability to learn and to maintain satisfactory relationships with peers and teachers. On the other hand, socially maladjusted children have serious social problems, which might include delinquency.

The government has established ten approved schools for boys and girls who are under age 16 and who are socially maladjusted, for the purpose of correcting delinquent behavior and providing education and training. Their teaching is based on a curriculum similar to that of the regular school with a strong emphasis on vocational training and self-reliance.

Educational Assessment and Resource Centers

The government has established 27 educational assessment and resource centers in special schools to help with early identification of special needs. They also counsel parents and assist in integration of handicapped children into ordinary schools through peripatetic services, preparation of equipment, and referrals to special schools and units for placement and to hospitals for further diagnosis and treatment. The centers also conduct seminars for teachers and parents and collect information about handicapped children. The services of these centers are provided by teachers, nurses, physiotherapists, occupational therapists, and social workers on a part-time basis.

In 1987, there were 780 special education teachers, of whom 408 were professionally trained. Those with training included 43 for visual handicaps, 135 for mental handicaps, and 230 for hearing impairments. Teachers of physically handicapped children have been given only inservice training. Until 1985, all special education programs were offered at Kamwenja and Highridge Teachers Colleges. In 1986, the Kenya Institute of Special Education (KISE) was established and took over the responsibility of training teachers for

special education.

Special education is administered by both governmental and private agencies. The Ministry of Education plays a key role in the management of formal education for the handicapped. It has professional staff at the headquarters who are responsible for the administration, curriculum, and supervision of special education. The Ministry of Health and Ministry of Culture and Social Services assist in provision of staff, equipment, and related services.

Voluntary agencies have also given considerable support toward the development and management of special education. The Kenya Society for the Blind, the Kenya Society for the Deaf, the Association for the Physically Disabled of Kenya, and the Kenya Society for the Mentally Handicapped all promote education and services for the handicapped. These agencies are affiliated with international bodies and are, therefore, able to enrich Kenya with ideas on the welfare of handicapped persons.

Teacher Training in Kenya

Teacher education programs are designed to produce qualified teachers for various cycles and levels of the national system of education and training in order to achieve the objectives and policies of education.

In the past, training of preprimary teachers was accomplished through short in-service courses by the various agencies that provide and manage preprimary schools. However, since 1985 the Ministry of Education has operated a two-year, inservice program for untrained preprimary school teachers. The course takes place during the school holidays and is conducted by staff from the district centers for early childhood education using a curriculum developed by the Kenya Institute of Education. The teacher trainees are examined and awarded teacher's certificates by the Ministry of Education.

In both the national and district centers for early childhood education the training program prepares personnel to staff various preschool institutions and involves the community in improving the quality of life of young children. The training program has drawn together large numbers of trainees and teachers from different environments in Kenya. This interaction has enabled those who prepare the program to be aware of the needs of young children in different environments.

Two levels of training are offered. The regular course enrolls working preschool teachers who have at least a KCPE. The alternative course enrolls working teachers who have undergone some primary education and have acquired basic literacy. Although English is the language of training in both courses, trainers are encouraged to use Kiswahili and/or mother tongues in their instruction.

There are a large number of untrained primary school leavers in Kenya. Presently, the aim of the government is to phase out as rapidly as possible all untrained teachers in the educational system by providing adequate preservice and in-service facilities. The preservice training is offered in 15 primary teacher training colleges. Student enrollment ranges from 420 in the smallest to 1,110 in the largest colleges. In 1986, the total enrollment was 12,760 students.

There are three grades or levels of primary school teachers, known as P3, P2, and P1. The preservice course for all grades is normally advertised in the local press. All candidates wishing to be considered for training as teachers are required to present themselves in person at their nearest zonal education office for registration. Each candidate must provide original academic certificates before being issued a registration form. Selection is based on the oral interviews and candidates' certificates and experience in teaching as untrained teachers.

The preservice course is two years in duration. During this time students are expected not only to acquire the skills and techniques for teaching various subjects, but also to update their academic knowledge in the 13 subjects taught in primary schools. Two-thirds of the training is devoted to methodology, while the remainder is content-related. Part of methodology work occurs during practice teaching. Continuous assessments are an important component of evaluation.

In the past, in-service training has been referred to as a "refresher course," "orientation course," "upgrading course," "crash program," and "induction course." The current name, however, is "in-service course." Courses for untrained teachers combine distance education and residential training during school holidays and weekends. Courses are also offered by radio through the Ministry of Education Media Service. Course work takes place over a period of three years. At the end of the second year, there is a semi-final examination. The final examination is taken at the end of the third year. A final teaching assessment by external examiners is undertaken during the last school term of the course.

Candidates who fail are permitted to repeat their examinations as many times as they wish or until they pass. In addition, single in-service courses are periodically offered to both trained and untrained teachers to highlight a problem area or a new development in the curriculum. Courses that deal with changes in the curriculum or in nationally recognized problem areas are organized by the Chief Inspector of Schools. Other courses are organized by the provincial education officers and the district education officers.

The main source of financial support for preschool programs is the Ministry of Education. However, this is not sufficient. In an attempt to deal with this problem, the Ministry has established a policy of partnership. The Ministry is responsible for the overall administration, provision of policy and professional guidance, provision of grants for training, provision of program staff at all levels, curriculum development, and research and evaluation in early childhood education.

Bilateral partners include the Bernard Van Leer Foundation, UNICEF, and the Aga Khan Foundation. The principal assistance from UNICEF and Aga Khan Foundation is in the form of grants to support the in-service course for teachers. This includes provision of materials and equipment for training and funds to hold community awareness meetings for improving children's health and welfare. UNICEF also provides motor vehicles in its respective district centers for early childhood education.

District partners include parent associations, welfare organizations, and private individuals. They are responsible for establishing and maintaining preschool institutions, and for programs concerned with children's health, nutrition, and care. They also provide salaries of the teachers in the schools they sponsor. At the district level, the local authorities are the strongest partners because they heavily subsidize the cost of the day-to-day operation of the preschool program.

Finally, the school milk and feeding programs provide a valuable service for primary school children in Kenya. The school milk program, instituted in 1979, supplies all primary children free milk. Currently, each child receives 0.2 liters of milk twice a week. More than 5.18 million children participate in this government-funded program.

The school feeding program is a joint project of the government and UN/FAO World Food Programme. It provides midday meals to primary and preprimary children in the arid and semi-arid districts of Kenya. The program started in 1981 in two regions, Turkana and West Pokot. It has been extended to other arid and semi-arid districts, which include Samburu, Baringo, Garissa, Mandera, Wajri, Narok, Kajiado, Marsabit, Lamu, Tana River, and a small part of Laikipia District. Recently, due to drought, parts of Machakos, Meru, Embu, and Kitui districts have also been brought into this program on an emergency basis.

References

Mdithi, et al. (1977). *Self-Help in Kenya: The case of Harambee.* Scandinavian Institute of African Studies, Uppsala.

Ministry of Education. (1987). *Education in Kenya: Information handbook.* Printed by Jomo Kenyatta Foundation.

Kamunge J.M. (1980). *Report of the presidential working party of education and manpower training for the next decade and beyond.* Government Printer, March.

Kipkorir, L. I. 1987. Innovations in Early Childhood Education and Care—The Kenya Experience. In *Early childhood education in Kenya: Implication and policy and practice* (p. 54). Jadini Seminar Report No. 31 of Sept. 4, 1984. Nairobi: Kenya Institute of Education.

EARLY CHILDHOOD EDUCATION IN LIBERIA

••••••••••◆••••••••

J. Nyanquoi Gormuyor
Cuttington University College
Monrovia, Liberia

This chapter provides a brief history of early childhood education, social policy, and legislation concerning the education and care of young children in Liberia. It also discusses recent initiatives in Liberia's early childhood education.

Liberia has two distinct systems of education: (1) the traditional system, founded on tribal lore or Moslem teachings, and (2) the modern system, centered on Western educational practices. The traditional system of education was the only means of educating children before the introduction of Western education by the Americo-Liberian settlers in the early 19th century.

The ethnic groups that inhabit Liberia came from different parts of Africa, migrating into the country at different times. The closeness of the settlements created and encouraged similarities in certain cultural practices. For example, certain ethnic groups found mainly in the north central and western parts of the country developed an organized system of education. These ethnic groups consist of the Vai, Gola, Mende, Lorma, Bassa, Kpelle, Gbandi, Kissi, Belle, and Dey, among others. The institutions they established are known as the *poro* (for boys) and the *sande* (for girls). These institutions culminate the training of the indigenous youth, which begins in the home.

The *poro* is conducted in a secluded grove, which is off-limits to females and noninitiates. Every male child, without exception, is eligible to attend the *poro*. There is no official age limit, but generally the boys should be able to perform some manipulative tasks. Once they enter the grove, they do not return and they must not be seen by any female or noninitiate until the end of the session, which used to be four years.

Among the aims of the *poro* are to preserve the culture and to enable the initiate to perform his assigned roles in society. Emphasis is placed on physical development, acquisition of fundamental skills essential to the survival of the individual, development of character, and appreciation of art. The boy must be strong and brave to defend his family and tribe at all times. The methods of instruction consist of discovery, role playing, observation, and imitation. The activities are centered on games, problem-solving, storytelling, learning by doing, etc.

The *sande* is the female counterpart of the *poro*. Like the *poro*, the *sande* is held in a secluded grove that is off-limits to males and noninitiates. Everything about the *poro* is the same for the *sande*, ex-

337

cept that it used to last three years. The girls are taught to perform the roles assigned to them by the tribe, that is, they must be loyal and faithful wives when they grow up.

Since 1962, the government issued certain rules and regulations to govern the *poro* and the *sande* societies so that they do not conflict with the Western-type schools. Among other things, these regulations stated that the *poro* and *sande* shall not remain in active groups for more than 18 months, and that it shall be unlawful for the *poro* and *sande* to forcefully admit for initiation any nonmember without the consent of the father or elderly family head who stands in for local parents. No *poro* or *sande* session, as a policy, shall conflict with the operation of local schools, which take precedence in the enrollment of boys and girls of school age. (Bureau of Folkways, Department of Interior, 1962: 3).

Introduction of Western Education

The first efforts toward establishing Western education in Liberia were made by individual members of the Americo-Liberian settlers and U.S. philanthropic organizations (*The African Repository*, XII, 1836). These settlers, who considered themselves missionaries, had the commitment to obey Christ's command to preach the gospel. They soon realized, however, that to accomplish this aim they had to teach the people to read and write so that they could read the scriptures themselves. As a result, the curriculum consisted of reading, writing, and arithmetic in addition to religious instruction. Vocational subjects were also taught, with the girls studying home arts while the boys learned basic agriculture skills and trades.

It is important to note that a majority of these early immigrants, having no formal education, were themselves barely literate. Some had taught themselves to read and write. One of the leading figures in this group was the Rev. Lott Carey. As a young man, he had learned to read a few chapters of the New Testament Bible with the aid of some fellow workers (*The African Repository*, XII, 1836).

When Reverend Carey arrived in Liberia with other immigrants, he focused on the education of the youth. His efforts were mainly directed toward teaching indigenous children who were adopted into settlers' families. His schools were partly supported by the Baptist Missionary Society of Richmond, Virginia. Because of the lack of knowledge about the interior of the country, efforts were limited to providing schools and schooling for the settler community and their descendants.

The lack of the formal education on the part of these early settlers played a significant role in determining the development of Western education in Liberia. Even at the time of repatriation, the American Colonization Society (ACS) did not include education in its plan (*ibid.*) This was one of the factors that hindered the growth of education in the early days of Liberia. But, when Jehundi Ashumun became agent of the colony and persisted in requesting the ACS to include education, the Board of Managers of the Society, on October 1, 1830, adopted the following resolutions:

> The Board of Managers of the American Colonization Society, anxious to extend the colony at Liberia, the blessing of useful knowledge, whereby all its inhabitants may eventually enjoy the means of developing their resources, of improving their moral and intellectual conditions, and of thus presenting to Africa, a model worthy of general imitation, consider the universal education of the children, as among the most effectual instruments of securing this objective.
>
> That to this end, schools fitted to the state of the colony, shall be forthwith established . . . ; in which reading, writing and arithmetic shall be taught to all the children, and such other branches as circumstances may from time to time render expedient.
>
> That . . . it will be proper to introduce as far as practicable, the Lancastrian mode of instruction (under this system, a single teacher taught several hundred pupils by using brighter pupils as monitors . . .); to use female instructors for the younger children . . . (*The African Repository* VI, 1836: 257–59).

This Lancastrian system was introduced into the colony because of the serious shortage of teachers and the low attraction to the teaching profession. The above resolutions further provided that the schools would be funded by the proceeds from licenses, fines, and taxes from real or personal properties. As well, $500 per year was promised by the board to be paid in provisions from the public store in the colony. These funds were, however, slow to come.

Finally, parents had to pay some of the cost of educating their children. It was believed that this would make them feel responsible for their children's education and at the same time justify the government's support of education.

Unfortunately, the board and the colonial government's efforts failed to usher in a firm foundation for education in the colony. Coupled with the earlier reasons that hindered the growth of education in the colony, the ACS regrettably did not want to take the full responsibility for education. It failed to pay the meager tax levied on it.

Another issue that exacerbated the situation was the lack of textbooks and school supplies. The agent, Ashmun, addressed himself to this issue when he proposed to the Board of Managers that "the want of school books is likewise a great impediment to the progress of elementary education in the colony." (*The African Repository* IV, 1836: 40). Later, he informed the board again that "there is at present a great want of school books and stationery" (*ibid.*).

These efforts failed to attract the necessary attention. As a result, many of the schools were closed by the colonial council. However, the board did not endorse these closures, and instead passed a resolution in 1834 "that the managers take proper steps to provide for the extension and permanent establishment of good common schools in the colony, so that every child may at least become acquainted with the first rudiments of education" (Huberich, 1947: 463).

Missions and the National Education Plan

The move by the board in 1834 began a new chapter in the development of education in Liberia. An appeal was made to Christian missions to come to Liberia to spread Christianity and "Western civilization" among the people in the colony. This could not have been possible without Western education. Thus, the 1830s saw the beginning of the progress of the work of Christian missions in the colony, which extended up to the 20th century.

The colonial government, realizing the importance of education and its inability to provide it, supported the missions by granting land for the construction of schools and the education of the children of the colony.

In 1839, a new constitution was established. It changed the status of the separate and scattered settlements to a commonwealth. As a result of the unity that consequently culminated into a common front, the settlers became more aware of the desire to educate their children. Little was done materially to realize this dream. However, as a government, they did make an effort by the promulgation of a series of measures concerning education. One such pronouncement was the Act Regulating Common Schools, passed in 1839. Below are excerpts of this pronouncement:

Sec. 1. Be it enacted by the Governor and Council of the Commonwealth of Liberia, in Legislature assembled, That there shall be established in each settlement a township . . . one common school, the same to be under the supervision or control of a school committee . . .
Sec. 2. . . . there shall be a teacher whose appointment shall come from the governor and school committee . . .
Sec. 3. . . . that at the sum of three dollars per year be paid . . . [by the student] parent or guardian of all those who may be admitted into these schools . . .
Sec. 5. . . . that each teacher of common schools shall receive for his services a sum not exceeding four hundred dollars per annum to be paid to him quarterly.
Sec. 8. . . . that all persons shall be bound by law to send their children to school, (provided their ages vary from five to twelve years), and whosoever fails to comply . . . shall . . . pay a fine of three dollars . . . to go into the hands of the school committee for the benefit of the school (Huberich, 1947: 1390–91).

This act was the first attempt made to establish a national education plan in Liberia. In reality, adequate funds were not available to implement the extensive public school system the Education Act demanded. Almost all of the schools were supported by religious and philanthropic organizations. All (16) of the teachers were foreign and the curriculum placed heavy emphasis on religious teaching (Roberts, et al., 1972).

The education census of 1843 revealed a total of 16 schools in the commonwealth; 11 were operated by the missionary Society of the Methodist Episcopal Church, two by the Baptist Church, one by the Presbyterian Church, and two by the commonwealth. There were a total of 562 students, of which 192 were indigenous children (Huberich, 1947).

Missions began to extend into the interior of the country, where they were encouraged by the government to establish schools for the education of more indigenous children. Up until 1960, these missions dominated the education of the tribal children in the interior while the government limited its efforts to providing education for children in the coastal counties.

The 1839 compulsory education act was reauthorized in 1841 and 1868. In 1912, it was completely revised. It provided for the age range of 6–12 years, making exceptions for children suffering from physical and mental disabilities. Schooling was not compulsory for the disabled (Azango, 1968). There is no available record concerning the provision of special education for them during this time.

It is also worthy to note, however, that though there exists in law a compulsory education act, little is done to enforce it. Thousands of school-age children are not attending school. The declaration of free public schools appeared in the law of 1912. However, it was not passed until 1944, at which time only elementary schools were made free (*ibid.*).

In 1912, measures were also taken to prohibit child labor, which was a common practice prior to this time. The passage of the child labor prohibition in 1912 was intended to ensure that every child benefited from the compulsory attendance law. The labor prohibition law states: "[I]t shall be unlawful for any person to employ or hire any child under the age of 16 years during the hours when he is required to attend school" (*ibid.*: 142). This law regrettably has not been enforced either. Many children can be seen in the streets selling merchandise and washing cars. In the hinterland, children are made to preform various tasks on farms.

Expansion of Education by Government

Public schools increased rapidly following World War II, and by 1960, there was high student enrollment and an increase in the number of teachers. The quality of education dropped, however, because teachers could not be properly trained and funds were not sufficient to provide the needed books and teaching aids. In 1960, the government called for a ten-year development program to improve standards as well as to expand

facilities. This plan also called for the establishment of teacher training institutions and the provision of scholarships for teacher training abroad (Roberts, et al. 1972).

The government's aim was universal elementary education during this period. However, this aim was often criticized because of the limited resources that had to be spent on providing a little education for a lot of children.

A reorganization of the school system in 1960 changed the system from the 8–4 system to the present 6–3–3. It was done in recognition of the fact that there exists a distinction between these various levels and as such they must be kept separate.

Preschool and Elementary Education

Preschool education in Liberia is offered mainly by private individuals. These people operate day care centers or nursery schools for children whose parents work in offices and industries in the urban areas. In addition, the Ministry of Education, through the Division of Preprimary Education, operates a day care center for children of market women of the Nancy B. Doe Market in Sinkor, Monrovia. This center, which charges a minimal fee of $3.50 per child per month, assists the market women with the care of their children while they are engaged in marketing activities. The center also teaches them skills necessary to prepare them for grade 1. It also provides them with food and other needed supplies. The center is co-sponsored by UNICEF, the Ministry of Education, and the Ministry of Health and Social Welfare (*Primary Education Bulletin*, 1988). The sponsors of the program intend to extend the opportunity of a day care center to other market women in other regions throughout Liberia. This will be a monumental achievement, since these services now exist only in Montserrado.

The Division of Preprimary Education has also embarked on a campaign to focus public attention on early childhood development activities. In April 1989, the division conducted, in two phases, a workshop on early childhood development. The workshop was sponsored by UNICEF. The participants discussed the need for and the utilization of both the human and material resources to promote early childhood development . . . support in establishing day care centers and alternative programs for urban slums and rural areas . . . goals and objectives of the approaches by different centers to early childhood development . . . the need for facilities and supplies for carrying out adequate education and child care in child care centers, and the production of materials for early childhood development (*Primary Education Bulletin*, 2(1): 8 (1989).

Kindergartens are found in almost every part of the country where there are elementary schools. They admit children from age 4 or younger depending on the child's readiness. They are operated both by the government and private individuals. In 1962, an attempt was made by the then Secretary of Education to abolish public kindergartens and to place them under private management because the government could not afford the cost of operation. Tuition fees are charged in private kindergartens, while registration and other miscellaneous fees are charged in public kindergartens.

The primary system consists of one to three years of preprimary education followed by six years of primary education. In theory, children should enter at age 6, but because many children do not have birth records, age is not a determinant in admission. Enrollments (grades 1–6) were estimated to be 146,508, in 1984, of which about 37 percent were in private schools. Approximately 37 percent of the students were female (Education and Human Resources Sector Assessment, Sept. 1988).

Enrollments in primary school declined by 37 percent between 1984–89, mainly as a result of the declining economic condition of Liberia and the high miscellaneous fees charged. In theory, primary education is free, but registration and other miscellaneous fees charged to attend a primary school are estimated at $38 per student (*ibid.*).

Other problems that beset primary education are the inavailability of instructional materials in schools due to high cost, under-qualified and unqualified teachers, and high drop-out rates. The Ministry of Education has tried to address these problems through a World Bank-funded textbook project and the USAID-funded project, the Primary Education Program (PEP).

PEP consists of an instructional system for Liberian primary schools. Programmed instructional materials are available for language, reading, mathematics, science, social studies, and health for grades 1 to 6. The ultimate aim of this program is to upgrade the quality of education in all public primary schools in Liberia by providing low-cost instructional materials, teacher training, and the supervision of classroom teachers (Primary Education Project, Brochure, 1987).

The Ministry of Education has identified primary education as one of its major priorities for development in its five-year development plan for 1990–95. There will be an intensive in-service teacher training program and supervision workshops to support this effort.

References

African Repository. (1836). 3: 22; 4, 40; 5, 257–59; 7, 22.

Azango, B. (1968). *Education laws of the republic of Liberia*. pp. 79, 141–42.

Bureau of Folkways. Department of Interior. (1962). p. 3.

Huberich, C. (1947). *The political and legislative history of Liberia*. pp. 463, 759, 1390, 1391. New York: Central Book Co.

IEES (Improving the Efficiency of Education Systems). (1988). Liberia: Education and human resources sector assessment, pp. 1–18.

Primary Education Bulletin (Bureau of Primary Education, Ministry of Education). 1988, 1989. 1(2), 4; 2(1), 8.

Primary Education Project: An Instructional System for Liberian Primary schools. (1987). pp. 1–2.

Roberts, T., et al. (1972). *U.S. Army Area Handbook for Liberia*. Washington, D.C.: U.S. Government Printing Office.

PRESCHOOL EDUCATION IN MALAYSIA

●●●●●●●●●●◆●●●●●●●●●

Rohaty Mohd Majzub
National University of Malaysia
Bangi, Selangor, Malaysia

Preschool education in Malaysia refers to the education of 4- to 6-year-olds in preschool centers. In Malaysia, preschool education is more popularly known as kindergarten (*tadika*). It operates separately from primary education, which begins at age 6 and is free from grade 1 to grade 6. Kindergartens are also conducted separately from nursery education, which serves children from birth to age 4. This chapter focuses on preschool education for children ages 4 to 6.

Preschool education centers in Malaysia are sponsored and organized by various groups, including governmental bodies, quasi-governmental agencies, and private organizations. In the early 1960s, preschool served only the children of the wealthy. Today, it is more popular and serves poor and disadvantaged families as well. The popularity of kindergartens is evident from statistics indicating that the enrollment in 1979 of 120,618, had increased by 1989 to 331,592.

In Malaysia, primary and secondary education is incorporated into the formal established educational structure. It is well-organized through an orderly administration with clear and specific rules and regulations which control and supervise the system. Unfortunately, preschool education does not have the same advantages or facilities. The regulations that exist for it are found in two documents: the Education Act of 1961 and the Education Method (kindergarten and nursery school regulation of 1972). The Education Method is restricted to matters regarding registration.

There is also diversity with respect to the philosophical orientations of preschool education, curriculum, teaching, and learning activities; the sponsoring agencies; and the fees for preschool education. Similarly, diversity exists concerning the academic and professional qualifications of preschool teachers and administrators. There is also a concern for the quality of preschool graduates entering the primary schools. The end product of preschool education is, therefore, marked by diversity in educational experience and academic readiness.

Development of Preschool Education

Kindergartens originated in Malaysia in the 1950s and 1960s. During that period, preschool education was organized by voluntary church organizations and individuals. Kindergartens were limited to the wealthy because of the high fees involved. However, in 1970 the Community Development Division (KEMAS) of the Ministry of National and Rural Development started model preschool centers known as the *tabikas*. KEMAS ("Kemajuan Masyarakat") became very active in developing preschool centers in rural areas. Other governmental and quasi-governmental agencies were also involved in preschool education. For example, the Federal Land Development Authority (FELDA) established a preschool in 1970 as part of its development strategy for settlers in the re-settlement schemes. In 1976, the National Unity Board (MPM) started a preschool with the objective of promoting national integration and unity among children of different ethnic origins in Malaysia. The Rubber Industry Small Holders Development Authority (RISDA) established preschools to improve the life of its settlers. The involvement of these agencies not only increased the number of preschool centers, but also widened the opportunities for preschool education among the disadvantaged. The Third Malaysia Plan (1976–80) also stressed the opportunities for preschool education for the disadvantaged.

In 1972, the role and contribution of the Ministry of Education became more defined. The Curriculum Development Center (CDC) of the Ministry of Education, with the sponsorship of Bernard Van Leer Foundation, undertook a remedial education project that culminated in the publication of *A Guide for Preschool Education* (1986). In addition, experimental preschool centers were set up by the CDC to test preschool goals and ideas.

In 1975, an international conference in preschool education was held with the help of Ford Foundation. To further promote preschool teacher training, the Sabah Foundation established an institute for preschool teachers at its child development center, to provide training for prospective preschool teachers. In 1976, the Specialist Teacher's Training Institute embarked on a scheme to train primary school teachers in preschool education. The Kindergarten Association of Malaysia, established in 1973, also conducted a training program for preschool teachers during school vacations.

Preschool seminars were also held in Malaysia, notably those organized by the Educational Planning and Research Division of the Ministry of Education with UNICEF funding. Preschool teacher training was also conducted in the Department of Human Development, Agriculture University in Serdang, and by the Faculty of Education, University Kebangsaan, Malaysia. In 1991, the Minister of Education, Anwar Ibrahim, announced that the Ministry of Education proposes to set up kindergarten classes in rural primary schools. This commitment implies that the Ministry will assume the responsibility of training kindergarten teachers.

Rapid growth in preschool education occurred in the 1980s: in 1979, there were 2,227 preschool centers, ten years later, the number of centers reached 6,959. Both the numbers of centers and children enrolled in preschool programs have tripled in this short time. In 1989, in terms of sponsoring agencies, KEMAS organized 4,256 preschool centers, compared with the private sector preschools totaling 1,392 centers. One of the major objectives of KEMAS is to redress the unequal educational opportunities that exist, especially in the rural areas.

The great demand for private kindergartens can be explained in terms of the higher awareness of the values of preschool education by urban parents. While KEMAS offered programs for 142,173 children, private kindergartens had enrollments of 132,328. Table 1 lists the percentage of preschools/kindergartens by agency. Governmental and semi-governmental agencies formed about 73 percent of centers.

It is evident from Table 1 that girls and boys have almost equal enrollment (168,631 males and 162,961 females). However, most teachers are female (147 preschool teachers are male). It can also be observed that private sector preschools have smaller classes than government preschools. In private sector preschools, several classes exist in one center.

The average number of children in centers is 34 for governmental agency preschools, 46 for quasi-governmental preschools, and 110 for private sector preschools. There is an average of one teacher per center in the government-agency-sponsored preschools compared with three or four teachers in private centers.

A factor in preschool centers in Malaysia is racial polarization. It was observed that Bumiputera

TABLE 1

Distribution of Preschool Centers According to Agencies, Preschoolers, Teachers, and Sex*

| Agencies | Preschoolers | | Teachers | | | |
	Male	Female	Male	Female	Class	Center
ABIM	5,526	4,764	0	498	362	204
BINA Sarawak	131	132	0	12	10	10
FELCRA*	79	76	0	14	7	6
FELDA*	8,920	8,961	0	672	526	208
KEMAS*	71,757	70,416	0	7,418	4,349	4,526
Police	563	520	0	47	35	29
Perpaduan						
(MPM)*	7,983	8,278	0	903	440	404
Private	68,266	64,062	47	5,388	4,679	1,392
JAIS	5,266	5,312	0	506	317	171
University	198	187	0	38	18	4
Sabah Foundation	63	65	0	13	6	1
PERKIM	179	188	0	15	15	4
Total:	168,931	162,961	47	15,524	10,764	6,959

* These belong to government-sponsored preschools.

Source: Education Planning and Research Division, Ministry of Education, Malaysia, 1984.

children (Malays) tend to go to government and quasi-government preschools, while Chinese and Indian parents favor sending their children to the private sector schools. A 1984 report demonstrated that only 4.1 percent of Chinese preschoolers and 22.7 percent Indian preschoolers were in government preschools compared with 85.4 percent of the Bumiputera preschoolers. One reason for these figures may be that a majority of Bumiputera children are found in the rural areas where government preschools abound, whereas the private centers are primarily urban (Status Report on Preschool Education, 1984). Figures also reveal that the private sector preschools are dominated by the Chinese, while the Indians appear to be evenly spread among the various kindergartens.

The choice of preschool centers is also determined by the socioeconomic status of the parents. The 1984 report also showed that the parents in most private kindergartens are likely to have a diploma or a degree. The distribution of children in preschool centers is also determined by the occupation of parents. In large towns, children whose parents are professionals are more likely to be in private kindergartens. Parents' occupation and income are less likely to be a variable in rural areas, where the choice is largely restricted to government centers.

Government and Quasi-Government Preschools

KEMAS, MPM, and FELDA are large-scale operators of preschool education. Other agencies include the Federal Land Consolidation and Rehabilitation Authority (FELCRA), the RISDA, the Ministry of Rural and Urban Development Sabah (KPBD), and the Aboriginal Affairs Department (JHEOA).

The 1984 status report noted the centralized and bureaucratic nature of preschool organization within the governmental and quasi-governmental agencies. Decisions made at the federal level take a long time to reach preschools. Lack of effective coordination and supervision has resulted in multiple interpretations of rules and regulations at all levels. The smooth operation of preschools depends on the discretion and commitment of officials at the periphery.

It is important to note that preschool education forms only a small part of the total community development strategy and programs of various governmental and quasi-governmental agencies. Because of this, the management of preschool education is only one responsibility and duty of officers in the agencies. It has been observed that most officials involved lack knowledge about preschool education. For example, an officer of KEMAS (the Supervisor of Family Development) not only supervises and coordinates preschool activities at the district level, he is also responsible for the management and supervision of such activities as the Rural Entrepreneur Program, the Beautiful Home Project, home economics classes, and other community training schemes. The Supervisor of Family Development also has to assume the role of headmaster in districts that have from 14 to 36 centers.

These officials must attend a special course organized by KEMAS before being appointed to their post. Unfortunately, the supervision of preschool centers and preschool education forms only a small portion of the course content.

As a result, government kindergartens have suffered. Poor and ineffective coordination and supervision have led to undesirable practices and the use of educationally unsuitable material and teaching aids. Weekend workshops, which should be conducted by the district supervisors, are often not held. The centers are poorly maintained. The communities are minimally involved in the continued growth and well-being of centers. In some cases, because government preschools lack a headmaster or headmistress (the officer assuming that role for a number of preschools), a teacher in the school often volunteers to perform that function.

Private Preschools

Private sector preschool centers are organized by individuals, religious organizations, or community associations. In community associations, a principal or head teacher is appointed to manage the center. While a preschool committee is appointed to oversee the general welfare and running of the center, including the appointment of teachers.

The number of classes in each unit in centers operated by individuals is generally less than those organized by an association. Depending on the number of classes, teachers are appointed to assist in the running of the center.

Coordination and supervision are not problems in private preschools. However, their is little agreement regarding curriculum or method among the private sector preschools. One difficulty is that not all centers are registered with the Ministry of Education and as a result they escape supervision. In any case, quality control and supervision are rarely done by Ministry officials. When visits are made, they are generally for the purpose of license application and inspection of physical premises. Visits usually occur only once every four to five years.

Preschools and Voluntary Organizations

Voluntary organizations—such as the Armed Forces, the Welfare Association, the Police Association, and others—provide preschool education as part of their community services. Each organization has an education committee, which appoints a principal who is responsible to the committee on matters relating to the preschool center.

The 1984 report on the status of preschools, observed that centers organized by voluntary organizations lacked clear policy guidelines. In addition, they tended to have difficulty recruiting suitable supervisors and administrators. As with centers operated by individuals, Ministry officials rarely visit these preschools.

Preschool Curricula

According to the 1984 status report, there are four main types of preschool curricula. First, is the official curriculum of governmental and quasi-governmental agencies, except for the Islam Foundations preschool. It is based on principles of child development with a heavy focus on the social life of children. However, there is no requirement that kindergartens implement the official curriculum.

The second type of curriculum focuses on mastery of reading, writing, and arithmetic. Academic readiness involves teaching such subjects as spelling, reading, language, writing, drawing and handicraft, arithmetic, physical education, and speech. The teaching of reading, writing, and arithmetic is done in a more systematic and structured approach. The curriculum offered in the preschool is quite similar to that of the new primary school curriculum.

The third type of curriculum focuses on the development of the whole child. The number of preschool centers in this category is rather small. The centers generally have very experienced and qualified administrators who are interested in preschool education. A more informal and relaxed learning climate exists.

The fourth type of curriculum is characterized by a lack of defined goals or objectives beyond mastery of reading, writing, and basic arithmetic. The classroom environment is very formal with homework routinely assigned. There is a reliance on commercially produced curriculum materials.

A major concern facing preschool education in Malaysia is curriculum duplication. The preschools that emphasize reading, writing, and arithmetic are in fact teaching the new primary

school curriculum for the primary schools. As a result, children are bored with their primary school experience. Private preschools have traditionally had an academic orientation, with retired primary school teachers making up the largest group of experienced teachers in the private sector. The problem of duplication arises because preschool teachers are unaware of the new primary school curriculum and preschools resist changing the formal school system.

The majority of rural preschools (i.e., those operated by governmental or voluntary agencies) use Bahasa Malaysia (the national language) as the language of instruction. However, the largely urban private preschools use English. Chinese and Tamil private kindergartens use Bahasa Malaysia and English, respectively.

The differences in goals and orientations among the various kindergartens in Malaysia, based on location, type, and medium of instruction, have implications for preschool policy development. For example, at issue is whether differences should be encouraged. Primary school teacher training programs must examine such issues as diversity as part of their program of study.

The effects of preschool tend to be greater among children from disadvantaged backgrounds.

TABLE 2

Academic Qualification of Teachers According to the Location of Kindergarten

Academic Qualification	Urban Areas (%/Number)	Rural Areas (%/Number)
Completed primary school education	5.0 (9)	5.7 (8)
Attended Islamic religious school	1.7 (3)	4.3 (6)
SRP/LCE	20.4 (37)	39.7 (56)
SPM/MCE	64.6 (17)	48.2 (68)
STP/HSC/diploma	6.0 (1)	0.7 (1)
University education	0.6 (1)	0.7 (1)
No response	1.7 (3)	0.7 (1)
TOTAL	100 (181)	100 (141)

Key: SRP=Sijil Rendah Pelajaran; LCE=Lower Certificate of Education; SPM=Sijil Pelajaran Malaysia; MCE=Malaysian Certificate of Education; STP=Sijil Tinggi Persekolahan; HSC=Higher School Certificate

Source: *Status Report on Preschool Education* (1984).

Children from these groups usually obtain significantly higher scores in the national language, mathematics, English, and Chinese. This is found to be true without regard to location of school (urban or rural) or type of preschool (private, agency, or government-sponsored).

Child Evaluation

The 1984 status study report observed that there do not seem to be any standardized evaluation methods or procedures in preschool centers to evaluate the children's development. In centers that focus on reading, writing, and arithmetic, monthly and term tests are usually given. Private preschools form the largest percentage of those who evaluate children's progress.

Preschool Teacher Training

In Malaysia, kindergartens prefer to recruit teachers with Sijil Pelajaran Malaysia or the Malaysian Certificate of Examination. According to the 1984 status report, more teachers in rural centers have only a primary education. (Table 2 compares the academic qualifications of teachers in urban and rural areas.)

Teacher Training

In Malaysia, teacher training colleges and universities do not offer training in early education. A variety of professional training programs of different quality and levels are conducted by various agencies that sponsor preschool education. These include FELDA, KEMAS, and the PTM (Kindergarten Association of Malaysia). FELDA conducted a six-month course for untrained FELDA preschool supervisors and teachers. Unlike FELDA, which trains only its own supervisors and teacher, KEMAS conducts a three-month course that serves its teachers as well as those of DARA (Development Authority for Pahang Tenggara), FELCRA, RISDA, JAIN (state Islamic religious departments), and MPM teachers. The Kindergarten Association of Malaysia (MTM) conducts a six-stage training program over a three-year period for private sector teachers and voluntary organizations. PTM also organizes short courses for beginning preschool teachers.

Table 3 shows the diversity of training programs in Malaysia. There is a need to coordinate the courses to offer a more unified view of preschool education.

TABLE 3

Distribution of Teachers According to Their Professional Qualifications

Professional Qualifications	Percentage/Number
Malaysian Association of Kindergartens Certificate	14.0 (45)
KEMAS Certificate	32.0 (106)
FELDA Certificate	4.7 (15)
Montessori Diploma	1.9 (6)
University Diploma with Preschool Education as a subject	1.2 (4)
MPM Certificate	0.3 (1)
Certificate From Foreign Institutions	0.9 (3)
Church Certificate	0.6 (2)
RISDA Certificate	1.9 (6)
Certificate in Special Education	10.9 (35)
Attending Training	8.7 (28)
Retired Teachers	2.5 (8)
No Professional Training	16.5 (53)
No Response	2.3 (9)
TOTAL	98.4 (321)

Source: Status Report on Preschool Education (1984).

Salaries of preschool teachers range from less than $150, to more than $600 per year. Quasi-governmental preschool teachers form the greatest percentage of those earning less than $150 (37 percent). Private sector teachers tend to have larger salaries.

Physical Facilities

Approximately 20 percent of the government centers use multi-purpose buildings, (e.g., community halls, mosques, former school canteens, or buildings belonging to boy scout associations and Rukun Tetangga Beat). These premises are generally unsafe for kindergarten children and are also subject to vandalism. Private sector kindergartens are more likely to own or rent buildings, homes, or terrace houses for the sole purpose of preschool education.

Government preschools rarely have sufficient teaching materials and furnishings. Private centers, on the other hand, are equipped with blackboards, books, abacus, and drawing boards. The higher the fees charged, the more able a center is to provide adequate facilities. Fees collected are often used to buy food and drinks, as well as to purchase teaching materials.

Government and quasi-government preschools may charge as little as $1 per month, whereas private urban preschool fees can reach as high as $100 a month.

Governmental funding for preschools, ranging from $500 to $4,000, is provided either on a yearly basis or as a start-up grant. Often, government schools receive equipment, such as stoves, cassette recorders, and teaching materials, instead of money. FELDA makes allocations to all its preschool centers. The state Religious Department also gives allocations to JAIN preschools. Donations do not constitute a major source of income for preschools.

Future of Early Education in Malaysia

The 1984 status report raised many concerns, which have been discussed at several national seminars on preschool education. In addition, the Ministry of Education and universities have expressed concern in matters pertaining to preschool education. The issues raised include the lack of definite curriculum orientation and objectives in preschools sponsored by different agencies. Proposals are now being prepared to create a uniform curriculum for all preschools in line with the national education philosophy.

A preschool curriculum for 4- to 6-year-olds, called the Garis Panduan Kurikulum Pra Sekolah Malaysia, has been developed by the Curriculum Development Center of the Ministry of Education. This is a curriculum package that is available for use in preschool centers. There are plans for the Curriculum Development Center and the Task Force on Preschool to undertake an evaluation of the curriculum.

Another major issue is preschool administration and management. There are two systems of management and administration in the preschools. Suggestions were made to ensure that preschool managers and administrators possess the relevant professional qualifications and are employed on a full-time basis.

The major study, *Status of Preschool Education in Malaysia*, also reveals a wide difference in training for preschool teachers. There is a need for a minimum academic qualification and a system of in-service training for working teachers.

Another important issue is the lack of registration and control of preschool centers. There is inadequate attention to regulations concerning the safety and health of the children. A lack of real control over fees has also led to a great discrepancy between those collected by private and government preschools. The private kindergartens are independently run and are not under the supervision of the government. Thus the private kindergartens are free to determine their fees, which can be very high, and to collect those fees. In addition, there is a lack of government officials to supervise and inspect the day-to-day operations of the kindergartens. This has created a polarization between the largely urban private schools and the rural government centers, thereby increasing the gap between the haves and the have nots in Malaysia.

References

Halim bin Ahmad. (1989). *Impact of preschool intervention on lower economic status children in Malaysia*. Unpublished Ph.D. dissertation. Ann Arbor, Michigan: University of Michigan.

Kurikulum Baru Sekolah Rendah. (1984). (New Primary School Curriculum) Kementerian Pelajaran Malaysia, Kuala Lumpur.

Laporan Kajian Gaya Pengajaran Guru Tadika Malaysia Masa Kini (Report on present teaching styles of preschool teachers). (1984). Bahagian perancangan dan Penyelidikan Pelajaran Kementerian Pelajaran Malaysia & UNICEF.

Laporan Kesan Pendidikan Preaekolah (Report on the Effects of Preschool Education). (n.d.). Bahagian Perancangan dan Penyelidikan Pelajaran kementerian Pelajaran Malaysia & UNICEF.

Ministry of Education. Statistics on Preschool (Data obtained from Educational Planning & Research Division). (1984). Kuala Lumpur, Malaysia.

———. (1984). *Status report of preschool education*. Educational Planning and Research Division, Ministry of Education Malaysia (in cooperation with UNICEF).

———. (1988). Education Act of 1961. (Kindergarten Regulations 1988). Malaysia.

Rohaty Mohd Majzub, Garis Panduan Kurikulum Pendidikan Prasekolah dan perkembangannya ke arah pembangunan, Laporan Seminar Kebangsaan Ke Arah Pembentukan Dasar Pendidikan Preaekolah (Proceedings of the Seminar of Policy Formulations of Preschool Education).

Rohaty Mohd Majzub. A study on the Priorities of kindergarten goals amongst experts, teachers and parents in Malaysia. (1984). Unpublished Ph.D. dissertation. Ann Arbor, Michigan: University of Michigan.

Rohaty Mohd Majzub. (1979). Isu-isu dalam Pendidikan Pra sekolah -pertimbangannya untuk Malaysia (Issues in preschool education—consideration for Malaysia) Laporan Seminar Penididkan Kebangsaan, June 1979.

Rohaty Mohd Majzub & Abu Bakar Nordin. (1989). *Pendidikan Pra Sekolah* (Preschool Education). Fajar Bakti, Kuala Lumpur.

EARLY EDUCATION IN THE MALTESE ISLANDS

• • • • • • • • • • ◆ • • • • • • • • •

Joseph A. Xerri
Primary Section
Department of Education
Malta

The Republic of Malta, situated in the middle of the Mediterranean sea, consists of three separate islands: Malta, Gozo, and Comino, with a total area of 316 square kilometers. With a population of 352,000, it is one of the most densely populated countries in Europe (over 1,000 persons per square kilometer). Malta has two official languages: Maltese and English. The semantic structure of Maltese is derived from Phoenician and Arabic, while its vocabulary includes many words of Roman and Anglo-Saxon origin due to its contact with western European culture.

Historical Background

Because of its strategic position in the Mediterranean, Malta has attracted a number of colonizers over the centuries. At different times, Malta has been colonized by the Phoenicians, Cartaginians, Romans, French, and British. Although Malta has enjoyed a certain measure of responsible government since 1921, the islands achieved full independence from Great Britain only in 1964. The result of this history of domination by foreign powers has affected both the culture and the language of Malta, which in turn has influenced its education. For example, Christianity, introduced to Malta by St. Paul in the first century, has played an important part in the setting up of the Maltese educational system.

Up to the end of the 18th century, elementary education was offered by religious orders (including the Jesuits who founded a college in 1553 that had a primary section) and some private teachers for the children of the wealthy. It was only at the end of 1799 that an attempt was made to provide elementary education for the masses. Napoleon Bonaparte, on route to Egypt, ousted the Knights of St. John from Malta. During his eight-day stay there, he initiated a reorganization of the administration of the islands. His first two edicts dealt with education.

Napoleon ordered the setting up of 15 elementary schools in Malta and Gozo to teach reading and writing, the French language, the elements of arithmetic and pilotage, the principles of morality, and the French constitution. The French authorities, however, did not have the opportunity to apply the edicts, since after only four months the Maltese rebelled against the French and ousted them from the islands with the help of Britain in 1800.

351

The major contribution of the English to Maltese education was the support of the Normal School Society, organized in 1819 by a group of Maltese and a wealthy English philanthropist under the patronage of the governor of the island. The Society organized and administered a number of public schools in Malta. However, in 1836 the British government ordered a Royal commission to inquire into Malta's affairs. The commissioners were asked to study the possibility of providing elementary education for the masses.

By that time the Normal School Society consisted of four schools with a total population of over 700 students. Some students were also attending private schools. The commissioners recommended that additional elementary schools be established to provide elementary education for the whole population. The schools were to be administered by the rector of the university. As a result, the number of schools had increased considerably by 1844. Their administration was eventually separated from that of the University and the Office of the Director of Primary Schools was created.

By 1850, the number of primary schools had grown to 28. However, only a small percentage of children attended them. Approximately one-sixtieth of the entire population of school-aged children attended the public schools, and another sixtieth, the private schools. The year 1850 also marked the beginning of a change from the monitorial system of Lancaster and Bell to the simultaneous system, and the opening of the first state-run infant schools.

Because schooling was not compulsory, many parents did not send their children to school. Many poor families with children who did attend school withdrew them as soon as they could work and contribute to the family income.

It was primarily because of a language issue that a second Royal Commission began an inquiry into the Maltese system of education in 1878. The commissioner found that 63 primary schools in Malta and 16 in Gozo were attended by 7,746 children. There were also about 100 private schools with an enrollment of approximately 2,000 children.

The curriculum in the primary schools consisted of instruction in Maltese, Italian, English, reading, grammar, spelling, writing, arithmetic, geography, religion, drawing (in urban schools),

sewing, and calisthenics (for girls), and physical drills (for boys). It was noted that the difficulty in mastering three languages was retarding progress in the primary schools.

The commission subsequently recommended that English instruction begin as soon as the children had learned to read Maltese, and Italian be taught only in the higher grades. Italian was also not to be taught within the regular school day. It could be taught after official school hours, in the evening, and on Saturday.

The introduction of these recommendations in 1880, although amended to include Italian in standards 3 and 4 (the highest classes in the primary schools), caused an uproar which resulted in what is known as the "language question."

When Britain colonized Malta, the language of the majority was Maltese. However, Maltese was regarded as a dialect by the local intelligentsia, who had cultivated the Italian language and culture for generations. As a result, Italian was the official language of Malta. and the language of the courts and the church. At first, the British government introduced English without enforcing its use. The commission's recommendations, however, caused widespread discontent. For the next 50 years, the language issue hampered progress in various fields, particularly education.

Toward the end of the 19th century, the British administrators attempted to resolve the issue by offering parents the right to choose Italian or English instruction for their children. For a variety of reasons, this was unsuccessful. Subsequently, in 1932 the British government decided to exclude Italian from the primary schools. Two years later, English and Maltese became the official languages.

In spite of all these difficulties, the number of schools and students continued to increase throughout the 19th century. According to the 1891 census, of the 37,000 children of school age (between ages 3 and 15), 13,400, or 35 percent, were registered in the public school system.

The population of Malta at the end of the 19th century was 177,736. At that time, there were 38 government-sponsored primary schools for boys and 39 for girls (including 15 attached to infant classes). There were 5, 645 boys, 6, 108 girls, and 921 infants enrolled in these schools, and average attendance was 4,532 for boys, 4,603 for girls, and

806 for infants.

More than 6,000 children were seeking admission into these schools, but they were not admitted due to the lack of accommodation. The granting of responsible government in 1921, which included the organization of a Ministry of Public Instruction with full responsibility for local education, resulted in accelerated progress in education.

In 1924, the Maltese Parliament enacted the Compulsory School Attendance Act, which obligated children who started primary school to continue to attend school until they finished the course. A school building program was also begun. However, flaws in the act soon became apparent. Children were obliged to attend school only if their parents registered them, so parents could opt not to register their children. Children could be absent for up to 25 percent of the school year. Parents were obliged to send their children up to the standard (year) that was available in their village, but in many villages classes were available only up to standard three, not the standard five that the courses consisted of. Also, children could be exempted from school if they were slow learners, and so forth. The result was widespread absenteeism, while a substantial number of parents kept their children at home. This contributed to the compulsory schooling issue, which had been debated since 1839.

A lack of human, physical, and financial resources made it difficult for the government to implement compulsory education, but in 1946 the Compulsory Education Ordinance was enacted. It obliged all parents of school-age children (i.e., ages 6 to 14) to send their children to school throughout the whole school year. Fines were levied against uncooperative parents.

Although the ordinance became law at the beginning of the 1946 school year, a lack of accommodations, school furniture, and teachers resulted in extremely low numbers of children in full-time attendance. Many children were able to attend only half-day. Selected private schools were provided with government funds for accommodating public school children. This makeshift situation prevailed until the 1950s, when a major school building program and the hiring of emergency teachers made it possible for the local authorities to finally be able to offer full-time schooling to all children. At this time, all students attending state primary schools were provided with free books, copybooks, and milk.

Current Legislation

In Malta, education is governed by legislation, as well as by the Constitution. Article 11 of the Constitution states: "Primary Education shall be compulsory and in State schools and shall be free from charge." The Constitution gives parents the right to withdraw their children from religion lessons until they are age 16, at which time the students have the right to decide whether to attend these lessons.

While education has been governed by the Constitution and laws since the 19th century, the principal legislation was enacted in 1946, 1974, and 1988. The 1946 Education Ordinance, which provides the outline of what education entails, combined with the 1946 Compulsory Education Ordinance, provides the foundation for the present education legislation.

Developments in the educational systems resulted in further legislation. The 1946 legislation was updated and included in the 1974 Education Act. It remained in force until 1988, when another act was approved by the Maltese Parliament.

The 1988 Education Act details the respective duties and rights of the state, the Ministry of Education, and parents. It gives the right to every Maltese citizen to "receive education and instruction without any distinction of age, sex, belief or economic means."

In specifying the duties and rights of the state, the Minister of Education, and parents, the act provides as follows:

• *Principal Duties of the State*: (1) to promote education and instruction; (2) to ensure the existence of a system of schools and of institutions accessible to all Maltese citizens catering to the full development of the whole person, including the ability of every person to work; and (3) to provide schools and institutions where they do not exist.

• *Principal Duties of Parents:* to send their children to school every school day starting from the first scholastic year the children are of compulsory age until the end of the scholastic year when they cease to be of compulsory age (i.e., ages 5 to 16), or until the end of any period the Minister prescribes by regulations.

• *Rights of Parents:* to decide on every matter that concerns the education of their children.

• *Rights of the State:* to establish a national minimum curriculum of studies as well as national minimum conditions for all schools and to ensure that all schools comply with them.

• *Rights of All Citizens:* (1) to apply for a license to establish a school; and (2) to appeal if their application is refused.

• *Right of the Minister of Education:* to inspect every school and supervise its administration.

On the issue of school licenses, the act requires the Minister to grant such a license to applications from the Catholic Church and any other voluntary society, religious or otherwise, of a nonprofit making character, as long as the applicants conform to the national minimum conditions. The Minister may grant licenses to other applicants if he deems this to be in the public interest.

In addition to the above general provisions, the act sets out provisions concerning the different levels of education. Those concerning early education are as follows.

• It is the duty of the state to provide primary education for children of Maltese citizens.

• It is the duty of the Minister to maintain, wherever possible, a school in every town and village and to provide transportation for pupils in outlying areas.

• It is the duty of the state to provide special schools for children who have special difficulties of a physical, mental, or psychological nature.

• It is the duty of the Minister to establish the curriculum for state schools, which may be different for different schools.

• It is the duty of the Minister to provide for Catholic education in state schools and to establish a Catholic religion curriculum in accordance with the dispositions of the bishops.

• It is the right of parents to stop their minor children from receiving religious instruction.

The act gives the state the option of providing schools for children who are under compulsory school age.

Administration of Education

Education in Malta had been the responsibility of the Ministry of Education (formerly of Instruction) since 1921 (with the exception of the years between 1933-47, and 1958-62 when the Constitution was suspended or revoked by the British government). However, the 1988 Education Act shifted this control from the Ministry to the state.

The Ministry, on behalf of the state, still administers the system and formulates and determines the national policies, including the national minimum curriculum and minimum conditions. The Ministry is also responsible for the curriculum, the methods of instruction and assessment, and the choice of textbooks in state schools.

The daily running of the Education Department, which includes all levels of education except the University, is the responsibility of the Director of Education. A number of assistant directors are in charge of different sectors and levels of education. One of these, generally known as assistant director (primaries), is responsible for all presecondary state schooling, including kindergarten and special schools.

Education officers (formerly known as school inspectors) report to the Minister of Education, through their superiors, regarding the operation of the school system. The main role of the officers is that of advisers and monitor. They carry out staff development through individual counseling and in-service courses. They are also asked to contribute to the planning of curricula, syllabi, and examination papers.

Each primary school is administered by a head of school helped by an assistant head (depending on the school population). Heads and assistant heads do not have teaching responsibilities, although they replace teachers when need arises and visit classes to give demonstration lessons and help teachers with their class.

Preprimary Education

State Kindergartens

Until 1975, the only preschool education provided in state schools was for 5-year-olds.

(Until 1988 compulsory schooling started at age 6.) However, the majority of parents traditionally sent their 3- and 4-year-olds to fee-paying private schools.

In 1975, the government embarked on an extensive program of preschool education, providing kindergarten centers for 4-year-old children. In 1988, this service was extended to 3-year-olds. Children are admitted on their third birthday, regardless of when this occurs in the school year.

Kindergarten centers are provided in every town and village in Malta and are attached to the primary school of the locality. The centers follow the same hours of operation as primary schools. However, attendance is not compulsory and parents are allowed to call for their children at any time of the day. In general, parents usually withdraw their children during the midday break.

The number of children in each group ranges from 15 to 20. Each group is led by a kindergarten assistant. Extra staff is available in centers to help children with special needs. Special needs children are also visited by educational psychologists and other specialists who advise kindergarten assistants on methods to assist children and their parents.

Aims of the Kindergarten System

One objective of kindergarten education is to give children the opportunity to socialize and develop their abilities under guidance. Another is to give children from homes lacking suitable educational opportunities the opportunity to develop and catch up with their peers who are not so deprived. Kindergarten should also prepare children in remote areas for entry into primary schools and provide relief for working mothers.

The National Curriculum for Preprimary School

At this level, although no formal teaching should take place, educational activities to develop the child's social attitudes, independence, and intellectual curiosity should be offered. By social attitudes, the Curriculum means the development of a sense of responsibility toward others. Independent attitudes refer to a child's ability to overcome shyness and excessive reserve. Children also display the ability to care for their clothes and learn how to attend to their needs. An attitude of intellectual curiosity refers to the child's ability to develop a reflective attitude and sense of aesthetics.

The "attitudes" are acquired through communicating by word or gesture, singing, playing, painting and forming figures, physical exercises, and rhythmics. Although neither reading, writing, nor mathematics should be formally taught, children should be familiar with the alphabet and with numbers in view of the formal teaching at the primary level.

The Daily Programs

The program is flexible, but there is sufficient regularity to satisfy children's love for routine and to make them feel settled and safe. Periods of activities alternate between quiet and active play. There is a regular mid-morning break, and time for directed group activities, such as story telling, singing, and drama. The play method is adopted for all the activities.

The kindergarten program primarily focuses on the social and emotional development of the child and the formation of good health habits. While children can choose their own activity, they are guided to achieve the greatest benefits possible from them. Children who repeat the same activity over a period of time are encouraged to try other activities.

Assessment

No formal assessment takes place at this level, but the kindergarten assistants are asked to evaluate children's work using the following guiding questions:

• Can children express themselves creatively through language, movement, and music?

• Do children want to learn about the environment by exploring, listening, discussing, touching, tasting, and smelling?

• Do children like to think, try to make generalizations, and solve problems?

• Do children work happily with adults and other children?

• Do children try to extend or broaden their knowledge about their world?

Primary Schooling

State Primary Schools

The transition from kindergarten to the primary level is at age 5 for both state and private schools. Every town and village of the Maltese Islands has at least one state primary school. In smaller villages, there is usually a single school for all grades (grades 1 to 6). In larger towns, there are two schools, one for grades 1 to 3 and a second for grades 4 to 6.

Children in grades 1 to 4 are grouped according to age. They generally remain with the same group until the end of grade 4. At this time they take a national examination which decides the stream they will be placed in. Promotion from one year to the next is automatic, and only in very exceptional cases, and after consultation with the parents, heads of school, teachers and the education officer in charge of special education, are children allowed to repeat a year.

The number of pupils in one class cannot exceed 30, but the average number of pupils is well below that and in small villages the teacher-pupil ratio is considerably lower. The vertical system (grade 1 pupils grouped with grade 2 pupils, etc.) is not practiced even if the number of students in a class is very small.

Each class is led by one teacher, who teaches all the subjects and is in charge of the class during the whole school day. However such subjects as art, physical education, music, and drama are also taught by specialists who visit schools on a rotating basis. In the case of children with learning difficulties, a remedial service is provided within the school.

During their six years of primary schooling, pupils are exposed to an integrated, child-centered curriculum involving the study of Maltese, English, mathematics, physical education, social studies (which includes history, geography, and environmental studies), science, religion, art and craft, music, and drama. In the first three years, the emphasis is on reading, writing, mathematics, Maltese, and English. More academic studies are introduced in the third and fourth years.

Assessment at the Primary Level

There is no formal assessment in the first four years. A student's progress is evaluated by the teacher on the basis of observation during the school year. Remarks are entered on the personal cumulative record card, which also includes other details, such as the pupil's emotional development, behavior, personality, etc. However, a school-based mid-year examination is held in grade 4 to prepare children for the end of the year national examination (all children in state schools write the same examination prepared by a board of examiners). Children are examined in religious studies (except for children who are withdrawn by their parents from the religion lessons), English, Maltese, mathematics, and social studies. In grades 5 and 6, children are streamed into classes based on ability as judged by the national examination results.

Additional Services in the Kindergarten and Primary School System

In addition to free tuition, kindergarten and primary school, pupils receive a variety of other services and benefits. These include free loan of textbooks, free writing materials, free mid-day break supervision, and free milk. Children in special schools are provided with a free hot meal during the mid-day break. In addition, a free medical and dental service is operated by the government Medical and Health Department, which provides constant checks on the health of all children in kindergarten centers and primary schools. These are carried out by schools' medical officers and nurses. All children are medically examined and granted a certificate before they are admitted into state schools.

The Media Education Center, which is run by the Department of Education, provides video materials for entertainment and educational purposes. The center also produces children's television and radio programs. These are broadcast on the local and national radio and television services. Most primary schools have a district library attached to them which is also used by the general public.

Special Education

Special Education in Malta began in 1956, ten years after education became compulsory. The first provisions were for hearing impaired children. The 1988 Education Act obliges parents of children of compulsory age, who suffer from a mental, emotional, or physical handicap, to register them and send them to a special school.

The existing provision consists of a varied system of special schools and services for children who are profoundly or minimally handicapped. There are six types of services available for handicapped children:

1. Special units for children with special needs, including children who have learning disabilities or emotional problems, the severely retarded, the visually impaired, the physically handicapped, and the hearing impaired.

2. Hospital programs for children who are receiving treatment at an institution, with teaching and play sessions being carried out by specially trained staff.

3. A resource service for chronically ill and homebound children, which is also provided to children who must be at home for long periods because of illness.

4. A resource service for the hearing impaired in normal schools, which is also extended to pupils not yet of statutory school age.

5. Special classes for educationally subnormal children in regular schools.

6. The Special Education Section is also involved in screening children with handicaps and emotional disturbances and in providing guidance and help to parents of handicapped children.

Private Preprimary and Primary Schools

Church schools, together with a few private ones, played an important role in the educational history of the Islands. They were the pioneers of schooling in Malta and they continue to make an important contribution toward educating the people. As of 1991, private schools serve about 25 percent of the children who attend primary (up to grade 3) and preprimary schools.

Two types of private schools exist for young children. First, are those administered by the Catholic Church and religious orders, commonly known as church schools. Second are those operated by individuals and in very rare cases by private enterprise. In 1988, a group of parents organized their own private school.

Most of the private, nonchurch schools offer preprimary schooling, although some of these have ventured into the primary sector. With the exception of one or two schools, the majority of these are small. Most have fewer than 60 students in one or two classes. On the other hand, church schools offer a variety of categories and levels of education. While some schools are solely for preprimary or primary, others include both primary and secondary levels.

Admission into the nonchurch schools is usually by registration. Since the most popular schools have extensive waiting lists, parents tend to register their children for these schools long before they are of school age.

Until 1988, each church school used its own criteria for admission. However, as the number of parents registering their children for admission into church schools continued to grow, many students were refused admission due to the limited space available. To establish common admission criteria for all their preprimary and primary schools, church authorities issued specific directives for admission in 1988.

According to the directives, children living in church homes for children, together with children who have siblings already attending a particular school, have first preference. In addition, ten percent of the enrollment is reserved for children who come from families with acute financial or marital difficulties. The remaining spaces are filled by a ballot system from among the applicants. Entry age in church schools follows that of state schools, (i.e., ages 3 and 4 in the preprimary and 5 in the primary schools). Children under age 3 are accepted by some of the other private, nonchurch schools.

Programs differ from one private school to the other, as well as from state schools. However, most of them follow the same general guidelines. These programs were reviewed to make them conform to the National Minimum Curriculum, which under the 1988 Education Act applies to private schools. The result was an agreement between the government and the Church rendering Church schooling free. Financial help will be provided by the government and the Church to make Church Primary Schools non-fee paying after January 1, 1992. Church Kindergarten Centers will be free after January 1, 1993. Secondary Church Schools are already free, and are supported in part by government financial aid.

All tuition for early age children in private schools, including church schools, is paid by parents. The schools are not financed by the state.

Assessment in Private Schools

Each private school has its own policy on assessment and streaming. Many private schools operate a system of tests and examinations at some level of the primary school. These tests and examinations are school-based. While some of these are used only for assessment purposes or to keep parents informed of their children's progress, others are used as basis for streaming children according to their level of achievement.

The Curriculum of Private Schools

Although the 1974 Education Act recognized the private sector when it stated that it was to provide an education "comparable to that of government schools," it was only in 1989 that a National Minimum Curriculum (NMC) binding on both state and private schools was issued.

NMC in Primary Schools

The first established curriculum was that of 1839. It was reformed in 1850 and made applicable to all state schools in 1858. Through the years the curriculum was reformed, updated, and rewritten, culminating in the 1989 NMC. The NMC states that formal instruction should start at the primary level and should center on the following five principles:

1. Good behavior and character formation:

• in the moral and religious field so that children may learn to act according to what is right, to love their citizens, and to revere God;

• in the social field, so that they learn how to conduct themselves in society;

• in the field of good health and hygiene, so that they learn how to maintain cleanliness and to take proper health care;

• in the field of self-control, so that they can cope with life;

• in the environmental field, so that they realize that they should appreciate and safeguard the earth; and

• in sporting spirit, so that they learn to behave well at play.

2. An acquisition of the tools of knowledge and expression through the teaching of:

• the Maltese and English languages, in the spoken, read, and written forms; and

• the value of numbers and mathematics.

3. An introduction to the culture of contemporary Malta, which includes:

• the study of history;

• an initiation into the appreciation of poetry, drama, and music;

• an initiation into the appreciation of figurative and applied arts;

• an explanation of folklore; and

• an understanding of the media.

4. An introduction to scientific knowledge, which includes:

• elements of physics, chemistry, and biology;

• elements of geography and environmental science;

• elementary notions about the human body; and

• elementary technological concepts.

5. Training in activity, creativity of thought and action:

• in recreational, sport, and leisure activities;

• self-expression in practical forms;

• work attitudes and the correct use of tools; and

• in interpreting the message of the mass media.

The second part of the curriculum provides guidelines for teaching methods and classroom strategies:

1.   *Time to be devoted to the several areas of teaching:* While the teacher should be careful to cover all five parts of the program of teaching, and while ensuring that the teaching in one part is integrated with that of other parts, a certain latitude is allowed in the allocation of time between one section and another. Although it is assumed that a high proportion of class time will be used to teach Maltese, English, and

mathematics, curriculum involving character formation should also be prominent.

2. *Teaching methods:* The best methods are those that stimulate active learning, use problem solving, and enable children to be successful and competent in their learning tasks. As a result, they will begin to enjoy learning and be motivated to learn.

3. *Homework:* Homework should be used for two specific reasons. First, to help children acquire the habit of performing on their own without the teacher assistance, and second to allow them to practice new skills. Homework should not be too long, too repetitive, or occupy too much of a child's free time.

4. *Concrete and visual aids should be promoted in class:* Teachers should ensure that all children actively participate in the lesson.

5. *Tests and examinations:* Tests and examinations should not be used to train children's memories, but rather used by teachers as tests of understanding and by the children as an opportunity to show their talents.

6. *Maltese will be the primary language of instruction:* The teacher should also use English in the classroom in order to accustom children to understand and speak the language. Children who speak English at home should receive English instruction in addition to Maltese.

In addition to the above guidelines, classroom strategies include the following:

• When children are involved in common activities where competition is a component, they should be taught to accept success and failure, to use the rules of fair play, and to act in a team spirit.

• During the years in primary school, children should be instructed in self-control, self-confidence, and self-reliance.

• The primary school system should be considered one continuous process and, therefore, while it is appropriate that areas one and two as stated above should be emphasized in the first years, the teacher should construct a program that includes all aspects of the NMC.

Primary School Programs in the NMC

Although the curriculum is regarded as an integrated entity, for the purpose of convenience and in order to maintain a general standard of efficiency, as well as to have a means of assessment (in view of annual national examination at the end of grade 4) educational authorities provide state schools with subject programs in the form of syllabi. The syllabi are flexible, however, and teachers are asked to adapt them to their class, taking into account the particular aptitudes, interests, and levels of achievement of their pupils. In view of the new curriculum, these programs are being revised.

Teacher Training

Preschool Teachers

Teachers in state kindergarten centers, known as kindergarten assistants, undergo a concentrated induction course in child development and teaching methods prior to their posting. Kindergarten assistants are also required to attend in-service courses periodically organized by the Education Department.

Preschool teachers in private schools have qualifications similar to those of teachers in state kindergarten centers. A number of nuns teach in the preprimary schools operated by the church, since almost all these schools are managed by female religious orders. The single exception are two primary schools operated by Christian Brothers.

Primary School Teachers

The basic qualification for primary school teachers is the four-year Bachelor of Education degree awarded by the University of Malta. Since the Faculty of Education was established only a few years ago, a large number of teachers in the primary schools received their teacher training in local teacher training colleges (for one to three years, depending on the time of attendance). The Education Department employs a number of casual teachers to compensate for a lack of regular teachers. Many of these are female teachers forced to "retire" from state schools after marriage.

The Department of Education and the Faculty of Education organize in-service courses for regular and casual teachers. Teachers usually attend these courses on voluntary basis. University diploma courses operated in the evening and organized by the Education Department help to update teachers.

While many teachers in church schools are members of religious orders, the majority are laymen who have received their training in training colleges or at the university. Others are employed on the strength of their academic qualifications.

The School, Community, and Family

The 1988 Education Act introduced school councils in state schools. The six member councils are elected annually. Councils are made up of three members elected by the parents who have children attending the school concerned, and three teachers elected by the teaching staff of that school. The chair is appointed by the Minister of Education, while the head of the School acts as secretary/treasurer of the council. The function of these "bodies corporate" include the administration of school assets and funds.

According to the same act, these councils cannot interfere with the teaching and the maintenance of discipline in schools, but they may request the Minister to include in the curriculum a particular course of studies in addition to those established by the Minister, who has the right to decide on such a request. Although not legally obliged, private schools are encouraged to adopt this system of school administration.

Many state schools also have a parents association whose members are also elected once a year. The parents' associations have their own federation. Private schools have separate parent-teacher associations, which are members of the Private Schools Parent-Teacher's Federation.

In most cases, parents are made to feel welcome and are encouraged to visit schools and to meet with the head of school and the class teachers. An official parents' day is held twice a year in primary schools, as well as prize days and other open days. Many schools issue school newsletters and bulletins to keep parents informed of school activities and decisions.

Resourceful parents are encouraged to help in school, especially in the organization of special events, such as prize days, exhibitions, and concerts. Some parents also assist in embellishing the school premises. In the kindergarten-nursery centers, parents are encouraged to take part in practical class activities as well as to participate in occasional class celebrations and children's out-of-school activities.

FAMILY POLICY AND PRESCHOOL PROGRAMS IN THE NETHERLANDS

• • • • • • • • • • ◆ • • • • • • • •

Elisabeth Singer
University of Amsterdam
Amsterdam, Netherlands

The Netherlands is a rich and highly developed country. It has approximately 15 million inhabitants, about 1.6 million of whom are children under age 9. To understand the facilities and intervention programs for parents and young children in the Netherlands, it is necessary to be aware of three important factors. First, there are few mothers with young children working outside the home. In 1987, roughly 6 percent of mothers with children under age 4 were employed for 21 hours or more per week; 18 percent worked for 20 hours or less; 76 percent had no employment at all outside the home.[1] However, it is expected that this percentage will increase in coming years. Second, the Dutch government has a family-oriented policy based on the assumptions that the father is the breadwinner, the mother devotes herself to family affairs, and young children belong at home. Third, direct intervention by the authorities in the care and education of children is condemned unless there is a suggestion of negligence or inability on the part of the parents to care for their children, or of child abuse. The facilities subsidized by the government are mainly directed toward family support and parent education. Day care programs are an exception to the rule in the Netherlands.

This chapter outlines the historical background to this traditional normative family policy and describes the most important facilities and programs currently available.

Brief History of Family Policy

The foundations of the present state policy on care and education of children are found in the 19th century. In the Netherlands, industrialization came relatively late, about 1870. At that time, due to an earlier period of economic decline, there was a large male labor reserve. It did not take long, as in England, before labor legislation was introduced. In 1871, the first laws to restrict child labor were established, and the restriction on the labor of married women followed in 1889. Labor legislation was mainly brought about by the enlightened bourgeois liberals and owners of industry who held out a normal family life along patriarchal lines to their male laborers. The patriarchal family was already deeply rooted in the culture in earlier centuries.[2] These facts—the large male labor reserve, the labor legislation right at the beginning of industrialization, and the existence of the patriarchal family—probably explain why a much lower proportion of women work outside the home in the Netherlands compared with other countries.

Until the 1970s, the proportion of registered working married women never rose much beyond 10% (part time workers included).[3] After World War II, a social security network was established in the Netherlands; it was centered on the father as the breadwinner of the family. In employment, his wages were supposed to be enough to support his family; in sickness, unemployment, old age, and death, his loss of wages was compensated by a benefit system. Furthermore, there were child benefits. Single mothers had no obligation to work for a living; in their case, the state takes over the father's role.[4]

But, in fact, there was also no right to economic independence for mothers. The lack of support for the working mothers, with a prenatal and postnatal leave of six weeks before and after childbirth, is in sharp contrast with the support system for the male breadwinner. It is only since 1989 that the right to a six-month, part-time, unpaid leave for mothers and fathers has been introduced. There are now also plans for extending the childbirth leave.[5]

The first interventions in the education of young children date from the 1820s, 50 years before industrialization.[6] They were intended for children of the poor and working classes. In sympathy with the ideas of the Enlightenment, bourgeois citizens tried to combat poverty through education. For this purpose, institutional child care in infant schools was used. Children from age 2 and older were gathered in large groups; over 200 children in one room was not uncommon. The main objectives of these infant schools were to keep young children off the street and to teach them obedience, morality, industry, devotion, and some knowledge. The number of infant schools remained severely limited until 1840. It was only in the second half of the 19th century that the infant school developed into a more frequently occurring facility, also used by the children of the middle class. The infant school progressively became a preparatory school for the elementary education. Over time, the opening hours were restricted to three and one-half hours in the morning and two hours in the afternoon, and the age of admission was raised to age 4.[7] Even so, it was only in 1965

that the infant school was recognized and fully subsidized by the government as part of the school system. Since that time, most Dutch children attend an infant school from age 4. The education plan for the 4-year-old is child-centered, with a strong emphasis on learning through play. Heinrich Pestalozzi, Friedrich Froebel, and Maria Montessori have all had a great influence in the Netherlands.

In 1901, a compulsory school age of 6 years was introduced. This age was lowered to age 5 in 1985 when infant and elementary schools were integrated. (See the following article by E. Mulder.)

In the 1970s, playgroups, a new form of institutional child care was introduced with an educational aim for children under infant school age.[8] In playgroups, children ages 2 and 3 play together under the care and guidance of two people trained in child care. The children usually attend the playgroups several times a week for three hours. The most important aims are the stimulation of cognitive, social, and emotional development. As of 1991, approximately one-third of all 2- and 3-year-olds attended a playgroup.[9]

A third form of institutional child care is day nurseries. They were first established near the end of the 19th century through the initiative of upper middle class women, including a few who were also feminists.[10] The day nurseries cared for the infants and babies of mothers forced by poverty to go to work, or those who, through social or medical circumstances, could not look after their children themselves. The founders of the day nurseries were alarmed by physicians' descriptions of the deplorable conditions of private care.[11] Until the end of the 1960s, day nurseries were oriented to mothers and children in "need." Since then, more children from "nonneedy" families have also been admitted. Nevertheless, the number of day nurseries was limited to only 268 in 1987, with a total capacity of 75 percent of all children from birth to age 4.[12]

The first initiatives in the "care for unmarried mothers" were closely related to the first day nurseries. In 1880, the first home for unmarried mothers and their children was established in the country.[13] The following decades witnessed the growth of a strong network of homes and clinics offering advice on pregnancy and childbirth, housing, finances, child care, adoption, and parental rights and responsibilities. The methods and procedures of these institutions were often based on a strong moral disapproval of the unmarried mothers. Some of these homes also offered child care in order to enable the mother to go out to work. The care for unmarried mothers changed considerably in the 1970s under the influence of a changing sexual morality, the availability of better contraception, and a welfare system allowing them more financial independence. Some of the homes and clinics were closed, and those remaining directed their attention to new areas, including "emergency help" for mother, father, and child and counseling and advice on divorce.

The single-parent family (primarily female led) has become a frequent and accepted phenomenon during the past 20 years in the Netherlands.[14] One in four marriages ends in divorce, and most children remain with the mother after the marriage has broken up, fathers forming one-parent families are still an exception.

The first health clinic for babies dates from 1901. During the entire 19th century until 1890, infant mortality in the Netherlands was extremely high: between 20 percent and 30 percent of all new born babies died in infancy. A decline, due to several factors, reduced the figure to 16 percent in 1900, 7 percent in 1920, and 1 percent in 1980.[15] The most important aim of these health clinics was the fight against infant mortality. Their numbers increased rapidly from the beginning of the 20th century. In the health clinics, infants and young children were medically screened by doctors, and mothers were given advice on feeding, sleep, hygiene, and upbringing by a team of doctor and district nurses. As of 1988, 96 percent of all infants and 80 percent of the 4-year-olds regularly attended a health clinic.[16]

During the 1920s and 1930s, various organizations were established to offer mothers advice on bringing up their children. Books, brochures, and magazines appeared, all in the field of child care and upbringing.[17] Exhibitions were held, and special courses on mothering were started. In the 1970s *speel-o-theken* (i.e., educational toy libraries) were introduced, offering information and the opportunity to borrow educational toys. Educational bureaus giving support and advice also sprang into existence and "coffee mornings" were organized for mothers. In addition, there was special home training for mothers to teach them how to play with their children. More effort is currently being made to include fathers in the information on child rearing.

The more psychotherapeutic forms of help for parents also have their origins in the 1920s and 1930s.[18] Until quite recently, this generally took place in child guidance clinics; but now this form of help has been integrated into the *Regionale Instellingen voor Ambulante Geestelijke Gezondheid* (RIAGG) (Regional Institution for Ambulatory Mental Health), covering the entire country. Courses for the parents are organized by the department of youth and (disease and disorder) prevention, which also arranges family therapy, individual behavior therapy, or conversation/discussion therapy for parents.

Furthermore, therapeutic day treatment is offered at 31 *medische kleuterdagverblijven* (MKD) (medical day care centers for young children) for children between 18 months and age 6, "whose otherwise normal development has been disturbed, or is in danger of being disturbed."[19] Besides the group teachers who work daily with the children, the MKDs can offer highly professional staff, including a psychologist, teacher, physiotherapist, speech therapist, children's specialist, and a social worker. In the evening and during the weekends, the children are at home with their parent(s). If the problems at home threaten to become too severe, the parents can have their children placed in foster homes on a voluntary basis.[20]

All the above-mentioned facilities are available on a voluntary basis; they work on the assumption that parents themselves sometimes feel in need of help, advice, and support. Apart from this form of voluntary help, the Netherlands also has a system of compulsory judicial help. The foundations for this were laid in 1901 when "child protection" was given a legal status in the form of laws specifically for children and young people (juvenile court).[21] If parents neglected or maltreated their children, the parental powers could be taken away, and the children could be make wards of the court and placed in care. These laws were established partly because of a feeling of social responsibility for the children. However, the wish to protect society from uneducated children who were likely to become criminals was also an important motive.

Besides placing the child in care, the magistrate of the juvenile court could, and still can, place the child "under special supervision." The child is then given a "family guardian," who also must help and support the parents. However, because of the large numbers of families needing guidance from these family guardians, and because of their position as uninvited social worker/judge, the help and support they can offer are often inadequate.

In the past, after being taken out of the family home, children would often end up in a children's home. Today, the chance of young children being placed with foster parents is much greater.[22] The government's policy is based on the theory that children function much better if they can grow up within a family. Financial considerations also play a central part, since fostering is voluntary and thus cheaper.

Since 1972, the Netherlands has had a system of *bureaus vertrouwensartsen* (confidential doctors) for dealing with reports of child abuse and neglect. Relatives, neighbors, teachers, and social workers can report to the bureau, anonymously if they wish, on any suspected child abuse or neglect. The report is then investigated by a team of doctors and social workers. On the basis of their findings, an effort is made to find help within the voluntary help network. If this is impossible, the magistrate of the juvenile court is contacted and a procedure of compulsory judicial help is started. During recent years, there has been a significant increase in public awareness of violence toward children within the family. Incest particularly has received a great deal of public attention,[23] which has led to a growing number of reports to the "confidential doctors."[24]

Parents, Professionals, and the State: Tensions in the System

The Dutch system is based on the assumption that parents are primarily responsible for the care and rearing of their children. In the Netherlands, "state upbringing" are words that invoke horror. However, this does not mean that the state has no influence on the definitions of "fatherhood," "motherhood," "normal family life," and "children's normal development." Quite the opposite is true.

First, the tensions apparent in the Netherlands between parental authority and state authority are channeled as a matter of course by a strong family support policy. Children are preferably approached through, and with the consent of, their parents. Parents are supported, influenced, and guided on a voluntary basis. To summarize, the family support policy consists of the following elements:

1. A welfare (social security) system based on the breadwinner and child benefits, thus guaranteeing families with children a minimum income.

2. An educational system consisting of playgroups for 2- and 3-year-olds, and schooling from the age of 4. Most Dutch children attend school from age 4. However, lunch time care and after-school care are either nonexistent or badly organized, which means that mothers have to be available at these times, noon to 2 p.m. and after 3 p.m. or 4 p.m.

3. An information and guidance system for parents (mothers) consisting of health clinics for nearly all children and *speel-o-theken* and advice bureaus offering help and advice on upbringing and courses for parents, all of which have a smaller range than the clinics.

4. A voluntary social work system for parents and children. The most usual form of help is that of therapeutic talks for parents with a psychologist, educational specialist, or social worker. If there are many problems at home, the parents can voluntarily have their child placed in a foster home. There is also therapeutic day care for children and a limited number of possibilities for 24-hour care for parents and children in a crisis situation.

5. "Confidential doctors" for dealing with reports of child abuse and neglect.

6. Day nurseries for the children of parents working outside the home and for children in problem situations. This facility is also marginal in the system in spite of the obvious need.

Besides the above-mentioned voluntary facilities, there is also a circuit of compulsory care in the form of the child protection (through juvenile courts) and the judicial foster care. However, removing parental authority (i.e., making a child a ward of the court) can be done only by the magistrate of the juvenile court, and then only in cases of very serious abuse or neglect.

Second, the tension surrounding state intervention in the care of children is further channeled by extending a large role in private initiative. Many of the previously mentioned facilities have developed from the initiatives of private citizens and church organizations. The management of these organizations eventually received subsidies from (local) government, but remained relatively independent and able to retain their own policies. Therefore, state influence was indirect.

This family support policy with a large private initiative, and with a clear division between voluntary and judicial help could, in itself, be an elegant solution to the numerous problems caused by state care of children. However, as the following illustrate, it is actually creating more tensions.

In practice it seems that families from the lower social classes had and still have a much greater chance of ending up in the judicial help circuit than others. Many parents and children have complained about the way they have been treated within the "child protection of juvenile courts." Besides which, it has become apparent that social workers in the voluntary system very often fail to recognize and treat child abuse, and the "talk/conversation methods" have often failed for families with many problems.[25]

The emphasis on private initiative has led to a jumble of facilities that often work at cross purposes. The result is a family that works at cross purposes. For example, a family may deal with two or three different organizations and not be meaningfully served by any. This situation led to the demand for more cooperation between these facilities. During the 1960s, the authorities felt a growing need to gain some control over the contents of the policies and the finances. The government refused to create new facilities for each newly discovered "need."[26]

The government's family policy is based on a traditional role pattern between fathers and mothers, on the breadwinners system assuming the role of housewife for the woman (the nursery schools, playgroups, courses for mothers), as well as the very short pregnancy leave allowed and the lack of child day care. This situation creates problems for mothers working outside the home and for their children.[27]

In the late 1960s, criticism of this kind was leveled at the government's family policy. The family was criticized from all sides, the existing facilities were inefficient and did not meet requirements, and there was a demand for more child care centers. However, by the late 1970s, a change took place. Instead of the call for child care centers, a preventive policy was launched, directed toward changes within the family. The latter is still the basis of the policy for the 1990s. However, it must be recognized by all that the expansion of facilities for children of working parents can no longer be halted.

The following discussion deals in more depth with the center-based programs, which have their origins in the 1970s, and the preventive programs, which played a central role in the policies of the 1980s. Finally, the development of child care at the beginning of the present decade is discussed.

Center-Based Programs

At the end of the 1960s institutionalized child care was rediscovered as an alternative for isolated and exclusive family care. The first and most radical criticism of the family was formulated by leftist students participating in the student revolts of the 1960s. They set up antiauthoritarian creches inspired by experiments and theories of Wilhelm Reich and Siegfried Bernfeld, German Freudo-Marxists of the 1920s, and by the German "Kinderladen," or antiauthoritarian creches. They objected both to the authoritarian power of the father in the family and the repression of sexual and aggressive impulses, and to the laissez-faire pedagogy because of their bureaucratic and hierarchical character as welfare institutions. In their own creches, they gave the children much freedom to experience the self-regulation of their impulses.

These antiauthoritarian creches were short lived and received little academic support. The issue of power in the relationship between parent and child remains today an under-researched theme in the country. Even the growing awareness of the role of power in abuse and violence toward children within the family has, as yet, brought no change. Research programs concerning child abuse are related more to "the pathology of the abusing parent" and look for "risk-factors" and "risk-groups."

The antiauthoritarian creches have, therefore, not led to programs subsidized by the authorities. However, perhaps there are remnants of this ideal in some of the "parent creches" set up and run by parents and volunteers.

The "second wave" of feminists also criticized

family care. They regarded creches as a necessary condition for allowing mothers to work or pursue activities outside the home. In their view, child care should be paid labor in state-subsidized creches.

In the 1970s and 1980s, the actions and demonstrations for day care met with little success. The authorities remained cautious and reserved on the subject, and the advocates of day care centers also received little support from the Dutch experts in child psychiatry and child development. Psychiatrists and psychoanalysts voiced strong doubts about creches, believing mothers should not pursue their own interests at their children's expense. Only recently has expert opinion begun to change. Using a modified version of John Bowlby's attachment theory, some developmental psychologists argue, in the interests of the child, for two or three primary caretakers instead of exclusive motherhood. But, in the Netherlands research by developmental psychologists on this topic in the context of day nurseries is almost nonexistent. Articles on the subject are mainly based on reviews of American research. The most recent developments in day care are discussed later in this chapter.

The third group criticizing the family upbringing at the end of the 1960s, were well-educated, middle-class mothers who had chosen to become housewives but who wanted more contacts for themselves and their children. These women were less radical in their criticism than the previous two groups. The result of their efforts was the essentially conservative playgroup movement. Playgroups were set up mainly by mothers and run by unpaid volunteers or (under)paid semi-professionals. The movement was very successful in gaining the support and approval of politicians, governments, and professional workers in child health care and psychiatry. Playgroups were quite cheap and their value for the development of children was emphasized. They relieved some of the tensions of motherhood without changing the mother image. On the contrary, in a way they intensified the mother's devotion to her child.

In many playgroups parental participation was, and still is, expected. There are parental meetings because, as workers in the playgroup, mothers have to professionalize themselves in child care. Coupled with the increase of playgroups was the demand for courses on the development of

toddlers for workers and volunteer parents. For the middle-class Dutch mother and father, "toddlerhood" was a new and hitherto unknown phase of development. In the early 1970s, new playgroups mushroomed all over the country. At this time about one-third of all 2- and 3-year-olds attend a playgroup. However, children from the middle class are over-represented. The playgroups were less popular with the parents from the lower social classes, and not at all popular with the parents or the ethnic minorities from Turkey and Morocco. It is quite likely that the "child-centered" and "free-play" oriented method does not coincide with what these parents want for their young children. Another obstacle could also be the financial contribution expected from parents.

A fourth stream of criticism against the family as exclusive caregiver came from the field of professional child care itself. Medical health-care workers and workers in child protection worried about their lack of access to children under age 4 (the age of enrollment in nursery schools was age 4). They asked playgroups to reveal the development of young children to the professional eye and to reach parents for parental education.[28] In the 1970s, some governmental experiments were set up to explore early detection and prevention of developmental disorders in young children. Within these experiments, playgroups were seen as screens for detecting disorders. In the case of greater problems, the child could, in cooperation with the parents, be seen by a multidisciplinary team of experts, drawn from the various facilities existing for parents and (young) children. This point is discussed later.

The final stream of criticism also came from professionals. Their criticism was directed against the child-rearing practices of the lower classes. They argued for day care centers and playgroups for children from disadvantaged families as a part of a system of compensatory programs.[29] As in other countries at the end of the 1960s, the Dutch government was interested in compensatory programs in order to give children from the lower classes more equal opportunities in the formal educational system. U.S. programs were imported and tried out. In 1970, the Proefkreche, an experimental day care center subsidized by the national government, started under the guidance of developmental psychologists to explore the effects of intervention on the cognitive development of disadvantaged children. Its publications about stimulating games with children in groups have been very influential. Many community centers organized playgroups in cooperation with larger educational projects for disadvantaged children in elementary schools. In addition to stimulating children's development, parental education was an important objective.[30]

In 1976 the results of research into the effects of the Proefkreche on intelligence and cognitive development were published. The exclusive interest in the effects on cognitive development symbolized the gap between this educational day care experiment and those day care centers demanded by feminists. In the latter, the question of disastrous effects on the mother-child attachment and emotional development dominated.

Though evidence suggested that children in the Proefkreche had better scores on cognitive tests than children reared exclusively at home, the results were not as decisive as had been expected. As a result, researchers suggested that intervention must begin earlier, with babies, and in the family instead of in child care centers.[31] As of 1991, playgroups for children from disadvantaged backgrounds are still organized by community centers. For Turkish, Moroccan, and Surinam children, experiments were started with "international day cares," where, with the help of additional subsidies, foreign group leaders could work. There are still center-based programs for disadvantaged children, but the emphasis has shifted to home-based programs. During the 1980s, very little academic research was carried out on center-based programs for disadvantaged children.

Prevention and Home-Based Programs

During the 1980s prevention and home-based programs had a central place in governmental policy and the academic world. Instead of a broad critique of the family, attention was directed to the "risk groups" and "problem families" and "problem children." Solutions were aimed at additional parental education programs and early recognition of help within the family. The slogan became to "offer help as early, as little, and as close to home as possible." Besides this, the cooperation between the various facilities and the restructuring of the available help were given priority. The government wanted to get rid of the jumble of facilities over which it had little or no control and which tended to work at cross purposes. The second slogan was therefore "cooperation, integration, and decentralization" to the council level.

The following discussion of programs developed in the last decade in the Netherlands is limited to the prevention policy and a few selected home-based programs.

One of the most important innovations during the past ten years has been the setting up of a system for the early detection of developmental disorders. The most important objective of this system is the prevention of children's and parents' problems in medical and psychosocial fields, and the ability to offer help at the earliest possible stage to prevent the situation from worsening. Prevention will supposedly lead to a saving of costs in child welfare, since fewer children will need the weightier and more expensive forms of help as they grow older.

Throughout the country, there are 42 regional bureaus for the early detection of developmental disorders. The task of these bureaus is to ensure cooperation among all the institutions and have people involved in child health care. These multidisciplinary cooperating teams have the job of coordinating the regional early detection of "screening" and setting up a registration system and so on. Apart from this, they also have the responsibility of helping all people working directly with children to become aware of the first signs of disorders. Through organizing courses and giving more information, these bureaus hope to teach parents, health workers, child care workers, general practitioners, and teachers to look at children "diagnostically" in order to detect problems and refer them to the multidisciplinary teams. The child care centers and children's clinics are seen as "finding places."

The initial experiences with this system have been moderately positive. In general, the preventive idea appeals to the various institutions and brings them more into line with one another. However, the more medically oriented tradition within the health clinics relates with great difficulty to the more psychotherapeutic traditions within other organizations.[32] Besides which, workers in the health clinics fear that more cooperation with severe forms of help could damage the confidential relationship with the patients.[33] Parents could be shocked by the suggestion that their problem could be placed before a multidisciplinary team. Questions are also raised by the problem-oriented approach to parents and children. For example, does the system detect problems or create them? Unfortunately, no evaluative research has been done into the effect, efficacy, and actual cost-savings of this approach.[34]

The government's prevention policy is strongly supported by developmental psychological and child-psychiatric research carried out in Dutch universities. Many of the research programs were designed to develop instruments and tests for early detection of psychosocial problems in children under age 8.[35] Epidemiological research is being carried out on the frequency of developmental disorders in Dutch children and within special categories, such as adopted children and children from one-parent families, etc.[36] Analyzing responsiveness and availability of mothers and attachment behavior in studies on mother-child interactions are most popular and connected to the question of how to discriminate normal from abnormal development. The attachment theories of Bowlby and Mary Ainsworth are extremely influential in the Netherlands.

Beside the system for early detection of developmental disorders, various versions of home training form an important new area of help available in the Netherlands. Home training is intended for children and parents from the ethnic minorities, as a support for cognitive development, and for parents of mentally retarded children and problem families threatened with the possibility of having a child placed in care.

As already stated, at the end of the 1970s the developmental psychologists and policymakers were very disappointed by the ambiguous effect of compensatory programs carried out in children's centers, on the language and cognitive development of children from the lower classes. Academics particularly became very interested in infant-stimulation programs. Mothers with babies between 9 and 12 months were taught to react positively as often as possible to signals given by the child to his or her initiatives to contact (responsiveness); and to take into account as much as possible the interests of the child, offering the opportunity to watch, listen, feel, smell, and experiment (stimulating behavior).[37] This approach is based on U.S. programs for infant stimulation, on theoretical learning/teaching principles, and on attachment theory. After three months of training, results were positive; the babies scored slightly higher on competence tests and tests for the speed of assimilation of information. As of 1991, more research is attempting to establish whether training in responsiveness has positive effects on the mothers and fathers, one-parent families, and parents from ethnic minorities. To date, very little has been made known about the results of this research.

Programs on information about playing at home have been developed for Turkish and Moroccan families.[38] Within these programs, families are selected by a district nurse and then visited by a semi-volunteer worker, who plays with the children at their home. The objective is to make these children familiar with the games and toys most Dutch children play with and that are important for cognitive development (e.g., building bricks, puzzles, books, and balls, etc.) In addition, the volunteer worker tries to interest the mothers, and even sometimes the fathers, in the games, and invites them to play with their children. From the first experiments with the program Information about Playing at Home, it has become apparent that Turkish and Moroccan parents will do a great deal to ensure that their children have better chances at school, and they valued the contact with the (Dutch) volunteer workers who played with their children and offered help and advice. It is unclear whether programs such as this will have a positive effect on the children. At this time, work is being done on the development of the program "Information on Games and Playing at Home," in various parts of the Netherlands.

The home training programs for parents whose children have been placed in care or are threatened with the possibility of this happening are very different.[39] Sometimes they involve mentally retarded children or children with behavioral problems. Occasionally, there is nothing wrong with the child, but the parents are unable to cope with the care and upbringing without extra help. The most important aims of these programs are to prevent children from being placed in care or to enable a child already in care to return home as quickly as possible. As far as the government is concerned, these programs have the possibility of being an inexpensive alternative to costly residential child care.

In general, these programs are based on the principle of offering intensive, brief help, in the home that involves the whole family. Use is made of video recording of the family, family therapy, and behaviorial therapy techniques and modeling. Most of the home training programs have been developed in Dutch universities or in cooperation with researchers. The first experiences with home training show that some parents are extremely well motivated and will do and learn anything to avoid having their child being placed in care. But, if the parents and children are less well motivated, the process is more difficult. In general, the following rule seems to apply: the more serious the family's problems, the less likely are the chances of success.

A third important change in policy during the last ten years concerns the fostering of children. If putting a child into care becomes unavoidable, the child should preferably be placed with a foster family instead of in a children's home. Families are presumed to offer the best possibilities for the child's development, especially the very young child. Besides which, the cost factor plays a very large role in that fostering is voluntary. Since 1984, the number of places in children's homes has been drastically reduced, and some homes have been closed altogether. National recruitment campaigns for foster parents were organized with some success. However, although many foster parents registered, this in itself is not a solution to all the problems surrounding foster care.[40]

In the early 1990s, it is easier to sum up the problems than to anticipate the solutions that will have to be sought during the coming years. There are many problems with the foster care system. One in four placements with foster families fails. A relatively large group of children (11 percent) will have been placed in more than five families before their tenth birthday. In addition, there are no clear guidelines on matching children to foster parents.

Recently, foster parents have united and organized themselves for the first time, and publicly aired their complaints. Many foster parents are dissatisfied with the counseling support given by social workers, and also with the amount of money they receive for expenses, which, they claim, rarely covers all the costs involved. They demand recognition as an important part of the child care service. The professionalization of foster care is still in its infancy in the Netherlands and the path it will take is impossible to predict.

Day Care

Governmental policy, as well as academic research, was, and still is, based on the family as the primary child care system. The care for children of parents working outside the home is very difficult within such a system and tradition. As already stated, until quite recently governmental policy and experts were reluctant to make changes, and actions undertaken by parents and the political pressure of women's organization met with very little success.[41] However, in the late 1980s, the situation began to change.[42] Due to the steady growth of the economy certain areas of business experienced a growing need for more female employees. In a short time, the number of creches in factories and businesses grew considerably, from practically none in 1985 to 160 in 1989.[43] Private enterprise quickly recognized an opportunity, and established nonsubsidized child care centers. Within a very short time, about 160 private child care centers were opened. The government has now also promised to carry out an expansion policy. Apart from economic and emancipatory moves, the United Europe of 1992 also forms an important impetus for the expansion policy. Without a change of policy, the Netherlands, with its very low percentage of women working outside the home, would form an exception to the rule when compared with other European countries. In 1989, there were 301 subsidized day care centers. Money has been made available to quadruple governmental spending on day care centers over the next four years. The federal funds will be transferred to the local government level. The councils can then decide for themselves what sort of child care they want: "guest parent" projects, a completely subsidized child day care service, a combination of creches provided by businesses and those subsidized by the council, or some other form of care. However, this expansion policy is mainly reserved for the children under age 4, which gives rise to the fear that the care of older children at lunch time and after school hours will remain a large problem.

The sudden quantitative growth of child day care raises many questions about the quality of this care. At the present time, councils are preparing regulations to ensure that a minimum standard of care is offered by all child day care centers. These include criteria for child workers: child ratios, the availability of outdoor play space, the amount of space per child indoors, hygiene, fire safety, etc. There is also an enormous growth of special courses within higher professional education, for child care workers and the management of child care facilities. Universities are also suddenly expressing their concern about the quality of the child care, and submitting research proposals on the subject.

In short, everything is changing, and in child care as in prevention programs, it is very difficult to say what things will look like in five years. Apart from that, it is unclear what the consequences of more and more mothers working outside the home will be for the above-mentioned facilities for families with young children. For instance, the recently established foster care system is voluntary. Will there be enough foster mothers available if working outside the home becomes normal for mothers? The father's responsibility toward his children will be appealed to. Otherwise mothers working outside the home will be overburdened by the triple task of a job, housekeeping, and child care. Will fathers be willing to respond to the appeal? It is more than likely that Dutch ideas and policies on the upbringing of children will have to change drastically during the coming ten years.

Notes

1. *Kinderopavang en arbeidsparticipatie van vrouwen*. Min. van Sociale Zaken en Werkgelegenheid, 1987, pp. 55–57.

2. Clerkx, L.E., Kinderen in het gezin. In *Gexinsgeschiedenis: vier eeuwen gezin in Nederland*. G.A. Looy (ed.) Van Gorcum: Assen, 1985.

3. S. Leydesdorff, *Verborgen arbied, vergeten arbeid*. Van Gorcum: Assen, 1977; C. Oudijk, *Sociale atlas van de vrouw 1983*. Staatsuitgeverij, Den Haag, 1983.

4. R.N.A. De kosten en opbrengsten van kinderen en huisvrouwen. In *Economisch Statistische Berrichten*, 14 mei 1986, pp. 485–489.

5. L. Pot, *Kinderopvang nu. Zorgen voor morgen*. Amsterdam 1988.

6. L.E. van Pijswijk-Clerkx, *Moeders, kinderen en kinderopvang*. Sun, Nijmegen, 1981, pp. 46–75; E. Soinger. *Kinderoopvang en de moeder-kinderlante*. Van loghum Slaterus, Deventer, 1989, pp. 53–81.

7. L.E. Clerkx, De afstoting van de bewaarfunktie uit het kleuteronderwijs. In: *Comenus* 13, 1984, pp. 3–24.

8. L.E. van Pijswijk-Clerkx, *Moeder, kinderen en kinderopvang*. Etc. pp. 264–298.

9. *Statistich Zakboek*, Centraal Buereau voor de Statistiek, 1987.

10. L.E. van Pijswijk-Clerkx, *Moeders, kinderen en kinderopvang*. Etc. pp. 76–99.

11. Van Bijswijk-Clerkx, *Moeders, kindergen en kinderopvang*. SUN, Nijmegen 1981, pp. 76–100.

12. CDS, *Statistisch Zabkoek 1987*, Den Haag, 1987.

13. B. Wiemann, Opkomst en neergang van de ongehuwde moederzorg in Nederland (1880–1985). In: *Amsterdams Sociologisch Tijdschrift 15*, 1988, 337–368.

14. B. Jansweijer, L. Pot, H.J. Groenendijk T H.M. Langeveld, *Haalbaar en betaalbaar: arbeid en kinderzorg na 1990*. Erasmus Universiteit Rotteerdam, 1988, pp. 14–16.

15. O. Vandenbroeche, F. van Poopel & A.M. van den Woude, De zuigelingen en kindersterfte in Belgie en Nederland in seculair perspectief. In: *Tijkschrift voor geschiedenis 94*, 1981, pp. 461–491.

16. *Preventie van spychosociale en pedagogische problematiek door het Kruiswerk*, Nationale Kruisvereniging, Bunnink, 1988.

17. L.E. van Rijswijk-Clerkx, *Moeders, kinderen en kingeropvang*. Etc. pp. 116–162; B. Singer, *Kinderopvang en de moeder-kindrelatie*. Etc. p. 27.

18. F.M. Gerards, *Psychosociale educatie: Een strategie voor preventie?* Herlen, 1984 (proeschrift), pp. 28–52.

19. J. Hermanns, Ontwikkeling in het Medisch Kleuterdagverblijf. In: *Maandblad voor Geestelijke Volksgezondheid*, dec. 1987.

20. M. van Ooyen-Houben T H. de Kort, *Meer jong kinderen in pleeggezinnen, del 1*. CWOK, Den Haag, 1987.

21. D. Roelands, *Kindergescherming in de maatschappij 1905–1980*. Ambo, Baarn, 1980, pp. 24–60; C. can Nijnatten, *Moeder justitia en harr kinderen*. Swets & Zitlinger, Lisse, 1986, pp. 8–53.

22. *Directie Kinderbescherming Verslag 1985/1986.* 1987, p. 78.

23. N. Drayer, *Seksueel misbruik van meisjes door verwanten.* Min. van Sociale Zaken en Werkgelegen heid, Den Haag, 1988.

24. *Bureau's Vertrouvensartsen inzake Kindermishandeling: gegevns uit de registatie 1988.* Rijswijk, WVC, 1989.

25. *Starnota Jeugdwelzinjnsbeleid.* Germangde Interdepartementale Werkgroep Jeugdelzjnsbeleid. Staatsuitgeverij, 's Gravenhag, 1974; *Tussen droom en daad,* Eindrapport van de Interdepartementale Werkgroep Ambulante en Preventieve Voorzieningen voor hulpverlening aan jeudgigen. Ministerie van W.V.C., Justitie en O.&. W. Rijswijk, 1984; *Interdepartementale Werkgroep Resisdentiele Voorzieningen.* Intermrapport ii, 's Staatsuitgheverij, Gravenhage, 1980.

26. Idem.

27. E. Singer, *Kindergopvang en de moeder-kindrelatie.*; L.Pot, *Kinderopvang nu. Zorgen voor morgen.*

28. B. Hengevld, Kleuters, kleuterspeelzalen, bedreigde kleuters, medische kleuterdagverblijven. In: *Katholiek gezondheidszorg,* 1968, pp. 426–429; *Starnota jeugdwelzijnsbeleid.* Gemengde Interdepartementale Werkgroep Jeugdwelzijnsbeleid. 's Gravenhage, Staatsuitgeverij, 1974.

29. D.T. Kohnstamm e.a., *Had de Proefkreche effect? Verslag van een wetenschappelijk onderzoek.* Dekker & Van de Vegt, Nijmegen, 1976.

30. E. Singer, Kansarme moeders en hun kinderen. In: *Nederlands tijdschrift voor opveoding, vorming en onderwijs* 1, 1985, pp. 57–65.

31. D.T. Kohstamm e.a., *Had de Proefkreche effect?*

32. M. de Winter, *Het voorspelbare kind.* Swets & Zietlinger, Lisse, 1986, pp. 58–63.

33. *Vroegtijdige onderkenning van psychosociale en pedagogische problemen bij kinderen van 0–7 jaar.* Landelijke Commissie VTO,

Publicatie nr. 9, Rijswijk, 1988; H. Tunnissen, Het swychologisch moederschap: de opkomst van het WTO-stelsel en de betekin van de peuterspeelizaal. In: *Kongresbundel Winteruniversiteit Vrouwenstudies 1983.* WUV, Nijmegen, 1983.

34. M. N. de Winter, *Het voorspelbare kind.* Swets & Zeitlinger, Lisse, 1986.

35. M. de Winter, *Het voorspelbare kind.* pp. 65–150; E. Singer, *Kinderopvang en do moeder-kindrelatie.* Etc. pp. 35–44.

36. F.C. Verhulst, *Mental health in Dutch children.* (Phd. Thesis) Rotterdam, 1985.

37. M. Riksen-Walraven, *Stimuering van de vroegkinderlijke ontwikkeling: een interventie-experiment.* Swets & Zeitlinger, Lisse, 1977.

38. *Project 'Spelvoorlichting aan huis',* Subsidieaanvraagf, Den Haag, augustus 1989.

39. P.H.M. van den Bogaart & P.M.A.E. Wintele, *Evaluatie van intensive thusibegeleiding (hometraining). Resultaten van een onderzoek onder tien experimentele projecten.* COJ, Leiden, 1988.

40. M. van Ooyen-Houben & H. de Kort, *Meer jonge kinderen in pleeggezinnen, deel 1 en 1.* CWOK, Den Haag, 1987; K.E.J. Hesser & A. van Hout, *Methodiekontwikkeling in de pleegzorg.* Hogeschool van Amsterdam, 1989; *Verslag symposium pleegzorg,* 29 september 1989 Bussem. Uitgave Brueau Landelikje Voorlichting van de Centrales voor Pleegzorg te Utrecht.

41. E. Singer, *Kinderopvang en de moeder-kindrelatie.* pp. 1–48.

42. L. Pot, *Kinderopvang nu. aorgen voor morgen.*

43. *FNV-emqiete (bedrijfs)kindergopvang in Nederland anno 1989.* FNV, Amsterdam 1989.

THE DEVELOPMENT OF PRIMARY EDUCATION IN THE NETHERLANDS

●●●●●●●●●◆●●●●●●●●

Ernst Mulder
University of Amsterdam
Amsterdam, Netherlands

To have a clear picture of the present organization of primary education in the Netherlands and of the recent Dutch educational policy, it is necessary to look at its origin. The modern Dutch educational system was born at the end of the 18th century. At that time the Netherlands, then the Republic of the Seventh United Provinces, once prosperous and powerful, was a nation in decline.

The country had lost its position of economic preeminence through a variety of causes. The deterioration of the staple market caused merchants to invest their accumulated wealth abroad, thus contributing to unemployment and poverty in the Netherlands, and in the 1780s attempts by the so-called Patriots to reform the government ended in a civil war, the occupation of Dutch territory by Prussia and the flight of many Patriots to France.

At the end of 1794, they returned with French troops and started the Batavian Revolution. In the resulting Batavian Republic, which lasted from 1795 to 1805, they immediately began to carry out their political program. This meant the introduction of a limited franchise, a constitution, and the centralization of government.

An important task of the central state was considered the organization of a national system of education. In 1799, the Agent of National Education was appointed, the first governmental official solely responsible for educational affairs in the Netherlands and as such the precursor of a Minister of Education. This official drafted the first national Education Act of 1801. As a result of political instabilities and some new constitutions, this act had to be reformulated in 1803 and 1806, but not substantially revised. The 1806 Education Act proved to be rather successful and remained operative for more than half a century.

The act had been strongly inspired by the ideas of the Society for the Public Benefit (Maatschappij tot Nut van't Algemeen). This was a private society, still in existence today, which operated on enlightened and moderate Protestant principles. Its members, mainly belonging to the bourgeoisie and with many ministers among them, tried to raise the moral and social level of the Netherlands, particularly by publishing booklets and leaflets. They wrote and argued about all kinds of social and political measures to be taken to relieve the fate of the lower classes in the Dutch community. They also took a great interest in the possibilities of popular education and many of the prize winning essays written for the Society were on this subject.

After 1795, when the prospects for reform seemed favorable, men of the Society began to put forward their ideas in the National Assembly. The affinity between the Society and the party of the Patriots, especially the moderate factions, made it easy to include the proposals of the Society in the drafts of the education acts. This surely contributed to making the act of 1806 the basis of "the most comprehensive educational system in Europe," (Schama, 1970: 589).

In the long run, this act brought some real improvements. First, it specified requirements teachers should meet before they were allowed to take a job. The Education Act also provided for the income of primary school teachers (to be paid for by the local government), so that they no longer depended on fees or other employment. Another important reform the act of 1806 initiated was the introduction of classroom instruction in contrast to the usual system of individuals learning by rote. Finally, under the act of 1806 the state appointed school inspectors. Their role was to ensure that the new national regulations were properly carried out, now that, after its disestablishment in the Batavian Republic, the Reformed Church was denied its traditional role in the control of the primary schools. Although many members of the inspectorate were ministers of this church, they now were selected because of their personal attitude to the new education. Their position made them central figures in the introduction and advancement of the education reforms in the early 19th century.

The act of 1806 did not create new kinds of primary education, but consolidated the existing system of public and private schools. In the first half of the 19th century, this meant a difference between schools that were financed by national or local authorities on the one hand and those funded by private bodies, like the Society, or by school fees. This distinction between public and private education would play a decisive role in the politics of Dutch primary education. The same is true with regard to the founding and maintaining of schools: this was not a responsibility of the state but of the cities, municipalities, corporations, and private persons.

After 1806, the Republic came under French rule and was finally annexed by France, and 1815 became the Kingdom of the Netherlands (including Belgium) after the defeat of Napoleon. The Education Act of 1806 survived, however, and in 1815 received the Royal assent. In many respects, the foundations were laid for a better primary education, but also for a serious political and ideological conflict. The influence of the Reformed Church on primary schools had officially come to an end as a result of its disestablishment. According to the act, education should be guided by general Christian principles and children should be taught "all social and Christian virtues." This was a rather vague formulation and growing numbers of orthodox Protestants, who already resented the loss of their influence on education, became dissatisfied with it, especially because the act explicitly instructed teachers to abstain from *any* dogmatic education. Roman Catholics, who since the Batavian Republic enjoyed equal rights in Dutch society, at first reacted positively to the general Christian character of the public primary school. But they also became more critical of it, because, among other things, in their view there were still too many Protestant primary school teachers and inspectors. Furthermore, however general the Christian character of the public school, it certainly was not Roman Catholic. Disagreement on primary education between the government and the Roman Catholics could have been influenced by a similar conflict between the government and the Roman Catholic clergy in the Southern Netherlands, that is, Belgium, on secondary education; this strife was one factor that eventually led to the Belgian secession from the Kingdom of the Netherlands in 1830. So Calvinists denounced public education as not Protestant enough and Roman Catholics as far too Protestant.

Orthodox Protestants especially, a minority in the Reformed Church, saw two ways to meet their objections to the general Christian public primary school. Some of them, like their political leader Groen van Prinsterer, tried to restore the situation to the way it was before 1795 when (for example, many schools taught their pupils the Calvinist Heidelberg Catechism). Others were inclined to found their own schools where they could teach their children along orthodox lines without state interference. But the government rejected these solutions, although the act of 1806 allowed private schools. For example, Jewish private schools were tolerated and even subsidized at the time. The authorities, however, withheld their permission as much as possible, probably because they first wanted to build up a good national system of primary education and certainly because as moderate, enlightened Protestants they detested the rigid Calvinists.

But the opposition against the existing system of public education rose. The government tried to save the 1806 act by permitting schools to consider the religious conviction of the local population. This erosion of the even vague Protestant-Christian character of the public education alarmed especially the orthodox Protestants, who became convinced that private denominational schools would be the only way to rescue religiously inspired primary education. They proved to be right. In 1848, the King, frightened by the revolutionary events all over Europe, "in one night turned from conservative into liberal" and the rising liberals came to power. In the new constitution of 1848, they included freedom of education.

Nevertheless, it took nine years of heated debate before a new education act was passed in 1857. This act again brought some real improvements: introduction of more subjects into the curriculum, a minimum salary for teachers, and a standard teacher-pupil ratio. In addition, the municipal authorities became the main executive in financial and organizational matters.

But the struggle over the religious character of primary education was not solved. The new act repeated the Christian and social virtues of the 1806 act, but stipulated that the teachers should abstain from any religious instruction because this could be offensive to pupils from another denominational background. Those who wanted religious education were allowed to found their own private schools without governmental permission, but also without governmental money. After a few years, the advocates of a Christian primary education concluded that the only way to achieve their goal was to start denominational private schools. Their most important issue for the next seventy years or so became to obtain state-aid for those schools, although they kept feeling a little ambivalent about it because of feared state-control.

In that political fight, known in Dutch historiography as the school struggle, the Roman Catholics took their side. Together they strove from maximum subsidy and minimum interference from the government. This struggle also played an important role in the political emancipation of orthodox Protestants and Roman Catholics.

After 1870, the liberals, who were still in power, tried to raise the level of public education, which went counter to their traditional policy of *laisser aller* (unwillingness to impose constraints). In the Education Act of 1876, the maximum number of pupils per teacher was reduced and the national government began to again subsidize public education. The private denominational schools viewed this as unfair competition because they were forced to meet the same educational standards as the public schools but without subsidy. Even worse, by paying their taxes they contributed to the public education they had not wanted. But the orthodox Protestants and Roman Catholics did not resign. On the contrary, they intensified their struggle and founded more denominational primary schools than ever.

Gradually the liberals began to realize that these schools provided for the wants of large groups of religious people and they began to think about concessions. At the same time, their power was waning so they had to reckon with the other (denominational) political parties. In a new Education Act of 1889, the denominational schools were granted some state aid and the amount was raised in the following decades. The liberals had accepted the principle of subsidy of private education; their main goal became to introduce compulsory education (from six to twelve years), which they achieved in 1900. This was a little late compared with the other Western countries, but enrollment in primary education was already more than 90 percent. Compulsory education met with resistance from orthodox Protestants and Roman Catholics because they saw in it the dreaded state interference in the decisions of parents. In this century, compulsory education has been gradually extended from six years in 1900, to ten years since the first half of the 1970s.

In 1917, a new constitution was passed which stipulated that the government was to take constant care of *all* primary education and that public and denominational education was to be financed equally by the state. Eventually, this meant a victory by the denominational political parties from the right. But there was a price to pay, that is, universal suffrage, which was a demand of the parties of the left, the liberals, and the socialists. This deal put an end to some eighty years of political struggle and solved two protracted problems in Dutch political life. (This is known as the pacification of Dutch politics.) The Primary Education Act of 1920 sealed the so-called financial equalization of public and denominational education. The ideal of 1806, one undivided school for one undivided nation, was dead and gone.

In the 1870s, more than 75 percent of all children in primary education attended public schools. In 1920, this percentage had already fallen to 55, and in the years after the financial equalization it fell even lower to a little more than 25 percent in the period from about 1945 till 1970. In the last two decades, this number rose again, but still only about one-third of all primary school children attend a nondenominational public school. So denomination education showed a remarkable development from a threatened minority to stable majority in half a century. The Roman Catholic schools did particularly well. In the 1920s, pupils in these schools outnumbered those in Protestant schools and they rose to a good 40 percent of all pupils in primary education. Today, about 35 percent attend a Roman Catholic primary school, some 30 percent a Protestant one and again some 30 percent a public, nondenominational school. The Dutch law not only allows denominational education financed by the government, but every kind of "particular" education (as is the literal translation of "bijzonder onderwijs"), denominational or nondenominational. This last category accounts for 2 percent to 5 percent of the pupils.

The settlement of educational affairs in the constitution of 1971 meant the consolidation and sanctioning of a Dutch system of primary education divided up into rather autonomous religious spheres. This system has been cherished by Protestants and Roman Catholics alike, and it is called the *verzuiling* (literally, polarization). Polarization was not limited to education, but it affected many sectors of Dutch society in the 20th century. As one Dutch historian described it, polarization meant

"the system of institutionalized segmentation according to which each religious or quasi-religious group, Protestant, Catholic, or humanist, was encouraged and subsidized by the state to create its own social world, comprising the entire existence of an individual from nursery schools to sporting club, trade union, university, hospital, broadcasting and television corporation, to the burial society" (Kossmann, 1978: 304).

The system of polarization has existed to this day and is particularly firmly entrenched in Dutch education. To promote their educational interests, the denominations brought about master organizations, which have been very powerful. Their influence has been evident in the regular consultations with the Minister of Education on almost every detail of educational policy. Together with denominational trade unions of teachers and with (orthodox) Protestant and Roman Catholic politicians, they have kept a close watch over what they have seen as the freedom of education: the freedom to found denominational schools with full financial state support but free from government interference as much as possible.

From time to time, critics have tried to point out the high costs of the system of financial equalization and of the obligation of local authorities to accept even very small denominational schools and to pay for them. These criticisms have always—and thus far successfully—been countered with an appeal to the freedom of education. But in the last few years even an orthodox Protestant Minister of Education has proposed another, more efficient system of so-called lump-sum financing, which should raise the quality of primary schools by creating more competition among them.

The strong position of denominational education and its fear of government interference have made it difficult for any Minister of Education to bring about reform. Therefore, from the 1920 act to World War II, the government had confined itself mainly to the finance and administration of primary education. Because of the peculiar polarized system, this was a complicated affair and the government took it seriously: in 1918 it created a Ministry of Education. This was also the beginning of an educational bureaucracy, which has been growing rapidly especially after 1945. Since the late 1960s, this Ministry has paid more and more attention to the innovation of primary education, which up to then had been the concern of some inspectors, teachers, and educational scientists.

This new, positive attitude of governmental officials and also of particular denominational politicians and Ministers toward reform has been affected by the increasing secularization of society and politics, but also by growing dissatisfaction with the existing primary education. Nevertheless, it took some twenty years to pass a new education act in 1981 (the first substantially new education act since 1920), which came into operation in 1985. In the meantime, since the end of the 1960s, the government, while working on new educational legislation, has tried to stimulate innovation by subsidizing national organizations that promote reform (e.g., by doing research and giving schools administrative support) and by building up a system of educational support (consisting of supporting organizations for achievement testing, for curriculum research and development, and for general and specific advice). These too indicate a growing government influence on the organization and content of primary education. Because they have benefitted from it at least as much as public education, even denominational politicians, boards, and educational organizations, always the first to point out the danger of state interference in education, have accepted and defended the extensive supportive system.

The Pedagogy of Primary Education

The Education Act of 1806 brought substantial improvements. It stipulated that teachers were allowed to practice their profession only when they had met specific requirements. This meant that the great majority of teachers received their professional training while working in the classroom as an apprentice. There already existed some private normal schools, founded by the Society of the Public Benefit, but these disappeared again and the development of national or local normal schools was very slow. Only after the 1857 act were more of these schools founded, but this proved to be not enough to train all those who wanted to teach at a primary school. So a system developed where teacher-apprentices worked in the classroom and

received their theoretical education in so-called normal courses, given by competent headmasters. These normal courses remained an important part of the training of primary school teachers until the Education Act of 1920, when they were concentrated in normal schools (or teacher training colleges). According to the polarized system, there were not only state normal schools, but also (orthodox) Protestant and Roman Catholic ones.

The programs of all these schools have been remarkably similar in outline through the last century: prospective teachers received a training in, the subject matter of primary education and in the psychology of child development, pedagogy, didactics, and social education. That is not to say that these reflected the changing opinion among educational scientists and educational spokesmen about educational reform, especially about new didactics. In the last twenty years, more and more attention is paid to special groups in the primary school, such as pupils with learning disabilities or from ethnic and cultural minorities.

The Act of 1806 also laid the foundation for a similar curriculum in every Dutch primary school and for the teaching method of classroom instruction that lasted for more than a century and a half. Pupils should be grouped by level of achievement and the teacher should lecture to a whole class. This was considered to be a necessary condition for the teachers to really explain the subject matter and for the pupils to really understand it. The subject matter itself consisted mainly of reading, writing, and arithmetic, with an emphasis on reading. In practice, teachers and textbooks laid great stress on moral instruction and especially on the virtue of obedience.

In the education acts of 1857 to the present, the subjects to be taught in primary schools were extended. Thus, the Dutch language, history, geography, biology and physics, drawing, music, gymnastics, manual training and needlework, and in the last decades before 1990 some mathematics and English became regular subjects in the curriculum.

Since the turn of the century, criticism of classroom instruction increased, especially among some members of the inspectorate, some education scientists, and some primary school teachers. They were evidently influenced by the international movement of progressive education and by individual reformers like Maria Montessori, Helen Parkhurst, John Dewey, Peter Petersen, and the Dutchmen Jan Ligthart and Kees Boeke. Some primary school teachers, inspired by their ideas and practices, tried to experiment in their own classrooms with group work, individual work, differentiation according to achievement (instead of to age), introduction of real life materials in the school curriculum, social education, and so on. These experiments, however, remained isolated cases, just as the schools of the educational innovators (or their followers) mentioned above. The system of teaching a whole class of children of the same age the same subject at the same time was there to remain for a little longer.

Despite the government's reluctance to stimulate reform, in the years after World War II the idea that primary education should be reformed had been growing stronger. At least three grounds for reform have been detected: (1) a need for innovation of the curriculum, (2) the large number of pupils who fall behind their peers or cannot reach the next grade, and (3) the presumed need to develop skills other than mere cognitive skills.

In the Act of 1981 the government tried to meet some of these criticisms, for example, by increasing the number of subjects in the curriculum. Another remarkable change the Act of 1981 brought was the integration of the nursery school (ages 4 to 6) and the primary school (ages 6 to 12) into one "basicschool," which means literally, basic school. As well, the beginning of compulsory education has been fixed at age 5 instead of 6, which dated from the Compulsory Education Act of 1900.

The idea behind this measure was to make the transition to the primary school easier for pupils and to create the possibility to prepare them better for the demands of primary education. This should prevent failure, drop out, and underachievement.

But, as mentioned above, there were reforms in primary education before the passing of the 1981 Act. Schools and individual teachers have always been allowed to experiment, within certain statutory limits, with timetables, didactic measures, educational materials, grouping, self-activity, individual teaching, and so on. Because this depended on the support of the inspectorate, the municipality, and the enthusiasm of schools and teachers, these experiments in educational innovation at first remained rather solitary classes. But gradually, especially since the end of the 1960s, more and more primary schools have introduced reforms so as to pay attention to internal differentiation according to individual achievement and aptitude, self-activity, group work, or didactic differentiation. As well, there was a growing interest among parents to send their children to Montessori schools, Dalton schools, Freinet schools, and other progressive schools. The rigorous system of uniform classroom instruction to age-grouped grades seems to be on its way out.

The Act of 1981 again offered the opportunity for a primary school to innovate its education, within certain limits. Each school has to draw up a working plan concerning the organization and content of the education for the eight-year period. The plan must include the educational aims of the school, the learning materials, didactic methods, organization of the school, grouping of pupils, means of evaluation, programs for problem pupils, and so on. Every two years, the local authorities, assisted by an inspector for primary education, must give their approval to this scheme. The regulations concerning the working plan leave room for a primary school to be unique and innovative, which is what actually happens.

Apart from the description of subject matter, the Act gives only rather general prescriptions for education in the basicschool. Primary education should stimulate not only the intellect, but also feeling; creativity; and social, cultural, and physical competence; and it should recognize the reality of the Netherlands as a multicultural society. But first, pupils must be given the opportunity to pass through an uninterrupted, continuous development, and education must be adapted to the development of each individual pupil as much as possible. Through the 1981 Act, the government has at least acknowledged some general principles of the progressive educators from the early 20th century.

Some Problems of Primary Education

When in 1900 children from ages 6 to 12 were compelled to attend a primary school, a group of mentally retarded, backward, or disabled children was revealed; before that they probably never came to school at all or they disappeared again silently. Compulsory education made the problem of children who needed special treatment visible, so to speak.

Schools for the deaf, the blind, and the mentally and physically disabled had existed for a long time, but schools for special education have only been founded since the turn of the century, especially in the cities and especially for mentally retarded children. In these schools, more or less specialized teachers tried to give pupils individual treatment. This treatment had sometimes been inspired by the Montessori method.

In the Education Act of 1920, special education was officially recognized by the government. Some thirty years later, in 1949, there existed already twelve types of special education; the schools for the mentally disabled or feeble-minded were the most numerous. Since then, special education has grown explosively in types, number of schools, and number of pupils. According to the polarized system in Dutch education there are public, Roman Catholic, and Protestant schools for special education. Public special education accounts for some 27 percent.

In the early years of this century, a few hundred pupils were enrolled in special education, in 1920 there were already 3,000; in 1950, 30,000; in 1970, 75,000; and today, more than 100,000 children visit a school for special education. The proportion of pupils in special education within the total number of children in primary education has also increased from almost 5 percent in 1970 to some 8 percent in 1990. This means that while the number of children in "normal" primary education has actually dropped, the number of children in special education has kept growing.

This development was reason for satisfaction and concern. Satisfaction because of the great possibilities for treatment and care of special needs children, concern because of the rising numbers of these children and of schools for special education.

In 1990, some 36 percent of the total number of children are enrolled in special education.

The sharp increase in special education is made up largely of schools for children with learning disorders and behavioral problems. These kinds of problems could be detected more easily since the development of intelligence tests and other psychological methods. Moreover, many learning disabilities seemed to be specific, that is limited to a certain area of competence (e.g., reading, or arithmetic, or small muscle control). These disabilities could be distinguished from general incapacity. So there has developed a differentiation in treatment in programs and sometimes in schools.

But together with the growth and refinement in the possibilities of treatment, the number of pupils that needed such special programs rose. Initially, it was up to the primary school teachers to observe a certain disability and to try to find an appropriate special program or school, although they were not trained for this aspect of their job. For this reason, there was a tendency to refer almost all pupils with learning disabilities and behaviorial problems to special schools. The result was an extensive system of special education, but also the separation of "normal" and "special" children.

This caused a debate about the desirability of the existing system. Special treatment by specifically trained teachers within the primary school was suggested as an alternative. Many children with minor disabilities, who were placed in special schools all too easily, could then stay in primary school and would not be segregated from their normal peers. This would mean a slowing of the growth of special education, while the burden of children who needed special programs would shift to the primary school. Indeed, although some primary school teachers qualified for remedial teaching, it seems that the need for a differentiated system of special education where children can be treated for specific disorders or disabilities will not decrease very much in the near future.

The government seems to recognize both: the objections against separation and differentiation, and the necessity of a good system of special education. The authorities have therefore developed a concept of the "broadening of care" of the primary school (i.e., the extension of possibilities and competence). This could be accomplished, for example, through a training program for primary school teachers that includes special educational programs to treat pupils with (minor) learning disabilities *within* the primary school. At the same time, special education could be strengthened qualitatively by better training of special school teachers. Thus, the activities in special education should concentrate on specialized, individual treatment, and the "broadening of care" should be aimed at the refinement of the working plan of the primary school and the improvement of the general didactic competence of primary school teachers.

Another, more recent problem in Dutch primary education is the growing number of pupils from cultural and ethnic minorities. After World War II, the Netherlands has known various groups of immigrants. Before that there lived only very small groups of foreign origin, like some Chinese, but they preferred to remain rather isolated. But since the 1950s, people from the (former) Dutch colonies, began to settle in the Low Countries: first those from Indonesia, and then those from Surinam and the Antilles. In the early 1960s, workers from the periphery of Europe came to the highly developed parts of the continent to supply the labor shortage and to earn a better living than in their native countries. People from Italy and Spain working in the Netherlands in the early 1960s were joined later in the decade by Turks and Moroccans. Since the economic crisis of the early 1970s, no additional foreign workers have been recruited. Yet, the number of immigrants rose because of the arrival of the families of the workers who already lived in the Netherlands. The labor migration changed into a family migration.

At first, the government thought that the foreign workers would leave again even after family reunion. But their stay proved to be rather permanent, in spite of their own wish to return to their native countries someday. This is true not only for the largest groups from the Mediterranean, the Turkish and Moroccan people, but also for the people of Surinam. In 1975, when Surinam became independent, about one-third of the Surinam population lived in the Netherlands and after the independence this number has fallen only slowly. Together with the Turks and the Moroccans, they make up the majority of all the cultural and ethnic minorities. In 1983, there were 152,000 Turks, 100,000 Moroccans, and 190,000 people from

Surinam. The total of people of ethnic groups in that year was 615,000. Slowly the authorities began to realize that Dutch society would be a multicultural society.

But this also created an educational problem: can the children from all these ethnic groups be treated just like the Dutch children? Obviously not, if only because of the language difficulties of children with another mother tongue. At first, the problem did not seem large. From 1970 to 1980, the percentage of children from cultural minorities in primary schools increased from just under 6 percent to almost 7 percent. But the numbers of Surinam and Antillian children dropped, while the numbers of Turkish and Moroccan children increased sharply to about 45 percent and 25 percent, respectively, of all minority children in primary education. Moreover, people from these ethnic groups are heavily concentrated in certain neighborhoods in the cities. This tendency has resulted in the distinction between what are called "black schools" and the "white schools," with a majority of white, mostly Dutch children.

That the Dutch primary school has not been prepared to give the children of ethnic and cultural minorities an adequate education is shown poignantly by the number of these children enrolled in special education. In 1988, 40 percent of all the Turkish and Moroccan children of primary school age (5 to 12) were enrolled in a school for special education, while they make up only 7 percent of the total primary-school-age population. The share of the Turkish and Moroccan children in the total population in special education was in 1988 29 percent and 26 percent respectively (CBS, Statistisch Zakboek (1988)). These very high numbers indicate a serious problem.

Since the 1970s, official policy concerning the education of children from ethnic and cultural minorities has been to try to integrate them into Dutch society and therefore into the Dutch educational system, although the authorities first thought about their education with an eye on returning these minorities to their native countries. Yet, some attention has been given to education in their own language and culture by specially appointed native teachers. But first these children should learn Dutch and the subject matter of the existing curriculum of the primary school.

From about 1980, the Dutch government has

recognized the cultural and ethnic minorities as immigrants who will stay permanently. Accordingly, the authorities have aimed their educational policy concerning these groups at the prevention of educational failure and the furthering of their participation in the educational system and in the Dutch society in general. What this actually means is that minority children can be placed in a regular class or grade in a primary school or in a special class to receive a more intensive program. For both situations, there are specially trained teachers to introduce them to Dutch language and culture. Special classes can particularly be found in schools with many minority children. A problem is the separation of children in these classes from the other children in the school, although from time to time they visit the corresponding age grades of the school. Another element in the government policy has been education in the language and culture of the ethnic groups themselves, not to prepare them to return to their native countries but to preserve identity and self-confidence. Unfortunately, the relationship between the mother tongue and the Dutch language and between the two cultures has never been articulated. The effect of the educational policy concerning minority children is still uncertain. Also, the prescription for every primary school that it should convey to its pupils the idea of a multicultural society and that every school should provide "intercultural education" shows good intentions, but this is only to state the problem, not to solve it. The place of minority children in primary education will be one of the great problems in Dutch education for the coming decades.

References

Kossmann, E. (1978). *The Low Countries, 1780–1940*. London: Oxford University Press.

Schama, S. (1970). Schools and politics in the Netherlands, 1796–1814. *The Historical Journal, 13*, 589.

EARLY CHILDHOOD EDUCATION IN NEW ZEALAND: THE WINDS OF CHANGE

• • • • • • • • • • ◆ • • • • • • • • • •

Anne B. Smith
University of Otago
Dunedin, New Zealand

"Educare" is a term being increasingly heard in the international early childhood world (Caldwell, 1989). It is used in this chapter to discuss the New Zealand early childhood system because it seems particularly appropriate at the present time. Current changes to the educational administration in New Zealand are (among other things) directed at producing a more integrated and equitably funded early childhood system. The importance of the concept of educare is that it recognizes the impossibility of separating care and education into services designated as providing mainly care or mainly education.

Educare is a term used to describe the continuum of supervised services with both social and educational goals, for the care and education of children from birth to age 7, in the temporary absence of their parents, in homes, early childhood centers, or primary schools. An integrated care and educational system for children under age 7 is an ideal toward which some progress is being made, particularly in provision for children under age 5, but which is not yet a reality. This chapter focuses on educare for children between birth and age 7 with the emphasis on provision for children under age 5.

Schooling in New Zealand is not compulsory until age 6, but more than 95 percent of New Zealand children first attend school on or near their fifth birthday. Most New Zealand children arrive at school having experienced early childhood educare. The first two years of school are spent in the junior school, and children enter the senior primary school (standard 1) at age 7 or 8. Ninety percent of 4-year-olds, 63 percent of 3-year-olds, and 20 percent of 2- and under 2-year-olds attend a childhood service (Burns, 1989: 12). There are 26 different varieties of early childhood centers in New Zealand, but the five main early childhood services are kindergartens, playcenters, child care centers, *kohanga reo* (i.e., Maori language nests where children are immersed in their mother tongue), and Pacific Island language nests. On October 1, 1989 a radical restructuring of early childhood, primary, and secondary education took place in New Zealand. This is discussed in this chapter following the description of the state of early childhood educare before the changeover.

Context of New Zealand Society

To understand New Zealand's educare provisions it is necessary to describe the history and current context of New Zealand education. New Zealand is a small country with a population of around 3.3 million. New Zealand consists of two major groups: Maori and non-Maori. New Zealand Maori, the first settlers of New Zealand who arrived in New Zealand from Polynesia somewhere between 900 A.D. and 1350 A.D., make up 12 percent of New Zealand's population. People of Maori descent comprise a larger proportion of younger age groups (the percentage of the non-Maori population that is under age 4 is 7.7 percent, while the comparable percentage for Maori is 13.3 percent). The non-Maori population is largely European (making up 80 percent of the total population); the next largest group is Pacific Islanders (3.5 percent of the total population) with small numbers of other non-European groups such as Chinese and Indian. New Zealand non-Maori settlement began after Captain Cook's visit in 1769 but it was not until after 1840 that systematic colonization began (Royal Commission Report, 1988; 1:4).

In 1840, the British Crown and New Zealand Maori chiefs signed a treaty that granted Britain sovereignty over New Zealand and allowed the Crown to be the sole buyer of land from the Maori in return for protection and Maori authority over land, resources, and other treasures (taonga). The Treaty of Waitangi has major significance for New Zealand society, and this has recently been accorded much more prominence. The needs and rights of the Maori people as tangata whenua (people of the land) are a major concern in New Zealand. A 1988 Royal Commission describes the treaty as "central to understandings of New Zealand society, its historical development and contemporary realities" (ibid., 2:17). The Royal Commission also states: "It [the Treaty] is not only an historical record upon which grievances for the past can be based, but more importantly we see it as a pro-active agreement with relevance to the twenty-first century and beyond" (ibid.).

The treaty is very important for social policy in education if it is interpreted broadly because it promises protection not only for the land but for the language, cultural, and social values of the Maori. Such a broad view has been reflected in recent legislation in education and early childhood educare has also been greatly influenced by the emphasis given to treaty principles in recent years. Indeed, the sweeping changes to education initiated in 1989 incorporate the Treaty of Waitangi in many ways (Deaker, 1990). For example, the 1989 Education Act states that every charter (i.e., a contract between schools or early childhood centers and the government) has to contain

policies and practices that reflect New Zealand's cultural diversity, and the unique position of the Maori culture; . . . [and take] . . . all the reasonable steps to ensure that instruction in tikanga Maori [Maori culture] and te reo Maori [the Maori language] are provided for full-time students whose parents ask for it.

The Minister of Education of the recently elected National government, Lockwood Smith, has stated that, in the future the former Labour government's goal of promoting the Treaty of Waitangi will be optional rather than compulsory for schools. However, he does not intend to change the legislation.

Like many Western countries, New Zealand's demographic characteristics have changed greatly in the last 20 years. New Zealanders are having fewer children, they live in a greater variety of family forms, and women participate more in paid employment in addition to their role in the family. The birth rate has declined rapidly since 1961, more rapidly for Maori than for non-Maori. (The New Zealand population of Maori descent has increased from 8.4 percent in 1961 to 12.4 percent in 1986). The total fertility rate for non-Maori is 1.9 births per woman and for Maori 2.2 births per woman.

Trends in marriage patterns have contributed to declining fertility with a major upward shift of age for entering first marriage and childbirth, decreases in the proportion of those who marry, increasing marital dissolution, increasing remarriage, and increasing fertility regulation (Cheyne, 1988). New Zealand has a high rate of ex-nuptial births (25 percent) but many of these are within stable de facto relationships. It is estimated that the percentage of single-parent families is 8 percent of all households and 14 percent of households with dependent children (Royal Commission Report, 1988, 1:151, 167). Such families are four times more likely to be headed by a female, to be a Maori, to have a low income, and to be disadvantaged with respect to income, housing, and basic amenities.

Women have increased their involvement in the labor force from 29 percent in 1945 to 53.3 percent by 1986. The greater participation of married women in the labor force is an important factor in their increased involvement. In 1986, 23 percent of women with children under age 5 worked full-time in paid employment, and 32 percent worked part-time (Burns, 1989: 13). New Zealand's parental leave legislation allows parents to take unpaid parental leave for up to one year. Parental leave entitles parents to return to their previous positions if they are still open or have preference over other applicants for similar positions.

New Zealand is experiencing a prolonged and continuing rise in unemployment, which affected 4.5 percent of the population in 1961, rose to 6.8 percent in 1986, and is currently 11 percent (*Otago Daily Times*, March 16, 1990). There is a higher rate of female unemployment (9.1 percent in 1986) than male (5.1 percent). The Maori rate of unemployment is higher (14.9 percent) than the non-Maori rate. Burns describes the current situation thus: "New Zealanders reel daily from news of company failures, corporate giants going into receivership. The news of another 100 jobs lost is no longer a matter of comment" (Burns, 1989: 1).

A centralized free, compulsory, and secular educational system was introduced in New Zealand with the Education Act of 1877 (Ewing, 1970). The New Zealand educational system has developed from a blend of 19th-century Scottish and English influences. But in the 20th century, progressive ideas came from many other countries. New Zealand's first Labour government came to power in 1937 bringing strong ideals of egalitarianism which have had a lasting influence. The Prime Minister and Minister of Education Peter Fraser's statement made in 1939 has been much quoted: "[E]very citizen . . . has a right to a free education for which he is best fitted, and in the fullest extent of his powers."

Services for Children Under Age 5

New Zealand has a diverse array of services for children under age 5. Even though future prospects are for more integrated services, currently the main early childhood movements fiercely guard their autonomy and individuality. They differ markedly as a result of their different histories, philosophies, and clientele. Procedures for governmental fund-

ing, training of staff, and administration also vary widely in the 26 different types of services. To provide a picture of educare in New Zealand, it is necessary to briefly describe some of the main strands in this complex weave of services.

Kindergartens

Kindergartens are the oldest early childhood service in New Zealand, having celebrated their 100th birthday in 1989. Kindergartens offer sessional programs for 3- and 4-year-olds. In 1989, kindergartens catered to the largest percentage of children under age 5 in early childhood educare (24,118, or 42 percent).

The kindergarten movement arose out of the charitable efforts of well-to-do women in Dunedin (a South Island city) to help the children of the poor during a depression. The movement emphasized the ideals of Friedrich Froebel and the idea that moral regeneration could occur through preschool education. The movement has had a profound long-term influence on early childhood education in New Zealand, because it was founded on the principle that preschool education should be free. Parents are not required to pay a fee, but most kindergartens ask them to give a donation toward expenses not covered by the government (85 percent of the total costs of the kindergartens are met by the government). Another long-term influence has been the link between voluntary organizations and the government. The government began to make contributions to kindergartens in 1904 and until recently kindergartens received the lion's share of governmental funding for early childhood education. In 1988–89, 69 percent of the governmental funding for early childhood (total 73 million NZ dollars—the New Zealand dollar is currently at U.S. $0.58) was spent on kindergartens. The kindergarten movement is probably the most homogenous of New Zealand's services for children under age 5, due to its support from (and control by) a centrally administered governmental education department in combination with a strong national body (the New Zealand Free Kindergarten Union) with firmly established policies for kindergartens all over New Zealand.

Like the majority of New Zealand's early childhood services, kindergartens are largely free-play programs where the child chooses among a variety of activities and the teacher's role is to support the child-initiated learning. Teachers are expected to interact frequently with children, and to play and arrange the learning environment in terms of space, objects, time, and people. Teachers tend to see the children's development in each of the social, intellectual, physical, and emotional spheres as equally important. A typical example of kindergarten general goals as expressed by a kindergarten teacher is as follows: To provide a program which is stimulating and creative, providing opportunity to develop socially, emotionally and intellectually. To provide an atmosphere that is homely and to encourage family interaction. Also to help parents understand their own children's development [through] observing at sessions (Meade, 1985: 36).

Kindergartens have been perceived by the public as somewhat more formal, disciplined, and school-oriented than playcenters or child care centers, although this perception is not supported by observational evidence (Meade, 1985; Smith, 1988). The usual (though not universal) structure of kindergartens is for two or three trained staff to work with a group of 40 children. A staffing scheme that ensures three teachers for every kindergarten is currently being phased in . Four-year-olds usually attend five morning sessions a week and 3-year-olds, three afternoon sessions a week. Kindergarten teachers are trained in state-supported colleges of education for three years. (Before 1987, kindergarten teachers were trained for 2 years, so the majority of kindergarten teachers currently have two years training.)

Some of the major problems for New Zealand kindergartens concern providing a quality service with the present teacher-child ratios, the necessity of providing more flexible hours and programs in response to parental needs in spite of the resistance to changing traditional patterns of organization, and lack of availability of places and trained staff in areas of high demand.

Playcenters

The playcenter movement is a parental cooperative movement that began in 1940. It catered in 1989 to the second largest number (24,199, or 23 percent) of children under age 5. It arose out of the needs of young women alone with children for

support in caring for children and out of a progressive educational movement (the New Educational Fellowship) based on the ideas of John Dewey and Susan Isaacs (among others). The playcenter movement has developed into a movement with strong educational ideals of cooperative community-based preschool education. It rejects the notion of the provision of a professional service for other people's children. Instead, playcenter sessions (usually offered two or three half-days a week) are staffed by parents who have various levels of training provided by the local playcenter organization. Playcenter sessions were originally mainly for 3- and 4-year-olds, but currently centers accept and receive funding for children from birth to age 5.

Playcenter supervisors are not paid a professional wage, but rather a modest honorarium for the sessions they lead. Their work is really voluntary because the playcenter movement does not wish to build up a core of professionals, but rather to train as many parents as possible who will make way for other parents as their own children reach school age. Playcenters still offer programs influenced greatly by the ideas of people such as Isaacs, with emphasis on children's spontaneous development through play in an environment of supportive adults. Structured adult-directed programs are frowned on, though a diverse array of play activities are provided for children. Ratios tend to be much more favorable than those in kindergartens, with 1:6 being the maximum especially if there are children under 2 1/2 years old present. Ratios in playcenters are more often around 1:3 for children under 2 1/2 years old—either a parent or a nominated parent substitute must be present. Many of the parents who work in playcenters have no training or only a small amount. Playcenters do, however, provide a variety of levels of training for people in the organization, from the level of a parent-helpers certificate to a national diploma.

Playcenters receive some governmental support for training, liaison, and programs, but parents also pay a fee. Playcenters in 1988–89 received 4.5 percent of the total governmental expenditure on early childhood education. The main current problem for playcenters has been lack of person power to provide the voluntary staffing of the centers, largely due to the movement of women back into the workforce while their children are young. There has been a gradual drop in numbers of children attending playcenters in recent years. Nonetheless, playcenters represent a powerful service voice and philosophy for progressive child-centered early childhood educare in New Zealand. Women who have contributed to the playcenter movement while their children were preschoolers often move to other early childhood services, and currently many have a major role in the new administration of early childhood educare.

Child Care

Child care services include a variety of programs for children from birth to age 5 in the absence of their parents. Child care centers catered to the third largest group of children under age 5 in 1989 (15,701, or 16 percent). Only slightly less than one-half of child care children are in full-day programs while the rest attend less than four hours a day. The approximate age division is that about one-third of child care children are under age 3, one-third are age 3, and one-third are age 4.

The first recorded child care center in New Zealand, established by Catholic nuns in Wellington in 1903, was also a philanthropic service for the poor with strong links to other welfare services, such as soup kitchens. It was not until 1960 that the government made any attempt to regulate the quality of child care centers. The child care regulations were initially administered by the Education Department, but between 1972 and 1986 were the responsibility of Social Welfare, before returning to Education again in 1986. The 1985 revisions of the regulations required each center supervisor to have a recognized training qualification: staff-child ratios in full-day programs of 1:4 for children under age 2, 1:5 for children over age 2, and 1:10 for 3- and 4-year-olds; and a group size no larger than 25 for any center with infants or 50 for centers without infants.

The changing role of women in New Zealand in the 1970s and 1980s resulted in a very rapid growth in the provision of child care services. Pressure from the women's movement also led to a considerable increase in the amount of governmental funding. The move of child care services from administration by Social Welfare to Education in 1986 reflected a landmark change in direction and attitude. The move was the result of years

of governmental reports and recommendations urging both more funding for child care and the recognition that child care provided both education and care for children under age 5. A trickle of governmental support in the form of subsidies for low-income families began in 1973. There were gradual increases in funding through the 1970s, but it was not until 1983 that much more substantial funding for child care developed and this was through the introduction of a scheme of grants for trained staff. While funding centers for trained staff was a large factor in improving the quality of child care centers, it led to problems in terms of lack of supply of trained staff.

Funding for child care in New Zealand is not limited to nonprofit centers. Private profit-making centers and voluntary or community child care services (largely provided by private owners or community organizations) have been largely funded by parents. In 1988, parents paid approximately 60 percent of the cost of child care and the government 40 percent. Child care services in 1988–89 received around 15 percent (about $10.5 million) of total early childhood educational funding. Since child care is a term that covers such a broad array of centers (including full-day child care centers, creches within workplaces and educational institutions, private and community kindergartens, Montessori and Steiner centers), it is almost impossible to generalize about the child care curriculum and program. There has been a much greater diversity of quality and of program philosophy within child care than within kindergarten, probably because of the much lower level of governmental support.

The perception that child care is more oriented to care than to education is changing. The integration of training for kindergarten and child care that took place in 1987 did much to change perceptions of child care as a care-oriented service, but these perceptions had already been undermined by the move of child care to Education in 1986. Since the first graduates of three-year courses did not appear until the end of 1990, it is likely that for many years only a small minority of child care staff will have three-year integrated training. Until the introduction of three-year training, one-year, full-time courses within colleges of education and field-based courses for people already working in centers provided by the New Zealand Childcare Association were the main training courses offered. About 70 percent of child care staff have some recognized qualifications, but these include a wide variety of courses (including primary teacher training). As demands for training for child care staff increase, many colleges of education are responding by providing courses for staff with older forms of training to upgrade their qualifications so that they are equivalent to a three-year diploma level.

Current issues for child care centers include the insufficient funding to pay staff a reasonable wage and to maintain standards of good quality child care; the lack of availability of training at the preservice level and for untrained staff currently working; and the lack of affordable and accessible child care services.

Te Kohanga Reo

In 1982, the *te kohanga reo* movement was born out of the Maori movement toward cultural renaissance, with the major aim of supporting and encouraging the use of Maori language and cultural values. By 1989, *kohanga reo* were the fourth largest provision for children under age 5 (11,125, or 11 percent). The 1988 Government Review of Te Kohanga Reo stated:

te kohanga reo sought to ensure that Maori was spoken to the children from the time of birth, literally, as the babes fed from the breast. Immersion in *te reo* Maori (language) and *nga tikanga* Maori (culture) were non-negotiable features of the innovation. They were the means to meet the challenge of reasserting the mana and daily use of *te reo* Maori and *nga tikanga* Maori in a society with such a strong monocultural bias (p.19).

Concerns for the educational development of Maoris in the 1960s (Bennet, 1985) identified early childhood education as the key to later educational progress. The Maori Education Foundation devoted considerable resources toward increasing the enrollment of Maori children in playcenters and kindergartens. Although there was a short-term increase in Maori enrollment at early childhood centers, this declined in the 1970s so that Maori children remained underrepresented in the preschool population and there was still a deep concern for their future (Government Review of Te Kohanga Reo, 1988; Smith and Swain, 1988). Increasingly, Maori people came to view Maori lack of progress in education as a result of the monoculturalism of the majority educational system, which resulted in feelings of alienation and loss of motivation in Maori children. The decline of the Maori language could certainly be attributed largely to educational practices of discouraging, and indeed punishing, children for speaking Maori. There is hope that Maori children's self-esteem and pride in their cultural heritage will be rediscovered through participating in *kohanga reo* and that this will turn around the current pattern of Maori underachievement.

One of the principles in the Treaty of Waitangi is *rangatiratanga*, which means Maori control over Maori people's lives and destiny. The *kohanga reo* movement fiercely insists on its own control and right to self-determination in the development of *kohanga reo*, according to the principles of the treaty. The growth of the *kohanga reo* movement has been the most rapid of any early childhood movement in New Zealand's history. From the first center opening in 1982, there were, in 1989, 534 centers.

Approximately 15 percent of all Maori children from birth to age 4 attend *kohanga reo*, and *kohanga reo* children comprise about 9 percent of all children in early childhood centers. About one-half of these children are age 2 or 3, and 7 percent of them are under age 1 (Government Review of Te Kohanga Reo, 1988). *Nga kohanga reo* are flexible programs (in size, premises, teacher-child ratios, and hours of opening), which vary in structure and operation according to the needs of the local community. The most important requirement of caregivers, usually older women, is that they be fluent Maori language speakers who are well-versed in Maori tradition and culture. Ninety percent of the adults involved with *kohanga reo* are not paid and many work on a part-time basis.

Another philosophical commitment is that *kohanga reo* be operated on a *whanau* (extended family) basis, so that the local family and community play a crucial part in the operation and support for centers. The *whanau* model views *kohanga reo* as a group responsibility so that all responsible should learn together under the training programs that operate in *kohanga reo*. The syllabus for training (known informally as "the Blue Book") provides information on preparation of food, bookkeeping, administration, and teaching programs.

Kohanga reo are somewhat less oriented toward free play than other early childhood centers (indeed this is explicitly rejected by some *kohanga reo*), and programs include more formal group activities and structured language teaching. It is significant that many *kohanga reo* programs take place in the *marae* (meeting house), which has deep spiritual importance for many Maori because it is seen as the home of their ancestors. The *marae* is also a place of great ceremonial significance to Maori and protocol unique to each tribe is followed carefully within it.

The administration and funding of *kohanga reo* is through the Department of Maori Affairs and the Te Kohanga Reo National Trust, not through the Department of Education. There was $13 million allocated to *nga kohanga reo* in 1988–89, which was divided among the more than 500 *kohanga reo* and paid as a bulk grant by the trust to the local management groups. Although funding came through the Maori affairs department, there were many links between *kohanga reo* and the Department of Education. For example, the Child Care Centre Regulations (which applied to any *kohanga reo* that were licensed centers) were administered by the Department of Education (until the restructuring); early childhood support and advisory officers were available to *nga kohanga reo*; and *kohanga reo* have been participants in local and national in-service courses.

Currently, the major problems for the *te kohanga reo* movement stem from the enormous pressure on the resources of Maori people to meet the pressing demand and the rapid growth in provision. The more fluent Maori speakers are needed to act as *kaiako* (teachers) in *kohanga reo* and sufficient funds are needed to pay for training staff while operating centers at the same time. There is also a major concern that children who have attended *kohanga reo* will lose their native language skills when they enter school unless follow-on programs to maintain the Maori language are provided.

Pacific Island Language Nests

The late 1980s also saw phenomenal growth in another movement designed to preserve minority mother tongue languages and cultural values: Pacific Island early childhood centers. Pacific Island people are the largest group of immigrants to New Zealand and New Zealand has close links with the Pacific, having had a history of colonial mandate over many Pacific Island nations. In some cases (e.g., Niue), there are more Pacific Islanders living in New Zealand than in the islands. Many Pacific Islanders have come to New Zealand seeking a better education and life-style for their children because of lack of opportunity at home. Pacific Islanders are concerned (Tamasese, Masoe-Clifford, and Ne'emia-Garwood, 1988) about problems of educational underachievement and concentration in unskilled jobs, but there is recent evidence of much improved retention rates at school and rates of participation in tertiary education.

Pacific Island children were shown in the late 1970s and early 1980s (Jamieson, 1979; Fenwick, Norman, and Leong, 1984) to be much less likely than European children to have attended preschool before entering school. For example, a 1984 study (Fenwick, Norman, and Leong, 1984) found that 47.5 percent of Pacific Island children had early childhood center experience compared to 85 percent of European children. A concern for Pacific Island children to have equitable learning opportunities and at the same time preserve their language and cultural identity has led to the development of Pacific Island language nests, where the indigenous language is used in the early childhood center (for example *aoga amata* are Samoan preschools and *te punanga reo* are Cook Island preschools). Pacific Island centers differ from *kohanga reo* in that their aim is not so much to revive a dying language as to preserve already fluent language and traditional values for immigrant groups. In 1989, the number of Pacific Island centers grew from 15 at the beginning of the year to 76 by June (Burns, 1989), illustrating the vigorous growth of this movement. Informal community centers including Pacific Island language nests had 5,602 (about 6 percent) children under age 5 in 1989. Pacific Island centers have been concerned with providing trained staff for the many centers being established, and have received some additional governmental support for training through the New Zealand Childcare Association's training scheme. Priority has recently been given to the support of Pacific Island language nests through sessional grants to nonprofit preschool groups, and $927,000 was approved in 1988 for such centers. Like *kohanga reo*, Pacific Island preschools include a great variety of types of center depending on the needs of the local community—from informal family playgroups and groups that meet for a couple of sessions a week, to full-time child care centers.

Family Day Care

Informal home-based child minding is an extensive out-of-sight form of provision for young children. Julian estimated in 1981 that there were approximately 35,000 children in such arrangements in New Zealand, often cared for in the homes of relatives, friends, or neighbors. There is no formal registration or supervision for private child minding in New Zealand. There are, however, several different supervised family day care schemes operating. Family day care schemes are defined here as supervised arrangements, where children are cared for in private homes with support and sometimes training from a social services agency or a community group. In 1985, there were 33 family day care schemes in New Zealand catering to about 5,000 children. All but two were administered by Barnardo's of New Zealand, an organization that emphasizes its role as providing a preventive social welfare service to families in need (Smith & Swain, 1988). Parents pay for family day care (about $2.50 to $3 an hour), but some subsidy comes from the government in the form of a project grant of $15,000 per scheme, per year. Normally, caregivers are paid at extremely low rates, often as low as $2 an hour, but family day care coordinators receive a professional wage. A form of family day care that usually only middle-class or professional families can afford has recently regained popularity; this is the use of professional nannies who look after children full-time in their own homes. New Zealand has two successful and popular "nanny schools" which train such caregivers. Currently, changes to the administration of early childhood educare draw family day care schemes into the network of state provision and accountability (supervised family day care schemes now receive state funding, but they are expected to meet reasonable quality standards).

Early Intervention for Children With Special Needs

According to Mitchell (1987), there has been a rapid and profound change in the provision of education for handicapped and at-risk infants, toddlers, and preschoolers in the last decade in New Zealand. In the 1970s, apart from the access to regular preschools, the principal provision for preschool children with special needs was from itinerant advisers to the deaf, two preschool groups for deaf children, and limited preschool provision by the Intellectually Handicapped Society (IHC) and Crippled Children Society (CCS). There was also access to speech therapy and cerebral palsy schools in a small number of cases. Provision for children under age 3 was extremely unusual (*ibid.*).

The 1970s saw an increase in concern for at-risk infants and infants with disabilities. Mitchell describes an era when the emphasis was on helping parents to cope with developmentally disabled children in their own homes. Beginning in 1973, the Department of Education began to staff groups for mildly handicapped preschoolers in regular kindergartens. By 1985, the number of special preschool groups had reached 40. In addition, there were four units for preschool deaf children and 31 special classes located in regular primary schools for preschool children with special needs. The Department also developed a special needs section of correspondence school to provide home-based programs for children under age 5, and appointed five advisers to work with parents and teachers of young handicapped children.

During the 1970s, a small number of early intervention programs for developmentally delayed infants developed in different parts of the country. An example of such a program is the Christchurch early intervention program (Ballard, 1988; Champion, 1985). It was initially developed for Down's syndrome infants but expanded to include children with other disabilities. Parents meet with their infants and an interdisciplinary team (including a psychologist and a physiotherapist) every week. Infants are regularly assessed and referred to specialists where necessary. Parents are encouraged to give extra stimulation and attention to their children according to a program based on a Piagetian process-oriented curriculum. From about age 3, the children are mainstreamed into regular kindergartens, playcenters, or child care centers, and visited by an itinerant teacher who provides support and suggestions for the regular teachers and for the parents at least once a week. The majority of children who have been through the program have not been successfully integrated into normal primary school.

The IHC did operate centers for mildly to profoundly intellectually handicapped preschoolers, although these are being phased out in favor of increasing children's access to existing community-based programs and support for parents at home. Mitchell (1987) described the Auckland Branch of IHC's program as based on formalized assessment, training, parental contact, and systematic evaluation. Groups of four to six children are assigned to one teacher, and children are regularly assessed on various developmental scales in order to determine broad teaching goals. Broad goals are broken down into smaller steps and goals are discussed in detail with parents, who are encouraged to continue group programs at home. Current IHC philosophy stresses that preschool children should receive, as of right, access to regular early childhood services with additional resources support provided for mainstreaming, rather than segregated provision.

Bray (1987) believes that quality early childhood provision for mildly handicapped children is essential if it is to be of any value. She was concerned about the difficulty in providing high-quality, carefully planned provision for children with a developmental delay in regular New Zealand preschools with a philosophy of unstructured and nondirected play and unfavorable staff-child ratios. The special groups within regular preschools were probably developed because of such consideration. Children with special needs are withdrawn at certain periods and taught by a special teacher, but at other times they are integrated into the regular program. Such an approach is not true mainstreaming, and it is likely that the children with special needs who are singled out for special attention may attract the negative expectations and labels associated with segregation. This approach has been referred to as "islands in the mainstream." Current opinion (Bray, 1990) is that early childhood centers should be staffed in such a way that children with special needs can share the regular program with the rest of the children. With full mainstreaming, it is crucial that every early childhood teacher receive the type of training that will enable her or him to provide individualized programming for developmentally delayed children within the same framework as that for other children in the center.

Mitchell (1987) identifies the main issues for early intervention in New Zealand as: (1) the movement away from a concern for categorizing types of disability to a more flexible approach; (2) the role of parents as agents or partners in teaching their children; (3) parents' access to medical and psychological records; (4) the need for parents' rights to be considered by professionals; (5) the lack of coordination in the administration of the plethora of early intervention services; and (6) how early intervention programs can be made more culturally sensitive.

A Canadian researcher who visited New Zealand's early intervention programs in 1986 commented that there was considerable variation in early intervention programs in different parts of the country in many characteristics (e.g., physical provision, funding, staff training, parental involvement, and programs (Brynelson, 1987). Programs operated in relative isolation from each other with little direction or support from funding sources. She found that many of the programs project an image of the participating children as "sick," deviant, or in need of sheltered and segregated treatment. She was surprised at the lack of an agency to coordinate early intervention programs and concluded that the variability she observed could be attributed to "a lack of direction, support and training opportunities for both professionals and parents involved in these services" (ibid., 73). Brynelson also felt that the separation of services for the handicapped infants from generic services contributed to the negative, categorical image, setting up the expectation of need for a sheltered, segregated existence.

Despite this unfavorable picture of early intervention in the mid-1980s, New Zealand has developed a strong philosophy of mainstreaming and commitment to early intervention for children with special needs. It is believed that children with disabilities should be educated in early childhood centers and schools alongside their peers, with appropriate resource support (Ballard, 1988; Mitchell, 1987). Mitchell argues that there is widespread agreement in the educational community that all children with special needs should be integrated into regular educational facilities, but he says that there is less than full support in the implementation of these views by the government's

Department of Education. A recent speech by the former Minister of Education (Goff, 1990) indicates the government was committed to mainstreaming, although he also said that special facilities would continue to exist. The former Minister also stated that there would be "a vastly increased emphasis . . . on early intervention" (ibid., 15) supported by the creation of 12 new district advisers' position in early intervention whose role would be to develop "flexible and coordinated" early intervention programs. Whether the new Special Education Service provides the necessary coordination and planning for early intervention recommended by Brynelson remains to be seen. The newly elected national government has already indicated that it is much less committed to mainstreaming than was the previous Labour regime.

One factor that should be influential in the provision of mainstreamed early education for children with special needs is a change in the law, which took effect in January 1990. The new Education Act states that people with special educational needs "have the same rights to enrol and receive education at state schools as people who do not." This means that starting on a child's fifth birthday, a child is entitled to free enrollment at any state school and cannot be denied that right.

Unfortunately, the Education Act refers to children who have reached the age of compulsory schools and does not cover children under age 6. It is therefore possible for children under age 5 to be denied access to state-supported early childhood centers. For example, in one case, a spina bifida child was denied admission to a regular preschool because of the child's disability (McArthur, 1990). The child was of normal intellectual development but because of the physical handicap did not have bladder and bowel control and had to wear diapers. The child was denied access on the grounds that all children had to be toilet-trained before they were accepted. This child's physical disability meant that she could not be toilet-trained. This example shows that children can still be excluded from early childhood educare programs because of a disability.

5- to 7-Year Olds: The Junior School

The primary education system in New Zealand is much more homogenous and centrally adminis-

tered than the early childhood system. For example, the central Department of Education (now the Ministry of Education) prescribes a national curriculum, sets regulations, approves expenditures, and sets national policy for education. Ten local education boards control the local appointment of teachers but are otherwise largely agents of the central Education Department (McLaren, 1974).

There are no formal administrative or professional links between early childhood services (for children under age 5) and junior classes within primary schools (for 5- to 7-year-olds). Primary teachers are trained in the same state colleges of education as early childhood (kindergarten and child care) teachers, but until recently there has been little in common in the courses taken by preschool and junior class teachers.

There is some evidence from educational historians of an influence from preschool to the primary school in the direction of encouraging the use of progressive ideas in the first years of school, such as more spontaneous and child-centered methods. The views of influential theorists as such Friedrich Froebel, Susan Isaacs, Dorothy Gardner, Maria Montessori, and Jean Piaget have at various times spread from the preschool to the primary sector (Cumming and Cumming, 1978: 181; Ewing, 1970: 80). A developmental approach (the so-called playway method) was introduced to New Zealand Junior Classes in the 1940s. Clarence Beeby, an influential researcher who became Director-General of Education in 1940, favored this approach. The Education Fellowship Conference held in 1937, which also influenced the birth of the playcenter movement, was one example of the progressive educational mood of the time and it clearly affected the direction of primary education in New Zealand. Susan Isaacs spoke at the conference (Walsh, 1982) about infant school practice in Britain with a strong emphasis on a developmental approach. A developmental approach has been defined as:

stimulating the learning of children through the pursuit of activities based on their own interests and related to the investigation and exploration of the world around them . . . [It] affords children an opportunity to develop their capacity to communicate by providing opportunities for using language and other modes of expression with understanding and for a variety of purposes (ibid. 5).

A developmental approach does not imply a "laissez-faire" method where children play without teacher intervention. Teachers are expected to have an important role in guiding children's learning. Children select activities but teachers are expected to have a clear idea of what they want the children to learn and to move around the classroom, observing children's work, giving help, guidance, inspiration, and security.

Dorothy Gardner, an important figure in early childhood education from England (*ibid.*, 2), visited New Zealand in 1968 and criticized the primary school for evolving away from developmental methods toward the teacher assuming a more dominant role so that "the teacher did far too much of the thinking and the children did far too little." There is no published data on the extent to which schools still have a developmental approach, but New Zealand primary schools have had a long tradition of activity-oriented methods and many junior classrooms would include at least an hour a day of free-choice developmental activities. Even the practice of children starting school at age 5, rather than having one or two entry points a year as is more common internationally, indicates a flexible, individualized approach to children.

One of the main goals of the early years of school is that every child should begin to acquire reading and writing skills (Clay, 1979). Reading programs in the first two years of school are based on language experience methods and shared book experiences (Smith, 1989). Language experience methods attempt to use the child's own experiences as the basis for the child's first reading. Children dictate to their teachers events out of their own experience, then the children trace over the teacher's letters, eventually copying the teacher's printing and writing their own sentences.

Shared book experiences involve the teacher reading regularly to a group of children or the class using a large-scale version of the book so that all the children can see the text. Reading is taught with a series of books published by the School Publications division of the Department of Education and supplied free to all schools. Recently an attractive new series of these books was developed relying on the use of natural language and stories that use the experience of a variety of cultural groups within New Zealand. The emphasis is on children's enjoyment (established by trials of the books) of stories by well-known children's authors who are widely published and read, rather than controlled vocabulary readers.

New Zealand has a strong philosophy of early intervention in the area of reading and language with the aim of ensuring that children who do not make initial progress catch up with other children before patterns of failure become established. The most influential figure in the junior school reading curriculum in New Zealand is Professor Marie Clay from Auckland University. Clay's reading recovery program is based on systematic observation of good readers and provides a one-to-one tutorial program for children who are not making sufficient progress after a year at school. Clay (1986) argues that waiting till children are in their third or fourth year at school before providing remedial instruction is ineffective because children have fallen far behind their peers by that time and have learned to practice errors. Reading recovery involves children receiving daily intensive tutoring, based on careful observation of each child's strengths in reading and the deliberate teaching of specific strategies, such as word analysis and self-correction, for a limited period of 13 to 14 weeks. Clay developed a training scheme for reading recovery teachers at Auckland College of Education. More than 1,100 primary schools provide reading recovery programs for 6-year-olds in New Zealand and reading recovery tutors are now based at 17 centers throughout the country (Department of Education, 1989).

There has recently been considerable controversy over the junior school mathematics curriculum in New Zealand (Young-Loveridge, 1989). Unlike the area of reading, where New Zealand achieves very well on an international level (Smith, 1989), New Zealand has performed rather poorly in mathematics. Young-Loveridge (1987, 1989) has pointed out that New Zealand has an interventionalist strategy in terms of reading, but it takes a "hands-off" approach to mathematics. A new mathematics syllabus (Beginning School Mathematics, or BSM) was recently introduced to the junior classroom in New Zealand. It is based on Piagetian approaches to teaching math, which emphasize the children's own interaction with materials and waits for logical operations to develop before introducing number activities. BSM includes rich ideas and materials from teachers to introduce children to mathematics through concrete experiences. Young-Loveridge has, however, criticized the new syllabus because it avoids introducing numerical concepts in favor of a general range of cognitive developmental activities (e.g., seriation and classification). Addition and subtraction are not introduced until year 3 (when children are age 7 or 8), and number work does not go above the number nine. Young-Loveridge cites considerable evidence, including her own New Zealand research, that many preschool and junior school children are quite capable of addition and subtraction and argues that logical abilities do not have to precede number concept learning. If teachers follow the BSM syllabus in a "lock-step" approach, Young-Loveridge argues that many children will not be challenged by mathematics and will likely lose interest. According to Young-Loveridge, number activities can be introduced through games, play activities, and activities related to daily living rather than through formal teaching.

The major issue for junior classes in New Zealand (other than the "reforms" to education administration) is teacher-child ratios. One of the Labour party's major election policies for education in 1984 was the introduction of 1:20 ratios in junior classes, a result of persistent lobbying from teacher groups (Wylie, 1987). Some new positions were added (200 in 1985, and 100 in 1986) and there was considerable increase in provision of reading recovery teachers, but there has been general disappointment that there has not been more progress toward a 1:20 ratio. According to Wylie (1987), the major stumbling block has been cost together with the arguments of Treasury that reducing the teacher-child ratio will not result in better learning.

The 1989 "Quiet Revolution" in Education

The events of 1988 to 1989 have been termed a "quiet revolution" (Burns, 1989). The description was first used by a political journalist, Colin James (1986), to describe massive changes introduced by the current government. In 1987, the Labour government returned to power in New Zealand. The previous Labour government had already radically reshaped its policies in many areas, such as tax, agriculture, and defense, and was moving away from centrally administered government departments toward smaller, more independent, devolved organizations (Burns, 1989). From 1988 on, the government turned its attention to the social services, including health, social welfare, and education. The Prime Minister of the time, David Lange, showed his determination and commitment to change by taking over the Education portfolio himself. (Since Lange resigned from Cabinet, Phil Goff has been the Minister of Education.) Lange several times stated that early childhood was seen as an investment in the future. For example, he stated: "Research shows that resources put into early childhood care and education have proven results. Not only do they enhance the individual child's learning, the advantages gained help create success in adult life. Improvements in this sector are an investment in the future" (*Lange*, 1989: iii).

The government had declared a commitment to improvements in early childhood education before its election in 1984, and there had already been some important changes (e.g., the move of child care to Education). But 1988 was to see a much more radical upheaval in education as the government commissioned three working groups to write major reports on education. The first (chaired by Brian Picot) dealt with primary and secondary education—*Administration for Excellence* (April 1988); the second (chaired by Gary Hawke) dealt with tertiary education (July 1988); and the third (chaired by Anne Meade) dealt with early childhood education and care—*Education to Be More* (August 1988). All three independent working party reports sought submissions from people interested in education, and were followed in late 1988 and early 1989 by three governmental reports which declared the government's intention to start the new system on October 1, 1989. The following discussion concentrates on Lange's 1989 reforms (i.e., the *Before Five* reforms) with a briefer discussion of Lange's 1988 reforms (i.e., *Tomorrow's Schools*).

The Picot report and *Tomorrow's Schools* argue that consumers need more control over and choice about schools. The recommendations are directed at reducing the amount of central administration of education in New Zealand. Schools are to be governed by boards of trustees (consisting largely of parents) that will employ a school principal and prepare a charter (or contract) setting out their aims. Bulk funding weighted according to local needs will be administered by boards of trustees. A much reduced central administration, the Ministry of Education, will replace the existing Department of Education and Education Boards. Schools will not receive bulk funding unless they can negotiate a charter with the Ministry of Education, and the charter has to incorporate national guidelines established by the Ministry. A review agency (i.e., the Education Review Office) will establish accountability of schools, by checking that schools implement their goals as set out in their charter.

Because the Picot report preceded the Meade report, to some extent the Picot model influenced the recommendations, since both reports have to mesh to form a logical overall structure for education. To a large extent central control was not as big an issue in the early childhood sector. With the exception of kindergarten (and even it shared control with a voluntary organization), control of early childhood educare was already devolved. The Meade report accepted many principles from the Picot report but gave more prominence to the role of early childhood services in providing for the educational needs of families and parents than did Picot. The Meade report was charged with advising the government on the respective roles of family, community, and government in providing care and education for infants and young children (under age 6). Some specific tasks were to look at the needs for more equitable access to early childhood educare and for more equitable funding and funding processes in early childhood services. It is these recommendations on funding that are likely to have the most far-reaching consequences for early childhood educare in New Zealand.

The Meade report proposed a structure of education administration that involved each early childhood educare organization setting up a charter of contract that sets out its aims and goals. Charters were to be developed by early childhood staff and parents according to their philosophies and local needs, but they were all to fulfill national guidelines that incorporate basic standards. Such national guidelines were to include standards of staffing, curriculum, advisory support, and minimum physical requirements. Any center organization with a charter (including home-based schemes) would be eligible for bulk funding from govern-

ment. Charter aims should set a higher level of quality than the minimum standards (required for licensing). Meade proposed that a board of trustees (consisting of parents and community) administer each center. The Ministry of Education would be the central body to provide funding and overall policy for early childhood educare, and would be involved in negotiating the charter. Accountability would be ensured by a review agency and support, advice, and in-service training provided by an autonomous early childhood development unit. A community education forum would identify and gather together community views, and a parent advocacy council would represent parents with particular difficulties in obtaining responsive service. (This was also recommended by the Picot report).

The Meade report also analyzed inequities of funding for different early childhood services and recommended a subsidy of $4 for all chartered services. Fee subsidies (through Social Welfare) for low-income families requiring child care would be continued and property loans would be available through the Ministry of Education. This would result in a slight increase in funding for kindergarten and a very substantial increase for most other early childhood services. It would also increase government spending on early childhood educare from around $73 million to at least $200 million.

The government's statement of intent, *Before Five*, adopted many of the Meade report's recommendations but submissions to the report (including those from other government bodies such as Treasury) influenced the government policy. A few notable changes were made, including the dropping of the idea of centers being managed locally by boards of trustees. *Before Five* announced that current management practices would be retained. This meant that existing community organizations could continue as before and that private operators did not have to have a management committee. Undoubtedly some strong lobbying went on by private operators against the ideas. *Before Five*, however, required management to prepare charters in consultation with local parents.

Another difference between Meade and *Before Five* was that Meade had recommended that advisory staff for special education be included in the early childhood development unit. Instead, *Before Five* said that a special education service (SES) (recommended by Picot), a free-standing self-administering body, should be set up for all educational services. The SES is to include specialist staff with expertise in early childhood education and knowledge of children with special needs. Previously, early childhood service had no right to special education advice and support, but sometimes received these by "grace and favor" through the education boards.

After the government issued its statements of intent in *Before Five* and *Tomorrow's Schools*, the government set up a series of implementation working parties to work out in much greater detail how the government's intentions could be translated into practice. This author chaired the working group on qualifications, training, and accreditation. The process was exhausting and for many of the working groups, exciting. It presented the opportunity to recommend major changes to the existing system that were likely to be implemented quickly. Working party members, who were from a diverse group of early childhood organizations, met over six weeks to develop recommendations. Although it was not always easy, a consensus was reached on the majority of issues. A draft report was presented to the Department. While not all working party reports were accepted in full by government, they provide a useful blueprint for the details of administering the very substantial changes that were introduced in October 1989.

Before Five did not specify how the government intends to fund early childhood services but it was later announced that to receive bulk government funding, centers would have to meet minimum standards and enter a charter agreement that would commit them to a higher than basic standard. The rate per child would depend on the number of contact hours and the age of the child. (The maximum government subsidy was 30 hours over seven days). For children under age 2, the rate of subsidy was $7.25 per hour, per child, or $21.71 per session (two and one-half to three hours), for children over age 2, the rate was $2.25 per hour, per child, or $6.75 per session. The arrangements for kindergartens (i.e., central funding of teachers' salaries and an operational grant) stay similar for two years but will move to the same system of hourly per child funding by 1994. This will fulfill the government's pledge to bring all early childhood services to the same level of funding as provided for kindergartens. Unfortunately, the national government has already frozen the phased increases to early childhood funding. Funding increases were already well underway when the Labour party lost, however. There was a substantial 65 percent increase in the funding of early childhood centers between 1989 when it was $73.8 million, and 1990 when it was $112.8 million.

The minimum requirements for staff-child ratios in all day centers are 1:5 for children under age 2 and 2:20 for children over age 2. In sessional centers, ratios of 1:5 for children under age 2, and 2:30 for children over 2 are required. The "quality objectives" for chartered centers are more stringent: 1:3 for children under 2, 1:5 for children over 2, and 1:6 for 3- to 5-year-olds. For sessional centers, quality objectives are the same for children under 3 but 1:10 for children over 3. The only minimum requirement for group size is that centers with infants may not have more than 25 children. These requirements are much less stringent than recommended by the working party dealing with standards of quality.

A stepwise process to upgrade training for early childhood staff was announced in August 1990. Despite the introduction of an integrated three-year training scheme for early childhood in 1987, many child care staff have lower levels of training than kindergarten staff and a substantial minority (about one-third) have none at all. By 2000, one-half or more staff in all chartered centers (except those run by parents) must have the equivalent of a three-year qualification. Staff with lower levels of training and experience will be given some credit for this and opportunities to take further courses to build on existing training will be provided. This decision was another essential step in improving the quality of early childhood centers in New Zealand.

In general, early childhood educare in New Zealand has greatly benefited from the changes to educational administration, although there are many difficulties still to be resolved. The changes have resulted in a move toward greater integration of services for the children under 5, the introduction of a more equitably funded system, and greater demands for good quality programs.

The two services where integration is most advanced are kindergarten and child care. Child care teachers have for many years been disadvantaged compared with kindergarten teachers (in rates of pay, hours of work, holidays, etc.), but the increase in funding has allowed the negotiation of major salary increases for child care teachers, so that they are approaching equity of pay rates with kindergarten teachers. One recent pay award for supervisors pays child care supervisors only 6 percent short of a kindergarten head teacher. The government now pays almost 50 percent of the cost of child care.

In addition, the two teacher unions (the Kindergarten Teachers Association and the Early Childhood Workers Union) were to be amalgamated in 1990. There are some concerns about kindergarten funding in future years, since the bulk funding arrangement (not to be fully implemented into kindergartens until 1993) depends on number of children actually present and does not provide funding for time when children are away in the holidays or when teachers are visiting parents and children in the home.

The playcenter movement has traditionally been very concerned with preserving its autonomy. It has resisted moves from the state to require accountability for government funding. The changes to educational administration leave many in the playcenter movement in a dilemma. They have the opportunity of greatly increased funding, but to receive it they must buy into a system with far greater quality controls and demands for accountability. They are actively lobbying against having to meet certain requirements, especially those concerned with physical standards (e.g., space or number of toilets) and trained staff. As an informal community-based movement, which has often used temporary space and makeshift facilities in a variety of areas, demands for upgrading facilities are considerable. In order to meet new charter standards, demand for training is also at an unprecedentedly high level in play centers. Additional funding would enable playcenters to pursue goals that they believe are important, such as providing more parental education and support courses. Whether additional funding results in paying the supervisors a professional wage remains

to be seen. While this would help solve the problem of attrition in the voluntary, largely female, labor force, it could change the nature of playcenters from being a parent cooperative movement. For playcenters, the reforms are not perceived as moving toward a partnership with parents but rather as an increase in state power. It is too early to see how these dilemmas will be resolved.

Nga Kohanga reo will not be included in the new integrated early childhood framework. They have chosen to remain separate and funded under the Maori Affairs Vote (also being devolved toward local control by *iwi*, or tribal, authorities). This preserves the Maori desire for autonomy and control over their own resources. The level of funding equals that being received by other early childhood services. It is important to note, though, that Treaty of Waitangi concerns also permeate the changes to early childhood educare in all centers as mentioned at the beginning of this chapter. All centers and schools must show that they acknowledge Maori values, customs, and practices, and the program will have to work on developing cross-cultural understanding. The impetus in the direction of biculturalism has, however, been greatly reduced by the new National government.

In November 1990, the Labour government, which had initiated these revolutionary changes in education, was massively defeated by the conservative National government. National election policy for early childhood had focused on promises for a new "parents as first teachers" scheme for the education of parents with babies, based on a similar scheme in Missouri, in the United States. Since coming to power, however, the phased-in funding increases to early childhood education have already been frozen, and more market-driven policies are likely to follow. It appears that many other reforms such as the transfer of responsibility of child care from social welfare to education are under question. The change in government has had a negative effect in the provision of early childhood services in New Zealand. Much of the new plans has been turned back: quality requirements, funding, and the unions have all suffered.

Note

I wish to acknowledge the assistance of colleagues who provided me with useful information, both from the university (such as Anne Bray, Glennys Faulds, Jude McArthur, and Janet Soler) and in the early childhood field (such as Carol Garden, Ro Parsons, Lyn Reggett, and Yvonne Sharpe).

References

Ballard, K. (1988). Mainstreaming. In Smith, A., *Understanding children's development: A New Zealand Perspective.* Wellington: Allen & Unwin/Port Nicholson Press.

Bennett, J. (1985). Early childhood care and education: Te Kohanga Reo. In *Early childhood forum: Keynote papers.* Wellington: Department of Education.

Bray, D. (1990). Director of New Zealand Institute for Mental Retardation. Personal Communication.

————. (1987). Provisions for "Backward Children." In D. Mitchell and N. Singh (Eds.), *Exceptional Children in New Zealand,* (pp. 248–59). Palmerston North: Dunmore Press.

Brynelsen, D. (1987). Report on early intervention programs in New Zealand. In D. Mitchell and C. Brown (Eds.), *Future directions for early intervention,* (pp. 9–36). Auckland, New Zealand: Down's Association.

Burns, V. (1989). Early childhood education in New Zealand—The quiet revolution. Unpublished paper presented to the Organization Mondiale de l'Education Prescholaire (OMEP), World Assembly and Congress, London, July 1989.

Caldwell, B. (1989). A comprehensive model for integrating child care and early childhood education. *Teachers College Record, 90,* 404–14.

Champion, P. (1985). *An investigation of the sensorimotor development of Down's syndrome infants involved in an ecologically based early intervention program: A longitudinal study.* Research Report No. 85–2. Christchurch: Education Department, Canterbury University.

Cheyne, C. (1988). Statistical profile of women in New Zealand. In *Future directions, report of the Royal Commission on social policy,* 3(1): 281–342.

Clay, M. (1986). *The early detection of reading difficulties.* Auckland: Heinemann Publishers.

————. (1979). *Reading: The patterning of complex human behavior* (2nd ed.). Auckland: Heinemann.

Cumming, I. & Cumming, A. (1978). *History of state education in New Zealand, 1840–1970.* Wellington: Pitman Pacific Books.

Deaker, M. (1990). Otago Schools and the Treaty of Waitangi. Paper delivered to Seminar on Treaty of Waitangi arranged by 1990 Commission at University of Otago.

Ewing, J. (1970). *The development of New Zealand primary school curriculum, 1877–1970.* Wellington: New Zealand Council for Educational Research.

Fenwick, P., Norman, H., & Leong, D. (1984). Attendance at preschool. Research Report Series, No. 31, ISSN 0111-8870. Wellington: Research and Statistics Division, Department of Education.

Fergusson, D., Horwood, L., & Gretton, M. (1984). Who doesn't get to preschool? *New Zealand Journal of Educational Studies, 16,* 168–76.

Goff, P. (Minister of Education) (Jan. 1990). Speech to 1990 South Pacific International Conference on Special Education, University of Auckland.

Hawke, G. (July 1988). *Report of the working group on post compulsory education and training.* Wellington: Government Printer.

James, C. (1986). *The quiet revolution.* Wellington: Allen & Unwin.

Jamieson, P. (1979). Who doesn't get to preschool in Newton? Set 1, Item 13.

Julian, R. (1981). *Brought to mind.* Wellington: New Zealand Council for Educational Research.

Lange, D. (Dec., 1989). *Before five: Early childhood care and education in New Zealand.* Wellington: Government Printer.

————. (Aug., 1988). *Tomorrow's schools: the reform of education administration in New Zealand.* Wellington: Government Printer.

McArthur, J. (1990). Personal communication.

McLaren, I. (1974). *Education in a small Democracy.* London: Routledge & Kegan Paul.

Meade, A. (1985). *The children can choose.* Wellington: New Zealand Council for Educational Research.

Meade, A. (Aug. 1988). (Chairperson) *Education to be more.* Report of the Early Childhood Care and Education Working Group. Wellington: Government Printer.

Mitchell, D. (1987). Early intervention. In D. Mitchell & N. Singh (Eds.), *Exceptional children in New Zealand,* (pp. 168–76). Palmerston North: Dunmore Press.

Picot, B. (April 1988). *Administering for excellence: Effective administration in education.* Wellington: Government Printer.

Report of the Royal Commission on Social Policy. (April 1988). *New Zealand Today* (Vol. 1) and *Future Directions* (Vol. 2). Wellington: Government Printer.

Report of the Government Review of Te Kohanga Reo (Sept., 1988). Wellington: Government Printer.

Report of Department of Education (EI). (1989). Wellington: Government Printer.

Smith, A. (1988). Education and care components in New Zealand childcare centers and kindergartens. *Australian Journal of Early Childhood, 3,* 31–36.

Smith, A., & Swain, P. (1988). *Childcare in New Zealand: People, programmes and politics.* Wellington: Allen & Unwin/Port Nicholson Press.

Walsh, J. (1982). What is a developmental approach? Unpublished paper presented to Teachers Refresher Course.

Wylie, C. (1987). Fleshing out the bones: the origins and development of the 1:20 teacher: pupil ratio in junior classes. Paper presented at Joint Conference of the Australian Association for Research in Education and the New Zealand Association for Research in Education.

Young-Loveridge, J. (1989). The development of children's number concepts: The first year of school. *New Zealand Journal of Education Studies, 24,* 47–64.

Young-Loveridge, J. (1987). Learning mathematics. *British Journal of Developmental Psychology, 5,* 155–67.

PRESCHOOL AND PRIMARY EDUCATION IN NIGERIA

• • • • • • • • • • ◆ • • • • • • • •

Joseph Aghenta and J. Nesin Omatseye
University of Benin
Benin City, Nigeria

The history of early childhood education in Nigeria can be traced to the preliterate era when fishing, hunting, and agriculture constituted the mainstay of the economy. Education at this time was informal, since there were no designated places and time for schooling, no timetables, no textbooks, and no other school paraphernalia. The teacher was either the children's mother or grandmother, who cared for them while others were working in the farm or elsewhere. The content of education was generally related to the practical life of the people. It had to do with interpersonal relationships as well as adjusting to the norms and mores of society in order to become a respectable member of the community.

Oral tradition constituted the mode of instruction in the old Nigerian society. Children were taught songs, told folktales, and instructed in the legends and stories about the warriors, animals, gods, and the ancestral spirits. Parents were careful to instill in their children, though instruction, a sense of belonging and achievement through hard work. Such was the kind of early childhood education available to the Nigerian child before the influence of Western education arrived in Africa in the early 16th century.

The first attempt to establish a primary school on the West Coast of Africa was made in 1515 by a group of Portuguese Christian missionaries in Warri and Benin. Their effort failed. It was not until 1842 that a Methodist missionary, Reverend Birch Freeman, successfully established the first primary school, in Badagry. The school, called the Nursery of the Infant Church, was funded and managed by the freed slaves from Sierra Leone. Shortly afterwards, other groups (e.g., the Church Missionary School of England, the Southern Baptists of the United States, and the Qua Iboe) established primary schools in Badagry, Iseyin, Ogbomosho Eket, and Uyo, respectively.

The founding and management of primary schools were solely in the hands of Christian missionary organizations during this period. It was not until the late 1800s that the colonial administration of Great Britain began to provide some grants-in-aid to the mission schools. As the government began to contribute to the funding of education, it understandably took more interest in the control of the emerging nation. This became apparent in the promulgation of the first education ordinance in 1882 for the territories of Lagos and the Gold Coast (now Ghana). Consequently, an inspectorate service was established to regulate education through examinations, grants for buildings and teachers' salaries, the awarding of certificates, and the establishment of local boards of education.

As a result of these activities, the government began to participate in the running of primary education in Nigeria. To provide access to education for non-Christians who were uncomfortable in the predominantly Christian schools, some public primary schools were established by the colonial administration. The first such school was built in Lagos in 1896 in response to the complaints of Muslims who felt that Christian teachers discriminated against their children in the mission schools.

Out of a total of forty governmental primary schools established in 1906, there were six in the west, eighteen in the central zone, and sixteen in the east. In Northern Nigeria, which was predominantly Muslim, the situation was different. The following categories of schools were proposed for the north:

• government-sponsored schools for Mallams (i.e., Muslim youths undertaking Islamic studies);

• schools for male children of traditional rulers and chiefs;

• secular schools for the children of ordinary citizens; and

• the cantonment schools for the children of civil servants from the coastal areas (nursery sections for working mothers and expatriates fell into this category).

The colonial administration decreed that no mission-type school should be built in the predominantly Muslim areas. Public schools located outside Muslim communities were also prohibited from teaching religious values.

When Nigeria became independent in 1960, it adopted a federal constitution that gave education expansion a great boost. Each regional government made education a priority. In 1951, there were 500,000 pupils in the east, 395,000 in the west, and 107,561 in the north. A decade later, the numbers rose to 1,430,514 in the east, 1,124,788 in the west, and 282,849 in the north. Indeed, in 1955, universal free primary education was introduced in the former Western Nigeria, and in 1957 Eastern Nigeria followed suit. These figures indicate how much importance each regional government attached to the development of education in Nigeria.

In view of the divergent educational policies adopted at the time by the regional governments, the east and west had a four-year junior primary program (consisting of infants 1 and 2), followed by four years of senior primary (standards 3–6). Secondary school education consisted of forms 1–6, culminating in the School Certificate. In the north, there were three stages: four years of junior primary 1–4, five years of middle school, and four years of secondary school. It was not until the introduction of nationwide, universal, free primary education in 1976, and the consequent launching of the National Policy on Education in 1977, that Nigeria adopted a uniform structure of 6–3–3–4.

The end of the Nigerian civil war in 1970 saw the beginning of the government's renewed interest in the control of schools. Before they were taken over by the various state governments, schools were mostly in the hands of private proprietors. Under the new arrangement, schools in the north were brought under the local education authorities, while southern schools were brought under the jurisdiction of both the school management boards and teaching service commissions. The management of primary education at the local government level is a joint effort of a Chief Inspector of Education (representing the State Ministry of Education) and representatives of the local government councils.

The 1980s witnessed a serious deterioration of primary education, prompting the federal government to take a critical look at the system in terms of funding, improvement of infrastructure, teachers' salaries, and provision of learning materials. Thus, in 1986, $15 million was provided for the rehabilitation of primary school buildings and provision of instructional materials nationwide. Two years later, another $43.47 million was made available for the same purpose. Since 1988, the federal government has taken over the payment of 65 percent of teachers' salaries in Nigerian primary schools. Each state and local government council must now match this with 35 percent to cover operating costs and physical development.

Social Policy and Legislation

Nigeria's social policy concerning education and care of the young is outlined in the Nigerian National Policy on Education. The focus is on developing the individual into a sound and effective citizen. The policy stresses equal educational opportunities at all levels. The educational aims and objectives of the policy are as follows:

1. the inculcation of the national consciousness and national unity;

2. the inculcation of the right type of values and attitudes for the survival of the individual and the Nigerian society;

3. the training of the mind in the understanding of the surrounding world; and

4. the acquisition of the appropriate skills, abilities, and competencies—both mental and physical—to equip the individual to live and contribute to the development of society.

Furthermore, the achievement of these objectives at the preprimary level should bring about a smooth transition from home to the school, and prepare the child for the primary level of education. In addition, adequate care and supervision of the children of working parents are to be provided. The preprimary education is to instill in the child the spirit of inquiry and creativity by exploring the environment; teach cooperation and team spirit; teach the rudiments of numbers, letters, colors, shapes, forms, etc., through play; and promote good habits, especially good health habits. Overall, the education is to introduce the children to social norms.

Since the success of the educational systems depends largely on the primary school experience, the government considers this level as the key. The policy, therefore, presents the general objectives of primary education as inculcating in children permanent literacy and numeracy, and the ability to communicate effectively; laying a sound foundation for scientific and reflective thinking; and teaching citizenship education as a basis for effective participation in and contribution to the life of the society. The primary education also seeks to provide character and moral training and to promote the development of social attitudes and the ability to adapt to the changing environment. The children are to be given opportunities to develop manipulative skills that will enable them to function effectively in society within the limits of their capacity and are to be provided with basic tools for further educational advancement, including preparation for trades and crafts of the locality (Federal Republic of Nigeria, 1969).

To accomplish the policy objectives, the federal government made primary education free and universal in 1976. It has yet to be made compulsory, although it is hoped that this will be accomplished in 1992. The establishment of libraries, government-owned book stores, publishing corporations, and agencies (e.g., the National Education Research and Development Council, and the Mathematics and Science Development Council) have also enhanced the social and educational development of the country.

Preschool Programs

Preschool education in Nigeria is more or less in the hands of private proprietors, rendering government involvement to the periphery. According to the Minister of Education, the concern of the federal and state governments in this sector is to improve standards and to encourage genuine private participation in providing adequate care and supervision for children (Federal Ministry of Education, 1987). Although there is no officially designed program for preschool children, early childhood educators in Nigeria have derived their own schemes from the state objectives of education for the country.

Before delving into the sphere of activities that would be found in a typical early childhood institution, it is relevant to mention that socioeconomic class is a major determinant of whose child is attracted to which institution. Basically, there are two types of preschool institutions: (1) the *Akara* school and (2) the traditional Western-type nursery and day care centers. The akara school is generally organized by primarily unemployed semiliterate adults who gather together the children of working parents in their neighborhood. Classes usually meet under a tree or in an uncompleted building for instruction in an informal setting. The children attracted to this school are usually from lower class families. They are left in the custody of the "teacher" while their parents are at work. Since there is no school uniform, no class register, and no timetable or rigid schedule of activities, the 3- to 5-year-olds learn just about whatever the teacher wants to teach them. They are offered *akara* (i.e., a Yoruba name for fried black-eyed beans) whenever the teacher tries to appease them and keep them quiet, hence the name, *akara* school.

The traditional Western-type nursery school has generally attracted children of the middle class and affluent parents who can afford the fairly high cost of such institutions. Activities in such schools include singing, dancing, drawing, listening to African folktales, and exploring with toys. These children are also taught the rudiments of numbers, letters, colors, shapes, forms, and other activities to retain their interest. Teachers generally endeavor to stress the importance of good health habits and effective communication. Although the national policy on education stresses the use of the child's mother tongue at this level, the English language remains the dominant means of communication.

By way of innovation, preschool educators in Nigeria have in recent times promoted the use of African toys and play objects in order to reflect the cultural environment of the children. Teachers are encouraged to take their pupils outdoors to see plants and animals in the compound. There is also a radical departure from the rigid control of children, both in the classroom and on the playground, so that children have more freedom to explore their natural environment. There is also a gradual departure from excessive use of foreign literature and influence. Meaningful stories (i.e., those that have relevance for African children) have become very popular at the preschool level.

As of 1991, approximately 15 percent of preprimary-aged children are enrolled in nursery schools. The majority of the few schools of this type that exist in Nigeria are in urban and semi-urban areas. Most preprimary children in Nigeria remain at home with their parents.

Organization and Curricula of Primary Education

Although the federal Ministry of Education does not operate primary schools, it plays an important role in the control of primary education. Each state government, including the Federal Capital Territory, has its own education laws governing the establishment and operation of primary schools in their areas of jurisdiction.

In every case, however, the state Ministry of Education has responsibility for quality control and maintenance of standards in all primary schools. The local government councils contribute to the payment of teachers' salaries and allowances, maintain the physical facilities, and provide instructional materials in some states. In recent years, most state governments have moved toward the establishment of school boards vested with the authority to manage government-owned primary schools. Education management committees have also been established at the local government level to supervise the grassroots activities. The chairman of the state school board, whose responsibility it is to monitor the activities at the grassroots level, in turn reports to the state Commissioner of Education.

The establishment of the National Commission for Primary Education, responsible for administering the payment of 65 percent of salaries paid to all primary school teachers in state-owned schools, has added a new dimension to the primary system. As a consequence, both state and local government councils now bear the remainder of the cost of providing infrastructures and materials for teaching and learning in the schools. The federal government's intervention is part of an overall policy of encouraging the transition from primary to the junior secondary schools, a goal no state government has yet been able to completely accomplish.

The curriculum of primary education, derived from the National Policy on Education (Federal Ministry of Education, 1978), includes the following subjects: language arts, mathematics, social studies, cultural arts, health and physical education, religious and moral instruction, agriculture, and home economics.

Special Education for Young Children

Each state of the federation has the responsibility of providing special education for all handicapped and gifted children. Schools for the blind, deaf and dumb, mentally retarded, and the gifted are to be found in different locations in each state. The Ministries of Education, Youth, and Social Development work cooperatively to construct, equip, and maintain these schools. In addition, corporations, business enterprises, and public-spirited individuals have from time to time donated generously to support the programs and activities of these institutions. Financing also occurs through fund-raising activities.

The children using the schools are usually from a background of poverty. Social and voluntary agencies are primarily responsible for operating and maintaining the institutions on behalf of state governments. Special schools owned and managed by private proprietors are closely supervised and monitored by the state Ministries of Education, Youth, and Social Development.

Training Programs for Teachers of Young Children

Although the private sector is entrusted with the responsibility for nursery education in Nigeria, the state is responsible for teacher training at both the preprimary and primary levels. For example, grades 2 and 3 teachers, who work at the nursery and primary school levels, receive their instruction at state teacher training colleges. In recent years, these schools have attracted the services of graduates of the Nigeria Certificate of Education (NCE), a postsecondary teacher education institution. Such university programs as the Associateship Certificate in Education (ACE), and diploma courses for teachers at the preprimary and primary education level, have further contributed to the quality of teacher training in Nigeria. High-quality certificate programs in nursery education and special education are offered at both the Ahmadu Bello University and the University of Ibadan.

Since postprimary institutions are not strong academically, postsecondary institutions have accepted the challenge of improving the teaching of mathematics, language arts, social studies, health and physical education, and pedagogy. To raise the quality of teachers, the National Policy on Education involves the phasing out of grades 2 and 3 teacher education institutions. The NCE has been adopted as the minimum teaching qualification for the country. Programs in colleges of education are being revamped and restructured to meet this requirement.

Parental Support and Educational Programs

The Nigerian government, like most others in the developing world, offers no direct financial assistance to parents in support of their children in nursery and primary schools. Since preprimary education is in the hands of private proprietors, only parents who can afford it send their children to nursery schools. Primary school education is free only at state schools, which are generally less equipped and more poorly staffed than the fee-paying private schools. The state assists mentally and physically handicapped children in special schools only by waiving their fees for room, board, and tuition. In fact, Nigeria's new approach to population management discourages assistance of any kind to families with more than four children.

Conclusion

Policy issues, curriculum and instruction, personnel, finance, management, and quality of primary education have all presented major problems in Nigeria. The problem of policy formation and implementation at the primary level is rooted in history. Preprimary and primary education was in the hands of the voluntary agencies, particularly missionary bodies, from 1884 to the early 1970s. More than one hundred different missions, communities, and private individuals offered primary schooling, and each executed its program in accordance with its own interests. In the 1950s, when regional government started to expand to the primary education system, in some cases making it free, it had to contend with the opposition of the voluntary agencies that saw their interests threatened.

The framework for state management of schools was fashioned by the Ashby Commission (1960), with the question of state control of education finally settled in the 1970s. Other commissions and committees on education also tried to lay a solid framework for state control of education, including Banjo Commission (1961), Dike Committee (1962), Ikoku Committee (1964), Taiwo

Committee (1968), and the National Curriculum Conference (1969). When the state assumed responsibility for primary and postprimary education in the 1970s, the objectives were to bring about central control, effective management, supervision of schools, relevance of the school curricula to national needs, better conditions of service for teachers in a unified and integrated service (intended to guarantee uniform standards), and fair distribution of educational opportunities. These objectives are yet to be realized. No sooner were schools taken over by the state, than some of the schools were returned to the owners in some parts of the country.

The launching of the National Policy on Education in 1977 has done much to rationalize educational policies in Nigeria, but the problems of lack of facilities, shortage of qualified teachers, poor funding, ineffective management and supervision of schools, and overall quality of primary education have not been solved. Indeed, such problems are aggravated by the ever-increasing population of primary-school-aged children.

Classrooms are overcrowded and some buildings are falling down as a result of poor maintenance and old age. With respect to staffing, most preprimary and primary schools are not staffed with teachers at the appropriate level. Teachers with an NCE who are therefore qualified to teach specialized subjects (e.g., home economics, agricultural science, and music) are not employed in great numbers. Though the National Policy on Education stipulates that at some future date the NCE will be the minimum qualification in primary schools, it does not appear this will be possible in the near future because of the depressed national economy. Although teachers at a lower level of training are available, turnover is high because of poor working conditions.

Reform has been attained in the area of curriculum, in that it is now relevant to national needs.

Local languages, history, geography, music, crafts, and agriculture are taught in addition to the traditional subjects of English, mathematics, and general knowledge.

Financing of primary education in Nigeria, like in many other developing countries, is a serious problem. There are two basic reasons for this: the poor state of the economy and a large population. There are an estimated 17 to 18 million children of primary school age in Nigeria. Nigeria is known to be spending about 3 percent of its gross national product on education, 48 percent of which is dedicated to primary education. In contrast, preprimary education is fee-paying and the enrollment ratio is only about 15 percent. While tuition in primary school is free, parents bear not less than 50 percent of the cost of books, uniforms, transportation, and midday meals. Federal, state, and local governments are being urged to do more in funding primary education so that parents can bear less financial responsibility. The federal government has been willing to assist the states in financing primary education.

Primary school management is ineffective, despite the creation of management boards. Although guidelines have been set and experienced head teachers appointed, there are still allegations of poor management. The situation is worsened by poor supervision by inspectors for the Ministry of Education. Head teachers often complain of inadequate funding and uncooperative teachers.

The problems outlined above seriously undermine the quality of primary education in Nigeria. As a result, private primary schools are of a much higher quality than those in the public system. Fortunately, Nigerians are concerned about the lack of quality because it represents most children's first contact with the educational system. Researchers and special committees are working to improve the quality of primary education in Nigeria.

References

Aghenta, J. (1990). *Primary school planning and administration in Nigeria since independence.* Paper presented at the NAEAP national conference toward a functional primary education in Nigeria. University of Jos, March 5–9, 1990.

Banjor, S. et al. (1961). *Report of the commission appointed to review the educational system of Western Nigeria.* Ibadan: Government Printer.

Dike, K., et al. (1962). *Report of the committee appointed to review the educational system of Eastern Nigeria.* Enugu: Government Printer.

Federal Government of Nigeria (with Ashby E., *et al.*). (1960). *Investment in education: the report of the commission on post school certificate and higher education in Nigeria.* Lagos: Federal Ministry of Education.

Federal Ministry of Education. (1978). *Blue print for the national policy on education.* Lagos: Federal Ministry of Information.

———. (1981). *National policy on education.* Lagos: Federal Ministry of Information.

———. (1987). *Guidelines for preprimary education.* Lagos: Federal Ministry of Information.

Federal Republic of Nigeria. (1969). *Report of the national curriculum conference.* Lagos: Federal Ministry of Education.

Ikoku, A., *et al.* (1964). *Report of the review of the educational system in Eastern Nigeria.* Enugu: Government Printer.

Onibokun, O., Okoye, N., Alao, A., & Onwunchekwa, J. (1981). *Nursery education* (ACE Series). Ibadan: Institute of Education, University of Ibadan.

Taiwo, C., *et al.* (1968). *Report of the committee on the review of primary education system in Western State of Nigeria.* Ibadan: Government Printer.

EARLY CHILDHOOD EDUCATION IN THE SULTANATE OF OMAN

• • • • • • • • • •◆• • • • • • • • • •

Thuwayba Al-Barwani
Sultan Qaboos University
Oman

The Sultanate of Oman is the second largest country in the Arabian peninsula, in terms of both area and indigenous population. However, before 1970, Oman was the least known and least developed nation in the peninsula.

Modern schooling in Oman started as early as 1897 when Peter Zwemer of the Arabian Mission started a school in Muscat that had four elementary grades and enrolled both male and female students. Since the school's goal was primarily mission work, the concentration was on Bible studies, with English, Arabic, history, and geography also being taught (Al-Dhahab, 1987).

Like most Muslim countries, Quaran schools (known as *kuttab* in Arabic) were the only form of education in Oman prior to the late 19th century. These schools are believed to have started shortly after Oman embraced Islam in 632 A.D. (*ibid.*).

Quaran schools spread throughout the Sultanate, though their exact number is not known. They provided basic education for children of both sexes under age 10. In addition to teaching Quaran and the principles of Islam (which was the main purpose of opening such schools), *kuttabs* also taught reading and writing of the Arabic language, and some elementary arithmetic (Mishad, 1984).

All *kuttab* schools were privately owned and operated. They usually did not have fixed or special buildings. Teaching took place in various locations, (e.g., under the shade of trees, in mosques, in teacher's homes, or in courtyards). Teachers were often selected to teach by virtue of their age, knowledge of Quaran, and good reputation in the community.

Kuttab schools co-existed with government-owned schools prior to the 1970s. They tended to be more community based, serving a broader cross section of the public than secular schools because secular schools were only in the large cities and enrolled selected students, while *kuttab* schools could be found in even the smallest villages in Oman.

Kuttabs are still in operation in Oman, but with the beginning of public education their importance has diminished. They now operate in the summer when public schools are closed, and some are open in the afternoons during regular school days. They also serve to keep young children busy when schools are off session.

The first public elementary school was started in 1914. Although the system offered admission to both boys and girls, the curriculum still resembled that of Quaran schools. (Al-Khahb, 1987).

In real terms though, modern education in Oman started in 1970 when Sultan Qaboos bin Said took over the leadership of the country. Before then, Oman, with a population of over one million, had only three primary schools which enrolled 909 students, mostly from wealthy families. The three schools were in the towns of Muscat (the capital), Muttrah, and Salalah (Mohammed, 1988). In the last two decades, Oman has made record achievements in the field of education. The country now has 370 primary schools and enrolls over 200,000 students (Ministry of Education and Youth, 1989).

Educational policies and targets are decided by the Council of Education and Vocational Training, which is chaired by the Ruler of Oman. The implementation of these policies is the responsibility of the Ministry of Education and Youth. The following is a summary of Oman's education policy:

1. Education is a universal right for all members of the Omani society. The government considers itself responsible for providing this education with all the possibilities and educational institutions at its disposal to meet each individual's need for education without limitations.

2. Each individual's abilities are to be developed unrestricted by time or place in order that each may learn and pursue educational goals throughout life. Each should be enabled to satisfy his or her needs for a uniform education covering all aspects of his or her personality and making him or her capable of effecting change in his or her environment.

3. The necessary manpower for all sectors is to be provided to promote the country's development plans and projects and to provide families and ancillary aids for specialized and higher education as may be consistent with Oman's development requirements.

4. The Omani individual is to be enlightened about his or her own country and the greater Arab motherland leading to his or her comprehension that unity and collaboration among the Arab people are sources of power for him or her.

5. Students are to be exposed to proper use of leisure time through suitable activities aimed at ensuring the welfare and progress of both the individual and the society in which he or she lives (Razik and El-Shibiny, 1986:30).

The first five-year development plan mainly concentrated on providing free education to all children ages 6 and above. Thus, during this period (1976–80), the Ministry of Education and Youth concentrated on the quantitative development of education.

The Omani educational system has three cycles: (1) the elementary cycle, which lasts six years; (2) the preparatory cycle, which lasts three years; and (3) the secondary cycle, lasting three years. Preschool education is not, therefore, part of the public school system.

Early Childhood Education in Oman: An Introduction

While great achievements have been made with regard to general education, one cannot claim similar successes in preschool education. Preschool education has been neither universalized nor made compulsory in Oman, though the demand for it seems to be increasing. With more and more women engaged in economic activities outside the home, coupled with an increasing awareness and appreciation for early learning, organized care for children in the form of the creche and kindergarten is becoming an important concern in the community. The UNICEF report of 1984 estimated the preschool-age population (3-5 years) to be roughly 9 percent of the total population (135,000 children). However, compared with the population, preschool facilities available in the country are scarce. Development council statistics (1986) indicate that there were 38,361 reported births in 1985. Babies born in this year would have been ready to join preschool in 1988, yet Ministry of Education statistics for that year indicate that only a small proportion (6.6 percent) of these children were actually enrolled in preschools.

Early childhood education in Oman can be divided into three distinct systems, each unconnected to the other. The preschool system includes day care centers and kindergartens, while the lower primary classes are contained within the formal school system.

Day Care Centers

Day care centers appeared in Oman in the mid-1970s with the influx of women into the workforce. However, no real governmental involvement was seen prior to the 1980s. Most day care centers that emerged in this period were privately initiated and existed independently. They were often geared to serve two major purposes: (1) to satisfy the need for the care of children of working mothers who had no other options and (2) to provide a special and intellectually stimulating environment for children.

A large demand for child care existed in the city of Muscat, where more women have joined the workforce. As for the other regions where the majority of the women were uneducated and did not work outside the home, the demand for day care centers was very low. The result was that most day care centers during this time were situated in the Muscat area. The establishment of these centers required only a certain amount of money to start the school. There were no governmental requirements to control the standard and quality of services rendered to children.

The first important step toward establishing an organized strategy for child care was taken in 1981 with the establishment of a Directorate General for Women's and Children's Affairs within the Ministry of Social Affairs and Labor. With this came an increased focus on the well-being of children—medically, socially, and educationally.

Also contributing to the quality of child care, a Royal Decree (1985) established the National Committee for Child Care. The committee was composed of members from Ministries of Social Affairs, Education and Youth, and Health. It was assigned the following responsibilities:

1. to prepare policy and strategies appropriate for child care;

2. to coordinate with Ministries and other governmental bodies in devising programs and projects related to child care;

3. to follow up on the application of policies related to child care;

4. to encourage field research and studies that provide data and more information about the needs of the child; and

5. to study issues related to the child that have been agreed upon in international, regional, and Arab forums so as to follow up on the application of the issues that have been agreed upon.

This Royal Decree was very symbolic in that it was the first important initiative to promote the well-being of children. The Directorate General of Women's and Children's Affairs was given the responsibility of supervising all day care centers in the country and of ensuring that required standards are maintained.

The first step taken to control day care centers was to require that all day care centers be registered with the Ministry of Social Affairs and Labor. Licenses were issued only to centers that met the rules and regulations of the Ministry. In February 1985, the first registered day care center was opened. By 1986 there were 11 registered centers and by 1989 there were 17 located in various regions of the Sultanate. The majority, however, are still in the Muscat area (Ministry of Social Affairs and Labor, 1990).

These centers generally enroll children ages 6 months to 4 years, and operate throughout the year from 7:00 a.m. to 3:00 p.m. (Official working hours in Oman are from 7:30 a.m. to 2:30 p.m.) Services offered in these centers most often include care-taking for the babies who are below learning age. The centers also seek to stimulate and socialize children. This is often done with children approximately 2 years and older. Play is interspersed with recitation of the Quaran, singing, drawing, and learning of numbers and alphabets. The centers also toilet train the children and teach them other habits considered important for survival in the society (e.g., obedience, cleanliness, and good learning habits).

Because the centers are privately owned, the government has not been able to interfere with regard to the fees charged. As a result, fees vary greatly depending on the type of services provided, for example extended hours, transportation, meals or care for children as young as 2 months old (civil servants receive two months of maternity leave). It is required that all day care centers assign a medical inspector to visit the children regularly and have available in the center all necessary first aid equipment. It is also required that the centers ensure that the proportion of caretakers to children is 1:6 (for babies between 6 months and 1 year) and 1:10 for children older than one year but less than age 4 (Al-Barwani, 1987).

The Directorate General of Women's and Children's Affairs also employs supervisors who visit the centers to ensure that conditions are appropriate for the well-being of children.

Kindergartens

While kindergartens in Oman are privately owned and operated, they are supervised centrally by the Department of Private Education at the Ministry of Education and Youth. Prior to 1973, there were no kindergartens in Oman. In 1980, there were only 17 kindergarten classes enrolling 396 children of both genders. By 1984, the number of kindergarten classes had reached 69 with a total enrollment of about 1,600 children (Ministry of Education, 1986). (See Table 1 for the development of kindergartens between 1969–70 to 1984–85.

Most kindergartens have no special buildings. Rather, they exist as part of private primary schools. Thus, in analyzing the development of preschool education in Oman, it is important to view growth in terms of the number of classes and students rather than number of schools.

Ministry of Education statistics indicate that there were 12 kindergartens in Oman in 1986–87 with a student population of 2,543, of which 1,479 were studying in Muscat area (Ministry of Education and Youth, 1986). By 1988–89, the number of classes had increased from 120 (as in 1986–87) to 132. The number of students also increased from 2,542 to 2,952. (Table 2 shows the distribution of

TABLE 1

Development of Kindergartens According to the Numbers of Schools, Classes, and Teachers From 1969–70 to 1984–85

	1969/70	1970/71	1971/72	1972/73	1973/74	1974/75	1975/76	1976/77
No. of schools	N.A.	N.A.	N.A.	N.A.	N.A.	N.A.	N.A.	N.A.
No. of classes	N.A.	N.A.	N.A.	N.A.	N.A.	2	4	2
Total no. of students	N.A.	N.A.	N.A.	N.A.	N.A.	42	160	54
No. of teachers	N.A.	N.A.	N.A.	N.A.	N.A.	N.A.	N.A.	N.A.
	1977/78	1978/79	1979/80	1980/81	1981/82	1982/83	1983/84	1984/85
No. of schools	N.A.	N.A.	N.A.	N.A.	5	3	2	10
No. of classes	2	4	5	17	24	39	37	69
Total no. of students	46	226	210	396	674	865	872	1642
No. of teachers	N.A.	N.A.	N.A.	N.A.	N.A.	35	37	81

Source: Statistical Yearbook of Education, 1985: 15

TABLE 2

Nationwide Distribution of Kindergartens According to Numbers of Classes, Students, and Teachers

Region	Number of Schools	Number of Classes	Number of Students			Number of Teachers	
			Male	Female	Total	Male	Female
Muscat	1	78	899	686	1,585	—	84
Batinah	1	20	296	188	484	—	18
Rustaq	1	5	73	43	116	—	5
Dakhliya	—	3	38	21	59	—	3
Sharqiya	2	4	53	39	92	—	5
Wusta	—	1	22	6	28	—	1
Dhahira	—	3	103	89	192	—	4
Ganubiya	3	15	255	141	396	—	14
Total	8	129	1,739	1,213	2,952	—	134

Source: Statistical Yearbook of Education, 1988–89:189.

kindergartens, according to the numbers of classes, students, and teachers in all regions of the Sultanate.)

Kindergartens in Oman have a two-year duration. They normally take children from ages 3 1/2 to 5 1/2. The study period is divided into two levels: the first level is the *rawdha* (in Arabic) and the second level is the *tamhidi*.

The Department of Private Education had a purely supervisory role prior to 1987. It registered the schools and ensured that they abided by the rules and regulations set by the Ministry. Inspections were carried out by supervisors who made annual visits to the schools.

In 1987, the Department published a handbook of rules and requirements for starting a kindergarten. In it were the guidelines that detailed all important information concerning teacher qualifications, class size, student-teacher ratio, dress code, hygiene, age range to be admitted, activities, and length of school day (Ministry of Education and Youth, 1987).

A ministerial decree legislated that the class size for kindergartens must not be more than 20 children per class and no male teachers should be employed to teach children of this age. However, the curriculum was left entirely to the discretion of the school administration. This was the government's first attempt at having some say in the running of the kindergartens.

In 1988, with permission from the Ministry of Education in Kuwait, Oman adopted and adapted (slightly) the books that were being used in Kuwaiti kindergartens. The first level has five books which concentrate on introducing important concepts and experiences (e.g., cleanliness, safety, and family). These concepts are introduced through drawing, coloring, and discussion.

The second level has also five books which deal with more cognitive concepts, such as distance, time, weight, size, shapes, relationships, differentiation, and matching. All these books are accompanied by comprehensive teacher's guides, which outline goals and objectives and suggested activities.

A child-centered philosophy seems to have guided the development of these materials. The curriculum is very much activity oriented and seems to concentrate more on concepts and experiences than on drilling the alphabets and words.

Similarly, the curriculum seems to encourage the teacher to expose children to real-life situations through field trips and presentations of actual objects in the classroom. Likewise, the teacher is encouraged to use activity centers where children are trained to select activities in which they are interested. The objective of the curriculum is to attain a balance among the cognitive, affective, and psychomotor domains (Ministry of Education and Youth, Muscat, 1988 and Ministry of Education, Kuwait, 1985).

The Ministry of Education in Oman has required that these books be used by all kindergartens. The schools must inform the Ministry of the number of books needed and the Ministry arranges with the publisher to provide them at the school's expense.

Prior to this mandate, each kindergarten was free to select and use its own materials, but with the mandate came a more technical, academic involvement. Ministry supervision now involves more than a mere check on whether the schools abide by the rules. Kindergartens now require guidance on how to use the books. This has become a huge burden on the small department which is ill equipped to fulfill such a responsibility.

Primary School Program

For purposes of this chapter, 8 years was set as the age limit for the period of early childhood education. This age coincides with the third grade at the primary level. This section therefore concentrates on the development of primary education for grades 1 through 3.

As indicated earlier, the period of the first five-year development plan between 1976 and 1980 witnessed quantitative expansion of the primary school system. This was especially true of the lower primary classes. This development plan aimed at providing education to all Omanis. The Ministry responded to the demand for education either by opening a school (if the student population justified it) or by providing a bus to transport students to a nearby school. At this time, the concern was to open as many schools as were needed irrespective of other considerations. Thus, one could find students learning in tents or in houses made of mud, fiberglass, or plywood.

TABLE 3

Development of Lower Primary Education According to Years and Gender (1978–79 to 1984–85)

Class	1978/79	1979/80	1980/81	1981/82	1982/83	1983/84	1984/85
				MALE			
1st Primary	11,659	11,375	12,797	13,251	15,922	18,370	1,983
2nd Primary	10,906	11,177	11,092	12,370	13,012	15,479	1,792
3rd Primary	8,685	10,291	10,607	10,953	12,182	12,831	1,512
				FEMALE			
1st Primary	7,062	6,735	8,535	9,289	12,642	15,615	1,822
2nd Primary	5,643	6,413	6,322	8,141	8,862	12,050	1,511
3rd Primary	4,078	5,076	5,947	6,051	7,764	8,465	1,159

Source: Statistical Yearbook of Education, 1985: 25

The second five-year development plan (1981-85) concentrated on upgrading the existing permanent schools by adding more classrooms and providing better educational facilities (libraries, laboratories, etc.) and replacing temporary schools with permanent ones. During this period, the concern was more on quality than quantity.

Gender segregation is practiced from the first primary grade although it is possible to find co-educational classes in small villages where there are not enough students to warrant opening separate schools for each sex.

Because of the large demand for education, the Ministry of Education and Youth decided to make optimum use of available school facilities. The result is a shift system in which the school buildings are used three times daily by different groups. Classes for young children are in the morning and in the afternoon while adults attend at nights. This has resulted in a short school day, which begins at 7:30 a.m. and ends at 12:00 noon, allowing the second group of children to start at 1:00 p.m. and end at 5:00 p.m.

While the general enrollment in the first three grades of the primary level increases annually, the proportional increase of girls is considerably lower. This can be explained by customs that deemphasize the importance of education for girls. Table 3 shows the development of education in the first three primary grades from 1978–79 through 1984–85 according to gender.

A look at Table 3 further reveals that while the annual intake gets higher (for both males and females), there is a considerable drop in student numbers as they move from one grade to the next. This can be explained by a high percentage of wastage, which is a typical problem in the lower primary classes. According to Razik (1984), wastage at this level is featured in high repeat and dropout figures and appears to be more evident at the first primary grade.

Table 4 shows the latest enrollment growth in the three grades according to regions. When Table 3 and 4 are compared, one notes the continued growth in student population with the gender gap getting narrower. Nevertheless, the decrease in student numbers as they move to higher grades continues to be evident. This seems to indicate that while there is development in the parental awareness and acceptance of the idea of education for girls, the dropout problem remains an important phenomenon in primary schools.

As a result of tremendous expansion, classes in Oman have become overcrowded with a teacher-student ratio as high as 1:45.

TABLE 4

Distribution of Grades 1, 2, and 3 Students According to Gender and Region (1988)

Region	Class 1		Class 2		Class 3	
	Male	Female	Male	Female	Male	Female
Muscat	4,091	4,007	3,983	3,876	3,750	3,752
Al Batinah	3,903	4,660	4,445	4,218	4,445	3,990
Rustaq	2,588	2,502	2,601	2,360	2,615	2,357
Dakhliya	3,139	2,752	2,793	2,539	3,021	2,590
Sharqiya	1,634	1,452	1,574	1,434	1,608	1,312
Musta	1,656	1,282	1,593	1,247	1,442	1,212
Dhahira	2,337	2,104	2,255	2,061	2,054	2,107
Ganubiya	2,024	1,869	1,950	1,689	1,841	1,708
Musandam	389	321	359	258	335	236
Total	21,761	20,949	21,553	19,682	21,111	19,264

Source: Statistical Yearbook of Education, 1989:81.

The curriculum is centrally prescribed by the curriculum department of the Ministry of Education and Youth. Initially, the curriculum used was Qatari but in 1978, an Omani curriculum was gradually phased in.

The main subjects taught at this level are Islamic education, Arabic, mathematics, general science, social studies, and vocational, technical, and scientific activities. Table 5 shows the distribution of weekly periods according to subjects taught and class level.

With the third five-year development plan came a search for efficiency in the Omani educational system. A critical evaluation of the curriculum, which was not considered previously, had become an important issue during this period. As a result, the primary school curriculum was evaluated and many important issues were raised.

Considering the problems that plagued the primary school system following the expansion period, various attempts were made to combat these problems during the second and third five-year development plans. These attempts included the following:

1. Cancellation of the final examination in the first three grades of the primary level. This was intended to reduce the amount of wastage that came about as a result of failure and repeating in lower classes.

Subjects Studied in the Lower Primary Grades

Subjects	1st Primary	2nd Primary	3rd Primary
Arabic	11	11	9
Social Studies*	1	1	2
General Science	2	2	3
Mathematics	5	5	5
English Language	—	—	—
Physical Education	2	2	2
Technical Education	1	1	1
Vocational Activities	—	—	2
Scientific Activities	1	1	—
Music	1	1	1
Total number of weekly periods	24	24	25

* Civics is taught in social studies periods; one period every two weeks.

Source: Statistical Yearbook of Education, 1987:9.

2.   Employment of more female teachers to teach children of both sexes at the lower primary classes. Female teachers were considered more effective at the lower levels.

3.   Encouragement of Omanis to enter the teaching profession and replace foreign teachers as fast as possible. This was seen to be very crucial at the primary level in general and lower primary classes in particular. It is estimated that by 1992 all primary classes will be taught by Omanis.

4.   Work toward a common curriculum for all Arabic Gulf Cooperation Council (AGCC) member countries. This was expected to result in a smoother transfer of Gulf nationals from one AGCC to another and the unified effort would result in a better and stronger curriculum.

Special Education Programs for Young Children

In 1981, the Ministry of Social Affairs and Labor issued a ministerial ordinance to establish the National Committee for the Care of the Handicapped. Among the objectives of this committee are the following:

1.   to determine the number of handicapped people in Oman and classify their handicap;

2.   to provide training courses that will help make the handicapped productive members of the society; and

3.   to provide the handicapped with all the services necessary to facilitate their optimal development.

This ordinance represented the government's first concern for the handicapped. Although a few centers were opened to rehabilitate the handicapped in the 1980s, it was not until 1989 that the first center for the care and rehabilitation of the handicapped children was established. The center was opened in Bidbid by the people of that city. They collected the handicapped children, provided the facilities, and asked the Ministry of Social Affairs to provide technical help for running the center.

The purpose of the center was to train the children and to teach them skills that would help them cope with life in the society, to provide older children with work skills, and to educate mothers of the handicapped children how to assist their children.

This center serves children from birth to age

14. Currently, there are 30 handicapped children at the center cared for by volunteers from Bidbid and the surrounding area. The center has no boarding facilities but transportation is provided to and from the center. Besides providing technical assistance, the Ministry also provides the specialized equipment (Ministry of Social Affairs and Labor, 1990). Sultan Qaboos University Hospital also contributes to the running of this center by providing a visiting pediatrician.

Studies are now under way to open another center for handicapped children in Salalah (the southern region).

Training Programs for Teachers of Young Children

Primary School Teachers

The Directorate of Teacher Education in the Ministry of Education and Youth was given responsibility for administering teacher education and training in 1983 (Razik and El-Shibiny, 1986). Its task involves both preservice and in-service preparation.

Preservice Preparation. The tremendous growth of education in the Sultanate since 1970 was achieved through three successive five-year development plans carried out by the Ministry of Education. When the first plan concentrated only on the quantitative development of the school system, there arose a huge gap between the supply and demand of teachers. The country had no option but to employ unqualified Omani teachers and recruit non-Omani's to teach in schools (usually from friendly Arab countries, such as Egypt, Jordan, Sudan, and Tunis).

The concern for quality in the second plan resulted in a need for trained Omani primary teachers. To meet this need, a three-year course for intermediate school leavers was established to train teachers for the lower classes of the primary level. Simultaneously, a one-year course to train secondary school graduates was begun.

The third plan (1986–90) witnessed a strengthening of the educational system. In this stage of development, an important step was taken toward raising the quality of future primary school teachers. A new two-year, post-secondary teacher's training college was established, phasing out the three-year institutes (Razik, and El-Shibiny, 1986).

Another measure taken to upgrade teaching was the Ministry of Education's initiative in 1983 to establish the intermediate colleges for male and female teachers. These colleges first admitted students in 1984–85 and accepted only secondary school graduates with good passing marks. The colleges follow the credit-hour system spread over a period of four semesters. The total number of credits required for graduation is 75. The program offered at the colleges is as follows:

• *General knowledge* (21 credit hours): Islamic culture, Arabic, English, social studies (Oman and Islamic civilization);

• *General skills and activities* (21 credits): art education, physical education, technical knowledge and skills (carpentry and metal work for boys and home economics for girls);

• *Behavioral knowledge* (22 credits): introduction to education, psychology, general methods of teaching, educational technology, evaluation and measurement, educational administration and supervision, methods of research, morals and ethics of teaching profession, environmental education, and teaching practice;

• *Primary school concentration* (mandatory for all students) (12 credits): developmental psychology, psychology of play, psychological and social counseling, psychiatry and adjustment, class management, general methods of teaching in the primary school; and

• *Subject matter concentration* (21 credits): methods of teaching the subject selected.

The specializations offered are Islamic studies, Arabic language, social studies, English, general science, and mathematics (Razik and El-Shibiny, 1986).

Students are certified to teach both the lower and upper primary classes. Contrary to the previous program where the student chose either to become a "classroom teacher," (being trained to teach all subjects and therefore teaching the lower classes) or to become a subject specialist (becoming specialized in one particular subject and becoming a teacher in the upper primary classes), this program offers all students a broad base and a specific area of specialization.

In 1985–86, the colleges enrolled a total of 657 students (343 males, 413 females). Today, the colleges enroll a total of 1,753 students distributed in six colleges located in four regions: in Muscat, Ganubiya (in the southern region), and Rustaq and Sharqiya (the eastern region). While Sharqiya has only a college for men and Rustaq one for women, Muscat and Ganubiya each have one college for men and one for women.

In 1989–90, the colleges graduated 851 students (463 males and 388 females).(Table 6 shows student enrollment in the six colleges according to regions and gender.)

TABLE 6

Distribution of Students at the Teachers Training Colleges According to Region and Gender

Region	Male	Female
Muscat	489	396
Ganubiya	155	104
Sharqiya	264	—
Rustaq	—	245
Total	908	745

Source: Statistical Yearbook of Education, 1989:166.

In-service Preparation. In-service training of Omani teachers began in 1973. This is accomplished mostly in the summer when the teachers are free to attend short courses, seminars, and meetings.

Among the important in-service programs is the basic training given to qualify teachers who have entered the profession without academic preparation. The curriculum for this program has three main components:

1.   development of knowledge—(exposure to new approaches, etc.);

2.   development of skills—where the teacher is shown how to write lesson plans, state objectives, select activities, design educational aids, select appropriate appraisal techniques, etc.; and

3.   development of attitudes—developing positive attitudes toward teaching, students, peers etc.,

Kindergarten and Day Care Centers Teachers

Because kindergartens are privately managed, the Ministry of Education and Youth does not have a program to prepare kindergarten teachers. However, the Department of Private Education has issued directives that specify the qualifications required for teachers at this level. Teachers must have one of the following qualifications:

1.   university degree with experience in the field of early childhood education;

2.   secondary school certificate, or its equivalent, with experience in early childhood education;

3.   secondary school certificate with a teaching certificate; or

4.   diploma from a teachers training college.

While these requirements are for Omani teachers, the expectations are higher for non-Omanis. Only those who have a university degree plus at least two years of experience, or a diploma (equivalent to a university degree) plus three years of experience, are to be employed.

In 1988, the Ministry of Social Affairs in cooperation with UNICEF began to train Omani secondary school girls to teach in day care centers. Four university graduates staffed the trainers program for day care and kindergarten teachers; 24 teachers have completed the program at this time. The second course was organized in January 1990 involving 32 secondary school graduates and three university graduates. This is envisioned to be a temporary solution until proper training is offered at either the teacher training colleges or the university.

References

Al-Barwani, T. (1987). Status of children in Oman. Paper presented at the conference Childhood in a Changing Society. Al-Ain University, Abudhabi.

Al-Dhahab, M. (1987). The historical development of education in Oman. From the first modern school 1893 to the first university 1986. Unpublished doctoral dissertation.

Al-Mishad, S. (1985). *The development of modern education in the Gulf*. London: Ithaca Press.

Darwish, M. (1984). *Situation analysis of children and women in the Sultanate of Oman*. Muscat: UNICEF.

Development Council. (1986). *Statistical Yearbook* (in Arabic). Muscat.

————. (1988). *Statistical Yearbook* (in Arabic). Muscat.

Ministry of Education and Youth. (1987). *Handbook for local private schools* (in Arabic). Muscat.

————. (1988). Child's Workbook (Books 1–10) (in Arabic). Muscat.

————. (1985). Teachers handbook on education and experiences for kindergarten (three books) (in Arabic). Kuwait.

Ministry of Social Affairs and Labor. (1987). *Report on child care programs and effort in Oman* (in Arabic). Muscat.

————. *Social care of children of Oman*. (in Arabic). Muscat.

Mohammed, J. (1988). Omani system of education. In Husen & Postlethwaite, eds., *International encyclopedia of Education* (15, 3657–60). United Kingdom: Pergamon Press.

Razik, T., & El-Shibiny, M. (1986). *The identification of teaching competencies; A study of Omani Primary Teachers*. Muscat: Ministry of Education and Youth.

Razik, T.A. (1984). *The international efficiency of the Omani educational system—A study of educational wastage*. Muscat: Ministry of Education and Youth.

PRESCHOOL EDUCATION IN RUSSIA

• • • • • • • • • • ◆ • • • • • • • •

Larisa A. Paramonova, Valentina D. Sych,
Larisa R. Anosova, Liubovj N. Pavlova, and Valentina M. Ivanova
Research Institute on Preschool Education
Moscow, Russia

Overview of Preschool Education in Russia

The first public kindergartens and creches in Russia were established as charity services in the prerevolutionary era. In 1914, there were 150 such charity preschools and creches serving 4,000 children. Some of the kindergartens used the grammar school curriculum in the preschool. Progressives, primarily women from the intelligentsia, assisted the teachers in applying the Froebelian system of early education. On the other hand, creches, serving mostly babies, were organized by some *zemstvos* (elective district councils) in villages during the harvest to permit women to work in the fields. They typically operated for 30 to 40 days a year.

Following 1917, and Lenin's initiatives to grant women the same property and parental rights as men, women were free to choose their profession and to receive an education. As a result, a child care system became necessary to ensure equal opportunity for women. Children's institutions and permanent teacher training programs were established throughout the country. As is evident from Table 1, growth in services was immediate and continuous.

TABLE 1

Growth of Preschool Facilities in Russia, 1917–90	
Year	*Number of Children*
1917	5,000
1940	1,953,000
1950	3,087,000
1970	9,000,000
1980	14,337,000
1990	17,354,000

In addition to the present-day figures, approximately one million children are enrolled in seasonal preschools in rural areas.

In Russia, the preschool period extends from birth to age 7. Children start school at ages 6 or 7, depending on their physical and mental development and their degree of school readiness. The focus of the preschool experience is to develop children's physical, intellectual, moral, and aesthetic abilities and to prepare them in a general way for school.

The legislated aim of preschool institutions is to function in "close cooperation with the family, carry out an all-round and harmonious education of the children, protect and strengthen their health, develop elementary practical skills and cultivate in children a love for work, take care of their aesthetic education, prepare them for school, teach them to respect the adults and love their socialist motherland and homeland."

Preschool institutions therefore exist to meet the demands of both the family and the society in rearing children. Facilities are sponsored by organizations ranging from public educational departments to factories to cooperative and collective farms. The main types of preschools in modern Russia are creches, creche kindergartens, and special kindergartens. Creches are child care institutions serving children from ages 3 to 7. More widespread are creche kindergartens, which combine care and education and enroll children up to school age (7 years). Special kindergartens, modeled on a sanatorium, have been established for frail children. They are generally located in pastoral settings or in the suburbs. They focus primarily on the children's health through a prescribed regimen of proper nutrition, long walks, games, and physical training.

Following a resolution of the Council of Ministers in 1984, a system of "school kindergartens" has been established to educate both preschool and school-aged children. School kindergartens are mainly found in sparsely populated rural areas.

Preschools use only purpose-specific or suitable existing buildings, which meet fire and safety codes and are sensitive to climatic, ecological, and cultural conditions. The number and composition of age groups vary according to the demand. Since 1982, new standards have resulted in larger program rooms and improved kitchen and medical facilities in preschools. In kindergartens for 12 or more groups of children, two dancing halls and two gymnasiums are provided. In northern communities and areas beyond the Polar Circle, kindergartens that serve more than 200 children have indoor swimming pools. The largest institutions, caring for 500–600 children, (i.e., those in cities and large settlements), have special facilities for meal preparation and storage as well as indoor swimming pools.

All preschools have special furniture, electrical equipment, sports equipment (e.g., skis, sleds, skates, and bicycles), and musical instruments. Children can choose from a variety of toys, games, construction sets, tools, and visual aids. Every kindergarten has a small but comprehensive library. Large numbers of children's books are published in Russia.

The length of the kindergarten day varies according to individual institutions and the parents' and children's needs. Preschool may function for five, six, or seven days per week, with children staying at the facility full-time with one or two days at home.

Because of the financial commitment of the state for kindergarten services, parents generally pay only 20 percent of the cost. A new fee structure has been in place since January 1990. A common fee was established based on the cost of one kindergarten visit (i.e., one day of care) regardless of the administrative attachment of the institution or the place of work or study of the parents. Therefore, all creches, creche kindergartens, and kindergartens in which a single visit is defined as less than 12 hours charge 60 copecks. Fees are waived for families whose total income is below the established subsistence level. In addition, parents with four or more children pay 50 percent of the regular fee. At their own expense, local executive committees of People's Deputies and individual sponsoring agencies can make further fee reductions.

To further support the family, motherhood, and children in Russia, a resolution in April 1990 granted a state allowance equal to the minimum wage to mothers caring for their children from birth to 18 months at home. The allowance is provided for each child under the age limit. The resolution supports young children and families in other ways as well. For instance, maternity leave has been extended to 56 days following the birth regardless of the number of days of leave prior to birth. Extended parental leave until the child is age 3 can be granted in full or partially to either parent, a grandparent, or another family member.

Women with children under age 14 can be granted a shortened workday or work week. Other provisions for mothers are additional leave time, preferential conditions of labor, reduced overtime, holiday and night work, and limited work-related trips from home. Working pregnant women must be provided with duties that are healthy and safe.

Teacher Training for the Preschool

Of the 1.6 million preschool teachers in Russia, 78.9 percent have higher and special secondary education. Preschool teachers with special secondary education have been trained at one of 313 vocational teacher training schools. They are taught anatomy, psychology, children's literature, methods of developing speech, physical training, singing, music, rhythmics, and general teaching methods. Further qualifications are available through teacher training institutes at the departments of preschool education, of which there are 101. Graduates generally function as kindergarten directors, senior teachers, and teachers in vocational schools. A recent development in preschool departments is a specialist training program in the areas of physical education, drawing, foreign language instruction, and psychology. The specialists work directly with children as well as act as consultants to teacher and parents. The new curriculum has a common year for all general education programs (e.g., anatomy, physiology, psychology, pedagogy, physical education, theory, and methods of language promotion). In their second year, students study teaching methodology for working with young children. In addition, more than 15 electives are available (e.g., rhythmics, choral singing, and puppet theater).

Higher education students also gain practical experience in kindergartens and in vocational teacher training schools. They may also have field experiences as inspectors or researchers for local educational bodies. Students are introduced to preschool education as a science, drawing on the research methods of social science, the pedagogical arts, and psychology.

Preschool Personnel

Large preschools have many teachers and educators headed by a director. Teachers, working with children in groups, play games, carry out lessons, and manage routines. A special music teacher is in charge of music education, which includes teaching music lessons, organizing festivals, and generally assisting educators in conducting morning exercises, music games, and dancing. The music teacher also consults with parents on music

education. A senior teacher is in charge of the whole process of teaching in the preschool, directing and controlling the work of the teaching and medical staff. Since 1985, the Certifying Commission has awarded the title "Teacher-Methodologist" to exemplary teachers, who are then paid a higher salary.

Children in national republics are taught in their mother tongue. Before the dissolution of the Soviet Union, all preschool education was governed by the Ministries of Education and their local bodies were under the authority of the department of preschool education of the State Committee of People's Education of the Soviet Union.

Preschool education is widely discussed in various publications (e.g., the journals *Preschool Education* and *Family and School*, newspapers such as *Family* and *Teacher's Paper*, and various similar publications in the republics).

Both scholarly works and textbooks on teaching methods are written by educational psychologists, many of whom work at the Institute of Preschool Education of the Academy of Pedagogical Sciences. The institute was established in 1960 by the academic A.V. Zaporozhets. Its goal is to promote excellence in both theoretical and applied research in preschool education. The institute coordinates the research activities of the various teacher training institutes of the republics, offers a doctoral program in education and developmental psychology, and promotes contact with foreign institutions. In 1989, the institute became a member of OMEP (International Organization for Preschool Education).

The institute also developed the curriculum followed in Russian preschool, the *Standard Educational Program for the Kindergarten*. National educational programs in the republics are developed on the basis of the standard program, with accommodation made for regional and geographic factors and the needs of individual preschool institutions.

Trends in the Development of Russian Preschool

An analysis of contemporary theory and practice of education in the kindergarten requires a survey of historical trends. Immediately following the October Revolution in 1917 a new system of public education was organized. The first level in the system was concerned with the care and education of preschool children. The founding of a system of state preschools was therefore a priority of the state.

The development of a theory and method of preschool education was a long and often difficult process. One the one hand, the theory of "spontaneous upbringing" was still dominant, while on the other, new studies demonstrated the necessity of purposeful instruction. In addition, the 1920s and 1930s witnessed great changes in theories of child development founded in Marxist-Leninist methodology.

A major contribution to the development of principles for Russian preschool education was a series of congresses on preschool education held 1919, 1921, 1924, and 1928. The result was a statement of purpose for preschool education, which is overall development of future citizens, as well as a critical evaluation of the theory of "spontaneous upbringing." The congresses demonstrated the need for a scientific foundation of preschool pedagogy based on Marxist methodology.

Major contributions to preschool pedagogy in this period were made by N.K. Krupskaya and A.S. Makarenko, who stressed the importance of the early years on future development and the importance of social interaction. Krupskaya emphasized that a Russian kindergarten ought to provide children with a broad education that includes not only an understanding of nature, the objective world, society and work, but also skill development. She advocated the investigation of children's abilities as well as of the methods of preschool instruction.

L.S. Vygotsky's theory of development also had an influence on preschools. He stressed that to promote development, education intervention should be oriented to the child's potential capacities (i.e., the "zone of proximal development"). His ideas about the value of social experience, and the important role of adults in this process, suggested the necessity of active pedagogical guidance of child education. In advocating a system of preschool education, Vygotsky was critical of simply drawing on the primary school model. Instead, he viewed a good program as one that draws on the child's

interests and age peculiarities. His approach helped educators and psychologists weigh the proportional value of social and biological factors in child development and determined the course of preschool research for decades.

Other studies were being simultaneously carried out under the supervision of N.M. Aksarina. They further demonstrated the need to provide education for young preschoolers and provided the groundwork for the development of a preschool curriculum and methodology.

E.I. Ticheeva, drawing on the principles developed by J.A. Comenius, H. Pestalozzi, and K.D. Ushinsky, developed a program of sensory development for children based on the use of didactic materials, geometrical figures, natural objects (e.g., pebbles and nuts), and didactic games. Further contributions were in the area of speech development and arts instruction.

In the 1930s and 1940s, statements were issued by the Communist Party of the Soviet Union (CPSU) Central Committee aimed at giving greater importance to the role of the kindergarten teacher in the educational process. At the same time, the official *Guide for the Kindergarten* was published, summarizing the contemporary themes of child rearing and education work and introducing special lessons for children. The lessons, however, were not then compulsory as they are now.

In practice, however, the kindergarten's role in early education was buried in the role of child care. The teacher was reduced to setting the stage for lessons, while children were responsible for their own learning. The main method consisted of providing tasks of a general character (e.g., "all children should draw vegetables" or "let's all of us make a house"). The teacher did not give specific instructions, but only advised and answered the questions of the children.

The studies of this period, conducted by such researchers as E.I. Ticheeva, F.M. Blecher, and B.I. Chtchapuridze, became more and more aimed at constructing didactic games, which in fact were more exercises than games, and didactic materials. Children investigated the materials, which contributed mainly to their sensory development.

The beginning of the 1950s marked a major change in the direction of research in preschool education. Research in the Department of Preschool

Education of the Institute of the Theory and History of Pedagogy under the supervision of A.P. Usova, as well as research conducted at the Institute of Teaching Methods by E.I. Monszon, A.I. Voskresenskaya, S.R. Redozubov, and I.F. Chemarev, resulted in a rethinking of the relationship of teaching method to curriculum content. As a result of their studies, it became clear that the optimal relationship of the contents and methods of instruction is when the method is subordinate to the content. If this relation is changed, the educational process is distorted. The studies also demonstrated that child rearing as well as educational functions should occur within this equation.

A.P. Usova concluded that a teacher needs a method of instruction that not only guides the separate actions of children, but their activity as a whole. This is accomplished through verbal and demonstrative explanations, consideration of children's history of experience, and their activity at the time. Usova advocated the use of collective, compulsory lessons, a format that came to dominate Russian kindergartens. Usova's ideas are expressed in the *Educational Program* (1953).

The introduction of systematic instruction and special lessons into kindergarten practice made it necessary to work out specific methods, contents, and techniques of preschool education. During the 1950s early 1960s, methods were developed in the areas of music (N.A. Vetlugina, 1953), movement (A.I. Bykova, 1955), language (O.I. Solovieva 1955), drawing and sculpture (M.P. Saculina, 1956), and mathematics (A.M. Leushina).

Usova developed her system further in *Education in the Kindergarten*, a treatise that has not lost its relevance. She distinguished two kinds of knowledge: that which children acquire themselves in everyday life and that which should be given to children through direct instruction. Usova demonstrated the possibilities for preschool children to learn skills.

While Usova considered the research stemming from *The Program of the Kindergarten* to be of great importance, some scholars criticized the use of systematized, teacher-led lessons in preschool education. E.A. Flerina, for example, was afraid that lessons could become an obstacle to development of creativity in children. However, studies carried out under the supervision of N.A. Vetlugina

have shown that continuous formation of creativity is possible if it is based on the firm knowledge, skills, and abilities acquired by children in the course of purposeful instruction.

The next body of research that contributed to Russian preschool education is represented by the studies of children's sensory development carried out in the 1960s at the Institute of Preschool Education (A.P.S. USSR) under the direction of A.V. Zaporozets and A.P. Usova (representative works are by L.A. Venger, N.N. Poddyakov, N.P. Sakulina, and V.N. Avanesova). These studies showed that the development of perception is founded in the child's acquisition of sensory standards (ethalones) (i.e., shapes, colors, sizes, and other properties of objects developed by human experience and having verbal representation) and the formation of perceptive actions. An important educational task, then is to teach children how to use generalized techniques while examining new objects. Sensory education is regarded as being closely interconnected with intellectual development and is successfully carried out in the course of different types of the child's productive activity (e.g., drawing and constructing). As such, it is entirely different from previous educational systems, where sensory education occurred through a series of monotonous exercises.

The result of the research mentioned above made it possible to create a new way of teaching children. A hierarchical system of actions, directed at examining objects, was used. This made it possible to develop a wholesome and at the same time a detailed image, as well as to encourage the process of object comparison and distinguishing of common properties. Didactic games were developed by L.A. Venter and E.G. Pilugina, aimed at the sensory education of younger and older preschool children. Thus, the research program made it possible to increase the level of sensory education at the kindergarten level.

At the end of the 1960s, the problem of intellectual development of children became the subject of intensive research. The psychological studies of cognitive processes in children (A.V. Zaporozets, V.V. Davidov, N.N. Poddyakov, and L.A. Venger) demonstrated that preschoolers are able through object-sensory activity to distinguish and reflect not only concrete objects and phenomena, but also the relations between them. The result was the basis for a new principle of selection and systematization of knowledge (N.N. Poddyakov). The content of this knowledge, described in the corresponding chapters of *Standard Educational Program for the Kindergarten* (1984), reflects the essential connections and interdependencies of the world sphere preferred by children. For example, certain systems of knowledge—such as "knowledge of animals and nature" (S.N. Nicolaeva and I.S. Fredkin), constructing (L.A. Paramonova), and "knowledge of the surrounding world" (V.N. Avanesova and V.I. Loginova)—are based on certain dependencies: the building of an animal's body depend on its environment; the life and growth of plants depends of the environmental factors; the structure of an object depends on its practical functions, etc. Such a profound intellectual understanding of objects and phenomena by children appeared to be possible only if the number of topics studied was considerably reduced (from two to three topics for each age group). A series of studies conducted under the supervision of N.N. Poddyakov demonstrated that the acquisition of this type of knowledge had a considerable effect on children's intellectual development.

The study of objects and phenomena in terms of their interrelationships leads to the discovery of their hidden properties and helps the children to acquire necessary cognitive strategies. The experimental data allowed researchers to work out forms of organizing children's activity. Thus, along with construction using a pattern, researchers used construction according to given conditions that forced children to think of different variations of the same object depending on its practical applications (e.g., a bridge across a "river" of a given width for transport or a bridge over a railway for pedestrians). This type of construction contributes to the development of the child's mind, creativity, ability to plan, and self-control, which is especially important in preparing the child for school learning. At the same time, it made possible an individualized approach to teaching children.

While developing elementary mathematical concepts, "construction" is aimed at helping the child go beyond immediate perceptions of things to the underlying mathematical relations.

Current studies of children's intellectual activity, creativity, and imagination are carried out at the Institute of Preschool Education (A.P.S., USSR) under the supervision of N.N. Poddyakov, V.V. Davidov, and L.A. Venger. For example, Poddyakov, who based his study on the dialectical character of cognitive processes, has suggested a method of increasing intellectual activity in children by introducing some new facts, thereby contradicting to a certain degree the system of interrelations already acquired by children. This method develops considerable cognitive interest in children and stimulates their reasoning processes.

The institute also conducts studies of children's speech development (initiated by the late F.A. Sochin), second language acquisition, language learning, grammar and reading instruction (according the principles developed by D.B. Elkonin), and various other subjects that contribute to the understanding of methods of teaching and child development.

One of the main criteria for success in teaching a preschool child is developed out of Vygotsky's thesis about the development of intellectual and emotional spheres. Specific conditions must be maintained during the lessons, stimulating positive emotions in children. There should be a general atmosphere of gaiety and creativity and praise should be given for even the smallest success of a child. There should also be an individualized approach to education, selecting problems and tasks relevant and satisfying to each child.

Curriculum

The *Educational Program for the Kindergarten* (1984), developed by the Research Institute of Preschool Education, is the compulsory, national curriculum for Russian kindergartens. It is to be used as the basis for developing programs of child care and education in the republics.

The philosophy underlying the program is that child development occurs through the process of various activities (e.g., play, work, classes, etc.), taking into consideration the developmental needs of preschoolers.

The program for each age group consists of two general components: "organization of life and child rearing" and "education during classes." In these programs, general aims of education and child rearing are described in order to orient the teacher toward the terminal qualitative objective, which should be gained at the final stage of education and may be viewed as the criterion for the program's success. For each age group, there is a list of class topics and related activities and resources for a one-week period. The aim of this research-based program is overall development of children.

Russian psychologists have viewed children's play as an activity that is essentially social in its content and structure (L.S. Vygotsky, A.N. Leontiev, and D.B. Elconin). As a result, the program aims specially at development of role-play at each genetic stage in accordance with the age characteristics of children. For example, with the group of 3-year-old children, the aim is to develop the ability to act within an imaginary and representative plane (substituting objects in play); for children of age 5, it is the ability to follow the rules of role behavior; while for 6-year-olds, it is the ability to coordinate individual plots in the process of role play.

The aims of children's physical development are represented in two chapters in the program: "Care and Maintenance of Health" and "Physical Culture." The first deals with the kindergarten's daily routine, recommending the development of a resistance to negative media influence and the benefits of physical training, gymnastics, and games. The second chapter aims at developing movement skills and physical abilities (e.g., dexterity, strength, speed, and coordination).

The program describes creche work with infants and it includes requirements for daily routines, motor development, play activities, guidance of practical activity, and language. In Russian pedagogy, the first two to three years of a child's life are traditionally called early childhood (infancy). This period is characterized by rapid physical and psychological development.

Because the program is aimed at providing a constant and continuous educational process, there are special sections devoted to infants organized by age. Separate sections describe education for each of years one and two. The third year is considered a transition period and is called the first junior kindergarten group. Children of this age, especially at the beginning of the school year, retain many characteristics of their infancy. By the end of the year, they become more and more socialized through the educational process.

A considerable amount of time in infant groups is devoted to child care and to the organization of everyday life. The program contains the requirements and rationale for routines.

The program is the practical realization of the modern scientifically substantiated pedagogy of infancy, and in particular it is based on recent research in the spheres of orientation activity, emotional and cognitive development, sensory skills, culture of thinking, and games and play. As an example of the link between research and practice, recent work has seen the implementation of a new set of materials in game playing: folk toys, tools, and construction sets.

Kindergarten teachers are given recommendations for evaluating the level of the program acquisition by children. According to their assessment, teachers organize year-end lessons to provide children with opportunities to demonstrate the use of their knowledge.

A more general evaluation of the program has shown both its positive and negative aspects. A positive result is a higher level of intellectual and speech development in children, knowledge in mathematics and grammar and elementary learning skills. The most important negative aspect is that the program "over-loads" with all sorts of knowledge. The volume of knowledge makes children's lives over-organized, the role of play as well as other self-directed activities is underestimated, the level of their emotional comfort decreases, and their health is damaged.

Three groups of children were able to be distinguished. The first and largest group consisted of children who mastered the program. The second group were those who did not master the program, while a third group could master even more complicated material. The program seemed to serve the "average child."

Two main findings—both weaknesses in the program—were specific to the republics. First, the standard program was used in its original form in kindergartens with children of different national origins. In addition, children were taught in Russian. In kindergartens where only the national language was used, the standard program was supplemented with additional materials connected to folk traditions. In the first case, the process of preschool education does not take into consideration the specific features of the surroundings, in the second case, the program becomes overloaded.

At present, researchers are working out a variety of experimental programs, with the goal of selecting the most effective for developing corresponding methods. The revised program will consider regional differences, the needs of preschool orphanages and children who do not attend kindergartens. All programs will have two levels of complexity: (1) the minimal program, which enables a child to reach the developmental level necessary for learning at school, and (2) the maximum program, which provides the child with additional opportunities for development.

Efforts are also being directed at developing methods for testing gifted children and detecting their special abilities. Creating optimal conditions for development of this category of children is one of the main problems of modern Russia.

The Kindergarten and the Family

The kindergarten and the family have common aims, which can be achieved only through cooperation. The kindergarten carefully preserves and develops the good qualities that a child acquires in the family. Unity of public education and education by the family are important principles of Russian preschool pedagogy.

The kindergarten helps young parents to bring up their children by giving them pedagogical advice. Different organizations and institutions contribute to the well-being of the young family. The mass media (both national and regional) organize meetings with specialists in education, psychology, medicine, and law for broadcast or written discussion. Innovative parents share their experience through family education.

National and local publishing houses issue many books and booklets on education for home reading. Among those are the *Set of Books for Family Reading*, *Parent's Library*, and the *Set of Parent's Books on Physical Training*. Also available are works by contemporary scientists, and the classics of Russian pedagogy and progressive teachers of the past.

Currently, the Russian family has a better opportunity than in the past to read translations of the works of foreign specialists on education and the family. The weekly publication of the Academy of Pedagogical Sciences, *The Family and School*, is very popular with the parents, as is *The Family*, the weekly of the Lenin Soviet Children's fund. The magazines *Health*, *Woman-Worker*, and *Woman-Peasant* also frequently have articles on education.

The mission of the all-union society called "Knowledge" is to help parents improve their understanding of pedagogy. Branches exist in all the union and autonomous republics, regions, town, and districts. Among the members of the society are lecturers on different subjects related to child rearing. The society organizes the People's Universities of Pedagogical Knowledge, public lectures, and a series of lectures for parents at their residence or workplace.

The Pedagogical Society also provides lectures. It has a network of branches at the republic and local levels. They encourage working teachers to write textbooks on family education. A network of institutions rendering genetic and sexual counseling and psychological help to the family is currently being organized.

Although intensive work in the area of parental education is being carried out, the effect is minimal. The main reason is the lack of involvement by the organizers of parents of children in the higher grades.

By contrast, the parents of kindergarten children get more purposeful, continuous, and systematic help. The preschool performs the function of the assistant in education for the family. Constant and close cooperation between the teachers and the parents guarantees the optimum conditions of life and education for children. The better the preschool establishment works, the greater authority it has with the parents and the greater is the educational effect for both parents and the children. The system of interconnection between the kindergarten and the family presupposes the teacher's understanding of the family and the family's understanding of public education.

PRESCHOOL AND PRIMARY EDUCATION IN SOUTH AFRICA

• • • • • • • • • • ◆ • • • • • • • • • •

Christoffel Jansen, Elsie Calitz,
Lydia Du Toit, Hester Grobler,
Annemarie Kotzé, Maria Lancaster,
Joan Orr, Aletta Smith, and
Elizabeth Swanepoel,
University of South Africa,
Pretoria, South Africa,

Before the discovery of gold and diamonds in South Africa during the second half of the 19th century, the population was largely rural, with agriculture as the main source of income. Households were to a great extent self-sufficient, with large families and the extended family system being the norm. Overall, the country was sparsely populated. This enabled each of the various cultural groups to pursue their traditional way of life, and there was little contact among different racial groups.

In this situation, children were raised at home in the care of the family. It was seen as the mother's duty to educate her children and to keep house for the family. Employment of women outside the home was virtually nonexistent.

The initial interest in preprimary education came about as a result of the British influence during the period of colonial rule (1806–1919). During this period, the pioneering efforts of Robert Owen, James Buchanan, and later, the Macmillan sisters were receiving much attention in Great Britain. Several schools for young children were founded during the 19th century. In Cape Town, a school for slave children and the children of the poor was founded in 1830 by William Buchanan, a son of James Buchanan, a teacher at Owen's nursery school in New Lanark, Scotland (Terblanche, 1966:9).

Schools were also established in Phillipstown and Bloemfontein in this period. Support for the founding of these schools was limited to the English-speaking section of the communities in the Cape and Natal provinces, with the exception of the Bloemfontein Infant School. No provision was made for preschool education in the education acts of the Zuid Afrikaansche Republiek (ZAR) and the Republic of the Orange Free State (OFS) in the 19th century. It can be assumed that no need was felt for such education (Potgieter, 1962:31). The kindergarten movement of the Anglo-Boer War was not acceptable to Afrikaners because of the avowed aim of Anglicization of the population (Verster, 1989:279). (During the Anglo-Boer War (1899–1902), when the so-called "Free Kindergarten" was the predominant form of infant education in England, Britain brought organized preschool education into the Transvaal and the Free State. Qualified English teachers had to instruct the young Afrikaners in English as part of the Anglicizing policy. The "Kindergarten," however, was a "nationally unfamiliar institution" and did not appeal to the Afrikaner [Verster, T.L. 1989:279].)

The increasing industrialization and urbanization in the early 20th century led to conditions conducive to the preschool education movement. During the early part of the 20th century, the Anglo-Boer War, World War I, the Depression (1929–35), and a severe drought (1933–36) caused great poverty and poor social conditions, particularly in the cities. The urban dweller suffered from overcrowding in poor housing, a lack of social services, and a variety of health hazards.

As was often the case in the rest of the world, a need arose to compensate young children for the educational opportunities lost due to their impoverished living conditions. The first school truly bearing the name nursery school in South Africa was founded by the Pretoria City Council in 1931. At this stage, nursery health classes had already been started in Johannesburg (Webber, 1958:2), and the Claremont Mothercraft Training Center was established in Cape Town in 1925 (Malherbe, 1977:360).

A large national conference on education was sponsored by the New Education Fellowship (NEF) in 1934. This gave a great impetus to the nursery school movement, since many influential speakers were invited from overseas, including John Dewey, who stressed the importance of early education.

As a result, the Nursery School Association of South Africa (NSASA) was formed in 1939. The NSASA continues to be active in the field of preschool education (ibid.:365). The NEF also formed local committees, which affiliated with the NSASA to promote the idea of preschool education (ibid.:362).

An example of this new interest in nursery education was the founding of the Eastern Suburbs Nursery School in 1937. Eastern Suburbs was a private school funded and administered by a committee of professional parents in Pretoria. However, according to Malherbe (ibid.:359) the development of nursery schools in South Africa originated primarily from two sources: (1) the English tradition of compensatory education to underprivileged children in city slums, and (2) the American tradition of serving privileged and professional groups as part of the research programs conducted in universities and colleges.

Although individual municipal authorities had given some financial grants to nursery schools, the state had not given official support before this time. However, in 1930 the Orange Free State (one of the four provinces in South Africa) made provision for the payment of teachers' salaries in schools situated in the suburbs where children's home circumstances were poor. Transvaal, the Cape Province, and Natal later followed this example (Verster, 1989:281).

During 1936, the Nursery School for African Children was opened under the protection of the Anglican Mission. A training school, where African women were given teacher training for nursery school teaching, was opened at the same time by the Anglican Mission in Sophiatown.

State Support and Control of Nursery Education

Control of nursery schools and day cares established during the early part of the 20th century was in the hands of private organizations and individuals within local communities. Starting in 1936, a small government subsidy, amounting to three pounds per child, was paid annually to schools that met government criteria (Potgieter, 1962:42).

Prepared to give some financial assistance to nursery schools in underprivileged areas, the state was not, however, prepared to recognize nursery schools as an integral part of the educational system, despite the recommendations of several commissions of inquiry (e.g., the Nicoll Commission, 1939; the Commission on Technical and Career Guidance, 1948; the De Villiers Commission, 1948) (Verster, 1989:285; Potgieter, 1962:44–49).

Education departments would not accept responsibility for nursery schools, reasoning that this was the responsibility of the Department of Social Welfare (Malherbe, 1977:367). There were also continued objections to the establishment of nursery schools based on the argument that nursery schools were usurping the task of parents. Only in exceptional circumstances, where the mother was obliged to work because of dire financial circumstances, was it felt that children should be sent to nursery school, in which case they "would be better off in a crèche where three meals a day are served, instead of one meal, as is the case in the nursery school" (Potgieter, 1962:46).

After repeated requests and evidence submitted by the NSASA to government commissions of inquiry (the Transvaal Commission, 1939; Natal Commission, 1946; Technical and Vocational Commission, 1948; OFS Commission, 1951), the need for and desirability of nursery school education were acknowledged. Nevertheless, it was not until 1969 that the state officially recognized nursery schools as part of the new National Education Act. However, the policy that preschool education should be optional and not free has been maintained to this day.

The National Education Act requires all nursery schools to be registered with the appropriate provincial department of education. All nursery schools, now preferably called preprimary schools, are to be registered. Each provincial department of education is responsible for the control and financial support of all the nursery schools in that province.

Legislation Related to Preprimary Schools

The above abbreviated historical background shows that the legislation dealing with the education and care of preschool children is not an integrated system. Rather, it is divided and subdivided among the various state, provincial, and municipal authorities. Current examples of legislation dealing with the care and education of preschool children are the Child Care Act (1983), the National Education Act (1988), ordinances of various provincial councils that specify health regulations, the manual of the Department of Health and Welfare (which sets standards for the physical, psychological, and social care of white children in places of care), and the White Paper on the Provision of Education (including preprimary education) (1983).

The White Paper consists of eleven principles relating to the education of young children:

1.   Equal opportunities for education, including equal standards in education, for every inhabitant, irrespective of race, color, creed, or sex, shall be the purposeful endeavor of the state.

2.   Education shall afford positive recognition of what is common as well as what is diverse in the religious and cultural way of life and the languages of the inhabitants.

3.   Education shall give positive recognition to the freedom of choice of the individual, parents, and organizations in the society.

4.   The provisions of education shall be directed in an educationally responsible manner to meet the needs of the individual as well as those of society and economic development, and shall, among other things, take into consideration the manpower needs of the country.

5.   Education shall endeavor to achieve positive relationships among the formal, nonformal, and informal aspects of education in the school, society, and family.

6.   The provisions of formal education shall be a responsibility of the state provided that the individual, parents, and organized society shall have a shared responsibility, choice, and voice in this matter.

7.   The private sector and the state shall have a shared responsibility for the provision of nonformal education.

8.   Provision shall be made for the establishment and state subsidization of private education within the system of providing education.

9.   In the provision of education, the processes of centralization and decentralization shall be reconciled organizationally and functionally.

10.   The professional status of the teacher and lecturer shall be recognized.

11.   Effective provision of education shall be based on continuing research.

Financial Support for Preprimary Education

Divisions in control over education have been a characteristic of education in South Africa since 1910 when the Union of South Africa was established. These divisions have also affected preprimary education. They have, in effect, given each province the freedom to make its own decision regarding the extent to which it supports and finances preprimary education.

The Cape Province, for example, concentrates on preprimary classes attached to the primary schools and to preprimary schools where the salaries of qualified teachers are paid by the education department. The Orange Free State has two categories of preprimary schools: (1) those that are subsidized and (2) those that are unsubsidized, or private. Preprimary schools are supervised by the province. The National Education Department also recognizes two types of schools, subsidized schools and private schools. A supervisory service for preprimary school exists in the National Education Department.

In the Transvaal, nursery schools have been subsidized since 1938, while specific criteria for subsidy have been in place since 1953. Four categories of schools are recognized in the Transvaal:

1. provincial preprimary schools, built and fully maintained by the Education Department;

2. provincially controlled preprimary schools (qualified teachers are employed by the education department);

3. subsidized schools (private, nonprofit, preprimary schools receive a per capita subsidy which has not been adjusted since 1975); and

4. private schools (which are run as a business to provide an income to the owner).

The Transvaal Education Department also provides a supervisory service for preprimary education.

The House of Delegates, which presents the budget for Indian education, makes provision for the financing of preprimary classes at primary schools as well as a number of subsidized preprimary programs. An inspector of preprimary education provides ongoing guidance. Both the subsidized schools and the preprimary supervisory service have existed for some time.

The House of Representatives, which presents the budget for education of colored persons, is currently establishing preprimary, or "bridging," classes and is also subsidizing a number of community schools.

The Department of Education and Training, which is responsible for the education of blacks, funds a number of community preprimary schools. The preprimary inspector provides guidance and encourages local authorities and communities to establish their own programs. Lack of adequate funding is a constant problem, due to the extensive demands of primary and secondary education.

Preschool Care in South Africa

The Department of Health outlines nine types of child care in *The Manual for Places of Care* (1988). Each is described below.

• A *full-day place of care* operates from approximately 7:00 a.m. to 5:00 p.m. In some cases, 24-hour care exists for the children of parents who work night shifts. A full-day place of care may, depending on the registration certificate, receive babies, preschool children, and school children.

• A *half-day place of care* provides child care during the morning or afternoon, and depending on the registration certificate, may receive babies, preschool children, and school children. A half-day is defined as four hours and therefore meals and rest periods are required.

• *Playgroups* operate for 3- and 4-year-olds for periods not exceeding four hours per day. Meals and rest periods are not required. The mothers of children who attend playgroups are usually not wage earners outside the home. The purpose of playgroups is to provide a social experience for the children.

• *Preprimary schools* function during regular school hours for children ages 3 and older. The registration and supervision of a preprimary school are exclusively the responsibility of the various education departments.

• *After-school centers* operate in the afternoon during school terms or quarters for school children. The center may also provide full-day care for school children during school holidays if provided for by the registration certificate.

• *Combination places of care* are also possible. The most common combination is the creche-as-preprimary school, which is subject to double registration. These centers combine an extended-day program for school children with a regular full-day program for children younger than age 3. These creches may also care for school children in the same building in the afternoon and during holidays. Double registration is required. A creche that provides after-school services cares for children of all age groups and requires only one registration.

• *Day-mother care* refers to people caring for a maximum of six preschool children (from birth to age 6) excluding their own children. Day-mothers are not subject to registration or inspection. They are encouraged through notices in the media to register with the Day-Mother Association which was formed in 1989. Local groups are encouraged to affiliate with it. Through the local and national associations, day-mothers are provided with information regarding basic safety measures and responsible "educare" practices.

Day-mothers must obtain a trade license from the local authority. Any day-mother caring for more than the maximum number of children is subject to local municipal health ordinances and inspection by the municipal department of health.

• *Schools for separate communities* are nursery education programs that are ethno-specific. (e.g., Jewish, Greek, German, and Muslim nursery schools). The program in these schools is usually highly structured with emphasis on the acquisition of religious or cultural knowledge and skills. Instruction is generally more formal in nature.

• *Multicultural schools* represent a growing movement within some state preprimary schools, as well as private preschools. A research project in 1989 revealed that a small number of such schools exist in the larger urban centers of Pretoria, Johannesburg, and Cape Town. The most formidable obstacle to these schools is the inability of teachers to communicate with the young black children in their home language.

Teacher Training for Preschool Education

The shortage of trained teachers in preschool education was one of the biggest problems in the early years of early childhood education.

The mothercraft movement was one early and important influence on preprimary teaching training in South Africa. For example, the Lady Buxton Mothercraft Center was established in 1925. The Union Department of Education started courses in mothercraft for girls at industrial schools and domestic schools during the 1930s, but it had difficulty finding suitably qualified teachers for these courses. During 1937, the Witwatersrand technical college started a course to train nursery school teachers and teachers in mothercraft, with the support and permission of the Minister of Education.

In 1945, the Buxton Preschool Training Center in Cape Town was given additional financial support to expand its training facilities. It was eventually renamed the Barkly House Training College for Nursery Education and still functions as a training college. In 1988, it was renamed again and is currently known as the Barkly House College of Education.

A curriculum for the National Certificate for Teachers of Preschool Education was established in 1938 and revised in 1952. In 1945, training colleges for preschool teachers were also classified as institutions for higher education. The University of Pretoria instituted a teacher's diploma in preschool education in 1940 and a degree in preschool education (combined with social work) about ten years later.

During the 1940s, the South African Board of Jewish Education also started training a number of Hebrew preschool teachers. This program, however, was not recognized by the education departments.

Professional Associations and Teacher Training

The NSASA was founded in 1939 (Verster, 1989:282). The original purpose of the association was to support "the interests of the pre-school children of South Africa, irrespective of race, class, politics or creed and excluded for its programme, political party or religious questions of a controversial nature" (Malherbe, 1977:365).

The present association has a membership throughout South Africa and is organized on a regional basis. In 1974, the NSASA changed its name to the South African Association of Early Childhood Education (SAAECE). It is also a member of the world association of early childhood education (OMEP).

The SAAECE has made significant contributions in the field of preschool education. For example, the association has attempted, with considerable success, to increase governmental recognition and financial support of nursery school. It has also been active in setting minimum standards for nursery schools. The association's standards were voluntary and were maintained through inspections for a period of twelve years. The standards became the criteria upon which the provincial education departments based the payment of subsidies (Potgieter, 1962).

Several publications of the NSASA have also served to promote preschool education. For example, the *Nursery School Handbook* (1942) contained specifications regarding the buildings, furniture, and equipment of nursery schools, and several editions of this book have been published.

The Transvaalse Vereniging vir Kleutero-pvoeding (The Transvaal Society for Preprimary Education) (TVKO) was established in 1944. The TVKO, an Afrikaans organization initially limited to the Transvaal province, currently draws members from several South African provinces. It was originally founded by an Afrikaans women's organization (i.e., the Suid-Afrikaanse Vrouefederasie) to provide nursery schools for disadvantaged Afrikaans children.

The TVKO has developed as a professional organization dedicated to maintaining and improving the professional image of the preprimary educator. Although differences between the TVKO and the SAAECE have become minimal over the years, it is generally easier to conduct the affairs of the organization (e.g., meetings, workshops, conferences, and symposia) in only one of the official languages. Both organizations have therefore continued to serve a useful purpose. In all matters of general interest to South Africa, (e.g., standards, teacher training, and financial support), the two organizations have repeatedly cooperated with success.

Day-mother associations, which formed following the formal recognition of the services of day-mothers by the Department of Health also promote professional development. They speak on behalf of members' interests, disseminate pertinent information to members, provide in-service training to members through lectures and seminars, and maintain an informal register of day-mothers whose services are available in a particular area. Local associations have their own standards and methods of inspection for day-mothers. Day-mothers registered with the national Day-Mother Association receive a certificate of registration and are entitled to advertise as a registered day-mother.

Development of Alternative Preschool Programs

The SAAECE, TVKO, and day-mother associations function within the traditional state, community, and school structures. However, preprimary education must be viewed against the rich backdrop of the population of South Africa. South Africa is composed of many different cultural, ethnic, and language groups. The population can also be differentiated economically. South Africa is not only in political transition, but it is also quickly becoming an urban society. Because the marketplace is predominantly Anglo and Western, the process of urbanization includes the adoption of Western cultural values and languages.

In addition, the black, economically disadvantaged population of South Africa is increasing dramatically. This presents a serious problem for the provision of preprimary education. To meet this need, self-help groups, home-based compensatory programs, and other educare programs have been developed in recent years. Some of these community-based organizations have purposely disassociated themselves from the structure of the South African state and church.

Organizations that have disassociated themselves from traditionally accepted norms and practices are described as "alternative." Vergnani, Van den Berg, and Short have listed a number of these organizations (1987:i–ii). Examples include the Grassroots Educare Trust, the Vumani Preschool Project, and the Van Leer Projects.

Current Issues in Preschool Education

The preschool facilities are inadequate to meet the needs of all population groups in South Africa, since South Africa has an exceptionally high birth rate. It is estimated that the population increases by one million per year. State funding and control should be expanded but due to the increasing demand for formal education, this seems unlikely. Privatization of state schools, subsidized educare, and employer-supported programs will be addressed.

According to Reilly and Hofmeyr (1983:105), the artificial division between custodial care and preprimary education creates a situation where it is not unusual for the lower qualified and low-salaried caregivers "to have little real insight into the needs of young children." On the other hand, the more highly qualified preprimary teacher presenting the half-day educational program to the children regards herself as being primarily concerned with the needs of the children and makes "little attempt to meet the needs of the working mothers." This dichotomy also exists within the creche as nursery school. This artificial division is detrimental to the child, the community, and preprimary education. Van den Berg and Vergnani (1987:5) comment as follows on this problem:

> State investment in pre-school provision comes largely via grants-in-aid, paid either by education departments or by welfare departments. Welfare grants are of such nature that they are available for very few children . . . available only for children in crèche-type operations, and do not extend to home-based programmes anyway.

The consequence of this situation, as pointed out by these researchers, is that the money available in the private sector is divided and that services are often duplicated to the detriment of the child. The immediate problem of the lack of funding is the inability to appoint and maintain a well-trained professional staff, which in turn can lead to programs that do not have the best educational standards.

The previous point immediately raises the question of standards. There are two types of standards, those concerning physical amenities and those concerning educational program standards. The former is simultaneously perceived as necessary as well as inhibiting, depending on the viewpoint. The proponents of the "emergency action" see standards as rigid, inhibiting, and especially designed to make the effective use of limited resources almost impossible. The more traditional viewpoint is that the nature of the child, as well as the prevention of malpractice, necessitates certain minimum standards. As far as educational standards are concerned, the absence of a control mechanism outside state schools results in a standard varying from excellent to appalling in terms of the stated educational aims.

Preschool Programs

Among the established, predominantly Westernized white preschools, there is a preference for a program based on the discovery learning model. The role of the teacher is indirect, and great care is taken in the planning of an environment conducive to exploration and discovery. Because of the climate of South Africa, a large portion of the daily program is spent in the playgrounds and outside the classrooms.

White preschool programs range from cogni-tive-developmental programs for 3- to 6-year-olds, to child care programs for children younger than age 3, to home-based, day-mother programs. Control of all of these facilities is shared by health authorities and the provincial education departments. The preprimary facilities within the state structure, therefore, vary according to the specific provincial education department. Although there seems to be a trend toward escalated academic demand in kindergarten and preschool and a downward extension of the primary curriculum, the programs profess to be planned along the lines of the "traditional" informal program. In some educational departments (e.g., the Cape Province Education Department), there are many preprimary groups attached to primary schools. In other departments, (e.g., Transvaal), there are a few state-controlled and state-subsidized schools, but the majority are private.

Private-sector preschools must register with the relevant education department. However, only the few private schools that receive a subsidy are subject to control of curriculum. In nonsubsidized programs, the curriculum usually depends on the specific training of the principal or the philosophy of the owner.

There are also some Montessori schools, as well as schools for specific cultural groups. In these schools, the content of the program is specifically structured to strengthen cultural ties. These schools are open to all children.

In contrast, programs for black, colored, and Asian children are generally of a compensatory nature. The educational system in South Africa often appears bewildering to outsiders. While the state-controlled educational system is conservative, authoritarian, and to a degree rigid, educational enterprises outside the state-controlled structures have almost unlimited freedom. Freedom exists in the appointment of staff, and procurement of funds, as well as in the area of curriculum. Van den Berg and Vergnani (1986:126) distinguish between child- and parent-oriented programs for black, colored, and Asian families.

Parent-oriented programs focus on parenting skills, the provision of physical care, prevention of child abuse, and home-based school readiness skills. The staff are trained paraprofessionals or qualified nurses or social workers.

The programs meet a great need in rural areas where poverty and abject educational neglect are the rule. Although there are farm schools for primary and secondary children, as well as mobile in-service training units of the department of education and training for primary and secondary teachers, no such facilities and services exist for preprimary children. Mothers in this group are usually illiterate and just as much in need of education as their young children.

Child-oriented programs include playgroups and creches. Workers in creches receive regular in-service training through lectures and workshops held by experienced qualified teachers from more affluent schools in white areas. The Grassroots Educational Trust is one of the few organizations that utilizes a recognized program, that of the High/Scope Foundation. Although emphasis is placed on the open-framework approach, there is a strong compensatory element in the areas of basic concepts, life-world extension, and language development.

Primary Schooling

Since 1981, schooling has been compulsory for all pupils from the first day of the school year wherein the pupil reaches age 7. Pupils who reach age 6 on or before June 30 of any year may be admitted to school provided that there is accommodation in that specific school. Younger children are admitted to school only in exceptional circumstances and then only with the permission of the director of education of the appropriate department. Primary education is subdivided into two phases: junior primary (three years: grade 1, grade 2, and standard 1) and senior primary (three years: standards 2, 3, and 4).

The school year extends from January to December, with admission only in January. The school year is divided into four terms, with approximately twelve weeks of vacation interspersed between the terms.

In the junior primary phase, children are taught according to their abilities and to maximize their potential. Although pupils are not tested for school readiness before admission to primary school, the program of the initial primary school education is geared toward school readiness and is applied, toward the end of this phase, in a differen-

tiated way. It attempts to bridge the physical, social, perceptual, and affective developmental handicaps pupils may have and to raise the level of learning readiness so that the child can meet the learning (cognitive) requirements of the school.

The teaching is planned to gradually and systematically change its emphasis from an initial informal teaching method to a more formal teaching approach. The prescribed teaching material is presented in a differentiated manner so that the learning needs of each child are accommodated. Children with serious problems are referred as soon as possible to the Educational Aid Service for further investigation and help.

Educational Aims of Primary Schools

Primary schools attempt to fulfill several educational objectives. They seek to develop in the child feelings of love for cooperation with all those in the school, security and safety in the school, and self-confidence and a positive self-image. They also attempt to develop an awareness in the child of himself or herself as a person among others, of his or her own interests and abilities, and of his or her environment. Primary schools also help the child to develop a time concept, a sex role identity, an appreciation for the beauty and wonder of creation, and deep-seated beliefs of the community, religious beliefs, and esteemed values. Other objectives of primary school include the development in the child of positive and realistic attitudes toward oneself, other persons, the environment, and the school, and with regard to the acceptance of authority.

Finally, primary schools attempt to help children acquire the following:

- psychomotor skills,

- communication skills,

- basic mathematical skills,

- intellectual skills (especially those emphasizing logical and creative thought),

- concept formation and memorization as learning skills,

- social skills, and

- self-discipline.

Primary School Curriculum

The needs, nature, and interests of the child, as well as his or her expectations regarding education, are addressed in the curriculum. Attention is then given to the following broad developmental areas:

• *physical domain:* motor movement and skills, co-ordination, perception, etc;

• *cognitive domain:* reading and writing skills, mathematical concepts, language, concentration, thinking skills, creativity, etc;

• *affective domain:* emotional stability, self-confidence, positive self-image;

• *social domain:* contact with others, socially acceptable behavior, communication skills, etc;

• *moral domain:* responsibility, norms, adherence to rules, and acceptance of discipline; and

• *spiritual domain:* spiritual preparedness, religion, etc.

Teachers are expected to provide each child the opportunity, according to his or her abilities, to develop optimally, and their teaching should make provision for this.

In junior primary classes, the curriculum consists of the compulsory examination subjects: first language, second language, mathematics, and environmental studies, as well as compulsory nonexamination subjects: religious instruction/right living and various expressive subjects.

• *first language:* Mother language (i.e., the home language of the child). About two-thirds of the available teaching time is spent on listening, reading, and speech. The remaining time is spent on written composition, word building, sounds, and poetry (grades 1 and 2), as well as spelling (standard 1).

• *second language:* English or Afrikaans, only listening and speaking (i.e., communication skills). In Standard 1, pupils are exposed to the written language.

• *mathematics:* Approximately 60 percent of the time is spent on oral work. All calculation, notes, and techniques follow concrete experiences.

• *environmental studies:* The content is selected from the life experiences of the child to serve as a basis for such subjects as history, geography, general science, and health education.

• *religious instruction:* Compulsory instruction based on the Bible as the Word of God is provided for Christians and provision is made for Jewish and Indian pupils to be educated in their religions.

• *expressive subjects:* physical education, art education, class music, and handwriting.

The length of the lesson periods depends on such factors as pupil activities and involvement during a lesson, the degree of difficulty of the material, the concentration required, and fatigue of the pupils. The periods are usually reasonably short and variation is essential. Some flexibility occurs regarding the length of a period and the integration of the subject content. Related activities follow closely to the timetable and more emphasis is placed on the whole rather than on specific subject topics.

Remedial Help

No general period exists where all pupils are involved in remedial work. Instead, the class teacher uses the principle of differentiation to help pupils who are experiencing problems, while the rest of the class continues with independent work. Experienced teachers, who have a qualification in remedial education, are available to help with the development of remedial programs for individual pupils.

Pupils who are unable to benefit from the normal classroom remedial help in first language and mathematics are referred to the Education Aid Services who offer programs and support for these children.

Children With Special Needs

Special education in the Republic of South Africa has a relatively short history compared with some Western countries. It was only in 1928 that schools for white handicapped children received state aid and much later (1963 for colored, 1965 for Indians, and 1979 for blacks) that the state assumed responsibility for special education for the other population groups. Formerly, such efforts were initiated and administered by churches and other welfare organizations. Although large-scale expansion and improvement of the provisions for the impaired have taken place since then, a qualitative and quantitative backlog still exists. This is especially true in the field of special education for the black population, largely due to financial, social, cultural, and political reasons.

"Children with special educational needs" is

an overall term that refers to all children who cannot benefit sufficiently from regular education and, therefore, need a modification of, or a supplementation to, regular education in order for them to optimally realize their potential. The term includes children with various forms of disabilities and developmentally impaired children, as well as gifted children. According to the Human Sciences Research Council (HSRC), the latter group cannot be regarded as either disabled or impaired, but nevertheless has special educational needs (1981:31). This chapter, however, does not discuss gifted children.

Disabled children who are categorized as children with special needs are aurally handicapped (i.e., deaf and hard of hearing), visually handicapped (i.e., blind and partially sighted), neurally handicapped (i.e., cerebral palsied and epileptic), physically handicapped or mentally handicapped, have learning disabilities, or exhibit autistic or psychotic conditions.

Children who are developmentally impaired include those who are chronically ill, educationally neglected, environmentally deprived, and emotionally and/or behaviorally disturbed.

Incidence of Disabilities and Impairments

Incidence figures for impaired children in South Africa are not likely to be lower than those of the prosperous developed countries. On the contrary, factors affecting the incidence of impairment in Third World populations may also increase incidence of impairments in South Africa. These factors include the following (HSRC, 1987:55–62):

- poverty, malnutrition, undernourishment;
- untreated childhood diseases (e.g., meningitis and encephalitis);
- untreated or neglected diseases (e.g., leprosy, poliomyelitis, and tuberculosis);
- uncontrolled viral diseases (e.g., German measles (rubella) and smallpox);
- cerebral malaria;
- the use of African medicines (known as "*muti*");
- neglect owing to the views of traditional communities (i.e., certain superstitions—for example, a bias against twins—that can lead to neglect);

- traditional birth customs and ignorance;
- poor hygiene, venereal diseases, parasitic infections; and
- population growth and population mobility.

Education of Children With Special Educational Needs

The education of children with special educational needs rests on the same philosophical principles as those that direct the education of unimpaired children and are referred to in the White Paper on the Provision of Education in South Africa (1983). Among other things, this provides that all children, including the impaired, are entitled to equal educational opportunities and that any form of discrimination based on race, culture, language, creed, sex, impairment, or social status is unacceptable (cf. HSRC, 1987:14).

In addition, the following principles also apply (HSRC, 1981:2, 201; HSRC, 1987:15):

- Children with particular educational needs should, where possible, be kept in the mainstream education while parallel education streams (i.e., special education) should be provided for children with exceptional educational needs.

- Education should be directed at the child in his or her totality and total existence within the context of space (i.e., family, social, and physical) environments and time (i.e., life span, past, present, future).

- The education should respect the individuality of each child and should take place in the least restrictive environment, enabling him or her to lead the most normal life possible.

Identification and Assessment

Identification of children with special educational needs may occur at any point—from conception through the first years of life. During the preschool years, the initial identification of moderate to severe forms of disabilities can be made pre-, peri, or postnatally by physicians, such as obstetricians and pediatricians.

Nurses and social workers also have an increasingly critical role in early identification. Identification is also done at private practices, private clinics, and clinics of city councils.

The coordination between the educational and medical fields is, however, insufficient. At the moment, no national high-risk register exists. The establishment of a coordinating body was, however, proposed by the HSRC (1987:160).

Children who reach school age without having been identified as having special educational needs (especially mildly disabled and developmentally impaired children) may be identified within the school system through the following procedures.

The Class Teacher. Class teachers play a significant role in the identification of children with special needs. To assist teachers of black children with this task, the Pupil Screening Scale was developed at the University of Witwatersrand. For the purpose of identification, a component of orthopedagogics (special education) has been introduced into all basic teacher training programs (Department of Education and Culture, 1989). Some education departments present in-service courses to equip their teachers with the necessary skills for identifying children with special needs.

Class teachers refer children with problems to the educational support services for comprehensive evaluations.

Educational Support Services. School clinics are separate functioning auxiliary service units geographically spread over the country in order to provide the most efficient service. They are responsible for the identification, assessment, provision of assistance, placement, and referral of pupils presenting problems. The staff, consisting of a school psychologist, remedial teacher, social worker, and speech therapist, functions on an interdisciplinary basis.

School Guidance. School guidance (including identification) is provided by specialized staff at the school. At the preprimary level, guidance is managed by traveling school clinic staff when requested to do so. At junior primary level, principals, heads of departments, and class teachers (tutor teachers) provide general guidance. Pupils with more serious problems are referred to the educational support services.

School Medical Services. The school medical service is a special auxiliary service at schools provided in conjunction with the concerned departments. The staff usually consists of a chief medical inspector, assistant medical inspectors, and school nurses. The aim of this service is mainly to identify pupils with physical and sensory defects. At the preschool level, medical services are provided by the local authorities. The aims are mainly prevention and identification of diseases and disabilities in children, as well as the rendering of advice on nutrition, development, and environmental hygiene.

Clinics at Schools for Special Education. Children may be referred to clinics attached to schools for special education for comprehensive assessments.

Educational Provisions

In describing the education of preprimary and primary school children with special educational needs, a distinction must be made between provisions within mainstream education and those outside the mainstream, namely, special education.

Mainstream Education. Children with special educational needs in mainstream education are generally those who are mildly disabled or developmentally impaired. Often they have not been identified before reaching the age for attending preprimary or primary schools. The following placement alternatives are available.

• *The Regular Classroom:* Children receive special aid in the regular classroom by the class teacher, who may be supported by the remedial teacher of staff of the school clinic.

• *Bridging Classes:* Concern about the extent of environmental deprivation and its detrimental effects on the achievements of school readiness has led to the gradual introduction to a period of preprimary basic compensatory education, called the bridging period, at primary schools for black, Indian, and colored children. The bridging period is provided free of charge and stretches over one or two years. At age 5, reached during the first half of the year, the bridging period may be entered voluntarily. At age 6, reached in the first half of the year, entry is compulsory. If the child is ready for school, his or her basic education begins, otherwise he or she enters the bridging program. At age 7, entry into basic education becomes compulsory. The bridging program is highly structured, teacher-directed, and developmental in approach. The primary objectives are the perceptual, cognitive, and language development of the child and the promotion of school readiness.

• *Aid Classes:* Aid classes exist at some primary schools. Children from the junior primary classes (ages 6 to 8) who experience specific learning problems may be referred to these classes for a year or longer. These classes consist of about ten to twelve pupils and teachers require a special training. The aim of these classes is to help the children to overcome their learning difficulties and to return to the regular classes.

• *Educational Support Services.* Children may be referred to the school clinic provided by the educational support services for individual aid.

• *Clinic Schools.* The clinic school is a supplementary service school where education of a more therapeutic nature is provided to emotionally maladjusted and behaviorally deviant pupils. This type of school serves both primary and secondary schools.

• *Hospital Schools.* Education is provided in a large hospital setting for children who have to be hospitalized.

Outside Mainstream Education. Children with severe handicaps are educated in separate schools outside the educational mainstream, called schools for special education. Special education in South Africa is legalized by various education acts and controlled and administrated by various state departments.

In the various acts for the different population groups, special education is, however, defined in a similar fashion, that is, special education is education of a specialized nature outside the normal mainstream. It includes the following:

• the psychological, medical, dental, paramedical, and therapeutical treatment (including the performance of surgical operations);

• the provision of artificial medical aids and apparatus;

• the care in a hospital and school hostel; and

• the provision of transport and physical care (HSRC, 1981:5).

Special education, with everything it includes, is offered free of charge in state-aided schools. The state supplies 95 percent of the costs, including buildings and teachers salaries. The sponsoring bodies are responsible for the remaining 5 percent of the costs.

Among the factors that characterize this form of education are the following:

• Disabled children may be admitted to special schools from age 3.

• Most schools for special education offer hostel facilities, since they may be situated far from the children's homes.

• Children who live close enough are transported to and from their homes by school buses.

• A multiprofessional team, consisting of members who are relevant for the particular disability, is responsible for assessing, programming, and treating the disabled child.

• Parental guidance and counseling facilities are provided.

• Children under age of 3 are treated on an outpatient basis for certain periods.

Although the above is theoretically true of the special education for all population groups, certain problems (e.g., lack of trained staff; insufficient funds; indifference, superstition, and illiteracy of parents; lack of community involvement, and conditions of unrest) lead to inadequate accommodations for impaired black children in terms of both quantity and quality (HSRC, 1987:72–73). (Table 1 shows the distribution of special education schools and classes in South Africa.)

TABLE 1

Distribution of Special Education Schools or Classes

Category	Blacks	Colored	Indians	Whites	Total
Deaf	19	2	3	5	29
Hard of hearing	0	0	0	1	1
Blind	12	1	1	1	15
Partially sighted	0	0	0	1	1
Physically disabled	18	2	0	4	24
Epileptic	0	1	0	3	4
Severe mental handicap	38	10	8	34	90
Autistic	0	1	0	2	3
Cerebral palsied	1	2	1	11	15
(including learning disabled)					
Total	88	19	13	62	182

Note: In addition to the above, industrial and reform schools cater to the education of pupils committed to state care by the Children's Act. These schools do not include young children.

Source: Compiled by authors from the various educational departments.

Curricula for Preprimary and Primary Special Education

Programs for disabled young children are basically the same as those for nondisabled preschoolers. They differ, however, in several aspects. First, the individual needs (strengths and weakness) of each child, as determined by a comprehensive assessment, are taken into account in the planning and presentation of the programs. Second, a supportive and child-directed environment is created by taking into account the child's physical, cognitive, and emotional needs. Acceptance of the child and a sense of security are promoted. The programs are success oriented. Third, the programs are more structured than those in regular preprimary education and are specialized in that they are planned and presented by specially trained personnel. Fourth, provision is made for an interdisciplinary approach to promote the perceptual, motor, language, cognitive, social, and self-care skills of the children. Fifth, the groups are small, with ten to twelve children in a class, and teachers are assisted by full-time class assistants. Finally, more effort is put into parental guidance and involvement than is usually the case with nondisabled preschoolers.

Teacher Training for Special Education

Apart from a compulsory component in special education in all basic teacher training programs, teachers can obtain an additional teacher's diploma for teaching in special schools. Such diplomas are offered by certain universities (e.g., the University of South Africa). The Department of Education and Training offers formal in-service training courses for black teachers to upgrade their qualifications. Most schools also provide informal in-service teacher training.

Training of Preschool Teachers

Teacher training in the early childhood education field occurs on a variety of levels, ranging from formal professional training at the tertiary level to the nonformal paraprofessional levels.

Tertiary-level Training

At this level, formal, professional teacher training occurs at the university or at teacher training colleges. In South Africa, the differences between the two types of institutions lie mainly in the authority invested in the university to confer a degree, while a teacher's training college may confer only a diploma.

Universities. Students who embark on preschool teacher training at South African universities must comply with normal university admission requirements. This entails a matriculation certificate or a certificate of full or conditional exemption from the matriculation examination. In essence, this involves a twelve-year schooling period.

Some universities offer a four-year Bachelor of Preprimary Education or combined Junior and Preprimary Education degree in association with the teacher's training colleges.

The University of South Africa offers a higher education diploma in preprimary education, which can also be attained at the post-graduate level, depending on the prior entrance qualifications of the student. To obtain entrance to this course, the student must hold a recognized teaching diploma that was issued after a four-year teacher training course, or hold a degree that complies with certain educational requirements regarding subjects included in the degree. This is regarded as a one-year higher education diploma. In some instances, however, it extends, because of the method of distance tuition, over a minimum period of two years.

This diploma provides initial preschool training for teachers and involves a ten-week compulsory practice teaching component at a registered preprimary school under the supervision of qualified preschool teachers. The course is unique in that it offers tuition in both English and Afrikaans through the medium of distance education to all population groups and as such is available to students who do not have access to residential universities or teacher's training colleges. Students can thus live anywhere in South Africa or in other countries in Africa or overseas.

The University of South Africa, in conjunction with the Pretoria College of Education, also offers a Bachelor of Primary Education, but this course is restricted to students registered at Pretoria College. This particular course has no preschool component.

Postgraduate Courses. Some universities grant a Bachelor's of Education degree with a preprimary specialization, which is equivalent to an Honors Degree. It is offered at the postgraduate level for candidates who hold an approved preprimary qualification. Some universities offer an Honors Degree in preprimary education. Master's and Doctoral degrees in education are offered at all universities with faculties of education.

Teacher Training Colleges. The training of preschool teachers occurs at various teacher's training colleges in South Africa. Generally, the courses combine both junior and preprimary education, and they extend over a three- or four-year period. On completion of these courses, the student is awarded a diploma in junior and preprimary education. Teaching practice for these courses is spread over the total period, with equal time usually being devoted to both junior and preprimary teaching practice. Normally, a minimum of ten weeks of teaching practice is completed in this period.

There are two exceptions to the rule of combined junior and preprimary teacher training in South Africa, although these might soon change to the combination junior/primary and preprimary courses. Barkly House College of Education in Claremont, Cape Town, as well as the Sallie Davis College of Education in Athlone, near Cape Town, still offer preprimary diplomas that do not include a junior primary component.

Various teacher's training colleges for further training offer upgrading courses for teachers who have the earlier two- and three-year diplomas in education. The College of Education for Further Training in Pretoria offers an upgrading to a fourth-year level, as well as a fifth year level in preprimary education.

Technical Colleges. Technical colleges offer formal, paraprofessional training for child care workers at most large centers in South Africa. They offer a course in child care, which qualifies the student as a teacher-aid. The entrance qualification for this course is standard 7 (or the equivalent of nine years of school). After three years of following this course, the student will attain the equivalent of standard 10, or twelve years of schooling. This course is also offered by means of distance tuition through TECHNISA (the Technical College of South Africa) to students around the country. A small component of practice teaching is also included in this course.

Nonformal Paraprofessional Training

Various institutions offer nonformal paraprofessional training for persons working in the day care field in South Africa. They include those discussed below:

The University of the Witwatersrand. The University of the Witwatersrand offers a course through its Department of External Studies. This course is geared to community workers, although it has a strong preschool, Montessori-based approach. It is not a formal teaching qualification and students receive a certificate of attendance on completion of the course.

Border Early Learning Center. Border Early Learning Center in East London services the border areas Ciskei and Transkei. Three training programs it provides for untrained preschool personnel are (1) the one-year educare teacher course, which holds weekly lectures/workshops for persons employed in the preschool field; (2) the PREST preschool training course, which is a two-week series of lectures, workshops, and observation visits for preschool personnel; and (3) the baby care training course, which is a one-year course for persons caring for children from birth to age 2. Lectures and workshops are presented once a week.

Early Learning Resource Unit (ELRU). The ELRU in Athlone in the Cape offers nonformal training programs designed to meet the needs of persons involved in different areas of early childhood education. ELRU issues its own certificates, which are not recognized by any governmental body but which are accepted by private management bodies. For ELRU, a certificate of competence means that participants completed satisfactorily all practical assignments during the course and that their practical assignments or training competence was evaluated in their work situation.

Parental Support and Educational Programs

Parental support groups and educational programs have been established mainly on private initiative and are maintained by private organizations. Many of the organizations have been established within specific church denominations and obviously aim at promoting specific principles, language, and culture. There are, however, just as many operating interdenominationally that are not bound to the promotion of any specific language or culture.

Many of the parental support groups originated from a very specific need (e.g., parents of autistic, cerebral palsy, deaf, or blind children, parents of twins, or single-parent families).

The overriding aim of these support groups is the protection of the child and the promotion of a healthy family life through parental support and community education programs. These groups fulfill a very definite need in the South African society. Education takes place on an informal basis through lectures, seminars, symposia, and workshops.

References

Department of Education and Culture (1989). *Criteria for the evaluation of South African qualifications for employment in education.*

Department of National Education (1988). *National Education policy: The teaching programmes for pre-tertiary education in South Africa.*

Department of National Health and Population Development. (1988). *His name is today. Report of the committee of inquiry into child mental health care services for children.* Pretoria: Department of National Health and Population Development.

Human Sciences Research Council. (1981). *Investigation into education. Report of the main committee: Provision of education in the RSA.* Pretoria: HSRC.

————. (1987). *Report of the Work Committee: Education for the black disabled.* Pretoria: HSRC.

Idenburg, P.J. (1975). *Theory of educational policy.* Groningen: H.D. Tjeek Willink.

Malherbe, E. (1977). *Education in South Africa.* Cape Town: Juta & Co.

Potgieter, D. (1962). *History of nursery schools for white children in South Africa.* Unpublished M. Ed-thesis. Potchefstroom University for Christian Higher Education.

Reilly, P. & Hofmeyr, E. (1983). *Preprimary Education in South Africa.* Pretoria: Human Sciences Research Council.

Republic of South Africa. (1983). White Paper on the Provision of Education in the Republic of South Africa. Pretoria: Government Printer.

————. (1983). The Child Care Act. Act 74 of 1983. Pretoria: Government Printer.

————. (1988). The National Education Act. Act 70 of 1988. Pretoria: Government Printer.

Schoeman, P. (1979). *Aspects of the Educational Philosophy.* Bloemfontein: Sacum Ltd.

Terblanche, J. (1955). *Kindergarten education in the Cape Province.*

Transvaal Education Department. (1985). *Manual for Preprimary Education.* Pretoria: TED.

Van den Berg, O., & Vergnani, T. (1987). *Door to the future.* Bellville: University of the Western Cape.

Vergnani, T., Van den Berg, O., & Short, A. (1987). Publications (Books) of the original manuscript. Vols. 1 & 2. See para. 7.3.1.

Verster, T. (1989). *A historical pedagogical investigation of infant education.* Pretoria: University of South Africa.

Webber, V.K. (1958). The development of nursery education in South Africa with particular reference to nursery schools 1930–1958. Unpublished B. Ed. thesis. Johannesburg: University of the Witwatersrand.

Zais, R. (1976). *Curriculum: Principles and foundations.* New York: Harper & Row.

PRESCHOOL EDUCATION IN SPAIN: HISTORICAL AND PRESENT PERSPECTIVES

• • • • • • • • • ◆ • • • • • • • •

Antonio Molero Pintado and
Maria del Mar del Pozo Andres
University of Alcalá
Guadalajara, Spain

The history of education in Spain, as in almost all countries, reflects the political and ideological evolution of the society. This chapter focuses primarily on preschool education, and references to primary education are generally related to the first grades of this educational level. Given the centralized character of the Spanish educational system, whose administrative component is the Ministry of Education and Science, this chapter discusses mainly "official instruction," which is the one organized, financed, and inspected by the state through this ministry. Along with this, there is also "private instruction" which, although it has some peculiarities, follows the models offered by the government. Since the constitution of 1978, however, Spain has initiated a decentralizing process, based on a new judicial concept that recognizes the competencies of specific regions to arrange and manage their own affairs.

Preschool and Primary Education in a Historical Context

Although schools and teachers in Spain have a long history, it was during approximately the 18th century that broad educational plans began to be designed as the inevitable fruit of that cultural environment. Nevertheless, it was not until the 19th century that these plans began to materialize in concrete legislative and institutional events. It was then that the public system of education began to emerge with financing and organization by the state, independent of private or religious support.

The basic system was organized around schools called "first letters." In studying this educational form at a concrete level, its contents, methods, and extensions, one studies the history of the state's attention to the problems of primary education as a whole according to the principle that such education should be accessible to and obligatory for all Spaniards. Within this general frame of developing primary education, the birth and early growth of preschool education represent a specific chapter— although intimately tied to the former. This chapter discusses these processes separately, although it is recognized that they converge at various important points.

Given the complexity and scope of this analysis, it is divided into two eras. The first encompasses the entire 19th century and the first third of the 20th century, including the period of the Second

Translated from Spanish by J. Bernhard.

Republic proclaimed in 1931. The second extends from that period to the present time. The most important legislation relating to infancy is also discussed.

Evolution of the Primary Educational System

At the beginning of the 19th century, the first major legislation that formally approaches the topic of education is the Constitution of 1812. Imbued with a liberal spirit, it distinctly addresses the issue of education: "In those towns of the monarchy, schools of first letters will be established in which children will be taught to read, write and count, as well as the catechism of the Catholic religion which will also include a brief exposition of the civic obligations." The constitution also adopts a planning criterion that marks the legislation of this century and a significant part of the present century: "The general plan of education will be uniform throughout the kingdom . . ."

The extremely absolutist tone that the king of this era, Fernando VII, gave to his politics prevented the realization of many of the constitutional plans. The General Plans and Regulations of Schools of First Letters, signed by Calomarde in 1825, was of more practical importance. The Calomarde plan is predominantly administrative and includes throughout its 207 articles important organizational, pedagogic, and professional aspects. Although the plan is rich in suggestions and proposals, many of these were not implemented because of lack of social support.

In the first third of the 20th century, two interesting initiatives, which are based on the ideas of various foreign authors, enriched attempts to structure the Spanish educational system. The first, which arose in 1806, was the Real Instituto Militar Pestalozziano (Royal Pestalozzi Military Institute). Its objective was to disseminate the educational system created by the Swiss pedagogue, Heinrich Pestalozzi. Unfortunately, this experience was short-lived and was terminated in 1808.

The second, undertaken in the following decade, was due to the private initiative of members of the nobility who founded a school at their own expense in order to apply the "Lancaster method." Joseph Lancaster had initiated this method in his native England, and it was particularly useful for schools in which there were numerous children for a single instructor. This method, along with that of Pestalozzi, was one of the most important precedents of the teacher-training institutions which were formalized three decades later. The year 1839 saw the first normal school of teachers begin to function in Spain in a regular and stable manner. Its first director, Pablo Montesino, who will be cited for other reasons, was responsible for developing this interesting project, which still exists.

However, the most important educational reform during the entire 19th century was the well-known Law of Public Instruction, promulgated in 1857 over the signature of the Minister of Development, Claudio Moyano. This law, of bureaucratic and administrative character, united the numerous limited regulations, which until that time had ruled education in Spain. The Moyano law organized the educational system with a centralist tone and tried to integrate all the levels and complementary services. It divided primary education into elementary and superior, the first of these being "obligatory for all Spaniards . . . from the ages of 6 to 9 years." The first elementary education was free for all children attending public schools whose parents could not pay. This state of poverty had to be justified through the certification of the local priest or mayor of the town.

From the time of the publication of the Moyano law until the end of the century, there are no novelties in the area of educational politics. Nevertheless, there was an abundant legislation which partially transformed the life of the schools. Without a doubt, the most innovative impulse beginning in 1876 was due to the ILE (Free Teaching Institution), a liberal, private initiative that involved several men who were neutral in terms of ideology and religion. The pedagogical renovation carried out by these men, headed by Francisco Giner de los Rios, is frequently recognized as the most outstanding educational effort in Spain until 1936, when the institution they founded was forced to disband due to the civil dispute in Spain during that year. Some conservative initiatives, such as that of Father Manjon, who worked toward popular education in Granada, are also worthy of mention.

In any case, during this time, various projects began to emerge that helped to form the public school system and to professionally define the work of the teachers. In 1883, a law established that the female teachers' salary, which up until that point was two-thirds of that of the male teachers, would be equal. In 1900, the Ministry of Public Instruction and Fine Arts was created, and in 1901 the state assumed the cost of paying primary education teachers, freeing the municipalities from this obligation. Perhaps due to these changes, in 1910, a public regulation changed the designation of elementary and superior schools to "national schools of primary education," thereby emphasizing the public nature of these centers. The age at which school was obligatory was fixed between 6 and 12 years, except in the preschools, which were not obligatory, and where children could attend beginning at age 3.

During this time, in the dynamic process of implementing the public school system, there was a constant ideological battle between the governmental parties as well as pressure from religious sectors. This battle continued, and the lack of any short- or long-term agreements hindered the establishment of a stable educational system. Also the economic difficulties of the state, permanently faced with internal or external wars, impeded giving greater attention to education. Well into the 20th century, the percentage of illiterates was substantial and the number of primary schools was insufficient to cover the demographic necessities of the country.

The proclamation of the Second Republic in April 1931, with the subsequent disappearance of the monarchical system, was a turning point in the process of school reform. The new republic included in its program the reform of the schools, and although the task completed was profound, it also opened other areas of conflict, mainly with the Catholic Church. This was the political and social background within which the pedagogical system developed.

Birth and Implementation of Preschool Education

The most remote lineage of preschool education in Spain must be situated at the beginning of the 19th century, but it was not an official initiative but a private one that led to this enterprise, in response to social needs. In fact, as in other European countries (although somewhat later), the interest of many families in taking their small children to specific places to be cared for during the day was evident, at this time in Spain. The preferred places were not schools but modest spaces (e.g., patios), and the person in charge of supervision was a woman popularly referred to as *amiga*, who had no professional qualifications whatsoever. It was therefore solely a service obtained by paying a small fee, without any type of formal instructional planning.

Nevertheless, with the passing of time, these rudimentary preschools became successful with the children, sometimes in the form of songs, memorization of prayers or biblical passages, and even an approximation of what today would be called prereading or prewriting activities. With a usually strict discipline, the *amiga* performed her duties, and without knowing it, was laying the first foundations of an important educational level. The first official and stable preschool opened in Madrid in 1839, thanks to a private philanthropic society as well as to the financial donation of the Spanish diplomat Juan Bautista Virio. In that same year, five schools opened in various neighborhoods in Madrid. Although many people were involved in this effort, the contribution of Pablo Montesino stands out, since he was able to use the experience he obtained during his years in exile in England. He even wrote a famous book entitled *Teachers' Manual for Preschools*, which was almost the only guide for teachers who wanted to dedicate themselves to this level.

Ten years after the opening of the Virio school, there were 95 preschool centers in Spain and some helpful support from the provinces. In 1849, the Virio school was affiliated with the state and was taken as a model school for future teachers who aspired to dedicate themselves to this specialty. During these years, the school was effectively developed by Jose Bonilla Lopez.

In 1853, a regulation was published regarding the provision of preschools. In it, for the first time, academic prerequisites of applicants were specified. These requisites included knowledge of the Christian doctrine, arithmetic, Spanish language, reading, writing, and some notions of geometry and song. The applicants were also required to complete a public practicum with children in front of the selection committee. The Law of Public

Instruction of 1857 (Moyano law) refers specifically to preschools, but not with the desired force, since they were not considered obligatory. Neither is the law stringent regarding the qualifications required for running these schools, which were inferior to those in the 1853 regulation cited above. The expansion process of the preschools was slow, but many provinces already had centers of this type.

The eruption of Froebelian thought in Spanish theory and pedagogical praxis appears around the middle of this century, as evidenced by certain articles about Friedrich Froebel in various magazines. This pedagogical stream was particularly noted in Madrid. In 1876, a chair of Froebelian Pedagogy was created in the Central Teachers Training College. This teaching was conveyed by a well-known professor, Pedro de Alcantara. Some time later and based on practical concerns, a preschool center was founded whose function was to experiment and disseminate Froebelian methodology. A man named Eugenio Bartolome y Mingo directed this center for about 50 years. Further study of the important task carried out by this school is absolutely necessary for a fundamental understanding of preschool education in Spain.

In the year 1882, there were some interesting developments in this area. One of these was a regulation determining that in the future, preschool instruction would be carried out exclusively by women. Another was the organization of a specialized teacher-training course which had the best training carried out until this time. Perhaps due to the first National Pedagogic Congress, in which many of these issues were discussed, there was a generally positive climate for such reforms.

In spite of this goodwill, the preschools did not generally improve throughout these years. Except for the model experiences cited, the preschool system was deficient, often considered without substance and as merely a preparation for the primary level. It remained noncompulsory and free for impoverished students, but the number of these schools and their resources remained scarce. Statistics from 1908 indicate there were 1,024 preschools in Spain, of which 458 were public, 508 private, and 58 subsidized. The rate of growth was slow. Eight years later, in 1916, the public schools numbered 479, an annual increase of 2.6 new

centers. The educational architecture was also badly constructed. There were large halls holding hundreds of children with the classic rows where the sexes were instructed separately, awaiting the teacher's instructions.

In 1922, there is an interesting initiative in the area of education aimed at helping women to fulfill their motherly tasks: the maternal schools. In the Royal Decree, the following objectives are cited: "1. The practical instruction and education of mothers and women in the care and education of children between the ages of 2 and 6, as well as the hygienic and pedagogical concepts related to spiritual life; 2. The care and assistance of children during this age."

The new centers were created as experimental, as a special section of a national school, with one or more teachers. These were open to women who were at least age 12 and had completed the first level of primary instruction. After this time, there were no further initiatives in this respect. Nevertheless, in 1932 a project of law presented to the Parliament established that the national schools will be divided into three groups: maternal schools for 2- to 5-year-olds, preschools for 5- to 8-year-olds, and primary for 8- to 14-year-olds. It is noted that the purpose of the legislation was to generalize maternal education definitively, regularize preschool education, and finally carry out compulsory education until age 14. Unfortunately, the political change of the time impeded the realization of the project.

Social Legislation and Support for Infancy

Given the initial vagueness in the term "social," it is necessary to clarify its content. It refers in this chapter to actions (legislative, institutional, and so on) directed at supporting and protecting infancy, or to the awakening of specific personal or collective values through education. The number of initiatives in this area is significant and heterogeneous. Although the classification of these initiatives is a difficult and subjective task, nevertheless, three large groups can be established to delineate most of the contributions: (1) institutional; (2) educational; and (3) complementary.

Institutional. In addition to the overall obligations of parents or tutors regarding their children's education cited above, there is an interesting piece of legislation regarding the protection of infancy. A law in 1878 established that those who required children younger than age 16 to perform any dangerous activities (e.g., such as those involved in acrobatics, bull fights, and circus performances), would be penalized by incarceration. Another law in 1903, established fines for parents whose children (minors) were found begging, wandering, or spending the night in public places. These diverse regulations were united in a law in 1904, which created a Superior Council of the Protection of Infancy. The council was created within the Governmental Ministry and had a local and provincial projection. The law states its goals as: "Under this law, children under ten years of age are protected in terms of physical and moral health, under the supervision of those in day care, school, shop, or asylum."

In general, all these regulations did not arise from specific educational institutions but rather from other governmental and judicial organs, so that they were broad in scope.

Educational. Spain has a long tradition of public and private establishments dedicated to the protection of underprivileged infants. In the early 19th century, the "schools of rescue" functioned to give the children some time of instruction as well as to initiate them into the trades. Later, these centers were called "hospices," in reality, authentic schools dependent on provincial and local governmental organs. Private initiative though mostly of a religious character, was also present in this task.

An interesting form of school support was the "summer camps" organized in beach or mountain areas, which served to enrich impoverished children's lives during vacation times. These initiatives were begun by the Pedagogical Museum, a center created in 1882, whose aim was the improvement of preschool education. In the same vein, other experiences such as the "open-air schools" must be mentioned. These temporary centers were used between the months of June and October to house pre-tubercular children, who also received pedagogical attention.

With the aim of favoring the precepts regarding compulsory education that were already established, there were various regulations in the early

part of the 20th century aimed at helping the education of the laborers. The dual aim was to facilitate the attendance at school, during part of the working day, of children who were working in a factory as well as to force industries with a certain number of workers to create and found schools for the children of the employees. In spite of the noble social sentiment of these measures, however, they were often ignored so that the state could not fulfill its own obligations.

Complementary. From 1900 on, there was an abundance of "complementary" services created to strengthen the usual tasks of the schools. The first of these initiatives is represented by the creation of the so-called canteens and school wardrobes. The canteens were a service that provided poor children with free breakfast, snack, and lunch. Initially, they were directed toward undernourished children, although in the long run they ended up as one more characteristic of the educational community. Their implementation was slow, and mainly in the large cities with industrial centers; in 1917, there were almost 150 canteens nationwide.

The school wardrobes had a similar social significance: to facilitate clothing for underprivileged children, although the actions of the state were usually limited to encouraging provincial and private initiatives to make donations. The establishment of school wardrobes was scarce due to economic difficulties, but contributed to reinforcing the role of the school as an organism receptive to basic social problems.

The desire of the legislators to instill in children a favorable attitude toward savings, and toward the moderate use of economic goods, led to the foundation in 1880 of the "School Savings Banks." Since this desire was not realized fully, in 1911, the topic resurfaced under different conditions: The "Educational Mutualities" arose and grew rapidly. Although the initial objective was to promote savings in general, it slowly expanded to the creation of other resources, such as libraries. Some schools initiated small-scale agricultural or farming experiences to familiarize children with the productive processes. In 1920, the service was made compulsory, which resulted in the improvement of traditional work methods. Educational programs in defense of nature and specifically the protection of birds and trees also existed.

As early as 1896, an educational regulation was aimed at awakening in children an attitude of social respect toward birds, animals, and plants. It was ordered that on all school doors there be a poster stating: "Children, do not deprive birds of their freedom, do not harm them or destroy their nests. God rewards children who protect birds, and the law prohibits that they be hunted, their nests destroyed, or their young taken away."

In this same sentiment, various initiatives were aimed at avoiding indiscriminate tree cutting in the mountains, the harming of urban gardens, and so on. As of 1915, it was established that a national holiday dedicated to trees would be created in all municipalities and that the children would be the principal collaborators.

The last aspect to be reviewed in this short synthesis refers to legislation regarding child abuse. As early as 1835, a law abolished the physical punishment of children. Another regulation approved in 1838 prohibited any punishment that would destroy a person's honor. In spite of these declarations, there was no explicit prohibition of physical abuse in the schools, but rather, it was considered an exceptional measure that the teacher could administer prudently. In 1918, the boundaries of this prudence were vaguely specified, suggesting such punishments as suspension of recess privileges and after-school detentions. In spite of the vagueness of these suggestions, these educational measures produced better practices for reducing disciplinary conflicts.

Contemporary Initiatives in the Preschool and Primary Environment

During the last half of this century, there have been important events related to the reform of the educational system. Each has its own cultural or political background, and its own ideological or social compromises. Some of these events are now briefly noted.

Between 1936 and 1939 Spain, suffered a civil war which had long-lasting negative consequences. Spain did not directly participate in World War II, but suffered its economic consequences. From this date until 1975, the government was run by General Franco, and the regime was run with a lack of freedom in many aspects of public life. Once the monarchy was reinstated in 1978, a democratic constitution was proclaimed that equates Spanish values of living with those of other countries in its cultural orbit. This is the political scenario in which its recent history has developed. The educational reforms are intimately tied to the events cited.

At the present time, the situation is as follows: In October 1990, the Spanish Parliament approved the LOGSE (Educational Law that governs the non-universitary levels). In this document, the education of infants and for children from birth to six years of age are not compulsory. The basic and compulsory education include ten years, divided in two levels: Primary Education, for children from 6 to 12 years old; and Compulsory Secondary Education, for adolescents from 12 to 16 years old. Two of the most important goals of this law are to fulfill the rules of the democratic Constitution of 1978 in relation to childhood and primary education, and to provide a framework that will equalize the values and objectives of the Spanish schools with those of the European Community educational institutions.

Specific Early Childhood Education Programs

The analysis of a program at any educational level assumes a condensed study of its principal elements. The following three areas must be addressed: organizational aspects, methodological criteria, and curricular plans. The discussion below describes preschool programs in Spain and introduces the historical antecedents necessary for a diachronic and global vision of this issue.

The first preschool centers, founded in Madrid in 1839, were named "rooms of infants," since even the promoters did not believe the term "school" to be an adequate designation for these large rooms in church basements or annexed to factories. Since the children attending these centers were mostly those of working mothers, the preschool centers operated from 7 a.m. to 5 p.m. These new institutions offered mothers a solution to the problem of the care and feeding of their children while they worked in shops and factories.

The official legislation implied that the creation of preschool centers was more an issue of charity and help for the working class than it was educational. In the public regulations published between 1839 and the Moyano law of 1857, these schools are called *"salles d'asile."*

In this context of a charitable and philanthropic approach, the organizational, curricular, and methodological aspects of preschool education were frequently forgotten. In 1853, the Spanish government published a decree regarding preschool education prescribing the space and areas that preschools should have: two rooms for children below age 2, one for cribs and the other for eating and drinking; three rooms for toddlers between ages 2 and 6, one for classroom activities, one for eating, and the third for games and gymnastic activities. Nevertheless, very few preschools adhered to the guidelines.

The introduction of Froebel's ideas around 1850 gave rise to a new understanding of the preschools. The centers of this educational level were no longer perceived as a mere repository for children of working mothers, but there was an awareness of the importance of the preschools as preparatory for primary education and as a means of broadening the instructive aspects. Thus, the legislation up to 1868 refers extensively to organizational and curricular aspects that must be considered in the preschools: age of attendance, available space, teacher-student ratio, instructional content, and schedules.

The largest qualitative step regarding the concept of preschool education was due to the publication of the General Law of Education in 1970. In this document, the specific character of this level is recognized and the fundamental objective is stated: the harmonious development of the child's personality. The emphasis is on the uniqueness of the preschool education centers, for which specific organizational, curricular, and methodological plans are formulated. Within this measure, there is a problem that has not yet been resolved in later reforms: the connection and coordination between this level and the first two grades of the general basic education (called the "initial cycle" as of 1981). The successive pedagogical, curricular, and methodological approaches in publications by the Spanish Ministry of Education and Science in 1971, 1973, 1979, and 1981 have been directed primarily at attaining a continuity in the programs attended by 3- to 6-year-olds.

During the last 20 years, the following types of institutions dedicated to the education of children from birth to age 6 have co-existed in Spain.

• *Infant Centers*. These are mostly private centers for children between 6 weeks to age 6. The emphasis is custodial rather than educational.

• *Maternal Schools*. These are day care centers for 2- and 3-year-olds, operating between 8 a.m. and 6 p.m. These schools are mostly private, although in the last few years the Ministry of Education has created many maternal schools. The focus is more educational than in the infant centers.

• *Infant Kindergartens*. These institutions for 2- and 3-year-olds are generally private and fulfill the same functions as the maternal schools.

• *Centers of Preschool Education*. These institutions are mostly run by the state and serve 4- and 5-year-olds. They tend to be incorporated into primary education, although they are often located in a different building.

Since 1987, the educational administration of Spain has embarked on a large-scale plan of re-form of all levels of instruction as specified in the dissemination of the LOGSE. The plan attaches special importance to preschool centers. The main objective of these centers is to provide children (whether or not their parents work) favorable experiences in their development that do not substitute for those of the family, but rather support and complement them. The qualitative advances in the organization of the centers of education for infants can be specified as follows:

• the establishment of a ratio of one teacher for every eight to ten children from birth to age three, and about twenty-five children for 3- to 6-year-olds;

• distribution of physical space in accordance with the needs of the children (e.g., places for rest, space for free movements, and different activity areas); and

• offering of a variety of educational materials for symbolic activities, the stimulation of affective, cognitive, and social development.

Methodological Criteria

During the first hundred years of existence, preschool centers in Spain were almost exclusively based on the following three methods of instruction.

1. Chronologically, during the entire 19th century, instruction was heavily influenced by the ideas

of English theorists, such as Robert Owen and Samuel Wilderspin. These methods were adapted to the socio-educational reality of Spain.

2.   Toward the end of the 19th century, Froebel's methodology began to be widely accepted, particularly in the central areas of Spain. Nevertheless, these ideas were severely criticized by teachers in Cataluña, particularly the well-known educator Julian Lopez Catalan. The major criticism related to the lack of novelty. It was argued that this method did not improve or contribute anything new to the Montesino system, and was not as well adapted to the preschool centers in Spain. The issue of religion was also problematic. While Montesino advocated Catholic education in the preschool, Froebel was inclined toward internalization of moral values in general. These various positions were debated in the First National Pedagogical Congress in 1882, and it was concluded that the Froebelian method should be accepted in all preschools in Spain.

3.   The method of Maria Montessori began to be practiced in Spain in 1914. The geographical area where the most expansion took place was limited to Cataluña and Valencia, and only a small number of schools were involved. Montessori herself conducted various courses on her method in Madrid and Barcelona between 1916 and 1935 and also supervised the organization of certain schools. In addition, the state administration began to acquire and distribute pedagogical materials to send them to all the preschools in Spain.

Following the civil war of 1936–39, the new ideological foundations of the Spanish government influenced the methodological conceptions of these schools. The Montessori experiences were abandoned, and the focus was on studying specific content areas (e.g., drawing, mathematics, music, language, and initiation into reading and writing).

Around 1970, a reform movement in the preschool educational system began. The General Law of Education had already made specific reference to the methods that should be utilized at this educational level: "They should be predominantly active to accomplish the development of spontaneity, creativity and responsibility." In addition, the Pedagogical Orientations for Preschool Education, published in July 1973, pointed to a new methodological concept that would transform curricular and pedagogical thought regarding the preschools: the concept of globalization. This method aims to get children to learn in successive stages, to resolve problems, and to elaborate on projects that require not only knowledge and experiences, but also attitudes, abilities, or feelings.

In the last 20 years, instruction that can be generalized has been the great methodological challenge assumed by the government in Spain. To support teachers in methodological reform, a wide range of courses, objectives, and suggestions regarding tasks and didactic models have been offered. One specific methodological suggestion involves the practice of activities that correspond to children's interests and that will help them to discover goals that are meaningful to them. Another suggestion is to substitute "projects" or a set of diverse, interrelated activities that have common goals or educational objectives, for the usual homework.

Curricular Foundations

Reviewing the history of the curriculum in a subject area or educational level allows one to evaluate the form in which the ideological viewpoints or sociological conceptions have historically influenced the transformation of educational practices. On the basis of this hypothesis, four types of curricular foundations in the history of preschool education in Spain are noted.

The first involves the model of the first preschools (1839–57), based on charity and assistance to working mothers, which presents a curriculum scarce in instructional content. The curricular foundation is tied to the development of good habits of behavior, the internalization of rules of moral and religious responsibilities. Toward this instructional goal, one sees the beginning of instruction in reading, writing, and arithmetic.

Next, the academic model that characterized the preschools in the second half of the 19th century gave way to a curriculum filled with materials and assignments that were inappropriate for the young age of the children at this educational level. For example, the curricular proposals of 1868 suggested religious and moral songs, Christian doctrine, history of Spain, knowledge of letters, syllables and works, counting and executing the basic mathematical operations, memorization of multiplication tables, and so on. This model was viewed favorably among the parents in the bourgeois and wealthy classes, who were impressed by the quantity and content that 4- to 6-year-olds could learn.

The third involves the dissemination of the new theoretical perspectives, such as those of Froebel, Montessori, and Decroly in the first third of the 20th century, which gave way to a new model of early childhood education that accounted for the child's developmental level and that emphasized clearly defined activities and sensory stimulation. In this way, the curricular design in 1878 combined the classic disciplines with new activities, such as conversations, songs, gymnastic games, gardening, agriculture, and botanic tasks.

Fourth, in the 1940s and 1950s, the academic model reappears with important variations regarding the conceptions of the 19th century: the new psychological currents have been incorporated, but greater importance is given to the integral development of the child, including affective and social aspects. (e.g., outdoor exercises, artistic education, language development, and social and religious education). In the 1960s, the obsession with reading and writing begins to disappear with the recognition that these skills depend on the child's physical and cognitive maturity, and are therefore inappropriate for this level. As a consequence, prereading and prewriting activities were included in the curriculum.

The General Law of Education of 1970 marked a new direction in the curricular design of preschool education. The text of this law indicated the following educational areas to be included within this level: games, language activities, rhythmic expression, observation of nature, logical and premathematical exercises, development of a community awareness, religious principles, and moral attitudes. Nevertheless, in spite of all these models, the principle of globalization, although desired as a guide in preschool education, did not result in any profound transformation of educational content. These continue to be structured in a more or less classical form in the various academic areas.

In LOGSE (1990), the curriculum in childhood education try to develop in children the following abilities:

1. Knowledge of their own bodies;
2. Social relations, by using different ways of expression and communication;
3. Observation and exploration of the family and social environment; and
4. Progressive autonomy in the usual activities.

Plans and Programs in the Training of Early Childhood Educators

Although the intent to regulate teacher training has a long history, the first official center aimed at training teachers began in 1839 with the inauguration of the first Central Normal School of Teachers of the Kingdom, whose model was progressively adopted in many provinces in Spain. With few interruptions, these schools still continue to operate.

In general, the title "teacher" was appropriate throughout the 19th century and part of the 20th century for teaching in both the preschool and primary levels. Nevertheless, there were always attempts to differentiate the two levels by the incorporation of specific knowledge related to the preschool level. As is demonstrated below, it seems that this tendency is most salient in the alternatives that have been proposed in the last half of the 20th century.

In 1931, it was proposed that student teachers in practicum experiences be paid, and that a Bachelor's degree would be required for admission to the normal schools. The specialization in preschool education would take place in the third year and so the title of teacher would enable graduates to teach at both the preschool and primary levels. The Law of Education of 1945, apart from declaring that the teachers in the maternal and preschool levels would be exclusively female, also established a special regulation that created prerequisites for admission into the teacher-training program. These included having worked as a primary teacher for at least one year, and competing in national exams that included written, oral, and practical exercises. The candidates, having already completed a report regarding educational organization, as well as child development courses, were highly accredited.

The law of 1970, which is presently in force, significantly changed the direction of this system of teacher training and access to the field of early childhood education. The normal schools were converted into degree-granting, undergraduate universities. The degree is valid for teaching at both the preschool and primary levels, and the only prerequisite is the competition in the national exams (which is not necessary to teach in private institutions).

In this new system, there are five areas of specialization, of which every center must teach a minimum of three, one of which must be in the preschool area. In spite of the academic freedom, which does not require that all universities in Spain give the identical training program, the degree in preschool education tends to consist of a first year of general education common to all education students, followed by two years of specialization. The curricular units that make up the last two years include the following: theory and history of preschool education, methods in early childhood education, psychology, developmental and educational psychology, the Spanish language, foreign languages, social sciences, mathematics, and the creative arts. This plan tends to be complemented by other optional courses, seminars, and workshops. In addition, the students complete at least four months of practical experiences during their training in selected preschool centers within the geographic area of the university.

Future Preschool and Primary Teachers

The Spanish universities, like the other educational levels, have experienced a period of effervescence in the last few years, motivated by impending reforms in their educational plans. Within this dynamic of change are the centers of teacher training, but the administrative-academic duality is not always resolved satisfactorily: practicing teachers are regulated by a governmental institution but the training of teachers is the responsibility of the university. Although both are units dependent on the Ministry of Education, there is sometimes a lack of harmony in the decision-making process.

In summary, the present situation is as follows: one law reorganizes the educational system, while other regulations revise the university-level training. Fifty-four percent of the curriculum is dictated by these regulations, with the remaining 46 percent autonomously dictated by each university. In addition, the new initiatives provide a wide range of activities for in-service training of practicing teachers. The set of ministerial measures points to a willingness to mobilize institutional and human resources to accomplish the objectives. Teacher training is viewed as a process that continues throughout the teaching career.

References

Alcantara Garcia, P. De: *Manual teórico-práctico de educación de párvulos según el método de los Jardines de la infancia de F. Froëbel.* Madrid, Lib. de Hernando y Cia., 3rd ed.; 1899.

Alcantara Garcia, P. De: *Froëbel y los Jardines de la infancia,* Madrid, Imp. de Anbau y Cía., 1874.

Alvarez de Canovas, J.: *Pedagogía del párvulo (Estudio del niño español).* Madrid, Espasa-Calpe, 2nd ed., 1950.

Alvarez de Canovas, J.: "Las escuelas de párvulos en España." *Bordón,* 17–18 (enero-febrero de 1951); pp. 20–33.

Andres Muñoz, C.: "El dibujo en las escuelas de párvulos." *Bordón,* 11 (marzo de 1950); pp. 9–18.

Becerro de Bengoa, R.: *La enseñanza en el siglo XX,* Madrid, Edmundo Capdeville, 1900.

Blanco Otero, M.: *Guarderías Infantiles y Escuelas maternales,* Madrid, Consejo Superior de Protección de Menores, 1963.

Bosch Marin, J.: *El niño preescolar ante la Ley de Educación,* Madrid, Real Academia de Medicina, 1970.

Cajide Val, J. y Doval Salgado, L.: "La educación preescolar: historia y prospectiva." *Educadores,* 129 (septiembre-octubre de 1984); pp. 511–521.

Cavero Nieto, M.: "En busca de la identidad de la escuela infantil: el curriculum y la programación," *De 0 a 8 años,* 12–13 (junio-julio de 1985); pp. 23–25.

Colmenar Orzaes, C.: "La mujer como educadora de párvulos. La formación de maestras en el método educativo de Froëbel en España," *Revista de Educación,* 290 (septiembre-diciembre de 1989); pp. 135–158.

Cossio, M.B.: *La enseñanza primaria en España,* Madrid. Fortanet, 1897.

Direccio General de Enseñanza Primaria: *La educación preescolar en España,* Madrid, Ministerio de Educación y Ciencia, 1967.

———— "Educación preescolar" (núm. monográfico), *Vida Escolar,* 135–137 (enero-marzo 1972).

———— "El ciclo inicial." Número monográfico, *Bordón,* 237 (marzo-abril de 1981); pp. 121–208.

———— *Enciclopedia de la Educación Preescolar,* Madrid, Diagonal/Santillana, 1986–87, 8 vols.

———— "Escuela Modelo de párvulos," *Anales de la Enseñanza,* 20 (20 de julio de 1879); p. 204–205.

Esteban Mateo, L. y Lazaro Lorente, L.M.: "Infants Schools in Spain (1838–1882): Notes for a research," en VAG, O. (ed.): *Conference papers for the 4th Session of the International Standing Conference for the History of Education*, Vol. 1, Budapest, Eótvós Lorand University, 1982; pp. 78–90.

Fernandez Sanchez, I.: *Programas de pedagogía para oposiciones a escuelas elementales y de párvulos*, Madrid, Imp. de J. Góngora y Alvárez, 1889.

Fernandez Sorio, J.M. y Mayordomo Perez, A.: "Perspectiva histórica de la protección a la infancia," *Historia de la Educación. Revista Interuniversitaria*, 3 (1984); pp. 191–124.

Fernandez Villabrille, F.: *La escuela de párvulos*, Madrid, Est. Tip. de Mellado, 1847.

Ferrant, A.: "El campo Plástico de los párvulos," *Bordón*, 38 (octubre de 1953); pp. 569 y ss.

Galindo Chavanel, M.A.: *Cómo coordinar el nivel Preescolar y el Ciclo Inicial*, Madrid, Escuela Española, 1981.

Garcia del Real, M.: "Nuestras escuelas de párvulos," *Revista de Pedagogia*, 22 (octubre de 1923); pp. 381–389.

Garcia Gabriel, M.R.: *Orentaciones técnias sobre el nuevo nivel preescolar*, Burgos, H. de Santiago Rodríguez, 1970.

Gil de Zarate, A.: *De la instrucción pública en España*, Tomo I, Madrid, Imp. del Colegio de Sordo-Mudos, 1855.

Gil Muñiz, A.: "Montesino a la luz de la moderna pedagogia de los párvulos," *Revista de Pedagogia*, 53 (1927); pp. 203–211.

Gonzalez Sanchez, R.: "Escuelas de párvulos," *El Magisterio Español*, 123 (25 de agosto de 1870).

Groizard y Coronado, C.: *La instrucción pública en España*, Salamanca, Est. Tip. de Ramón Esteban, 1899.

——— "Jardín modelo de niños," *Anales de la Enseñanza*, 13 (10 de mayo de 1879); pp. 120 y ss.

——— "La educación preescolar." Número monográfico, *Revista de Ciencias de la Educación*, 79 (julio–septiembre de 1974); pp. 281–501.

Lopez Catalan, J.: *El froebelianismo puor y neto. Breve historia de dos arrepentidos*, Barcelona, Lib. de Juan y Antonio Bastinos, 1887.

Lopez Catalan, J.: *El arte de educar. Curso completo de pedagogia teórico-práctica aplicada a las escuelas de párvulos*, 4 vols., Barcelona, Imp. de J. Jesús, 1864–67.

Maillo, A.: *Manual de educación de párvulos*, Burgos, H. de Santiago Rodríguez, 2nd ed., 1966.

Martinez Medrano, E.: *La educación preescolar, a examen*, Zaragoza, Instituto de Ciencias de la Educación de la Universidad de Zaragoza, 1982.

Medina de la Fuente, A.: *Educación de párvulos*, Barcelona, Labor, 1962.

Meseguer Gonell, M.: *Estudio crítico sobre la instrucción primaria en España*, Castellón, Imp. Roviro Hnos., 1882.

M.E.C.: *Borrador del anteproyecto de la Ley de Ordenación General del Sistema Educativo* (L.O.G.S.E.), Madrid, Ministerio de Educación y Ciencia, 1990.

M.E.C.: *Educación Infantil*, Madrid, Servicio de Publicaciones del Ministerio de Educación y Ciencia, 1989.

M.E.C.: *Educación Preescolar*, Madrid, Servicio de Publicaciones del Ministerio de Educación y Ciencia, 1972.

M.E.C.: *Educación Primaria*, Madrid, Servicio de Publicaciones del Ministerio de Educación y Ciencia, 1989.

M.E.C.: *Ejemplificaiones del diseño curricular base (Infantil y Primaria)*, 2 vols., Madrid, Servicio de Publicaciones del Ministerio de Educación y Ciencia, 1989.

M.E.C.: *La educación preescolar: teoria y práctica*, Madrid, Servicio de Publicaciones del Ministerio de Educación y Ciencia, 1982.

M.E.C.: *Libro blanco para la reforma del sistema educativo*, Madrid, Servicio de Publicaciones del Ministerio de Educación y Ciencia, 1989.

M.E.C.: *Plan de investigación educativa y de formación del profesorado*, Madrid, Servicio de Publicaciones del Ministerio de Educación y Ciencia, 1989.

M.E.C.: *Programas renovados de Educación Preescolar y Ciclo Inicial*, Madrid, Escuela Española, 1981.

M.E.C.: *Proyecto para la reforma de la enseñanza. Educación infantil, primaria, secundaria y profesional. Propuesta para debate*. Madrid, Servicio de Publicaciones del Ministerio de Educación y Ciencia, 1987.

Montesino, P.: *Manual para los maestros de escuelas de párvulos*. Madrid, Imp. Nacional, 1840.

Navarro Higueras, J.: *La escuela de párvulos. Orientaciones didácticas y temas desarrollados*, Madrid, Escuela Española, 8th ed., 1970.

Pereyra, M.: "Educación, salud y filantropia: el origen de las colonias escolares de vacaciones de España," *Historia de la Educación. Revista Interuniversitaria*, 1 (1982); pp. 145–168.

"Preescolar y Cicio Preparatorio." Número monográfico, *Vida Escolar*, 201 (enero–febrero de 1979); pp. 2–83.

Piquer, I.J.: "Misión y limitaciones de los parvularios de suburbio," *Pro Infancia y Juventud*, 29 (septiembre-octubre de 1953); pp. 158 y ss.

Pozo Pardo, A. y Andres Muñoz, C.: "Educación preescolar." Número monográfico, *Bordón*, 43 (marzo de 1954); pp. 159–242.

Prieto Garcia-Tuñon, A.: "La programación de la actividad escolar en educación preescolar y en el Ciclo Inicial de E.G.B.," *Aula Abierta*, 32 (mayo de 1981); pp. 46–76.

Puig Alvarez, E.: "La música y el canto en la edad preescolar," *Bordón*, 37 (mayo de 1953); pp. 475–486.

Quecedo, D.: *Reflexiones sobre la educación de párvulos y consejos a las maestras y jardineras de infancia*, Burgos, H. de Santiago Rodríguez, 2nd ed., 1971.

Ruiz Berrio, J.: "Les Jardins de l'Enfance (kindergarten) en Spagne avant 1.882), en VAG, O. (ed.): *Conference papers for the 4th Session of the International Standing Conference for the History of Education*, Vol. 2, Budapest, Eótvós Lorand University, 1982; pp. 125–134.

Salvat Espasa, M.: *El kindergarten*, Barcelona, Salvat, 1932.

Sama, J.: *Montesino y sus doctrinas pedagógicas*, Barcelona, Lib. Bastinos, 1888.

Sama, J.: "D. Pablo Montesino. La Instrucción primaria en 1.808 y su desarollo posterior," *Boletin de la Institución Libre de Enseñanza*, 271 (1888); pp. 133–139.

Sanchez Fernandez, P.: "La Educación Preescolar en España en el momento actual," *Vida Escolar*, 220–221 (septiembre-diciembre de 1982); pp. 78–89.

Sanchidrian Blanco, M.C.: "Las escuelas de párvulos de la Fábrico Nacional de Tabacos de Madrid (1841-1859)," *Historia de la Educación. Revista Interuniversitaria*, 2 (1983);

pp. 77–86.

Serrano, L.: *La Pedagogia Montessori. Estudio informativo y critico*, Madrid, Lib. y ed. Hernando, 1915.

Solana, E.: *Maria Montessori. Exposición critica de sus métodos de educación y enseñanza*, Madrid, El Magisterio Español, 3rd ed., 1932.

Sureda, B.: *Pablo Montesino: Liberalismo y educación en España*, Palma de Mallorca, Prensa Universitaria, 1984.

Tiana Ferrer, A.: "Educación obligatoria, asistencia escolar y trabajo infantil en España en el primer tercio del siglo XX," *Historia de la Educación, Revista Interuniversitaria*, 6, (1987); pp. 43–60.

Varios Autores: *El Ciclo Inicial en la Educación Básica*, Madrid, Santillana, 1981.

Varios Autores: *Proyecto 5/B*, 10 vols., Madrid, Narcea, 1980.

Viñao Frago, A.: "Una cuestión actual: sobre el academicismo en la enseñanza preescolar en el siglo XIX," *Historia de la Educación. Revista Interuniversitaria*, 2 (1983); pp. 179–188.

Xandri y Pich, J.: *La pedagogia montessoriana*, Madrid, Yagües, 1936.

EARLY CHILDHOOD EDUCATION IN THE SUDAN

● ● ● ● ● ● ● ● ● ● ● ◆ ● ● ● ● ● ● ● ● ● ●

Gasim Badri
Ahfad University for Women
Omdurman, Sudan

The Sudan is the largest country in Africa with an area of almost one million square miles. This is almost one-quarter the area of Europe or almost one-third the size of the United States. Its population, however, is only about 22 million.

Ethnologically, the Sudan is composed of several groups. The people of the Northern and Central Zones are a mixture of Arabs and Africans. The result of this mixture is that the Northern Sudanese are negroid physically yet Arabic in culture. The Southern Sudan has remained beyond the reach of Arab influence and is composed of different purely African tribes, each with its own language and customs.

This diversified ethnicity, which presently poses problems for the country, will hopefully be a factor contributing to its strength in the future. Moreover, these ethnic differences mean that each group has its own customs and traditions, which are reflected in how each group treats its young children. This alone makes the task of early childhood education important not only for the sake of the individual child, but also as a means for the unification of the Sudan. Although it is beyond the scope of this chapter, to delve into the philosophical-political issues of the role of education in national unity, it

can be said that education in the Sudan faces formidable problems and, yet, offers great hopes for the unity of the country.

History and Development of Modern Education in Sudan

This section familiarizes the reader with the history and development of modern education in the Sudan. It also describes the development of kindergarten education.

Formal schooling in the Sudan has passed through five distinct periods: the early Muslim era, the period of the Turco-Egyptian occupation, the Mahdist national state, the Anglo-Egyptian colonial administration, and the present post-colonial national period.

After the spread of Islam in Northern and Central Sudan in the mid-16th century, education followed the traditional Islamic model, that is, the study of the Quran. The task of education was carried out by the *faki*, in his *khalwa* (school). A unique feature of the *khalwa* is that it has no age limit for the students. The ages of its population range between 7 and the late teens. In some cases, the older students are given some teaching responsibilities, and the brighter ones opened their own *khalwas*. So the *khalwas*, in a way, serve as a teacher's training institute as well.

Because the number of *khalwas* has always been rather small, few children can find places in them. The *faki* is more than a teacher. He has a free hand over his students and can virtually do anything to them. Corporal punishment, for example, was the rule and not the exception in these institutions, and rote learning was the mode of teaching (Badri, 1969).

Under Turco-Egyptian rule (1821–85) the *khalwa* continued to exist as before, but the government soon realized that it needed a different type of educated man. In 1853, the new administration opened the first primary school in Khartoum (Hill, 1959). Provincial schools were slow to follow. It took nearly 15 years to open other schools outside Khartoum (*ibid.*). In these schools the pupils studied the Quran, Arabic, Turkish, and arithmetic (*ibid.*). The number of pupils in the Khartoum school was less than one hundred and all of them were children of government employees (*ibid.*).

Other forms of education in this period were sponsored by Latin Christian missionaries who became active in the Sudan during the second half of the last century. In their endeavor to spread the Christian faith, missionaries opened schools in different parts of the country during the 1870s (*ibid.*). It was in these schools that the genesis of genuine child care started. Music, play, and drawing were introduced into the curriculum of these schools (Tonyolo, 1958).

Irrespective of these innovations in education, whether on the part of the government or that of the Christian missions, the *khalwa* remained the major form of education, and the majority of the Sudanese children who became educated were graduates of the *khalwas* and not the other forms of school.

The third phase in the development of education in the Sudan was the Mahdist period (1885–98). The Mahdiayya was a religious-national revolution that drove the Egyptians headlong from the Sudan. During this period, education once more depended solely on traditional means—the *khalwa* and its *faki*. All other schools withered away in the contemptuous blast of Mahdism. The Mahdist state, however, was unable to maintain itself against

the European imperialism of the late 19th century. At the turn of the century, the Sudan came under Anglo-Egyptian rule or, as it is called, the Condominium Administration.

Under the Condominium (1898–1955), education was again modernized and brought even more into western lines, a feature that characterizes Sudanese education to the present day. The new government from the very beginning felt a need to educate the indigenous population so as to employ Sudanese in the expanding administrative machine.

Sir James Currie, who was appointed Director of Education in 1900, laid down the educational policy of the new regime. He sought to provide vernacular elementary schools to enable the masses "to understand the elements of the system of government," technical schools "to train a small class of competent artisans," and an intermediate school to train elementary schoolmasters and "to provide small administrative classes for entry to the government services" (Holt, 1961: 119–20).

Moreover, work was resumed that had been interrupted during the Mahdiyya. It was in the missionary schools that the first kindergartens were founded. In the first decade of this century, the Catholic mission established schools in Khartoum and Omdurman to which kindergartens were attached. The second attempt in kindergarten education was soon carried out in the Coptic College in Khartoum, a school that mainly served the Egyptian community. In all these schools the local language, Arabic, was the medium of instruction. The English language was introduced in the higher classes.

However, the first kindergarten opened by the Sudanese was not established until 1930. Like the Catholic and Coptic kindergartens, it was also attached to an elementary school.

In spite of the westernization of official education in the Sudan during the Condominium, the *khalwa* remained an important agent of education. According to the statistical reports for 1930, some 11.5 percent of the boys of school age were receiving some kind of education. If the *khalwa* is excluded, the figure becomes a mere 3.5 percent. Even when the Condominium administration came to an end in the mid-1950s, the percentage of boys in elementary schools did not reach 10 percent, and that for girls was much less.

Since independence in 1956, the Sudanese have made enormous strides in education. (See Table 1.) The number of schools for both boys and girls has rapidly multiplied. However, the national government has focused mainly on increasing the number of schools. All the expansion that has taken place and the planning for the future have been geared toward expanding the existing forms of education, that is, the elementary, intermediate, and secondary. There is no provision, as yet, in the plans of the Ministry of Education for opening any preschool institutions.

The present situation of early childhood education in the Sudan, as far as the government is concerned, is not different from that of the Condominium administration. The present government has assumed no responsibility for opening kindergartens or nursery schools under the Ministry of Education. The task of preschool education has been left to the initiative of the people and private organizations.

TABLE 1

Progress of Primary Education, 1956–86

Year	Boys	Girls	Total
1956	79,996	26,581	106,577
1959	200,156	65,306	265,462
1962	262,611	113,571	376,182
1965	274,980	149,697	424,677
1968	388,549	184,074	572,623
1971	630,869	301,058	931,927
1974	851,191	406,148	1,257,339
1977	828,364	504,148	1,332,512
1980	873,054	591,173	1,464,227
1983	943,814	655,367	1,599,181
1986	1,081,295	749,282	1,830,577

Source: Author

Preschool Programs

Today there are four types of early childhood education facilities in the country: (1) privately owned elementary school kindergartens, (2) privately owned kindergartens or nurseries, (3) the department of social welfare kindergartens, and (4) association kindergartens.

The school kindergarten is the oldest of the four. As mentioned earlier, the first was started in the early 1900s by the Catholic mission. These kindergartens, which are attached to missionary primary schools, are very few in number (six or seven). In most cases, only children of the rich can afford them. These kindergartens emphasize discipline and the teaching of reading, writing, and arithmetic. Music and singing are also included in the curriculum. The social atmosphere of such kindergartens, particularly those run by the Catholic mission, is very rigid. The kindergarten is, in effect, a downward extension of grade 1.

The second type of early childhood education center is founded on the individual initiative of certain women. These kindergartens began to appear in large cities. They are of two subtypes. The first, and the majority, operate in private homes or in rented houses. In most cases, there is no space for the children to play in, there are no adequate toilet facilities, and the rooms are not properly ventilated. Moreover, the women in charge of these kindergartens have no professional training. These facilities are more akin to playgroups, child care, or baby-sitting services than to a nursery school or kindergarten. There is no curriculum to be followed and no objectives to be achieved; children are merely safeguarded from harming themselves while playing.

In the second category of institution, which consists of a mere three or four kindergartens in the entire nation, facilities are better and staff is better prepared. The schools are housed in special buildings, some staff have received some training, and they engage the children in a wider range of activities than undirected play.

The third type is the form of kindergarten established by the department of social welfare in the early 1970s in Khartoum. There are 12 such kindergartens. Each is assigned a small corner in a youth center of a family club. All 12 have the same daily timetable, which is drawn up in the headquarters of the department. Some of the staff have received in-service training in the form of a few general lectures on child development. Such training is minimal at best.

The fourth and most recent type is the kindergarten opened by different associations of workers in both the governmental and the private sectors. These kindergartens usually cater to the children of the members of the association. Most are housed in the association's club (a building used in the evening by the members of the association for social purposes). These kindergartens are similar to those of the social welfare kindergartens in that what they offer the children reflects the level of training of the staff working in them.

All four types of early childhood education are found in Khartoum and other big cities. In most of the rural areas, the *khalwa* is still the only means of education while in a few rural places where an elementary school exist, the *khalwa* becomes a sort of a preschool center. Moreover, the number of existing early childhood education centers is still very small. In 1986, for example, there were about 81,237 children in such centers while the population of the elementary school was nearly two million (*Educational Statistics*, 1986–87).

There are signs that both government and the public are giving more attention to preschool education. The Ministry of Education in 1976 appointed a national committee to look into preschool education with the intention of expanding early childhood education. However, most of the recommendations of this committee have not yet been implemented. The situation of preschool education in the Sudan today leaves much to be desired. Although there is increased awareness of the importance of preschool education, very little has been done to reflect this in practice. The Ministry of Education is still not willing to assume the full responsibility for opening kindergartens in its schools, let alone establishing independent kindergartens.

Another problem facing the proper development of kindergartens in the country is the lack of training institutions for kindergarten teachers. Most of the teachers who work in kindergartens, as mentioned earlier, have no professional training. To rectify this, the Ministry of Social Welfare, with the help of UNICEF, opened a center for the training of kindergarten teachers in 1983. The center provides a six-month training course in child development, nutrition, art, music, and the production of teaching materials. The participants in the course are usually drawn from teachers who have spent some years working in kindergartens. From the follow-up of the participants in the

course, it was felt that the duration of the course is rather short. A plan to increase the course to one year is now under consideration.

The other facility that provides training for early childhood education teachers is the Ahfad University for Women. A nongovernmental institution established in 1966, the Ahfad University for Women, offers a bachelor's degree in preschool education. However, many graduates do not opt to work in kindergartens because of low salaries. Recently, some graduates have opened their own kindergartens and some are employed by the associations kindergartens, also recently opened.

Ahfad University for Women also trains women from rural areas. These village women come into Ahfad through the university's Rural Extension program and receive up to six months of training, including knowledge of how to set up a kindergarten in their village.

Primary School Programs

Modern schools were introduced to the Sudan during the Turco-Egyptian period. Primary education today covers the first six years of schooling. Children are admitted when they reach age 7. The curriculum of the primary school emphasizes reading, writing, and arithmetic, and religious knowledge. Science, history, and geography are introduced in the upper classes of the primary school. Learning is very traditional and the teacher, rather than the child, is the center of the classroom. Furthermore, classes are large, with nearly one hundred children in a class in some schools in metropolitan areas.

Even more alarming are the statistics for primary education. Although the National Strategy of General Education, drawn up in 1977, called for achieving universal primary education by 1990, only 55 percent of the school-age children are in schools. There is a wide discrepancy between rural and urban areas and between different regions of the country. While in big cities nearly 90 percent of the children enter primary schools, less than 40 percent find the opportunity in rural areas. In some regions, over 90 percent of children attend grade 1, while in other regions the percentage is a mere 12 percent (*Educational Statistics,* 1986–87). Given the existing political and economic situations of the country, universal primary education seems to be a goal beyond the reach of the Sudan in the near future.

Special Education

Special education in the Sudan is limited. The few institutes there are were established, and are often still operated, by voluntary groups. (See Table 2.) There is one institution for the deaf and hearing impaired, established by the Sudanese Society of the Deaf nearly two decades ago. This institute cares for children from kindergarten age through primary school (ages 5–13). It is now operated by the Ministry of School Welfare, and its teachers are seconded from the Ministry of Education.

A second institute is the Noor Institute for Blind Children. The institute serves as a primary and intermediate school (grades 1–9). Again, although founded by voluntary efforts, it is now administered by the Ministry of Social Welfare and staffed by teachers from the Ministry of Education.

Both institutes follow the same curriculum found in the mainstream schools of the Ministry of Education. Few of the teachers have special training. Another problem is that teachers in those institutes, even those who were specially trained, are subject to transfer to any other school by the Ministry of Education. This arbitrary transfer creates a high turnover of teachers and hence instability in the institutes.

The third institute of special education is found in Atbara, a city about 150 miles north of Khartoum. It is the Broad Horizons Institute for the mentally retarded. It was the first institute for the mentally retarded in the country. Again, voluntary efforts played the leading role in establishing this institute, and only later did the Ministries of Social Welfare and Education help run it by providing the teaching staff.

The fourth institute is the Sakina Institute for the Mentally Retarded and Physically Handicapped. It was established through the voluntary efforts of Dr. Faisal Makki Amien, a gynecologist, in the mid-1980s. This institute, as its name indicates, caters to children with different types of disabilities, and the children in it cover a wide age range (from ages 6 to youth in their teens). The institute has both its

TABLE 2
Number of Children in Special Education Institutes

Number of Institutes	Number of Children		
	Boys	Girls	Total
Institute for the Hearing Impaired	36	51	87
Noor Institute for Blind Children	39	11	50
Broad Horizons Institute	69	53	122
Sakina Institute for the Mentally Retarded and Physically Handicapped	68	39	107

Source: Educational Statistics, 1986–1987.

own staff and teachers from the Ministries of Education and Social Welfare.

The pattern of support of institutes for children needing special education is an increasing shift from support by private, voluntary groups to the Ministries of Social Welfare and Education. While the public support is not great, clearly the central government has accepted some responsibilities for special education. Recently, for example, the Ministry of Education established a directorate of special education in the Ministry.

As has been stated, there is little training for the teachers who work in the institutes. However, there is some in-service training by specialists from Europe and the Americas who were trained in Egypt. Again, Ahfad University for Women took the initiative in providing training in the area of special education. In 1983, a special education curriculum was established in Ahfad. Part of that training includes a 12-week practicum for the students, with each student spending four weeks at three different institutes. A few of the graduates have taken positions in the institutes, thus bringing new trained teachers into the system.

Teacher Training

Teachers in the Sudan are trained in different institutions depending on the level of school they wish to teach. For primary school, teacher training takes place in one of 24 teacher's training institutes for boys and girls (*Educational Statistics*, 1986–87). The students come to the institutes after they finish intermediate school (grade 9) and they are given four years of training. The first three years concentrate on academic subjects, and the final year on educational subjects and teaching methodology. The graduate is expected to teach all subjects in the primary schools.

Due to the rapid expansion in primary education, the supply of trained teachers is lagging behind and, to make up for the shortage, the Ministry of Education has started to employ graduates of secondary schools as teachers. Moreover, the system of in-service training was introduced to help in upgrading the levels of both trained and untrained teachers. There are now 41 such training institutes. Despite all these efforts, however, primary school teachers need to improve in quantity and quality.

Other Resources

Apart from formal schooling, the rearing of children in the Sudan is the sole responsibility of the family. Parents are not provided with any parent educational programs. Even in radio and television programs directed toward family matters, issues related to the education of children are virtually ignored. These programs usually concentrate on health issues. However, there is clear awareness in many parts of the Sudan of the importance of parental involvement in promoting the development of their young children. Plans for new primary kindergartens included parents not only in the program but also in planning the kindergarten. The Ministry of Education brings rural women into training institutes from time to time for training in child development. The Rural Extension program at Ahfad both brings women in

and sends staff out to villages to teach early childhood education and parental involvement.

Ahfad University for Women has taken the leadership in addressing the issue of parental involvement in the development of young children. It does this by incorporating parental involvement concepts in its early childhood education program and by focusing research on the issue. After studying child-rearing practices in the Sudan to determine what parents were doing and what they need to do to enhance the development of their young children (Badri, 1978), Badri and Grotberg conducted an experiment in 1984–85 involving 240 families, with one-half receiving information and demonstrations from Ahfad students on early stimulation activities. After a nine-week intervention, posttests were administered on both experimental and control groups, with significant gains in development made by the children in the experimental group (Grotberg and Badri, 1986).

Future of Early Education in the Sudan

The situation of early childhood education in the Sudan is not as advanced as is desirable, with early childhood education struggling to find a place in the Sudan's educational system. The Ministry of Education, although accepting the ideas of kindergartens since the 1970s, is unwilling to take the steps necessary to open kindergartens in its existing schools. It is simply maintaining its old role as the licensing authority for those who want to open kindergartens. However, the issue of early childhood education is not ignored in the Sudan. Rather it tends to be limited to the private sector as the source for new ideas about early childhood and special education.

References

Badri, B. (1969). *The Memoirs of Babiker Badri*. London: Oxford University Press.

Badri, G. (1978). *Child rearing practices in the Sudan: Implications for parent-education*. Unpublished Ph.D. dissertation, University of California, Santa Barbara.

Beshir, M.O. (1969). *Educational development in the Sudan, 1898–1956*, Oxford: Clarendon Press.

Educational statistics 1986–87. Ministry of Education, Khartoum.

Grotberg, E., & Badri, G. (1986). "The effects of early stimulation by Sudanese Mothers: An Experiment," *The Ahfad Journal*, 3(1), 3–16.

Hill, R. (1959). *Egypt in the Sudan, 1821–1881*, London: Oxford University Press.

Holt, P.M. (1961). *A modern history of the Sudan*, New York: Grove Press.

Tonyolo, E. (1958). *The role of the Catholic missionaries in the geographical and anthropological discoveries in the Sudan 1842–1889.* (Arabic text). Khartoum.

EARLY CHILDHOOD EDUCATION IN SWAZILAND

• • • • • • • • • ◆ • • • • • • • •

Marissa Rollnick
University of Swaziland
Kwaluseni, Swaziland

Early childhood education in Swaziland spans two sectors of the Swaziland educational system: the preschool sector and the earliest segment of the formal system. These are discussed separately in this chapter, since the approach and scope of each differs enormously.

The Kingdom of Swaziland is a small country in the east of Southern Africa, covering an area of 17,364 square kilometers. The country can be comfortably crossed in 12 hours by motor vehicle. Swaziland is a landlocked country, surrounded by South Africa on the north, west, and south, and by Mozambique on the east. Geographically, the country can be divided into four regions: the Highveld, Middleveld, Lowveld, and Lubombo plateau, each of which has its own climatic characteristics.

The country attained independence from Britain in 1968 and is still a member of the Commonwealth. Because of the long period of colonial rule, there has been a large British influence on the country's educational system. Running parallel to this is the fact that Swaziland is a traditional society, ruled by a monarch, and this too has influenced the education in the country.

According to the 1986 population census (Central Statistical Office, 1989), the population of Swaziland was 712,131, of whom 31,072 were living outside Swaziland. Assuming a population growth of 3.4 percent per annum, the resident population (at the end of 1989) was about 746,380. Since the absentee population is predominantly male, the percentage of females in the resident population is 53 percent.

Swaziland's population shows a typical third-world structure, with 47 percent of its population below age of 15. This chapter discusses two groups of children. It deals first with children of preschool age (i.e., children ages approximately 3 to 6.) Projecting the results of the 1986 census, again at 3.4 percent growth per annum, there were about 101,500 children of this age in the country at the end of 1989. The second group of children are those of school age. The population cohort of this group is harder to determine, since the ages at school vary enormously. In fact, it is not uncommon to find teenagers in these grades.

The control of the educational system in Swaziland is vested in the Ministry of Education, which concentrates the vast majority of its resources, in both manpower and expenditure, into the formal sector. Informal education and adult education in the Ministry are the responsibility of one senior inspector, and preschool education is the responsibility of one primary inspector.

The school system in Swaziland is highly competitive. It is freely acknowledged that some schools are better than others and the first big hurdle in the formal educational system is to secure a place at a good school in grade 1. It is not uncommon for schools to interview prospective children for admission to their grade 1 classes. This has consequences for the nature of preschool education in the country. Parents often "shop" around for a preschool that they feel will prepare their children well for school. They also expect the preschool's activities to be directed solely toward preparing children for school.

History of Preschool Education in Swaziland

Preschool education for Swazi children is a relatively recent phenomenon. While expatriate wives have been organizing nursery schools for their children and for those of their friends since the 1940s, the government began to take an interest in preschool education in 1970 when the first preschool program was launched by the then Ministry of Local Administration. The major objectives of this program were to release mothers from child care responsibilities and to facilitate national development and social welfare of the children. Under this program, government funds were used to construct 18 new preschools between 1975 and 1978 (Magagula, 1987).

In 1979, the preschool program was transferred to the Ministry of Education. By this time, there were 64 preschools in the country with an enrollment of 2,867 (Tyobeka, 1986). This represented about 5.7 percent of the age group at that time. Since 1979, the preschool system has continued to grow, both through the involvement of UNICEF (Magagula, 1987) and through extensive private initiatives (Tyobeka, 1986).

Data on primary school enrollments show three distinct periods: a period of slow growth from 1979 to 1983, a period of fast growth from 1983 to 1986, and a leveling-off period from 1986 to 1989. The increase in growth during the second period can be attributed to the active involvement

of UNICEF in the program and the support of the inspectors and teacher leaders from the Ministry of Education. The leveling off in more recent years is due to many schools closing down due to lack of funds, and new ones taking their place.

In 1985, the National Education Review Commission (NERCOM) published a major policy statement on education that identified several serious problems in the preschool system. These included uneven distribution of schools throughout the country, severe financial problems in the schools, lack of trained teachers, overcrowding, and lack of resources (NERCOM, 1985). In view of these problems, the commission recommended, among other things, that preschool education be made free for all children and that preschools be located within two kilometers of the pupil's home. Furthermore, it called for a standardized national curriculum and a program to train preschool teachers.

Establishing free preschools for all children throughout the country appears somewhat unrealistic, since even at the primary school level, the country is unable to provide free schooling. However, progress has been made in training teachers and in the construction of a national curriculum.

Preschool

Preschool Teacher Training

In 1981, UNICEF sent 11 preschool teachers to Israel for training. By 1983, another seven teachers had been trained at the National Baptist Preschool in Swaziland and three at the Montessori Institute in Kenya. It was clear by this time that the rate of teacher training was not keeping pace with the rate of expansion of the preschool system, and several local training options were being considered, including asking Israeli teacher trainers to conduct local courses for large numbers of trainers (Kibria, Mwamwerda, and Otaala, 1984).

Finally, a curriculum for in-service and preservice training of preschool teachers was drawn up by Allen (1985). Subsequently, the Swaziland Bahais initiated a program of preschool teacher training, based in Mbabane, Hlatikulu, and Manzini. The first 70 graduates of the in-service program graduated in December 1988 (Nxumalo, 1988).

Another 22 were undergoing preservice training in Hlatikulu, and 70 began the program in 1989 and graduated in 1991. The training program is based on the new preschool curriculum plan (Allen, Kuhbor, and Nxumalo, 1988).

Preschool Curriculum

The preschool curriculum was published in 1988, after being tested and revised. Most of the information in this section is drawn from this document, though it is not easy to assess how far this written curriculum reflects actual practice in schools.

The document begins by outlining the objectives of the preschool program in Swaziland. These are the following:

1. to promote the healthy physical growth and development of the children;

2. to promote the socialization of children;

3. to promote the mental development of children through appropriate activities;

4. to assist and to provide for children's emotional development and meet their needs for affection;

5. to aid the development of communication skills in children through speech, listening, and other modes of expression;

6. to promote desirable attitudes and values in children and motivate them to learn and enjoy school;

7. to encourage moral and spiritual development (i.e., good character) in children;

8. to promote an understanding and appreciation of Swazi culture; and

9. to attempt to diagnose common disabilities in children and take corrective or referral action.

These aims are comprehensive, taking into account the children's mental, physical, and emotional needs. The content of the curriculum reflects this.

The structure of the program is in line with current thinking about the nature of preschool programs, that is to say, learning should be through play. Children should not be taught to read and write, though many prereading and writing activities are included. Several aspects of the program require such resources as books, toys, and art materials.

Subject areas are divided into language arts, mathematics, and science areas. There is also a section on moral/social education. Health and

physical development are also emphasized in the curriculum. A sample timetable is provided in the curriculum, running from 8:00 a.m. to 12:30 p.m. Time for music, traditional dance, and structured and unstructured play periods is included. The schools tend to provide food between 10:00 a.m. and 11:00 a.m., followed by a rest between 11:00 a.m. and noon. In many cases, the preschool day ends at this time.

Exactly one-half of the preschools in the country receive aid from the World Food Program and this aid is slightly more concentrated in the rural areas.

The curriculum does not state which language should be used in preschools, but phrases such as "awareness of the function of language within his own culture" suggest that the preschools should make no attempt to teach the children to speak English. Nhlengethwa (1990) found, however, that schools were generally trying to promote English. This is thought to be because of the role preschools play in preparing children for formal schooling. Surprisingly, several parents felt that the children's mother tongue was being neglected and advocated more use of it.

Nhlengethwa also found that there was a high degree of pupil participation in the preschool program. Teachers in the formal sector actually complained that pupils who had been to preschool were more difficult to control because they were not as well adapted to the rigidity of formal schooling.

The training of teachers alone is not enough to guarantee effective implementation of the program described above. Tyobeka (1986 and 1989) reports that several schools, even those with trained preschool teachers, attempt to teach the pupils to write and read, thereby anticipating the activities of formal schooling. This is thought to be due to the fact that mothers see preschool mainly as a preparation for school and not necessarily as a means of freeing them from child care. This is particularly illustrated by the fact that most preschools offer only a morning program and mothers frequently entrust the care of other children to other adults at home when child care is required.

However, their determination to see their children receive this education is apparent. Unlike many other development projects, where people tend to rely on the government to do everything, the preschool system has grown with minimal governmental assistance and support.

Current Situation

Before examining specific areas, it is useful to look at the nationwide distribution of preschools and enrollment. There were about 101,500 children of preschool age in Swaziland at the end of 1989, and the total enrollment in preschools was 10,270. This represents 10.1 percent of the age group. Magagula (1986), found an enrollment of 7,855 in 1986. This represented 8.5 percent of the age group at the time. Hence, there was an increase in enrollment over that three-year period. In spite of this, 10.1 percent is low. Nearly 90 percent of the children in Swaziland are not receiving preschool education. This is especially low when compared with the 51 percent of 5- to 7-year-olds in the formal system (Central Statistical Office, 1989 and 1988).

The distribution of the preschools in the country is uneven, favoring the metropolitan areas. The two biggest towns in Swaziland are in the Manzini and Hhohho districts, and these areas are clearly better serviced with preschools. The situation has improved slightly since 1986 (Magagula, 1987). It should also be noted that the growth of schools in the country has not been smooth. Rollnick (1990) found that some 10 to 20 schools had closed down, while more than 50 new schools had opened.

Rollnick (1990) found that most preschools throughout the country are registered with the Ministry of Education. In theory, this should make it easy for the inspectorate to keep a register of schools and to ask for yearly returns, as is the case in the formal school system. However, at present there is only one inspector to look after all the interests of the 256 preschools in the country.

Ownership of preschools is primarily by communities and private individuals or companies. Urban preschools tend to be owned by a private individual and are often operated in private homes, whereas rural preschools are generally community owned. Hence, preschool committees predominate in the rural areas. There are four towns in the country that have been established purely to serve a large industry. In these towns, preschools tend to be owned by companies. Significantly, only one preschool in the whole country claims to be owned by the government. In the absence of governmental input, this represents a major nongovernmental initiative in Swaziland.

Forty-one percent of preschools are less than three years old. The number of schools had only increased by 21 percent since 1989, meaning some schools must have closed down while others have opened. This points to the unstable nature of some of the preschools.

In general, preschool buildings are made of modern materials, although about 12 percent of the schools are made from traditional materials, such as mud and stick. The mud buildings with thatched roofs have an advantage of good insulation, but do not have as long a life span as those made with modern materials.

The buildings in the rural areas tend to be newer than those in the urban areas. This is probably because there are fewer existing permanent buildings in the rural areas and new ones have to be built, increasing the capital cost of establishing preschools. However, in many cases buildings are not built specifically for preschools, and those establishing schools make use of buildings that were previously used (and sometimes still are used) for other purposes.

Since 1986 the percentage of schools of all types using tap water has decreased. Twenty percent of schools have water sources that are more than one kilometer from the school. The fact that the number of urban schools getting water from sources other than taps increased by 130 percent since 1986 probably points to the establishment of preschools in urban informal settlements.

Ninety-six percent of the schools have toilets, but more than one-half of these are pit latrines, which are difficult to keep clean. More than one-half the preschools in the country do not have suitable furniture.

There are substantially more storybooks in the preschools now than there were in 1986. Over half of the schools in the country have adequate numbers of storybooks. Most of the increase has been due to a increase in the number of books in rural areas. There are, however, fewer workbooks than there were three years ago. This could be due to the fact that workbooks cannot be reused and therefore require a recurrent input of money, whereas storybooks can be reused.

Overall, the funding of preschools is extremely precarious. Preschools in Swaziland are funded almost entirely by school fees. More than one-half of the preschools charge less than $5 per month per child. This is the main source of funding for most of the schools. This can be confirmed by the fact that the figures for the total income of the school are consistent with those of the fees charged and the average number of pupils per school.

Conservative estimates put the annual inflation rate in Swaziland since 1986 at about 15 percent. The figures reflected in Rollnick (1990) for school fees and school income are not very different in absolute terms from those of 1986. This means that there has been a decrease of fees and income in real terms.

The situation is far worse in the rural areas, where more than 80 percent of the schools charge less than $5 per month. Even in the urban areas, over 60 percent of the schools charge less than $10 per month. Eighteen percent of schools receive a small contribution from the government toward teachers salaries, but the number of schools receiving this contribution is not growing much every year.

Urban schools tend to have more pupils per school, but in general large preschools are rare. Nationally the average number of pupils per school is 40. The average for urban areas is 47, while that for rural areas is 36.

Nationally there is a pupil-teacher ratio of 26.4:1, which is unacceptably high for the preschool level. The ratio is even higher in the rural areas. The situation improves slightly when teaching assistants are considered. A more realistic representation of the ratio, including both teachers and teaching assistants, is 18.5:1 nationally and varies less between urban and rural areas than the other figures quoted.

The majority of preschool children are between ages 4 and 5. This underlines the extent to which parents see preschool as a preparation for school, rather than as child-minding institutions.

The average number of teachers per school has increased slightly since 1986, but remains small at 1.5. Most schools are staffed by a single teacher. This strengthens the picture of preschools in Swaziland as predominantly small enterprises.

Since 1989, there has been a marked improvement in the teachers' level of education. The percentage of teachers not holding at least a Junior Certificate (grade 10, regarded in the country as the minimum acceptable qualification) decreased from 37 percent in 1986 to 11 percent in 1989. For teaching assistants, this figure dropped from 42 percent in 1986 to 25 percent for 1989. This represents important progress toward staffing the preschools with trained teachers.

The percentage of teachers with more than one year of training increased from 39 percent in 1986 to 44 percent in 1989. However, the percentage of untrained teachers has not changed much since 1986. This is possibly due to the large number of new schools opening. However, a large proportion of teaching assistants remains untrained or undertrained. There is also a tendency for urban teachers to be better trained than their rural counterparts. More than one-half of the teachers have been teaching for more than three years. The turnover rate of teachers over a three-year period is about 27 percent.

Salaries of preschool teachers have increased marginally in absolute terms since 1986, but have not kept pace with inflation. The extremely low salaries are a consequence of the shaky financial standing of most of the schools and account to some extent for the instability in the staff referred to above. In the rural areas about one-quarter of the teaching staff are working for a salary considered below the legal minimum salary in Swaziland. The salaries are so low in some cases that teachers can be considered doing voluntary work.

Although the preschool system is largely privately run, there is a small input from government in the form of an inspector and four teacher leaders. With the help of the Bahais (a religious group), a preschool curriculum and teacher training curriculum have been developed. The objectives of the preschool program have been stated above. Parents, however, have a much narrower view of the program. Only three of the nine stated objectives can be said to directly address the expectations of the parents. Because preschools are privately run, and are in many cases answerable to parents, the teaching in the schools tends to concentrate on the aspects of preschool education that relate directly to preparation for formal schooling. The absence of resources, such as books and toys, tends to make this instruction very teacher centered.

The preschool system in the country is growing quickly, but without substantial financial backing or sufficient central control. Both of these elements will be required in the future for healthy growth of the system. The 1985 NERCOM report called for a strengthening of the preschool inspectorate and the establishment of posts for teachers in the preschools. This now seems extremely unlikely in view of the Fifth National Development Plan (Economic Planning Office, 1990). The section on preschool education states:

> The purpose of the preschool education program is to provide care and supervision for children aged 3–5 years and to prepare them for primary education by providing a stimulating environment in a formal education structure. Over the plan period, the Ministry aims to encourage communities and private organizations to undertake and participate in the preschool programs and to promote parental interest and involvement in their child's education.
>
> Preschools not only prepare children for entry to formal schools, but also serve as health centers where health measures such as vaccinations and medical check ups are provided.

This is a clear indication that very little assistance can be expected from government during the plan period. It is thus necessary for organizations with large financial resources, such as UNICEF and companies, to provide assistance to the preschool system.

A firmer financial base for the preschool system would mean a more stable teaching staff, more resources in the schools, and a higher standard of health and nutrition for the pupils. All this will result in a higher quality of education in the preschools. There also needs to be support for teacher training. Efforts that have been made since 1989 have certainly borne fruit in this regard.

Some progress has been made toward achieving the NERCOM recommendations, but most of them are still to be implemented. Some may be rather ambitious, considering the limited resources of government, but others are realistic objectives and need to be realized. Rollnick (1990) and Magagula (1987) have both called for the implementation of these proposals. Table 1 shows the NERCOM recommendations and the state of their implementation.

It is clear that the cry for more preschool support has not been sufficiently heard. Preschools are largely initiated, organized, and run by women. It is possible that the largely male decision making bodies are not sufficiently aware of the importance of this type of education.

Early Formal Schooling

There has been considerable expansion of the school system in Swaziland since independence. This growth has been accompanied by a consolida-

TABLE 1

Success in Implementing NERCOM Proposals in Preschools

	Recommendation	Implementation
1.	Establish free preschool*	Not implemented
2.	Locate preschool within 2 km of child's home*	Not implemented
3.	Establish directives on operation of schools	Implemented
4.	Strengthen administration	Not implemented
5.	Formulate a national curriculum	Implemented
6.	Institute teacher training	Implemented P/T
7.	Provide governmental assistance	Not implemented
8.	Establish criteria for building schools	Not implemented
9.	Establish teacher posts	Not implemented
10.	Promote community involvement	Implemented
11.	Allow for the government to provide materials	Not implemented

*Thought to be ambitious

TABLE 2

	Average and Expected Age of Pupils, 1988.		
	Primary Education		
Grade	Average Age		Expected Age*
	Male	Female	
1	7.5	7.3	6
2	8.9	8.6	7
3	10.2	9.8	8
4	11.5	10.9	9
5	12.3	12.1	10
6	13.6	12.7	11
7	14.8	14.0	12

Source: Central Statistical Office (1988).

*The expected age is calculated from a pupil who progresses without repetition through the system, starting grade 1 at age 6.

TABLE 3

Retention Rates in the School System, 1988	
Grade	Percentage of Pupils in the System
1	100
2	86.0
3	77.7
4	68.1
5	60.5
6	55.9
7	50.4

Source: Calculated from Central Statistical Office data (1988).

tion of the teaching force, in terms of both numbers and qualifications. Since 1968 there has been a tendency toward larger numbers of pupils per school. The distribution of girls and boys in the schools has undergone a change since 1968, in that the statistics show a move toward an equal distribution of the sexes in the schools.

The overall picture seems to be that despite disadvantages and heavier domestic responsibilities, girls are making good headway in the educational system. School pupils on the average tend to be old for their class, as can be seen from Table 2.

Table 2 shows that pupils in primary school tend to be approximately two years too old for their class. Also, girls tend to be younger than boys. This can be attributed to the fact that boys are kept at home to herd cattle and sent to school at an older age.

The figures in Table 2 do not entirely show what is an enormous age range in each class. For example, the ages of pupils in grade 1 range from under age 6 to age 16 and those in grade 2 from under age 6 to age 18. Although there are relatively few pupils in these classes over age 14, the difficulties for a teacher teaching such an age range are immense.

Dropouts and Wastage

Dropouts in the educational system are a problem. Enrollments are concentrated at the primary level and dropouts occur steadily throughout the system. Particularly large numbers of dropouts are observed at the obvious selection points where public examinations are held. The most disturbing factor is that most dropouts occur in the first three years of education, before the pupils have become literate in their own language. Table 3 confirms this.

The picture has improved greatly since 1985 when a study on school dropouts was carried out by the Ministry of Education (1986). Reporting on this study, Nsibande (1986) found that more than one-half the children had dropped out by grade 4. At the primary level, the reasons for pupils dropping out were found to be more related to parental problems.

Primary Teacher Training

In 1988 there were 4,665 primary teachers in the country. Table 4 shows the composition of this group by qualification and sex.

As is the case in many countries, the majority of primary teachers in Swaziland are women (80 percent). The majority of teachers are holders of the PTC or its equivalent (60 percent), while 38 percent hold the PLC or its equivalent, a qualifica-

TABLE 4

Primary School Teachers by Qualification and Sex

Sex	Graduate	Postmatric + training	Prematric + training		Uncertified	Total
			PTC*	PLC**		
Male	7	47	662	303	2	921
Female	20	90	2,139	1,482	13	3,744
Total	27	137	2,801	1,785	15	4,665

Source: Central Statistical Office (1988).

* PTC includes all holders of Primary Teacher's Certificates and Primary Higher Certificates.

** PLC includes all holders of Primary Lower Certificates and Primary Lower Upgrading Certificates.

tion that is considered outdated. The PTC requires a two-year teacher training after Junior Certificate (Grade 10), while the PLC requires two-year post-grade 8 training. This means that at present only 3.5 percent of primary teachers in the country have a post "O" level (grade 12) qualification. This picture should change quite radically from 1989 onwards since the entry qualification and primary teacher's course has been changed at the country's teacher training colleges. Primary teacher training leads now to a three-year post "O" level (grade 12) Primary Teacher's Diploma. This will make a considerable difference to the quality of teaching in the primary system.

The primary school teaching force in Swaziland is relatively stable, with a fair number of experienced teachers; 44 percent have more than ten years of teaching experience (Central Statistical Office, 1988).

Teacher Pupil Ratios and Facilities

The average number of pupils per teaching room in primary school is 40 nationally, and the average number of pupils per qualified teacher is 32. These numbers appear to be favorable, but they hide a great unevenness in the system where generally classes are much bigger, particularly in the lower classes. It is not uncommon to find lower primary classes of 60 pupils and more.

Primary schools in the country are very short of facilities. Of the 477 schools existing in 1987,

there were only four wood workshops, one metal workshop, 94 home economics rooms, 42 agriculture rooms, and 223 head teachers' offices. A shortfall of 2,334 teachers' houses was also reported (Ministry of Education, 1989).

Primary School Curriculum

Pupils in the lower grades in Swaziland study a wide range of subjects. The Ministry of Education prescribes syllabi for SiSwati, English, mathematics, science, agriculture, social studies, religious knowledge (Christian in orientation), home economics, music, and physical education. At this level, the medium of instruction is expected to be SiSwati with a gradual transition to English. Governmental policy states that after grade 4, the medium of instruction should be English.

There are locally developed materials for the primary schools from the National Curriculum Center and these are widely used throughout the country. Infusion workshops are held to introduce the teachers to these new materials. Research (e.g., Luhlanga, 1990) indicates that the teaching is very teacher centered. This is attributed to large classes, lack of materials, and inadequate teacher training.

Problems in Early Education

The 1985 recommendations of the NERCOM highlight some of the problems of the primary educational system. In the long term, the commission recommended that an eight-year primary course be introduced, with the first four years being tuition free. Despite intentions in this direction after independence (Magagula and Putsoa, 1986), parents still pay fees for schooling. Sentongo (1987) estimated that parents of pupils were paying 25 percent of the cost of primary education. Fees vary widely from school to school and contribution to building funds means that parents are paying for capital costs as well as recurrent ones. The fees are not correlated in any way with the quality of the school. Some better endowed schools charge less than poorly equipped schools. Apart from "voluntary" levies, which vary from E150 to E500, Sentongo estimates that primary school fees average about E150 per year at the lower primary level (E3=$1.00). This represents a sizable proportion of most rural parents' income. A second problem is class size and classroom space, which has been discussed above.

Another severe problem is that many rural children have to walk long distances to school, frequently setting out at sunrise with very little food in their stomachs. Many schools operate feeding schemes to alleviate this situation.

Future of Early Education

Many basic problems at this level of education need to be addressed. One of the most pressing problems is access to schooling. Grades 1 to 3 in the formal system should serve children ages 6 to 8. Projections from the 1986 census (Central Statistical Office, 1989) indicate that there were 69,227 children of this age group in 1988. Of these, 50,905, or 73 percent, were in the formal system. This means that over one-quarter of the children in the country are not benefitting from education at this stage.

Successive development plans have seen the concept of universal free primary education becoming gradually diluted, first by dropping the "free" from universal free primary education, making it universal primary education. This has not been achieved, largely due to financial constraints. The Fourth National Development Plan period calls for universal primary education to be implemented and for a ten-year basic education.

Since the publication of the NERCOM report, few of its recommendations have been implemented. (See Table 5.) The few recommendations that have been implemented were implemented by institutions or individuals rather than the government. Many of these, such as four years of free primary education, are highly desirable and feasible.

TABLE 5

Success in Implementing NERCOM Proposals at Primary Level

Area	Recommendation	Implementation
Primary School	8-year primary system	Not implemented
	First four years free	Not implemented
	Smaller class sizes	Not implemented
	English medium after grade 3	Not implemented
	Emphasis on practical arts	Not implemented
	Continuous assessment	Not implemented
Teacher Training	Screening of applicants to teacher training	Implemented
	3-year teacher training	Implemented
(Primary)	Enforce probationary period	Not implemented

Source: NERCOM, 1986 (inquiries by author).

References

Allen, I., Kuhbor, M., & Nxumalo, B. (1988). *A national preschool curriculum plan.* Mbabane: UNICEF/Ministry of Education.

Allen, I. (1985). *The development of a national core curriculum for preschool staff development in Swaziland.* Ministry of Education/UNICEF.

Central Statistical Office. (1988). *Education statistics, 1988.* Mbabane: Government of Swaziland.

———. (1989). *Highlights of the 1986 population census.* Mbabane: Swaziland Government.

Economic Planning Office. (1990). *Development plan, 1990/91–1992/93.* Mbabane: Government of Swaziland.

Kibria, G., Mwamwenda, T., & Otaala, B. (1983). *Report of the regional preschool teacher trainers intensive workshop.* Held at the University of Botswana, Gaborone, Botswana, December 5–16.

Luhlanga, H. (1990). *An investigation into the problems encountered by primary school teachers in teaching science in Swaziland.* Unpublished B.Ed. Dissertation, Kwaluseni: University of Swaziland.

Magagula, C., & Putsoa, B. (1986). *Educational policies in Swaziland: An historical account and critical appraisal.* Unpublished paper, SIER 89/002, Kwaluseni.

Magagula, C. (1987). *An inventory of preschools in Swaziland.* Mbabane: UNICEF.

Ministry of Education. (1986). *Wastage in the educational system.* Mbabane: Education Research and Planning Department.

———. (1985). *Reform through dialogue: Report of the National Education Review Commission.* Mbabane: Government of Swaziland.

Nhlengethwa, T. (1990). *Evaluation of a national core curriculum for preschool staff development.* Unpublished report, Swaziland Institute for Educational Research. Kwaluseni: University of Swaziland.

Nsibande, D. (1986). *Failure at school: statistical dimensions of repetition and dropout in primary and secondary education in Swaziland.* Paper presented at a seminar on social dimensions of child guidance, Mbabane, September 8–12.

Nxumalo, B. (1988). *Swaziland early childhood development project: Preschools 1988 report.* Ministry of Education.

Rollnick, M. (1990). *An updated inventory of preschools in Swaziland.* Mbabane: UNICEF.

Sentongo, C. (1987). *Private costs of education.* Mbabane: Ministry of Education.

Tyobeka J. (1986). *Community preschool education in Swaziland.* Paris: UNESCO.

———. (1989). *Rural development in the Southern lowveld: An appraisal of the Elulakeni Rural Development Program.* Kwaluseni: Social Science Research Unit at the University of Swaziland.

EARLY CHILDHOOD EDUCATION IN TAIWAN

• • • • • • • • • ◆ • • • • • • • •

Hui-Ling Wendy Pan
National Taiwan Normal University
Taipei, Taiwan, Republic of China

Early childhood education is experiencing tremendous growth in Taiwan, principally as a result of the increasing numbers of women joining the labor force and the interest of parents in the correct rearing of young children. In 1950, there were only 28 kindergartens, by 1988, there were 2,548. The result has been the creation of an early education system that includes relevant legislation, curricula, teaching methods, equipment, and teacher's training programs.

This chapter provides a general overview of early childhood education in Taiwan. After the historical development is introduced, the types of institutions, their administrative control and financing, curriculum, instruction, and teacher training are discussed. Finally, the unique features of Taiwan's early childhood education system are highlighted and future directions are articulated.

Two types of institutions for preprimary children exist in Taiwan. Nursery schools (day care centers) serve children ages one month to age 6. Children under age 2 are cared for in the infant section, while children ages 2 to 6 attend the children's section. In contrast, kindergartens admit only children from ages 4 to 6. The following describes the evolution of these two separate systems.

Evolution of the Kindergarten

The preschool in the Chinese educational system assumed its present shape only recently. In the late Ching Dynasty (the last dynasty in China, 1644–1912), preschool became part of the school system. Prior to this most young children were cared for at home. The family rather than the school was responsible for educating and rearing young children. Although more that 80 years have passed since the first preschools were established, they remain a neglected aspect of the educational system. In this context, the Preschool Education Act of 1981 may be viewed as a milestone.

There are five identifiable stages in the development of the kindergartens (Lu, 1987).

The Initial Stage

In 1902, the earliest known preschool, called *meng yang yuan*, was founded. Children ages 3 to 7 attended for four hours daily, participating in play, songs, conversation, and the making of handicrafts (Chang, 1988). The curriculum of *meng yang yuan* was borrowed from Japanese preschools of the period. Some Christian kindergartens also existed, which used essentially Western materials and curricula.

471

The Transitional Stage

When the Republic of China was founded in 1912, educational reforms ensured equal opportunity to schooling for girls and boys. The number of preschools increased following the Educational Law of 1912 and the Primary School Law of 1916. The Primary School Law particularly had an impact on preschools in the areas of curriculum and administration, and standards for teachers, class size, and equipment.

Also during this period, John Dewey and Bertrand Russell visited China. The impact was profound and preschool education in this period was characterized by a desire to imitate that of Western countries.

Stage of Construction

With the introduction of the "New School System" in 1922, *meng yang yuan* was renamed "kindergarten." Its status in the school system has assumed a downward spiral since that time. In 1939, the Temporary Curriculum Standard for Kindergartens was issued. After two years of experimentation, the permanent curriculum was established (1942). The curriculum has undergone several revisions in the last half century.

Stage of Development

Following 1949, the Chinese government moved to Taiwan. Subsequently, a number of government and private initiatives resulted in a rapid growth in the preschool movement. However, the Taiwan system has been dominated by foreign influences, ideas, and philosophies. From the beginning, when the first kindergarten borrowed a Japanese curriculum, to the present, when Western visions of preschool education are prevalent, Taiwan kindergartens have been influenced by foreign educational ideas. Although some educators have attempted to integrate Chinese and Western practices to create the ideal program for modern Chinese children, the attempts have not been successful.

Evolution of Nursery School

In contrast with the educational role of the kindergartens, which is administered by the Ministry of Education, nursery schools in Taiwan serve a child care function. As in many countries, they have their origins in orphan asylums. The first formal nursery school was established in 1931 in Shanghai as an experimental institute for the children of laborers (Ding, 1974). The first public nursery school was established in 1942 in the Chiang-Si province. Following these pioneering efforts, nursery schools were set up nationwide.

After the Chinese government moved to Taiwan, nursery schools, as child welfare programs, were administered by the Ministry of Interior. Important legislative initiatives over the years regarding the programs were the Regulations for the Establishment of Nursery Schools (1955, revised in 1981) and Equipment Criteria for Nursery Schools (1973, revised in 1981).

Because different ministries are responsible for the two types of preschools in Taiwan, there are two sets of standards and regulations governing them. They have separate aims, standards for teacher training, criteria for class size, and curricula.

Modern Kindergarten and Nursery School

The most rapid growth in the number of kindergartens in Taiwan has occurred during the past 40 years. In 1988, 248,498 children were enrolled in 2,548 kindergartens (Educational Statistics, 1989). After 1960, the enrollment in the private sector kindergartens surpassed that of the public sector (see Table 1). In fact, the number of public kindergartens actually declined in the early 1960s. While in 1960 there were 358 public kindergartens, the figure decreased to 201 in 1965. The number increased slightly to 404 in 1980. However, by 1985 the number was one-half that of 1960. By the late 1980s, the public system had again recovered.

Private kindergartens, on the other hand, have continued to increase in number over the years and as a result, the private sector has dominated early education in Taiwan. The government's reluctance to fully develop a public system of preschools, in spite of the demand caused by an increasing need for child care, is partly responsible for the strong private sector. As a result there are ten times more children enrolled in private kindergartens than in public kindergartens.

TABLE 1
Number of Kindergartens, Enrollment, and Classes

Year	Kindergartens			Enrollment			Classes		
	Total	Public	Private	Total	Public	Private	Total	Public	Private
1950	28	—	—	17,111	—	—	397	—	—
1951	203	177	26	21,531	7,735	3,796	510	410	100
1955	413	297	116	46,390	28,503	17,887	1,039	607	432
1960	675	358	322	79,702	35,863	43,839	1,883	766	1,117
1965	555	201	354	78,878	24,143	54,735	1,833	534	1,299
1970	570	218	352	91,984	25,560	66,424	2,075	567	1,508
1975	762	273	489	117,990	29,342	88,648	2,796	651	2,145
1980	1,186	404	782	178,216	44,934	133,282	4,592	1,065	3,527
1985	2,210	158	2,052	234,674	17,895	216,815	7,668	553	7,115
1988	2,548	678	1,870	248,498	47,765	200,733	8,366	1,615	6,751

Source: Ministry of Education, Educational Statistics of the Republic of China (Taipei, 1989).

The teacher-pupil ratio, as a measure of preschool quality, has also been subject to changes over the past 40 years (see Table 2). Although significant improvements have been made in this regard, the average number of teachers in each class still does not meet the standards of the Preschool Act. Table 3 presents the data concerning the quantity development of nursery schools.

There are three kinds of nursery schools in Taiwan: the general, rural, and harvest. The harvest nursery, established to provide care for the children of farmers, had a significant role prior to 1970 (see Table 3). However, its current status is precarious, having served only 150 children in 1988. The general and rural nurseries have shown a reverse trend, increasing rapidly over the past 20 years.

TABLE 2
Children, Teachers Per Class, and Pupil-Teacher Ratio

Year	Children Per Class			Teachers Per Class			Pupil-Teacher Ratio		
	Total	Public	Private	Total	Public	Private	Total	Public	Private
1951	42.22	43.26	37.96	.37	.34	.51	113.32	127.59	74.43
1955	44.65	46.96	41.41	.94	.75	1.22	47.34	63.06	33.88
1960	42.33	46.82	39.25	1.07	.93	1.17	39.46	50.30	33.54
1965	43.03	45.21	42.14	1.10	1.04	1.13	38.99	43.66	37.23
1970	44.33	45.08	44.05	1.11	1.04	1.13	40.12	43.54	38.94
1975	42.20	45.07	41.33	1.27	1.06	1.33	33.25	42.65	30.98
1980	38.81	42.19	37.79	1.46	1.17	1.54	26.64	36.03	24.49
1985	30.60	32.29	30.47	1.63	1.39	1.65	18.82	23.31	18.52
1988	29.70	29.58	29.73	1.61	1.49	1.64	18.48	19.84	18.18

Source: Calculated from Table 1.

TABLE 3

Number of Nurseries and Children Enrolled

			General Nurseries		Rural Nurseries		Classses	
Year	Total Number	Public	Private	Number of Children	Number of Nurseries	Number of Children	Class	Number of Children
1965	171	4	167	17,632	154	17,020	2,339	107,173
1970	213	5	208	22,748	738	38,217	750	33,394
1975	480	7	473	44,668	1,251	61,703	10	300
1980	742	12	730	76,488	2,186	108,921	10	300
1985	1,207	15	1,192	97,646	2,834	132,873	5	292
1988	1,423	18	1,405	120,702	2,824	127,242	5	150

Source: Statistics Abstract of Interior of the Republic of China (1989).

TABLE 4

Kindergarten Teachers by Year

		Teachers	
Year	Total	Public	Private
1950	144	—	—
1951	190	51	139
1955	980	452	528
1960	2,020	713	1,307
1965	2,023	533	1,470
1970	2,293	587	1,706
1975	3,549	688	2,861
1980	6,690	1,247	5,443
1985	12,471	766	11,705
1988	13,446	2,047	11,039

Increasing percentage from 1950 to 1988 is 9237.5 percent.

Source: Ministry of Education, Educational Statistics of the Republic of China (Taipei, 1988).

TABLE 5

Children Enrolled in Different Types of Institutions

Year	Kindergarten		General and Rural Nurseries		Total
1977	135,232	49.7%	136,862	50.3%	272,094
1980	178,216	49.0%	185,409	51.3%	363,625
1985	234,674	50.4%	230,519	49.6%	465,193
1988	284,498	50.1%	247,944	49.9%	532,442

Source: Statistics Abstract of Interior of the Republic of China (1989), Ministry of Education, Educational Statistics of the ROC (Taipei, 1989).

TABLE 6

Populations of 3- to 5-Year-Olds

Year	Age 3	Age 4	Age 5	Total
1977	359,457	360,043	372,093	1,091,593
1980	420,754	366,436	359,297	1,146,487
1985	409,048	405,115	415,328	1,229,491
1988	365,061	377,468	396,841	1,139,370

Source: Ministry of Interior, (1982); 1987 Taiwan-Fukien Demographic Fact Book, the Republic of China.

TABLE 7

Enrollment Rates for Preschool Children

Year	Kindergarten	General and Rural Nurseries	Total
1977	12.39	12.54	24.93
1980	15.54	16.17	31.71
1985	19.09	18.75	37.84
1988	21.81	21.76	43.57

Source: Calculated from Tables 5 and 6.

Administrative Control and Financing

All education in Taiwan is centralized. According to the Chinese Constitution, each level of government—municipal, provincial, and central—must contribute to a certain percentage of the budget for education, science, and culture. The majority of the central government's contribution is directed to higher education, while the other levels of government provide the remaining components of the school system.

Public preschools, however, receive only a small fraction of the overall education expenditures. In 1987–88, 99.7 percent of money spent on preschool was from the private sector (Ministry of Education, 1989). It is evident from this lack of financial support that the preschool is neglected in the public education system.

Curriculum And Instruction

According to the Preschool Education Act, the objectives of kindergarten education are to promote children's physical and mental health; to foster good habits, morals, and values; to enrich their lives; and to foster cooperation. The curriculum is divided into five areas: health, play, music, work, language, and common sense (i.e., nature, social, and mathematics concepts).

While nursery schools were established to provide child care, the function has shifted to include education. The objectives for nursery care, found in the *Manual of Education and Care in the Nursery School* (1979), are the same as those for kindergarten outlined above.

Although play should be viewed as a method and not a subject, traditional ideas of teaching mean that teachers instruct children in the knowledge that they think is important. An illustration of this phenomenon is revealed in a survey of preschool education (Sinyee Foundation, 1987) in which it was found that 75 percent of the 337 schools visited included writing in the curriculum.

Four major teaching methods, described below, are used in Taiwan kindergartens (Lin, 1987; Lu, 1988):

• *Traditional Teaching*. This method is teacher-centered; with children being passive learners. It is the major method used by today's preschool teachers.

• *Group Teaching.* This method was derived from the discovery teaching method, which was so constrained by the limited space that sufficient learning areas were impossible to arrange, so the group teaching method was used.

• *Center-Based Learning.* A center-based program is organized around a number of curriculum centers (science, language, dramatic arts, and so on) that exist independently in the classroom. Center-based classrooms are founded on the notion that children learn through discovery; that is, children will explore the various centers, make cognitive connections, etc., largely without teacher intervention.

• *Area Learning and Unit Activity Combined.* A number of preschools attempted to teach specific curriculum units within a center based program. However, they were largely unsuccessful because of the inability of many teachers to integrate the various learning units in a way meaningful to the children.

Experimental Programs

Subsequent to the Chinese Central Government's move to Taiwan, there have been five kinds of experimental programs that have dominated early childhood at different periods. Each is discussed below.

Five-Finger Activity Teaching

Five-finger activity teaching was initiated by Ho-Chin Cheng in 1940. The Ministry of Education tested the curriculum in the kindergarten attached to the Taiwan Provincial Girl's Junior Normal College. The "five-fingers" refer to health, the social world, science, the arts, and language. The spirit of the method is to integrate the five activities as a single learning unit. Experimentation continued from 1953 to 1959. The impact of the five-fingers method has been profound. The method is still in use in some kindergartens (Lu, 1988).

Behavioral Curriculum

Shen-Men Chang developed the behavioral curriculum in 1938. It was to become the dominant method during the years 1960 to 1967. Shen-Men Chang devoted himself to integrating Chinese culture and modern science with early childhood education. His influence has been so great that a popular saying proclaims that "before Shen-Men Chang, there was no early childhood education in China." He advocated what was essentially a child-centered approach, developing children both physically and mentally in order to foster their ability to absorb experience and thereby adapt to the environment. For Shen-Men Chang, living is education and the practice of living in the kindergarten is expressed by the behavioral curriculum. The curriculum originates in the daily experience of life as lived. Such experiences as sweeping, cleaning, raising chickens, or planting corn or flowers provide the activities through which children develop true knowledge.

Integrated-Unit Program

This program, initiated in 1965 and terminated in 1970, was influenced by the trend in both primary and secondary education in Taiwan to break down the artificial borders between individual subjects and promote learning through the design of integrated units.

Discovery Teaching

In 1970, H. Borke, the wife of a visiting U.S. scholar, introduced the concept of discovery learning. The method was subsequently adopted by three kindergartens in Taipei starting in 1971. However, constrained by high teacher-child ratios, limited resources, and traditional ideas of teaching, the discovery method had a limited life span.

Science Education Experiment

In 1980, the Ministry of Education launched a science education policy, which included the kindergarten as the first level. The Science Education Center of the National Taiwan Normal University therefore was assigned the task of developing an experimental program of kindergarten science education in 1981. A total of 21 kindergartens were involved in the project.

Teacher Training in Taiwan

Different training programs exist for teachers in kindergartens and nursery schools. Kindergarten teachers must be graduates of a department of preschool teacher training in a normal junior college, a related department for preschool teacher training in a college or university, or a senior secondary school having earned more than 20 credits in preschool education at a designated school (Ministry of Education, 1988).

Nursery teachers may have a kindergarten or primary school certificate, or specialized nursery school training in a department of child welfare at a college or a university, preschool teacher training, or related department at a normal or vocational school; or secondary school training with a concentration in preschool education (Ministry of Interior, 1981). It is also possible to qualify as a nursery teacher by completing a six-month training program combined with two years of experience in a nursery school. The various training institutions are described in more detail below.

Normal Schools. Following Taiwan's independence from Japanese colonization, preschool educational programs were established in three normal schools. However, they were discontinued when the programs were upgraded to five-year junior normal colleges in 1960. Although the colleges offered a preschool program, enrollment was low. The reason for the minimal interest on the part of students was the low prestige of kindergarten teaching and the focus of colleges on the primary level. The result was a shortage of teachers for kindergartens. In response, the Ministry of Education established an in-service training program in three colleges to raise the professional standards of existing kindergarten teachers.

While in-service training relieved the immediate problem of a teacher shortage, the overall quality of teachers did not improve. The program was subsequently discontinued and replaced by a two-year, part-time program for graduates of the initial training. The revised program became responsible for over one-third of kindergarten teachers in Taiwan (Ministry of Education, 1984). In 1987, all nine normal colleges in Taiwan were upgraded to teacher colleges. Two-year, full-time preschool programs, recruiting graduates from secondary schools, were established to train kindergarten teachers. These programs may become the most significant source of kindergarten teachers in the future.

In addition to training kindergarten teachers, junior normal colleges offered in-service programs for nursery teachers from 1978 to 1985. Most nursery school teachers currently working in Taiwan are graduates of this program.

A few related departments in colleges and universities, (e.g., home economics, and child and youth welfare), train preschool teachers. Combined, the programs train only a small number of preschool teachers (Ministry of Education, 1984).

Senior Secondary Education Programs. There are 35 high schools and vocational schools, that have nursery teacher training programs. This is currently the largest source of new nursery teachers.

Current Status of Early Childhood Education in Taiwan

There are some features of early childhood education in Taiwan that are unique. Although the kindergarten and nursery schools were initiated with different aims, their roles have now merged. Both emphasize the education of young children. In addition, the two types of programs serve almost the same number of Taiwanese children and the same age group. Although nursery schools are available for children from one month of age, most children under age 3 are cared for in the home or by babysitters. While children should be between ages 4 and 6 to attend kindergartens, the rule is often violated in practice, resulting in many programs recruiting 3-year-olds. In addition, although two ministries are involved in administering preschool programs, their goals and objectives for early education are similar.

Another unique aspect of early education in Taiwan has been the uneven development of the public and private systems. The government delayed a planned policy despite the increasing need brought on by women working outside the home. Today, state expenditures on preschool education account for only .3 percent of the total.

The number of children enrolled in all preschool programs is lower than that for Western countries. However, the number may be deceiving because only certified programs are included in the enrollment statistics.

The curriculum in most preschools is oriented toward the teaching of subjects. In theory, kindergarten and nursery schools should emphasize a more broad education as articulated in legislation. However, traditional educational ideologies prevent many teachers from adopting a more integrated method.

For many years, Chinese educators have attempted to construct a preschool model suitable for Chinese children. Since the founding of the Republic, progressive educational ideas have exerted an influence on the theory and practice of Chinese education. Friedrich Froebel, Maria Montessori, and Jean Piaget remain the three most influential figures in the field of early childhood education. However, although Froebelian and Montessori materials may be found in some kindergartens, and Piaget's ideas are espoused, the understanding of their philosophies tends to be confused and superficial. Consequently, some educators desire the creation of a more responsible, uniquely Chinese preschool model that nevertheless draws on the best of Western educational thought.

Future Directions

The two types of preschools—kindergartens and nursery schools—were originally established for different reasons and to serve different clients. However, in modern Taiwan their roles have overlapped. The preschool system therefore needs to be restructured so that children under age 3 attend nursery schools and children ages three to six attend kindergarten. Innovations may be near in that the Ministry of Education launched a ten-year developmental plan that will include the 5- to 6-years olds in the primary level, compulsory education system.

Four-year programs for preschool teacher training in teacher's colleges should be created. In addition, departments of early childhood education should be set up in other colleges and universities.

Because the field of early childhood education in Taiwan is in the development stage, a research center is necessary for the planning of a system, legislation, teaching methods, and curriculum. The creation of a model of preschool education that will serve the needs of Chinese children warrants the attention of educators in Taiwan.

References

Chang, S. (1988). The development of nursery school in our country in the past forty years. In *Bulletin of the National Institute of Education Materials*, Vol. 13. Taipei: National Institute of Educational Materials.

Chen, H. (1988). The developmental direction of early childhood education in our country. In *Bulletin of the National Institute of Educational Materials*, Vol. 13. Taipei: National Institute of Educational Materials.

Ding, B. (1974). *Child welfare*. Taipei: Singshau.

Hwang, Y. (1986). From the international trend of development to project our country's innovation in education. In Chinese Educational Association (Ed.), *The trend and prospect of educational innovation*. Taipei: Taiwan Bookstore.

Hsieh, U. (1987). Investigation of the trends of early childhood education of Taiwan. In Fong-Tai Foundation (Ed.). *Early Childhood Education in the Changing Society*.

Jeng, M. (1987). *The comparative study of preschool systems*. Kaoshuiang: Fuwen.

Ju, J. (1986). *Preschool education*. Taipei: Wunang.

Lai, C. (1984). The survey study of kindergarten affiliated to kindergarten. In *Bulletin of the Provincial Taichung Teacher College, 14*, 1–24. Taipei: Provincial Taichung Teacher College.

Lai, Y. (1978). The survey study of preschool education in eastern area in Taiwan. In *Bulletin of the Provincial Taidong Teacher College, 14*, 1–24. Taipei: Provincial Taidong Teacher College.

Lin, H. (1984). Review of development of early childhood education in Taiwan, the Republic of China—From viewpoint of equality of educational opportunities. *Bulletin of National Taiwan Normal University, 29*, 175–205.

Lin, Y. (1987). The developmental directions of early childhood education in our country. In *Bulletin of the Provincial Taipei Teacher College, 14*, 1–24. Taipei: Provincial Taipei Teacher College.

Lo, S. (1988). The aims and functions of early childhood education in six countries: the comparison of the Republic of China, America, England, France, and West Germany. In *Bulletin of the National Institute of Educational Material*, Vol. 13. Taipei: National Institute of Educational Material.

Lu, S. (1987). Preschool in Republic of China. In the Chinese Comparative Education Society (Ed.), *The comparative study of early childhood education*. Taipei: Taiwan Bookstore.

———. (1988). The teaching materials and methods of early childhood education in our country in the past forty years. In *Bulletin of the National Institute of Education Materials*, Vol. 13. Taipei: National Institute of Educational Materials.

Ministry of Education. (1984). *Survey study of kindergarten education in the Republic of China*. Taipei: Ministry of Education

———. (1987). *Curriculum standard for kindergarten*. Taipei: Ministry of Education.

———. (1989). *Educational statistics of the Republic of China*. Taipei: Ministry of Education.

———. (1989). *Education in the Republic of China*. Taipei: Ministry of Education.

Ministry of Interior. (1981). *Establishment regulations for nursery school*. Taipei: Ministry of Interior.

———. (1989). *Statistics Abstract of Interior of the Republic of China*. Taipei: Ministry of Interior.

Sinyee Foundation. (1987). *Interview survey report of kindergarten and nursery school*. Taipei: Sinyee Foundation.

Tsai, S. (1988). The teacher's training of early childhood education in our country in the past forty years. In *Bulletin of the National Institute of Education Materials*, Vol. 13. Taipei: National Institute of Education Materials.

Wang, J. (1987). The curriculum of early childhood education in our country in the past forty years. In *Bulletin of the National Institute of Education Materials*, Vol. 13. Taipei: National Institute of Education Materials.

———. (1987). The current status and prospect of early childhood education in our country. *Guidance of Primary Education*, 27, (1), 45–77.

EARLY CHILDHOOD EDUCATION AND CARE IN TURKEY

• • • • • • • • • ◆ • • • • • • • •

Tanju Gürkan
University of Ankara
Ankara, Turkey

The Turkish educational system is based on the principles of fulfillment of the needs of the individual and society, the right to education, equality of opportunity, continuity, a devotion to Atatürk's revolution and principles, nationality in the Atatürk's sense, democratic education, secularity, scientific research, planning, co-education of girls and boys, and the collaboration of school and family. The current centralized system is the product of a long history.

Formal education in the Turkish educational system consists of preschool, primary school, secondary school, and higher instruction.

Early childhood education encompasses the period from birth to compulsory school age, which is age 5. Primary education takes place from ages 6 to 14. The first five years of this period is referred to as primary school and the last three years as secondary. A further distinction takes place within primary school. The first three years of the five years is the first term of primary school and the last two years is the second term. A primary school diploma is awarded to those who complete the first five years of the primary education, that is, the first stage. At age 5, children have the option of attending an infant class within the primary schools. This popular service is not compulsory.

State Policies Related to Children

Social policies related to children historically have been influenced both by Islam and by principles of social justice. For example, it is a tradition in Turkish history for the state to care for orphans.

Since 1923, the year of the founding of the Turkish Republic, policies relating to children have always been in harmony with that of the state. In 1949, a law was passed regarding the protection of children in need. It was revised in 1957. In the planned development periods, beginning in 1960s, the health, education, care, and protection of the child from birth have been regarded as the most valuable investments for the future of the country.

The first five-year plan (1963–67) stressed the training of professionals. The improvement of mother-child nursing homes, an equal distribution of these institutions, population planning, child care, and nourishment were the subjects of importance. In addition, the care and education of children in need of protective services, delinquent children, and the education of maladjusted and mentally retarded children were considered in this plan.

The second five-year plan (1968–72) stressed

481

family planning and providing adequate food and nourishment. In this plan, basic education was considered to include preschool and primary school education. Preschool education was aimed at children between ages 3 and 6. In the informal education programs, priority was given to "woman's education." The need for parental education was critical. At this time, various other public relief organizations were formed.

The third five-year plan (1973–77) emphasized the need to raise the quality of education at all levels to reflect modern developments and standards. Because of limited financial resources, the Ministry of Education, and other relevant institutions, developed a model for preschool education, with the expectation that the private sector would work within this framework.

The fourth five-year plan (1978–83) aimed at expanding health services to the entire population and providing mother and child care and planning within health services. Pilot preschools were started in depressed urban areas with the children of laborers.

In addition, an attempt was made to improve conditions in some of the most crowded primary schools. It was not uncommon to have two or three shifts of students each day, and more than 60 students in a classroom. In all levels, there was an attempt to change education from memorization to a focus on the development of personality.

The fifth five-year plan (1985–89) focused on the learning of useful knowledge and skills at all levels, and there was a goal of increasing attendance of 5- and 6-year-olds in schools to 10 percent. Although noncompulsory infant classes were attached to schools in this plan, state and private sector enterprises were encouraged to establish kindergartens and nurseries. In addition, provisions were made for handicapped children between ages 4 and 6 to attend preschool programs. It had been anticipated that in 1988–89, vaccination would be available in all health institutions for children starting from birth.

Importance has been given to Turkish educational programs for the 788,000 "guest workers'" children between birth and age 19 in order to protect their national identity and to aid their development. These are children of Turkish parents who have sought work in neighboring countries, the largest group being 544,000 living in West Germany.

Another aim has been to use attractive and quality texts and materials in the primary school, and to improve the quality and quantity of public and children's libraries. For the 3- to 7-year age group, a series of films is to be prepared and updated every six months.

Finally, a policy group was established in 1989 under the name "Family, Woman, and Child" to provide leadership in the field and to develop family policy.

Evolution of Early Childhood Education

During the Ottoman Empire, minorities and foreigners established kindergartens for their children. The first attempt at formal early education could be the infant schools established during the reign of Sultan Mehmet the Conqueror. In these schools, children between ages 6 and 12 were educated together. The purpose was to provide religious instruction in the Koran.

In addition to the infant schools, there were *darül-hüffaz*, another form of primary education. The aim was to take advantage of young children's ability to memorize and to train them to recite the text of the Koran by heart, called *hafiz*.

A radical attempt to establish schools coordinated with state interests was attempted during the Ottoman Empire. Dated 1869, the Regulation of General Education viewed primary education as consisting of two stages, each lasting three years. The *mekteb-i iptidaiyye* (primary school) was compulsory for both boys and girls. In these tuition-free schools, reading and writing, arithmetic, religion, history, geography, handicrafts, and other basics were taught. The second stage, the *mekteb-i rüsdiyye* (grammar school, or upper primary school) offered instruction in reciting the Koran, religion, Turkish, Arabic, arithmetic, geography, Turkish and Islamic history, calligraphy, and agriculture. Persian, drawing, geometry, and health care were also taught.

In the 20th century, a section of the Temporary Primary Education Code, introduced in 1913, ordered the establishment of kindergartens throughout the country as the first stage of primary schools. The age of children to be admitted to the kindergarten, methods to be applied, materials, and basic principles were outlined. Following the setting of regulations for kindergartens in 1915, an increase in the number of kindergartens and infant classes was recorded.

The educational system of the Turkish Republic assumed its present shape with a series of reforms dating to 1924. In that year, the Education Unity Code provided the foundation of the secular and democratic school. The system adopted the 5+3+3 model as its basic structure (refers to the division of schooling by level).

Within the modern system, primary education was viewed as being of utmost importance. An indication of this commitment is the popular use of the system. In 1987–88, 96 percent of the population of Turkey had attended primary schools.

In the Primary Education Code of 1961 it was outlined that preschool education was considered noncompulsory and that providing preschool education could be organized by municipalities, private administration, and the state. In 1962, the Regulation of Kindergartens and Infant Classes was issued, delineating the aim of these schools and classes, standards, administration, and the conditions of acceptance.

The Basic National Education Code of 1973 was the first code to consider all levels of education from primary education to the university as an integrated whole. In it, preschool education was again defined as the noncompulsory education of children not at the age of primary education. The aim and duties of preschool education, in conformity with the general goals and principles of national education, are as follows:

• to provide for children's physical, mental, and emotional development, and to ensure correct habit formation;

• to prepare children for primary education;

• to establish a social setting for children from disadvantaged families; and

• to ensure that children speak Turkish in a correct and pleasant manner.

At the Tenth National Education Board, which met in 1981, a further step was taken to integrate the school system while maintaining the internal structure and content of the program. It was at this time that an 8+3 model was introduced.

At the Eleventh National Education Board meeting in 1982, it was decided:

• to raise preschool attendance to 10 percent;

• to develop the physical and social setting standards necessary for the preschool education studies;

• to provide a sufficient number of personnel to execute guidance and inspection duties in the preschool institutions; and

• to bring the educational instruments and materials related to preschool education to a sufficient level to meet the demand.

Training of Preschool Teachers

There were several developments in preschool teacher training in the pre-Republic years. The 1896 Regulation of General Education established a teacher training system named "A Guide for the Kindergarten Teachers." In 1915, the first school for kindergarten teachers, The Nursery Teacher School, was established in Istanbul and offered a one-year program, but it closed in 1919. The school reopened, offering a two-year training program, during the Republican era in the 1927–28 school year. It closed again in 1933. The Girls Technical Higher Teacher School, established in Ankara in 1935, became one of the main preschool teacher training institutions.

In the 1961 Primary Education and Teaching Code it was stated that graduates from teachers' schools, graduates from special departments to be opened solely for this purpose, or those who attended equivalent schools abroad can be appointed as preschool teachers. This code recommended training of kindergarten teachers in special education.

The 1973 National Education Basic Code stated that teachers must be university graduates regardless of their level of schooling. Appointing graduates from the Child Development and Education departments of vocational high schools as kindergarten teachers, a practice dating from 1961, stopped in 1973.

With the 1982 Higher Education Code, all teacher training institutes, including those for preschool education, were brought into the administration of universities. A two-year, pre-license program was instituted for preschool teachers (in 1989–90, this became a four-year program).

Training of Primary School Teachers

The Temporary Primary Education code issued in 1926 proclaimed that in each province a primary education teacher training school was to be opened. But in the year the Republic was founded, there were only 20 such schools. These training schools did not even meet the urban demand for teachers. In time, implementations were made to train village teachers. The most important of these was the establishing of secondary schools for village teachers (köy enstit üleri) in 1939. The aim was to train village children to be teachers. The policy of two systems of teacher training, the village and the city, continued until 1953. After this date, all institutions training teachers were combined under the name "primary education teacher school."

Other attempts to meet the demand for primary teachers were the use of "reserve officer teachers," and "temporary teachers," as well as the practice of hiring high school and commerce school graduates.

Present State of Early Childhood Education

Preschool Education

Preschool education refers to the period prior to compulsory schooling. In general, institutions serving children from birth to age 3 are called creches (which can extend to age 6), those for 3- to 6-year-olds are called kindergartens, and those that exist within the primary school for 5- and 6-year-olds are called infant classes.

Preschool education services are administered by the Ministries of Education (kindergartens, infant classes, and experimental kindergartens), Labor and Social Security (creches and day care centers in work places), Social Services, and the Society for the Protection of Children (other creches and day care centers). By law, workplaces that employ more than 300 workers must provide a creche or a day care service for the children of workers.

Private kindergartens, day care centers, and creches can also be found in the major urban centers. These are established by the permission of either the Ministries of Education, or Social Services or the Society for the Protection of Children, and also inspected by them. Other preschool institutions may be established in factories and work places as a social service. These are not subject to external control. In some universities, there are experimental preschools or creches for the employees.

Most children, however, are not cared for by an institution but are instead looked after by their mother, or an aunt or grandmother if their mother works. Some working mothers leave their children with a maid within or outside the home.

In total, only 1.4 percent of preschool age children are in any type of program. The goal is to increase this to 10 percent. Within the administration of the Ministry of Education there are 23 kindergartens (enrollment of 2,406), 2,715 infant classes (enrollment of 85,855), and 314 experimental kindergartens (enrollment of 8,969); 5,741 children are enrolled in the 161 private kindergartens established with the permission of the Ministry.

An additional 6,880 children are cared for in creches and day care centers under official supervision (there are 460 officially recognized private creches). Thirty-three creches and day care centers are in hospitals and 15 kindergartens are in the universities. The number of institutions established according to the 1973 Breast Feeding Rooms and Creches Regulation (making work places creches mandatory in companies of a certain size) is 67. In state enterprises, factories, and work places, 262 day care centers care for an additional 17,321 children.

Preschool Curriculum and Programs

The preschool education program was prepared by a group of teachers from the Ministry of Education General Directorate of Primary Schooling, and the Girls Technical Schooling General Directorate, members of the Gazi University Faculty of Child Development and House Economy

Department, and kindergarten and infant class teachers. The program was introduced on a trial basis in the 1989–90 school year. Intended to be flexible in its application, the program focuses on the development of the whole child. See Tables 1 to 4 for samples of kindergarten activities.

Preschool Teachers and Other Personnel

Personnel employed in preschool education institutions are to include a director, assistant director, department chief, teacher, psychologist or social services expert, clerk, health personnel, cook, and others. In practice, however, not all schools have a full complement of personnel as listed.

Related Establishments and Publications

The oldest association founded in Turkey in the field of preschool education is the Association for the Development of Preschool Education in Turkey. Founded in 1967, the association has been a part of Preschool Education World Organization (OMEP) since 1971. The purpose of the association is to stimulate public interest in the importance and necessity of preschool education. Since 1968, the association has been publishing a magazine called *Preschool Education*.

The Children Houses Foundation, established in the 1980s, has its headquarters in Antalya. The foundation establishes preschool institutions in various establishments and after operating them for some time, transfers them to the original owners. The organization also sponsors conferences, seminars, and parental education programs.

A publication and marketing company called YA-PA has been organizing a preschool education seminar in various counties since 1984. Presentations at each of these seminars, which have brought together professionals from throughout Turkey, have been published in book form. YA-PA also publishes materials for preschool children.

The original publication on preschool education is the preschool education magazine published by Preschool Education Development Association of Turkey. There are various other publications issued by the Ministry of Education.

TABLE 1
Sample Daily Activities Chart for Full-Day Kindergarten

Hours	Activities
8:00 a.m.–10:00 a.m.	Arrival, cleaning and health check, free play
10:00 a.m.–10:15 a.m.	Preparation for snack
10:15 a.m.–10:30 a.m.	Snack
10:30 a.m.–10:45 a.m.	Clean up
10:45 a.m.–11:15 a.m.	Turkish language instruction
11:15 a.m.–11:30 a.m.	Play
11:30 a.m.–11:45 a.m.	Music
11:45 a.m.–12:00	Toilet, cleaning, getting ready for lunch
12:00–12:45 p.m.	Lunch
12:45 p.m.–1:00 p.m.	Clean up
1:00 p.m.–1:15 p.m.	Preparation for rest
1:15 p.m.–3:00 p.m.	Rest
3:00 p.m.–3:15 p.m.	Clean up
3:15 p.m.–3:30 p.m.	Snack
3:30 p.m.–3:45 p.m.	Clean up
3:45 p.m.–4:15 p.m.	Preparatory training for reading and writing
4:15 p.m.–5:45 p.m.	Play
5:45 p.m.–6:00 p.m.	Preparation for going home

TABLE 2
Sample Daily Activities Chart for Half-Day Kindergarten

Hours	Activities
8:00 a.m.–9:45 a.m.	Arrival, cleaning, and health check
	Free play
9:45 a.m.–10:00 a.m.	Preparation for snack
10:00 a.m.–10:15 a.m.	Snack
10:15 a.m.–10:30 a.m.	Clean up
10:30 a.m.–11:00 a.m.	Turkish language
11:00 a.m.–11:30 a.m.	Play
11:30 a.m.–11:45 a.m.	Music
11:45 a.m.–12:15 p.m.	Preparatory training for reading and writing
12:15 p.m.–12:30 p.m.	Preparation for going home

TABLE 3
Sample Themes in Preschool Programs for 4- to 5-Year Olds

- My school
- Our homes and our families
- My friends and I
- October 29 Republic Day
- Autumn
- November 10 and Atatürk
- Our bodies
- Our health
- Winter
- New year
- Sky
- Communication equipment
- Transportation vehicles
- April 23, national Independence and Children Day
- Spring
- Holiday of Ramadan
- Poultry
- Holiday of sacrifice
- Summer
- Traffic
- Forest
- Fire
- Village
- Earthquake
- Erosion and floods
- Plants
- Electrical equipment
- Heating equipment
- Shopping
- Animals (e.g., land animals, domestic animals, farm animals, sea and inland water animals)

TABLE 4
Days and Weeks to Be Celebrated or Remembered in Preschools

Event	Date
Day of protection of animals	October 4
World Children Day	First Monday of October
Red Moon Week	October 29–November 4
Week of World Children's Books	Begins the second Monday of November
Week of Atatürk	November 10–16
Teachers Day	November 24
Savings, Investment, and National Product Week	December 12–16
Energy Saving Week	Begins the second Monday of January
Week to Foster Activities Against Smoking and Alcohol	March 1–7
Forest Week	March 21–26
Health Week	April 7–13
Tourism Week	April 15–22
Traffic Week	Begins the first Saturday of May
Mother's Day	Second Sunday of May

Primary Education

Primary education in Turkey covers the education of children between ages 6 and 14. This education is free in the state schools, and the first five years, known as primary, are compulsory. Those who finish primary school receive a primary school diploma.

In Turkey, primary education is the responsibility of Ministry of Education. There are two classification of primary schools: urban and rural. In the village schools, the school day is shorter. In some village schools, one teacher teaches more than one class in the same room. This is known as a "combined class." A variation is "dual education," (i.e., a shared classroom and teacher but for different hours in the day).

There are also primary schools operated by the private sector with the permission of the Ministry of Education. These schools are concentrated in large cities. A few of these private schools belong to foreigners and to minorities.

The current education program has been in force since 1968. It was designed to promote a common understanding of goals and methods, and to increase productivity in the schools having regular and dual education. Table 5 provides examples from the daily activity charts in the program.

Related Establishments and Publications

The Education Council, within the Ministry of Education, prepares curricula for the primary school and prepares or selects textbooks. The council does not have the same function at the secondary level.

The Turkish Education Association (TED) conducts research in education at all levels. The association also publishes *The Education and Science Magazine* and holds scientific meetings on various subjects.

There are also publications printed by the Ministry of Education oriented to primary school teachers. In addition, publications such as *Education While Living* and *Contemporary Education and*

TABLE 5

Distribution Chart of Primary School Weekly Subjects

	Classes				
Subjects	I	II	III	IV	V
Turkish	10	10	10	6	6
Mathematics	5	5	5	4	4
Sciences	—	—	—	4	4
Social Sciences	—	—	—	3	3
Life Sciences	5	5	5	—	—
Religion and Morals	—	—	—	2	2
Painting and Handcraft	1	1	1	2	2
Music	1	1	1	1	1
Physical Training	3	3	3	3	3
TOTAL	25	25	25	25	25

Psychology often address issues in primary education.

Special Education

The development of special education in Turkey differs according to the type of handicap. Special education services were started in 1889 with the education of those with hearing defects. But is was not until 1951 that special education became a formal part of the Ministry of Education. The Turkish Constitution also makes provisions for special education for preschool age children.

Visual Impairment

A section for visually impaired children was opened in the school for the deaf established in Istanbul in 1889. In 1921, a private association founded a school for deaf children and blind children. The school was taken over by the Ministry of Health and Social Welfare in 1924, and subsequently by the Ministry of Education in 1950. In 1951, the section for the blind moved to Ankara.

Since the 1970s, the number of schools for the blind has increased. Today, schools for the blind are administered by the Special Teaching and Guidance Department Directorate within the Ministry of Education. There are nine schools for visually impaired (six primary, two primary and secondary combined, and one secondary) with a total enrollment of 836.

Hearing Impairment

The education of deaf children started in Istanbul in 1889. In 1912, the students were transferred to the alms-house until it closed in 1926. At this time, the students were sent to the schools for the deaf in Izmir. The education of the deaf has been provided by the Ministry of Education since 1951. Currently, there are 29 schools for the deaf with an enrollment at the primary level of 4,366. The focus in the schools, starting from grade 4, is on handicrafts and vocational training. There are also two primary schools for those who are hard of hearing operated by the Ministry of Education, and 72 classes for the deaf in the regular primary schools.

Mentally Retarded Children

The education of mentally retarded children started in 1952 with special preparatory classes opened in two primary schools in Ankara. In these classes, a different teaching program is applied to the children and a primary school diploma is awarded to those who graduate. In 1982, a labor school was opened with the aim of teaching a skill to those who finish special preparatory classes.

In addition, there is a primary school in Istanbul for children who are difficult to educate (established in 1969). For the teachable mentally retarded, there is a state-run school in Ankara (opened in 1987). Some private schools offer programs in the large cities for retarded children. There are no schools for severely retarded children.

Maladjusted Children

The first institution for the education of maladjusted children was opened in Istanbul as a primary school in 1952. But after a short while this school changed its focus to care for children in need of protection. From 1969–87, the Anadolu Hisari Special Education Primary School and Training House operated in Istanbul to serve maladjusted young children.

Services are offered in several counties through the Guidance and Research Centers, the National Education Directorates, and the psychiatric clinics of hospitals.

Physically Handicapped Children

Institutions for the physically handicapped are limited. In 1974, a school for physically handicapped opened in Ankara. At present, there are 84 students in the primary section of this school.

Gifted Children

After the foundation of the Republic and until 1950, the tendency was to send gifted children abroad for study. After 1964, these children were accommodated in Turkey in science high schools. Admission to the schools is based on a test.

There are no regular publications related to special education other than textbooks, booklets, and essays written by university instructors, related ministries, and professionals. The preparation of a Guidance Booklet for the Teacher and the Family on Special Education has yet to be prepared by the Ministry of Education.

Goals of Early Education

The goals in the field of early childhood education in Turkey include raising enrollment to 10 percent of the population in preschool and to 100 percent in primary level and ending dual education in primary and secondary education. Reducing the number of children in classes is also an issue. As a first step, it is recommended that class size be a maximum of 40 students. To this end, priority should be given to areas where dual education and crowded classes are an ongoing problem, and where urbanization is extensive.

Equipping schools with materials, modern laboratories, and computers is another goal; as is making preschools a priority in areas of intensive industrialization. Other targets include increasing (1) the number of infant classes in primary schools; (2) the number of handicapped children in preschools to 5 percent; (3) the number of handicapped children at the primary level to 5 percent; and (4) the collaboration between teachers and experts in special education with the universities. Offering special programs and services to gifted and talented children and promoting parental education are also areas that have been identified as important.

References

Cicioglu, H. (1982). *Primary and secondary instruction in the Republic of Turkey.* Ankara: Ankara University, Publications of the Faculty of Language, History, and Geography No: 332.

Danisoglu, E. (1989). *State policies related to children in development plans and yearly programmes, The state of children in Turkey.* Ankara: UNESCO

Doganay, A. (1988). *Problems of curriculum and teaching in the transformation of two-year education institutions to education colleges.* M.A. Thesis, Ankara University. Ankara: Institute of Social Sciences.

Gürkan, T. (1981). *Development and evaluation of preschool education curriculum in Turkey.* Ph.D. Dissertation. Ankara University, Faculty of Education. Ankara.

————. (1987). *Evaluation of 5-year application in basic education.* Ankara: Ankara University, Publications of the Faculty of Educational Sciences No. 155.

Gürkan, T., Küçükahmet, L., Kisakürek, M., & Hakan, A. (1987). *Primary school curriculum and teaching methods.* Ankara: Anatolia University, Publications of Open Education Faculty No. 189.

Kagitcibasi, C. (1989). *Interaction within families and the development of the child—State of children in Turkey:* Ankara: UNESCO.

Kaya, Y. (1989). *A new look at our educational system.* Ankara: Science Publication.

Konanc, E. (1989). *Protection of children in Turkish law.* Ankara: UNESCO.

Kut, S. (1989). *Children who need protection in Turkey—State of children in Turkey*. Ankara: UNESCO.

The Magazine of Preschool Education. (1989). Ayyildiz Publication No. 33. Ankara.

Ministry of Education. (1981). *Tenth National Education Board*. Ankara: Publication of Ministry of Education.

———. (1982). *Eleventh National Education Board*. Ankara: Publication of Ministry of Education.

———. (1984). *Regulation of kindergartens and infant classes within the Ministry of Education*. Ankara: Publication of the Ministry of Education.

———. (1986). *Law and regulations related to special education*. Ankara: Publication of the Ministry of Education.

———. (1987). *Institutions of private education*. Ankara: Publication of the Ministry of Education.

———. (1987). *Primary school program*. Ankara: Publication of the Ministry of Education.

———. (1987). *Rules of the work school for educable children*. Ankara: Publication of the Ministry of Education.

———. (1987). *The ten-year plan and the content of special education and guidance services*. Ankara: Publication of the Ministry of Education.

———. (1988). *Twelfth National Education Board*. Ankara: Publication of the Ministry of Education.

———. (1988). *The function of teachers and education experts within the Ministry of Education*. Ankara: Publication of the Ministry of Education.

———. (1989). *Preschool education curriculum*. Ankara: Publication of the Ministry of Education.

———. (1989). *Preschool teacher's guide*. Istanbul: Publication of the Ministry of Education.

Özsoy, Y., Özyürek, M., & Eripek, S. (1988). *Introduction to special education*. Ankara: Karatepe Publications.

Türkoglu, A. (1988). *Problems encountered in curriculum applications in higher education schools*. Adana: Cukurova University, Publications of Education Faculty No. 1.

Varis, F. (1988). *Introduction to educational sciences*. Ankara: Ankara University, Publications of the Faculty of Educational Sciences No. 159.

YA-PA Sixth Preschool Education Seminar. (1986). Ankara: YA-PA Publication.

YA-PA Seventh Preschool Education Seminar. (1987). Ankara: YA-PA Publication.

Yavuzer, H. (1989). *Psycho-pedagogical results created by interaction within families and factors external to family—State of children in Turkey*. Ankara: UNESCO.

Yücel, A., & Demiral, Ö. (1989). *Child and education—State of children in Turkey*. Ankara: UNESCO.

PRIMARY EDUCATION IN THE UNITED ARAB EMIRATES

●●●●●●●●●●◆●●●●●●●●●●

Mahmoud Ahmed Ajjawi
College of Education
United Arab Emirates University
United Arab Emirates

The United Arab Emirates (UAE) is a newly established developing country. It became an independent state on December 2, 1971, through the union of seven emirates: Abu Dhabi, Dubai, Sharjah, Ajman, Um-Al-Quwain, Ras Al-Kheimah, and Al-Fujeirah. Before 1971, the UAE was a British colony for 150 years. The UAE lies on the Arabian Gulf and has borders with the Sultanate of Oman, Saudi Arabia, and Qatar. It has an area of 83,600 square kilometers and a population of 1,622,464 according to the 1985 census.

The citizens of the UAE are estimated to be only about 20 percent of the total population of the country. The rest of the population comes from all over the world, but mainly from the Arab countries. This demographic diversity has left its marks on the UAE's systems of education. Non-Arabs have their own private schools which follow the curricula of their respective countries. Citizens and Arabs send their children to government schools, as well as to some Arabic private schools. This chapter deals only with primary education in government schools in the UAE. After a brief historical introduction, this chapter first discusses the kindergarten level, which is for children between ages 4 and 6, and the lower elementary level which

covers the first three grades of school and is for children between ages 6 and 8.

Education in the UAE: A Brief History

Education in the UAE started at the turn of the century (Abdullah, Mohammed, 1981; Ajjawi, Mahmoud, 1986). This short history of education can be divided according to the level of development into three phases.

The first phase, from 1905 to 1953, saw the development of the Al-Matawha schools. Because the purpose of these schools was religious, the teachers, had a deep understanding of Islam. Their main role was to teach students to read and write, and their curriculum was the Holy Quran. Financed by wealthy merchants, the schools opened and closed according to the financial status of the merchant. There was never more than four such schools in operation at the same time.

The second phase, from 1953 to 1971, witnessed the beginning of formal education. Schools were divided into levels, and the curriculum included all subjects taught in today's schools. Education was financed and staffed by the govern-

TABLE 1

Education in the UAE in 1971–72 and 1989–90

Year	Number of schools	Classes	Students	Teachers & Administrators
1971–72	74	1,024	32,862	1,585
1989–90	473	8,948	245,953	15,317
Increase rate (%)	639	873	748	966

Source: Ministry of Education statistical yearbooks.

ments of Kuwait, Qatar, and Egypt. The educational system in the emirates, except Abu Dhabi, followed the Kuwaiti system. In Abu Dhabi, education started in the mid-1960s and was financed by the local government of Abu Dhabi from its oil revenues. Education in Abu Dhabi followed the Jordanian system and teachers came mainly from Bahrain and Jordan.

The third phase covers the period from independence in 1971 until the present. The Ministry of Education was established in January 1972, and took over the educational system. Financing education became the responsibility of the state.

The development of education in the UAE in the last 18 years has been tremendous due to rapid political and socioeconomic developments. These developments include the establishment of the union state, the flow of oil, and the social demand on education. To face the demand on education, the Ministry of Education continued to cooperate with other Arab states to provide its schools with qualified teachers and administrators. Table 1 compares the status of education in 1971–72 with that of 1989–90.

The budget of the Ministry of Education in 1971 was 62 million dirhams and in 1991 it was almost two billion dirhams (3.7 dirhams=$1.00).

Kindergarten

Kindergarten in the UAE is free but not compulsory. It is divided into two years. The first year admits children between ages 4 and 5 and the second year admits children between ages 5 and 6. Admission at the kindergarten level, unlike all other levels, is restricted to citizens only.

The first kindergarten in the UAE opened in 1968 by the local government of Abu Dhabi. Despite this recent history, kindergartens have spread nationwide. Table 2 shows the development of kindergartens between 1972 and 1990 with respect to schools, classes, children, and teachers.

Because the total number of citizens between the ages 4–6 is unknown, the percentage of children attending kindergarten is also unknown. The government has not universalized this level, and doing so is not one of the objectives of the Ministry of Education.

Kindergartens are co-educational, although only females can be teachers. The number of male children and female children are almost the same. (i.e., 8,150 males, 8,278 females).

Academic qualifications for most teachers and administrators are low. Table 3 shows the status of teachers and administrators according to qualification and nationality in 1988–89. Only 22.21 percent of all teachers and administrators hold a first university degree. None specializes in kindergarten education. The rest hold either a secondary school certificate or are graduates of teacher education centers with two-year study programs. Teachers who are citizens comprise 54.6 percent, whereas the rest come from other Arab countries and 87 percent of them have qualifications less than the Bachelor's degree.

Most administrators (i.e., 87.69 percent) are citizens, the rest are Arabs. This high percentage of citizens as administrators is a new trend in education in the UAE. It began after the Ministry of Education nationalized the educational system

TABLE 2

Development of Kindergartens

Year	Number of schools	Classes	Children	Teachers & Administrators
1972–73	11	93	3,276	312
1989–90	42	598	16,428	1,029
Rate of increase (%)	381	643	501	379

Source: Ministry of Education statistical yearbooks.

beginning with headmasters and headmistresses and then the teaching staff.

The lower elementary level in the UAE is free and compulsory. It includes the first three grades of school. A child whose age is 6 or will be 6 by the end of December in that year is admitted to grade 1. Children age 5 1/2 are also admitted on condition that they have studied two years at the kindergarten level. Admission at this level is open to citizens and Arabs who work for the federal government or any local government bureau, while

children of parents working in the private sector have to go to private schools. Education at this level is not co-educational except in some rural areas where the number of students is too small to open one school for boys, and one for girls. In any case, the number of such schools is very limited.

Prior to independence in 1971, educational opportunities for citizens were very limited. Schools were not capable of admitting all children between the ages of 6 and 8. When the Ministry of Education was established in 1972, it found that over 70

TABLE 3

Kindergarten Teachers and Administrators According to Qualifications and Nationality

	Secondary School Certificates (SSC)	Two Years after SSC	B.A. Degree	Total
Teachers				
Citizens	356	3	54	413
Noncitizens (Arabs)	33	255	63	351
Administrators				
Citizens	67	19	85	171
Noncitizens (Arabs)	6	7	11	24
Total	462	284	213	959

Source: Ministry of Education statistical yearbook

percent of the males and 90 percent of the females over age 10 were illiterate. The capacity of schools did not exceed 40 percent of all children between ages 6 and 11.

To reverse the situation, the government implemented a series of incentives to attract students to the school system. Among those measures were the following:

• a monthly salary for every student attending school (which are no longer available);

• transportation for students to and from school;

• fresh hot meal at school (no longer available);

• money for clothing; and

• textbooks, workbooks, and all the stationery needed.

These measures were supported by a social welfare system through which low-income citizens, the elderly, divorcees, and others were given a monthly salary to motivate them to keep their children at schools.

In the last 18 years, elementary education in the UAE has been universalized. In fact, the UAE is one of the few Arab countries to achieve that goal.

Elementary education in the UAE has developed tremendously. Table 4 compares the status of elementary education in 1972 with that in 1990 in terms of schools, classes, students, and teachers, and administrators.

TABLE 4
Status of Elementary Education in 1972 and 1989*

Year	Schools	Classes	Students	Teachers & Administrators
1972–73	82	905	30,577	1,584
1989–90	198	5,436	148,865	9,246
Increase rate (%)	241	600	486	584

*Figures in this table include all elementary grades from 1–6.

The table shows that the ratio of students to classes is 27.39 students per class. This ratio differs in cities and rural areas. While the table shows that the average student-teacher ratio is 27.39 the ratio generally decreases in rural classrooms and increases in the cities.

The Ministry of Education statistics do not separate the lower elementary level (grades 1–3) from the upper elementary level (grades 4–6) except for number of students and classes. The 1989–90 figures show that the number of students in grades 1–3 is 79,676 students, of which 49,862 (24,907 males, 24,955 females) are citizens and 29,814 students are noncitizens. This means that male and female citizens are almost equal in number. The number of classes at the lower elementary level is 2,944. Thus the average number of students in each class in 27.06 students.

The distribution of students, teachers, administrators, and technical staff according to nationality and gender is illustrated in Table 5.

Table 5 shows that the numbers of male and female citizens at the elementary level are almost equal. In fact, the enrollment of females in the educational system in UAE is considered one of the great achievements of the union state. Females before 1971 were deprived of such educational opportunities. Citizens from 64.05 percent of all students are at the elementary levels. Others come from the Arab countries and are the children of Arab nationals working for the federal government or the local governments of the seven emirates. Non-Arabs normally go to their own schools.

Table 5 also shows that the percentage of citizen-teachers is very low compared with the total number of teachers at the elementary level (24.39 percent). The low percentage of male-citizens working in the teaching profession is a serious problem facing the Ministry of Education. (This problem is discussed later under the teacher-education programs.) The rest of the teachers come from Arab countries, mainly Egypt, Jordan, Syria, and Palestine.

The percentage of citizens as administrators and technical staff is 59.06 percent of the total. This percentage is higher than that of teachers because

TABLE 5

Students, Teachers, and Administrators According to Nationality and Gender in Elementary Schools in 1989–90

	Citizens			Noncitizens			Total		Grand Total
	M	F	Total	M	F	Total	M	F	
Students	47,656	47,691	95,347	27,482	26,036	53,518	75,138	73,727	148,865
Teachers	251	1,769	2,020	3,555	2,697	6,252	3,806	4,466	8,272
Administrators & Technical Staff	240	767	1,007	472	226	698	712	993	1,705

* These figures include all grades at the elementary level (1–6).

the Ministry of Education gave priority to nationalizing the top positions at schools, namely headmasters and their deputies.

Organization and the Curricula

Kindergarten

The kindergarten level in the UAE is free but not compulsory. Schools are co-educational but teachers, administrators, and others employees are female. This level is for citizens only.

School employees in the UAE are divided into four categories:

1.   the teaching staff;

2.   the administrative staff, which includes the headmaster or mistress, the deputy, secretary, accountant, general services, and the storekeeper;

3.   the technical staff, which includes the social specialist, activities specialist, librarian, and science and language lab specialists; and

4.   other employees (e.g., security guards, gardeners, and janitors).

Each school does not necessarily have all four categories nor do schools have an equal number of employees. Categories and employees depend on the level and size of the school. The kindergartens, for example, do not have lab specialists, an accountant, or a storekeeper.

Salaries of the teaching staff, administrators, and technical staff follow the degree system. That is to say, salaries of all B.A. degree holders are the same irrespective of the level at which they teach or work.

Lower Elementary Level

The lower elementary level is free and compulsory. It is not co-educational and the staff of each school follows the sex of students, except in some rural areas where the number of students is not enough to have two separate schools. Admission at this level is open to citizens and noncitizens as long as their parents work for the federal or local governments.

The description given to the kindergarten concerning the employees and salary applies also to the lower elementary level.

Objectives of Primary Education

Kindergarten

The Ministry of Education has set the following objectives for the kindergarten level:

• helping the child to recognize the principles of good Islamic conduct;

• developing the child's feelings of belonging to his or her homeland;

• helping the child adjust to the social life of schools;

• helping the children to acquire good habits of cleanliness and discipline;

• enriching the child's language and developing his or her verbal skills;

• encouraging the child's self-expression through music and the arts;

• satisfying the child's needs for activity, curiosity, and providing them with the experiences that help them recognize material elements in their environment;

• developing the child's senses, skills, aptitudes, and powers;

• developing the child's feelings about himself or herself, and assisting him or her acquire the skills of cooperation, self-discipline, and movement;

• fulfilling the child's feelings for security and belongingness; and

• providing the child with all the opportunities to play individually and with his or her peers.

Lower Elementary Level

The Education Law states the following objectives for the elementary level (grades 1–6):

• developing Islamic doctrine and the students firm belief in it;

• helping the student to appreciate beautiful things in the world and love nature, and developing the student's powers of observation and imagination;

• acquiring discipline and perseverance;

• acquiring the habit of scientific thinking;

• developing motives for learning, acquiring knowledge, and curiosity, in addition to developing interests;

• helping the student to have stable mental health; and

• developing the student's skills and consciousness as a citizen by knowing his or her rights and duties.

The Curricula

Kindergarten

School at the kindergarten starts at 8 a.m. and it ends at 12 noon. Each day consists of six periods,

one is for a hot meal at 10 a.m. followed by half an hour of rest. Each period lasts for one-half hour. The weekly timetable includes two periods for sports, two for drawing, two for music, and one for free activities. Each of these subjects is taught by a special teacher. The rest of the periods during the week are spent on the instructional units of the curriculum.

The kindergarten curriculum in the UAE is a core-curriculum. That is to say, it consists of certain units from which knowledge in different areas is introduced. The curriculum consists of ten units divided equally in the two-year kindergarten program. During the first year (i.e., ages 4–5), the units are (1) my kindergarten, (2) the family, (3) the desert, (4) myself and others, and (5) the zoo.

During the second year (i.e., ages 5–6), the units are (1) the sea, (2) professionals, (3) the fruit and vegetable market, (4) animals, and (5) transportation. The content of each unit is taken from the local environment. Children of the UAE are normally familiar with these topics.

The teacher's handbook tells the teachers how to teach each unit and what knowledge should be transmitted. It also tells them about the techniques and methods to be used in transmitting that knowledge. Knowledge taught in each unit revolves around the following areas: Islamic education, Arabic language, mathematics, science, art, music, and body movement.

The handbook makes it clear that children are not supposed to be taught in a formal setting, as is the case at upper levels. Neither are they supposed to be taught to read and write. In this respect, their knowledge is restricted to the recognition of the alphabet. Field trips, play, pictures, singing, etc. are the techniques used to enrich the children's knowledge.

Lower Elementary Level

The school day at the lower elementary level starts at 7:30 a.m. and ends at 12:00 noon. Students study five periods a day, each for 45 minutes. There is a five-minute rest between periods. There is also a 20-minute rest after the third period. The overall number of periods per week is 30. Table 6 shows subjects taught and the load for each subject per week.

TABLE 6

Lower Elementary Subjects

Subject	Number of Periods/Week
Islamic education	5
Arabic language	12
Mathematics	5
Science	2
Art education	2
Physical education	2
Music	2
Total	30

The Ministry of Education follows the class-teacher system. The class-teacher teaches the first four subjects listed in Table 6 and the rest are taught by special teachers. The number of periods per week applies to the three grades of the lower elementary level. In some selected schools, it is 34. The extra periods are for the English language. The Ministry is experimenting with teaching English from grade 1, and this project will be evaluated. Presently, English is being taught beginning at grade 4 or the elementary level.

The subjects taught and their loads show that Arabic amounts to 40 percent of all periods. That is because Arabic is the official language of the country and the mother tongue of its citizens. Arabic is used in mathematics and Islamic education, and each carries 16.67 percent of all periods per week. Each of the other subjects has 6.67 percent of the total load.

The evaluation for the lower elementary level is organized by a ministerial law passed in 1988. The scholastic year is divided into two semesters: the first is from September 15–January 15, and it accounts for 50 percent of the total marks of the year. This percentage comes from three monthly tests. The same applies to the second semester. The final results of the first semester are added to those of the second semester and divided by 2. This means that evaluation is continuous throughout the year. It is also divided into five ranks: A—distinction (90–100), B—very good (80–89), C—good (70–79), D—satisfactory (60–69), and F—weak (below 60).

The student passes and is promoted to a higher grade if he or she receives satisfactory or more in at least three of the four main subjects (i.e., Arabic,

Islamic education, mathematics, and science). Each school has a special committee consisting of the headmaster, the class teacher, and the social specialist to study the cases of those who fail. This committee decides the action to be taken in each case: promotion, repeating the grade, or transferring the student to the special education class in the school.

Special Education

There are two types of special education programs in the UAE. The first is for the severe mentally or physically handicapped and for the sensory impaired (deaf and blind). This program has its own institutions, which are run by the Ministry of Labor and Social Welfare. The second type is for mildly handicapped children and is part of the school system run by the Ministry of Education.

The second program is rather new. Special education classes at schools started in the scholastic year 1979–80. Children in such classes are of five categories:

1. slow learners;

2. educable mentally retarded children;

3. children with specific learning disabilities;

4. children with mild sensory weakness or environmental deprivation; or

5. mild behaviorally disturbed children.

Special education classes are available only at the lower elementary level. Their main purpose is to help students overcome their learning and behavioral problems, thus enabling them to return to their regular classes at the school.

Results of the scholastic year 1988–89 show that there were 720 students (359 females, 361 males) in ninety special education classes. Each class has a teacher trained in special education techniques. Of the 242 students who passed the final exams (35 percent), 132 were females (37 percent) and 110 males (30 percent). Students who pass are either promoted to higher grades or transferred back to their original classes.

Teachers of special education classes follow the following principles:

• use of individualized teaching in addition to group teaching;

• emphasize the development of children's aptitudes to learn;

• teach from the concrete to the abstract;

• teach lessons through a series of short sessions; and

• repeat and revise in order to reinforce advancement in learning.

The special education section at the Ministry of Education lacks trained professionals and well-established assessment tools and procedures. At present, the Ministry of Education, with the cooperation of the Department of Special Education at the UAE University, has formed a joint committee whose task is to upgrade special education services with special reference to integrated educational settings within public schools.

Teacher Education Programs in the UAE

A good percentage of the teachers at the kindergarten and lower elementary levels are not nationals, but are from other Arab countries. In fact, education in the UAE would have never developed without the help and support of the other Arab countries.

After the establishment of the union state, demands on education increased; thus, more teachers were needed, causing the Ministry to turn to other Arab countries. Teaching offered high salaries and introduced other benefits (e.g., air tickets, accommodations, and bonuses) to attract more and better teachers.

Education in the UAE depended completely on Arab teachers until 1979, when the Ministry of Education started its own teacher education program: a two-year, in-service training program after the Secondary School Certificate. The purpose was to nationalize the teaching profession. Nationals were appointed as teachers, teaching during the school day and studying in the afternoon. For six years, the program concentrated on training subject teachers to the upper-elementary level. By the end of those six years, the program had trained 119 male teachers and 684 female teachers.

In 1984, the program shifted its emphasis from training subject teachers to the training of class teachers and kindergarten teachers. Two years later, new areas of specialization were introduced to the program: family education, art education, secretarial work, and lab specialists. Table 7 shows the number of graduates in each field according to sex and the year of graduation.

The table shows that the total number of graduates is 2497. In addition to this, 388 will graduate at the end of 1990. The number of male graduates is only 276 (13.4%) of the total number of graduates.

In 1988, the Ministry decided to stop the program of class teachers and kindergarten teachers due to several reasons. Among them were that the quality of teachers coming to the program was not satisfactory, the program was not academically solid, and the program was not in harmony with the contemporary trend in teacher education, (i.e., having university graduates specialized in kindergarten and elementary education as teachers at both levels). In addition, surveys conducted by the Ministry showed that the quality of education at the elementary level was deteriorating mainly because of the poor quality of teachers.

Due to the importance of primary education in the future educational career of children, and the importance of good quality teachers at the primary levels, the Ministry of Education has decided to retrain all graduates of the in-service training program at the UAE University. A long-term plan has been set with the cooperation of the College of Education. The first phase of the plan aims at retraining the class teachers. In 1989–90, 657 class teachers began their university studies at the tutorial external centers of the university, which are located throughout the emirates. The program implemented is the same curriculum as the class teacher program at the College of Education.

Teacher Education Program at the University

The UAE University was established in 1977–78. The College of Education was one of the first four colleges of the university. As of 1991, the university included eight colleges with an enrollment of 8,423 students and 500 staff members.

The College of Education programs from 1977–78 to 1985–86 were restricted to graduate teachers for the secondary level and specialists in education and psychology. In 1985–86, the programs of the

TABLE 7

Number of Graduates in Different Fields According to Sex

Year of Graduation	Class Teachers		Kindergarten Teachers	Family Education	Art Education	Secretarial Work		Librarian	Lab	
	M	F	F	F	F	M	F	F	F	Total
1985	40	389	95	—	—	—	—	—	—	524
1986	54	317	89	—	—	—	—	—	—	460
1987	76	240	85	—	—	12	77	—	—	490
1988	—	—	—	—	—	55	121	—	—	176
1989	48	219	100	63	29	—	—	—	—	459
1990	—	—	—	29	118	—	116	61	64	388
TOTAL	218	1,165	369	92	147	67	314	61	64	2,497

college underwent radical changes, new programs were introduced, and others were dropped.

The College of Education presently includes the following departments: Education, Special Education, Psychology, and Physical Education. The Department of Education includes the following programs:

• family education (for graduate female teachers at all levels);

• art education (for graduate teachers at all levels);

• kindergarten program (for graduate teachers at the kindergarten level);

• elementary education (for graduate class teachers at the lower elementary level and subject teachers at the upper-elementary level); and

• teacher education (for graduate teachers in all fields of study at the secondary level).

The outlines of the program are as follows:

• 21 credit hours in basic skills (includes Arabic, English, mathematics, computer science, and techniques of scientific research);

• 15 credit hours as university requirements or general culture;

• 18 credit hours as college requirements (includes courses in education and psychology);

• 72 credit hours in the field of specialization (includes required courses (18), support courses (12), and practical training, the practical training is for one semester when students finish their coursework, they will spend four months in actual teaching); and

• 6 credit hours as free courses.

The total credit hours required for graduation is 132 credit hours.

Despite all the changes, teacher education programs face important problems. First, the admission policy of the College of Education is not based on the students' interests but rather on the government's objectives of nationalizing the teaching profession. The government's policy has lead to the increase in total enrollment at the college by 33 percent annually. As of 1991, the total number of female students at the College of Education is 2,320, or 39.48 percent of the total number of female students at the university.

Second, the achievement level of most of the students admitted to the College of Education at the secondary school certificate is very low. The average needed to enroll at the college is 60 percent and it is one of the lowest at the university.

Third, as a result of the admission policy, the percentage of students who have academic warnings (who are on academic probation) is about 40 percent of the total number of students at the College of Education. This is the highest at the university.

Fourth, the number of male students admitted to the College of Education is very low compared with the number of females. Even after admission, male students usually transfer from the college, or withdraw from the university, or even seek a job outside the Ministry of Education after graduation.

The 1989–90 statistics show that the College of Education has 224 male students and 2,320 females in all its programs. The number of male students in the class teacher program is only *two* students, while there are 61 females in the program. Admission to the kindergarten program is restricted to females only and their total number is 284 students.

Male nationals show little interest in teaching profession for several reasons. First, the income is low compared with other professions in the society. Second, teachers are not as highly respected as they once were. Third, other jobs are available that provide better salaries and better social status (e.g., the police force, the army, and the oil companies). In addition, there is the ambiguity about the future of the teacher, as well as the fact that the teaching profession is highly demanding compared with others (Rasheed, Ajjawi, and Mutaweh, 1987).

The high percentages of probation and of withdrawal of students means that there is a high percentage of waste, especially in light of the fact that the total cost of education for every student of the university is about U.S. $12,000 annually.

This reality, combined with the lack of interest in teaching, means that the objectives of the government to nationalize the teaching professions by the year 2000 will not be met. If the current trend persists, male schools could not be nationalized in the coming half century.

Conclusion

Since the UAE universalized primary education in 1971, special efforts have been given to provide educational opportunities to the deprived, namely women and people in rural areas. The UAE has also established a university where citizens could continue their higher education free of all expenses. The university provides its students with free boarding, free meals, free textbooks, and free transportation. The government also guarantees every graduate a job.

Despite all these achievements, education in the UAE especially primary education, has to overcome many difficulties. The first task is to improve the quality of education. As is the case in many countries, the quality of education in the UAE does not match the development in quantity. Priority has been given to providing every citizen, of all ages, with an opportunity of education to the extent that little attention has been given to quality.

The second task is to prepare and train nationals to become teachers. Most teachers at the primary level are not well qualified. In addition, male nationals are not interested in the teaching profession. Retraining class teachers has started, but measures must be taken to entice male citizens into the teaching profession. The College of Education must also take measures to attract the best students to its teacher education programs.

Another is to minimize the waste in education. The percentage of dropout at the lower elementary level is 2 percent, whereas the percentage of failure is 8 percent, and it increases at higher levels.

The first step to improving the educational system have been taken. The Ministry of Education has formed joint committees with the College of Education to evaluate the education system and suggest how to improve it. This is a long-term process, but what really matters is that it has started.

References

Abdullah, M. (1981). The United Arab Emirates, Kuwait: Dar-Al-Qalam. p. 150.

Ajjawai, M. (1986). The development of education in the UAE 1905–1971. University of Kuwait: Dirasat Al Kahaleej Wal-Jazirah Al-Arabia, January 1986.

College of Education Catalog 1986–1990. Abu Dhabi UAE University, pp. 49–67.

Ibrahim, A. (1988). Teacher's guide to the application of instructional units. Ministry of Education, 3rd Ed.

Ministry of Education. Statistical Report 1973–74.

————. Department of Educational Planning. (1983) Education in the UAE in the last twelve years.

————. Department of In-service Training. (1983). The In-service Training Program, Facts and Figures.

————. Department of Information. Teaching Staff, Administrators according to Academic Qualification 1988–1990. (Computer print-out).

————. Department of Information. Preliminary Statistical Report, 1989–1990.

Rasheed, F., Ajjawi, M., & Mutaweh, H. (1987). Education in the U.A.E. Society. Al-Ain: The Bookshop.

CONTESTED TERRAIN: EARLY CHILDHOOD EDUCATION IN THE UNITED STATES

• • • • • • • • • • ◆ • • • • • • • • •

Steven A. Gelb and Kathryn D. Bishop
University of San Diego
San Diego, United States of America

It is a challenge to focus on preschool, primary, and early childhood special education in the United States in the same chapter. That is because the field of early childhood education (ECE) has never penetrated elementary and special education to the degree that many early childhood educators have wished, and these three areas, for many reasons, have remained fairly distinct from one another. With the exception of the early twentieth-century Progressive era, the "developmental" play-centered curriculum favored by U.S. heirs to the romantic Froebelian tradition has not been embraced by the educational establishment. This is in spite of early educators' long-standing commitment to transform elementary education from the bottom up. Prekindergarten and primary education especially have been worlds apart in aims, curricula, methods, and organization. And the gulf between the fields of ECE and special education at both the prekindergarten and primary levels has been greater still.

Presently, the education and care of young children has reemerged as a focus of national attention in the United States. This has been a response to increasing numbers of women entering the work force and to the exacerbation of social problems—including a well-documented deterioration of children's physical and social health under the "benign neglect" policies of the Reagan-Bush and Bush-Quayle administrations (Children's Defense Fund, 1990)—combined with optimistic appraisals of promising (but still inconclusive) research about the potential long-term benefits of ECE (Barnett & Escobar, 1987).

The renewed attention has been a mixed blessing. Ironically, in the light of its historical mission, the field of ECE now continues to struggle not only to influence primary education to appreciate children's spontaneous activities, but also to defend against the encroachment of didactic elementary school practices in kindergarten and in pre-kindergarten education (Kagan and Zigler, 1987). Today, the terrain of early childhood is contested between advocates of "developmentally appropriate practice" that is aimed at facilitating the growth of "the whole child" (Bredekamp, 1987) and those—primarily with identifications outside of the field—who are caught up in national movements toward competency-based instruction, mastery learning, the consumption of corporate-produced and marketed basal readers and workbooks (Goodman, et al., 1988) and, above all, the use of standardized multiple-choice tests scores to measure educational progress and to guide curriculum development (Kamii, 1990).

The present situation cannot be adequately discussed without describing its development. Therefore, this chapter begins with a broad overview of the history of ECE in the United States. It then describes prevailing models of teacher training and curriculum models in both regular ECE and early childhood special education; due to the size and diversity of the United States presentation is selective. The chapter concludes with a discussion of current issues in the field and a list of resources.

History of ECE in the United States

Establishment of the Kindergarten

Although the importance of self-directed play in U.S. ECE has been emphasized since the late nineteenth century, it has not always been so. Before 1830, ECE in the United States was shaped by Calvinism and its doctrine that children, as heirs to the human condition, are innately depraved. The purpose of early education was to prepare children for conversion through religious teachings, and suppression of the will was a central educational goal. The curriculum was based on the Bible and the "catechetical method"—drill on religious doctrine—was the educational method of choice. Calvinists advised parents to banish all play materials because children's desire for them was a sign of depravity and unbridled willfulness (Shapiro, 1983).

By the early nineteenth century, such notions were challenged both by the ascendance of faculty psychology (whereby mental capacity consisted of discrete abilities that could be exercised like muscles) and by evangelical Protestantism (which rejected the doctrine of original sin and depravity). Moral training was understood to be central to education but submission of the will was neither necessary nor desirable, since proper training was sufficient to develop healthy habits. In contrast to the earlier era, play was valued highly. An author writing in the *American Journal of Education* in 1829 commented that "a clearer light is falling on the subject of early education, and our methods of attempting to gain access to the mind are becoming more congenial, more intellectual, more cheerful" (quoted in Shapiro, 1983: 12).

The 1830s saw the establishment in Boston of an infant school movement following the English model. These schools, which were based on the teachings of James Buchanan and Samuel Wilderspin, were primarily intended to elevate the children of poor families. Although they were relatively lively places for their period, they were still a far cry from the post-Froebelian schools that followed later in the century. Lessons continued to be by rote, and it was necessary for children to maintain suitably serious facial expressions or else risk calling down their teacher's wrath (Kilpatrick, 1916).

The kindergarten took root in the United States after its introduction by German disciples of Froebel, who fled to the United States to escape the aftermath of the Revolution of 1848. The first U.S. kindergarten was begun in 1855, in Watertown, Wisconsin, by Margarethe Schurz, who had recently arrived from Germany. For the next two decades the kindergarten movement remained the province of the German-American community. In 1870, there were 11 kindergartens in the United States and only one of them was English-speaking (White and Burka, 1987).

The period from 1870 to 1900, however, saw rapid expansion of the kindergarten movement for many reasons. First, it was spurred by the stirring of a women's movement. For women in the United States, just as for many in Europe, the kindergarten movement offered an outlet for the expression of a "female ethic of cooperation, nurture, and community . . . consciously advocated as a redeeming alternative to the patriarchal values of competition and aggression" (Allen, 1988: 30). Second, kindergartens were seen as a remedy for social problems. In the late nineteenth-century, life in the United States was undergoing transformation from the personal, relatively slow pace of the small town environment to a more centralized, bureaucratic, and impersonal organization that was developing to service an increasingly industrialized and corporation-dominated economy. Consequently, many in the United States believed that the social fabric itself was unraveling as evidenced by the growth of urban poverty and crime (Wiebe, 1967).

Their discomfort was further exacerbated by a shift in immigration patterns. At the end of the nineteenth century, newcomers from southern and eastern Europe began to outnumber those from northern and western Europe and the new arrivals were characterized as inferior by the descendants of the earlier immigrants (Solomon, 1956). As a result, many perceived the need to rapidly "Americanize" the children of the new immigrants.

The charity kindergarten movement of the 1870s and 1880s was begun out of concern for the lives of the children of the urban immigrant poor. By the 1880s, more than 1,000 charity kindergartens had been established to provide Froebelian education for young children and comprehensive services for their families, including parental education; provision of hot lunches, clothing, and shoes; and, in some cases, solicitations of donations to keep families who had fallen behind in their rent from being evicted (Ross, 1976).

As the perceived threat of social problems grew, kindergarten became increasingly marketed as a means of social control. By 1893, Sarah Cooper, a leader of the San Francisco charity kindergarten movement, declared flatly that "the design of the kindergarten was to prevent crime" (cited in Ross, 1976: 36). For others, kindergarten was seen as a way to undercut the subversive potential of the working class while assimilating immigrant cultures into the U.S. mainstream (Allen, 1988).

The center of kindergarten expansion after 1873 was St. Louis, Missouri. In that year, the first public school kindergarten in the United States was opened there under the direction of Froebelian-trained Susan Blow and Superintendent William Torrey Harris. The St. Louis program became the model that other urban school districts emulated in the following decades.

For Blow, the focus of the kindergarten was the happiness of each child; for Harris, it was to fit the child to a future role in an industrial economy (Ross, 1976). Harris, who was influenced more by Hegel than by Froebel, opposed the kindergarten movement's tolerance and enthusiasm for the "gushing hilarity" of childhood, which could not, in his view, advance intellectual development (cited in Shapiro, 1983: 59). Thus, at its inception, the public kindergarten embodied a conflict of aims that still resonates today.

By 1900, the kindergarten movement was well on its way to becoming institutionalized. Fifty normal schools (i.e., postsecondary schools that trained teachers) created kindergarten departments between 1890 and 1900. Despite even this rapid growth in training facilities, there was still a shortage of trained teachers (Ross, 1976). By 1914, every major urban center in the United States had a public kindergarten, although only a small minority of eligible children were served.

Yet all was not as kindergarten advocates had hoped it would be. Kindergarten teachers found that conditions in the public schools were frequently inferior to those associated with the charity kindergartens. They complained of being sometimes assigned to the worst room in a building, often without light, ventilation, or access to child-sized toilets. And because they were expected to teach two sessions a day instead of one, there was little or no opportunity to conduct home visits, to hold meetings for mothers, or to continue increasing their own knowledge and skills. Finally, they were under increasing pressure to provide academic lessons to prepare children for the primary level (Ross, 1976).

Along with the expansion of kindergartens, a split developed within the movement. An orthodox group, led by Susan Blow, identified itself closely with Froebel and defended his teachings against what it saw as distortions and corruptions. At the same time, the child study movement—initiated by G. Stanley Hall in the 1890s with the purpose of discovering generalizable laws about child development—led many to critically examine Froebelian practice and to recommend its reconstruction. Hence, a second group of early childhood educators, led by Patty Hill of Teacher's College, opposed Froebelian orthodoxy and argued for change, innovation, and a looser adherence to Froebel's teachings.

Blow's group was clearly fighting a rearguard action. There was no chance that strict Froebelianism, with its mystical and religious foundations, could survive in a twentieth-century American context that increasingly saw science and its methods as the ultimate arbiter of educational aims, curricula, and methods. The lasting legacy of the child study movement was the link it forged between the new science of psychology and education (Zenderland, 1988), and this movement was reflected in U.S. thought on ECE.

Kilpatrick's (1916) influential criticism of Froebel's educational philosophy was a point of transit between nineteenth- and twentieth-century U.S. approaches to early education. Arguing on the basis of modern psychology, Kilpatrick attacked Froebel's pantheism, his symbolism, his "law of opposites," and the orthodox use of his "gifts" and "occupations." He urged teacher training institutions to cease using Froebel's books as teacher training texts.

For Kilpatrick, Froebel's important contribution had been to create an educational institution that centered learning on the "joyous activity" of the child. That example, and challenge, according to Kilpatrick, was now to be carried to the rest of education. It was time for kindergarten to become one with the elementary school, to give up its separate existence—even its name—in order that "Froebel's kindergarten will continue to live yet more abundantly" (Kilpatrick, 1916: 208).

Thus, the field of ECE in the United States moved gradually away from associations with religion, mysticism, feminism, and/or political and social reform, and toward the centrality of developmental psychology as its organizing principle. Today, 75 years later, Kilpatrick's assessment of Froebel could be considered current, but his prediction that Froebel's spirit would escape the vessel of the kindergarten and transform the entire elementary school has not happened. In the last decade of the twentieth century, the influence is in the other direction.

History of the Nursery School Movement

The nursery school movement in the United States began in the 1910s at a time when most kindergartens were already attached to schools and had become primarily educational in their focus. This movement, unlike the charity kindergarten movement of the late nineteenth century, was aimed at middle-class mothers and children. Three types of nursery schools were introduced in the 1920s: (1) family-oriented nurseries, (2) child-welfare-oriented nurseries, and (3) research-oriented preschools (White and Burka, 1987).

The family-oriented schools were the outgrowth of parental groups formed through the child study movement, and they provided group experiences for children and parenting skills for their mothers. They tended to be run as cooperatives. In contrast, the child-welfare nurseries, which were imported from England, were oriented more toward the middle class than they had been in their country of origin (White and Burka, 1987). They included comprehensive programs in health, nutrition, and parental education. The National Committee on Nursery Education, begun in 1925 by promoters of this philosophy, has since grown into the National Association for the Education of Young Children (NAEYC), the largest and most important early childhood association in the United States today.

Finally, research-oriented preschools attached to universities, such as Columbia University's Teachers College, the University of Minnesota, and the University of Iowa, were also established in the 1920s. In one case, this direction of development was reversed. A laboratory school begun in New York City by the Bureau of Educational Experiments grew into a respected and influential postsecondary institution, New York City's Bank Street College (Antler, 1987).

The U.S. nursery school movement continued to expand from the 1920s to the 1950s. Influenced by Dewey, Freud, and Montessori, it continued to elaborate a progressive educational philosophy whose aim was often described as teaching "the whole child." The curriculum principles developed by the movement have been summarized as: "(1) Play is a basic mode for thinking in early childhood. (2) An important aspect of the teacher's role is to exploit the ongoing daily encounters, physical and social, as material for stimulating thinking processes. (3) The cognitive search for relationships should be stimulated through providing varied multiple opportunities for the children's direct, active contact with the people and the processes of their environment" (Biber, 1977: 47).

Yet because the nursery school movement was middle-class-oriented, this curriculum was generally available only as a luxury in programs for those who could afford it.

It was this received wisdom of the early childhood field—which was arrived at after experimentation, innovation, and struggle (Biber, 1977)—that was ironically labeled "traditional" when renewed interest in ECE in the 1960s led to an explosion of new program models. Before describing that critically important decade, it is necessary to discuss the final, often neglected strand of U.S. early childhood history: child care.

History of Child Care

The roots of the current child-care crisis in the United States lie in the nation's historical ambivalence toward nonmaternal care, which, until very recently, was not understood as educative in aim (Scarr and Weinberg, 1986). Americans have long viewed child care as a "necessary evil," a temporary support to bridge short-term needs in times of crisis (Phillips and Zigler, 1987: 10). Throughout the nation's history, leaders have argued that child care dissolves family ties, reduces mothers' sense of responsibility to their children, makes mothers lazy, lessens fathers' desire to be the sole breadwinner, and—the lazy-mother argument notwithstanding—reduces men's salaries because it encourages women to compete against them in the job market (Steinfels, 1973). Therefore, child care has received support only when it was perceived to be in the interest of other goals, such as redeeming the poor, providing jobs for the unemployed, or aiding a war effort. When such needs have been met or abandoned, so has support for child care.

In the late nineteenth century, as the charity kindergarten movement developed, a parallel day-nursery movement grew to provide care for the children of poor mothers who, because of their husband's inadequate earnings, death, or desertion, had to work long hours in factory mills. Previously, such children had remained alone or had been placed in orphanages. But growing fear of the anarchic potential caused by the disruption and exploitation of family life in the country's industrializing economy led to support for child care. Centers were established to save poor children, and society, from the "evil" influences of the urban slums they lived in (Steinfels, 1973).

Unlike the kindergartens, the primary concern of the day nurseries was providing physical care for children; the day often began with a bath for all the children. Centers were run by "matrons"—instead of trained kindergarten teachers—who were responsible for cooking, laundry, and housekeeping as well as for child care. Although some day nurseries reported using Froebel's teaching methods, many did not and the care provided was more custodial than educational (Steinfels, 1973).

The overall effort of the day-nursery movement was to restore traditional family life. Success, as the movement defined it, would not have brought the establishment and institutionalization of a network of high-quality child-care facilities, but rather an end to the need for child care itself, along with the social problems that created the need. The day nursery was a charity service and, by definition, it served mothers with problems.

Initially, in the late nineteenth century, mothers were not seen to be the cause of their problems. Instead, they were seen as victims of either shiftless or alcoholic men, poverty, or other external circumstances. But that changed in the 1920s along with the colonization of day care by social workers. Now families' needs for child care were no longer understood to be circumstantial but instead symptoms of an inner pathology. Day care and casework walked hand-in-hand and families requesting care often had to accept a pathology designation in order to receive services (Steinfels, 1973).

A decade later, in the Great Depression of the 1930s, child care was expanded for the purpose of creating jobs for unemployed teachers, nurses, and cooks. Providing daily care to children was a secondary goal. By 1937, the Works Project Administration (WPA) set up under President Franklin Roosevelt's Federal Economic Recovery Act had created 1,900 centers which served 40,000 children. However, these were dismantled when the special legislation that authorized their establishment expired (Phillips and Zigler, 1987).

An even more elaborate government-sponsored child-care system was established during World War II and was similarly dismantled at the end of the war. In the 1940s the war-created labor shortage led to a rapid mobilization of women workers and to an immediate large scale need for care of their children. By the end of the war, federal and state governments had invested over $50 million in child-care centers serving more than 1.5

million children. But with the return of peacetime, public support of child care was again withdrawn, and, with the consolidation of the "feminine mystique" (Friedan, 1963), and the absence of a new crisis to justify it, again viewed as anti-family and un-American.

An opportunity to reverse this policy was lost in the early 1970s, despite the heightened need for child care that had resulted from mushrooming numbers of women entering the work force in ensuing decades. In December 1971, President Richard Nixon vetoed the Comprehensive Child Development Act, which had been passed by both houses of the U.S. Congress and which would have established a comprehensive developmental child-care program for both the poor and the middle class. The Nixon administration would not "weaken families" by supporting "communal approaches to childrearing over against the family-centered approach" (cited in Phillips and Zigler, 1987: 15). Later attempts to pass comprehensive child-care bills were defeated in 1975 and 1979 through oppositional campaigns that appropriated the same argument (Phillips and Zigler, 1987).

Many argue that the crisis in the current child-care system is due to the makeshift system that has grown up in the absence of a federal policy. The symptoms of this crisis include (1) large numbers of children in unregulated, unlicensed extra-familial care, (2) low wages and high turnover of child-care workers, and (3) increasing numbers of "latch-key" children (i.e., elementary-school-age children who spend their time after school without adult supervision). In 1981, after a 13-year struggle to establish federal interagency day care requirements, all federal standards for child care were suspended. At the same time, the federal government cut back its support for programs so that funding, in real terms, was less than one-half that provided in 1977 (Phillips and Zigler, 1987). The creation of a voluntary early childhood program accreditation system in the mid-1980s by NAEYC was, in part, a response to the abdication of a federal governmental role in setting standards and policy for child care, a problem that early educators had been lamenting since at least the 1920s (Forest, 1927).

But as the 1990s begin, there is widespread recognition in the United States that ECE and child care are not separate issues and must be considered jointly. At the same time, as the numbers of single-parent and two-working-parent families have grown, Americans have been moving away from the earlier equating of the need for child care with family pathology. Again comprehensive child-care measures were passed by both houses of Congress in 1989, but died when a compromise bill could not be agreed on. The 1990 Congress passed, and President Bush signed into law, a bill authorizing the disbursement of child care and Development Block Grants to the states, intended to strengthen early childhood development and before- and after-school child care. However, President Bush vetoed a bill that would have allowed parents six weeks of leave from work following the birth of a child.

History of Head Start

The development of the Head Start Program, which was established in 1964 and is still operating, has been the most significant happening in U.S. ECE since the arrival of Froebel's disciples in the nineteenth century. As "one of the most ambitious, influential, and controversial social programs in the country's history" (Scarr and Weinberg, 1986: 1143), Head Start mobilized attention, support, and a national commitment to ECE in an unprecedented fashion (Biber, 1979). Ironically, since its original purpose was to overcome cognitive deficiencies in children caused by parents caught in a "cycle of poverty," it resulted in Americans of all classes wanting their children to reap the benefits of ECE before they entered kindergarten.

For a brief period in the early 1960s, Americans stopped taking for granted the existence of large blocks of poverty in an otherwise affluent nation. The War on Poverty was fought under President Lyndon B. Johnson between 1964 and 1968, and then abandoned by subsequent administrations, which preferred a policy of benign neglect. Yet Head Start, almost alone among the programs conceived during the War on Poverty, has survived and has received its first largest funding increases in decades.

The War on Poverty conceived of hardship as an individual problem rather than as a structural issue related to discrimination or to the availability of jobs, housing, medical care, and social services.

The economically deprived were seen as "cultur-ally deprived," and Head Start was one of several programs aimed at fixing their inner "deficits." As one authority noted, Head Start "was a creative, innovative effort to interrupt the cycle of poverty, the nearly inevitable sequence of *poor parenting* which leads to children with social and intellectual deficits, which in turn leads to poor school per-formance, joblessness and poverty, leading again to high risk births, *inappropriate parenting*, and so continues the cycle" (Cooke, 1979: xxiii, emphasis added).

Early childhood had already received some attention in the late 1950s after the Soviet Union launched *Sputnik* and Americans responded by seeking ways to become more educationally competitive in the Cold War. In the early 1960s, two influential books, J. McVicker Hunt's *Intelligence and Experience* and Benjamin Bloom's *Stability and Change in Human Characteristics*, convinced many that early development was critically important to the formation of adult intelligence and that intel-ligence was highly responsive to environmental intervention.

Head Start was initiated as a community action program under the Economic Opportunity Act of 1964. Its aim was to: (1) improve children's physi-cal health and physical skills; (2) enhance their emotional and social development; (3) improve their cognitive skills, especially the use of language and concepts; (4) establish attitudes and expecta-tions that would lead to success in future learning; (5) help children relate more positively to their families, and vice-versa; (6) help children and their families develop "responsible" attitudes toward society and also encourage society to help its poor; and (7) enhance the self-respect and sense of dignity of the child and family (White and Burka, 1987).

Head Start was also seen as a rallying point around which the socially and economically marginalized might be empowered. It was hoped that Head Start, as a comprehensive program, would coordinate fragmented social services in inner cities and even lead to reform in the quality of public schools. Also, it was hoped that parental efficacy in advocating for their children would increase through their involvement in the Head Start program.

On May 18, 1965, President Johnson an-nounced the approval of 1,676 Head Start projects, which would create 9,508 centers to serve 375,842 children (White & Burka, 1987). Incredibly, the plan to meet all of the Head Start goals was originally telescoped into a summer program for children before their entry in kindergarten. The implausibility of doing so much in such a short period was recognized during Head Start's first summer of operation and programs were thereaf-ter modified to run throughout much of the year.

Although Head Start was founded to meet the needs of "the whole child" (Biber, 1979), it included funds for curriculum experimentation and, as a result, wound up implementing a number of diverse program models. Some, such as the highly didactic Direct Instruction Model of Bereiter and Engelmann (1966), made no pretence of following in the footsteps of the Froebelian/progressive/nursery traditions. Other important models included the High/Scope Cognitively Oriented Curriculum, based on the theory of Piaget (Weikart, et al., 1971); the Darcee Model, which is teacher directed, highly sequenced, fast paced, and didactic (Gray, et al., 1966); the sense-training method of Maria Montessori; and the Bank Street Model (often called, to the chagrin of its supporters, the "tradi-tional" nursery model). The diversity of these models precludes any specific model being closely identified with the Head Start Program (Miller, 1979).

Nor is it possible to say which program was most effective in meeting Head Start's goals, despite great expenditures of effort and money to compare programs. Different models excelled in different areas but none was superior in all areas, and the overall interpretation of the many studies on Head Start makes the total picture exceedingly complex (Goodwin and Driscoll, 1980; Miller, 1979).

A significant problem in assessing the impact of these models was the narrowly focused range of measurement instruments that were used in most of the studies. Changes in children's cognitive development were almost always assessed, but other Head Start goals—including enhancing children's physical, social, and emotional devel-opment and having programs serve as centers of community action, coordinators of social services, and catalysts for school reform—were neglected.

And although the modification of intelligence quotient (IQ) was not even a Head Start Program goal, many programs nonetheless reported IQ changes as program effects (White and Burka, 1987). When higher IQ scores following Head Start participation were shown to decline a few years after children left the program, some observers concluded that the programs had failed entirely. Arthur Jensen's (1969) widely cited *Harvard Educational Review* article, with its clearly drawn implication that race and class differences in school performance are of genetic origin, was among the most widely read. At least partly as a response to such reports, Head Start, only a year later, found itself in a fight for survival when the Office of Management and Budget attempted to eliminate its funding. It survived, but within the political climate of the 1970s, received appropriations that did not keep pace with inflation (Condry, 1983).

The debate over Head Start took a new turn in the late 1970s when long-term positive effects on child development were reported from longitudinal studies that followed poor, primarily African-American children who had received preschool intervention and compared them with comparable groups of controls that had not been in preschool. The comparisons showed that experimental children had higher scores on intelligence tests for up to four years after attending preschool, did better in elementary school arithmetic and reading, were less likely to be placed in special education programs or remedial classes, were more likely to graduate from high school, and had higher self-esteem and higher occupational aspirations (Lazar, 1983).

In the wake of these findings, a new national consensus has emerged that Head Start is a cost-effective program that should be supported and extended. Congressional debate on Head Start appropriations are now sprinkled with references to the well-publicized outcomes of the longitudinal studies. Although at present Head Start serves fewer than one in six children who are eligible (Children's Defense Fund, 1990), it is likely that a much larger proportion of poor children will be served in the future. A bill to greatly expand Head Start funding was passed by the U.S. Congress in 1991 in which Head Start programs across the nation received increased funding enabling them to expand significantly their programs and services.

Head Start has been important to ECE in the United States for the following reasons: (1) it makes ECE the focus of national attention by investing it with the power to redeem the lives of impoverished children; (2) it generates a massive increase in research on child development and early education because social science researchers, particularly psychologists, focus on those areas in response to grant initiatives by government and foundations; (3) it builds a consensus that early education is beneficial for all children, and crucial for those from impoverished families; and (4) it effectively uses a comprehensive, family-centered approach influenced ECE generally to further involve parents in early education.

Teacher Training

It is difficult to generalize about ECE teacher training in the United States, first because the 50 states and the District of Columbia each have autonomy to set their own standards for teachers in public schools. Second, the regulation of teachers working in nonpublic facilities below the kindergarten level is typically not monitored by the state educational agency responsible for teacher certification, but instead by an administrative entity responsible for either social services or health. Standards in this underpaid and underregulated sector are frequently minimal, when they exist at all. Only 24 states require preservice training for teachers of children age 4 and younger (McCarthy, 1988).

This section begins by describing the range of certification programs defined by the various states and then discusses community college programs and the Child Development Associate (CDA) Program, which generally prepares teachers to work with preschool children in settings not affiliated with public schools.

Certification Programs

Thirty-two states and the District of Columbia have established specific ECE certification for teachers of young children in public schools. However, there is little uniformity among the states in what is meant by ECE. Some states define it as encompassing birth through age 4, others ages 5 through 9, and still others ages 3 through 8

(McCarthy, 1988). It is common for teachers prepared to teach at the elementary level to teach at the kindergarten level without any special preparatory coursework (Lamme, McMillan and Clark, 1983).

One reason for the unwillingness to reach a uniform definition of ECE is perceived administrative efficiency. Many principals of schools with kindergarten through grade 6 want to have the ability to assign their teachers to any level within their building. Shrinking elementary enrollments in the early 1980s led many of them to assign elementary teachers to kindergarten placements. There is strong resistance to certification that would divide the elementary school into smaller units, notwithstanding early childhood educators' wish that ECE certification should end at age 7 or 8 (Lamme, MacMillan and Clark, 1983).

Moreover, the distinction between primary and upper elementary education is not heavily emphasized in the United States. Frequently, elementary curricula are organized on a grade 1-to-4 or grade 1-to-6 model. The federal government's Center for Educational Statistics does not even identify primary school as a separate educational entity alongside the kindergarten, elementary, middle, junior, and senior high levels (U.S. Department of Education, 1988).

In all states, certificates are granted to those who earn a baccalaureate degree and graduate from an approved teacher training program. Recently, there has also been a well-publicized alternative certification movement that would give teacher candidates credit for life experiences and get them into classrooms more quickly, but very few teachers have been trained in this fashion (Bradley, 1990). Applicants to approved programs are screened by undergraduate grade point average—2.5 on a 4-point scale is a common cutoff—and by tests of "basic skills" that assess literacy and general knowledge. Twenty-eight states require teacher candidates to pass the written National Teacher Exam or their own exam before obtaining certification (McCarthy, 1988).

Thirteen states do not offer early childhood certification but have add-on endorsements that teachers may obtain on top of their elementary school certification. The requirements for such endorsements range from a minimum of two

courses in ECE to a maximum of 15–18 semester hours and student teaching experience (McCarthy, 1988).

Teacher certification in the United States typically involves coursework that culminates in a one-semester teaching experience. The requirements at the University of San Diego (USD) for elementary teaching are presented here, not because they are typical—there is far too much diversity in the United States for any program to be so considered—but to provide a specific example of requirements from an institution in the nation's most populous state. [Readers interested in learning about especially innovative models of ECE teacher preparation should consult Perry (1990).] USD students are required to take 24 units in education, which amounts to four semester courses and one semester-long full-time student teaching experience. The four required courses—Philosophy and Cultural Foundations, Psychological Foundations, Curriculum and Methods of Teaching, and Methods of Teaching Reading—are each three credits. Student teaching is awarded the other 12 units. Also, students are introduced to real classrooms prior to the student teaching experience through 24 required one-hour observations and two 60-hour field experiences.

Upon completion of the program and the baccalaureate degree, students are awarded California probationary certification, which allows them to teach from kindergarten to grade 6. To obtain a "clear credential," students must return within five years for 30 semester units of post-baccalaureate coursework in an approved program. Many other states have similar "fifth year" training requirements for beginning teachers.

Public school teacher training is viewed as problematical by U.S. early childhood educators for the following reasons: (1) there is little reciprocity from state to state because of the lack of commonality in definitions of ECE; (2) there is insufficient emphasis on training teachers to work with children below age 5, and even less to train them to work with those below age 3; and (3) overall, programs fail to meet the standards for training early childhood teachers that have been recommended by the NAEYC (McCarthy, 1988; NAEYC, 1982).

Community Colleges

Early childhood professionals are even less satisfied with the situation regarding teacher training below the kindergarten level. As mentioned earlier, standards at this level are created and monitored by state departments of social services or health, and not by departments of education. Where requirements for preservice training exist—and they do in only 24 states—they require much less preparation than for certification (McCarthy, 1988). California, one of the states with the most stringent standards, requires teachers to have completed 12 postsecondary units in child development and early education, the equivalent of only four courses. More typical are the 26 states that require no training or preservice experience for teachers (Kuykendall, 1990).

Because wages are so low and benefits so inadequate in community child-care jobs, such work is generally shunned by certified teachers, who may easily earn twice as much in the public school system. Child-care programs often recruit workers whose training was completed in less prestigious (but not necessarily inferior) settings than four-year colleges and universities.

Therefore, community or junior colleges that offer two-year programs leading to associate arts degrees are important in training teachers for preschool education. Such institutions usually cater to working adults, and because they are lower priced than four-year colleges, are attended by a more diverse clientele. Also, many community colleges operate child-care facilities that are centers for parental education as well as for teacher training.

The graduate of the two-year program is typically qualified to begin work as an assistant teacher in child care or as a head teacher after one year of experience. Many graduates of community colleges obtain work as aides in public school kindergarten classrooms while others become family day care providers (Liu, 1985). Because community college child development graduates are frequently from a social class that has experienced fewer career opportunities, they are, according to Liu (1985), more resigned to the low status and pay in the field than are the primarily middle-class European Americans who attend four-year programs in colleges and universities. In this way, ECE teacher training reflects and perpetuates the racial and social stratification that pervades U.S. society.

Child Development Associate Credential

Another important avenue for training preschool teachers is the Child Development Associate (CDA) Program. This comprehensive training program was established in the early 1970s and, until recently, was formally associated with the NAEYC. It is now operated by the Council for Early Childhood Professional Recognition (Phillips, 1990).

The CDA Program is based on the "whole child" nurturing philosophy of education, updated and adapted for use with adults. Although the program is competency-based, assessment is qualitative and complex and emphasizes demonstration of skill with children. The relationship between CDA advisers and candidates for the CDA credential is close and the amount and quality of feedback that candidates receive in their training exceed that teachers receive in most certification programs. The CDA Program takes pride that its graduates—80 percent of whom work in Head Start Programs (Phillips, 1990)—usually report increased self-esteem as a result of participation in the program (Perry, 1990).

Community colleges and the CDA Program are operating, however, in an increasingly difficult context. As wages for child-care workers continue to stagnate far below salaries for workers with comparable amounts of training in other fields, it becomes more difficult to attract teacher candidates. And trained teachers continue to leave the field for more lucrative areas.

Curriculum Models

The availability of federal support for curriculum planning and experimentation in the national Head Start and Follow Through Programs (initiated in 1967, it is a program to help disadvantaged children from kindergarten through grade 3) has resulted in careful elaboration of distinct ECE curriculum models in the United States. Initially, such models were pitted against each other in "horse race" research to discover which "works best." When it was shown that different models excelled on different measures, but none on all measures, the debate attenuated, although recently it has shown signs of being reignited in a more focused form (Powell, 1987).

Unfortunately, a more needed debate on what purposes curricula should work toward (Gibson, 1986)—as opposed to the philosophically unqualified and therefore unanswerable question of "what works"—has not received as much attention. This is largely because ECE has aligned itself closely with the discipline of psychology and its assumptions that "facts" can be separated from "values," and that science is the best arbiter of educational aims. Early Childhood educators in the United States do not find problematic such oft-stated goals as "to help each child to reach her or his potential" or "to help children attain universal developmental milestones" (see, e.g., DeVries and Kohlberg, 1990). With the exception of Suransky (1981), one finds in the U.S. ECE literature little sense of the post-Foucaldian awareness that supposedly neutral goals and methods of the helping professions can be aligned with larger, frequently oppressive social projects.

High/Scope Cognitively Oriented Curriculum

The High/Scope Cognitively Oriented Curriculum is perhaps the single best-known ECE curriculum model in the United States today. It developed from the Perry Preschool Project of Ypsilanti, Michigan, in 1962, to help poor African-American students become successful in public school. The organization responsible for the model—the High/Scope Educational Foundation—has been extraordinarily successful in popularizing its findings that preschool participation is of lasting benefit to program participants (Schweinhart and Weikart, 1983). Publicity about this project has been of great importance in convincing Americans that ECE is cost-effective for the amelioration of social problems (Barnett and Escobar, 1987) and undoubtedly helped in the recent successful drive to increase Head Start appropriations.

The Cognitively Oriented Curriculum is explicitly derived from the developmental theory of Jean Piaget. Like most North American early childhood educators, the model's authors' approach

to Piaget is uncritical (Woodill, 1988). They implicitly accept Piaget's notion that the end of development is scientific thinking and work to organize that habit of mind as early as possible, in a manner appropriate for the age of the child: "In a sense children are expected to learn by the scientific method of observation and inference, at a level of sophistication consistent with their development" (Weikart and Schweinhart, 1987: 255). The model does not emphasize social or emotional goals.

The High/Scope Curriculum assumes that children are active initiators of their own learning experiences, and in this regard it is similar to the "traditional" nursery school model that is now most closely associated with the Bank Street School of Education (discussed below). However, the model is also distinct because of its emphasis on cognition. A consistent daily routine is organized around students being given the opportunity to plan activities, to carry them out, and finally to think about and represent achievements (or "plan-do-review," as model authors call this cycle). Teachers strive to develop a style of questioning that extends children's thinking, yet remains naturally conversational. Cognitive areas that are emphasized include language, representation, classification, seriation, mathematics, and spatial and temporal relationships.

Although the model was initially developed for work with poor minority children in the United States, it has been adapted for handicapped children, for U.S. children whose first language is Spanish, and for use with children in South America, Africa, and India. The model's authors make the noteworthy statement that the curriculum "is essentially democratic in operation, adaptable to local culture and language, and open to use by thoughtful adults everywhere" (Weikart and Schweinhart, 1987: 255).

Bank Street Model

The Bank Street Model is more theoretically eclectic—although its advocates prefer the adjective integrative (Biber, 1984)—than the High/Scope Model, which is circumscribed by Piaget's work. The Developmental Interaction Model, as the Bank Street Model is also called, is heir to the rich progressive tradition initiated by John Dewey and elaborated by such progressive ECE pioneers as Lucy Sprague Mitchell, Carolyn Pratt, and Harriet Johnson. It is also strongly influenced by psycho-analysis, especially through the work of Susan Isaacs and Erik Erikson, and by work on cognitive development, including the work of Piaget. This complexity makes the Bank Street Model less tidy than others that are more narrowly conceived and more difficult to describe simply. Perhaps for these reasons it was dismissed as "traditional" by some in the 1960s and is still misunderstood by others as "just letting the kids play."

The Bank Street approach begins with the assumption that the major developmental sequences discussed separately by various theorists— (e.g., cognitive/linguistic, psycho-social, moral) are interdependent and must be treated as such in educational planning. Bank Street authors argue that education should be integrative and interactionist, and contrast this approach with other models that focus on "the primacy of one system rather than the other" (Biber, 1984: 288). In planning, Bank Street teachers are to consider a particular strategy's potential effects on all areas of development; they are charged to educate the "whole child."

While other programs have defined their mission simply as preparing children for success in school, Bank Street, as befits its progressive history, has bucked that trend and instead focuses on enhancing children's "current psychological adaptation" (Zimiles, 1987: 163). Its broad goals include promoting autonomy and psychological well-being by developing the child's self-concept as a learner and fostering self-expression and a sense of competence (Zimiles, 1987). Cognitive competence is considered important, not for itself, but as an essential element in children's overall development and emotional well-being. Individual rates of development are respected, and there is no push to have children reading or computing at an early age, nor to make progress in a lockstep fashion.

Like the High/Scope Model, the Bank Street Model assumes that children are active initiators who learn best through their own playful explorations of the world. They are given a wide variety of materials to explore, including blocks, clay, dress-up clothes, paint, sand and water tables, games, and books. Teacher-made and student-made materials are highly valued. Following Dewey, there is great emphasis on seeing relationships and real-world applications, and these are sought through the development of units derived from themes of interest to the children. And, as might be expected from a model influenced by psycho-analysis, there is also an emphasis on having teachers establish a safe, warm, and nurturing relationship with children. The Bank Street tradition is probably the strongest influence in U.S. ECE and most teachers, whether or not they can name the model, accept its basic assumptions.

One aspect of the tradition—the notion that schools should work to build a more just social order—has received less and less emphasis during this century. Political commitment has been replaced with an allegiance to promoting "universals" of human development. It is frequently forgotten that the model derives from earlier work by Carolyn Pratt and others, who aimed at building schools that were to be a "synthesis of art and politics" (Antler, 1987: 241) and that such work developed before most of the research in psychology—that is now cited as the model's foundation—was completed.

Direct Instruction Model

The Direct Instruction Model, a derivative of applied behavioral psychology, is without question the most notorious member of the U.S. family of early childhood curriculum models, although special educators are quite receptive to it. The model has many advocates but few of them share the commitment to "developmentally appropriate" ECE that has been elaborated by NAEYC (discussed below). On the other hand, Direct Instruction advocates are likely to view post-Froebelian ECE as naive, unscientific, and unfocused, and therefore unsuited to meet the needs of poor, disadvantaged children.

The model was created by Carl Bereiter and Siegfried Engelmann (1966) but more recently has been identified with Engelmann and Wesley Becker. Its goals are to help children meet age- or grade-established objectives in arithmetic, language, and reading. The model breaks these areas down into component skills, which are precisely specified and sequentially presented. Teaching is carefully scripted so that all students may have material presented to them in the most effective way possible. Teacher improvisation is therefore discouraged.

Rapid presentation of stimuli, positive reinforcement for correct responses, and repetition drive the program. In small groups, children respond in loud clear voices to questions presented at a rate of nine to 12 per minute (Gersten and George, 1990). The rapidity of presentation is intended to hold students' interest. Repetition is provided so that the students will gain fluency in whatever objective is being taught; up to 20 examples may be presented for some concepts. The program is structured to provide all students with successful experiences and to eliminate mistakes, which are seen to be without educational value.

Opponents of such programs argue that they are not developmental because they place inappropriate academic expectations on children before they are ready for them (Elkind, 1981). Supporters argue, however, that the program is not stressful because it allows children to achieve success, that it keeps them active while responding in small groups, and moreover, that in a full-day program there is plenty of time remaining to allow children to engage in traditional early childhood activities (Gersten and George, 1990). It is certainly true, however, that in the name of efficiency the Direct Instruction Program ignores critical goals of education in favor of a "no-frills" approach that aligns teaching with management.

Yet the behavioral approach is quite viable in a school context that is driven, increasingly, by the need to demonstrate educational progress on standardized tests (Kamii, 1990). U.S. primary education is today dominated by programs narrowly conceived to improve test scores. Increasingly, curricula are analyzed for presentation in small, sequential pieces that are taught through the use of worksheets or workbooks. And the materials themselves closely resemble the standardized achievement tests whose scores are published in U.S. newspapers to compare schools, districts, and states: they ask children to read test-like directions and to answer multiple-choice questions, thereby providing them with practice in making neatly marked answer sheets.

For example, a worksheet adopted for use at the grade-3 level in one large California city asks students to: "Read the sentence in the box. On the dotted line, write out the word with the missing letters. Now choose the letter or letters needed to spell the word correctly and fill in the bubble next to the one you choose." A typical item that follows is: "I found a ro__ on the beach." Students must fill in an answer bubble by choosing between "ck," "k," "c," and "kc," and then write the complete word on the dotted line beside the bubbles. Math, science, and social studies worksheets present knowledge in a comparably fragmented and decontextualized fashion.

"Developmentally Appropriate" Practice

The broad guidelines recently published by NAEYC as "developmentally appropriate" practice represent the consensual wisdom of the U.S. field of ECE. Age appropriateness is defined by respect for the "universal, predictable sequences of growth and change that occur in children during the first 9 years of life" (Bredekamp, 1987: 2). Individual appropriateness is said to exist when teachers respond sensitively to the "uniqueness" of each child.

The guidelines assume that play is the "primary vehicle" for children's development and also its best indicator (Bredekamp, 1987: 2). Therefore, provision and support for children's play are viewed as essential components of a quality program. Consequently, the guidelines explicitly criticize programs, such as Direct Instruction, that use scripted, formal methods to teach academic skills to young children. NAEYC believes that the curriculum should be integrated rather than focused on narrow academic goals, that it should provide children with opportunities for active exploration, and that it should be modified not only on the basis of individual differences but also so as to be sensitive to family and cultural backgrounds (Bredekamp, 1987).

Other important indicators of developmental appropriateness are the quality of the adult-child relationship, the ratio of adults to children, and group size. Adults are expected to respond quickly and sensitively to children's needs and wishes, to be openly communicative, and to be genuinely respectful of children. Adult-child ratios of one to three are recommended for infants, one to six for toddlers, one to ten for children ages 4 and 5, and one to 13 for children ages 6 to 8. Corresponding maximum group size recommendations are three infants, 12 toddlers, 20 4- and 5-year olds, and 25 6- through 8-year-olds. These figures reflect concern in the United States for implementing a highly individualized program (Tobin, Wu, and Davidson, 1989).

In 1984, in response to the absence of standards from the federal government and in an attempt to upgrade and professionalize the field of early childhood, NAEYC initiated a voluntary accreditation program based on the principles of developmentally appropriate practice. Accreditation is implemented by the National Academy of Early Childhood Programs, a division of NAEYC. Programs seeking accreditation begin by obtaining academy materials to conduct a self-study. If and when the program is ready to initiate the next step in the accreditation process, it sends the results of its study to the academy, which then arranges for a site visit by a trained "validator." The validator assesses whether the information presented to the academy is accurate. Then, based on the information in the validator's report, a three-member commission determines whether to award accreditation. Accreditation is valid for three years (*Accreditation Criteria and Procedures,* 1984).

Emerging Curricular Trends

Two international curricular movements that are of growing importance to primary education in the United States are cooperative learning approach and the whole-language approach to the development of literacy (Hollifield, 1989). Both of these movements are seen by many as having the potential to revitalize the curriculum and to restructure schools in a more democratic fashion (Edelsky, Altwerger, and Flores, 1990; Sapon-Shevin and Schniedewind, 1991).

The cooperative learning movement seeks to eliminate the typically competitive goal structure of schools by having students work together in small heterogeneous groups in which there is both individual accountability and positive interdependence. Students are responsible for themselves and for the learning of others in their group. Some of the cooperative learning models that have been popularized in the United States promote intergroup competition. The benefits of these approaches are

that they allow students to control their own learning, teach them valuable social skills, and help members of different groups (e.g., academic skill, race, gender, class) to develop supportive relationships and reduce stereotyping, even as students learn as much or more than they would have in traditionally structured classrooms (Slavin, et al., 1985).

However, some long-time cooperative learning advocates see a danger in the speed with which U.S. educators are jumping on this bandwagon. They argue that cooperative learning should be more than a new technique grafted onto the body of existing educational practice, that is, more than a new way to enable students to have more fun while completing more worksheets in less time. In the context of a society that is ideologically committed to competition, they view cooperative learning as having the potential to facilitate large-scale educational and social change. Yet they wonder whether it will be implemented as "liberatory praxis" or instead marketed and consumed as context-free "hamburger helpers" (Sapon-Shevin, 1990).

Whole language is also a hot bandwagon in the United States, as attested to by the number of school districts endorsing the approach and publishers producing books in this area (Edelsky, Altwerger, and Flores, 1990). Its basic premise is that reading and writing are meaningful activities that cannot be effectively taught in isolation from their natural social contexts and purposeful uses. The emphasis on the word "whole" helps to distinguish this approach from the "fragmented, isolated"—critical words used by whole language advocates—approach, which teaches reading through drills on language parts, such as letters, syllables, words, and grammar rules. Whole language advocates view such activities as context-poor, desocialized exercises with a misapplied focus on the form of written language rather than on its meaning and uses (Edelsky, Altwerger, and Flores, 1990).

Whole language teachers give students many opportunities to consume and create written language in a print-rich environment. At the preschool level, students frequently have stories read to them and may create newspapers by drawing pictures and dictating stories to teachers. They may also have read to them notes that were composed by parents and included in their lunch boxes. At the primary level, students are encouraged to write journals and stories and to share them with others, and to read quality literature (not basal readers) with easy and predictable content. Children's ideas and interests are considered the heart of the curriculum and therefore teachers resist the use of mass-produced materials (Schickedanz, 1986).

In the U.S., this approach is currently more compatible with preschool education than it is with primary school education, with its more narrowly academic focus. As public schools have recently and rapidly moved to incorporate whole language into their programs, they have assimilated into it older, more didactic methods of teaching, creating such oxymorons as "whole language" flash cards, pocket charts, or basal readers (Edelsky, Altwerger, and Flores, 1990). This would appear to make it more difficult for teachers to emerge as the critical "politicized professionals, working to take control of their own professional lives" that whole language advocates suggest they need to become (Edelsky, Altwerger, and Flores, 1990: 1).

Parental Involvement and Parental Education

Early childhood educators in the United States have historically viewed parental involvement in early education as important. The charity kindergarten movement of the late nineteenth century developed a comprehensive, family orientation that included parental education and the provision of many social services for urban families living in poverty. In the early twentieth century, many middle-class parents argued that all mothers, not just poor ones, should be trained in parenting skills and involved in their children's schooling (Schlossman, 1976). Their movement led to a rapid increase in membership in the National Congress of Parents and Teachers in the years after World War I. Today, in the recent wake of Head Start's family-centered approach, it is taken for granted that parental involvement is an essential component for quality early educational programs (Bronfenbrenner, 1976), although actual practices vary widely among programs.

Currently, many U.S. programs include home visits with parents. In some cases, such visits,

conducted perhaps once or twice a year, are for the purpose of establishing a link between the school and the home and for helping teachers gain a deeper understanding of their students. Other programs, especially those that describe themselves as being in the business of "early intervention," have more ambitious goals for home visits, which may be the primary, or exclusive, site of early education (see section later in this chapter). Some programs train parents to be teachers of their children (Shearer & Shearer, 1972). Others reject such a redirection of the parents' role and instead work to support the family through the facilitation of caregivers' and children's involvement in mutually satisfying interactions (Bromwich, 1981).

It is customary in the United States for preschool and primary school programs to invite parents to schools for parental evenings. Most programs hold an open house within a few months after the school year begins in September so that parents may explore their child's classroom and materials. Many invite parents to discuss educational or child developmental issues, following the presentation of a film or speaker on a specific topic. Others plan activities for parents and children to enjoy together (Honig, 1979).

One of the best developed models of parental involvement and education is the Head Start Program, which involves parents as policy makers and as participants in the classroom. Typical Head Start Programs involve parents in a decision-making capacity on advisory committees; one-half of the Head Start policy committee, for example, must be composed of currently enrolled Head Start parents (Berger, 1987). Parents are encouraged to work in the classroom and to further their education through the Child Development Associate Program (see earlier section on teacher training). Many current Head Start teachers entered the field of ECE in this way (Benson and Peters, 1988).

Many U.S. parents are highly motivated to learn more about parenting, and bookstores generally contain many books devoted to parenting issues. Indeed, since 1900, U.S. middle-class parents have been inundated with "scientific" advice on how to raise their children properly, although the precise counsel offered has shifted over time (Wrigley, 1989). The phenomenal sales of Dr. Benjamin Spock's *Baby and Child Care*, which by

1975 had already sold 20 million copies, is evidence of U.S. parents' need for advice and reassurance from experts (Zuckerman, 1975). The book's success is ironic, since its message is that parents should trust their own instincts rather than look to experts to tell them how to parent (Zuckerman, 1975).

Early Childhood Special Education

The fields of ECE and early childhood special education have evolved separately. While special educators in the United States are trained in behavioral, data-based methods of teaching, their ECE counterparts are more likely to be encouraged to use nondirective methods to stimulate discovery learning. And while the field of regular ECE is wholly committed to theory as the basis of practice, special education has remained largely atheoretical. The two groups read different authors and attend different professional meetings. Yet both areas are increasingly committed to the proposition that typical and atypical young children should be educated together for both groups' benefit. A dialogue and subsequent rapprochement are needed so that regular and special early educators may collaborate on this project. Such a dialogue would require both camps to challenge some of their basic assumptions.

Legal Mandates

In the United States, early childhood special education encompasses children from birth to age 5 who are considered "at risk" for developing, or who have been diagnosed as having, a disability. Early childhood special education has, for the most part, followed the movement of special education services for all children with disabilities. Many legal cases (e.g., *Mills v. Board of Education of the District of Columbia*, 1972; *Pennsylvania Association for Retarded Children v. Commonwealth of Pennsylvania*, 1971) and social influences (e.g., Civil Rights Movement and parental organizations) have led to legislative action mandating specific educational services.

The most significant legislation for educational services for children with disabilities in the United States is Public Law No. 94–142, entitled the Education for All Handicapped Children Act. Prior to its passage in 1975, services for these children were minimal at best and were typically provided in segregated, "handicapped only" facilities. Basic educational services for many children with disabilities were denied. Public Law No. 94–142, allowed children over age 3 to have equal access to public education. The act defines the framework for educational services as including:

• the right to a free appropriate public education for all children;

• education in the least restrictive environment (i.e., education alongside nondisabled peers to the maximum extent possible);

• nondiscriminatory testing, classification, and placement;

• due process procedures;

• parental involvement; and

• an individualized educational program (IEP) (i.e., the delineation of present level of performance, short- and long-term objectives, amount and context of integration, and designated services). (*Federal Register*, 1977).

Advocates also called for Section 504 of the Rehabilitation Act of 1973 to be applied to school-age children. Section 504 states that no individual who is disabled shall be excluded, by reason of disability, from participation or benefits, or be subjected to any discrimination in any program or activity receiving federal funds (Public Law No. 93–112, 1973). Section 504 affected educational, vocational, recreational, and welfare programs. This law resulted primarily in modifying the physical features of buildings (e.g., installing ramps and elevators, expanding doorways, lowering drinking fountains, and converting bathroom spaces) so that independent access to community buildings and services was possible for individuals with disabilities.

Besides legislation to support all people with disabilities, there are laws pertaining specifically to early childhood special education services. The Handicapped Children's Early Education Assistance Act (Public Law No. 90–583, 1973) established funds to develop and improve early childhood special education services and supported demonstration projects throughout the country. The Economic Opportunity Amendments (Public Law

No. 92–424, 1972) mandated that Head Start Programs provide services to children with disabilities who are from low-income families.

In 1986, the rights provided to school-age children through Public Law No. 94–142 were extended to include children from birth to age 5. This law—Public Law No. 99–457, The Education of the Handicapped Amendments—mandates services for preschoolers (ages 3–5) by the 1990–91 school year. In addition to providing preschool services, Public Law No. 99–457 establishes on the federal level a state grant program for services to children from birth to age 2 who are developmentally delayed or who are at risk for developmental delays. Participation in the program is optional for states. To be eligible to receive funds from the federal government to provide services, each state must have the following components in place:

• Definition of "developmentally delayed";

• Timetable for provision of services in the state;

• Multidisciplinary needs evaluation of children and families;

• Individualized family service plan (IFSP) and case management services;

• Child find and referral system;

• Public awareness plans;

• Central directory of services and resources;

• Personnel development system;

• Single line of authority in a lead agency established by the governor for administration, fiscal responsibility, resource coordination, etc.;

• Policies for working with local service providers;

• Procedures for reimbursement of funds;

• Procedural safeguards; and

• Data compilation system on programs (California IFSP Study Project, 1990).

Families

Although Public Law No. 99–457 allows federal funding and provides mandates for services, one of the most important shifts in this legislation is the requirement of a written IFSP as opposed to the IEP that is required for school-age children under Public Law No. 94–142. This is a significant change in that the focus, shifts from being child-centered (IEP) to being family centered (IFSP). Specifically, the IFSP must include the following:

• A statement of the child's present level of functioning in the speech/language, cognition, motor, self-help, and psychological areas;

• A statement of the family's strengths and needs that relate to stimulating the child's development;

• A statement of major outcomes expected to be achieved by the child's family;

• The criteria, procedures, and timelines for determining progress;

• The specific early intervention services necessary to meet the needs of the child and family;

• The projected dates for initiation of these services and their expected duration;

• The name of the case manager; and

• Procedures for transition from early intervention into the preschool program (Lowenthal, 1988: 58).

The focus on the family is expanded to include such designated services as parent training and counseling, and case management services involving the parents as well as the children. The IFSP is intended not only to provide services and instruction to families but to ensure parental input and greater parent-professional collaboration. The importance of the family as a unique entity is stressed, encouraging professionals to become familiar with the life-styles, values, culture, supports, resources, interests, and priorities of each family. The stated goal is not to change and mold families into what they "should be," but rather to understand and work with them, nonjudgmentally, as they are. The intent is to maximize support and collaboration so that a long-term relationship is founded that will enhance the development of the child with a disability.

One challenge to increasing family involvement is the balance professionals must maintain in trying to supportively involve parents and family members without overburdening them. When families are striving for basic emotional and physical survival, professionals unreasonably expect them to sacrifice their overall needs for the sake of early education (Turnbull and Turnbull, 1990). Turnbull and Turnbull (1990) suggest that there be some guidelines for involving families in early childhood services, including:

• making the curriculum relevant to the individual child, family, peers, and community;

• using parents as full partners for educational planning and decision making;

• systematizing communication between family and professionals; and

• incorporating the child's skill development into the family's typical daily routines (p.114).

Early interventionists work with families to gain a better understanding of the individual family system. By doing so, service providers hope to prevent the "burnout" parents often experience as the child with a disability grows older and their energy has been depleted.

Various models of providing services that include families in early intervention programs have been demonstrated and reviewed by the California IFSP Study Project (1990). Although the *multi-agency approach* is similar to existing early intervention programs, it incorporates an additional coordinating group for community planning and implementation. This approach supports multiple points of entry (e.g., school district, case management agency, medical facility) into the early intervention system with a highly coordinated network of referrals, placement, and follow-up. The approach encourages flexibility and ongoing communication between the myriad of local level service providers and case managers.

The *inter-agency approach* channels entry into the early intervention system through a local interagency coordinating council. When an agency receives a referral, it then becomes responsible for involving other relevant service providers in the IFSP process. The council is then responsible for developing, implementing, and monitoring service delivery systems and local resources for that family. The council maintains responsibility for facilitating the involvement of all appropriate agencies and individuals in the IFSP.

The *trans-agency approach* develops a community-based transagency team, which includes state agencies and parental facilitators representing the local community. This team serves as the consistent single point of entry for early intervention services and remains the coordinating body in that community as well as in facilitating the IFSP process.

All of these approaches have demonstrated success in facilitating the IFSP and coordinating services effectively. Regardless of the way the services are coordinated, however, each approach emphasizes the active involvement of parents and caretakers in the decision-making process.

Services for families reflect a wide range of needs. Common areas of service provided to families have been identified as: sharing general information, support, and/or counseling; obtaining specific skills or information through training; being assisted with parent-child interactions, and becoming familiar with community resources (Hanson and Lynch, 1989). Others have outlined the strategies of parental intervention (Hanson and Krenz, 1986). They view the process as involving the steps of alerting (i.e., calling attention to certain issues or concerns), guiding (i.e., providing information, modeling, etc.), practicing (i.e., trying out the strategies), and assessing (i.e., analyzing, receiving feedback). The sequential incorporation of these strategies facilitates active parental involvement with their child and necessitates a working relationship between parents and professionals. Again, this working relationship is considered successful only if both parties share an understanding of the child's needs and goals as a member of the family.

Program Philosophical Bases

There are three primary models of early intervention service delivery: the medical model, the developmental model, and the functional model. The *medical model* is typically experienced first by families. In it, the key players and decision makers are physicians, therapists, and nurses. The model focuses on the prevention of additional health impairments and the "cure" of the disabling condition. Although essential in emergencies, the medical model is less effective for educational purposes. In the earlier history of early intervention programs, the medical field took the lead. Now, it is more commonly recognized that the medical field and those making medical decisions are limited in their ability to develop and provide comprehensive services that extend beyond short-term survival needs. Service providers who follow non-medical-model philosophies seek physicians and relevant medical professionals as representatives and solicit input on planning teams. However, they take a more comprehensive approach than do medical workers to the needs of children and families.

The *developmental model* is based on an understanding of normal child development and assumes that children will learn when they are developmentally ready to learn (Ackerman and Moore, 1976). Programs reflecting the developmental model are less teacher-directed and facilitate the child's own physical, cognitive, and social-emotional development through play, peer interactions, problem solving, and exposure to diverse activities. A developmental program looks much like any typical early childhood program and includes activity centers and emphasis on child-initiated activity. Although this popular model has demonstrated positive impacts on the development of young children with mild disabilities as well as those who are considered "at risk," for developing mild disabilities effectiveness of the developmental model for children with more moderate to severe disabilities is unclear.

The *functional model* (also referred to as the ecological model) was developed and implemented with children who have severe disabilities. It has been elaborated by Lou Brown and his colleagues at the University of Wisconsin, Madison. Because children with severe disabilities learn at a much slower rate and have difficulty generalizing information across settings, the model's educational focus is on teaching functional skills that children would use in their current or future daily routines. Functional skills can be determined by asking the question, "If the child is not able to do this task by herself, will someone else have to do it for her?" (Brown, et al., 1979). For example, if a child is asked to put pegs in a peg board and does not do it, no one else would have to do it for her, therefore putting pegs in a peg board is not considered a functional skill. However, if a child is not able to feed or dress herself, someone would have to do that for her, therefore self-feeding and self-dressing are functional skills and would be taught in this model. This model considers the current and subsequent environments of children with disabilities and focuses on vocational, domestic, recreational, leisure, and community life domains

(Brown, et al., 1979). Infused into these curricular areas are the basic skills of communication, motor, academic, and social competence (Falvey, 1989).

Although the functional model was developed for use with older school-age children and adolescents, it was quickly adopted by early interventionists. The concern about using the functional model with very young children is that it circumvents natural development in favor of structured tasks. Currently, early intervention programs are seeking to blend the developmental and functional models. To offer an effective program for children with disabilities it is vital that early interventionists have a strong basis of knowledge in child development, specific disabilities, diverse cultural backgrounds, and family involvement.

In practice, early childhood special education programs in the United States are either center-based or home-based, and either child-oriented or parent-oriented (Thurman and Widerstrom, 1985). Infant services tend to be more home-based and parent-oriented, allowing learning for the parent and child to occur in the natural environment of the home in the most individualized manner. Frequently home-based programs allow a teacher to spend several hours a week in the family's home providing information and hands-on training to family members. From ages 3 to 6, services become primarily center-based with a greater orientation toward the child. Although there are some programs that strictly adhere to certain models or methods of service delivery, most programs attempt to provide the broadest range of services so that the needs of families and children can be met. For example, most center-based programs are scheduled so that teachers also have the opportunity to work in the home with parents and children.

Integration

Historically, children with disabilities were provided services in segregated or "handicapped only" environments. However, the value of integrating children who have disabilities into environments that include peers of the same age who are nondisabled is great. The benefits for children with disabilities include interaction and friendships with peers of the same age, normalized activities and greater opportunities to participate in the community, higher expectations, and richer environments. For children without disabilities, the benefits include an appreciation of individual differences, diverse friendships, and cooperative learning opportunities.

Some families (Turnbull and Turnbull, 1990) and professionals (Stainback and Stainback, 1990; Lipsky and Gartner, 1989) believe that the potential of children and adults with disabilities can never be met unless they are involved in meaningful, ongoing interactions and activities with nondisabled peers. Public Law No. 94–142 requires educational services for children with disabilities to be provided alongside nondisabled peers to the maximum extent possible. This enables regular and special educators and administrators to plan and deliver services in a collaborative manner to promote the most effective educational services for all students.

Hanson and Lynch (1989), however, caution against indiscriminate full integration of infants and toddlers with disabilities. They acknowledge that large segregated institutional settings are of no benefit to young children, and argue instead for home or day care educational settings. However, they caution that if the developmental philosophy is followed, children with and without disabilities may not benefit from exposure to each other due to differing developmental levels. Also, they feel that for some parents of infants or toddlers with disabilities, seeing other children without disabilities is "a source of sadness" (p. 41). Hanson and Hanline (1989), on the other hand, stress the importance of play and social interaction for infants and toddlers. Some benefits of integration for young children include the enhancement of communication, attention, social behavior, and learning skills (Hanson and Hanline, 1989). Parental needs and preferences should be considered along with the needs and preferences of the child when making placement decisions.

Best Practice Components

Over the past ten years, most of the focus in early childhood special education has been on isolated interventions as opposed to model program development. Public Law No. 99–457 has brought renewed attention to the development of early childhood special education programs. Although the passage of the law has provided mandates and funding for service provision, the specific program components have yet to be delineated. There are, however, current best-practice guidelines and optimal program components identified in the literature and in some demonstration programs.

Guidelines for best practices as identified by McDonnell and Hardman (1988) include services for children with disabilities that are integrated, comprehensive, normalized, adaptable, peer and family-referenced, and outcome-based. These guidelines suggest that all out-of-home intervention be provided in generic early childhood service programs. Pawl (1990) emphasizes the important relationship between providing child-care services and providing early intervention services. By supporting existing child-care services with special education expertise all children can benefit, and community support for all families can be established.

Hanson and Lynch (1989) suggest that the components of an optimal early childhood intervention model program be as follows:

• Program philosophy that is theoretically based and procedurally well defined.

• Staff who have been well trained and have the educational expertise as well as the personal sensitivity to work effectively with children and families.

• Identification and referral processes that are incorporated across all community resources.

• Assessment procedures that identify the strengths and needs of children and their families.

• Curriculum that is individualized and recognizes developmental sequences as functional goals, objectives, and activities.

• Family involvement that reflects each family's culture, needs, and priorities, with the goal of family involvement being empowerment.

• Transition services, which enable families and service providers to plan for future environments, and ongoing support from school and community resources.

• Provision for the health and safety of every child and, in addition, the family members and the service providers. Beyond standard safety factors, other considerations and procedures may be necessary for specific health issues, such as infections caused by cytomegalovirus (CMV), acquired immune deficiency syndrome (AIDS), or rubella.

• Program administration and management that ensure the effectiveness and efficiency of the program.

• Program evaluation and outcome measures to assure that what is supposed to be done is being done.

Implementation of these components establishes the foundation for providing effective early childhood special education services. Within each of these components it is necessary to incorporate the current best practices in instructional methodology, communication strategies, curriculum development, data collection and analysis, and collaboration.

Teacher Credentialing

The U.S. federal government does not require special credentials for early childhood special education. Teachers are required to obtain either a learning handicapped, severely handicapped, or other specialist credential. These specialist credentials focus on providing special education services to school-age children but rarely provide specific information in the area of early childhood. Many colleges and universities offer an emphasis or master's degree program in early childhood special education, which is acquired in addition to the basic special education credential.

Independent of the federal governmental regulations, 25 states now require some type of license, approval, certificate, or credential for early childhood specialists. But because there is no reciprocity between states, a certificate obtained in one state is not honored in another.

Part of the reason for the lack of credential requirements, as with the regular early childhood credential, is that school officials want the freedom to place teachers in any age category and would be more restricted by an early childhood credential. Another reason is that early childhood special educators have not agreed on a set of competencies or professional standards. The Early Childhood Education Division of the Council of Exceptional Children has developed professional standards that are separate for children from birth to age 3 and ages 3 to 6. These competencies differ from standard special education requirements in that they include a knowledge of normal child development, typical early childhood activities and curriculum, and extensive cooperation and collaboration with families. Teachers are expected to have the knowledge and ability to use play-based activities to foster skill-building, as opposed to the structured activities used in more traditional educational settings. With the passage of Public Law No. 99–457, there may be renewed discussion and greater support for a standard early childhood special education credential.

Current Issues

The increased national attention now focused on ECE has increased the salience of many contested issues facing the field. These are currently being played out within the larger social context of concerns in the United States over deteriorating conditions for families and children; the troubled state of the economy (especially the size of the budget deficit and the unfavorable balance of trade); the state of the educational system, which is now widely viewed as incapable of adequately preparing students for the future; and the changing demographics of the country's young (increasingly poor and minority) in a climate of growing racial intolerance and tension. The debate over the issues is framed by a conviction by most Americans that ECE can be a partial solution to these problems.

Future of the Kindergarten and Preschool

Although kindergarten is still voluntary in most states, it is now attended by 93 percent of U.S. children (Hollifield, 1989). However, the identity of the kindergarten, which had until recently maintained its distinctness from the rest of the elementary school, is now being eroded and is even in danger of disappearing (Walsh, 1989). The kindergarten curriculum is becoming more centralized (controlled by giant publishing firms); more narrowly academically focused; and more driven by pressures for accountability, as defined by scores on standardized tests. Elementary school principals freely admit that today's kindergarten resembles the grade 1 of yesteryear (Hollifield, 1989; Walsh, 1989), even as the kindergarten day is being extended from a one-half day to a full day in many parts of the country (Olsen and Zigler, 1989).

Associated with the erosion of kindergarten has been the use of the Gesell School Readiness Screening Test to identify children who are not "mature enough" to enter kindergarten, and the retention of children who have completed kindergarten but who are not considered to have made enough progress to justify promoting them to grade 1. The Gesell test is now widely condemned within the ECE profession because it has been shown to be technically inadequate (Meisels, 1987) and because, in any case, early child educators would prefer that kindergartens remain flexible enough to meet the needs of developmentally diverse children (Willer and Bredekamp, 1990). The screening is symptomatic of increased academic pressures on the kindergarten, as are rising kindergarten retention rates. Nonpromotion helps districts appear to have high standards even though retention has been shown to be unhelpful to children (Holmes and Matthews, 1984).

A significant problem associated with these trends is that they make it more difficult for early childhood programs to move toward the integration of handicapped young children. Teachers and administrators under pressure to standardize curricula and pupils will understandably resist the inclusion of students who will make the achievement of those goals more difficult. And if handicapped children are included in such rigid, nonindividualized programs, it will not be to the children's benefit.

Academic pressures are being extended down to preschools now as well. If children are not ready for formal academic instruction in kindergarten, some argue that they should have more solid preparation at earlier levels of schooling. Elementary school practices could become more widely implemented in preschools as public schools increasingly expand into this area. By 1983, 5.7 million preprimary children were enrolled in public school programs often targeted at "high risk" or special needs children (Hollifield, 1989). And once aligned with public schools, preschools are hostage to the need to raise students' scores on standardized tests, a concern, which has increasingly come to drive U.S. schooling (Kamii, 1990). Despite educators' opposition to this trend, it is likely to continue as long as merit pay increases for principals and school district superintendents are based on standardized tests scores.

Child-Care Crisis

The mounting U.S. crisis in child care is partly responsible for making the early years "far more precarious and less safe for millions of America's children" (Johnson, 1989: 10) than they have been previously. Child-care workers, by their low wages, subsidize child-care costs. They are a demoralized group whose yearly turnover rate now stands at an astonishing 41 percent (Daniel, 1990). In the words of one director, child care in the United States is now "an industry drowning" (Daniel, 1990: 23).

The burden falls most heavily on the poor, who in the absence of an adequate number of sliding scale positions, are asked to pay substantially the same rates as affluent parents who can afford much more. Instead, many place their children in "unlicensed, unregulated, and underground" family day care homes (Ayers, 1989: 40). Others leave their children to care for themselves. And the number of families in this predicament continues to grow. Twelve and one-half million, or 20 percent of U.S. children, now live in families whose incomes are below the federal poverty line (Meisler and Fulwood, 1990).

The child-care crisis is especially onerous for parents of infants. It is predicted that by 2000, the mothers of four out of five infants below age 1 will be working (Krause-Eheart and Leavitt, 1989). Because there are presently so few facilities to care for infants, the great majority spend their time in family day care homes, many of which are part of the underpaid, unregulated network already alluded to.

Developmentally Appropriate Practice

Quality programming, as defined by U.S. early educators, is rooted in the educational tradition extending from Rousseau to Froebel. In the 1980s, the profession, through NAEYC, did much to clearly present (and promote) the consensual wisdom of the field (Bredekamp, 1987). However, ECE in the United States has not yet begun to address the problems that inhere in its claim that its recommendations for best practice unproblematically spring from universally applicable stages of human development.

Any theory of development must justify the shift from describing what "is" to prescribing what "ought to be" (Bernstein, 1986), and that movement is inescapably value laden and political. The study of human development is best conceived of as a "policy science" (Bruner, 1986: 20) that demands explicit definition of the value presuppositions that underlie recommendations for practice. Otherwise, theorists succumb to the "dangers of universalizing and hypostatizing what may only be well entrenched cultural ideals . . . for theories of moral and social development have been ethnocentric, logocentric, and phallocentric" (Bernstein, 1986: 9).

Many aspects of "developmentally appropriate" teaching in the United States, such as adults being intensely communicative with young children, intervening in children's fights, maintaining relatively small groups and high adult-child ratios—practices that promote individualism—are derived from a sociocultural agenda, and not, as it is implied, objective truths about human development (see, e.g., Gardner, 1989; Tobin, Yu, and Davidson, 1989). Many special educators doubt that "de-velopmental" practice alone will best serve some special populations.

It is no longer adequate to claim that any particular version of theory and practice is universal and timeless. Workers in ECE should be encouraged to develop a critical stance toward the developmental research that they now cite as if it were synthesized outside of the personal histories and social contexts of the theorists with whom it is identified (Woodill, 1988). As Bruner (1986) pointed out, "[W]ithout explicit value presuppositions, we will fall into the habit of forming implicit ones and lose such power as we might have either in furthering or opposing the values of the culture in which we find ourselves" (p. 27). Because early educators in the United States now appear to be engaged in a climactic struggle over the future of early education, they would do well to break that habit.

References

Ackerman, P. R., Jr., & Moore, M. G. (1976). Delivery of educational services to preschool handicapped children. In T. Tjossem (Ed.), *Intervention strategies for high-risk infants and young children* (pp. 669–88). Baltimore: University Park Press.

Allen, A. T. (1988). "Let us live with our children": Kindergarten movements in Germany and the United States, 1840–1914. *History of Education Quarterly, 28,* 23–48.

Antler, J. (1987). *Lucy Sprague Mitchell: The making of a modern woman.* New Haven, CN: Yale University.

Ayers, W. (1989). *The good preschool teacher.* New York: Teachers College Press.

Barnett, W. S., & Escobar, C. M. (1987). The economics of early educational intervention: A review. *Review of Educational Research, 57,* 387–414.

Benson, M. S., & Peters, D. L. (1988). The child development associate: Competence, training, and professionalism. *Early Development and Care, 38,* 57–68.

Bereiter, C., & Engelmann, S. (1966). *Teaching disadvantaged children in the preschool.* Englewood Cliffs, NJ: Prentice-Hall.

Berger, E. H. (1987). *Parents as partners in education.* Columbus, OH: Merrill.

Bernstein, R. J. (1986). The question of moral and social development. In L. Cirillo & S. Wapner (Eds.), *Value presuppositions in theories of human development* (pp. 1–18). Hillsdale, NJ: Lawrence Erlbaum Associates.

Biber, B. (1977). Cognition in historical perspective. In B. Spodek & H. Walberg (Eds.), *Early childhood education: Insights and issues* (pp. 41–64). Berkeley, CA: McCutchan.

———. (1979). Introduction. In E. Zigler & J. Valentine (Eds.), *Project Head Start* (pp. 155–61). New York: Free Press.

———. (1984). *Early education and psychological development.* New Haven, CN: Yale University.

Bradley, A. (1990, June 20). Despite growth of alternative routes, few teachers have earned credentials. *Education Week,* p. 9.

Bredekamp, S. (Ed.). (1987). *Developmentally appropriate practice in early childhood programs serving children from birth through age 8.* Washington, DC: National Association for the Education of Young Children.

Bromwich, R. (1981). *Working with parents and infants: An interactional approach.* Baltimore: University Park Press.

Bronfenbrenner, U. (1976). Is early intervention effective? Facts and principles of early intervention: a summary. In A. M. Clarke & A. D. B. Clarke (Eds.), *Early experience: Myth and evidence* (pp. 247–56). New York: Free Press.

Brown, L., Branston, M. B., Hamre-Nietupski, S., Pumpian, I., Certo, N., & Gruenwald, L. (1979). A strategy for developing chronological age-appropriate and functional curricular content for severely handicapped adolescents and young adults. *The Journal of Special Education, 13,* 81–90.

Brown, L., Branston-McLean, M., Baumgart, D., Vincent, L., Falvey, M., & Schroeder, J. (1979). Using the characteristics of current and subsequent least restrictive environments in the development of curricular content for severely handicapped students. *AAESPA Review, 4,* 407–24.

Bruner, J. (1986). Value presupposition of developmental theory. In L. Cirillo & S. Wapner (Eds.), *Value presuppositions in theories of human development* (pp. 19–28). Hillsdale, NJ: Lawrence Erlbaum Associates.

California IFSP Study Project (1990). *Implementing individualized family service plans in California: Final report.* San Diego, CA: San Diego State University, Department of Special Education.

Children's Defense Fund (1990). *Children 1990: A report card, briefing book, and action primer.* Washington, DC: Author.

Condry, S. (1983). History and background of preschool intervention programs and the consortium for longitudinal studies. In Consortium for Longitudinal Studies (Ed.), *As the twig is bent . . . Lasting effects of preschool programs* (pp. 1–31). Hillsdale, NJ: Lawrence Erlbaum Associates.

Cooke, R. E. (1979). Introduction. In E. Zigler & J. Valentine (Eds.), *Project Head Start* (pp. xxiii–xxvi). New York: Free Press.

Daniel, J. (1990). Child care: An endangered industry. *Young Children, 45*(4), 23–26.

Day, B. D. (1988). What's happening in early childhood programs across the United States? In C. Warger (Ed.), *A resource guide to public school early childhood programs* (pp. 3–31). Alexandria, VA: Association for Supervision and Curriculum Development.

DeVries, R., & Kohlberg, L. (1990). *Constructivist early education: Overview and comparison with other programs.* Washington, DC: National Association for the Education of Young Children.

Edelsky, C., Altwerger, B., & Flores, B. (1990). *Whole language: What's the difference?* Portsmouth, NH: Heinemann.

Elkind, D. (1981). *The hurried child: Growing up too fast too soon.* Reading, MA: Addison-Wesley.

Falvey, M. A. (1989). *Community-based curriculum: Instructional strategies for students with severe handicaps* (2nd ed.). Baltimore, MD: Paul H. Brookes.

Federal Register. (1977, Aug. 23). Education of handicapped children: Implementation of Part B of EHA, Public Law No. 94–142, Education for All Handicapped Children Act of 1975. Washington, DC: U.S. Department of Education.

Forest, I. (1927). *Preschool education: A historical and critical study.* New York: Macmillan.

Friedan, B. (1963). *The feminine mystique.* New York: Dell.

Gardner, H. (1989). *To open minds: Chinese clues to the dilemma of contemporary education.* New York: Basic Books.

Gersten, R. , & George, N. (1990). Teaching reading and mathematics to at-risk students in kindergarten: What we have learned from field research. In C. Seefeldt (Ed.), *Continuing issues in early childhood education* (pp. 245–59). Columbus, OH: Merrill.

Gibson, R. (1986). *Critical theory and education.* London: Hodder & Staughton.

Goodman, K. S., Shannon, P., Freeman, Y. S., & Murphy, S. (1988). *Report card on basal readers.* Katonah, NY: Richard C. Owen.

Goodwin, W. L., & Driscoll, L. A. (1980). *Handbook for measurement and evaluation in early childhood education.* San Francisco: Jossey-Bass.

Gray, S. W., Ramsey, B. K., Klaus, R. A., & Forrester, B. J. (1966). *Before first grade.* New York: Teachers College Press.

Hanson, M. J., & Hanline, M. F. (1989). Integration options for the very young. In R. Gaylord-Ross (Ed.), *Integration strategies for students with handicaps.* Baltimore, MD: Paul H. Brookes.

Hanson, M. J., & Krenz, M. S. (1986). *Supporting parent-child interactions: A guide for early intervention program personnel.* San Francisco: San Francisco State University, Department of Special Education.

Hanson, M. J., & Lynch, E. W. (1989). *Early intervention: implementing child and family services for infants and toddlers who are at risk or disabled.* Austin, TX: Pro-Ed.

Hollifield, J. (1989). *Children learning in groups and other trends in elementary and early childhood education.* Urbana, IL: ERIC Clearinghouse on Elementary and Early Childhood Education.

Holmes, C. T., & Matthews, K. M. (1984). The effects of nonpromotion on elementary and junior high school students: A meta-analysis. *Review of Educational Research, 54,* 225–36.

Honig, A. S. (1979). *Parent involvement in early education.* Washington, DC: National Association for the Education of Young Children.

Jensen, A. R. (1969). How much can we boost I.Q. and scholastic achievement? *Harvard Educational Review, 39,* 1–123.

Johnson, J. (1989, Oct. 2). Childhood is not safe for most children, Congress is warned. *New York Times* (National Edition), p. A10.

Kagan, S. L., & Zigler, E. F. (Eds.). (1987). *Early schooling: The national debate.* New Haven, CN: Yale University.

Kamii, C. (Ed.). (1990). *Achievement testing in the early grades: The games grown-ups play.* Washington, DC: National Association for the Education of Young Children.

Kilpatrick, W. H. (1916). *Froebel's kindergarten principles.* New York: Macmillan.

Kuykendall, J. (1990). Child development: Directors shouldn't leave home without it. *Young Children, 45*(5), 47–50.

Krause-Eheart, B., & Leavitt, R. L. (1989). Family day care: Discrepancies between intended and observed caregiving practices. *Early Childhood Research Quarterly, 4,* 145–62.

Lamme, L. L., McMillan, M. R., & Clark, B. H. (1983). Early childhood teacher certification: A national survey. *Journal of Teacher Education, 34,* 44–47.

Lazar, I. (1983). Discussion and implications of the findings. In Consortium for Longitudinal Studies (Ed.), *As the twig is bent . . . Lasting effects of preschool programs* (pp. 461–66). Hillsdale, NJ: Lawrence Erlbaum Associates.

Lipsky, D. K. & Gartner, A. (1989). *Beyond separate education: Quality education for all.* Baltimore, MD: Paul H. Brookes.

Liu, K. C. (1985). Child care training in community and junior colleges. (ERIC Document Reproduction Service No. ED 306 017).

Lowenthal, B. (1988). United States Public Law 99–457: An ounce of prevention. *Exceptional Child, 35*(1), 57–60.

McCarthy, J. (1988). *State certification of early childhood teachers: An analysis of the 50 states and the District of Columbia.* Washington, DC: National Association for the Education of Young Children.

McDonnell, A., & Hardman, M. (1988). A synthesis of "best practice" guidelines for early childhood services. *Journal of the Division for Early Childhood, 12,* 328–41.

Meisels, S. J. (1987). Uses and abuses of developmental screening and school readiness testing. *Young Children, 42*(2), 4–6.

Meisler, S., & Fulwood, S. (1990, July 15). Economic gap bodes ill for U.S. *Los Angeles Times,* pp. A1, A22–23.

Miller, L. (1979). Development of curriculum models in Head

Start. In E. Zigler & J. Valentine (Eds.), *Project Head Start: A legacy of the War on Poverty* (pp. 195–220). New York: Free Press.

Mills v. *Board of Education of the District of Columbia*, 348 F. Supp. 866 (D.D.C. 1972).

National Association for the Education of Young Children (1982). *Early Childhood Teacher Education Guidelines for Four- and Five-Year Programs*. Washington, DC: National Association for the Education of Young Children.

———. (1984). *Accreditation Criteria and Procedures*. Washington, DC: Author.

Olsen, D., & Zigler, E. (1989). An assessment of the all-day kindergarten movement. *Early Childhood Research Quarterly, 4*, 167–86.

Pawl, J. H. (1990). Infants in day care: Reflections on experiences, expectations, and relationships. *Zero to Three, 10*(3), 1–6.

Pennsylvania Association for Retarded Children (PARC) v. Commonwealth of Pennsylvania, Civil Action No. 71–42 (1971).

Perry, G. (1990). Alternative modes of teacher preparation. In C. Seefeldt (Ed.), *Continuing issues in early childhood education* (pp. 173–200). Columbus, OH: Merrill.

Phillips, C. B. (1990). The child development associate program: Entering a new era. *Young Children, 45*(3), 24–27.

Phillips, D., & Zigler, E. (1987). The checkered history of federal child care regulation. In E. Z. Rothkopf (Ed.), *Review of Research in Education* (Vol. 14) (pp. 3–41). Washington, DC: American Educational Research Association.

Powell, D. R. (1987). Comparing preschool curricula and practices: The state of research. In S. L. Kagan & E. F. Zigler (Eds.), *Early schooling: The national debate* (pp. 190–211). New Haven, CN: Yale University.

Public law no. 90–583, Handicapped children's early education assistance act. (1973). Washington, DC: U.S. Department of Education.

Public law no. 92–424, Economic opportunity amendments. (1972). Washington, DC: U.S. Department of Education.

Public law no. 93–112, Rehabilitation act of 1973, section 504. (1973). Washington, DC: U.S. Department of Rehabilitation Services.

Public law no. 94–142, The education for all handicapped children act of 1975. (1975). Washington, DC: U.S. Department of Education.

Public law no. 99–457, The education of the handicapped act amendments of 1986. (1986). Washington, DC: U.S. Department of Education.

Ross, E. D. (1976). *The kindergarten crusade: The establishment of preschool education in the United States*. Athens, OH: Ohio University.

Sapon-Shevin, M. (1990, April). Cooperative learning: Liberatory praxis or hamburger helper? How we collude in our own disempowerment. Paper presented at the meeting of the American Educational Research Association, Boston.

Sapon-Shevin, M., & Schniedewind, N. (1991). Cooperative learning as empowering pedagogy. In C. Sleeter (Ed.), *Empowerment through multicultural education*. Albany, NY: State University of New York.

Scarr, S., & Weinberg, R. A. (1986). The early childhood enterprise: Care and education of the young. *American Psychologist 41*, 1140–46.

Schickedanz, J. A. (1986). *More Than the ABCs: The early stages of reading and writing*. Washington, DC: National Association for the Education of Young Children.

Schlossman, S. L. (1976). Before Home Start: Notes toward a history of parent education in America, 1897–1929. *Harvard Educational Review, 46*, 436–67.

Schweinhart, L. J. & Weikart, D. (1983). The effects of the Perry Preschool Program on youths through age 15—A summary. In Consortium for Longitudinal Studies (Ed.), *As the twig is bent . . . Lasting effects of preschool programs* (pp. 71–101). Hillsdale, NJ: Lawrence Erlbaum Associates.

Shapiro, M. S. (1983). *Child's garden: The kindergarten movement from Froebel to Dewey*. University Park, PA: Pennsylvania State University.

Shearer, M., & Shearer, D. (1972). The Portage Project: A model for early childhood education. *Exceptional Children, 36*, 210–17.

Slavin, R. E., et al. (Eds.). (1985). *Learning to cooperate, cooperating to learn*. New York: Plenum.

Solomon, B. (1956). *Ancestors and immigrants: A changing New England tradition*. Cambridge: Harvard University.

Stainback, W. & Stainback, S. (1990). *Support networks for inclusive schooling: Interdependent integrated education*. Baltimore, MD: Paul H. Brookes.

Steinfels, M. (1973). *Who's minding the children: The history and politics of day care in America*. New York: Simon & Schuster.

Suransky, V. P. (1981). *The erosion of childhood*. Chicago: University of Chicago.

Thurman, S. K., & Widerstrom, A. H. (1985). *Young children with special needs: A developmental and ecological approach*. Boston, MA: Allyn & Bacon.

Tobin, J. J., Wu, D. Y. H., & Davidson, D. H. (1989). *Preschool in three cultures*. New Haven, CN: Yale University.

Turnbull, A. P., & Turnbull, H. R. (1990). *Families, professionals, and exceptionality: A special partnership* (2nd ed.). Columbus, OH: Merrill.

U. S. Department of Education (1988). *Digest of Educational Statistics 1988*. Washington, DC: U.S. Government Printing Office.

Walsh, D. J. (1989). Changes in kindergarten: Why here? Why now? *Early Childhood Research Quarterly, 4*, 377–91.

Weikart, D. P., Rogers, L., Adcock, C., & McClelland, D. (1971). *The cognitively oriented curriculum*. Urbana, IL: University of Illinois.

Weikart, D. P., & Schweinhart, L. J. (1987). The high scope cognitively oriented curriculum in early education. In J. L. Roopnarine & J. E. Johnson (Eds.), *Approaches to early childhood education* (pp. 253–68). Columbus, OH: Merrill.

White, S., & Burka, S. L. (1987). Early education: Programs, traditions, and policies. In Ernst Z. Rothkopf (Ed.), *Review of Research in Education* (Vol. 14) (pp. 43–91). Washington, DC: American Educational Research Association.

Wiebe, R. H. (1967). *The search for order, 1877–1920*. New York: Hill & Wang.

Willer, B., & Bredekamp, S. (1990). Redefining readiness: An essential requisite for educational reform. *Young Children, 45*(5), 22–25.

Woodill, G. (1988). Influences on the development of Piaget's early thought. *Canadian Children, 13*, 1–16.

Wrigley, J. (1989). Do young children need intellectual stimulation? Experts' advice to parents, 1900–1985. *History of Education Quarterly, 29*, 41–75.

Zenderland, L. (1988). Education, evangelism, and the origin of clinical psychology: The child-study legacy. *Journal of the History of the Behavioral Sciences, 24*, 152–65.

Zimiles, H. (1987). The Bank Street approach. In J. L. Roopnarine & J. E. Johnson (Eds.), *Approaches to early childhood education* (pp. 163–78). Columbus, OH: Merrill.

Zuckerman, M. (1975). Dr. Spock: The confidence man. In C. E. Rosenberg (Ed.), *The family in history* (pp. 179–207). Philadelphia: University of Pennsylvania.

EARLY CHILDHOOD EDUCATION IN THE YEMEN REPUBLIC

• • • • • • • • • • • ◆ • • • • • • • • •

Azza Ghanem, Amat Al-Razzak A. Hummed Al Hawri,
Waheeba Al-Fakih, and Mohammed A. Al-Soofi
Sana'a University
Sana'a, Yemen Arab Republic

The Yemen Arab Republic (YAR) has undergone many changes in the almost 30 years since the Republic replaced the monarchy in 1962. The change in the governmental and political structures led to the espousal of new philosophies which were progressive, humanitarian, and developmental. It was realized that education may hold an answer for some of the countries problems. Illiteracy, however, remains a problem, especially among women. A 1982 report estimated that while 75.8 percent of males were illiterate, the figure was 98 percent for females.[1] More recently, this figure has been supported by Amran (1988).[2]

Thus, since the revolution, primary basic education has been given priority. The population census of 1986 indicated that the total YAR population was 9.25 million with a male-female ratio of 97:100 (which includes one million men working abroad).[3] The average family size increased from 5.1 in 1975 to 5.7 in 1986. Most important for educational planning is that currently 20 percent of the population are under age 5, and nearly 50 percent are under age 14.[4] The YAR therefore has a large proportion of young people in need of educational services.

The YAR covers an area of 200,000 square kilometers[5] and is divided into four major physical geographical zones: the coastal lowlands that extend along the length of the country bordering the Red Sea, the middle plateau characterized by rugged landscape and valleys, the high central mountainous plateau, and the eastern, semi-desert, sparsely populated escarpment. This physical topography makes communications and transport extremely arduous and makes parents reluctant to send their young children on foot to the distant, scattered schools.

The country is divided for administrative purposes into 11 major provinces, which are subdivided into smaller districts. The rural population constitutes approximately 80 percent of the population living mostly in scattered villages. The Swiss Report (1978) estimated that in 1975 there were 11,000 settlements with 100 to 500 inhabitants.[6] This fact is extremely important in planning schooling services for rural areas.

School enrollment has increased immensely in the last few years. In 1987–88, there were nearly 49,000 children in secondary schools, 174,000 in preparatory schools, and over one million in primary schools (grades 1 to 6).[7] Although the primary stage is the only compulsory level by YAR law, no action is taken if a parent chooses not to send a child to school.

In particular, enrollments at the primary stage increased tenfold within 20 years, from 61,000 in 1962 to over one million in 1987. In actual fact, examination of age-group figures shows that there should have been approximately 1.3 million children in primary schools in 1987. The rapid increase demonstrates a growing interest in education. However, there is still a large proportion of girls that do not attend school and large numbers of children who drop out.

The third five-year plan (1985–90) set a goal to increase male and female enrollments by 35 percent and 72 percent, respectively, at the primary level. Interestingly, in 1985–86, females represented 19 percent of the total primary enrollments.[8] A study has shown that the largest drop-out rate occurs after the first year of primary schooling. From 1974–82 drop-out after grade 1 averaged 32 percent for boys and 34 percent for girls.[9] The rate is lower for succeeding years. This educational wastage may be due to the fact that promotion to the next level depends on passing transfer exams at the end of each year.

Many problems face the primary education system. Issues include the content of the curriculum, lack of interesting teaching methods and attractive books or other visual aids, differences in pupils' ages in the same class due to repetition of classes, drop-outs and long absences, lack of facilities and basic requirements (e.g., desks and chairs), and above all, a lack of well-trained, qualified teachers to meet the growing student enrollment.

Preschool Education in Yemen

Recently, much attention has focused on studies of childhood by educators and psychologists. Caring for children has become a good indicator of the developmental level of a society. The way children are brought up has an important impact on the future.

Preschool education is the basic education for each individual in society. The first six years of a child's life are crucial for the healthy development of emotions, social skills, and intellect. In recent years, the Arab world has given more attention to

children in order to improve their status educationally, socially, and culturally, as well as to raise their level of health. Children's programs in the Arab world are in accordance with the International Declaration of Child Rights issued by the United Nations in 1959, which concurs that a well-developed child is a sign of a good society.[10]

In addition, the increased attention given to children is due to the changes in cultural, social, and economic standards. These changes led to the founding of many educational organizations that promote preschool education. However, preschool education is generally viewed as less important than that of later years. Its inferior status has retarded the development of preschools and kindergartens. The system is small, with no clear goals or consensus regarding a proper curriculum or method.[11]

However, efforts have begun to place children's programs within national development plans. In 1987, the Arabian Committee for Childhood and Development, a nongovernmental organization, was established. Its main goal is to support Arab children's issues on the national level through the provision of knowledge and services. The committee invited all Arab countries to establish their own councils to implement their suggestion.[12] The YAR, in forming a council, has begun to focus much more attention on preschool education. The main goal is to provide necessary services for children, (e.g., health care) and to impart social and cultural values and valuable knowledge. The services also help working women by taking care of their children.

Kindergartens

Before describing preschool education in the YAR, it is helpful to define some terms in this field. *Preschool education* includes all kinds of care provided to children from birth until age 6, prior to the first class in primary school. Nursery schools and kindergartens are two types of preschool education. *Nursery schools* provide child care from birth to age 3. *Kindergartens* are educational programs for children ages 3 to 6. Their focus is on providing activities that lead to healthy, well-rounded development. Most of the following discussion concerns kindergartens. The few nurseries that exist in the YAR are in kindergartens, which allocate one or two rooms for taking care of infants.

The main goals of kindergartens are as follows[13]:

1. to enable the child to acquire morals and values, including those of Islam;

2. to help the child be responsible and independent;

3. to help the child achieve a well-developed personality socially, ethically, mentally, hygienically, and emotionally;

4. to develop in the child basic skills (e.g., talking, reading, and moving);

5. to provide the child with time for play activities to encourage using his or her abilities and expanding his or her interests; and

6. to help the child to adjust to a school environment and to prepare him or her for primary school.

There are three types of kindergartens in the YAR (Private Education Decree, 1981). Government kindergartens are established by the Ministry of Social Affairs and Education. Private kindergartens also exist and are established by a member of the community or nongovernmental organization. Finally, private kindergartens for foreign children are established by some foreign embassies or committees.

The kindergartens were started in the YAR in 1972, with the first in Taiz City. Two years later, another kindergarten appeared in Hodeida. The number of kindergartens increased slowly during the 1970s. Although there was no official supervision for the early kindergartens, more attention has been focused on preschool education during the past ten years. Because the government has included preschool education programs in a national development plan, kindergartens have been established in Sana'a, Taiz, and Hodeida. There are no preschool programs in rural areas.

The increase in the number of kindergartens led to the Ministry of Education attempting to regulate and organize private and preschool programs in 1981. The legislation identified goals and philosophy for kindergarten education.[14]

There were about 27 kindergartens, both private and public, in the YAR as of mid-1990. It is necessary to receive permission from the Ministry of Education and Ministry of Social Affairs to open such schools. However, actual supervision is by the Ministry of Social Affairs.

There were approximately 2,600 children enrolled in the 25 kindergartens, however, this number is not constant each year, because of the absence, sickness, or moving away of children. This number is very small compared with the numbers of pupils entering grade 1 in the primary school every year. There were over 260,000 pupils in grade 1 of the primary school in 1988.[15] The majority of children cannot enter kindergartens or preprimary educational programs. The small number of kindergarten places prevents many children from getting educational experiences before grade 1.

Funding of Preschool Education

There is no free preschool education in the YAR. Registration fees must be paid prior to the child's attendance. The fee differs from one kindergarten to another according to whether it is sponsored by the government or a foreign diplomatic mission, or is privately operated. Tuition fees, higher in private kindergartens than in government, are paid monthly. Government kindergartens depend on a registration fee, tuition fee, and grants from the government and international organizations to cover costs.[16]

Curricula and Methodology

In visiting kindergartens in the YAR it is evident that most schools have similar programs and teaching methods. Similarities and differences are not of great importance because the main goal for kindergarten is the complete development of the child's personality in terms of abilities, skills, and attitudes. It provides children with basic knowledge about education, ethics, and social values. It prepares children to enter primary school.

Most kindergartens have some learning activities and educational games, music, and songs. Differences in curricula and teaching methods appear in the ways they meet specific behavioral objectives. Most official and private kindergartens in the YAR have the same plans and programs. Private kindergartens for foreign children, (e.g., Pakistani, American, and British kindergartens), have some differences. They focus on learning English besides Arabic and Islamic education. There are no family education programs for kindergarten children and parents in the YAR.

Curricula in kindergartens in the YAR is both formal and informal.[17] The academic curriculum includes textbooks and school experiences. Activities in language, science, religion, and ethics are part of the academic curriculum. Alphabet learning, letter and number naming, and writing are learned by using different aids, such as drawings. Activities are concentrated in the last year in kindergartens. There is no definite curriculum prepared by the Ministry of Education or the Ministry of Social Affairs. Therefore, the programs depend on the personal experience of the director. It was found that most curricula used in the Yemeni kindergartens are imported from other Arab countries, such as Lebanon and Egypt.

Extra-curricular activities, including plays, music, songs, videos, and films, depend on the interest of the teachers. Informal learning activities result from the social interactions between children and staff. Field trips and parties are examples of these activities. They help children adjust to the kindergartens and ease the transition to primary schools.

Teaching methods draw on traditional ideas, such as rote memory work, as well as on innovative processes, such as play and guided discovery. The latter seems more appropriate and relevant to children's experience. Instructional aids in kindergartens are video, pictures, and cubic games.

Finally, it can be said that governmental efforts in this area are increasing in the YAR. This is evident in the establishment of more kindergartens, the encouragement of their staff, and supervision

of programs. The government also sponsors conferences and seminars on the topic of children's issues.

Primary Education

The YAR aims to achieve universal primary education by 1995. However, the size of the undertaking is large; in the mid-1980s one-half of all school-aged children were not enrolled in school.[18] Primary education also faces social, economical, and geographical difficulties. There are also gender inequities. Girls form only about 24 percent of the total population of school children in the YAR.

In rural areas, schools are often located far from a portion of the population. While the urban population forms only about 20 percent of the total, one-half of all schools are in urban areas.[19] However, the overall growth in primary education has increased rapidly since 1962 (see Table 1).

Pupil Enrollment and Period of Study

Pupils study at the primary level for six years beginning at age 6. In remote areas, starting recently, children can be accepted in grade 1 of primary school at any time between ages 6 and 9. In urban areas, children tend to enroll when they are age 5 because of the lack of kindergarten and preschool services. Education at this stage is co-educational, and it is rare to find gender-segregated schools despite the Education Act's ruling that there should be separate schools for boys and girls.

The primary stage has special importance,

TABLE 1

Growth of Pupils, Classrooms, and Schools at the Primary Level in the YAR, 1962–89

Year	Number of Pupils	Number of Schools	Number of Classrooms	Number of Teachers
1962–63	61,335	10	27	1,332
1966–67	63,366	712	1,385	1,336
1970–71	88,217	847	1,927	1,780
1974–75	333,784	1,883	7,310	5,773
1978–79	351,386	2,075	3,028	5,830
1982–83	663,312	4,706	2,028	13,165
1986–87	985,421	5,964	22,653	18,193
1988–89	1,141,615	6,740	37,898	23,903

Source: Educational Statistics (1989).

since it is the base on which future education depends, and because it is compulsory for all children. In addition, it replaced the old schools (*kuttab*) which existed before 1962.[20] According to the Education Act, primary education is free and compulsory, from ages 6 to 12. The government has devoted more of its resources to this initial stage than any other.

The aim is to give pupils the principles of the Islamic faith and good morals, in addition to the instructional aims of reading, writing, and mathematics in the first three grades. In the next three grades, the child is taught Arabic grammar and the basic principles of science and social studies, in addition to general knowledge and skills and an awareness of duty in society.

Pupils must pass a general and comprehensive examinations at the end of the sixth school year in order to go to the next preparatory stage. Moreover, promotion from one grade to the next is subject to passing exams.

Special Education Programs and Services

Special education services in the YAR are limited. Those that exist are in segregated centers in the main cities of Sana'a, Taiz, and Hodeida.

In Sana'a, there is a center for blind children established by the Ministry of Social Affairs in 1967. The center has graduated 30 young men from its primary school program. Currently, there are 74 boys and five girls enrolled. While all but six boys are residents in the school, the girls live at home and commute to school. The average age for the boys is 17 and for the girls 13. The wide range of ages means that young children live with adults at the center.

The Home for the Disabled is also in Sana'a; it is run by nuns and supported by government funds and donations. There are no educational services and residential care is provided for approximately 100 physically disabled persons, inclusive of 30 children under age 10. In 1989, a school for deaf and mentally retarded children, called The Home for Mental Retardation and Vocational Rehabilitation, was established in Sana'a as a day school. Seventy boys and 15 girls have enrolled, but the total number may reach 3,000 by

the end of 1991. At least 20 of the 85 are between ages 7 and 10 and study a school curriculum while the others receive vocational training.

The Home for Social Guidance is a residential school in Sana'a for delinquent boys and those with behavior problems. Schooling is a major aim, as is vocational training and behavioral reform. There are 130 boys in the Sanaa home, 84 in the Hodeida branch, 52 in the Taiz branch, 50 in the Ibb branch, and 12 in the Saada branch. The ages range from 7 to 16, but most of the boys are between 7 and 12. There are no such services for girls. In addition to these services there is a school for deaf and dumb children in Hodeida but no figures were available as to the numbers enrolled.

Kindergarten Teacher Education

Although all kindergartens are established according to Ministry of Education legislations, there is no reference to the qualifications required for teaching in the schools. All that is stipulated is that the administration of such schools be assigned to a person who meets the "educational conditions," without specifying what was meant by such conditions.[21]

Although the establishment of infants and nursery schools started as early as 1972, there is as yet no institution to train teachers for nursery schools. The qualifications of teachers in infant and nursery schools are diverse. None of the teachers working in such schools is professionally qualified in preschool education, apart from the in-service training that a few receive.

In a report made by the Department of Women and Children in the Ministry of Social Affairs, based on visits to fourteen of the schools located in Sana'a, it was pointed out that 13 percent of the teachers hold primary school certificates, 15 percent hold preparatory school certificates, 37 percent hold secondary school certificates, and 34 percent hold university degrees.

Among these teachers only 35 percent received training courses organized by the Ministry of Social Affairs before they were assigned to such work. These teachers are working in public nursery schools. According to the report, many of the teachers who received training courses no longer work in nursery schools. As the report states: "[T]here is in an urgent need for training courses like those of public schools."[22] The general lack of experience and education is reflected in the teacher's focus on direct instruction.

The Department of Women and Children has affirmed that the objective of kindergartens can be achieved only if training courses are provided for teachers in both private and public kindergartens[23]; as a result, it has proposed a training program.

Primary Teacher Training

The first Initial Teacher Training Institute for boys at the preparatory stage (the three years after primary school) was established in 1964 in Sana'a. In 1966, a second Initial Institute was opened in Taiz. The institutes consisted of classes attached to secondary schools. In 1967, two additional Initial Institutes for boys were opened, one in Hodeida and the other in Ibb.[24]

Initial Institutes accepted pupils with primary school certificates. The period of study was three years, after which they were awarded an "initial diploma," equivalent to a preparatory school certificate, qualifying them as teachers in the primary level. The first group of nine students graduated in 1967. Two institutes for girls were established in 1967, one in Sana'a and the other in Taiz.[25]

In 1968–69, the Primary Teacher's Training Institutes were started. Two institutes, in Sana'a and Taiz, were opened with 37 student teachers. This type of institute is called "general teacher training." It accepts preparatory school graduates for three years, after which they are granted a certificate called a general diploma, which is equivalent to the general secondary school certificate.[26]

Since 1970, the Ministry of Education has announced various reforms directed at primary teacher training, with the goal of increasing the number of candidates. Up to 1982 however, all of these plans were either withdrawn before they were implemented or after a short trial period. The following are four examples of failed initiatives.

1. In 1970, the system of Initial Teacher Training Institutes for boys was abolished only to be reestablished in 1974.

2. In 1974, the Initial Diploma Course was extended to four years, and diverse other reforms were announced, in a General Education Decree by the Ministry of Education, but these changes were not implemented.

3. In 1976, on the basis of a suggestion made by the UNESCO Education Development Project, the Initial Diploma and the General Diploma courses were each reduced in length to two years, but after being tried in two cities, the system was abolished in 1978.

4. In 1978, a new additional route for entry to primary school teaching was announced, a one-year course for secondary school certificate holders leading to a Special Diploma, but this course was not implemented.

Therefore, in 1982 the system was very similar to that which had been in operation in 1970.

Teacher Training Institute Goals

The objectives of teacher training institutes were established by the 1978 decree that regulated the then existing Initial and General programs.[27] They include the goal that Yemeni teachers will be able to take an effective role in serving the surrounding community. Their role is not limited to performing their educational duties within the school environment. In addition, whenever possible teachers should be a member of the province in which they teach to ensure the stability of teachers. Teachers are also encouraged to pursue professional training at the university level. Therefore, teachers from the middle class are especially targeted. Finally, the training programs should contribute to the modernization of primary schools through the use of institute-based practice teaching schools.

Teaching Training Institute Curriculum

Because of the demise of the Initial Institute, only the General Institute's curriculum is described here.[28] The curriculum is concerned with the personal, professional, and cultural development of the student. The program offers a foundation in teaching methods and opportunities for teaching practice. The curriculum is divided into academic, professional, and cultural subjects.[29]

The Initial Institutes were abolished for several reasons,[30] including the short period of preservice training and the young age of the graduates. The Initial Institutes functioned mostly as a feeder school for the General Institutes.

In 1982–83 they were replaced by a system of five years of training and education after the primary level instead of three. The new five-year plan was established with the following aims[31]:

1.   increasing the channels that provide the teacher training institutes with student teachers;

2.   achieving a balance between the number of enrolled primary school pupils and the number of students enrolled in teacher training institutes;

3.   intensive preparation of primary school teach-

ers and meeting the needs of provinces; and

4.   upgrading the overall standard of primary school education.

The government is trying to overcome the acute shortages of qualified Yemeni teachers and the reluctance of students to attend the existing teacher training institutes. Therefore, the government issued a resolution in 1985 that obliges secondary school leavers to teach in primary schools for one year as a national service. About one-half of the Yemeni primary teachers in 1987–88 were in this category.[32] The In-Service Training Centre in the Ministry of Education offers a short training program for two weeks during the summer holiday before assigning secondary school leavers to primary schools.[33]

Notes

1. *Eradication of Illiteracy Report.* YAR: Ministry of Education, 1982.

2. Amran, A. "Arab world population today and in the future," *UNFPA Report*, 1988.

3. Population Census 1986. Central Planning Organization Report, YAR.

4. The Five-Year Health Plan, 1987–91. Ministry of Health, YAR.

5. *Statistical Year Book.* 1981. YAR.

6. The Swiss Report. 1978. Central Planning Organization, YAR.

7. Educational Statistics. 1987–88. Ministry of Education, YAR.

8. The Third Five-Year Plan for Social and Economic Development. 1987–91.

9. The Dynamics of Enrollment and Educational Wastage. Educational Research and Development Center. Sana'a, YAR.

10. Al-Ebrahin, H. (1987). Arabic Council for Childhood and Development: Great Mission and Great Hope, Arab Childhood.

11. Arabic Council for Childhood and Development. (1989). *Analytical Study of Kindergartens in Arab World.* Cairo.

12. Arabic Council for Child and Development (1987).

13. Ministry of Education, Curricula Department. (1990). *Educational Aims for Kindergarten School.* Sana'a, YAR.

14. Ministry of Education Legal Department (1981). *Decree No. 37 Concerning the Organization of Private Education.* Sana'a, YAR.

15. Ministry of Education, Educational Statistics Department. (1988). *Statistics and Planning for the Year 1987/1988.* Sana'a, YAR.

16. Ministry of Social Affairs, Women and Child Department. (1989). *A Comprehensive Report on Evaluating Public and Private Kindergartens.* Sana'a, YAR.

17. Arab Organization for Education Culture and Science, Education Development. (1986). *Kindergartens in the Arab World.* Tunis.

18. Ministry of Education. Educational Statistics, 1987.

19. Central Planning Organization. Statistical Year Book 1985, p. 65.

20. Traditional religious classes which grew near mosques, or under trees without planned curricula or trained teachers. This kind of educational service was the only chance for the children before 1962 and was known as *Meilama.*

21. Ministry of Education, Curricula Department. (1990). Report concerning the organization of Private Education. Sana'a, YAR.

22. Ministry of Social Affairs, Women and Child Department. (1989). A comprehensive report on the evaluation of public and private kindergartens. Sana'a, YAR.

23. Ibid.

24. Ba' abbad, A. (1982). *Analytical Study of Some Problems of Education and Teachers in YAR.* Sana'a University.

25. Ibid.

26. Ibid.

27. Ministry of Education. (1978). Regulations of Teacher Training Institutes. Sana'a, YAR.

28. Ministry of Education, Teacher Training Institutes Department. (1984). Memo No. 2 Regarding the Modification of the Name of Principles of Education Subject in the General Teacher Training Institutes. Sana'a, YAR.

29. Ibid.

30. Ministry of Education. (1980). The Syllabuses of Initial and General Teaching Training Institutes. Sana'a, YAR.

31. Qubaki, A. Teaching Training Institutes Department. (Undated). Introductory Study of Establishing Teacher Training Institutes (Five-Year System).

32. UNESCO. (1989). Yemen Arab Republic, Debarment Needs of the Educational Sector. Pan's.

33. Ministry of Education, In-service Training Center. (1989). The detailed program of the training course for secondary school graduates who are obliged to teach in primary school. Sana'a, YAR.

COMPARATIVE EARLY CHILDHOOD EDUCATION—AN ENGLISH BIBLIOGRAPHY

• • • • • • • • • • ◆ • • • • • • • • •

The following citations include references to works in English that either take an overview of early childhood education in a particular country or that are based on a comparison of early childhood education in two or more countries.

Adams, C. & Winston, K. (1980). *Mother at work: Public policies in the U.S., Sweden, and China.* New York: Longman.

Adams, M., & Coulibaly, M. (1985). African traditional pedagogy in a modern perspective. *Prospects: Quarterly Review of Education, 15* (2), 275–80.

Ainslie, R. (Ed.). (1984). *The child and the day care setting.* New York: Praeger.

Al Arrayed, M. (1989). *Education in Bahrain: Problems and progress.* London: Ithaca Press.

Al-Misnad, S. (1986). *The development of modern education in Bahrain, Kuwait, and Qatar with special references of the education of women.* London: Ithaca Press.

Ali, A. & Akubue, A. (1988). Nigerian primary schools' compliance with Nigeria national policy on education: An evaluation of continuous assessment practices. *Evaluation Review, 12* (6), 625–37.

Allen, A. (1988). "Let us live with our children": Kindergarten movements in Germany and the United States, 1840–1914. *History of Education Quarterly, 28,* 23–48.

———. (1986). Gardens of children, gardens of God: Kindergartens and day-care centers in nineteenth-century Germany. *Journal of Social History, 19* (3), 433–50.

Almy, M. (1975). *Early childhood education at work.* New York: McGraw-Hill.

Andreolo, R. (1977). *Cooperation between parents, pre-school, and the community: The "Organi Collegiali" in Italy.* Strasbourg, France: Council of Europe.

Aries, P. (1962). *Centuries of childhood: A social history of family life.* New York: Knopf.

Ashby, G. (1980). Preschool education in Queensland, Australia—A systems approach. In L. Katz, (Ed.), *Current Topics in Early Childhood Education,* Vol. 3. Norwood, NJ: Ablex.

Askling, B. (1979). *Training of preschool teachers in Sweden: Current structures and some development trends.* Stockholm: Swedish Institute.

Auerbach, J. (1988). *In the business of child care: Employer initiatives and working women.* New York: Praeger.

Austin, G. (1976). *Early childhood education: An international perspective.* New York: Academic Press.

Bashizi, B. (1979). Day-care centers in Senegal: A woman's initiative. *Assignment Children.* 47–48, 165–71.

Beekman, D. (1978). *The mechanical baby: A popular history of the theory and practice of childrearing.* New York: New American Library.

Bell, P. (1988). *Early childhood education: Teacher behavior from a cross cultural perspective: Further observations.* ERIC Document ED 307 057. [Austria, India, Russia, Zimbabwe].

Belsky, J., & Steinberg, L. (1978). The effects of daycare: a critical review. In *Child Development, 49,* 929–49.

Ben Ari, E. (1987). Disputing about day-care: Care-taking roles in a Japanese day nursery. *International Journal of Sociology of the Family. 17,* (2), 197–215.

Benavot, A. & Riddle, P. (1988). The expansion of primary education, 1870–1940: Trends and issues. *Sociology of Education, 61* (3), 191–210.

Biber, B. (1984). *Early childhood education and psychological development*. New Haven, CT: Yale University Press.

Bihr, J. (1975). Kindergarten education: Past, present and future. *School and Community, 62*, 24–32.

Bixler-Marquez, D. (1986). Educating migrant children in Mexico. *Educational Leadership, 43* (5), 78–79.

Bobeith, N. (1983). *A cultural history of education in the Arab world with special reference to the Arabian gulf region.* ERIC Document ED 239 933.

Boegehaold, B., Cuffaro, H., Hooks, W., & Klopf, G. (Eds.). (1977). *Education before five.* New York: Bank Street College.

Boocock, S. (1987). *Changing definitions of childhood: Cross-cultural comparisons.* ERIC Document ED 304 205. [Japan and United States].

Bone, M. (1977). *Pre-school children and their needs for day care.* London: HMSO.

Borstelmann, L. (1976). *Changing concepts of childrearing, 1920s–1950s: Parental research, parental guidance, social issues.* ERIC Document ED 127 010.

Braun, S. & Edwards, E. (1972). *History and theory of early childhood education.* Worthington, OH: Charles A. Jones.

Bridgeland, W. & Duane, E. (1986). *Child care spokespeople in three countries: A comparison between Sweden, Canada and the United States.* ERIC Document ED 291 540.

Broadfoot, P. (1987). Teachers' conceptions of their professional responsibility: Some international comparisons. *Comparative Education. 23*, (3), 287–301.

Bronfenbrenner, U. (1970). *Two worlds of childhood: USA and USSR.* New York: Russell Sage Foundation.

Brown, B. (1985). Head Start: How research changed public policy. *Young Children, 40* (5), 9–13.

Burgess, C. (1984). Public schooling: A historical perspective. *Childhood Education, 61*, (2), 107–14.

Burnett, J. (1982). *Destiny obscure: Autobiographies of childhood, education and family from the 1820s to the 1920s.* Harmondworth, England: Penguin.

Cable, M. (1975). *The little darlings: A history of child rearing in America.* New York: Scribner.

Catarsi, E. (Ed.). (1985). *Twentieth-century pre-school education.* Milan: Franco Angeli.

Chazan, M. (1978). *International research in early childhood education.* Slough, England: NFER Publishing.

Chenier, N. (1984). Toward universality: An historical overview of the evolution of education, health care, day care, and maternity leave. In *Financing child care: Future arrangements.* Ottawa: Status of Women Canada.

Chowdhury, K. (1984). *Efforts in universalization of primary education: The case of Bangladesh. Occasional Papers Series, Number 12.* New York: Publications Department, Comparative Education Center.

Clarke, A. (1982). *Daycare.* Cambridge, MA: Harvard University Press.

Clarke, A. & Clarke, A. (1976). *Early experience: Myth and evidence.* London: Open Books.

Cleverly, J. & Philips, D. (1986). *Visions of childhood: Influential models from Locke to Spock.* New York: Teachers College Press.

Cochran, M. (1977). A comparison of group day and family child-rearing patterns in Sweden. *Child Development, 48,* (2), 702–07.

Cochrane, J. (1981). *The one-room school in Canada.* ERIC ED 264 064.

Cohen, B. (1988). *Caring for children: Services and policies for childcare and equal opportunities in the United Kingdom.* London: Family Policies Studies Centre.

Cole, M. (1983). Whitelands training college and the development of the kindergarten system in the second part of the 19th century. *Early Childhood Development and Care, 10,* 187–98.

Compendium of information on intercultural education schemes in Europe. Education of migrants' children. (1983). Strasbourg, France: Council for Cultural Cooperation.

Cooke, K., London, J., Edwards, R., & Rose-Lizée, R. (1986). *Report of the task force on child care.* Ottawa: Government of Canada.

Corbett, B. (1968). *The public school kindergarten in Ontario, 1883 to 1967.* Doctoral Thesis, University of Toronto.

———. (1989). *A century of kindergarten education in Ontario.* Toronto: Froebel Foundation.

Corn, S. (1982). *Past and present child care in Israel.* ERIC Document ED 234 903.

Council of Europe. (1976). *Factors which influence the integration of migrants' children into pre-school education in France.* Strasbourg, France: Council of Europe.

———. (1977). *Co-operation between parents, pre-school and the community.* Strasbourg, France: Council of Europe.

———. (1979). *Priorities in pre-school education.* Strasbourg, France: Council of Europe.

———. (1982–83). *Conference on primary education in Western Europe: Aims, problems and trends.* Document from the Innovation in Primary Education Project. Strasbourg, France: Council of Europe.

———. (1983). *Symposium on innovation in primary education in Western Europe.* Document from the Innovation in Primary Education Project. Strasbourg, France: Council of Europe.

———. (1983–84). *Symposium on Innovation in Primary Education in Western Europe.* Document from the Innovation in Primary Education Project. Strasbourg, France: Council of Europe.

———. (1984). *Primary education in Belgium.* Document from the Innovation in Primary Education Project. Strasbourg, France: Council of Europe.

———. (1984). *Primary education in Denmark.* Document from the Innovation in Primary Education Project. Strasbourg, France: Council of Europe.

———. (1984). *Primary education in France.* Document from the Innovation in Primary Education Project. Strasbourg, France: Council of Europe.

———. (1984, 1988). *Primary education in Iceland.* Document from the Innovation in Primary Education Project. Strasbourg, France: Council of Europe.

———. (1984). *Primary education in Liechtenstein.* Document

from the Innovation in Primary Education Project. Strasbourg, France: Council of Europe.

———. (1984). *Primary education in Luxembourg.* Document from the Innovation in Primary Education Project. Strasbourg, France: Council of Europe.

———. (1984). *Primary education in Portugal.* Document from the Innovation in Primary Education Project. Strasbourg, France: Council of Europe.

———. (1984). *Primary education in Switzerland.* Document from the Innovation in Primary Education Project. Strasbourg, France: Council of Europe.

———. (1984). *Primary education in Turkey.* Document from the Innovation in Primary Education Project. Strasbourg, France: Council of Europe.

———. (1984, 1986, 1988). *Primary education in Malta.* Document from the Innovation in Primary Education Project. Strasbourg, France: Council of Europe.

———. (1984, 1988). *Primary education in Austria.* Document from the Innovation in Primary Education Project. Strasbourg, France: Council of Europe.

———. (1984, 1988). *Primary education in Cyprus.* Document from the Innovation in Primary Education Project. Strasbourg, France: Council of Europe.

———. (1984, 1988). *Primary education in Finland.* Document from the Innovation in Primary Education Project. Strasbourg, France: Council of Europe.

———. (1984, 1988). *Primary education in Sweden.* Document from the Innovation in Primary Education Project. Strasbourg, France: Council of Europe.

———. (1984, 1988). *Primary education in the United Kingdom.* Document from the Innovation in Primary Education Project. Strasbourg, France: Council of Europe.

———. (1984). *Symposium on the management of innovation in primary education.* Document from the Innovation in Primary Education Project. Strasbourg, France: Council of Europe.

———. (1985). *Primary education in Greece.* Document from the Innovation in Primary Education Project. Strasbourg, France: Council of Europe.

———. (1985). *Symposium on children with special needs in the primary school.* Document from the Innovation in Primary Education Project. Strasbourg, France: Council of Europe.

———. (1985). *The relationship between the primary school and underprivileged families.* Document from the Innovation in Primary Education Project. Strasbourg, France: Council of Europe.

———. (1986). *Co-operation between school and family.* Document from the Innovation in Primary Education Project. Strasbourg, France: Council of Europe.

———. (1986). *Children with special needs in the primary school symposium—1985.* Document from the Innovation in Primary Education Project. Strasbourg, France: Council of Europe.

———. (1986). *Primary education in Norway.* Document from the Innovation in Primary Education Project. Strasbourg, France: Council of Europe.

———. (1986). *Educational research workshop on reading and writing skills in primary education.* Document from the Innovation in Primary Education Project. Strasbourg, France: Council of Europe.

———. (1986). *Expectations at secondary level and trends in primary education in Europe.* Document from the Innovation in Primary Education Project. Strasbourg, France: Council of Europe.

———. (1986). *Co-ordinated school work in Iceland.* Case Study. Document from the Innovation in Primary Education Project. Strasbourg, France: Council of Europe.

———. (1986). *Science and technology in the primary school symposium—1986.* Document from the Innovation in Primary Education Project. Strasbourg, France: Council of Europe.

———. (1986). *Primary education in the Netherlands.* Document from the Innovation in Primary Education Project. Strasbourg, France: Council of Europe.

———. (1987). *New challenges for teachers and their education.* Standing Conference of European Ministers of Education. Strasbourg, France: Council of Europe.

———. (1987–88). *Innovation in primary education—the final conference. General report.* Document from the Innovation in Primary Education Project. Strasbourg, France: Council of Europe.

———. (1987). *Primary education in Italy.* Document from the Innovation in Primary Education Project. Strasbourg, France: Council of Europe.

———. (1988). *The contact school plan. Visit to the Swedish contact school.* Document from the Innovation in Primary Education Project. Strasbourg, France: Council of Europe.

———. (1988). *Innovation in primary education. Final report.* Document from the Innovation in Primary Education Project. Strasbourg, France: Council of Europe.

———. (1988). *Primary education in Sweden. Project No. 8: Innovation in Primary Education.* ERIC Document ED 295 745.

———. (1988). *Primary education in the United Kingdom. Project No. 8: Innovation in primary education.* ERIC Document ED 297 850.

———. (1988). *Primary education in Austria. Project No. 8: Innovation in primary education.* ERIC Document ED 295 747.

———. (1988). *School improvement from within: The contact school plan.* Document from the Innovation in Primary Education Project. Strasbourg, France: Council of Europe.

———. (1988). *Topic work in the primary school.* European teacher's seminar Report 1988. Document from the Innovation in Primary Education Project. Strasbourg, France: Council of Europe.

———. (1989). *40th Council of Europe Teachers' Seminar on Human Rights education in pre-primary schools.* Strasbourg, France: Council of Europe.

———. (1990). *Dissemination of the project's findings. 7th national seminar. Greece, Delphi, Sept. 1988.* Document from the Innovation in Primary Education Project. Strasbourg, France: Council of Europe.

Cremin, L. (1961). *The transformation of the school: Progressivism in American education, 1876–1957.* New York: Knopf.

———. (1970). *American education: The colonial experience, 1607–1783.* New York: Harper and Row.

Csapo, M. (1984). Preschool special education in Hungary. *Early Child Development and Care, 14* (3–4), 251–68.

———. (1983). Special education in Hungary: An overview of historical development. *B.C. Journal of Special Education*, 7, (2), 181–96.

———. (1984). Special education in the USSR: Trends and accomplishments. *Remedial and Special Education (RASE)*, 5, (2), 5–15.

———. (1984). Preschool special education in Hungary. *Early Child Development and Care*, 14 (3–4), 251–68.

———. (1986). Zimbabwe: Emerging problems of education and special education. *International Journal of Special Education*. 1(2), 141–46.

Darroch, A. & Ornstein, M. (1984). Family and household in nineteenth century Canada: Regional patterns and regional economics. *Journal of Family History*, 9, 158–77.

Das, J. (1979). *Cognitive processes in children: Consideration for a cross-national perspective*. Paris: UNESCO.

Davies, B. (1982). *Life in the classroom and playground: The accounts of primary school children*. London: Routledge and Kegan Paul.

Davis, G. (1979). *Childhood and history in America*. New York: Psychohistory Press.

Deasy, D. (1978). *Education under six*. London: Croom Helm.

Deller (Pollard), J. (1988). *Family day care internationally: A literature review*. Toronto: Queen's Printer.

de Mause, L. (1974). *The history of childhood*. New York: Psychohistory Press.

de Mezerville, G. & Monge, G. (1981). *An Information guide to rehabilitation and special education in Costa Rica*. ERIC Document ED 218 860.

Diniz, F., & Kropveld, P. (Eds.) (1983). *Teacher training and special education in the eighties*. Association for Teacher Education in Europe.

Dolman, D. (1987). Education of the hearing impaired on the island of Jamaica. Programs in action. *Volta Review*, 89 (6), 287–92.

Donzelot, J. (1979). *The policing of families*. New York: Pantheon Books.

Downey, M. (1986). The children of yesterday. *Social Education*, 50 (4), 260–65.

———. (1986). The history of childhood: An annotated bibliography. *Social Education*, 50 (4), 292–93.

———. (1986). Teaching the history of childhood. *Social Education*, 50 (4), 262–67.

Downs, R. (1975). *Heinrich Pestalozzi: Father of modern pedagogy*. Boston: Twayne.

Doxey, I. (1990). *Child care and education: Canadian dimensions*. Toronto: Nelson.

Elder, G. (1981). History of the family: The discovery of complexity. *Journal of Marriage and the Family*, 43, 514–19.

Eliot, A. (1972). Nursery schools fifty years ago. *Young Children*, 27, 208–13.

Elkind, D. (1973). Preschool instruction: Enrichment or instruction? In B. Spodek (Ed.)., *Early childhood education*. Englewood Cliffs, NJ: Prentice-Hall.

———. (1976). *Child development and education: A Piagetian perspective*. New York: Oxford University Press.

Elvin, Lionel, Ed. (1981). *The educational systems in the European community: A guide*. ERIC Document ED 220 993.

Endsley, R., & Bradbard, M. (1981). *Quality day care: A handbook of choices for parents and caregivers*. Englewood Cliffs, NJ: Prentice Hall.

Enloe, W., & Lewin, P. (1987). The cooperative spirit in Japanese primary education. *Educational Forum*, 51 (3), 233–47.

Etaugh, C. (1980). Effects of nonmaternal care on children. *American Psychologist*, 35, 309–19.

Eurydice. (1986). *The Greek education system*. ERIC Document ED 284 789.

Evans, E. (1975). *Contemporary influences in early childhood education*. New York: McGraw-Hill.

———. (1982). Curriculum models and early childhood education. In B. Spodek (Ed.)., *Handbook of Research in Early Childhood Education*. (pp. 107–34). New York: Free Press.

Fein, G. & Clarke-Stewart, A. (1973). *Day care in context*. New York: John Wiley.

Finkelstein, B. (1975). Pedagogy as intrusion: Teaching values in popular primary schools in nineteenth-century America. *History of Childhood Quarterly*, 2 (3), 349–78.

———. (1985). Schooling and the discovery of latency in nineteenth-century America. *Journal of Psychohistory*, 13 (1), 3–12.

———. (1989). *Governing the young: Teacher behavior in popular primary schools in 19th century United States*. New York: The Falmer Press.

Finkelstein, B. (Ed.). (1979). *Regulated children/liberated children: Education in psychohistorical perspective*. New York: Psychohistory Press.

Fisher, S. (1979). *The Commonwealth Caribbean: A study of the educational system of the Commonwealth Caribbean and a guide to the academic placement of students in educational institutions of the United States*. ERIC Document ED 249 886.

Fogel, A., & Melson, G., (Eds.). (1986). *Origins of nurturance: Developmental, biological and cultural perspectives on caregiving*. Hillsdale, NJ: L. Erlbaum Associates.

Frey, J. (1988). *A study of the educational system of Iraq and a guide to the academic placement of students in educational institutions of the United States*. ERIC Document ED 304 404.

Fuchs, R. (1984). *Abandoned children: Foundlings and child welfare in 19th century France*. Albany: State University of New York Press.

Fuller, B. (1986). Is primary school quality eroding in the third world? *Comparative Education Review*, 30 (4), 491–507.

Garvey-Mwazi, K. (1983). Nambia. *Integrated Education*. 20 (6), 25–28.

Gathorne-Hardy, J. (1972). *The rise and fall of the British nanny*. London: Weidenfeld and Nicolson.

Genovesi, G., (Ed.). (1986). *Compulsory education: Schools, pupils, teachers, programs and methods*. ERIC Document ED 279 099.

———. (1986). *Introduction, development and extension of compulsory education. Conference papers for the 8th session of the international standing conference for the history of education (Parma, Italy, Sept. 3–6, 1986)*. Eric Document ED 279 098.

Gidney, R., & Millar, W. (1985). From voluntarism to state schooling: The creation of the public school system in Ontario. *Canadian Historical Review*, Dec., 443–73.

Goutard, M. (1980). *Preschool education in the European Community*. Brussels: Commission of the European Communities.

Greenleaf, B. (1978). *Children through the ages: A history of childhood*. New York: McGraw-Hill.

Hardyment, C. (1983). *Dream babies: Child care from Locke to Spock*. London: Cape.

Harrigan, P. (1986). A comparative perspective on recent trends in the history of education of Canada. *History of Education Quarterly, 26* (1), 71–86.

Harris, N. (1983). The Carondelet Historic Center and Susan. C. Blow: Preserving kindergarten history. *Childhood Education, 59,* 336–38.

Haskell, A., & Lewis, S. (1971). *Infantilial: The archaeology of the nursery*. London: Dennis Dobson.

Haskins, R., & Norwood, D. (1983). *Parent education and public policy*. NJ:ABLEX.

Hawes, J., & Hiner, N., (Eds.). (1985). *American childhood: A research guide and historical handbook*. Westport, CT: Greenwood Press.

Hendry, J. (1986). Kindergartens and the transition from home to school education. *Comparative Education, 22* (1), 53–58. [Japanese preschool education].

Hewes, D. (1985). *Compensatory early childhood education: Froebelian origins and outcomes*. ERIC ED 264 980.

————. (1985). More on early child history. *International Journal of Early Childhood, 17* (1), 9–13.

Hewett, M. (1984). *A guide to the study of childhood, 1820–1920*. New York: Strong Museum.

Hochmaulova, D., & Tencl, L. (1979). Care of pre-school children in Czechoslovakia. *Demosta, 12* (2), 38–40.

Hofferth, S., & Phillips, D., (1987). Child care in the United States, 1970 to 1995. *Journal of Marriage and the Family, 49,* 559–71.

Holowinsky, I. (1981). Research and education of exceptional children in the Ukrainian USSR. *Journal of Special Education, 15* (1), 91–96.

Hultaker, O. (1982). Forms of child-care in Sweden: Experiences and acceptance. *Journal of Comparative Family Studies. 13* (2), 209–19.

Immigrants' children at school. (1987). Paris, France: Organization for Economic Cooperation and Development, Centre for Educational Research and Innovation.

Institute of International Education. (1986). *Regional education profile: Asia. China, Hong Kong, Macau, Thailand, Indonesia, Malaysia, Brunei*. ERIC Document ED 272 047.

Ishigak-Emiko, H. (1986). *A comparative study of educational environments of preschool children in Japan and Israel*. ERIC Document ED 297 414.

Jasik, L., & Horowitra, R. (1983). On-the-spot course on early childhood education in Phitsanulok, Thailand. Mount Carmel International Training Centre for Community Development. ERIC Document ED 242 404.

Johansson, J. (1984). Knowledge traditions in the education of pre-school teachers [Sweden]. *Western European Education, 16* (2), 75–84.

Juan, S. (1985). The Yoji Gakuen: The Suzuki philosophy in the preschool. *Childhood Education, 62* (1), 38–39.

Kaplan-Sanoff, M., & Yablino-Magrid, R., (Eds.). (1981). *Exploring early childhood education*. New York: MacMillan.

Kessel, F., & Siegel, A. (1983). *The child and other cultural inventions*. New York: Praeger.

Khandekar, M. (1979). Policies for children's services in the eighties: Some suggestions. *Indian Journal of Social Work, 40* (3), 333–43.

Kidd, M. (1978). Day care in other countries. In G. Ross, (Ed.)., *Good day care*. Toronto: Women's Educational Press.

Kojima, H. (1986). Japanese concepts of child development for the mid-17th to the mid-19th century. *International Journal of Behavioral Development, 9* (3), 315–29.

Kopmels, D. (1988). *The contact school plan: School improvement from within*. Project No. 8: Innovation in Primary Education. Strasbourg, France: Council for Cultural Cooperation.

Ladd-Taylor, M. (1986). *Raising a baby the government way: Mothers' letters to the Children's Bureau, 1915–1932*. New Brunswick, NJ: Rutgers University Press.

Lande, J., & Scarr, S. (Eds.). (1988). *The future of child care in the United States*. Hillsdale, N.J.: Erlbaum.

Langford, P., & Sebastian, P., (Eds.). (1979). *Early childhood education and care in Australia*. Kew, Victoria: Australian Interaction Press.

LaPierre, L. (1980). *To herald a child: The report of the commission of inquiry into the education of the young child*. Toronto: OPSMTF.

Leigh, A. (1980). Policy research and reviewing services for under fives. *Social Policy and Administration, 14* (2), 151–63.

Leira, A. (1987). *Day care for children in Denmark, Norway, and Sweden*. Oslo, Norway: Institute for Social Research.

Lewis, C. (1988). Japanese first-grade classrooms: Implications for U.S. theory and research. *Comparative Education Review, 32* (2), 159–72.

Lieberman, A. (1978). Psychology and day care. *Social Research, 45* (3), 416–51.

Liegeois, J. (1984). *The training of teachers of gypsy children.* Council of Europe Teachers' Seminar (20th Donaueschingen, Federal Republic of Germany, June 20–25, 1983). Strasbourg, France: Council for Cultural Cooperation.

Liesch, J. (Ed.). (1982). *Comparative perspectives on futures in education. Proceedings of the annual conference of the Australian comparative and international education society*. ERIC Document ED 268 212. [India].

Lorence-Kot, B. (1985). *Child-rearing and reform: A study of the nobility in 18th century Poland*. Westport, CT.: Greenwood Press.

Maas, J. & Criel, G. (1982). *Distribution of primary school enrollments in Eastern Africa. World Bank Staff Working Papers Number 511*. ERIC Document ED 243 571.

MacDonald, K. (1986). Developmental models and early experience. *International Journal of Behavioral Development, 9* (2), 175–90.

Magne, O. (1988). Hearing impaired children in Swedish education. *International Journal of Special Education, 3* (1), 81–87.

Marradi, T. (1982). The nursery school ten years later. *Western European Education, 14* (3), 49–67.

Mbanba, A. (1981). A diagnostic analysis of the education

system in Nambia. *United Nations Education, Scientific, and Cultural Organization.* ERIC Document ED 238 088.

McGaffey, W. (1982). Education, religion and social structure in Zaire. *Anthropology and Education Quarterly.* 13 (3), 238–50.

Mead, M., & Wolfenstein, M. (1955). *Childhood in contemporary cultures.* Chicago: University of Chicago Press.

Meijnen, G. (1987). From six to twelve. Different school careers in primary education. *Zeitschrift fur Sozialisationsforschung und Erziehungssoziologie,* 7 (3), 209–25.

Melhuish, E., & Moss, P. (1991). *Day care for young children: International perspectives.* London: Routledge.

Mellor, E. (1990). *Stepping stones: The development of early childhood services in Australia.* Sydney: Harcourt, Brace, Jovanovich.

Mendelievich, E., (Ed.) (1980). *Children at work.* Geneva, Switzerland: International Labour Office.

Menges, R. (1977). *The international teacher: Controller, manager, helper.* California: Brooks/Cole. Co.

Meyers, P. (1985). Primary schoolteachers in nineteenth century France: A study of professionalization through conflict. *History of Education Quarterly,* 25 (2), 21–40.

Mialaret, G. (1976). *World survey of preschool education.* Paris: UNESCO.

Millie, A. (1986). The past, present and future for the early childhood education researcher. *Early Childhood Research Quarterly,* 1 (1), 1–13.

Moolgaokar, L. (1979). Children's programmes in villages: Some unresolved problems. *Indian Journal of Social Work.* 40 (3), 323–31.

Morley, D. (1979). The CHILD-to-child programme. *Assignment Children.* 47–48, 172–85.

Mosha, H. (1986). A reassessment of the indicators of primary education quality in developing countries: Emerging evidence from Tanzania. *International Review of Education,* 34 (1), 17–45.

Moskoff, W. (1982). The problem of the "double burden" in Romania. *International Journal of Comparative Sociology,* 23 (1–2), 79–88.

Moss, P. (1988). *Childcare and equality of opportunity: Consolidated report of the European childcare network.* Brussels: European Commission.

Myers, W. (1989). Urban working children: A comparison of four surveys from South America. *International Labour Review,* 128 (3), 321–35.

Nakielska, C. (1988). *Determinants of outstanding success in education: An investigation among finalists of competitions in Polish language and mathematics for pupils in Polish primary education.* ERIC Document ED 301 309.

Nashif, H. (1986). *Preschool education in the Arab world.* London: Croom Helm.

National Institute for Educational Research (Tokyo, Japan). (1986). *Elementary/primary school curriculum in Asia and the Pacific. National reports: Volume 1.* ERIC Document ED 297 432. [Australia, Bangladesh, China, India, Indonesia, Japan, Malaysia, Nepal].

———. (1986). *Elementary/primary curriculum in Asia and the Pacific. National reports: Volume II.* ERIC Document ED 297 433.

New forms of preschool education. Final report of a study group meeting (New Delhi, April 1983). (1983). ERIC Document ED 251 169. [Afghanistan, China, India, Maldives, Nepal, Sri Lanka].

OECD. (1978). *Pre-school education: Reports from five research projects.* Paris: OECD.

———. (1980). *Children and society: Issues for preschool reforms.* Paris: OECD.

Oggenfuss, A. (1988). *Primary education in Switzerland. Project No. 8: Innovation in Primary Education.* ERIC Document ED 297 870. Council for Cultural Cooperation, Strasbourg, France.

Olmstead, P., & Weikart, D. (Eds.). (1989). *How nations serve young children: Profiles of child care and education in 14 countries.* Ypsilanti, MI: High Scope Press.

Olsson, N., & and Sellebjerg, A. (1985). *Stockholm's day care centres: 1974–1984.* Sweden: Stockholm Real Estate Office; Sweden: Stockholm Social Services Administration.

Omwake, E. (1971). Preschool programs in historical perspective. *Interchange,* 2 (2), 27–40.

Opravilova, E. (Ed.). (1984). *Preschool education 1981: Selective bibliography.* ERIC ED 264 936 (See also ERIC ED 250 056).

———. (1987). *Preschool education: Selective bibliography of 1984, Part 1 and Part 2. Information Bulletin.* ERIC Document ED 291 458 and ED 281 609.

Osborn, D. (1980). *Early childhood education in historical perspective.* Athens, GA: Education Associates.

Overman, S. (1983). Work and play in America: Three centuries of commentary. *Physical Education,* 40, 180–90.

Owen, S. (1988). The "unobjectionable" service: A legislative history of childminding. Unpublished manuscript. Bromley in Kent, Great Britain: National Childminding Association.

Oxepham, J. (1984). New opportunities for change in primary schooling? *Comparative Education,* 20 (2), 209–21.

Pahud, D., & Besson, F. (1985). Special education in Switzerland: Historical reflections and current applications. *Journal of the Division for Early Childhood,* 9 (3), 222–29.

Paul, U. (1986). Participation of local communities in the financing of education in Guyana. *Prospects: Quarterly Review of Education,* 16 (3), 377–87.

Pearse, R. (1982). *Primary schools in the lands of Padi and Palm or the western primary school in revolution: Fiji and Java.* ERIC Document ED 268 220.

Persaud, G. (1983). *Moral education and the primary school curriculum: A comparative review of case studies of selected Latin American and Caribbean countries.* ERIC Document ED 239 932.

Peters, D. (1980). Social science and social policy and the care of young children: Head Start and after. *Journal of Applied Developmental Psychology,* 1(1), 7–27.

Petri, A. (1984). *Elementary education in the People's Republic of China.* ERIC Document ED 248 022.

Pieterse, M. (Ed.). (1988). *Early intervention for children with disabilities: The Australian experience.* ERIC Document ED 308 674.

Pinchbeck, I., & Hewitt, M. (1969). *Children in English society, Volume 1: From Tudor times to the eighteenth century.* Toronto: University of Toronto Press.

————. (1973). *Children in English society, Volume 2: From the eighteenth century to the Childrens Act of 1948.* Toronto: University of Toronto Press.

Pollock, L. (1984). *Forgotten children: Parent-child relations from 1500 to 1900.* Cambridge: Cambridge University Press.

Preschool education: A review of policy, practise and research. (1981). Canberra: Australian Department of Education. Australian Government Publishing Service.

Preventing school failure: The relationship between preschool and primary education. Proceedings of a workshop in preschool research. (1981). Ottawa: International Development Research Centre.

Primary and secondary education in Sweden. Fact sheets on Sweden. (1984). Stockholm: Swedish Institution.

Psacharopoulos, G. (1980). *The economics of early childhood services.* Paris: OECD.

Randall, M. (1978). Notes from Cuba: 1976. In K. Ross, (Ed.)., *Good day care.* Toronto: Women's Educational Press.

Rasheed, M., & and Hengst, H. (1983). Improving education in the Arabian gulf region. *Journal of Thought, 18* (2), 97–103.

Regional education profiles: Asia, China, Hong Kong, Macau, Thailand, Indonesia, Malaysia, Brunei. (1986). New York: Institute of International Education [Hong Kong].

Reid, S. (1985). *The Samoan child in Samoa and in Hawaii.* ERIC Document ED 257 929.

Robinson, N., Robinson, H., Darling, M., & Holm, G. (1979). *A world of children: Daycare and preschool institutions.* Monterey, CA: Brooks/Cole.

Roby, P. (1975). Shared parenting: Perspectives from other nations. *School Review, 83* (3), 415–31.

Roden, G. (1988). Handicapped immigrant preschool children in Sweden. *Western-European-Education, 20* (3), 95–107.

Role of parents in the education of children of preschool age in tropical Africa, India and Maghreb countries. (1980). ERIC Document ED 226 818. [Algeria, Cameroon, Central African Republic, India, Tamil, Nadu, Ivory Coast, Kinship, Senegal].

Ross, E. (1976). *The kindergarten crusade: The establishment of preschool education in the United States.* Athens, OH: Ohio University Press.

Rothman, S. (1973). Other people's children: The day care experience in America. *Public Interest, 30,* 11–27.

Rudzinski, E. (1986). Whatever happened to the comprehensive school movement in Austria? *Comparative Education, 22* (3), 283–95.

Ruggie, M. (1984). *The state and working women: A comparative study of Britain and Sweden.* Princeton, NJ: Princeton University Press.

Sadli, S. (1979). *Changing patterns of child-rearing practices: An Indonesian study.* Paris: UNESCO.

Saraceno, C. (1984). Shifts in public and private boundaries: Women as mothers and service workers in Italian daycare. *Feminist Studies, 10,* 1.

————. (1984). The social construction of childhood: Child care & education policies in Italy and the United States. *Social Problems, 31,* (3), 351–63.

Savas, U. (1986). *Early childhood education in Turkish Gecekondu.* ERIC Document ED 296 791.

Scarr, S. (1984). *Mother care, other care.* New York: Basic Books.

Schulz, P. (1978). Day care in Canada: 1850–1962. In K. Ross, (Ed.)., *Good day care.* Toronto: Women's Press.

Scott, H. (1977). Women's place in socialist society: The case of Eastern Europe. *Social Policy, 7* (5), 32–35.

Sestini, E. (1985). Preschool policies and programmes in low income countries. *International Journal of Early Childhood, 17* (1), 23–28.

Shapiro, M. (1983). *Child's garden: The kindergarten movement from Froebel to Dewey.* University Park, PA: Pennsylvania State University.

Sifuna, D. (1986). The vocational curriculum in primary education in Kenya: An evaluation. *Prospects, 16* (1), 125–34.

Sijelmassi, M. (1979). *Certain cultural and social aspects of children in some Arab countries.* Paris: UNESCO.

Sobeith, N. (1984). *Dependence and interdependence in education in the Arab world in the pre-colonial, colonial periods: The historical perspective.* ERIC Document ED 244 861.

Sommerville, J. (1982). *The rise and fall of childhood.* Beverly Hills, CA: Sage.

Spodek, B. (1973). *Early childhood education.* Englewood Cliffs, NJ: Prentice-Hall.

————. (1985). Early childhood education's past as prologue: Roots of contemporary concerns. *Young Children, 40* (5), 3–7.

Sponseller, D. (1980). *National child care policy: Past and present influences on future directions.* ERIC Document ED 211 181.

Stamp, R. (1983). *The schools of Ontario: 1876–1976.* Toronto: Mosby.

Steinfels, M. (1973). *Who's minding the children: The history and politics of day care in America.* New York: Simon & Schuster.

Stenholm, B. (1984). *The Swedish school system.* Stockholm: Swedish Institution.

Strader, W. (1984). The historical perspective of parent education as it relates to early childhood education. *Early Child Development and Care, 15* (4), 315–48.

Sutherland, N. (1976). *Children in English-Canadian society.* Toronto: University of Toronto Press.

Suvannus, S. (1981). Special education in Thailand. *B.C. Journal of Special Education, 5* (2), 158–63.

Thompson, D. (1985). *An overview of comparative and international perspectives of early childhood education in six selected countries: An annotated bibliography.* ERIC Document ED 282 621. [China, England, India, Israel, Scandinavia, USSR].

Tobin, J., Wu, D., & Davidson, D. (1989). *Preschool in three cultures: Japan, China, and the United States.* New Haven, CT: Yale University Press.

Tozaki, N., & Shimizu, H. (1987). Special classes for underachievers and mentally retarded children in the Taisho era: A resurvey of the schools listed in the two reports published by the ministry of education. *Japanese Journal of Special Education, 25* (2), 39–49.

Turgonyi, J. (1977). Pre-school education and working mothers in Hungary. *Prospects, 7* (4), 540–48.

UNESCO. (1979). *Wastage in primary education: A statistical study of trends and patterns in repetition and drop-out.* Paris:

UNESCO.

———. (1983). *New forms of pre-school education. Final report of a study group meeting.* ERIC Document ED 251 169.

———. (1984). *The drop-out problem in primary education: Towards universalization of primary education in Asia and the Pacific—Some case studies: China, India, Peninsular Malaysia, Socialist Republic of Vietnam, Sir Lanka, and Thailand.* ERIC Document ED 256 640.

———. (1984). *Towards universalization of primary education in Asia and the Pacific: Country studies.* ERIC Document ED 274 445. [Bangladesh, China, India, Indonesia, Korea, Nepal, Pakistan, Papua New Guinea, Philippines, Sri Lanka, Thailand, Vietnam].

———. (1984). *Towards universalization of primary education in Asia and the Pacific: country studies—Indonesia.* ERIC Document ED 274 450.

———. (1984). *Towards universalization of primary education in Asia and the Pacific: Country studies—Pakistan.* ERIC Document ED 274 452.

———. (1986). *Education of girls in Asia and the Pacific: Report of the regional review meeting on the situation of education of girls for universalization of primary education (Bangkok, Thailand, Nov. 19–28, 1985).* ERIC Document ED 285 798.

UNICEF, Nairobi. (1980). *Survey of basic education in Eastern Africa.* ERIC Document ED 237 257.

UNICEF. (1980). *Survey of basic education in Eastern Africa.* ERIC Document ED 237 257. [Madagascar, Burundi, Comores, Ethiopia, Mauritius, Botswana, Kenya, Lesotho, Swaziland, Tanzania, Zambia, Malawi, Somalia].

Uyanga, J. (1980). Rural-urban differences in child care and breastfeeding behaviour in Southeastern Nigeria. *Social Science and Medicine, 14D* (1), Mar. 23–29.

van der Eyken, W. (1982). *The education of three-to-eight year olds in Europe in the eighties.* Slough, England: NFER—Nelson.

Vanderberghe, R. (1985). *The renewed primary school in Belgium: The local innovation policy and institutionalization of innovations.* ERIC Document ED 259 445.

Vandewalker, N. (1971). *The kindergarten in American education.* New York: Arno Press.

Wagner, D. (1983). *Child development and international development: Research policy interfaces.* San Francisco: Jossey-Bass.

Wagner, M., & Wagner, M. (1976). *The Danish national child care system: A successful system as model for the reconstruction of American child care.* Boulder, CO: Westview Press.

Wald, K. (1978). *Children of Che: Childcare and education in Cuba.* Palo Alto, CA: Ramparts Press.

Weber, E. (1984). *Ideas influencing early education.* New York: Teacher's College Press.

Whitbread, N. (1972). *The evolution of the nursery-infant school: A history of infant and nursery education in Britain, 1800–1970.* London: Routledge & Kegan Paul.

Winter, C. (1984). *The provision of appropriate education in selected southern African countries: Malawi, Zimbabwe, Nambia and the "independent" South African homelands.* ERIC Document ED 260 143.

Wishy, B. (1968). *The child and the republic: The dawn of modern American child nurturance.* Philadelphia: University of Pennsylvania Press.

Wolfe, A. (1989). The day-care dilemma: A Scandinavian perspective. *Public Interest, 95,* 14–23.

Woodhead, M. (1979). *Preschool education in Western Europe: Issues, policies and trends.* London: Longman.

Woodill, G. (1986). The European roots of early childhood education in North America. *International Journal of Early Childhood, 18,* 1.

World of Daycare (1984). *Child resource world review.* Berkeley, CA: International Child Resource.

Yates, B. (1984). Comparative education and the third world: The nineteenth century revisited. *Comparative Education Review, 28* (4), 533–49. [Zaire].

Zelizer, V. (1985). *Pricing the priceless child: The changing social value of children.* New York: Basic Books.

BIOGRAPHIES OF CONTRIBUTORS

• • • • • • • • • ◆ • • • • • • • •

Editors

Dr. Gary A. Woodill, Ed.D., is Professor of Early Childhood Education at Ryerson Polytechnic Institute, Toronto, Canada. His 1984 doctoral thesis from the Ontario Institute for Studies in Education was a critical examination of preschool special education in the province of Ontario. He has written a number of articles on the history and practice of special education and early childhood education, on computers and young children, and on social-emotional development.

Dr. Judith K. Bernhard, Ph.D., teaches in the School of Early Childhood Education, Ryerson Polytechnic Institute, Toronto, Canada. She was born in Santiago, Chile and emigrated to Canada in 1973. Her recently completed doctoral thesis was on gender differences among preschoolers in the use of computers. Her research interests include the assessment of linguistically and culturally diverse children, and gender equity issues in education.

Lawrence Prochner, M.A., is a doctoral student at the Ontario Institute for Studies in Education, Toronto, Ontario. He is also an instructor in the School of Early Childhood Education, Ryerson Polytechnic Institute, Toronto, Canada. His re-

search interests include comparative early education and the history of day care in Canada.

Albania

Professor Bedri Dedja is a member of the Academy of Sciences of the People's Socialist Republic of Albania. Professor Dedja is an instructor at Tirana University, and an author of a number of published works on early childhood education.

Antigua

Dr. Patricia Canning, Ph.D., C.Psych., recently assumed the position of Associate Dean of Research and Development, Faculty of Education, Memorial University of Newfoundland, St. John's, Newfoundland, Canada. Previously she was Professor of Child Study at Mount Saint Vincent University, Halifax, Nova Scotia, Canada. She has had extensive experience developing teacher-training programs for early childhood educators in Canada and the Caribbean, including Antigua. She has published articles on the professionalization of child care, young children with special needs, program development, and cross-cultural education. Her current research focuses on the development of resource information for parents of, and professionals working with, young children with special needs, the integration of children with special needs into preschool, and an examination of the effects of the quality of child care on children's development.

Dr. Edris Bird, Ed.D. received her training at the University of West Indies, the University of London and the Ontario Institute for Studies in Education in Toronto, Ontario. She has over 40 years of experience in teacher training in Antigua. Current projects include the development of early childhood education training programs in Antigua and Barbuda.

Argentina

Professor Carlos Héctor Hurtado teaches Education Sciences at the National University of Córdoba, Argentina. He has numerous publications on popular and rural education in Latin America, held several governmental posts in education, and has participated in a variety of research projects of national significance in Argentina.

Australia

Dr. S. Vianne McLean has been an early childhood teacher, advisor and lecturer, and currently is Head of the Department of Care and Education, School of Early Childhood Studies, Queensland University of Technology. She has worked in several states of Australia and in Arizona, USA, where she completed a Ph.D. at Arizona State University.

Professor Barbara Piscitelli, M.Ed., is a lecturer in the Department of Care and Education and coordinator of the Graduate Diploma of Education (Early Childhood) at Queensland University of Technology. She is currently working on a biography of a prominent Australian art educator.

Professor Gail Halliwell, M.S., is a senior lecturer in the School of Early Childhood Studies, Queensland University of Technology. She holds a master's degree from the University of Illinois at Urbana-Champaign. Her current research interests include teachers' personal, practical knowledge about implementing the curriculum in early childhood settings. She is particularly interested in the application of early childhood curriculum approaches in primary school settings.

Professor Gerald F. Ashby is the Head of the School of Early Childhood Studies, Queensland University of Technology. He is a respected figure in Australian early childhood education and special education fields. Recent work has included the establishment of a national data base on special education services.

Austria

Dr. Wilhelm Wolf is head of the department of Primary Education at Oberrat University. Dr. Wolf is involved in works examining minority schools and pilot projects in the field of compulsory education in the Federal Ministry of Education, Arts, and Sports in Vienna. Dr. Wolf is the author of several publications in primary education.

Bahrain

Dr. May Al-Arrayed Shirawi is an assistant professor in the College of Education at the Arabian Gulf University. She was educated at the American College and Bahrain University, from which she obtained her B.A. with distinction. She received her Ph.D. in Education from Durham University, England. Dr. May Al-Arrayed Shirawi is also the author of several publications in education.

Belgium

Dr. Marc Depaepe is a professor of History of Education at the Catholic University of Leuven. He is Secretary of the I.S.C.H.E. (International Standing Conference of the History of Education) and has published in the areas of the history of primary education in Belgium, theory and methodology of the history of education, and the history of education sciences. He is a member of the editorial board of *Paedagogica Historica* (an international journal for the history of Education), and of *Pedagogisch Tijdschrift* (a Belgian-Dutch educational journal).

Dr. Ferre Laevers is a professor of Early Childhood Education at the Catholic University of Leuven. He publishes on early childhood and elementary education and is a member of the editorial board of *Pedagogisch Tijdschrift* (a Belgian-Dutch educational journal).

Dr. George Meuris is a professor in the Faculty of Psychology and Education Sciences at the Catholic University of Louvain and head of the experimental pedagogy unit at that university. His research and publications are in the areas of the history of education, comparative education and teacher training.

Botswana

Dr. John H. Yoder is Coordinator of Graduate Studies in the Faculty of Education and Senior Lecturer in the Department of Primary Education at the University of Botswana. He holds a Ph.D from the University of Virginia. Dr. Yoder has conducted research and published in the areas of special education and gifted education.

Ruth Monau, M.Ed., is a lecturer in the Department of Primary Education, Faculty of Education. She received her Master's of Education degree from Ohio University. Her research interests lie mainly in early childhood education and primary education, and she has also done a consultancy on "Day Care Center Programs in Botswana".

Brazil

Dr. Lucia Regina Goulart Vilarinho is an associate professor of education at the Federal University of Rio de Janeiro. She is also an author of a book on didactics and several articles on the teaching-learning process, including the area of alphabetization.

Bulgaria

Dr. Plamen Radev, Ph.D., is an associate professor at the University of Plovdiv in Bulgaria. As a member of the European Association of History of Social and Behavioral Sciences, Dr. Radev researches the history of early childhood education and contemporary educational technologies.

Canada

Dr. Andrew Biemiller, M.Sc, Ph.D., is an associate professor at the Institute of Child Study, University of Toronto, and the Department of Applied Psychology, Ontario Institute for Studies in Education. He is the author of several papers on day care effects, early childhood research in Canada, and early childhood programs in Canada.

Dr. Ellen M. Regan is a professor in the Applied Psychology Department, Ontario Institute for Studies in Education. Her research interests include beliefs/implicit theories of early childhood practitioners and exploring dimensions of child centered practice.

Dr. Donna Lero is Associate Professor of Child Studies in the Department of Family Studies at the University of Guelph where she teaches courses in child development, child and family poverty, and family policy. She is currently Project Director for the Canadian National Child Care Study, a large-scale comprehensive study of Canadian families and their child care arrangements.

Chile

Professor Selma Simonstein Fuentes teaches curriculum studies in the School of Education, Central University, San Bernardo, Chile.

Professor Maria Cristina Varas Aceituno teaches philosophy in the School of Education, Central University, San Bernardo, Chile.

Professor Mario Zambrano Bobadilla teaches in the School of Education at Central University, San Bernardo, Chile.

Professor Hernan Ahumada Aldoney has 25 years experience working in the educational system in Chile. His research interests are in special education. He is a professor of education at the Universidad Metropolitana de Ciencias.

Professor Shelma Soto Sanchez is a professor in the School of Education, Central University, San Bernardo, Chile.

China

Zihixin Laing is Associate Professor and Director, Division of Preschool Education, in the Department of Education, Beijing Normal University. She has published widely on preschool moral education, and children's play.

Lijuan Pang is Assistant Professor, the Division of Preschool Education, Department of Education, Beijing Normal University. She has published in the area of child psychology and education.

Costa Rica

Professor Irma Zúñiga Leon holds a Licentiate in Education, a Bachelor in Education (Preschool) and a Bachelor of Education (Pedagogy of Communication) from the University of Costa Rica and the National University respectively. She is coordinator and professor of several courses at the Preschool Education Training program at the National University and author of several publications.

Cyprus

Dr. Antonis Papadopoulos is the Director of Primary Education at the Ministry of Education. He is very active as the chairman and vice-chairman of several educational associations and the School for Parents. Dr. Papadopoulos is the author of three books and many articles in the area of education.

Finland

Dr. Mikko Ojala, Ph.D. Phil., is an associate professor of Early Childhood Education and the National Leader of IEA Preprimary Project. His interests/achievements in the field of early childhood education as a researcher and author are extensive.

Dr. Martti T. Kuikka, Ph.D. Phil., is an associate professor in the Department of Education at the University of Helsinki. Dr. Kuikka's interests in early childhood education concentrates on the historical development in Finland and in Europe.

France

Dr. Marie-Thérèse Le Normand is a director of research, INSERM (Institut National de Santé et Recherche Medicale), in Paris, France. She is a psycholinguist who specializes in severe speech and language disorders in young children, and has published widely in this field.

Germany

Prof. Dr. Hans A. Horn is a professor of education at the Institute of Elementary and Early Childhood Education, University of Frankfurt. His research interests include the history of early childhood and primary education, cooperation between kindergarten and primary schools and multicultural education in kindergarten and primary school.

Prof. Dr. Arnulf Hopf teaches teacher training, elementary education, and theories of socialization at the C.V. Ossietzky University, Oldenberg. He has published several books on education, including *Theory and Practice of Education in Sexuality,* Dortmund, 1990.

Ghana

Dr. George Q. Collison was head of the Department of Science Education and dean of the Faculty of Education in the University of Cape Coast from 1979 to 1990. His research and writing has been in the area of science curriculum at the primary level.

Great Britain

Audrey Curtis, M.Sc., is Senior Lecturer in Child Development in the Department of Child Development and Primary Education, Institute of Education, University of London. She is a longstanding member of OMEP and has lectured in many countries on preschool education. She has published numerous articles in journals and teacher magazines in Australia, China, Japan, Poland, Bulgaria, Yugoslavia and the United Kingdom.

Hong Kong

Dr. Silvia Opper is a developmental psychologist at the University of Hong Kong where she is Lecturer in Education and Director of the M.Ed. program in Early Childhood Education. After undergraduate studies at Geneva University with Jean Piaget and Barbel Inhelder, she completed her Ph.D. at Cornell University using a Piagetian framework for her dissertation on Thai children. During this period she co-authored, with Herbert Ginsburg, *An Introduction to Piaget's Theory of Intellectual Development.* She is currently the Hong Kong National Research Coordinator of a cross-national study sponsored by the International Association for the study of Educational Achievement, IEA, on 4-year old children in countries around the world.

Hungary

Dr. Suzanne Hunyady is Dean of the Budapest Teachers' Training College. Éva Knoll Pereszlényi and Agnes Szilágyi also teach at the Budapest Teachers' Training College.

India

Dr. Venita Kaul is a Reader in the Early Childhood Education Unit of the Department of Preschool and Elementary Education at the National Council of Educational Research and Training in New Delhi. Dr. Kaul has been working in the area of early childhood education continuously since 1975, training teachers and teacher educators, developing teaching/learning materials and curriculum, and designing extension programs for early childhood educators in India. Dr. Kaul has published extensively in the areas of children's play and special needs.

Iran

Dr. Mohamad Yamani Douzi Sorkhabi obtained his doctorate from the University of Paris (Sorbonne). He is currently an assistant professor in the Faculty of Education Sciences and Psychology at the Shahid Beheshti University, Tehran, Iran. He has published several articles on primary education in Iran.

Dr. Zahra Sabbaghian, is Head of the Department of Education at Shahid Beheshti University in Iran. Dr. Sabbaghian's research interests include program design for early childhood education.

Israel

Dr. Rina Micholwitz is Director of Early Childhood Education, Ministry of Education, Tel Aviv.

Italy

Dr. Caterina Cicogna obtained her doctorate in Developmental Psychology in 1977 from the University of Padova, Italy, following which she was appointed superintendent of elementary schools in the Verona area of Italy. She was later seconded to the Ministry of Foreign Affairs in Rome, and placed in charge of education abroad at the elementary level. In 1983 she was transferred to the Consulate General of Italy in Toronto, Canada, where her duties currently include the role of educational consultant and advisor to Heritage Language Program instructors.

Japan

Dr. Isaaki Noguchi, is a professor in the Department of Pre-school Education, at Hirosaki University. Dr. Noguchi's research interests include the training of pre-school teachers and the history of kindergarten education in Japan.

Sumie Ogawa, M.Ed, is an associate professor at Tochigi Junior College at Kokugakuin University. Professor Ogawa's research interests focus on the training of pre-school teachers and the history of kindergarten education in Japan.

Dr. Santaro Hashimoto, Ph.D., teaches at Hirosaki University. Dr. Hashimoto's research interests include the training of teachers and the education of mentally handicapped children.

Tomoyoshi Yoshikawa, M.Ed., teaches at the School of Allied Medical Sciences, Hirosaki University. Research interests include the training of nursery teachers and the history of education.

Kenya

Professor George Godia is the Director of the Center for Human Resource Development and an associate professor of Education, Moi University. Professor Godia is presently working on a proposal to start a degree program in early childhood education (pre-primary education) at Moi University.

Liberia

J. Nyanquoi Gormuyor is a lecturer in the Education Division of Cuttington University College, Monrovia, Liberia.

Malaysia

Dr. Rohaty Mohd Majzub lectures in the Faculty of Education at the National University Malaysia. An early childhood education specialist, Dr. Majzub is the author of a widely used text on preschool education in Malaysia.

Malta

Joseph A. Xerri is an education officer (Primary Sector) in the Department of Education in Malta. His research interests focus on the history of education in Malta. He lectures at in-service courses for kindergarten and primary teachers.

Netherlands

Dr. Ernst Mulder teaches at the University of Amsterdam, Department of Pedagogical Sciences. He is the author of *Principle and Profession: Pedagogy at the University in the Netherlands, 1900-1940,* as well as several articles on the history of western education and educational science, 19th and 20th centuries.

Dr. Elisabeth Singer is associated with the University of Amsterdam, Department of Pedagogical Sciences. She carries out research in the field of day care institutions and family life, and the social-emotional development of young children.

New Zealand

Dr. Anne B. Smith is an associate professor of education at the University of Otago, Dunedin, New Zealand. She is a developmental psychologist with a particular interest in the effects of early childhood experiences on social development. Dr. Smith has also had considerable involvement in early childhood policy development, and has published two books, one on child development and one (with David Swain) on child care in New Zealand.

Nigeria

Prof. Dr. Joseph A. Aghenta, is the former Head of the Department of Educational Administration and Foundations of the University of Benin, State Commission of Education. Dr. Aghenta's research interests lie in the historical foundations of Early childhood education in Nigeria.

Dr. J. Nesin Omatseye, Ed.D., is a senior lecturer and former acting head of the Department of Educational Administration and Foundations, as well as Acting Director, Institute of Education, University of Benin and Proprietor of Silver Spring Demonstration School (nursery and primary). Dr.

Omatseye's research interests are in the philosophical dimensions of early childhood education in Nigeria.

Oman

Dr. Thuwayba Al-Barwani, Ed.D., is an assistant professor of education and director of the Center of Educational Research at the College of Education and Islamic Sciences, Sultan Qaboos University. Dr. Al-Barwani's research interests include early childhood education, adult education and women studies.

Russia

Dr. Larisa A. Paramonova is a doctor of pedagogy, vice director of the Institute for Preschool Education of the Academy of Pedagogical Science of the USSR and a specialist in preschool didactics. Dr. Larisa R. Anosova is a doctor of psycholinguistics, senior scientific worker of the Institute for Preschool Education, assistant professor of the Additional Teacher Training Institute of the Federative Republic of Russia. She is a specialist in psychology of child language, teaching language to young children, aesthetics, children's literature.

Dr. Valentina D. Sych is a doctor of pedagogy, senior scientific worker of the Institute for Preschool Education, and specialist in Aesthetical Education and Education through mass media.

Dr. Liubovj N. Pavlova is a doctor of pedagogy, Laboratory Chief of the Institute for Preschool Education, and specialist in baby and infant care and education.

Dr. Valentina M. Ivanova is a doctor of pedagogy, senior scientific worker of the Institute for Preschool Education, specialist in the education in the family.

South Africa

Prof. Dr. C.P. Jansen, D.Ed., is Director of the Institute for Educational Research at the University of South Africa. Dr. Jansen's special interests and achievements are in the fields of philosophy of science, science education, research methodology and curriculum research.

Dr. E.M. Calitz, Ed.D., is Senior Lecturer in the Department of Didactics at the University of South

Africa. Dr. Calitz's special interests are in the fields of multicultural teaching in the preprimary school and the development of a structured informal curriculum for use in schools/institutes with untrained non-professional educare workers.

Prof. Lydia Du Toit, Ed.D., is a professor in the Department of Orthopedagogics of the University of South Africa. Her special interests and achievements are in the fields of special education in general, mental handicap, early intervention, parent guidance, compensatory education, and teacher training.

Prof. H.M. Grobler, M.Ed., is a senior lecturer (preprimary education) in the Department of Didactics at the University of South Africa. Her special interest is in the teaching of music in the preprimary school system.

Prof. Annemarie Kotzé, B.Ed., was for many years the head of a preprimary school. She is now a lecturer of the history of education at the University of South Africa. Prof. Kotzé's special interests are in the preprimary education and involvement of authorities at various levels as well as charitable organizations in preprimary education.

Dr. M.M. Lancaster, Ph.D., is Chief Researcher at the Bureau for Curriculum Development of the Transvaal Education Department. Dr. Lancaster's research interests and achievements are in the field of introductory reading, with emphasis on the different approaches, methods, and strategies of teaching and reading.

Prof. J.P. Orr, B.A.(Hons.), is a lecturer in the Department of Didactics at the University of South Africa. Her special interests are non-formal paraprofessional training in early childhood educare and health aspects of early childhood education.

Prof. A.M. Smith, M.Ed., is a Lecturer in the Department of Orthopedagogics at the University of South Africa. Her research interests focus on young children with special educational needs with special reference to handicapped children, learning disabilities, high risk infants, chronically ill children, and children with terminal illnesses.

Prof. E.M. Swanepoel has two D.Ed. degrees. Dr. Swanepoel is an associate professor in the Department of Fundamental Pedagogics at the University of South Africa. Her special interests are in the fields of the crèche as an educational institution, and learning and development of the infant.

Spain

Dr. Antonio Molero Pintado is a professor of theory and history of education at the University of Alcalá de Henares in Guadalajara, Spain. His primary interest is the contemporary Spanish history of education. He is the director of several research projects including the history of in-service teacher training in Spain from 1840-1990.

Professor Maria del Mar del Pozo Andres teaches theory and history of education at the University of Alcalá de Henares in Guadalajara, Spain. Her current research projects include a historical study of the introduction of Froeblian methods into Spain.

Sudan

Dr. Gasim Badri is the Dean, Ahfad University of Women and a professor of psychology and early childhood education. Dr. Badri's research interests include parent education related to the enhancement of children's cognitive abilities and child abuse.

Swaziland

Dr. Marissa Rollnick holds a Ph.D in Science Education from the University of the Witwatersrand. She lived in Swaziland for fifteen years, working in teacher training at both the teachers' college and the university, where she was involved with training primary and secondary teachers. She is the author of *An Inventory of Preschools in Swaziland*, a report commissioned by UNICEF, and a contributor to the 1990 *Situation Analysis on Women and Children in Swaziland*, also produced by UNICEF. In September 1990 she joined the chemistry department of the University of the Witwatersrand as a director.

Taiwan

Dr. Hui-Ling Wendy Pan is an associate professor, Department of Education, and Secretary-General, the Chinese Comparative Education Society, Taipei, Taiwan.

Turkey

Dr. Tanju Gürkan is currently an associate professor at the Faculty of Education Sciences of Ankara University. She is the chairperson of the board of an experimental kindergarten operated by the Faculty of Education Sciences. Her main research interests are developmental characteristics of young children, and curriculum development for both early childhood education and early childhood teacher training. Dr. Gürkan is also the author of several published works.

United Arab Emirates

Dr. Mahmoud Ahmed Ajjawi is an associate professor, College of Education, United Arab Emirates University. He has published a number of books and articles on the training of elementary school teachers.

United States of America

Dr. Steven A. Gelb is Director of the Manchester Family Child Development Center and Assistant Professor in the School of Education at the University of San Diego. He has written extensively on the history of psychology and is currently interested in critical perspectives on developmental theory.

Kathryn D. Bishop is an assistant professor in the School of Education at the University of San Diego where she is responsible for the graduate teacher credentialling program in the area of severe handicaps. She is presently completing her doctoral studies in the joint program at the UniversityUniversity, Los Angeles.

Yemen

Dr. Azza Ghanem is a lecturer at Sana'a University in Educational Psychology and Special Education. She has many publications concerning handicapped children in Yemen.

Dr. Mohammed A. Al-Soofi is Lecturer in the Faculty of Education, Sana'a University and is head of that faculty's research unit. He is a member of the panel of referees of the Journal of Education for Teaching (JET), published in Britain. He has published on educational research methodology and teacher training.

Dr. Waheeba Al-fakih is Director of the Foundations of Education Department, Sana'a University. Her publications have focused on the education of girls in Yemen and on universal primary schooling in Yemen.

Dr. Amat Al-Razzak A. Hummed Al-Hawri is Lecturer of Curricula and Teaching Methods in the Faculty of Education and Head of the Department of Arabic Studies at the Sana'a University. She has done research on reading in primary school and on the evaluation of primary teacher education programs.

INDEX

Higher education 13, 242

Hill, Patty Smith 139, 505

History (of early childhood education) 3–10, 15, 21–23, 25, 39–41, 50–55, 75–77, 79, 86–89, 93–96, 106, 129, 135–142, 155–156, 159, 165–166, 169–174, 175–176, 181–182, 193–195, 205–208, 214, 217, 223–224, 231–234, 239, 242, 249–251, 259–260, 265–266, 269, 271, 277, 284, 293–294, 311, 317–319, 351–353, 361–364, 373–377, 384–387, 399–400, 407–408, 417, 419–424, 425–426, 433, 441–450, 453–456, 462, 471–472, 481–483, 487–488, 491–492, 504–510

History education 22, 26, 106, 185, 187, 199, 214, 239, 265, 330, 356, 358, 377, 433, 448, 456, 482

Holidays 27, 122, 211, 239

Holmes, Edwin 234

Home care. *See* Family day care

Home economics 126, 330, 346, 402, 415, 478

Home Start 245

Home visitors 243

Homework 211

Hong Kong 249–258

Hospitalized children 37, 60, 81, 165, 194, 242, 357, 436

Hungary 225, 259–273

Hurons 4

Hunt, J. McVicker 509

Hygiene. *See* Health of children

Ideology 12–14, 295

Illegitimate children 221

Illiteracy. *See* Literacy

Illyrians 21

Immigrant children 16, 106, 505

India 14, 16, 275–292

Industrialization, effects of on childhood education 6, 7, 361, 426

Infant care 13, 190, 23, 55, 147, 157, 195, 206, 209, 221, 444–445, 524

Infant mortality 7, 31, 205, 363

Infant schools 6, 22, 35, 93, 121, 225, 231, 259, 362, 482, 484

Infant stimulation programs 368

Infanticide 4

Initiation schools 120

Integration of children with disabilities 8, 16, 81, 87, 109, 188–189, 200, 211, 219, 225, 245, 314–315, 379–380, 391, 434, 435, 513, 518, 521–522, 524

Intellectual handicaps. *See* Mental handicaps

Intelligence testing 7, 379, 510

Interest centers 98, 99

Iran 293–305

Isaacs, Susan 51, 386, 392, 514

Islam. *See* Muslim religion and childhood education

Israel 307–309

Italy 311–315

Itard, Jean 7, 8, 208

Itinerant teachers 44

Jamaica 35

Japan 12, 317–325, 472

Jensen, Arthur 519

Jesuits 5, 159, 351

Jewish education 294, 307–309, 375, 429

Johnson, Harriet 514

Kagisano 114

Katsarov, Dimitar 139

Kenya 327–336

Kergomard, Pauline 206

Kilpatrick, William 140, 506

Kindergarten 7, 14, 15; Albania 22, 23, 24; Argentina 39–47; Australia 49, 52, 58–60; Austria 83, 84; Bahrain 87–89; Belgium 94; Bulgaria 141; Canada 147, 149; Chile 155–156; China 170; Finland 194; Germany 218; Ghana 228; Hong Kong 249, 252; Hungary 261, 269–271; Iran 299–300; Israel 307–308; Italy 312; Japan 317–320; Liberia 341; Malaysia 343; Malta 354–355; New Zealand 385, 395; Oman 408, 410–414; Russia 417, 420; South Africa 425; Sudan 455–456; Taiwan 471–472; Turkey 484; United Arab Emirates 492–495; United States 504–506, 523; Yemen 530–531

Kinderladen movement 218

Knitting schools 6, 205

Kodály, Zoltán 260

Kohanga reo (Maori preschools) 14, 383, 388, 397

Krupskaya, N.K. 420

La Mettrie, Julien 8

Labarca, Amanda 155

Labarca, don Guillermo 155

Laboratory schools 7, 506

Lancaster, Joseph 5, 6, 136, 338, 442

Lane, Homer 234

Language education 22, 23, 24, 80, 87, 106, 126, 141, 172–173, 185, 187, 199, 213, 214, 239, 242, 252, 266, 267, 295, 315, 320, 330, 341, 356, 358, 377, 402, 413, 415, 421, 422, 433, 448, 449, 450, 463, 468, 475, 476, 482, 513, 514, 532, 533

Latch-key children 508

Lawrence, Esther 232

Learning disabilities 167, 219, 377, 379, 497

Least restrictive environment 64

Legislation 40, 84, 105, 140, 156, 160, 166, 169, 170, 177, 182, 194, 197, 198, 200, 207, 227, 232, 233, 239, 250, 260, 265, 266, 269, 270, 271, 311, 318, 353, 373–378, 379, 384, 385, 392, 427, 442, 443–444, 446, 447, 449, 472, 481, 482, 483, 484, 497, 508, 510, 518, 533

Lenin, V.I. 417